# Temporary Economic Crises



In traditional theory of economic crisis, and in all its manifestations, there is no fundamental difference between economic disorder and economic crisis: the two types of economic turmoil are both considered temporary states.

This book is a methodical study of deep-seated causes of economic crises. The aim of the book is to explain the key difference between economic disorder and economic crisis. Its key argument is that economic disorder is a permanent condition, whereas economic crises are a series of transitory periods. Economic crises, unlike economic disorders, are acute and frenzied volatilities that are unpredictable and short-lived. Humans cannot survive in a condition of perpetual economic crises but can only accommodate life under unremitting economic disorders. The book also explores the root cause of economic crisis. Unlike the received wisdom in economics, this book looks at the root cause of such hysterical economic turbulences as a result of an innate propensity of human fallibility. The final section of this book looks at the ramifications of this alternative perspective on macroeconomic policy formation and implementation.

This book is a major contribution to the literature on economic disorder and crises and will be of great interest to readers of economic theory, philosophy of economics, and the history of economic thought.

**Shahzavar Karimzadi** is Senior Lecturer in Economics at the University of Hertfordshire Business School, UK.

## Routledge Frontiers of Political Economy

**Macroeconomic Modelling, Economic Policy and Methodology**
Economics at the Edge
*Edited by Mikael Randrup Byrialsen, Hamid Raza and Finn Olesen*

**Economics, Anthropology and the Origin of Money as a Bargaining Counter**
*Patrick Spread*

**Bernard Schmitt's Quantum Macroeconomic Analysis**
*Alvaro Cencini*

**Blockchain and the Commons**
*Vangelis Papadimitropoulos*

**Globalization and the Decline of American Power**
The Political Economy of the American Fall
*Cyrus Bina*

**Marx and *Le Capital***
Evaluation, History, Reception
*Edited by Marcello Musto*

**Permanent Economic Disorder**
*Shahzavar Karimzadi*

**Temporary Economic Crises**
*Shahzavar Karimzadi*

**Money and Capital**
A Critique of Monetary Thought, the Dollar and Post-Capitalism
*Laurent Baronian*

For more information about this series, please visit: www.routledge.com/Routledge-Frontiers-of-Political-Economy/book-series/SE0345

# Temporary Economic Crises

Shahzavar Karimzadi

Routledge
Taylor & Francis Group
LONDON AND NEW YORK

First published 2023
by Routledge
4 Park Square, Milton Park, Abingdon, Oxon OX14 4RN

and by Routledge
605 Third Avenue, New York, NY 10158

*Routledge is an imprint of the Taylor & Francis Group, an informa business*



*British Library Cataloguing-in-Publication Data*
A catalogue record for this book is available from the British Library

ISBN: 978-1-032-38697-3 (hbk)
ISBN: 978-1-032-38698-0 (pbk)
ISBN: 978-1-003-34635-7 (ebk)

DOI: 10.4324/9781003346357

Typeset in Bembo
by codeMantra

# Contents

*Acknowledgements* vii

**Introduction** 1

**1 Cyclonic ebbs and flows of trade** 11

*Introduction 11*
*From prudent to enthusiast and deranged traders 14*
*The Dutch tulip crusaders 22*
*National sovereignty and the state finance 33*
*The end of the medieval era 42*
*Equality before the guillotine 51*
*Power of appropriation and expropriation 56*
*Conclusion 64*

**2 High and low times of industrialization** 67

*Introduction 67*
*The cradle of industrialization 69*
*Banking and money economy 74*
*Great wars, revolutions, and depressions 80*
*Hyperinflation and economic depression 89*
*Empires and the Frankenstein states 97*
*The generations of wars 112*
*The pandemic of globalization 119*
*Conclusion 134*

**3 Crypto-economy and trade cycle** 138

*Introduction 138*
*The last decades of the last millennium 139*
*The new right and the old left 148*
*The 2007–2008 credit depression 154*

*Altruistic or self-serving subprime mortgage* 161
*The predatory financial products* 168
*Conclusion* 174

4 **Over-trading, trade cycles, and crises** 178
*Introduction* 178
*Parting with self-imposed blind faith* 180
*From trade to over-trading* 183
*Consolidation of three trends* 187
*No poor on nature's banquet* 194
*The original model of capitalism* 201
*From trade cycle to economic crisis* 207
*Two crises and three illusory capitalisms* 215
*Conclusion* 221

5 **Economic crises and human propensity to extremism** 224
*Introduction* 224
*The root cause of the economic crisis* 226
*Human propensity to extremism* 231
*Monotheism, the extreme end of beliefs* 238
*Atrocities – consigned to oblivion* 246
*Embedded extremism in economics* 252
*Conclusion* 256

6 **Coping with unknowns and human follies** 259
*Introduction* 259
*Digression from fatalism* 262
*Every person can acquire knowledge* 267
*Perfect and imperfect truths* 272
*Liberty and pursuit of self-interest* 279
*Economics of might is right* 289
*Fixed known and the changing unknown* 294
*Permissible and impermissible boundaries* 304
*Extremism and survival* 313
*The end, the means and adaptability* 322
*Conclusion* 334

*Bibliography* 339
*Index* 359

# Acknowledgements

I would like to express my sincere gratitude to Connor Hayes for reading Chapter 6 and for his valuable comments. My deep appreciation goes to my partner, Angela Harvey, for drawing my attention to the many shortcomings in the first draft of the book. I wish to thank Frank Currie for his constant support with my teaching. My thanks are also due to Radio Gwank for permission to use their interview with ND. Last but foremost, I am indebted to Andy Humphries from Routledge, the publisher, for his continuous help and guidance.

# Introduction

Human history is blighted by the plague of extremism: the occupying of one community by another and the enslavement of the defeated community, imprisonment, torture and killing of the heretics, complete violation of women's rights – the list of such extreme atrocities is endless. In other spheres of society, we find the rule of tyranny by kings, queens, emperors, military dictators, oligarchs, theocratic rulers, and other undemocratic rulers. Most organized human societies have fallen victim to imperial conquest and colonization one way or another. To this day many human societies are wrecked and deformed by idiotic religious wars and intolerance. In these societies, mindless obedience to unfounded religious fairy tales is the dominant order of the power structure. In this haunted reign of irrationality, there are rulers and their subjects that are easily taken in and are ready to kill and be killed for their beliefs. Our world is still dominated by all sorts of discrimination and phobias. Racial, sexual, age, and class discrimination are endemic in all repressive societies. There is a prevalence of ignorance amid a profusion of knowledge. The extent of the division of labour, employment, and specialization are stretched to the most extreme boundaries of possibilities, during which the most essential and basic knowledge, skills, ethical values, justice, freedom, equality, human relations, history, and cooperation are generally neglected and overlooked. Economists write about the economics of one country without having any basic knowledge of the colonial geopolitical construction of that country. The culture that has enslaved women is put on a par with the culture that strives for gender equality and empowerment. The economic prescriptions offered for both cultures by the hegemonic discourse are impossible to tell apart.

The impetus that sways in the realm of systematic ignorance, during boundless opportunities for learning, is the curtailment of knowledge to securing one's job. Learning, by and large, is not for the sake of acquiring knowledge and understanding but for other ends. In politics, it is not conviction that rules but career enhancement. Journalism is dominated by those who are promoting power, prestige, status, and wealth of big businesses and powerful rulers of the establishment rather than digging into secrets, corruption, and crimes of those in power to inform the public. The cost of being on

DOI: 10.4324/9781003346357-1

the side of truth can be very high for those seeking truth. There are very few learned and clever individuals who refuse to be a part of the development and construction of weapons of mass destruction, provided they are offered very attractive income packages. Sales of weapons to the most despotic and violent regimes are the norm; the environment is taken for granted. The long-term survival of humanity depends on the environment. When it comes to making easy money, the destruction of the environment is easily ignored: the dominant rule of conduct is the use of any means to achieve the cited goals. In ruling economics, humanity is not the end but a means to achieve the goals of power and wealth. Despite the progress of economics during the Age of Enlightenment, economics as a discipline has failed to progress and develop in keeping with natural sciences or even with law, politics, and ethics.

The Age of Enlightenment was a keyhole for humanity to recognize its many follies. One of its main achievements, however, was that it made humanity the ultimate source of judgement about what is right and wrong, and what is true and false. The individual and the community, both local and global, became responsible for what they are. In this respect, it was a big, but not a complete step to secede from the dark ages. Instituting humans as their own maker has been critical to human progress; it liberated human destiny as something that is predetermined. Huminites' fate is in their own hands and is written by humans. By virtue of this breakthrough, each person is the source of their knowledge and of one's moral conduct. A rational being cannot be a captive of destiny. Because of gaining a free hand in one's own freewill, science was liberated from religion, magic, and witchcraft. By means of scientific methodology, critical outlook, and analysis, science and technology were advanced. Countless scientific and technological inventions and discoveries have been made by such methods that once were unthinkable or were considered heretical as an intervention into the work of divinity. It was the age of reason that freed humanity from religion and absolute rule. In its demand for democratic secularism, it separated the state from religion and put an end to the reign of theocracy. It empowered people to represent themselves in a representative government that is elected because of the free choice of the people. As a by-product of this movement, freedom of beliefs, faiths, and conscience did not require validation by any other source, be it from either scientific or non-scientific perspectives. Everyone is the master of their own internal contemplation and inspection. Freedom of belief is the cornerstone of religious tolerance. It is not a complete panacea to religious intolerance because religion, by its very nature, is sectarian, but it is a significant antidote to the alleviating of religious extremism that has been the cause of untold bloodshed, cruelty, and destruction in history.

It was during the Enlightenment that the institution of law was released from divinity, kings, and priests: people became makers of their own laws. The rule of law was not from above but from the common people and arbitrary rules were discarded. No individual was sinful from birth. The maxim of the presumption of innocence until it is proved otherwise before a fair and public trial set aside the concept of cardinal sin. The Age of Enlightenment barred the state from the use of torture or taking a human life for any type of penal offence. It exposed the source of political tyranny and revealed that the concentration of political power in one entity (a divinity), one individual (a king or a military dictator), or one institution (a political party, i.e., the Communist party) is the source of tyranny and dictatorship. The wisdom of the age taught us that it is in the nature of the state to abuse its power if it is not under the control of law. Constitutional government was suggested to reduce the extreme abuses of state power. The excesses of state power were limited by separating the three branches of state power, namely: the legislative, the executive, and the judiciary branches. The independence of the judiciary has become the cornerstone for safeguarding liberty, fairness, and the rule of law and democracy in democratic nations.

It was the age of reason that rescued humanity from being the means in serving divinities, religions, ideologies, and rulers to become an end in itself. Each individual, for being a human, became an end that could not be exploited for any end as a means by any power or source. It was during this period that equal rights was discussed and was demanded. It was during this period that the institution of slavery was questioned and discarded, and it was also during this period that the occupation, colonization, and subjugation of other nations were rejected. It was also said that all these rights would not be materialized without freedom of thought, expression, and association. What followed, i.e., secular democratic governments, freedom, free press, rule of law, gender equality, formation of independent political parties, workers' associations and unions, human rights, equal opportunity, and religious tolerance, was a result of the interaction of all these events, movements, ideas, and outlooks. Therefore, the rational, secular, democratic, and humane upheaval that was initiated during the Age of Enlightenment had more success in the realm of scientific endeavour, the dominion of politics, and the sphere of morality compared to the world of economics. These successes are best demonstrated in secular democratic nations. Economics, as a discipline, despite its claim as the "crown of social sciences," has been left behind in its progress, effects, and outcome. Some of the success in the field of study of economics has been due to the success of natural sciences, the formation of a secular liberal democratic government, freedom of expression, and the observance of rational and humane morality.

The excesses in economics – extreme behaviour – cannot be contained entirely by the prevailing economic schools of thought: in respect to containing extremism, economics lags behind politics, law, and ethics. Extremism can only be moderated and managed relatively in an open, transparent, and accountable democratic environment that is based on the rule of law with an independent judiciary system. Economics is not an exception to this general outlook; thus, what is needed is a democratic economy to contain the excesses and extremism in economics. Economic growth can happen in any theocratic, fascist, totalitarian, and tyrannical state and colonial geopolitical structure; the ebbs and flows of the economy are not exclusive to any of these systems. Upward and downward fluctuations occur in all types of economic systems. Their economies go through phases of recovery: expansion, peak, decline, and trough; thus, economic growth that always ends in all these economic configurations in decline and contraction cannot be a criterion of success. In the majority of cases, economic growth, under such economic configurations, is at the cost of human life, freedom, happiness, well-being, and the environment. The actual and future potential of human economic activities, growth, prosperity, well-being, peace, security, and happiness under the rule of a despotic criminal state is taken to be very much alike, as in a representative secular democratic government that operates in a rational, humane, open, and accountable manner.

Economic crises are transitory developments. They belong to organized markets. All organized markets have experienced one or another form of crisis. From the Dutch tulip mania to the 1929 Great Depression to the 2007 global financial crisis, they all have been the work of organized markets. The longest and the deepest of these crises were the Great Depression that started with the wall street crash in 1929 and lasted until 1937 (Stabile 2005: 91). The second greatest economic crisis was the 2007 global credit crunch that lasted until 2009 (Knoop 2015: 313). All other economic crises have been for a shorter length of time. The Dutch tulip crisis only lasted about one year from 1636 to 1637. There has not been a permanent economic crisis. Neither has there been a global economic crisis that has destroyed all sectors of the economy in every part of the world. In organized markets, economic crises can only be limited to certain sectors of the economy and certain locals or regions but not to all locals and regions of the world. The reason for that is there can never be equal economic development in all parts of the world. The idea of global economic crises that all sectors of economy collapse at once and forever is a mere fallacy.

There is a clear dividing line between economic disorder, economic crisis, and economic decline. Economic disorder is a permanent order. The subject of permanent economic disorder has been discussed extensively in my book, *Permanent Economic Disorder* (2023). The vitality of any economy is not something that goes forever. All economies eventually slow down and decline. This is a long-term process provided that the economy is not destroyed by external forces such as natural disasters or forceful occupation and war. In contrast to economic disorders and declines, economic crises are transitory events. Each economic crisis, irrespective of its form, cannot breakdown abruptly and systematically all sectors of the economy and all economic activities permanently at the rate beyond which there will be no turning point. In the worst case scenario, human survival depends on food, shelter, and protection. Most of human occupations revolve around such activities. Furthermore, economic crisis is not tantamount to total loss of habitat (land), technology, institutions, infrastructures, and social, legal, political, cultural, and moral structures. The niches of rebounding and revival are embedded in all these human endeavours. If economic crises were permanent and worldwide, seeping into every sector of economy simultaneously, such circumstances would trigger the extinction of the human species. This scenario does not leave any viable natural range for human preservation. Economic crises do not obliterate the things that are vital for human life even for a short period. They do not drive human beings to extinction.

Economic crises are serious local and regional economic disruptions but they are not comparable to catastrophes such as deadly pandemic diseases, ice ages, volcanic eruptions, and the consequences of asteroid collisions. Moreover, the worst economic meltdown does not terminate the entire economy. It is not like the permanent exposure of human body to all sorts of deadly radiation and toxicity. In short, economic crises do not destroy all parts of the economy once and for all. For this reason, there is scope for repairing many damaged parts of the economy even during the deepest point of economic depression. The three prescriptions proposed by economists, hitherto, to diagnose economic disorders and crises are about the recognition of different symptoms and different failures in different presupposed variations of economic structures. Those in line with classical economics see a body of the economy with the possibility of over-production in certain sectors, which are self-healing. Those under Keynes's influence see a body of the economy that is dominated by organized markets that can collapse and need a helping hand to recover. Those affiliated to Marxian thought see a diseased body in which its organs one by one, because of irrevocable logic of history, stop working until there is total failure of all its organs.

In the prevailing theories of economic crises, crises are disconnected from the subject who is at the helm of the act. Economic agents (people) do and act. They are the doers and the actors. Economic crises are manifestation of human actions. Such activities are in-built constituent part of the actual doers and the actors. It is the doer and the actor who goes astray and the rest will follow. But often the finger is pointed at the capitalist economy, financial markets, institutions, instruments, governments, regulations, trade unions, management, ideology, economic doctrines, greed, inequality, interest rates, external factors and circumstances, and others as the real offenders. There can be no doubt that all these factors play a role in the gestation and delivery of crises but the subject behind all such actions is humankind. Granted that the diagnoses are made according to the given economic causes cited above, the treatment prescribed cannot be compatible with the misidentified form of economic defects. As the economic malfunctions and policies are in conflict, the objective of preventing and curing economic crises cannot be achieved.

Each economic crisis is a cocktail of events and a compound repository for a number of inextricable elements. The elements that are bounded up with each economic crisis are as follows: (a) all economic crises fall under the realm of contingent truths. A contingent truth could be false, a truth that has the possibility in itself that it could not have happened at the time and place that it did. There is no contradiction in saying that Charles Darwin's voyage on the Beagle, instead of 1832–36, was at another time and place. Against this truth, we have the necessary truth that can be no other than as it is. It is possible for an economic crisis not to become a fact at the time and in the place as it does. But a triangle can be no other but a triangle. A triangle must and will always have three angles. An economic crisis is not also an analytical truth. The truth of crisis does not derive from the arrangements and the virtue of the meaning of the terms in its definition but it occurs within certain historical, social, psychological, and economic conditions. (b) There is no uniformity in economic crises. The envelope of history contains the past, the present, and the future. What is observed and recorded in the past and at the present will never be a perfect refection of the bygone history. Besides, the future is always unobserved and unrecorded. If there were a perfect uniformity of events in a perfect linear circular motion then unobserved and unrecorded future would fit perfectly well with the past. Since there is no regularity in the inner parts of history from its past to the present and the future, predicting the unobserved from the observed is tantamount to projecting the past into the future and expecting the future and the past to match exactly, piece by piece in stages. But the course of history does not follow a uniform path. Hume raised serious doubt as to the form of reasoning that relies for its validity on constant conjunctions, a doubt that came to be known as the problem of induction.

Hume's objection to inductive reasoning has two dimensions. First, he contends that extending observed to unobserved and subsequently forming a general law that is applicable to all possible worlds is rationally unfounded. In other words, inductive reasoning cannot be corroborated by deductive reasoning. Second, we cannot prove the connection of cause and effect directly. The repeated concurrence of two events is not necessarily connected in a cause-and-effect relationship. This connection is not provable. (c) Economic crises occur at the time of extreme economic and social instability and uncertainty. In times of extremisms, such as during the wars and revolutions, rationalism and judicious judgements will become less attractive to a great number of people. This is the time that the imposters, charlatans, demagogues, and zealots gain ascendency over the reasonable, informed, well-rounded, and clear-sighted people. It is the time that covert deception will also become permissible. For example, the authorities in charge and their ideologues, and the captains of the markets do not tell the whole truth about the economy. Such actions are sanctioned by tacit agreement and unspoken legal and moral norms. For instance, if such individuals say that this or that market, economy, or stock market is on the verge of collapse, their acknowledgement of the fact will precipitate the collapse of that market. (d) Last but not the least, with financial crises, when most economic agents are convinced of the collapse of a market, the collapse will become a reality. Consider the case of the share price of one company. Whenever most economic agents are convinced that the share prices of this company will fall, this will happen. The outcome has got nothing to do with reality and viability of such a company or market. Nevertheless, this is what we can see in organized markets.

This book consists of six chapters. Chapters 1–4 are bonded together under one common theme. These chapters are devoted to the subject of trade. The common precursor of all theories of economic disorder and crisis, in essence, is trade. Strictly speaking, it is about either the fact that there is too much trade or too little trade in different stages of economic development. For purposes of clarity, the sort, scope, and scale of trade in the mercantilist period were different from trade during the Industrial Revolution and from modern contemporary trade. The requirements, implications, institutions, organizations, and the legal and technological framework of trade in these periods are not the same. In these four chapters, we shall decipher the evolving relationship between changes in the conditions of trade and the mutation of the concept of the trade cycle from trade disorder to the business cycle and, in time, into economic crisis.

Chapter 1, "Cyclonic ebbs and flows of trade," seeks to discover the genesis of trade disorder; the disorder is present at the very moment trade was first initiated. It is the trade's birth defect. Needless to say, in nothing, there is no trade; equally, out of abundance, people do not trade. The act of trade entails that there is a shortage of two goods or services. When goods and services are scarce, people do trade. In order to get what they need, they exchange something that is relatively less needed for each counterparty on either side of the exchange. Thus, scarcity is the most fundamental and root cause of trade disorder; Hesiod, the ancient Greek economist, has pointed to this fact. In addition, there have always been numerous natural, social, institutional, cultural, technological, practical, and religious obstructions to trade.

For about two millennia, the teaching of Aristotle and the clergy dominated trade activities. Obtaining wealth was divided into natural and unnatural ways; this was a major barrier to the growth of trade. Many biblical canons also disapprove of the acquisition of wealth since it distances individuals from their chief service, which is to serve God. Money, the language of communicating trade, was graded as the gravest mortal sin – the root of all evils. Hindrances of these sorts against trade were too many for so long, which are indicative of long-lasting trade disorders. The ancient Egyptians were well aware of trade fluctuations. They symbolized bad years and good years with seven lean cows followed by seven fat ones. The good years represented good harvests and the bad years, poor harvests and crop failures. That is to say that in prosperous years, trade revived and proliferated, and during bad, lean cows, trade dwindled and stagnated. This chapter is centred upon the social, institutional, customary, and natural restrictions that can cause trade turmoil. We take the seventeenth century as the crossroads – the defining juncture for trade to break away from many of the old restrictions – and the rise of different challenges to the trade cycles.

Chapter 2, "High and low times of industrialization," concentrates on the Industrial Revolution. This chapter sets out the broad social, economic, technological, institutional, and cultural changes that have profoundly transformed humans' way of life as a consequence of this grand upheaval. The Industrial Revolution, in its early stages, brought great progress but also great poverty. It increased the gap between rich and poor and the relative inequality between the working class and the wealthy classes. It established an industrial order with rapid industrial production, causing a sharp division of labour and employment. During this period, masses of people left their traditional jobs and way of life, and migrated to towns and cities, leading to concentration and urbanization of the population. The dispossessed population gathered in factories and were transformed into factory workers who were progressively de-skilled by being assigned to and specialized in one simple task. The modern factory system dismembered the elements of production to a sequence of simple tasks and specialized labour in performing one task, hence leading to an enormous increase in the productivity of machines and labour.

The Industrial Revolution created the industrial working class. It initiated mass production and mass consumption and was the cause of the greatest expansion in international trade until that period. Family self-sufficiency was destroyed at the fastest rate in human history up to that point, and more and more people became dependent upon the works and products of other people. British imperial growth, hegemony, and pre-eminence were on the back of becoming "the workshop of the world." Side by side with the unrivalled rapid economic growth, a very complex credit system, financial markets, institutions, instruments, and forms of money emerged and developed. With all such drastic transformations, the forms of economic disorder and crises have also altered. In this chapter, we shall see an account of how this momentous landmark in human history impacted upon the trade fluctuations and the interpretations that were offered for the industrial production cycles.

All things considered, the modern developed economies are not what the economy of England was during the Industrial Revolution, nor has the process of industrialization been the same for all other developed economies. Modern developed and democratic nations have very little in common with the economy of England back then. The whole constellation of economic, social, political, legal, cultural, and technological institutions is profoundly different. Changes and transformations, as deep as they are, are mutually dependent and reinforcing. The Industrial Revolution had more in common with the medieval economy than the economy that is dominated by internet technology. Given this reality, the forms of economic crisis are not going to be the same as they were in the developed commercial economies of the seventeenth century or the industrialized economies of the nineteenth century. The subject of our analysis in Chapter 3, "Crypto-economy and trade cycle," is to assess such transformations and the forms of trade cycles that emerge from new changes in these economies. The World Wide Web (WWW) has been the most profound technological invention of the late twentieth century; in a very short time, it has created a global village. It has connected different parts of the world and reduced time and space in just one click. The WWW has created the global market, producers and consumers, a global library, university, credit system, institutions and forms of money, and global social and cultural interactions. Above all, it has created unlimited functionality and possibilities; thus, this chapter deals with the crypto-economy. It studies the ebb and flow of the emerging electronic economy. It will dig into the rise of the global e-credit system, and the wax and wane of this emerging market. This chapter will evaluate the 2007–2008 global credit crunch in the light of the rise of the e-credit system, the digital form of money, and the crypto-economy.

Chapter 4, "Over-trading, trade cycles, and crises," traces the evolutionary process of transformation of the idea of over-trading into business cycles, and business cycles into economic crises. Humans, from the very beginning, were confronted with natural calamities – drought, famine, floods, earthquakes, volcanic eruptions, tsunamis, typhoons, pestilence, and wild and deadly animals. They were engaged in communal rivalries and wars. They were experiencing the good times and the bad – the prosperous years, when it was good for agriculture, hunting, fishing, and gathering fruits, and the bad years of drought, war, and displacement; the times that were too hot and the times that were too cold, too rainy or no rain at all. Therefore, long before the age of systematic thinking and the construction of ideas to make sense of the world, masses were cognizant about the bad times and the times of hardship caused by natural disasters, war, social and political unrest, and cultural, institutional, legal, and technological inadequacies. The times of trouble and the times of peace, security, and prosperity cannot be disregarded easily: humans are thinkers, dreamers, inventors, makers, and discoverers. Humans can invent things that are real and things that are imaginary, and fight for and over the two. We can dream, fantasize, and envisage the best and the worst of all possible worlds. We can live in false hopes and myths. Humans can invent language and use it for their progress, and they can invent a belief and kill their fellow humans who entertain a different faith or conviction. They can invent a gun to conquer and use the same gun to defend their territory. The point is that on the same grounds, economists from the early novice commentators to the modern experts are not oblivious to what may be described as "normal" and "abnormal" times.

Fluctuations in the means of existence are very real. The force of circumstances is unbeatable; the early economists were not dismissive of this fact. They referred to it as the presence of "sterile" activity – an unusual level of poverty, damaging regulations and policies, productive and unproductive labour, a usury credit system, inflationary spirals, debasing coins, over- and under-extension of credit, and inconvertibility forms of money – the list goes on and on. Furthermore, they were not heedless of the disproportionality of production of different goods, and occasional speculative mania, as well as the temporary lack of effective demand. These ebbs and flows of trade are described as over- and under-trading. The tulip mania, John Law's monetary experiments, and the Mississippi speculation were defined within the context of the over-trading scenario, but such trade disruptions were said to be consistent with the laissez-faire system, and irregularities resolve themselves automatically. As modern industrialized economies developed further, production, distribution, division of employment, credit markets, institutions, and instruments became more complex. Theories of over- and under-trading were unable to convince later generations of economists as to the accurate description of economic fluctuations. Theories of trade cycles – business cycles – are the extension of ideas of initial under- and over-trading. The 1929 Wall Street crash was a historical turning point in the evolution of the trade cycle into an economic crisis. All theories of economic crisis ever since are anchored to the concept of capitalism. In this chapter, we shall critically examine this process of transition from over- and under-trading to trade cycles, and then into an economic crisis that is primarily based on the pre-supposition of capitalism.

The last two chapters, 5 and 6, focus on two central questions about economic crises. Chapter 5 provides a competing explanation compared to the ones proposed hitherto. In line with a different interpretation of the economic crisis, Chapter 6 presents an alternative adjusting mechanism and adaptive strategy of coping with the economic crisis. Chapter 5, "Economic crises and human propensity to extremism," puts forward a different account of the main causes of economic crisis. It outlines what is unique about humans: humans are the most complex living species on the earth. Organized economic activities are one feature of this distinguishing trait of human beings. Humans are neither the captives of their instincts nor entirely the hostages of the events. They can imagine, think, reason, plan, and act. These capabilities can go either way: human intelligence is a double-edged weapon. It can be put hard at work for advancing truth or untruth; it can be preoccupied with right or wrong. A person can choose to use their intelligence either way. Above all, this double-edged sword can be scaled up into extremism. This chapter unravels the question of the human propensity to extremism. It is said that propensity to extremism is a common trait of human behaviour. Economics is a human affair that is vital to human existence. As economic activities are human activities, economic crises are another form of expression of the human propensity to extremism in economic affairs.

Chapter 6, "Coping with unknowns and human follies," is the concluding chapter. This chapter recapitulates and sums up all the arguments that have been developed in the preceding chapters. It will be argued that there is no universal remedy and everlasting cure for economic disorders and crises. Economic crises are part and parcel of natural circumstances and human dispositions. Such behaviours are the reflections and the articulation of human propensity to extremism and the means that they construct to achieve their set ends at a given time. The more effective policy for the best outcomes of coping with unknowns and human follies, and adapting to the rapidly changing conditions, is moving hand in hand with advances in other fields of human endeavours, such as advances in science, technology, politics, law, ethics, culture, and institutions. The best and most feasible outcome to deal with such contingencies is freedom. It is with freedom that humans put to use their rational factuality most effectively. This is how the actual potential of each individual can be utilized more fully, and the economy will also be democratized, and the excesses of economic activities can more effectively be alleviated and moderated.

# 1 Cyclonic ebbs and flows of trade

## Introduction

Economic problems have a long history. A history that goes back to the ascent of humanity. For a very long time, in highly ordered and hierarchical social relations of production, many elements of the economy were among the biggest taboos. Homer viewed trade "as a secondary, and inferior, way of acquiring wealth" (Backhouse 2002: 11). One of the most widely accepted economic principles today is the principle of scarcity. It is considered to be the most fundamental and the root cause of all economic problems. The most refined account of it is crystallized in Lionel Robbins's (1898–1984) definition of economics. Robbins defines economics as "the science which studies human behaviour as a relationship between ends and scarce means which have alternative uses" (Robbins 1952: 16). Perhaps, he articulated the problem most elegantly, but he was not the first who revealed the secret of scarcity. Hesiod (750–650 BC), known as the first economist, has referred to this problem in the eighth century BC (Rothbard 2006: 8). Hesiod noted: "the gods keep men's food concealed: otherwise, you would easily work even in a day enough to provide you for the whole year without working" (Hesiod 1988: 38).

The description of ancient writers about economic problems is usually tainted with mysticism and oriental rituals but that does not erase their lead at the contest. The economic reforms that Solon introduced in Athens, in the sixth century BC, particularly on property law and currency reforms, were because of the urgency of the economic problems of the time (Backhouse 2002: 14). Xenophon pointed out that a person cannot be skilled and efficient in every employment. He contrasted the division of labour and specialization in towns and villages and linked greater productivity in towns to the division and specialization of employment. Xenophon, including the other two Socratic philosophers, Plato and Aristotle, did not think of their contemporary social and economic organizations as the only cradle for a good life and economy. In their worldview better existence was possible in a better society. The custodian of a good life was rationalism. Professing that one could organize an efficient society and economy according to rational principles. Asserting

DOI: 10.4324/9781003346357-2

that a good life is a life which we can live rationally. With this in mind, they declared that their vision and outline of their ideal society is subject to a number of prerequisites. A good life is feasible in a city-state where the acquisition of wealth is conducted through natural means, where goods that cannot be produced at home are imported, and where there is an ideal state in charge. Plato drew the outline of the ideal state in his *Republic*, whereas, in his extensive collected writings, Aristotle set out his vision of the constitution of natural economy and natural ways of obtaining wealth.

The biblical economics shared many of the ancient Greek economic doctrines. Land in biblical teaching does not belong to people. Our presence on earth is only temporary. Acquisition of wealth was condemned as it directed the attention of individuals away from god. Serving God and acquiring more wealth stood opposite to each other. Partial devotion to god was a sin. In addition, the Old Testament set side by side acquisition of wealth with dishonesty and exploitation of the weak and poor. The prophet Amos proclaimed that the wealth seekers "grind the destitute and plunder the humble" (Amos 8: 4–6). Many ancient thinkers and moralists also rejected the act of charging interest on loans. This was the time when the loans were predominately for consumption purposes. The debtors who defaulted in the payment of a loan and the interest were reduced to slavery. In view of this fact, their objection to the practice of lending is hardly surprising. This view dominated economic thinking for several millenniums. Aristotle articulated a flawed but widely influential and long-lasting argument against lending money at interest. His argument dominated the theory of credit for over two millenniums.

The Old Testament forbade charging interest on loans to the Jews. The New Testament went a step backwards. Under no circumstance lending money at interest in the New Testament is allowed. Koran has adopted the latter approach. The pursuit of money here in a religious context is seen as the cause of misery. Money is said to be the "root of all evil." We find many references to economic problems in all major ancient texts. The code of Hammurabi is one of them. The sixth Babylonian king, Hammurabi (1792–50 BC), in 1754 BC issued a decree containing 282 case laws. Among these laws, there were economic provisions about slavery, debt, trade, tariffs, and prices. Along the same line, the economy was central to the rise and fall of the Roman Empire. In the third century the population of the empire:

> fell by a third, partly due to the plague that was brought in by eastern invaders. The supply of gold fell, possibly because there were no longer new imperial conquests … given that the Empire was held together only by the army and that there were many people in the cities who needed to be pacified with the distribution of food, taxation rose … Some of the money needed was raised by debasing the coinage. In the time of Augustus coins were pure silver, but by 250 AD the silver content had fallen to 40 percent, and by 270 to 4 percent.
>
> (Backhouse 2002: 30)

Leaving natural scarcity of resources and natural disasters aside, economic crises commence from the time when for the first time one group of people (a tribe) forcefully occupied the land and enslaved and subjugated people of another group or tribe. In its mature form, this came about when one nation occupied another nation and exploited the Native persons and looted their resources. The formation of and continuation of empires are a perfect specimen of the manifestation of economic crises. Colonialism is the other side of imperialism. There are two sides to each empire's growth and prosperity. One is from the eye of the victor. The economic growth, which is due to their territorial expansion and exploitation of their colonies, is seen as the confirmation of the legitimacy of their empire. In this calculation exploitation, marginalization and destruction of the subjugated nations are rarely deliberated. Above all, the potential opportunities that are lost from being conquered and enslaved are never mentioned.

Throughout human history the faiths that have a claim to universal authority have kept their close alliance with emperors or became the heads of empires. The most malevolent empires have been the ones that are armed with the power of universal divinity. In an imperial theocracy, there is no limit in divine sovereignty and its right to vengeful conquests. Within the realm of theocracy, the economy is a subordinate of the religion. No economy under such conditions can utilize its full potential. Most specifically the colonized people, those working and particularly women, will bear the brunt of the excesses under the command of theocratic empires. At a time when half of the population, women, are excluded from economic activity or prevented from utilizing their full potential, talk of slight and brief economic growth would lose its meaning. The exclusion of half of the population from social and economic activity is nothing but a deep economic crisis. When an economy is regulated by irrational policies, customs, and outdated behaviour and habits, we cannot speak of a good and efficient economy. In this type of administration of economy, most people cannot fulfil their full potential. An economy where economic organizations, institutions, technology, legal framework, distribution of income, and social relations are kept grossly underdeveloped, this economy would be in a deep and ongoing crisis. In an economy where efficient management of resources and factors of production is absent, where there is no security, no protection, and no rule of law, this economy is in crisis. Suffice to say that economies underperform when they lack a democratic economic system and a democratic political system.

This and the next two chapters will address the concept of economic crisis in general. The focus of the study in these chapters is on the main events that have transformed modern economies and major crises since the seventeenth century. The aims in this chapter are fourfold: first, it is to investigate the root cause and development of different economic crises in the seventeenth and eighteenth centuries; second, to explain each event and crisis in the context of its specific location and its historical context; third, to explore what constitutes the essence of each crisis; fourth, to provide a synopsis of the impacts of each crisis. The chapter is divided into six sections. The first section briefly explores the ascent of mass trade and money economy. This covers the epoch that laid the foundations of the modern economic era. The second section peruses into the case of the Dutch tulip hysteria. We take this episode as a starting event for excessive trade in the early modern commercial economic system. The third section is on the formation of the first sovereign national state in its modern sense, the state finance, and early modern national debt. The fourth section is a diversion from our main theme. It traces the pathway of the end of the medieval era that laid the groundwork for the formation of exclusive crises that are specific to modern developed economies. The fifth section is on French revolutions and their impacts on modern economies, state finance, and monetary disorders and crises. The sixth section surveys the discrete power of the old undemocratic state and modern democratic states in the appropriation of private and public assets and the implications of abuse of this legal entitlement on the economy.

## From prudent to enthusiast and deranged traders

Trade emanates from the exchange of surplus products and out of necessity. The term "crisis" has an affinity with word trade. Crisis refers to "a crossroad: it is the point where things could go either of two different ways" (Graeber 2012: 177). Trade is a crossroads. It is the exchange of two commodities or a commodity with a medium of exchange. In ancient times and for most of the medieval times traders and workers held a low social status. Agriculture, however, "escaped the contempt and the censure of Greek and Roman writers" (Gray 1957: 14).

The discovery of agriculture and farming altered the course of human history. Domestication of crops and animals resulted in permanent human settlements, i.e., the formation of villages, towns, and cities. The stationary settlements were a turning point in enabling larger communities to preserve and store food for emergencies and longer times. Little wonder that land in the ancient time was designated as sacred. In Ancient Egypt, farming was a holy activity and land was at the centre of this sacred activity (Hughes 1992: 12). In ancient India, cattle were raised to the status of a deity. We find the same level of glorification of land in other ancient cultures. In China, the God of land and the God of cereals were venerated equally (Zhuo 2018: 36). Animal husbandry was the measure of power and wealth in Ancient Greece and in Rome farmers were among the most admired social groups (de Herrera 2006: 27).

Agriculture has kept its relative importance to the present day. But the same cannot be said about trade. The position of trade has ebbed and flowed with political ideologies "in tandem with the technological innovations of land and sea transport" (Bernstein 2009: 8). Trade, in effect, is a unity of opposites. It enhances economic activity, growth, and prosperity but at the same time it increases the level of individual dependency and vulnerability to others. If we were to choose one historic date for modern world trade, that would be Christopher Columbus's second voyage to the new world in 1493. This event was synchronous with both extreme plenty and scarcity. At once the colonization of the new world brought plenty for Europe, especially for the Spanish, Portuguese, and other European imperial powers down the line. Concurrent with that incident the native population of the conquered world was deprived of everything they had including the right to live. Those who were saved from the butchery of conquistadors "died like fish in a bucket" from the new diseases introduced by the colonists (Crosby Jr 2003: 21).

The hallmark of all empires is floating between two extremes of decadence and deprivation. Gaius Plinius Secundus (23–79 AD), known as Pliny, attributed the fall of the Roman Empire to its decadence. Side by side with usurping the gold and silver of its colonies, Rome extended its conquests, conspicuous waste, and opulence parades. Hand in hand with the enlargement of the empire went the level of its conspicuous waste. Pliny noted that Emperor Nero burnt more perfume in a day than the amount produced in a year in Arabia (Pliny 1968: 83).

Not long after colonization of the new world several trading syndicates were set up in the captured territories. In 1505 monopoly trading syndicates were charted in England. These companies were granted the right to ship wool to Sicily, Tripoli, Cypress, and other places. On the way back they brought spices, silks, and carpets. The Muscovy was charted in 1555. This was followed by the formation of the Eastland Company in 1579 and the Levant in 1581. The economic structure of nations that were more open to new experiments in Europe altered after the colonization of the new world. The treasures of the new world placed Europe into a higher orbit of economic conversion compared to Asia. The influx of precious metals "rapidly revolutionized the trade, commerce, and the finance of Europe" (Gray 1957: 66 and 71). The ample overflow of most marketable mediums of exchange transformed the economy of these quarters into a money-dependent economy. Subsequently, the bountiful supply and standardization of money into more convenient forms greatly facilitated all sorts of transactions including payments of taxes, international trade, and the accumulation of wealth.

Business cycles are none other than the property of trade in a money economy. Often, the trade cycle, the economic cycle, and the business cycle are used synonymously. The fact is they are not one and the same. These economic behaviours and events do neither convey the same meaning nor share a common historical beginning. From the ascent of humans to the present day, humanity has always intermittently encountered economic cycles. Economic cycles can also be triggered by natural processes that are beyond human control. The ascent of humans and the ascent of trade can be traced back to two different periods in history. Humans preceded trade by thousands of years. The development of the human species, Homo sapiens, is dated to over 300,000 years ago. About 15,000 years ago our ancestors began to domesticate wild animals. The hunters and gatherers in central Asia first domesticated dogs. A few thousand years later, about 9,500 BC in the Neolithic period, they started agriculture and domesticated other animals such as goats and other cattle. Therefore, any sense of trade if it existed must have started in a very primitive way after the domestication of animals and the invention of agriculture and farming. However, these developments in themselves were not sufficient for trade to take place. Trade in the true sense of the word requires a relatively developed division of labour that can create surplus products and the establishment of the institution of private property to give somewhat legal backing of ownership of surplus products to be traded against each other.

Therefore, the history of economic cycles goes back to the ascent of humans. The hunters and gatherers were exposed and completely dependent on the natural environment in which they were surrounded. They were at the mercy of their tribe and the very rudimentary tools for hunting and gathering food. For these groups, economic cycles were too frequent. Any extreme change in weather, from extreme heat or cold, to disease and loss of territory could have devastated the entire community. Fleeting rises or falls of the population within such communities in times gone by rest on the overwhelming erratic power of nature over wide open and helpless people. Economic cycles and human history run in parallel timelines. However, trade cycles have a fairly short history. The trade cycle is tied up with trade but not with any size of the trade. For the trade cycles to be consequential and have any tangible impact, first there must be a sizable population with a considerable division of employment and specialization and most members of the population should be dependent on goods and services that are supplied by others.

We cannot home in on the date in which the first trade had taken place; however, we can explain the necessary conditions under which trade between traders can take place. The three necessary and sufficient preconditions for trade to take place are given as follows: first, sufficient division of labour and employment that specializes in different individuals to carry on different tasks to such a level that will result in the production of surplus products. The second precondition is the establishment of the institution of private property ownership. The third precondition is the willingness to exchange one's surplus products with someone who has the product that the counterparty wants and is ready to exchange their product with the counterparty's product. If we assume the origin of trade to be concurrent with the domestication of animals and the establishment of agriculture, then trade cycles were in the beginning at mercy of natural forces. Over time as the human population increased, the institutions of private property spread extensively, there was more division of labour, and the state and religion held sway over the society. Thus, the state, religion, and technical progress were added to factors that instigated trade cycles. All the more so were the state and religious wars and conquests. These malpractices uprooted communities, plundered their resources, and caused forced mass migration. Those whose rights were breached, if indeed they survive, had to start a new life and economy all over again. Thus, the history of trade cycles goes back to the time soon after the exchange of surplus products turned into a defining factor in the daily life of different communities scattered in different parts of the world. The ancient scriptures referred to the cycles of famine and plenty. In the Old Testament, it is labelled as the fat years and the lean years. In Genesis, it recounts the Pharaoh's dream in which the Pharaoh witnesses seven fat cows and seven emaciated cows coming out of the river Nile. Then the skinny cows eat up the fat cows. Joseph interpreted the Pharaoh's dream as seven years of prosperity followed by seven years of scarcity and misery (Chorafas 2015: 1).

Every populated, organized, and complex society has experienced and will experience economic fluctuations. We do not have any written records of most of such fluctuations. What has been left from ancient times and even the Middle Ages is sparse and inaccurate anecdotal chronicles. There are three main reasons for this. Human societies predominantly relied, for most of their history, mainly on the production for self-consumption than for exchange. Second, during this long period of economic and trade fluctuations, it was dominated by natural disasters and wars. The third reason has been the supremacy of religion in the ancient and medieval worlds. After an entire population succumbed completely to divinity, this inevitably leads to debilitation. Free will and action have no place under the sovereignty of the super being. It is the super being then who determines the course of events, who fixes the natural order, and who decides the destiny of everyone else. It is the belief that whatever happens is inevitable, as decreed in providence, that prevents people from observing, examining, and understanding the events surrounding them objectively. It precluded them to see and act otherwise than what the priests and the rulers dictated as the divine wish and plan. Those who put a foot outside this fatalistic worldview and used a bit of their free will and intelligence were branded heretics and were punished severely. In view of this any attempt to describe economic and trade cycles and to highlight the years of scarcity, famine, poverty, and misery as being caused by wars or the wrong policies of rulers was tantamount to heresy and against divine law and order.

There are numerous indications of business cycles in the early settled and populous human societies. Hammurabi's legal system is a case in point. In about 1800 BC Hammurabi ordered the first royal mandate on credit, in the first recorded legal codes, in Babylon. Many of these legal codes were laid down to regulate credit and prices. The edict put a cap on the maximum interest rate that moneylenders could charge on lending money. The edict set ceilings on the interest rates charged on the two most marketable forms of money, grain and silver. The caps were enforced, and the breach of the writ resulted in severe punishments. During the decline and the fall of the Babylon Empire, in the fifth century BC, the minimum interest on silver loans was about 40 per cent. In India, the Laws of Manu around 2400 BC set the maximum interest that lenders could charge. This was about 24 per cent. These events occurred in the Bronze Age (2400–1200 BC). A period of major changes that marked the rise and fall of the Aegean Sea golden age. In this period the population of the Aegean Sea increased, and its economy flourished. It was during this time that the Lydians invented coins as a new form of money.

Among the earliest recorded economic crises, we have Athens's credit crisis in 594 BC. It was this crisis that brought Solon (630–560 BC) into power. Solon was a poet, and it is said that his credit reforms saved the Greek Empire from collapse. At the time he assumed leadership, farmers were tied up with crippling and exorbitant debts. Farmers were starved but defiant. The repercussions of this high debt were the loss of personal freedom and security. In almost all societies at that time, debt bondage was a normal practice. The creditors enslaved the debtors if the debtors were unable to pay their debts on time. The moneylenders could not just enslave the debtors, but they could also abduct members of their families and sell them in overseas markets. The Solon's edict did not lift the interest rate caps but it banned personal slavery, cancelled many debts, and freed those enslaved for debt. His credit reforms also tackled inflation that was out of control and restored the value of drachma by depreciating its value by 25 per cent.

Xenophon of Athens (died in 354 BC) was probably the first ancient Greek philosopher and historian who spoke of business cycles. The type of cycle that he referred to is the one that is triggered by war. In his last work, *Ways and Means* (354 BC), written shortly after the Peloponnesian War, Xenophon writes about the post-war financial difficulties in Athens. His remedy is Keynesian as he called for the city's authorities to boost investment, in housing and in the foreign sectors. The Roman senator and historian, Publius Cornelius Tacitus (died in 117 AD), talked about another form of the cycle that is set off by mounting sovereign debts. The economic downturn, he argued, is the result of excessive and unsustainable Empire's borrowings. He cited the law of Twelve Tables in the fourth century BC to support his claim. This law was ratified in 450 BC and granted legal protection to lower classes by setting a ceiling for the payment of interest. Tacitus also referred to the 33 AD debt crisis during the reign of Tiberius.

The invention and use of different forms of money disseminate apace with the growth of population, division of employment, the proliferation of production of surplus products, and the dispersion of private property ownership. The precept that "money is the root of all evil" was a readdressed response of the victims of extortionate interest rates against the ill use of money by moneylenders. The edict is false. Not to mention that it is not illuminating. Nonetheless, it has historical significance. It stands at the centre of the development of the theory of money, interest, and financial crisis. Many lines of economic crises lead up to it. The general feeling of the time, when borrowing at usurious rates for consumption was high, was that it played its part in the popularization of such sophisticated idioms. All forms of money can be misused. Each form is the product of its age. Money consolidates all kinds of power. The consolidation of power goes side by side with corruption, violence, and exploitation. Money can buy any horror and repulsive acts. The monetary crisis is born with forms of money. Each form of money is open to misuse. There has not been a form of money in the history of money that has not been misused either by private individuals or by the state. Such cases are not rare either. Below we will provide some historical examples to show the symbiotic relationships between money and monetary crises.

China is a good case study for the evolution of different forms of money and monetary disorders. It has been a relatively highly populated part of the world with a very structured and hierarchical society. Consecutive ruthless states have ruled for several millennia. One generally accepted medium of exchange in the fourteenth century BC was cowry shells. In 1375 BC P'an Kang, a king from the Shang dynasty, "rebuked his Ministers for their greed in hoarding cowries and gems" (Einzig 1951: 254). The monetary disorders thrived to such a high rate in ancient China that during the Zhou dynasty, King Tcheng ordered his officials to issue a monetary decree to regulate the use of different forms of money. As a result of which copper rings became legal currency. On many occasions, Chinese authorities in ancient China issued different types of coins or demonetized the types of coins in circulation because of counterfeiting and large circulation of counterfeited forms of money overshadowing full-bodied forms of money. Wuzhu five grain coin was issued in 118 BC in the Han dynasty to replace banking coins (Williams 1997: 136). It was not long after that the Wuzhu lost most of its value through counterfeiting. In 48 BC Wuzhu was demonetized and people turned to commodity money with full intrinsic value such as silk and grain (Einzig 1951: 256). Gong Yu, a Chinese moral thinker, also saw the root of all evil in money. In about 45 BC, he commented that "the rich hoard housefuls of coins, and yet are never satisfied ... The merchants seek profit ... That is why evil cannot be banned. It arises entirely from money" (quoted from Williams 1997: 155). As soon as silk and grain became legal tenders, the fraudsters began to experiment with new methods of deception, i.e., enhanced the weight of grain by soaking it and stretching the length of silk by spinning it thinly (Williams 1997: 156).

Chinese were the first to invent and use paper money. Paper money like most of the other forms of money was invented out of the needs of trade. It was invented amid a monetary crisis. As the existing forms of money cannot overcome the surmounting requirements of the ever-increasing scale and volume of trade, new forms of money are invented. Necessity is two parents in one body. It is the mother of invention and the father of destruction. The first paper forms of money were issued under the reign of Hien-Tsung (806–21) in the ninth century. It was called "flying money." This form of money was redeemable by metallic money (Ederer 1964: 92). The Song dynasty (960–1279) stretched the frontiers of trade to different parts of China. The invention of paper money was a primary requirement for this expansion but it also greatly aided the growth of trade networks. Chinese rulers found a loophole in the issuance of paper money to exploit. That was the issue of fiat money. A form of money that was not backed by precious metals. Taking advantage of the loophole started with a fractional issuance of fiat currency during the Chengtsung rule (997–1022). As this form of paper money had no intrinsic value and its value was less certain, it was designated as "changelings" form of money (Ederer 1964: 92). The emission of unbacked paper money escalated to fund the wars as Chinese rulers resorted to issuing large sums of paper money to pay for the war machine and upkeep of their administration.

The Jin dynasty in 1189 issued the first form of fiat money (Williams 1997: 149). This effort was unsuccessful. The fiat money lost its value quickly. Minting the silver coins to restore the value of the currency did not only improve the situation but it caused a high rate of inflation (Mote 1999: 284). The Mongols invaded China in 1206 and ruled all of China from 1279 to 1368. They too adopted a paper form of money. The Mongol dynasty issued paper money first in 1260. By making the use of gold, silver, and copper forms of money illegal, they forced the public to use paper money. It was at this time that Marco Polo (1254–1324) went to China. He visited China during the reign of Kublai Khan (1215–94) and stayed there from 1275 to 1295. Among the strange things that he observed in China and reported on when he returned to Venice was the use of paper money in China. In his book, he noted that the paper money was signed by officials and stamped by the emperor. He went to say that "the way it is wrought is such that you might say he hath the secret of alchemy in perfection" (Polo 1874: 409).

The Mongol colonists were iron-fisted rulers. They were very strict about their rules including their laws about the use of paper money. But as soon as other sources of raising money to finance their lavish expenditures and war adventures drained, they resorted to issuing more paper notes. A Chinese historian, Man-Twan-Lin, described personally experiencing a period of the issue of a large number of inconvertible notes and hence a drastic drop in the purchasing power of money in China (Groseclose 1961: 118). The Ming dynasty (1368–1644) replaced the Yuan dynasty in 1368. They also tried to adopt the paper money. Their best form was known as the "precious note of the Great Ming." These notes could not be exchanged with precious metal. Paper money in China depreciated over time and by 1399 it became worthless. Hun-Wu tried to revive the fiat currency, but his attempt was in vain. Widespread hyperinflation deepened the currency crisis in the decades following the fifteenth century and destroyed people's trust in paper currency and subsequently put an end to the system of use of paper money in China.

Metallic money by its very nature is susceptible to being debased. There has not been any form of metallic money which has not been debased. The temptation for making a profit by debasing coins is very high. Despite the strict penalties laid down against debasing coins, certain individuals breached the law and tempered with the contents of coins. The price of defying these rules was the death penalty but this did not prevent many from taking the risk. Nicholas Oresme (c.1320–82), the fourteenth-century French theologian and philosopher who was deeply influenced by Aristotle's ideas of trade, described three ways to make a profit from money – "one is the art of the money-changer, banking or exchange, another is usury, the third alteration of coinage. The first way is contemptible, the second bad and the third worse" (Oresme 2009: 27).

Throughout the history of coin forms of money, all sorts of ingenious tricks were concocted and laboured to debase the coins. Two ingenious methods and tricks of the trade to tamper with coins were clipping and sweating coins. They clipped small pieces from the edges of coins. In the case of sweating, they put coins in leather bags and shook the bags violently to collect the leftover dust from the coins (Munro 2016: 30). Many other methods were contrived to augment the value of coins. Gresham's law was a by-product of an astute discerning of such practices. A practice whose history goes back to time immemorial. The ancient writers talked about the power and effect of the circulation of bad money on good money. However, it was Henry D. Macleod (1821–1902) who attributed the idea that counterfeit coins keep genuine coins out of circulation to Thomas Gresham. The economist who popularized the Gresham principle was Stanley Jevons (Flynn and Roper 1982: 219). Thomas Gresham (c.1519–79) was the founder of the Royal Exchange in England. The law associated after his name says that "bad money drives out good." The date of Gresham's law is said to be 1558. But we find an expression of the same law in Nicolaus Copernicus essay on coinage, which was written 1525 or even earlier than this date in the work of Oresme (Kindleberger 1997: 43).

The relationship between fraud and money is symbiotic. Money in all its forms, each form in its own time, is open to abuse. In fact, the invention of each form of money goes with the temptation to create more of it. One ingenious method used to invent or discover new forms of money was the gimmick of Alchemy. The alchemists were believed to have magical power. They consumed their time in search of a cure for eternal life and a new form of money out of worthless metals. The alchemists hoped to transform base metals into precious metals. By means of wizardry, they believed they could create superior forms of money, i.e., to transform lead into gold. Paradoxically, Isaac Newton, an icon of modern science, was a faithful Alchemist. He devoted 30 years of his life to the witchcraft of alchemy, trying to turn the base metals into gold. Newton was also the Master of the Royal Mint from 1696 to 1727. Appointing the greatest scientist of his time as the Master of the Royal Mint for over 30 years shows the growing importance of money in this period. The increasing importance of the role of money in the economy accelerated the wheel of counterfeiting and the invention of new forms of money. The French monarchs debased the livre in 1519, 1532, 1549, 1561, and every year except 1576 between 1571 and 1577. Henry VIII, during the period of the great debasement, from 1542 to 1551, debased his currency several times and raised a quarter of his revenue from reducing the metal content of his currency.

As the gate of American bountiful treasure was opened wide to the bounty hunters of Europe, the Spanish colonists looted the silver of Potosi (now in Bolivia) and flooded the growing economies of Europe. The monetary units in the upcoming economies of Europe were eroded severely. The main reason for this inflationary spiral was an overflow of precious metals after the conquest of America. Other factors that contributed to the erosion of the monetary units were debasing, clipping, sweating, financing war mercenaries, low economic productivity, population growth, and series of epidemics that occurred during this period. This was not a typical period. Inflationary crises were not also ordinary inflation. One of the most acute observers of monetary matters who noted this extraordinary time was Jean Bodin, the French political philosopher. He, unlike another French thinker, Jehan de Malestriot, saw inflation not as an illusion but a pervasive problem in Europe. In Bodin's list, the influx of precious metals from the new world eclipses other causes of high inflation in sixteenth-century Europe.

## The Dutch tulip crusaders

The leading economies in the seventeenth century were the northern European economies, in particular, the Netherlands after it gained its independence from Spain. Gold and silver were dominant forms of money in these economies. The Thirty Years War from 1618 to 1648 was another great defining event of the century. It is noted as "one of the most destructive wars in European history" in which eight million people lost their lives (Wilson 2008: 554). To get hold of more coins (the principal money) to finance the war, men of power turned to the art of counterfeiting. The Holy Roman Empire outpaced the rest in this contest. The five years from 1618 to 1623 are characterized as "kipper and wiper." The German states were involved extensively in debasing their currencies to finance the war. Kipper and wiper was a systematic and widespread practice of clipping coins, melting good quality coins, mixing them with inferior metals, and rigging weight scales to get more pure coins. The practice extended to all German states. Each state tried to get as many good coins from other states as possible, then meltdown the good coins with inferior metals, and return them to the original state either to exchange them with good coins or to buy food or other goods. The practice ruined the monetary system of these states and resulted in hyperinflation. During the war:

> good coins disappeared from circulation, while taxes were paid with debased currency. The real value of civic revenue fell by nearly 30 per cent in Naumberg. Prices soared as traders demanded sackfuls of bad coins for staple commodities: the cost of a loaf of bread jumped 700 per cent in Franconia between 1619 and 1622.
>
> (Wilson 2011: 797)

The Dutch supremacy in the seventeenth century was deep-rooted in the long decades of Dutch people struggling for their independence from Spain. A portion of history of this period is linked with the city of Antwerp. Before it fell to Spanish troops in 1585, it was the commercial capital of lower countries in Europe. Other countries, in particular Portuguese, used it as the outlet for their merchandise (pepper and spice) in the sixteenth century. The Dutch revolt against Spanish colonialism and the religious strife ended the commercial dominance of Antwerp by 1585. The bloody warfare resulted in the exodus of many merchants, artisans, textile workers, and Calvinists to the northern provinces of the Netherlands. This influx of population added to the urbanization and ever-growing population of the Netherlands northern parts. From 1500 to 1650, the population of these regions almost tripled. This reinvigorated many sectors of the Dutch economy. The textile production at the beginning of the seventeenth century was about 50,000 pieces per year. It grew to 130,000 pieces in the 1660s. The fishing industry was another fast-growing industry during this period. In the first half of the seventeenth century, on average per year, the herring caught was over 30,000 metric tonnes. The same went for the overseas colonial trade and the tobacco processing industry. Subsequently, Amsterdam replaced Antwerp as a Europe centre for refining sugar. In 1605 the number of sugar refineries in Amsterdam was said to be about three and by 1660 their number increased to 60 refineries (Cipolla 2003: 199).

Modern industrialized economies owe much to the Dutch economic head start. It was the Dutch economy that changed the economic landscape radically. The Dutch economic transformation is a landmark in the history of economic development. It marks the beginning of a new economic system. The Dutch succeeded in spreading their international network of trade from the Baltic trade, the "mother trade" to east and south. They were among the first nations to set up conglomerate companies, the United East India Company in 1602 and the Dutch West India Company in 1621. These were joint-stock companies that held monopoly rights to trade in Asia and America. The East India Company started with an initial capital of about 6.5 million guilders and 1,800 shareholders and 17 directors. The directors were the largest shareholders of the company. The Dutch East India Company also founded the Amsterdam Stock Exchange market in 1602. These companies were governments of the territories which fell under the sphere of their trading monopoly. The Dutch founded the exchange bank in 1609. The functions of the bank were limited initially to deposit-taking and exchange but from 1614 onwards it was lending money. The bank's deposits were less than one million guilders in 1611 but by 1700 its deposits increased over 16 million guilders.

Interest rates in the seventeenth century in Holland were lowest in Europe. In addition, the Dutch emancipated themselves from the "usury laws" (Homer 1963: 173). The rate of interest paid on the public loan at the beginning of the century was 8 per cent and it was reduced to 4 per cent by 1655 (Park 2005: 80). Low rates of interest, free trade, and decentralization of government liberated the Dutch economy from the medieval restrictions. The Dutch Republic, during the period considered, was the most democratic nation in the world. Each region of the republic was relatively autonomous. The democratic principle was not limited to the decentralization of the political system. One could also detect embryos of other democratic norms in law, economy, and culture. Grotius's rule of law based on natural law is a case in point. The idea that everyone is entitled to certain natural laws that should be safeguarded and enforced by the state. This was his solution to end conflicts, and to institute peace and stability. It is self-evident that there cannot be any long-term economic prosperity without peace and stability. These radical changes in the seventeenth century transformed the Dutch economy into the most dynamic and democratic economy in the world.

Opting for Protestantism diminished harsh Catholic restrictions on production, trade, commerce, and credit. Protestantism was more relaxed on such matters. It also "made virtues of the selfish, egoistic, and acquisitive motives" less objectionable (Hunt 2002: 31). It confronted the economic rigidities of the feudal agrarian economy. Breaking from the feudal agrarian economy meant to challenge head-on the conventions of peasant households, the rural bonds, and the canonical laws. This was a way of life, a world that debarred most of the population from any tangible progress. It kept people in the same conditions they were born in. Individual social and economic positions were fixed and prearranged. The scope of economic activities was limited to agriculture. Family ties reigned. Individual initiatives were rebuked and castigated. It was a time when the real producers were heavily taxed, the economy was heavily regulated, trade and industrial activities were looked down, interest rates were kept artificially high, and international trade was severely restricted.

The Dutch golden age was the dawn of a new era. It was the cradle of the modern, democratic, political, and economic world. With all shortcomings of a pioneer movement, the Dutch age was the beginning of a new phase in human history. Dutch introduced the concept of democratic law after 80 years of struggle for independence from Spain. Not all laws were legitimate prior to its independence. For example, the Spanish colonial law imposed on the Dutch nation was an illegitimate law. The only legitimate law was one that the citizens of a free nation, free of colonialism and occupation, can make and enforce. That is the bedrock of any democratic law. This bedrock was the contribution of Dutch independence. There are many prerequisites for a political, legal, and economic system of a free nation to be fully democratic. We will look at this point in detail in the next chapter. In the seventeenth century, the Dutch republic was not only the centre of the new economy, but was the centre of new ideas about political philosophy, legal and moral debates, and culture. Northern Netherlands was one of the first centres that called for religious freedom and reforms. It was where the Brothers of the Common Life started. Desiderius Erasmus (1469–1536) was from this region. He was born in Rotterdam. Erasmus looked back at the past and wrote critically. In contrasting the Greek approach to that of the scholastic approach, he found one to be the work of free thought and the other the work of the blind mind. As in the latter approach, he considered the idea of predestination to be one among many blind conformities. The custodian of this approach was, in his view, the Pope and his entire ecclesiastic apparatus. The Calvinists refugees from France after 1560 influenced the thinking in Northern Netherlands against dogmatism and religious fanaticism that reigned through these countries (Tucker 2018: 32–33).

The seventeenth century was the Dutch republic world primacy. The Dutch nation was the first nation that gained her independence, in the modern sense of the term, from the Spanish Empire. The Dutch war of independence lasted for 80 years, from 1568 to 1648. After gaining her independence, the northern and southern parts of the Netherlands formed the Dutch republic. Dutch independence was of paramount importance to the idea of a democratic government, the legitimacy of political authority, rule of law, economic liberty, and transaction, and for the influence of enlightened thinkers and ideas. First and foremost, it questioned the legitimacy of imperial rule. In short, it for the first time in theory and practice repudiated laws imposed on a subjugated nation by a colonial power. The Dutch independence inaugurated the enlightened idea that a free nation, regardless of its size, population, level of development, and power, is entitled to determine its own laws and future. This step forward was a sharp turning point against the presupposed principle that might is right. Dutch independence was the precursor of democratic law and state. It heralded the quest for the prerequisites for a democratic law and a state. Hugo Grotius (1583–1645), the Dutch jurist, was a product of this period. Long years of war of independence, religious conflicts and reformation filled his entire lifetime. Grotius arrived at the conclusion that war cannot be natural. The most palpable demonstration of this view is in his theory of natural law. On this basis national sovereignty is natural. It is an incontrovertible truth, whereas colonialism is a product of force and occupation. Thus, it is contrary to the law of nature. Grotius's legal, moral, and political theories laid out the foundations of the Dutch Republic and modern international law.

One of the greatest ethicists of the modern age was the product of this period. The Dutch philosopher and rationalist, Benedict Spinoza (1632–77), was a product of this period. Spinoza was an original thinker. He was born in a Jewish family but soon found his own moral position in conflict with that of Judaism and other institutionalized theistic religions. The Portuguese Jews (Marronos) fled the Inquisition and sought sanctuary in Holland in the sixteenth century. Spinoza's father, Michael, was a prominent member of Synagogue elders in Amsterdam. His mother died when he was six years old, and his father died in 1654. He passed his inheritance to his sister. To meet his basic daily necessities, he worked as a grinder of optical lenses. In 1656, he was excommunicated from the Synagogue and was accused of advocating heretical views and apostasy. It was a century later that Spinoza's philosophy was put under the category of pantheism. The idea of pantheism goes back to ancient times. There is no consensus on one form of pantheism. Many variations of it are to be found in the ancient and medieval philosophy and religions. The term first was used by Irish thinker John Toland in 1705. Pantheism in its origin has a Greek root. It is composed of two parts: pan, which means all and Theos, which means God. In a nutshell, Pantheism is the view that there is one whole that contains everything and every thought. It consists of the whole cosmos. The pantheists equate everything to God, and nothing exists outside it. Spinoza wrote his greatest book the *Ethics* (1664–65) with this tacitly assumed prerequisite in mind. The book was published posthumously in 1677. In this book, Spinoza sought to explain ethics rationally and logically. In his approach, the realm of reason and realm of virtue rests on the same foundation. They share the same structure that can be explained, demonstrated, and proved in a form of geometrical order. This period also produced a long list of artists, among whom are the greatest of Dutch artists such as Rembrandt, Adam Willaerts, Johannes Vermeer, Frans Hales, and many more.

The tulip mania (1636–37) was one element among many elements described above about the Dutch socio-economic and political structure in the seventeenth century. It was an integral component of increasing Dutch confidence in securing not just their political liberty but also economic liberty. The answer lies in their faith in their everlasting decentralized national government and uninterrupted political and economic stability. The source of the tulip mania was also to be found in greater individual political and economic freedom. It was because of the weakening of religion restrictions and progress in individual rights and rationalization of the rule of law and moral conduct that many individuals overstepped the prevailing medieval circumscriptions and carried to excess and overexerted whatever was new. The medieval rules, moral conduct, and customs overtime lost their domination. Land, labour, capital, entrepreneurism, science, and technology were emancipated from the grip of religion, medieval scholasticism, and feudal constraints. The concerns were gradually discharged from the canons of the archaic institutions and obsolete beliefs and rehabilitated as matters of individual concern. The medieval taxes and usury laws gave way to free wage labour, markets, and free trade. Another contributory factor in Dutch economic and political transformation in the seventeenth century was the role of emigrants. The emigrants out of necessity discarded the old habits, culture, and prohibitions and accepted a variety of different new jobs to make ends meet. Work and trade became their top priorities. Subsequently, the Dutch established the largest economy, the international network of maritime trade, the first and the largest stock exchange market, and the first joint-stock companies. To this, we must add their greater hopes and expectations about the future. That this situation will last forever or even will get better. The rush to buy tulips and sell it at a higher price in an organized market was something new. Any individual was capable and allowed to buy and sell. Traders could not only see the profit they could make in the marketplace but were attracted to further their socio-economic position. The thing that attracts the attention of the crowd is the soaring profit but not the unseen narcissistic nature of the act. The more profit one can make from such transactions the more one gets self-involved and egoistic. This propensity is one of human's greatest follies. Tulip craze was one of these human follies. Other cardinal follies that the entire century was engulfed with, that in the metaphysics of economics are left unsaid, were long and bloody wars, colonialism, slave trade, displacement, and religious conflicts.

Let us now turn to the story of tulip mania. The wild tulips grow in the Karatau Mountains in Kazakhstan. Somehow the flower found its way to Turkey and in the Ottoman rulers' gardens. The empire was established in 1299. The rulers of the empire, in equal measure, were fond of Islam and tulips. Little wonder that they picked tulips out of the crowd of flowers as the symbol of god. It was said that God in Arabic script looks a lot like the shape of the flower. With that portrayal, the flower was granted a holy status. So, it was not a coincidence that the tulip acquired its divinity status and became the sole property of emperors. Turning it into a holy and imperial flower dislodged it from a common flower and detached it from the common masses. Its high status decimated its earthy qualities. With that being said, the tulip found its way to Holland at the end of the sixteenth century. In no time it also became a symbol of status and wealth in Holland. The demand for these rare exotic flowers grew quickly. The flower attracted people from all walks of life. The lure was not only because the tulip was exotic, exquisite, and holy but also because it made sellers good money. The news that anybody could make money by buying tulip bulbs and selling them immediately at a higher price was too tempting to resist. This was something new. Economic freedom for any individual to trade and make money was the dawn of a new era in economic development. The trend in Holland then was why not make the most of the new liberty in trade. The rush that ended in the stampede began in the summer 1636. Obviously, the real traders and the insiders were in a better position. These groups of people were relatively more informed, either through reading, experience, or because of their position. As for the imitators, they had none of those advantages. Worst of all the latter social groups were latecomers but far more intrigued and bewitched by the fever that infested the events than any other motive.

From 1633 the price of tulips kept rising continuously until their prices plummeted in 1637. The rarest tulips were in the greatest demand. The irony of it all was that the rarest tulips were virus-infected plants. The tulip bulbs in this category could fetch many times more to its weight in gold. At this time, it is said the richest man in Holland had about 400,000 guilders. A successful tulip trader could make 40,000–60,000 guilders in a year. During 1636–37, a rare tulip could be sold for 2,500 guilders, almost 16.5 times the yearly income of a skilled worker. Between December 1636 and January 1637, prices of some tulips rose over 1,000 per cent. Buying and reselling of the same tulips went on in the same spot many times without the parties seeing the actual bulbs or exchanging the actual bulbs. The practice of exchange was not real. The reality was quickly replaced by delusion. This becomes more obvious when we compare the prices of some goods and incomes of different social groups in the first decades of the seventeenth century. Guilder, the unit of currency of the Dutch Republic then, consisted of 20 stuivers. In 1620, six and a half stuivers could get you a £12 loaf of bread. Thirteen guilders could fetch you one tonne of herring in 1636. A cloth shearer in 1633 in Amsterdam only could get 18 stuivers. The annual income of a carpenter in 1630 was 250 guilders, and that of an average merchant was about 1,500 guilders.

This was a new era with its specific facets. First and foremost, the tulip was a new product in Holland. The Dutch public and state expectations were open to new adventures and possibilities. Their vision of self-advancement, to do better and to get better, exceeded that of medieval economies. To get rich for a working person was not a cardinal sin anymore. The fad of getting rich took over and preoccupied the minds of a few individuals first and soon the craze was widespread and swept the nation. The population was obsessed with tulips and intoxicated with the hunger of getting rich. The frenzied trade in tulip bulbs went out of control and became an endemic compulsion. It became socially and morally acceptable for everyone to get rich. This was democracy in trade at the extreme. The idea was that any person can buy cheap and sell at a higher price. The dream was enticing and very infectious. The delusion that all economic agents in the market are equal spread through the public consciousness at an alarming rate. In truth, trade is not a level playing field. It can be mutually beneficial, but it is not a fair play that is acted impartially with equal chance. In the background, there was the middle class that was growing fast, adding fuel to the fire of passion of getting rich backed up by their recent experience of climbing the social ladder. Other contributory factors that exacerbated the speed of change of the socio-economic environment were the rate of innovations in financial markets, institutions, and instruments in Holland during this period.

Indispensable to a deeper understanding and to unlocking the secret of the tulip mania were several important events that took place in the background preceding the crash in Holland. A new comet was discovered in 1618. One ramification of this event was that this could hardly be judged or be attributed to any myth or religious hunch. It was real. It is even more important to know that this was the year that the Thirty Years War, a religious war predominantly in central Europe among the Protestant and Catholic states, started. The war (1618–59) destroyed communities, dislocated people, and the course and centres of the trade. The protracted conflict increased military repression and augmented the total tax burden. It plunged Western Europe into revolution and religious conflict on one hand and on the other heightened the struggle for emancipation from social, political, and economic stagnation, despotism, and fanaticism. All these were not compatible with modernity. Besides, the good old days of the Spanish Empire were over. In 1640 the Catalonian and Portuguese revolted against Spanish colonial rule.

Portuguese revolt succeeded and the Catalonia movement failed. Andalusia revolted in 1641 and Naples and Masaniella in 1647. The Dutch war of independence succeeded in 1649 that led to the formation of the united provinces of the Netherlands. From 1648 to 1653 we had the puritan revolution in England. In the same period, France was going through the Frondes revolts. An English preacher described this period in 1643 as "days of shaking" (quoted from Trevor-Roper 1959: 31).

The size and composition of Holland's debt in 1600 was 5,495,375 Dutch guilders. This sum represented 35.2 per cent of life annuities, 34.9 per cent of redeemable annuities, and 29.9 per cent of bills. A decade later in 1610, the debt had almost tripled to 15,033,902 guilders. Out of this, 41 per cent were life annuities, 58 per cent redeemable annuities, and 1 per cent bills. The following decade, in 1620, it increased to 18,152,668 guilders, consisting of 44 per cent life annuities, 52.8 per cent redeemable annuities, and 3.2 per cent of bills. By 1630, Holland's debt more than doubled compared to a decade earlier. It increased to 45,824,564 guilders. The share of life annuities was 19 per cent, that of redeemable annuities 71 per cent, and that of bills 10 per cent. In the year before the tulip crisis, 1635, Holland's debt was 70,360,171 guilders. The share of life annuities was 12.9 per cent, that of redeemable annuities 53.6 per cent, and that of bills 33.5 per cent. During the two years of the crisis, it increased to 75,697,063 in 1636 and to 80,334,235 guilders in 1637. The composition of debt in 1636 was 12 per cent life annuities, 50.5 per cent redeemable annuities, and 37.5 per cent bills. For the year 1637, life annuities were about 11.4 per cent, redeemable annuities were 48.1 per cent, and bills were 40.5 per cent (Gelderblom and Jonker 2011: 29–30).

We must not also lose sight of the demographic trend in the seventeenth century in Europe. There is much to be said about the demographic changes that had occurred in Europe. Many factors played a part in this demographic transition. Most specifically, famines, religious wars, and plague reduced the population of the Mediterranean region. From 1600 to 1650, the population of Italy reduced by 16 per cent and Spain by 14 per cent. The region under the domination of the Holy Roman Empire declined by 35 per cent and the whole of Europe by 5 per cent. However, the maritime provinces of the Netherland and England were the exception to the trend. Their population continued to grow until 1660 (Vries 2009: 159–60).

In 1600 France was the only country with a long-standing high surplus balance of trade. Except with Italy, it had a trade surplus with all its other trading partners. This resulted in a net accumulation of surplus bullion and hence excessive money supply in France. But as the route of the trade changed from Leyon-Genoa to the Atlantic coast, the bullion ended in the hands of Dutch merchants (Vries 2009: 172–73). For about two decades from 1590 to 1610, Genoa lost its financial and commercial supremacy and Amsterdam replaced it. Amsterdam not only became the centre of the European economy but became the centre of the world economy (Vries 2009: 175). By 1650, the Dutch were sending about 280 ships just across the Atlantic, the highest number than any other country at the time. The Dutch in the seventeenth century substituted the Italian and Spanish traders and diverted the European trade to Atlantic and North (Kindleberger 1998: 11). It was no wonder that the banking sector followed the trade. Wherever the trade went, banks went with it. It was not by chance that the pioneering Italian bankers transferred their businesses from Florentines to Lyons and Antwerp (Kindleberger 1998: 13). It was then that the modern world trade was shaped, and the modern nation-state was born. The long-lasting era that was founded on "shared core of faith, tradition, and authority" stumbled upon with much opposition. These disruptions also shook the secure foundation of the "theology's age-old hegemony" (Israel 2001: 3–4).

Seventeenth century laid the foundations of modern democratic Europe and modern European economies. This would not have been possible without the formation of the nation-state in its true sense of the word. The formation of a nation is a historical process. At some point in their history people who inhabit and congregate at certain locations develop a common history, culture, language, habits, values, arts, legal and moral codes, and behaviour. This sense of belonging is one of the most pivotal factors for the social and economic development and well-being of not only the nation in question but the peace and well-being of the entire community of nations in the long run. The idea that each nation – small or large, rich or poor, weak or powerful, developed or underdeveloped – has equal rights was recognized for the first time in the seventeenth century. The Dutch Republic was a serious departure from the past political arrangements. It was a leap of creative thinking and a hallmark in the construction of a representative democratic state. The Dutch liberation from Imperial Spain endorsed this right, and it was a seminal factor in the self-actualization of the Dutch nation, their optimism, economic progress, and prosperity in the seventeenth century.

The Dutch tulip crash was the result of interactions of the cited forces, factors, events, expectations, and innovations. All of which were recent. This was a modern move, a transformation passage, and a revolutionary era that set the trend for the democratization of trade. The central message of the trend was at variance with the prevailing custom of the time. It altered the usual status of traders. Economic liberation improved the social status of the traders and drew more people to buy and sell goods and services. To this end, credit was rescued from the stringent conditions of the land of sin and brought under the jurisdiction of virtue. The market for trading on margins grew steadily. Traders used margin debts to increase their potential profits. The idea of future contracts was not new, but it was the first time being applied widely in organized markets. Aristotle in his book *The Politics* clearly describes the process of a future contract. In his tale of the Thales of Miletus, he writes:

> deducing from his knowledge of the stars that there would be a good crop of olives, while it was still winter and he had a little money to spare, he used it to pay deposits on all the oil-pressed in Miletus and Chios,

> thus securing their hire. This cost him only a small sum, as there were no other bidders. Then the time of the olive-harvest came and, as there was a sudden and simultaneous demand for oil-presses, he hired them out at any price he liked to ask.
>
> (Aristotle 1970: 48)

Futures contracts in Holland in the seventeenth century were neither standardized nor regulated. As is aptly described in Aristotle's extract, a futures contract is an agreement between two parties either to buy or sell a particular asset of a certain quality at a predetermined price and a pre-set date sometime in the future. The buyers of contracts pay only a small percentage of the price of the underlying asset to control the whole asset. This brings us to the mystique of trading on margin. Strangely enough, the price paid to control the underlying asset, which could be less than 5 per cent, can also be borrowed money. In the case of the tulip fiasco, the tulip bulbs in most demand, in most cases, did not exist at the time of signing the contract.

Towards the last decade of the seventeenth century, Joseph Penso de la Vega (1650–92) provided a vivid description of trading in the Amsterdam Stock Exchange in his book *Confusion de Confusiones* (1688). In this book, he likens the passion of trading in the stock market to that of religious passion. De la Vega argued that when this passion gets a commanding position over everything else, it breaks all other norms, orders, or laws. When speculation runs the show, the craving to make a fortune becomes endemic. The emulation of the golden touch spreads quickly and widely. He wrote, "if one were to lead a stranger through the streets of Amsterdam and ask him where he was, he would answer, "Among Speculators," for there is no corner [in the city] where one does not talk of shares" (De La Vega 1996: 188). He described the trade in the Amsterdam stock exchange as trading of the wind or the windhandel trade. His frame of reference was goods like Herring. One could buy and sell with a small amount of initial margin Herring before they were caught, and it was the same with other goods such as grain before they were sown and harvested. There was no barrier in exchange for speculators. The speculative gain laid down the law. De la Vega despised acts of speculation in business. He considered speculators as lacking moral fibre and the plague of his day. He saw salvation in eradicating speculators. On this subject, he commented:

> All schools of philosophy teach that the soul is nobler than the body, life nobler than death, and the existent nobler than the non-existent. But, as for the stock exchange, I approve the paradoxical opinion of the Platonic musician that the non-existent is better than the existent. I think it much better not to be a speculator.
>
> (Del la Vega 1996: 211)

It is a common experience that in due course avaricious buying ends in panic selling. This was what happened in the cradle of the modern derivatives market, in the Amsterdam Stock Exchange, in 1636–37. Prices of some Tulip bulbs rose by 1,000 per cent from December 1636 to January 1637. Such a startling increase of price was a fertile breeding ground to entice and seduce the gullible, the misguided, the conceited, and the hyper-excited utopian swindlers to join the deranged parade. Most of the newcomers had no or very little possession. Those with a little possession bewitched with the flare of speculative trend pawned whatever they had and invested at the height of the market. Many borrowed when interest rate hit its climax and joined the herd of swindlers and the self-assured. The emerging climate created a favourable terrain, a hotbed for fraudsters, hoaxers, charlatans, embezzlers, and other criminals to cash in on the troubled time. The tulip inferno produced a lucrative market for the thieves in Amsterdam. The thieves raided the tulip fields at night, stole the valuable bulbs, and some of the bulbs looted were the very bulbs that they had sold in the future market earlier. The unintended repercussion of this was the formation of another market, a market for the alarm system. That, in turn, increased the price of bulbs due to the increase in the cost of security and the inordinate anxiety that infested the city.

The speculative market rests on the belief that one can sell at a higher price and the expectation of making an even higher profit in the next round of buying and selling. The vision of uninterrupted higher returns in the future rounds is an insatiable enchantment. A compulsive predisposition that has no limit. It is a strong desire that when put into motion, it accelerates side by side with the velocity of exchange and the pace of speculative profit. The desire is indescribable. Making a profit has no end. Speculative trends start slowly. At each stage of its progression, it finds its powerful allies, economic and political justifications. What is much more important is the speed by which more people want to get rich quicker and quicker over time. The pace quickens to the day when the turning point is unavoidable. The pattern of overdoing remains irrepressible until the time of the crash. As the pace of trade accelerates most buyers know that they are being cheated but are equally confident that there are other enchanted buyers out there who are ready to be ripped off. The peak of the speculative cycle is not a well-defined destination. As the drivers of the market do not know the endpoint, they enter a territory that has no way of going back or forward. At the height of the market, amid plenty, the potentials fail to materialize. Sellers cannot find buyers at desirable prices. The frenzied selling occurs amid of overabundance and market dissipation. The bubble bursts and the sudden break starts the stampede. At this point everyone rushed to sell their Tulips. The crash hit hardest those who had borrowed, pawned their entire possessions, or mortgaged whatever they had and did not buy the actual bulbs but the right to buy.

The soaring prices are a display of the fermentation of the overexcited nervy of both buyers and sellers. Something, a craze, that is not sustainable for long. The democratic speculation, the wishful thinking that everyone can take part in cheating each other and this will be advantageous to all, is merely a delusion. The myth is based on the display of wealth, superstition, and the fallacy that wealth can be created from thin air or everyone can get rich quickly just by double-dealing. Tulips did not lose their religious aura in Holland. It just converted its religion to Christianity. In the seventeenth century in the Netherlands, the tulip symbolized the amalgamation of a magical power of divinity, love, alcohol, and the display of wealth. The highest standard of living then in Europe was in Holland. The tulip fitted well to their Calvinism worldview. The tulip was well-suited to their strict form of Christianity and as a symbol of wealth. God and wealth were fused and revered in one exotic flower.

This is what happened on 5 February 1637. The tulip traders congregated at the saleroom in Alkmaar. The auction of tulip bulbs began. The trade started as normal with steady bidding and gradually the bidding got more frenzied. The price of a single bulb rose rapidly and approached 200 guilders. It soon climbed to 400, 600 and then passed a thousand guilders. The rarer varieties were even sold for over 2,000 guilders. The sale of tulip, at the end of the auction in one day, rose to 90,000 guilders. With such a stroke of luck, no one could dare question the prospective returns in the market and reproach those who wanted to make fortunes. The market crashed however, but the collapse of the tulip market was relatively short-lived. The crisis did not cripple the entire Dutch economy. After this passing set-back, the Dutch economy recovered. It was not the Tulip conquest of the Netherlands that destroyed the Dutch economy but the French colonization of the Dutch nation that destroyed the supremacy of the Dutch economy in the seventeenth century. The French revolutionary occupied Belgium in 1794 and a year later conquered and colonized Luxembourg and the Netherland. The rest is history.

## National sovereignty and the state finance

One of the defining characteristics of the modern era is the formation of the democratic nation-state. The birth of the democratic state has been an evolving process, a process neither smooth nor complete. Over the course of time, the institution of the democratic state has outworn, reawaken, restored, recuperated, reconstituted, repudiated, and overrun. The Dutch Republic was the first democratic nation-state. This was the product of over 80 years of the Dutch liberation struggle against the Spanish Empire. In the seventeenth century, the Dutch nation laid the ground rules for the present-day democratic nation-states. National sovereignty and state finance are two sides of the same coin. By its very nature, a democratic state is from the people and for the people. It is duty-bound to the provision of certain socio-economic, political, and legal rights. It is liable to national defence, enforcement of justice, freedom, rule of law, and raising the standard of living and welfare of its citizens. These entitlements cost money. The modern state finances cut both ways. Public finance is tied up with innovation in new forms of money, in the creation of new financial markets, institutions, and instruments. At the same time, it has triggered new challenges. This section discusses the rise of the democratic sovereign state, public budgeting and finance, and the role they have played in economic crisis and disorder.

The idea of a sovereign nation-state is an offshoot of the sixteenth and seventeenth centuries. Two opposing tendencies of thinking have merged side by side about the sovereign nation-state. The first one was articulated by a French jurist, Jean Bodin (c.1529–96), and an English political philosopher, Thomas Hobbes. Both authors argued for the absolute power of the monarch as the head of the nation-state. The monarch is said to be the trustee and custodian of the whole nation. Bodin professed that "sovereignty is the most high, absolute, and perpetual power the citizens and subjects in commonweale ... that is to say; The greatest power to command" (Bodin 1962: 84). Along the same lines, Hobbes argued that a viable national sovereignty is only applicable if it is instituted in an absolute sovereign power. Otherwise, there will be no sovereignty at all (Korab-karpowicz 2012: 171).

The counter-argument to view was proposed by two other contemporary thinkers. They were the German Jurist and philosopher, Johannes Althusius (1557–1638) and Samuel Pufendorf (1632–94). Personal experience and education of both thinkers were instrumental in the fermentation of their understanding of the structure of nation-state. Althusius completed his education in law and philosophy in Switzerland. The political order in Switzerland was a confederate state. The beginning of this system went as far back to the year 1291. Althusius argued that people create different social associations in different circumstances. The most basic form of human association is a family; the next is voluntary cooperation; then the formation of communities, provinces, and finally the state. A move from one form of association to the next and eventually many necessitates social associations. These complex associations are compelled to enter multiple social contracts. Implicit in Althusius's belief is the idea that absolute sovereignty is contrary to human nature. This is because:

> no man is self-sufficient, or adequately endowed by nature ... Politics is the art of associating men for the purpose of establishing, cultivating, and conserving social life among them. Hence it is called 'symbiotic.' The subject matter of politics is, therefore, association in which the symbiotes pledge themselves to each other by explicit or tacit agreement, to mutual communication of whatever is useful and necessary for the harmonious exercise of social life.
>
> (Althusius 2005: 27)

Samuel Pufendorf was well acquainted with the work of Dutch jurist Hugo Grotius. Both are egalitarian thinkers. All human beings, in their opinion, are equal by nature. Pufendorf worked as a tutor for the Swedish ambassador in Copenhagen. When the war broke out between Denmark and Sweden in 1658, he was detained and put behind bars for eight months. The war and the Dutch liberation experience had exerted a major influence on his character and shaped his vision of human nature and his political philosophy. It is hard to imagine a modern democratic state without the contributions of the Dutch independence from Spain in the seventeenth century. The Dutch initiated their liberation struggle against the Spanish Empire in 1568. To make their movement more effective, in 1579 an alliance of seven provinces of the Dutch nation called Union, with similar goals, was formed. After 80 years of the liberation war, in 1648 the Dutch nation became independent. It was a federal state, which altered the traditional political and legal landscape. The political structure was neither a city-state nor a despotic absolute monarchy. It was a loose federation. The federation units and cities enjoyed considerable autonomy. It was a ground-breaking and visionary political system that was "local in its economic and political organization" (Westermann 1996: 21). The Dutch nation then ranked the world's most free nation. In this loose political arrangement laid the foundations of modern fundamental civil liberties.

Against this background, Pufendorf wrote his influential book, *The Law of Nature and Nations* (1672). In this book, he defended the ideas of natural rights, popular sovereignty, and perpetual peace. Reasoning from his deep conviction in equality, he deduced that it is in humanity to be free and to live in peace. In consideration of the foregoing qualifications and by appeal to his experience he recommended the confederation system as the most suitable political order because it is consistent in nature and it can guarantee unity and peace. Pufendorf described his ideal form of government as "systems of states" that do not fit within a conventional centralized sovereign state. A confederation system "consists of several states bound to each by a perpetual treaty" (quoted from Schutze 2009: 18). This form of political structure is more expedient as human beings are social and such political order not only diminishes the advances of tyranny but also delegates power to the smaller sovereign states.

In this section, we take the Dutch republic as our reference point for the origin of the modern democratic nation-state. This point of departure is essential for this study. All forms of the dictatorial political system, imperial, colonial, totalitarian, and theocratic, are inherently illegitimate. However, economic growth and disorder are not exclusive to one type of political system. There can be economic growth in all forms of fascist, totalitarian, theocratic, and colonial states. Economies also grew in ancient slave systems. Be that as it may, in undemocratic societies where the fundamental civil, political, legal, economic, and cultural rights of most people are violated and people live in a climate of fear, by the very nature of these conditions, the economic potential of these countries and the abilities of their citizens cannot be fully utilized. Irrespective of their occasional economic growth, these countries live in a state of perpetual instability and substandard economic performance. Sooner or later such types of political structures descend into social, political, cultural, legal, and economic decay, turmoil, and civil war. The aim of this section is to explain the economic crisis and disorder in democratic nations. For this reason, we need to look briefly at the nations and the events that first laid the foundations of democratic state, society, and economy. As noted earlier, in the strict sense, the place to start and explain the rise of a modern democratic nation can be no other than the Dutch republic in the seventeenth century.

The invention of the democratic state, at the stage of social and economic development which came into being, was a necessity. In turn, the need for a national democratic state gradually altered the socio-political, cultural, and legal foundations of the old political structure. The Dutch were the pioneers of the democratic state. They created a relatively free and open society that was safer for refugees and free from war. Suffice to say that it is not slavery and tyranny that brings the best out of humanity but freedom and security that can most effectively utilize the potential of everyone in a society. The independent Dutch republic lasted until the 1780s. The Union of Utrecht, which was formed in 1579, was a league of several "sovereign "provinces" which agreed to give up their sovereign rights in a few limited areas, chiefly defence, taxation, and foreign policy" (Israel 1998: 276). The Union of Utrecht was a confederacy. Each unit of the confederacy had its own independent government. Not just each independent province but also each city and its inhabitants were equal before the law and were given equal rights of protection to exercise their customs and beliefs freely. The power of the federal authority was extended to that of the Union of Utrecht in the 1590s. It was extended to territorial administration, shipping, and religion. Cities, urban life, the formation of a sizable middle class, individual freedom, rule of law, and a loose confederacy were the key prerequisites to the Dutch republic success. The sovereign authority started from the bottom up. This free and secure climate enabled the Dutch to construct the most liberal institutional framework, the largest economy, and a naval and commercial network in the seventeenth century. It made the Dutch the wealthiest nation and a world power.

Daniel Defoe referred to the position of Dutch in the world then as

> the Middle Persons in Trade, the Factors, and Brokers of Europe … they buy again to sell again, take in to send out, and the greatest part of their vast commerce consists in being supplied from all parts of the world that they may supply all the world again.
>
> (Defoe 1728: 192)

Josiah Child (1630–99), a leading proponent of mercantilism, saw the secret of Dutch success in their free trade policy and low interest rate policy. He wrote, it

> is the *Causa Causans* of all the other causes of Riches in that People; and that if interest of Money were with us [in England] reduced to the same rate it is with them [Dutch], it would in a short time render us as rich and considerable in Trade as they now are.
>
> (Child 1997: 109)

Moreover, Holland in the seventeenth century was the safest harbour for critical thinkers and political dissidents of Europe. Among those who found a hideaway in Holland were John Locke, Spinoza, and Descartes. All these great thinkers benefited from the liberal climate of Dutch society. Spinoza attributed the prosperity and greatness of the city of Amsterdam to political rights, civil liberties, and different communities living side by side in harmony. He declared:

> take the city of Amsterdam, which enjoys the fruits of this freedom, to its own considerable prosperity and the admiration of the world. In this flourishing state, a city of the highest renown, men of every race and sect live in complete harmony.
>
> (Spinoza 1991: 298)

The most critical element for free trade in the seventeenth century was access to the sea. It meant that for early modern global trade to be viable, the maritime power and the sea-based empires' exclusive control over the great oceans had to be broken. It meant to break up the Spanish-Portuguese maritime empires. The Portuguese controlled the trade in Asia and Africa and the Spanish controlled the trade in the Caribbean and America. Hugo Grotius objected to the domination of the sea and argued,

> can the vast, boundless sea be the appanage of one Kingdome alone … Can anyone Nation have the right to prevent other nations … Can any Nation give away what it never owned, or discovered what already belonged to someone else? Does a manifest injustice of long-standing create a specific right.
>
> (Grotius 1916: 4)

Adam Smith also attributed the economic prosperity in a United Netherlands to its relative free trade policy. He said, "Holland, in the proportion of the extent of the land and the number of its inhabitants, by far the richest country in Europe, has, accordingly, the greatest share of the carrying trade in Europe" (Smith 1986: 473). As with any new advance, free trade was pushed to its extremes. It was extended to free trade in humans. The Dutch were the first who shipped and traded slaves in America.

Our understanding of liberal democracy would be incomplete without referring to another momentous event in the seventeenth century. That was England's revolution in 1688–89. The revolution removed James II within three years of insurgency, from 1685 to 1688. James II wanted to rule without the parliament as an absolute monarch. He suspended the parliament and selected his cronies as the members of Parliament and used the laws of treason and sedition to get rid of his adversaries and judges. William of Orange, the Dutch son-in-law of King James II, invaded England and overthrew the King. The abdication of James II and the crowning of his daughter Mary and son-in-law as the queen and king of England was a major transition in political rights and liberty in England. For the new king and queen to be ordained, they had to agree with the Bill of Rights. Parliament passed this Bill on 16 December 1689. The Bill limited the power of the king, it separated the powers of the state and guaranteed freedom of speech. It prevented the King from interfering in the law and the king to act as a judge or set up a court. The king was also prevented from introducing new forms of taxation without the approval of parliament and the Bill made Parliament the sovereign legislative body of the land.

The chief distinguishing mark of the Bill of Rights in England was that it limited the uncontrolled power of the monarch. It stripped the absolute power of the monarchy and stopped it from being worshipped as a supreme being, as a deity or the representative of a deity that is ordained to have dominion over all his subjects. It is vital to know that depriving the monarchy of the rank of a celestial deity, with total devotion from his subjects, and grounding him in a temporal, mundane, and earthly place was a revolutionary development. With this radical political development, the exorbitant power and prestige of the king who was the embodiment of a deity were confined to the demands of the common people. This was a profound social and political change. It opened society to dissentient voices and a divergence of ideas. Greater freedom of expression and individual liberty drew people to debate, discuss, and criticize matters of common concern openly with no fear of retribution. The economy was one of these objects of common concern. The expression of individual liberty in the field of economy was free trade.

The nature of politics is conflict. This conflict exists between different social groups who have different economic, political, religious, cultural, institutional, military, and information power. The state can be the usurper or the arbiter of this power. It can make the public subservient to its will or can be subservient to the will of the public. Gillin upholds that the roots of democracy are "to be found in the struggle between classes with opposing interests. Whether it be in France or in England" (Gillin 1919: 710). It is the latter case that is the object of our discussion here. A representative government is a democratic compromise among conflicting power interests. The Dutch Republic was one of the first steps in abolishing the old auto-theocratic and colonial political systems. In a nutshell, it partially eradicated all types of absolute monocracy and passed the power into a democratically constituted national state.

Dutch independence and the English revolution paved the way for American independence and its modern state. One of the distinctive characteristics of the American state from its beginning was religious tolerance. The American state was the first state that ended national religion. This fact is mainly attributed to the influence of the Dutch who settled in America and introduced religious liberty and made it popular. The Dutch set up their colony in the seventeenth century in North America and called it New Netherland. This colony covered the area from Delaware to the Hudson River valleys. Complying with religious tolerance, initially, was a matter of expediency. Gradually the newcomers with different religious affiliations from England, Scotland, Ireland, Germany, France, and other European countries joined the Dutch. Living and working with the Dutch exposed the Dutch pluralistic and pliant way of life to those who had a more puritanical and rigid belief. The Dutch prescription instead of the endless bloody religious strife was a more convenient way out for all these diverse nationalities and believers. Hence, they surrendered to the Dutch way of life. What the American declaration of independence achieved was to promote religious freedom as a matter of expediency to a principle of right and obligation. But the root of religious tolerance goes back to the confederation of Dutch provinces. This was one aspect of the Dutch republic that the English dissidents such as John Locke learned from personal experience while living in exile in Holland. We find the influence of Dutch religious liberty on the Act of Toleration (1689) in England soon after the Glorious Revolution (Bangs 2010). The freedom of belief laid the foundations of freedom of thought and expression. But for this freedom to be safeguarded, you need the protection of the rule of law.

The overriding pretext behind the English 1688 revolution was law. The proponents of the revolution accused the monarch, James II, of subverting the law. Their appeal was to a higher law, the supreme law. For that, they needed to define what this higher law and the legitimacy of this supreme law was. The contention was that James II saw himself as the maker of the law by virtue of the fact that he represented the divinity. The proponents of the Parliament questioned this authority. It was a battle over the issue of "whose power … and power to do what" (Russell 1990: 138). The issue of law was central to the 1688 revolution. What took place in this regard was not just a landmark transformation in England's political and legal system but a profound paradigm shift in human political organization. After the revolution and because of the revolution the "monarch became limited" and the authority of parliament, in a series of steps, overshadowed the power of the king (Harris 2006: 494). The declaration of the American independence emanated from the strength of the aforesaid ideas and events.

Party politics stemmed from freedom of thought and association. A representative government entails mobilization and participation of a nation's citizens. Each nation is composed of various interest groups. For these groups to express their preferences on a common agenda, they need political parties. It was in England where such political parties were formed in the seventeenth century. These parties, in their very rudimentary forms, were rooted in sectarian religion. The two parties that resulted from the English glorious revolution were the Whigs and the Tories. The former, the Protestants, backed the 1688 revolution and parliament; the latter, the Tories, were followers of the Anglican Church and were pro-monarchy.

The American independence was a successor of the Dutch Republic and the English revolution. The declaration of independence in 1776 was not only a mirror reflection of these two momentous events but also a synthesis of the two historic upheavals. It was one of the greatest political achievements of the age of enlightenment. The leaders of the American Revolution were the disciples of reason and the principle of natural law. They advocated the application of the law of nature to improve human societies. These leaders were the "off-spring of the eighteenth century" intellectual environment. The founding Fathers of the United States were immersed in "the teaching of their age" (Kaplan 1956: 31). These leaders were students of Hobbes, Locke, and Roussos's principle of a social contract. Locke published his *Two Treatises on Government* anonymously in 1688. The introduction to the book was written after the revolution. The introduction gives the impression that the book was written in defence and justification of the glorious revolution. The book was written in 1681, during the Exclusion Crisis. The book tries to refute the objections to rebellion against tyranny. Locke argues that the right to resist a tyrannical authority is neither a breach of divine law nor is it socially subversive. He refutes the divine right of the king to rule in the first treatise and in the second Treatise he presents his rationale for the need to have a government. Starting with the premise that there is no government in the state of nature but that natural rights exist even where there is no government. These rights exist for the reason of being a living thing. For example, the right to live and stay alive; the right of safety, self-defence, and self-protection; and the right of finding the means to survive are rights that are tied to one's existence and not to the existence of any government. Locke reasons that the institution of government comes into being because the state of nature is a deprived, perilous, exposed, and uncertain mode of existence. The government is a social contract between people and their rulers for the people to give up some of their rights and for the government to use its privilege of authority to maintain law and order and the safety of its citizens.

Locke's view of social contract differs from Hobbes's idea. Locke does not believe that people are inherently self-fish and violent. Besides, life in the state of nature in his opinion is not as Hobbes described as "solitary, poor, nasty, brutish, and short." For Locke, there is a mutually constitutive relationship between individuals' natural rights, moral autonomy, and individual liberty. He accepts Hobbes's view of government as the maintainer of peace and order but rejects his view of letting the state have absolute power. For Locke, it is natural and morally permissible for people to rebel and overthrow their rulers if their natural rights – the right to life, liberty, and property – are violated. Unlike Hobbes, Locke sees the power of a governed is being decided by the consent of those governed. The French thinkers and philosophers in the eighteenth century made extensive use of Grotius and Locke's idea of natural law. They used the idea of natural rights as their frame of reference and their leading light to advance their idea of progress. Provided that the rights to life, liberty, and property are guaranteed, and the government is elected by the consent of those they govern, a more equal, just, harmonious, and prosperous society can be established – because people by nature are good and cooperative. They are equipped with the power of reason and modern science to develop and progress. This was the approach that was embraced and applied in many walks of life by the Philosophes.

Montesquieu in his ground-breaking book *The Spirits of Laws* (1748) repudiated the conventional view of the law. In this seminal and widely influential work, he spelled out different types of government that correspond to different kinds of the constitution. Each type is claiming to comply with the rule of law and the principle of justice. Montesquieu maintained that there can be "no greater tyranny than that which is perpetrated under the shield of the law and in the name of justice" (quoted from Gould and Pate 2016: 27). Montesquieu saw, as Locke did, a hidden danger in the exercise of political power. The danger occurs when the political power is concentrated in the hand of one individual, institution, or agency. This concentration of power will always result in tyranny. Locke was also conscious of this danger, but his prognosis was half-hearted and inconclusive. He only saw the prevention of liberty in the absence of division of the legislative power between the parliament and the monarchy. For Montesquieu, Locke's division of power cannot effectively safeguard liberty and guarantee the rule of law. Montesquieu reasoned that for a "moderate government" to be effective it is "necessary to combine the several powers; to regulate, temper, and set them in motion; to give as it were ballast to one in order to enable it to counterpoise the other" (quoted from Gordon 2003: 86). Montesquieu's verdict to separate powers into legislative, executive, and judicial functions was a compelling conviction. The separation of powers between different organs serves as the most effective mechanism for the constitution of liberty and rule of law. It creates an intergovernmental system of checks and balances that prevents the domination of one branch of government on another and restrains the government from undue exercise and misuse of power.

Voltaire was inspired by English thinkers. His chief target was unreason and repression. He fostered the belief that the source of truth is nature, which can be discovered by means of reason. Voltaire campaigned against the absolute power of state and religion. He opposed the abuses of powers in France "especially arbitrary court judgments, cruel punishments, and religious persecutions … which he judged to be the inevitable results of authoritarian rule" (Woods 2009: 400). Voltaire identified three main obstacles to liberty and human progress. These are the state arbitrary rule, the parasitic clergy, and the reactionary academia. This being so he advocated that the presence of these barriers is not compatible with individual liberty, equality, and civil rights. Another polymath and deeply learned French intellectual of the age of enlightenment was Denis Diderot. He was the chief editor of the Encyclopedie (1745–72). What Diderot dreaded the most was men who are "created by religion." Those men who claim sole rights to truth. Diderot was a committed disciple of the Socratic Method. His quest for truth begins with scepticism. He doubted, disputed, and rejected what he considered to be illusory and absurd. He professed that "scepticism is the first step towards truth." Jean-Jacques Rousseau was another leading figure of the French enlightenment movement. He embarked on his quest from human nature. His core argument rests on the claim that humans are good by nature but can be corrupted by society. Along with being instinctively good people are "born free" but everywhere they are "in chain." In the past, in the state of nature, human nature and nature were in harmony. But it is contemporary societies that have alienated humanity from its true nature. Although Rousseau resented modern societies, he did not rule out the likelihood of an "ideal society" manifesting itself from these societies. The prospect and practicality of such a society hang on a social contract that Rousseau expounded in his best-known work, *The Social Contract* (1762). A book that led to brand him a heretic and forced him to flee France.

## The end of the medieval era

The transition from the medieval period to the modern era is a period of constant war. There were wars of religion, wars within different sects of religion, wars of colonization, wars of national liberation, and civil wars. The end of the medieval period marked the end of the long-lasting imperial power of the Church of Rome. The long-feared ecclesiastical gerontocracy that clung to power for so long and being far removed from reality and was gradually detached from the political scene. The battle was long and bloody. The church did everything in its power to guard its authority and privileges. In the end, it lost the battle. The dissolution of the Church of Rome was a great advance in speaking one's mind. It was an event of historic proportions. European wars of religion were the struggle of the world of modernity to emancipate itself from the grip of the church and absolute monarchs. Most freethinkers of the age of enlightenment, for a well-founded fear of persecution, admitted to being believers but rejected the church excesses. Many professed a belief in Deism. The list of freethinkers who were deists is long. We find among this list names of thinkers like John Locke, Leibniz, Kant, Voltaire, George Washington, Benjamin Franklin, and Thomas Jefferson.

The Renaissance created a new social and political environment for the Ancient Deism to revive. The basic tenet of Deism is the precept that human beings are not a distinct entity detached from nature. Religion is a human activity. As such, it was argued that it must be embedded in nature. For many Deists some religions' core principles are innate. This type of religious knowledge is inborn. The rest of religious knowledge is acquired through reason, religious scripts, or revelation. Deists believe in the real world, which has a creator. They believe that after the creation of the world, the creator has left it to us to seek the truth about the world. Furthermore, the world is real and orderly, and this means there is a purpose and reason to get to the truth. This perspective puts the Deists on the firing line of orthodox religions. For the Deists if religion is true then it must be rational. Religion cannot be true if it is not in harmony with nature. This meant direct confrontation with canonical scriptures and clerical rule. The Deistic movement implicitly questioned the authority and validity of religion. The movement asked for tolerance and plurality of beliefs, but this request could not be fulfilled without surgical amputation of religion from the state. Curbing the rule of the few in parts of Europe and North America enables many critical thinkers to speak their minds. The result was that reason triumphed over myth and superstition.

Doubts were cast on the validity of matters that were sacrosanct. Benedict Spinoza questioned the validity of miracles, the revelation, and the alleged descent of morality from divinity. All freethinkers repudiated the authority of clergy and monarchy. Locke wrote,

> men will always differ on religious questions and rival parties will continue to quarrel and wage war on each other unless the establishment of equal liberty for all provides a bond of mutual charity by which all may be brought together into one body.
>
> (Locke 1978: 689)

Gotthold Ephraim Lessing (1729–81), the German dramatist, pleaded for freedom of conscience. Hume argued that "superstition is an enemy to civil liberty" (Hume 1998: 42). In his satire, *Candide* (1759), Voltaire remarked that "superstition sets the whole world in flames." Thomas Clarkson (1760–1846), an evangelical Anglican and one of the leading opponents of slavery, professed that God has not "made an order of beings, with such mental qualities and powers, for the sole purpose of being used as *beasts*, or *instruments* of labour" (Clarkson and Cugoano 2010: 202 – italics in original). Paul Henri Thiery d'Holbach (1723–89), who wrote for Enyclopedie mostly on scientific matters, accused religion and clergy for depriving people of happiness. He argued that

> oppressed by the double yoke of spiritual and temporal power, it has been impossible for the people to be happy. Religion became sacred, and men have had no other Morality than what their legislators and priests brought from the unknown regions of heaven. The human mind feared truth and disdained reason, in order to follow authority.
>
> (Holbach 2013: 5)

It was not just doubts being cast on the validity of the absolute rule of theocracy but also the absolute rule of monarchy. These objections were intelligible since they were followed by a solution. Abbé' de Saint-Pierre (1658–1743), in his book *Project for Settling an Everlasting Peace* (1712), proposed federalism as the most effective political structure and mechanism for perpetual peace. Emmanuel Kant was attracted to this idea. In his work, *Toward Perpetual Peace* (1795), Kant described the process of achieving lasting peace in Europe. He wrote:

> A condition of peace among men living near one another is not a state of nature (*status naturalis*), which is much rather a condition of war, that is, it involves the constant threat of an outbreak of hostilities even if this does not always occur. A condition of peace must therefore be *established*; for suspension of hostilities is not yet assurance of peace, and unless such assurance is afforded one neighbour by another (as can happen only in a *lawful* condition) the former who has called upon the latter for it, can treat him as an enemy.
>
> (Kant 1996: 322 – Italics in original)

Kant stated that when there is an absence of a set of conditions peace may not result. Perpetual peace can sustain itself if its prerequisites are in place. For Kant, the basic requirements for long-lasting peace are civil constitution and a republican constitution. However, the civil constitution is ineffective in the absence of freedom. When all members of a society are equal in their freedom, they become equal citizens subject to common legislation. Moreover, international peace is contingent on equal rights given to all nations regardless of their size and strength. It is contingent on judicial equality before international law. For this situation to materialize, Kant suggested the federation of free nations, the League of Nations. In this scheme all nations are treated alike, enjoy the same rights and protections under the international constitution. The whole scheme, however, is a subsidiary of two cardinal principles. Most importantly, "the right of human beings must be held sacred, however great a sacrifice this may cost the ruling power … all politics must bend its knee before right" (Kant 1996: 347). Next is "the idea of the right of nations presupposes the *separation* of many neighbouring states independent of one another … in accordance with the idea of reason" (Kant 1996: 336 – Italics in original).

In economics, Physiocracy is believed to be the first insightful perspective in economics. The school was founded in France in the mid-eighteenth century by Francois Quesnay. In a seminal article, which was published in Encyclopaedia in 1756, Quesnay expounded the central tenets of the school. The term "Physiocracy" means "the rule of nature." The school saw the economy as an integral part of nature. It is said that as in the rest of nature, the economy has its own natural laws. So, letting the economy to operate naturally would set it in conformity with nature. Little wonder that they strictly adhered to the science of their time. They advocated a laissez-faire policy and opposed the mercantilists' restrictions and regulations against free commerce and trade. The Physiocrats accepted freedom of trade as a matter of course that is in harmony with the law of nature.

It was against the backdrop of these social, economic, political, and scientific events and upheavals that the American and the French republics were formed. The Anglo-Saxons who colonized North America demanded the same rights as those rights that their compatriots enjoyed at the metropole after the 1688 revolution. From 1700 to 1763, the 13 English colonies grew on their own. England needed funds to finance its wars with the French and the Native persons. The American colonies were compelled to accept the financial burdens of the British protracted imperial war. In 1763 the parliament in England passed several laws to raise funds for England's expansionist policy in North America. Patrick Henry (1736–99), a lawyer and politician, set up a campaign in 1763 against the British taxation policy in America. The British imposed the Stamp Act on the American colonists and raised tax rates on many items including wills and newspapers. As was to be expected this act exacerbated an already uncompromising situation. The British policy to pay for the costs of their wars in America united the colonists, who opposed the policy, based on one main demand and that was the idea of no taxation without representation. The colonists argued that the right to tax should not be in the hand of the metropole, in London. It should be the responsibility of each periphery assembly to decide what tax rates their citizens should pay. The enmity divide built daily until the irreconcilable conflict advanced to a level that the differences among the two sides could not be reconciled.

The leader of American liberation, on 4 July 1776, declared American independence from Britain. The declaration of American independence marks the beginning of a new era. It resulted in an epoch-making political transformation, the formation of a constitutional government. Besides other determined factors such as economic, scientific, and cultural transformations, the formation of the American republic was about a century-long cultivation of intellectual debates, discussion, and criticism, and a break from all previous systems of government and economy. The American republic harvested the fruits, good or bad, of the age of enlightenment. A constitutional civil republic would not have been possible unless there was a radical break from the past. One problem the founders of the American Republic were immediately confronted with, after they set up their resistance, was the absence of a legal source to rely on, to justify the legality of their demand. Great Britain had no constitution. Therefore, the law could be twisted in any direction to serve the interest of the ruling establishment. In the thick of the revolution, in May 1776, the founders of the new state passed the resolution of the Continental Congress, declaring independence from Britain, and asked each colony to set up a new government. This move was justified from the principle inherited from the enlightenment movement and was claimed to be in accordance with "the laws of Nature and of Nature's God" (quoted from Reck 1991: 730).

The colonists of the 13 pioneering states in America were British. Over a century of separation, they claimed to have formed a distinctive national identity from that of the British. On that basis, they demanded the right of self-determination and then erected their government on the principle of popular sovereignty. This was the English popular demand in the revolution of 1688. The revolution reoriented the ultimate power from the king and clergy to the people as the sovereign and the supreme power. It altered the standard by which the legitimacy of a government is measured. The canon of legitimacy was altered to the consent of the governed. The American state was founded on this parameter, on the ideas of John Locke. In *Second Treatise of Civil Government*, Locke described the requirements of an ideal political society and how it can be formed. On this point, he said:

> For when any number of men have, by the consent of every individual, made a community; they have thereby made that community one body, with a power to act as one body, which is only by the will and determination of the majority. For that which acts any community, being only the consent of the individuals of it, and it is one body must move one way, it is necessary the body should move that way whither the greater force carries it, which is the consent of the majority.
>
> (Locke 1948: 48)

In addition, the American declaration of independence rested on the Lockean distinction of society and government. For Locke "the dissolution of the society" is always harmful. This being the case the destruction of society is indefensible, whereas "the dissolution of government" is justified if a government does not have the consent of the governed. To this David Hume added that "as force is always on the side of the governed, the governors have nothing to support them but opinion; therefore, on opinion only that government is founded" (Hume 1953: 24).

The declaration of independence in its opening paragraphs provides five distinctively clear and indivisible requirements for a legitimate government. It describes them as self-evident truths. These are "all men are created equal," they have natural and "unalienable Rights." Governments acquire "their just powers from the consent of governed," and are responsible for the "safety and happiness" of their subject. In addition, "whenever any Form of Government becomes destructive … it is the right of the People to alter or abolish it, and to institute a new government" that derives its just power from the consent of the governed. However, the founders of America met two challenges soon after the declaration of independence. They knew that popular sovereignty was the right way to go but they questioned how they were going to implement such an aspiration. Compounding this problem was one they inherited, the British unwritten constitution. One of the most creative periods of debate for laying the foundation for a democratic government in history was from the time of the declaration of American independence during 1776–1789. The question was how to put in practice liberty, the sovereignty of the people, and the rule of law. The American revolutionaries discovered the solution in the "constitutional convention." Palmer elucidated this point by saying that the constitutional convention:

> embodied the sovereignty of the people. The people chose it for a specific purpose, not to govern, but to set up institutions of government. The convention, acting as the sovereign people, proceeded to draft a constitution and a declaration of rights ... It was thus the constitution that created the powers of government, defined their scope, gave them legality, and balanced them one against another.
>
> (Palmer 1959: 215)

The constitutional convention was the device whereby it instituted people at the centre of political society. People became sovereign and by their free will they set up their constitutional conventions, which in turn ratified the people's constitution. This meant the formation of a government by people, making and legislating laws by people, and the appointment of the political representatives by people. The constitutional convention created a law above the government. The constitution became the highest law that limited the power of the state and laid out the duties and responsibilities for all branches of government and declared the rights of free citizens. One important contingency that sprung from this was that of a constitutional government.

Broadly speaking, the idea of constitutional government was not new by any means. The principle of constitutional government goes back to Lycurgus' constitutional reform in the eighth century BC. Lycurgus (800–730 BC) was an original thinker and a figure of historical importance. His name is mentioned as one of 23 top influential lawgivers of all time, in the chamber of the US House of Representatives. When King Eumenos died, Lycurgus' brother Polydektes succeeded to the throne. It was not long after this that Polydektes also passed away and Lycurgus became king. The story goes that when his brother died his widow was expecting a baby. His brother's widow made a marriage proposal to Lycurgus, with one condition, that they kill her unborn child. Lycurgus accepted the marriage proposal only in words believing that otherwise she would kill the child. When the child was born, he took the baby to Agora, and declared that the boy to be the king of Sparta. To avoid bloodshed after this proclamation, Lycurgus went to Egypt, Libya, India, Spain, and Crete. During this time, he studied the history and political systems of governments in these parts of the world. After many years spending time abroad, Lycurgus returned to his nephew Charilaos, then the King of Sparta.

Lycurgus' extensive comparative study of different political systems convinced him of the great need for reforming the Spartan political system. With his deeds, Lycurgus proved the validity of his reforms and ideas. To convince the Spartans about the applicability of his reforms, he got two puppies. He fed one of them very well and the other one trained for hunting. When the puppies grew up, he gathered the people and showed them that the first puppy was useless. He carried out the whole plot to put in place his constitutional reforms. The rich opposed these reforms. On one occasion in Agora, he was hit in the eye and lost his eye. Lycurgus saved Alkander, the youth responsible for this action. Alkander then became one of the most devoted disciples of Lycurgus for the rest of his life. After the Spartans accepted these new laws, he asked that the people of Sparta never change these laws until he returned once more. Lycurgus never returned for the fear that if he did return, they would change the laws. By reforming the Spartan political constitution, Lycurgus created a system of law that lasted for about five centuries. After studying and observing the political institutions of the nations he visited, he arrived at the conclusion that a balanced political constitution could serve his aim of restoration of absolute equality among citizens of Sparta. The three essential elements of an effective government that Lycurgus recognized were a monarchy, democracy, and aristocracy. His political reforms aimed at combining the merits of these different elements and interest groups and creating a balanced political order to neutralize the excesses of all sides.

The Spartan mixed constitution (rhetra) was the model of the constitution that Plato and Aristotle wished to adopt for their political society. The mixed constitution, in their view, safeguards against two extreme forms of the constitution, the direct rule of people (Athenian democracy) and the constitution of tyranny. Plato divided the primary types of the constitution into two forms. He called them the "mother forms" constitution. One of these constitutions is "monarch and the other "democracy." Persian constitution represented the first and the Athenians the second extreme. In the former type, there is no freedom and in the latter there is. Other forms of constitutions derive from these two mother forms (Morrow 1993: 521). Plato considered the mixed constitution as an ideal form of constitution for Greek city-states.

By far the most elaborate and detailed classification of the political constitution in ancient times was proposed by Aristotle. He identified six forms of the constitution: monarchy, aristocracy, politeia, democracy, oligarchy, and tyranny. The basis of this classification rests on who are the rulers and whose interests they serve. He described each constitution based on those two principles. For instance, in a monarchy there is one ruler; in an aristocracy, there is the rule of a few; and in a polity, there is the rule of many. In the view of the foregoing, he added that any of these constitutions can be as effective as the other but at the same time each is open to the risk of despotism and tyranny. The latter pitfall arises when public interest is substituted with the pursuit of private interest. Aristotle insisted that mixed constitutions are not susceptible to this danger since they:

> will turn the balance and prevent the extravagances of the opposing extremes. For this reason, it is a happy state of affairs when those who take part in the life of the state have a moderate but adequate amount of property; for where one set of people possesses a great deal and the other nothing, the result is either extreme democracy or unmixed oligarchy or a tyranny due to the excesses of the other two.
>
> (Aristotle 1970: 173)

One of the ancient classic accounts of the mixed constitution is by a Greek historian, Polybius (c.203–120 BC). In book six of his *Histories*, he discusses the merits of the Roman constitution. The Roman constitution is his model constitution. For many years Polybius was a hostage in Rome and one of the advisors to Scipio Aemilianus, Cicero's hero. The Roman constitution was like the Lycurgus constitution of Sparta. It was a mixed constitution with some elements of monarchy, aristocracy, and democracy. A combination of all these elements in one republic, for Polybius, was the best form of government. It should be borne in mind that the most perfect constitution that Polybius advocated was one where the political power was shared equally by a monarchy, aristocracy, and democracy. This was the constitution that was put into practice at the time of the Hannibalic war. Contrary to Aristotle's view, Polybius believed that the absence of a mixed constitution would inevitably result in mob rule, oligarchy, and tyranny. But mixed constitutions ensure "sufficient checks and balances." Moreover, the division of power ensures greater social and political stability. Ideas of Polybius on the mixed constitution and the case study of the Roman Republic were very influential in the American constitution. This was admitted by the founders of the republic. John Adams wrote that Polybius "writings were in the contemplation of those who framed the American constitutions" (Adams 1797: 169). Following in the steps of Adams, Alexander Hamilton in *Federalist* number 34 wrote that the Roman Republic "attained to the utmost height of human greatness."

All the founders of the American Republic were children of the new age. Their political ideas were inspired above all by ideas of Machiavelli, James Harrington (1611–77), Hobbes, John Locke, Montesquieu, Hume, Rousseau, and many other forerunners of the age of enlightenment. These founders with the help of "the light from both the candle of reason and the lamp of experience … endeavoured to formulate the best constitution for their time and situation" (Reck 1991: 745). Their ideal polity was the one proposed by these thinkers. A system of political society that is based on the principles of "representations instead of collections of people – a total separation of the executive from the legislative power, and of the judicial from both – and a balance in the legislature, by three independent branches" (Adams 2003:

109). Montesquieu's division of power was instrumental in defeating the anti-federalist argument. In *The Spirit of Law*, Montesquieu distinguishes between three systems of governments: the republican, the despotic, and the monarchy. The republican system can be democratic or aristocratic. The republican government is based on the principle of virtue, the despotic government on fear, and the monarchy on honour. In the *Federalist*, number nine, Alexander Hamilton used Montesquieu division of systems of government and political power in advancing his federalist agenda (Reck 1991: 745–46).

Montesquieu's separation of powers was for the following reasons: (1) there cannot be political liberty without separation of powers. There is political liberty

> only when there is no abuse of power. But constant experience shows us that every man invested with power is apt to abuse it and to carry his authority as far as it will go. Is it not strange, though true, to say that virtue itself has a need for limits? To prevent this abuse, it is necessary from the very nature of things that power should be a check to power.
>
> (Montesquieu 2011: 150)

(2) A government turns despotic if checks and balances are not instituted with its three constituent parts. These are "three sorts of power: the legislative, the executive to things defended on the law of nations, and the executive in regard to matters that depend on the civil law" (Montesquieu 2011: 151). (3) Despotism and tyranny remain in charge unless the judiciary system is set independent. Montesquieu contended:

> there is no liberty if the judiciary power is not separated from the legislative and executive. Were it joined with the legislative, the life and liberty of the subject would be exposed to arbitrary control; for the judge would be then the legislator. When it joined the executive power, the judge might behave with violence and oppression. There would be the end of everything, were the same man or the same body, whether of the nobles or of the people, to exercise those three powers, that of enacting laws, that of executing the public resolutions, and of trying the causes of individuals.
>
> (Montesquieu 2011: 152)

The founders of the new republic opted for the doctrine of the separation of powers and a constitutional republic. John Adams associated "the generation and corruption of governments" to human nature (Adams 1797: 175). He related it to human passion that constantly gravitates to the same undesirable behaviour. This causes political instability and his remedy for this was a mixed constitution. He argued a government with no limited power

> by swelling beyond its due bounds, might degenerate into the vice that is congenial to it, and that while each of them were mutually acted upon the *opposite powers*, no one part might incline any way, or *outweigh* the rest; but the commonwealth, being equally *posed* and *balanced*, like a *ship* or wagon, acted upon by contrary powers, might long remain in the same situation.
>
> (Adams 1851: 223 – Italics in original)

James Madison, another principal architect of the American constitution, laid much stress on the necessity of the separation of powers. In *Federalist* 51, he asked the question "what is government" and then he explained it is:

> the greatest of all reflections on human nature? If men were angels, no government would be necessary. If angels were to govern men, neither external nor internal controls on government would be necessary. In framing a government which is to be administered by men over men, the great difficulty lies in this: you must first enable the government to control the government; and in the next place oblige it to control itself. A dependence on the people is no doubt, the primary control on the government; but experience has taught mankind the necessary precautions.
>
> (Federalist 51: 322)

This is how a government controlled by law was born. Its essence is captured in the Declaration of American Independence. The declaration reads as follows:

> We hold these truths to be self-evident, that all men are created equal, that they are endowed by their Creator with certain unalienable rights that among these are Life, Liberty, and the pursuit of Happiness. To secure these rights, Governments are instituted among Men, deriving their just powers from the consent of the governed. That whenever any Form of Government becomes destructive of these ends, it is the Right of the People to alter or to abolish it, and to institute new government, laying its foundation on such principles and organizing its powers in such form, as to them shall seem most likely to affect their Safety and Happiness.
>
> (Tsesis 2012: 321)

## Equality before the guillotine

The last king of France Louis XVI (1754–93) was executed by means of the guillotine on 21 January 1793. His queen, Marie-Antoinette (1755–93), also had her head chopped off by the same means on 16 October 1793. This means of decapitating the heads of enemies of the state, the heretics, and the convicts was not unique to France. Similar devices had been employed in other parts of Europe including England and Scotland for putting to death the criminals of aristocratic descent. What the French revolution did as part of the right to its fair trial was the legal equality of beheading. It treated equally by law the method of execution for all those who were condemned to death. The universal equality was the rallying cry of the 1789 French revolution. In the National Assembly of France in 1789 a law was passed for capital punishment. The National Assembly endorsed Joseph-Ignace Guillotine (1738–1814), a physician's proposal. The method ratified was by "means of a machine." This device for beheading the accused, called Guillotine, after the name of its inventor has been eternalized as the symbol of the Reign of Terror in France.

The French revolution was inspired by the ideals of the age of enlightenment and the American Revolution. It was a movement against the unrestrained power of nobility and clergy and the demand for the "rights of man." It intended to end the old regime. For many centuries almost all the King's associates, ministers, top clergy, and governors, in France, were from the Nobel social classes. The French Revolution stood against such privileges. Denis Diderot, a co-founder and chief editor of Encyclopedie, published an article in his Encyclopedie in 1751. In this article, *Political Authority*, he questioned the authority of the monarchy. He pointed out that the ultimate source of political authority is "people." It is by people's consent and for their interest. Diderot commented that the power of the state must be controlled by law and the relationship between the state and its subject must be based on a well-defined "social contract." De Jaucourt in another article, *Natural Equality*, in Encyclopedie (1755) defined natural liberty as "the constitution of human nature" that is "common to all men." Therefore, by 1789, Rousseau's ideas of "social contract," Voltaire ideas of "liberty," Montesquieu principles of "division of power," the experience of the American war of Independence, and the ideas of natural law, equality, and fraternity formed a web of a deeply held beliefs that impacted and involved all strands of French society. It was these compelling and contagious ideas of "the rights of man," of liberty, equality, and fraternity, and "hatred of the aristocracy" as the "deepest motivating force" that resulted in the 1789 French revolution.

The Parisian enacted the message of the "general will" of people on 14 July 1789 by seizing the Bastille, symbolizing the radical break with the old despotic regime. As the ideals of the enlightenment were put in front of the movement, the French revolution was approved by most of the forerunners of enlightenment across Europe. Among these thinkers, writers, philosophers, and poets were Herder, Goethe, Fichet, Kant, Schiller, Thomas Paine, Burns, Wordsworth, Blake, Coleridge, Mary Wollstonecraft, and William Wilberforce.

The last French Estates-General was summoned by the last French king on 5 May 1789. The tradition of the Estates-General went back to 10 April

1302 when it was for the first time convened at Notre-Dame. It consisted of the orders of the realm, the nobility, the clergy, and the representatives of the people. With gradual ascendance of the absolute power of the monarchy, this tradition was set aside and the last one was held during the financial crisis and the fever of the revolution. In the last meeting of the Estates-General, the privileged social groups, the Nobles, and the clergy had lost some of their traditional power and the representative of the Third Estate took advantage of the situation and formed the revolutionary National Assembly on 17 June 1789. This ended the supremacy of monarchy and clergy in France. At last, the French people were represented in their national assembly. The National Assembly reduced the status of the clergy and nobility to that of the Third Estate. This move was followed by the fall of the Bastille on 14 July 1789. The Parisian formed the National Guard of 48,000 men to protect their Assembly. The guard was led by Marquis de Lafayette (1757–1834), a veteran of the American Revolution. The whole event dismantled the Old Regime. The Assembly substituted the king as the state and the lawmaker. There were 745 deputies in the Constituent Assembly who were elected for a period of two years. The Assembly carried out a series of radical reforms from 1789 to 1791 that paralyzed the old regime completely. Its targets were the nobility and the clergy who were exempt from paying tax under the old regime.

On 26 August 1789, the Assembly passed the Declaration of the Rights of Man. Article 1 of the Declaration reads: "men are born and remain free and equal in … rights; social distinctions can only be based on public utility." The period of moderate reforms was very short. The Assembly abolished the Catholic Church and in 1790 it confiscated the Church lands and stopped its tithes. Soon after the mobs took the law into their own hands and polarizations among revolutionaries between the left and the right kept increasing. Maximilien de Robespierre (1758–94) represented the extreme left. He was a staunch follower of Rousseau and summed up the will and virtue of the French republic and the public in himself. On the opposite was Lafayette. The Jacobins gradually extended their control over the Assembly and by May 1792 seized control over the Assembly. Following this move on 20 September 1792 the Legislative Assembly was dismissed and, in its place, the National Convention, similar to that of the US constitutional Convention, was instituted. The convention created the French Republic and ended the reign of the monarchy in France.

The revolutionary regime introduced a uniform system of justice, a civil court, trial by jury, and ended the medieval penal system and torture. It ended the practice of torture by breaking the accused on the wheel. Jean Calas was one of the victims of this method of torture who was crashed on the wheel in 1762. It was Voltaire who brought Calas case to the public attention. The phase of radical reforms was over by July 1793. The reign of terror crushed the revolution's ideals of reason and consent, something that came to its head between July 1793 and July 1794 (Palmer 1971: 113). On the slightest suspicion of opposition to the state, the citizens were arbitrarily arrested, detained, or killed with total impunity. About half a million people are estimated to have been detained during this period (Jones 1988: 115). Whoever was accused was condemned to death. From September 1793 to July 1794 about 17,000 were condemned to death. The victims of terror included the leaders of the revolution, such as Camille Desmoulins (1760–94), the poet Andre Chenier, one of the most progressive and enlightened philosophers, Condorcet (1743–94), and the famous chemist Antoine Lavoisier (1743–94). Between June and July of 1794, in Paris, 1,376 people were guillotined.

No revolution is neutral. Extremism is the second nature of every violent political revolution. Revolution is an extreme panacea to extreme conditions and passions. An upheaval that gravitates on a mirage of a dreamland, in a time of great turmoil and desperation if not constrained and obligated by a democratic political and social contract or charter, will end in disaster. There are two sides to every violent revolution. These are extreme hate and extreme adoration. On the one side there is the love for the ideal world of complete freedom, justice, equality, truth, civility, opulence, and harmony. On the opposite side is the tainted hate for the old system. In a violent revolution the zeal, zest, and frenzy wrath of those who defend the old regime, and their interests are surmounted by the greater force of hate of those who discard and replace the old system. The devotion, fever, ecstasy, ferocity, and aberration of the situation nurture extreme lunacy from both sides.

Blinded by the flame of the fanaticism of the extreme situation, there will be paranoid zealots from both sides who will commit the grisliest crimes against humanity. Revolutionary wars would fail when they lack a provisory safeguard as a safety measure for the post-conflict reconciliation and peacebuilding. Blind dedication and incitement of hatred and violence is a fertile environment for the growth of demagogues and warlords. Precarious situations such as violent revolutions, without cover, are in vulnerable situations. Without an interim backup, they fall into hands of another form of absolute dictatorship. The potential harms can, in part, be mitigated by an informed freedom charter that is rational, humane, and democratic. A roadmap that is level-headed, judicious, far-sighted, liberal, accommodating, amiable, and fair. We find many of these attributes in the Declaration of American Independence. The success of the American Revolution, as one of the few successful revolutions in history, is mainly credited to this guidance document and the safety plan of action. In the absence of such a roadmap, the revolutionary zealots, who tend to be the least informed and have a very minor or no role in the revolution, gradually prevail over the committed, well-informed, good-intentioned, fair-minded, prudent, sincere, and earnest drivers of revolution. In the event of a lack of preventative measures, i.e., a democratic liberation charter, the intense and powerful passion for change will ferment obstinacy, prejudice, urgency, delusion, psychosis, and blood lust that will be elevated to mob rule with unpredictable far-reaching disastrous consequences like those that had been witnessed in the French revolution.

After four years of radical and drastic change, the French revolution was plunged into a period of widespread savagery and terror. This period started on 5 September 1793 and ended on 27 July 1794. Maximilien Robespierre (1758–94), a radical Jacobin, was at the head of the French revolutionary government. Captivated and misguided by Rousseau's ideas, Robespierre launched his war to safeguard the ideals of the revolution: the principle of equality, freedom, justice, and fraternity with diligent and unyielding cruelty and bloodshed. These ideals were not those that were safeguarded. Instead, the priority shifted to the protection of the new order and rulers. As Robespierre took over, he made terror "the order of the day" (Schechter 2018: 203). The savagery of his reign only lasted for about a year and after that, he was removed from power and executed by his old comrades on 27 July 1794.

The changes that took place during this period were drastic and dramatic among leading European nations and in North America. The ancient regimes were overthrown but patriarchal social, political, and economic orders persisted well into the future. The privileges of the nobility, clergy, and the newly emerging military and merchants' classes recovered and were promoted. There was not much tangible improvement in working masses, women, and slaves' conditions. This is not all. Most of the leading thinkers of enlightenment did not believe in gender equality and some even remained slave owners. Locke asserted that men are superior to women because they are "the abler and stronger" (Locke 1969: 161). Kant purported that in marriage a man is "the party to direct" and woman "to obey." Moreover, in his estimate women are not suited for "laborious learning or painful pondering" (Baron 1997: 167). Rousseau alleged that women are wrong when they complain about "the inequality of man-made laws. When she tries to usurp our rights, she is our inferior" (Lauren 2011: 33). In the same way, it was assumed that it is part of the order of nature for the poor social classes to stay wherever they are and for the slaves to obey.

Oddly enough, with all its shortcomings the era of enlightenment did foster the right of gender equality. In Britain, this quest started with Thomas Hobbes and completed with Jeremy Bentham. Misogyny, Bentham contested, cannot stand up to rational justification. He remarked that contrary to the popular belief, complete equality of gender is natural. Thomas Paine wrote that through the ages women were "robbed of freedom of will by the law … Man with regard to them has been either an insensible husband or an oppressor" (Paine 1894: 62). In France, Claude Andrien Helvetus (1715–71) argued that there is no difference in natural and intellectual abilities between men and women. He put the blame on women's lack of progress, lack of opportunity, and exclusion from education. Marquis de Condorcet, another French philosopher, expressed the same sentiment and called for equal rights for women.

Few women that had the chance of being educated raised their voice against the general treatment of women in society. Among the most influential critical thinkers was Mary Wollstonecraft (1759–97). In her book *Vindication of the Rights of Women* (1792), she denounced women's long-lasting repression and articulated their voice for equality of rights. She deliberated that "women would not always remember they were women if they were allowed to acquire more understanding" (Wollstonecraft 2009: 210). Olympe de Gouges, one of the victims of the Reign of Terror, expressed disapproval of the French declaration of the Rights of Man. In her view, the revolution was devoted merely to the rights of men. To counter discrimination, she wrote her influential work entitled *Declaration of the Rights of Man and the Female Citizen*. The critical issue at hand under these circumstances is how we can have social and economic progress when women who constitute half of the population are excluded from political, economic, and public life. Where the slaves and the working population, most of the population, were disfranchised and were denied their fundamental citizenship rights, badge of equality is a futile hope. When they do not consent, with intent, they are prevented from exercising their free will and excluded from utilizing their full potential. One then can cast doubt with sufficient grounds on the tenability of such economic order. Until these citizens are not emancipated and entitled to exercise their fundamental rights, talk about an economy that is free from chronic disorder is null and void.

## Power of appropriation and expropriation

An absolute ruler can confiscate his subjects' asset at will. Individuals' consent evaporates entirely under such circumstances. The boundless power of an absolute ruler is exacerbated when it is sanctioned by a subservient religion. A vivid and illuminating example of the unrestrained discretion of the sovereign was the thing that James I (1566–1625), the king of Scotland as James VI and the first Stuart king of England, was longing for. In his speech to representatives of houses of commons and lords on Wednesday 21 March 1609, he described the rule of monarchy as "the supremist thing upon earth: For Kings are not only God's Lieutenants on earth, and sit upon God's throne, but even by God himself, they are called Gods" (James VI and I 1986: 107). In view of the foregoing, the state is not bound by the rule of law and there can be no checks on the state power. When this happens, the state enjoys complete impunity to appropriate private assets, debase the full-bodied medium of exchange, print paper money at will, or subjugate other nations and plunder their resources to finance its expenditures. All these methods of state finance, either collectively or individually, have been applied one way or another by undemocratic states over the course of history.

Sources of revenue for the old states, which were mostly empires and theocratic, came from looting, misappropriating the assets of their citizens or robbing the assets of people they conquered, debasing the coinage, confiscation of land, and a variety of exorbitant taxes that they imposed on the people under their authority. Borrowing was few and far between as everything including the life of the citizens belonged to the emperor or other less significant tyrant rulers. For those theocratic imperial states of Abrahamic theology, judo-Christian and Islam, charging interest on loans was either banned or partially restricted. In the modern democratic world, the power of the state is restricted by the rule of law. The state is not the representative of any deity with unlimited power over life and possessions of its subject. The modern democratic states initiated borrowing in a big way on interest to finance public expenditures and laid the foundations of modern money and capital markets. The Dutch state, after the Dutch nation gained its independence in the modern era, brought public finance under the rule of law. But it was not long after its independence that the French occupied Holland and ended the Dutch national sovereignty.

The Dutch republic lost its leading continental and world power after the Franco-Dutch War (1672–78). Louis XIV (1638–1715) declared war on the Dutch and the French army comprising 120,000 military personnel invaded the Dutch republic in the spring of 1672. The war lasted until 1678. With the Nijmegen peace treaty, the Golden Age of the Dutch republic ended, and France replaced Dutch as the world power. France as the most powerful nation in Europe had the largest army, the most advanced economy, and the largest population. The French population in 1700 was 19.2 million. The population of its closest competitor, Britain, at the same year was 6.9 million. By 1780 the French population increased to 25.6 million and the British population to 9 million. French foreign trade was £9 million in 1700 and 22 million in 1780. For the same years, Britain's foreign trade was 13 million in 1700 and 23 million in 1780. Given 1700 as the base year, the agricultural output in France in 1780 was 155 million, for Britain it was 126 million. The industrial output for France was £454 million and for Britain, it was £197 million. As for the total production it was £169 million for France and £167 million for Britain (Rostow 1975).

It was in the last decades of the eighteenth century that the Industrial Revolution took off in England and subsequently England led the way for industrialization. We can understand the crisis of the industrial economy better if we look at crises closely through the prism of the industrialization of the British economy. This will be the main subject of our analysis in the next chapter. Nef argues that "the rate of industrial change from about 1735 to 1785 was no more rapid in Great Britain than in France" (Nef 1943: 5). France also for most of the century was edging ahead of Britain in scientific knowledge, innovations, and discoveries. The number of patents granted in France in the first half of the century was considerably higher than they were in England.

France extended its hegemony over Europe through its successes during the war in the eighteenth century. In the first decade and half of the century, France was preoccupied with the war of the Spanish succession (1701–14). The powerful French absolute monarch, Louis VIX, died a year later in 1715. His reign is marked by a continuous state of war. Financing unremitting wars that no longer were parochial but world-wide necessitated different sources of finance from what was commonly practised for ages. The traditional methods of war finance in the form of taxation, compulsory loans, debasing of coins, confiscation of private wealth, seizure, and looting and plundering of a foreign land were inadequate. Funding mercenary armies, using such methods including a war booty, could not quench the insatiable thirst of the colonial expansion of the European pacemaker colonialists in the eighteenth century. All methods of public finance under the reign of the absolute monarchy were arbitrary and the tax rates were set willy-nilly by the king. Innovative methods of public finance owed much to the ongoing war. Public deficit due to the wars, for the most part of the second half of the seventeenth century, in France was financed by short- and long-term loans. After the war, the remaining short-term loans were converted to long-term loans at lower interest rates in line with the falling rates of interest (Velde 2006: 10). Jean-Baptise Colbert (1619–83), the distinguished finance minister of Louis XIV from 1661 to 1683, converted such debts in 1680, 1698, and 1699. But even this method was not sufficient to finance the swelling costs of wars. New conditions required new financial experiments.

The main source of revenue in peacetime was tax revenue. The total tax revenue for the selected peacetime years 1683, 1700, 1715, and 1725 was 116.0, 112.1, 165.6, and 191.1 million, respectively (Velde 2006: 6). Another source of some significance was seigniorage. But such sources were short of war demand finance. Colbert abolished seigniorage in 1676. The revenue from the demonetization of coins, the forced coinage, not just was short-lived but also was the cause of greater monetary instability. French demonetized their coins in 1709, 1718, 1720, and 1726 (Velde 2006: 12). Out of the eight times recoinage from 1690 to 1726, five of them (in 1690, 1693, 1701, 1704, and 1709) were during wartime and the other three (in 1715, 1718, and 1726) were during peacetime.

By eighteenth century France became the dominant power in Europe. The French economy was growing. The time was ready for new ideas to improve state finance. Louis XIV ruled the largest population in Europe, three times more than that of the Spanish population. The French economy was in better shape than its competitors. It comes as no surprise that in the eighteenth century France conducted the first modern monetary experiments and produced the first systematic school of economic thought. In 1756 Francois Quesnay, the founder of physiocratic school, published his celebrated article about circular flow of income. The school advocated "the rule of nature" in the economy and sought the origin of all wealth in land. Adam Smith met the leaders of the school and was influenced by their ideas. With the publication of his monumental work *The Wealth of Nations* (1776), Smith shortened the duration of physiocrats' influence. The essence of physiocracy economic theory was best articulated by Jaques-Claud-Marie Vincent de Gournay (1712–59). He remarked that

> commercial liberty does not consist of whatever one wishes. The goal of the state is to have useful commerce. To have useful commerce,

> restrictions and prohibitions are necessary … It is commonly said that commerce needs both liberty and protection, but between them, liberty is more useful.
>
> (quoted from Horn 2015: 96)

The economic and political conditions in the second decade of the eighteenth century were predisposed to accommodating unconventional monetary experiments. The case in point was John Law's fiscal trials. Law (1671–1929) was a Scottish economist, banker, and founder of monetary economics. His father was a Goldsmith banker who died in 1688 when John Law was only 13 years of age. For being prepared to assume the family business he studied economics at the age of 14. The parochial family business was too insular to tame Law's overambitious goals. So, he left for London where he spent most of his time gambling and filled his spare time studying mathematics and economics. He killed Edward Wilson in a duel on 9 April 1694. Law was tried and found guilty of manslaughter. He was imprisoned but he succeeded in escaping from prison and fleeing to Amsterdam. The city of Amsterdam then was unparalleled for its economic, financial, banking, and monetary developments. After ten years in exile, he returned to his homeland Scotland where he wrote his book *Money and Trade Considered* (1705). At the same time, he proposed an innovative banking and money supply system to the Scottish Parliament, which was not accepted. The union acts of 1706 and 1707, the former passed by Parliament of England and the latter by Parliament of Scotland, forced Law once again to go into exile.

Law left for France in 1712–13. He presented his plan to the French government. Given the circumstances of French public finance, then Law's plan was very attractive. Louis XIV numerous wars were too costly, and the French government was trapped in a very heavy debt burden. With that said, the French government permitted Law to execute his monetary plan and reduce public debt in 1716. Law's monetary antidotes and prognoses were far ahead of his time. His efforts, in the end, proved to be in vain. His drastic measures to rectify the financial difficulties of France produced more heat than light. Even though his ideas of using more effective forms of money, the endogenous supply of money, the banking system, and the central bank were innovative, they were ill-timed. They were ill-matched with the legal, cultural, political, institutional, and technological confinement of the French and the world economy then. But desperate times called for drastic measures. The French rulers saw no cause for alarm and were mesmerized by Law's proposals. His proposal for a national bank was agreed with great deal of enthusiasm. That led to the creation of the General Bank in 1716. This was a private bank. The main function of the bank was to create credit and issue the paper form of money to repay the state debts. It was proposed that the notes should be backed by land or precious metals. The venture had a good start. To throw the full backing of the state behind the bank's paper money, Law renamed the bank to the Royal Bank in 1718. Law became the Controller General of the bank. The good days of Law's venture lasted until the downfall of the Mississippi scheme. This scheme aimed to develop French colonies in America.

To develop the colony of Louisiana, Law launched a new venture. He set up a company, the company of the West. For its initial capital, Law offered a share to the public payable in billets d'Etat. This comprised the company asset. For its working capital, he relied on the accrued interest. For paying interest Law proposed another plan, the monopoly of a tobacco farm. After a series of mergers and acquisitions, the French Indies company was formed. The intention of this plan was to cover interest payments with the lease price. Law brought both the bank and the company under his control. In summer 1719 he thought of another scheme. The Indies Company was given two additional responsibilities: to manage mint and tax collection. In August 1719, he cancelled the old lease and replaced it with another lease on the General Farms. Following this Law aimed for lowering the interest rate to refinance the public debt. The company had the state, the Royal Bank, and Law's prestige backing. What is more, it issued shares at very attractive prices. The whole scheme seemed very lucrative and up-and-coming. It grew so fast.

All the prospects in Louisiana were much exaggerated. The scheme stood on a perilous edge and at the mercy of circumstance. The forces of adversity were creeping in and the demise of the scheme was unavoidable. A frenzied speculative trend triggered the fall of the company in 1719. As a result of this, the share price increased from 500 in 1719 to 18,000 livres during the first half of 1720. This success encouraged Law to merge the General Bank to the Indies Company. By this manoeuvre, Law aimed at achieving the main objective of his scheme. That was to finance public debts. In selling company shares for the state securities, billets d'etat, not only did he contemplate increasing share prices through state backing but also increasing the demand for state securities. Law sold his scheme as a win-win partnership that every partner in the scheme could gain from taking part in the scheme. The fact was that the relationship was mutually reinforcing but in the opposite direction. The increasing price of government security and the company shares fed each other in opposite ways. On one hand, it resulted in a frenzied spiral of the speculative market. During this hue and cry, it substituted illusion with reality. At the same time, the speculative fever was inflated with the injection of ever more fiat money and credit. The spell broke when the hope, the buoyant speculation, and the issue of paper money and credit were detached from the underlying economic fundamentals. The scheme intended to achieve three objectives. These were to raise cheap funds to finance the national debt. The way to do that was to convert public debt into company equity. Second, company equity was secured by its monopoly to collect tax in France. Finally, for the scheme to last, there was one way forward. That is a continuous rise in share prices by means of intervention and manipulation.

For this purpose, the amalgamation of Royal Bank with the Louisiana Company became handy. The bank kept issuing notes and circulating them in the economy. Unrestrained injection of notes into the market fed the share prices, and the fascination of rising prices and making money out of thin air was too addictive. Law had a monopoly over the company, the national bank, and virtually the state. He was the driver of the whole system. He used his position to set one part of the machine for or against other parts. His early successes in handling the system made him overconfident to the point of losing his sense of reality. In addition to the cited responsibilities, Law was appointed as the finance minister in January 1720. At first, everything seemed to go according to his plan. The share prices kept rising at the back of monetizing debt on the top of more debts. Foreign exchange depreciated and the inflation rate was receding. It was not long before Law recognized the predicament, he was in, but the problem was too large to be overturned. When rising inflation depreciated the paper money, Law partially demonetized gold and silver. This was an attempt to stabilize the value of the paper form of money, but the attempt was in vain. By May 1720 Law lost control over events. France lost trust in Law's scheme and the run on the bank began. In the summer of 1720 Law's scheme was no longer. The value of the company plummeted and by 1721, the company lost 97 per cent of its market capitalization. Law's monetary skills hit a dead end. Nothing could save him from a fall from grace. He became a liability. For fear of reprisal from the mob, Law fled France for Brussels then moved to Rome, Copenhagen, and London. He died, broke, in December 1720 in Venice. His originality as a monetary thinker is noted by eminent economists such as Marx, Marshall, and Schumpeter (Bilginsoy 2015: 31). The Mississippi episode and the South Sea Bubble occurred at the same time. The effects of these frenzied speculations rippled throughout Europe. These events reversed the direction of the French economy from a relatively open and liberal economy into an inwardly, overregulated, and lethargic economy. The French school, the Physiocrats, was a response to such conditions.

One of many causes of the 1789 French revolution was the outstanding national debt (Hamilton 1947: 124). France contributed to the war of the American Revolution. It backed the American colonies both financially and in armed forces to break away from Britain. The French financial aid to the American Revolution is estimated to be over one billion livres (Chaline and Kowalski 2018: 57). Their involvement in the American Revolution increased the French public debt considerably. Convening the States-General of 1789 was chiefly due to the budgetary constraints. Extending the financial burden to the clergy and the nobility also deterred and drove back such natural allies from the old regime. Taxing these influential social groups united them with numerous strata of the labouring population against the ruling class. The situation was made worse in July 1788 because of the poor harvest and a hailstorm (White 1995: 223). After the revolution, the extreme events were followed by extreme responses. The old system of taxation was dismantled, and the budget deficit kept widening. It was under 100 million livres in 1788 and by 1790 it increased to 364 million livres (White 1995: 240). For the new regime to hold onto power, it required new sources of finance. In addition to securitizing properties, the revolutionary regime confiscated and sold the properties of the monarchy and the church from 14 to 17 May 1790. The French revolutionaries issued paper bills (assignat) – a paper form of money from 1789 to 1796 to finance their growing fiscal deficits (White 1995: 242). The over-issue of assignat resulted in the devaluation of assignats and inflation. For crashing counterrevolutionary forces and exporting the revolution, even the issue of assignats was inadequate. So, it was decided to finance the national debt from abroad in the name of exporting the revolution. With this in view, France invaded Belgium in 1792 and confiscated considerable resources as war booty. This was followed by a decree on 15 December 1792 to appropriate Belgium properties. A coup on 27 July 1794 terminated the government of the Terror. However, the fiscal problems persisted in the new regime. In another coup on 9 November 1799, Napoleon came to power. He financed his government expenditures through his conquests. It is estimated that during the period 1799–1814 he confiscated about 785 million francs from the conquered land (White 1995: 251).

One of the distinct features of modern democratic states is their system of taxation. However, taxation did not begin with the formation of the democratic state. Imposing tax has no one root but many. Its origin is lost in the mists of time. One thing is clear. It may safely be said that all empires were built in part on taxation revenue – side by side on plundering the resources of the lands they conquered. The rulers levied a range of taxes to pay for constructions of palaces, to fund wars and their luxurious lifestyles. Gunter Dreyer, an archaeologist, and his team in the 1980s unearthed clay tablets from the tomb of King Scorpion I of ancient Egypt that dates to 3200 and 3300 BC (Jones-Hunt 2011: 225). These were records of tax levied on linen and oil. The Egyptians also taxed grain, the use of the Nile for transportation, foreign trade, and livestock. In ancient times, Chinese too levied taxes – on rice wine, tea, tobacco, land, salt, gold, and other precious metals to finance the construction of the great wall, the imperial court, and religious ceremonies. In ancient Greece foreign residents paid a poll tax, and market traders paid indirect taxes. During the war, people paid taxes directly and after the war, these taxes were cancelled. The Romans adopted the Hellenic taxation system and raised a greater portion of their tax revenue from land. By 167 BC, levying taxes on Roman citizens was abolished. Instead, taxes were levied on the colonies.

We also find a detailed account of tax payment in two of the ancient Indian literary works, the Manusmriti which dates to 1250 BC and the Arthasastra which dates to 300 BC. In the former work, we find the instruction to the monarchs about rules of taxation. The traders and artisans were instructed to pay 1/5 of their profits in silver and gold as tax. For agriculturalists, it was 1/6, 1/8, and 1/10 of their products. In the Arthasastra, it is noted that certain social groups such as students, poor, sick, and aged were exempt from paying tax. In the Bible, the tax payment is as "tithing," a duty that people paid to the temples. The formation of empires and imperial states and wars has widened the imposition of the broad range of compulsory levies both on their subjects and on those who they subjugated. Ibn Khaldun (1332–1406), an Arab scholar and historian of the medieval era in his book the *Muqaddimah* (1375), noted the increasing importance of levy taxes to big governments and imperial rule in his time. He commented:

> cultural enterprises grow the number of individual imposts [forms of tax] and assessment mounts. In consequence, the tax revenue … increases … [people's] customs and needs become more varied because of the prosperity and luxury in which they have become immersed. As a result, the individual imposts and assessments upon the subjects, agricultural laborers, farmers, and all the other taxpayers increase. Every individual impost assessment is greatly increased, in order to obtain a higher tax revenue.
>
> (Khaldun 2005: 230)

Taxation in all its forms is a compulsory levy. It is mandatory. Every state's fiscal capacity is limited. Most of the fiscal burdens often fall on the public. Whoever bears the burden of a form of tax is unrequited. One's tax liability is independent of the assistant that one may receive. Slavery and slave labour are the two most extreme forms of taxation. In its first form, the individual has no independent identity. The slave owner owns their slave totally. Slavery in Roman law was considered as "an institution of the law of nations by which … a person is subjected to the dominion of another" (quoted from Finkelman 2012: 106). In the second form whatever one produces goes to whoever is in control of one's entire labour. In despotic political systems, compliance is unconditional. The taxpayers must comply as they are commanded. A taxpayer consent to what rates they can pay to the state coffers is taken out of the relationship. The history of the tyrant rulers is littered with many examples of levying atrocious taxes that not only devastated the lives of their subjects but also led to the downfall of their own rule. Since the invention of taxation, there has developed a struggle between those who impose the tax and the subjects who bear the burden of taxation. To mitigate the burden of taxation there has been an ongoing democratic struggle of masses until the formation of national democratic governments. The Magna Carta in 1215 limited the king's power to tax in England. It enacted that "no scutage or aid shall be imposed on our kingdom without the common consent of our kingdom" (quoted from Fryde 2001: 143). The Bill of Rights during the 1689 revolution narrowed the state power to tax even more. The Bill declared that "levying money for or to the use of the Crown by the pretence of prerogative without grant of parliament, for a longer time, or in other manner than the same is or shall be granted, is illegal" (Harlow and Rawlings 2006: 605).

The taxation system has evolved and is evolving. In the American War of Independence, mandatory taxation became a fundamental right. The

American Revolution infused taxation as an imperative standard of the legitimacy of the democratic government – proclaiming that there can be no legitimate democratic government without public consent to pay tax. During the course of revolution, the Magna Carta edict of "no taxation without consent" became a rallying cry. It is said that John Hamden in 1637 was the author of the statement that "taxation without representation is tyranny" (Kean 2011: 274). Whatever its origin, it was James Otis (1725–83), a lawyer, who applied the edict at the right time and place. In requesting the same rights for all British subjects, Otis argued that "no parts of His Majesty's dominions can be taxed without their consent" (quoted from Fell 2004: 235). This expression was reinvented into "no taxation without representation" that acted as catalysts in the victory of American liberation. It was the year of the American Revolution (1776) that Adam Smith also published his ground-breaking book in economics, the *Wealth of Nations*. In this book, Smith defined four democratic principles of taxation. These principles are as follows: (1) "The subject of every state ought to contribute to the support of the government, as nearly as possible in proportion to their respective abilities." He added that it is not "unreasonable for the rich to contribute to public revenue not only in proportion to their income but something more than that proportion." (2) "The tax which each individual is bound to pay ought to be certain and not arbitrary. The time of payment, the manner of payment, the quantity to be paid, ought to be clear and plain to the contributor, and to every other person." (3) "Every tax ought to be levied at the time or in the manner, in which it is most convenient for the contributor to pay it." (4) "Every tax ought to be so contrived as both to take out and to keep out of the pockets of the people as little as possible over and above what it brings into the public treasury of the state" (Smith 1804: 258–60).

## Conclusion

The main foundations of the modern world were laid in the seventeenth and eighteenth centuries in Europe. Contemporary advanced economies are inconceivable without the profound scientific, economic, political, legal, institutional, cultural, and technological transformations that took place most specifically in Holland, France, England, and the United States of America in these interim centuries. These centuries changed the nature and the course of economic disorders and crises from what they had been in the previous centuries and millenniums. The fact is history does not halt. With the passage of time, everything changes. But there is a distinction between ordinary changes and historical changes. The age of enlightenment was a historical change. It was a passing age from agriculture to industry, from superstition to science and reason, from theocracy to democracy, from bondage to individual liberty, from muddled thoughts to clear thoughts, from pursuit of self-interest as vice to pursuit of self-interest as virtue, from forced loans to secured loans, and from restricted trade to free trade.

Before we pass any final judgement about this time, we need to look at this period as a distinct break from the past. It is a mistaken precept to perceive any transitional period as only good old days or only bad old days. Revolutionary periods are fraught with unexpected dangers and are teeming with all sorts of possibilities and opportunities. To place the whole idea of economic crisis upon a proper footing would lead us nowhere if it is not examined in a wider historical context. It is generally admitted that during this period we entered a new epoch in human history. The new system of production, exchange, and distribution that came into existence in the seventeenth and eighteenth centuries is a populated commercial and industrial system that is marked by a complex division of employment and the application of science and technology. It is a trade and money economy.

The genesis of modern financial engineering was in the seventeenth and eighteenth centuries. The force of circumstances compelled people of wealth, power, and knowledge to invent different financial institutions, markets, and instruments to meet the needs of their time. These changes gradually cast off the old deep-rooted prejudices, habits, customs, regulations, and beliefs. These changes, for their part, quickened the wheels of commerce and trade. The speed of change outpaced any other period preceding it. In general, everything is in a state of flux. But the pace of transformation in the seventeenth and eighteenth centuries was to the extent that the like of which cannot be found prior to this period. The acceleration of the pace of change was more consequential than revolutionary changes. This was the age that shattered the stagnant medieval era with the speed never seen before. Furthermore, the new changes triggered the pace of change to accelerate as time went by. This was the era of the inception of joint-stock investment and organized stock markets. The Amsterdam Stocks Exchange was established in 1602 where the Dutch East India Company offered its stocks to the public and where its shares were traded. The London Stock Exchange was founded in 1773 but for several decades before the foundation of the London Stock Market, there were organized security markets in London. There was a growth in joint-stock companies that publicly issued shares and traded on secondary markets. Amsterdam and London were the commercial and financial centres of the world during this period. This was an era of the formation of the first central banks.

The expansion of trade and industry paved the way for the development of the banking sector and the invention of new forms of money. The habits of investments and supply of money took a new form. The banking system initiated the endogenous supply of money and experimentation in discovering new forms of money led to the use of fiat money. To finance the revolution, the American revolutionaries issued the Continental Currency from 1775 to 1783. This was issued in paper bills – a representative, a token, form of money. The excessive issue of Continental Currency made it worthless after 1780. The French revolutionaries also issued fiat money, the inconvertible "assignats" to finance their day-to-day expenditures from 1789 to 1796. The excessive issue of assignats also led to the end of its circulation. This was the age when the sovereign borrowing had evolved. The source of borrowing of the monarchic and theocratic states of medieval time was mostly from personal borrowing and forced loans. The modern nation-states that emerged during the age of enlightenment extended the social, economic, and legal scope and scale of the state. Enacting these responsibilities required regular sources of finance. This is how modern sources of state finance, money, and capital markets developed and thrived. This is also the era of the unfolding of economic theories and the birth of economic schools of thought. As all these activities were new, they were overdone.

There is no complete knowledge about the economic crisis that will continue to hold good in the future. What took place during the early stages of the economies of the modern world is materially different from the latter stages of economic transitions. What is regular is, in fact, the irregularity of economic crises. The future is never like the past. There is no rationally secure foundation for all generations of people to be psychologically constituted in the same mode or to live and think in the same way and under the same conditions. Revealing the secrets of one crisis at one time in history does not follow in the unlocking of the secrets of all economic crises, always and everywhere. There is no more to the crisis than its time of happening. A period in the past can never fit into another period at the present or in the future. This is the striking feature of all economic crises. The hallmark of each crisis is specific to its time and conditions or else the society and economy will remain fixed in time and with conditions that are immutable. The organizations and order of society and the economy are constantly changing. Economic crises occur neither under the veil of ignorance nor under the blanket of know-it-all. Empirical generalizations, in the case of economic crises, are not verifiable but effortlessly falsifiable. As no two crises are identical, economic crises, contrary to the prevailing theories of crisis, are devoid of general laws. No economic crisis is verifiable in the light of any other crisis either in the past or at the same time in another location.

# 2 High and low times of industrialization

## Introduction

The phrase "Industrial Revolution" was coined by Louis Guillaume, a French diplomat in 1799 (Ross 2008: 9). These two words also appeared in Peter Gaskell's book, *The Manufacturing Population of England*, in 1833 and a decade later in Friedrich Engels' book, *The Condition of the Working Class in England*, in 1844. In his book, Engels links the rise of the proletariat class with the Industrial Revolution. He argued that "the invention of the steam-engine and of machinery for working cotton … gave rise … to an industrial revolution, a revolution which altered the whole civil society" (Engels 2008: 1). The latter two authors fittingly associate the genesis of the modern industrial economy with England. One century that represents the Industrial Revolution is no other than the nineteenth century. The Industrial Revolution was a momentous landmark in human history. It was a defining moment, a radical break with the medieval past and the beginning of a new era. Britain reigned supreme in the nineteenth century on the back of the Industrial Revolution. There were many factors that contributed to the revolution to take place in England. The examination of all determinants is beyond the scope of this chapter. In this chapter, we will merely briefly refer to the primary prerequisites that led to industrialization to take root in England.

The Industrial Revolution was a process, not a discrete event. Many enabling aspects of British society, fostered over many centuries, paved the way to the right conditions that were conducive to one of the most profound structural transformations in human society. It needs to be said that each revolutionary transformation breeds its distinct economic disorders and crises. Industrial economic fluctuations are distinct features of economies that are in the process of industrial development or are industrialized. Industrial economic fluctuation is the subject of inquiry of this chapter. England is the architect of this type of economic fluctuations. Out of the three pioneering nations, the Dutch, the French, and the English that broke away from the medieval agrarian economy, England seized the opportunity and complete the break. The Dutch led the way in the seventeenth century but the French imperial conquest cut short their economic advances. France was the

DOI: 10.4324/9781003346357-3

wealthiest and most populated nation in the eighteenth century but missed out on the chance.

Chapter 2 is divided into seven sections. The first section, "The cradle of industrialization," is devoted to a synoptic discussion of the Industrial Revolution. England, a couple of centuries prior to the revolution, was a small and minor country at the north-western fringe of Europe. The Industrial Revolution catapulted it to the master of the world. The process of industrialization is a wide terrain. In this section, we will only focus on the aspects of industrialization that are related to the object of this book. As a turning point, the Industrial Revolution first changed the landscape of Britain and subsequently the world. Modern industrialized economies are the outgrowth of the Industrial Revolution. What the revolution achieved was the acceleration of division of labour to a degree that had never been experienced in the pre-industrial era. The revolution had transformed the techniques and mode of production by applying science and technology, i.e., steam-driven machinery in factory production. Consequently, it gradually destroyed family and communal dependent existence and normalized dependency on wage labour. It standardized class structure and institutionalized the increasing gap between the rich and the poor. It caused rapid growth in the economy, population, markets, colonialism, technology, production of commodities for mass consumption, and monetary instruments and institutions.

Indeed, the Industrial Revolution was a multidimensional process. One of its characteristics was its drastic impacts on money and the banking system. The second section, "Banking and money economy," explores the structural changes and their repercussions that took place in the realms of forms of money and banking system that were different from other previous periods. In the next sections, we follow the evolution of the process of industrialization and probe some of its effects that are the precursors of economic disorders and crisis in modern economies. The third section looks at great wars and revolutions that are integral parts of the setup of the economic system and business organizations based on domination and control of markets. The fourth section provides an outline of hyperinflation and economic depression. In this section, we put more emphasis on the nature of modern states, which are also a by-product of the process of industrialization. Modern states play a significant role in the economy. Raising their revenues and their expenditures is critical during economic cycles.

One area that rarely cited in mainstream economics is the Frankenstein states. These states were created artificially by European empires at the end of their demise. The fifth section, "Empires and the Frankenstein states," will demonstrate with the help of one case study the destructive nature of these imperial legacies and the perpetual political-economic crises that these countries cannot escape from so long as they are kept in the same colonial political structure. The sixth section is on the generation gap and the role that this gap can play in the economy. It is argued that the generations that experience long-lasting wars, civil wars or wars between nations, in particular world wars, their outlook about life, work, and future can never be the same as the generations that live in a free and open society in peace and prosperity. This is one of the most crucial factors for economic and social transformation that is overlooked generally in economics. The last section is on the role of the paradigm shift in economics. In the part on the pandemic of globalization, we take globalization as our example to show that economic ideas, right or wrong, can come and go like any other form of fashion. As soon as a trendy idea submerges into the mainstream economic narrative, it receives its licence of legitimacy. Regardless of its validity, it would then be defended and consolidated in the reigning teaching setup and the world outlook.

## The cradle of industrialization

Certain facts of political, economic, and legal conditions paved the road to industrialization in England that France and Holland either lacked or were deprived of it. The overriding factor that instigated industrialization in England was the greater legal, political, property, and security rights that people individually enjoyed compared to its rivals, France and Holland. The story of these rights went to several centuries back. These rights were constituted in the 1086 Domesday Book, in the Magna Carta (1215), in the 1689 Bill of Rights, and in the Great Reform Act of 1832. In 1066 the Normans led by Willian the conqueror (1027–87) conquered England. William ordered the most comprehensive census then to be taken. The data of people and their assets in England were recorded in two books known as Domesday Book. This exercise was intended to spread and strengthen the political and economic power of the Normans over England. The census unintendedly shaped the English national unity and their national common law. This process was greatly promoted in the reigns of Henry I (1100–35) and Henry II (1154–89). Instead of diverse local courts, the royal judges travelled to different parts of the country to adjudicate disputed matters, which were recorded and used as a precedent for solving similar disputes in other parts of the country (Perry 2013: 145). The adjudication based on the principle of precedent evolved and replaced the local customary laws and eventually formed a common national law. This unified legal framework and order was significantly more consistent and less biased than the former segregated judicial system. The gradual mutation of this unintended decree ultimately laid the foundation of the modern legal system of justice of Britain and the US.

The combination of several events in thirteenth-century England gave birth to a new legal document that reinforced individual rights in England. The weaknesses of the authority of the reign of King John (1199–1216) were the gateway to these rights. At the end of his reign, King John encountered many serious challenges to his power that made it impossible for him to continue to rule with the same force and authority. He lost Normandy to France in 1204. Pope Innocent III excommunicated him and closed England churches. His Barons capitalized on his vulnerabilities and became united and stood against him. The civil war and all these challenges diminished King John's authority considerably. The defeated King saw no way out of his ever-worsening troubles. So, he conceded to the demands of his barons and signed a peace treaty with them. The King lost and his barons gained additional liberties. These liberties were granted in a document that was written in 1215 and became to be known as Magna Carta or the Great Charter. The whole decree comprises 4,000 words. Some of these rights that were granted to the barons inadvertently upgraded the rights and liberties of the common people. Jerome K. Jerome (1859–1927) described Magna Carta as "England's temple of liberty" (Jerome 2007: 127). Alfred Denning (1899–1999), the renowned British jurist, held it as "the foundation of the freedom of the individual against the arbitrary authority of the despot" (quoted from Weir and Beetham 20005: 23).

For our analysis in this section, the clauses 39 and 40 of the Magna Carta are of interest. In these clauses, the king disclaimed his power to arbitrary arrest of individuals. He made the sale of justice illegal and guaranteed equal justice by the means of the right to trial by jury. The charter declared that no unlawful dues "shall be imposed ... except by the common consent of our kingdom." The most important by-product of the Magna Carta was the protection of a free man. In this respect, it states "no free-man shall be taken or imprisoned ... save by the lawful judgment of his peers or by the law of land" (quoted from Perry 2013: 145). Magna Carta was not only a significant step in the process to codify English law, but it guaranteed the right against arbitrary arrest and for trial by jury for every individual. The charter was a very powerful instrument to assemble against the king's arbitrary authority in 1230 and for the Parliamentarian to question the Stuart kings for their absolute power in 1620.

The other two events that created the political and legal conditions for economic industrialization were the 1689 Bill of Rights and the Great Reform Act of 1832. Both these changes were acts of the parliament. The Bill of Rights defined basic civil rights and limited the inherited rights of the king. The toleration act (1689) gave the right of religious freedom to all Protestants, whereas the Triennial Act (1694) was passed to hold general elections every three years. The Bill laid the first basic step of reducing the arbitrary power of the government. The Representation of the People Act 1832 was out of the fear of revolution. Many MPs in the House of Commons expressed their fear of revolution without some electoral reforms. The reforms that were undertaken were narrow and conservative. Nevertheless, the electoral system broadened its votes to the middle classes and its parliamentary seats to the central and northern regions of England. The Act only partially extended the franchise to small farmers and shopkeepers and enabled the householders with the rental of ten pounds per year to vote. The Act excluded women and workers from voting. The important thing about the Act was the fact that it galvanized all sides of the conflict. Those who were in favour and those who against the act. The open clash between these opposing views created a new culture in the world of politics. Those in favour called for popular constitutional reforms and the conformists were against the reforms. The contest between these opposing forces paved the way for elections, party-based adversarial system of voting, national politics, and, subsequently, modern representative democracy.

The Industrial Revolution was a structural economic transformation. It was a major shift in mode, method, and social relations of production and distribution that introduced the large-scale industry by applying science and technology in production. The impacts of industrialization have been far-reaching. In the pre-industrial era, society and economy were stagnant. The land was the source of economic activities and land ownership determined the social hierarchy. Production and distribution were organized around the family. Most people lived in the countryside and were poor. The division of labour was hereditary and social mobility very rare. Life was slow, locked in conventions and all sorts of rigidities (Deane 1967: 12–13).

On this as on many other major transformations in human history, the factors that brought the change are numerous and they go back a long way in the past. Moreover, these factors will always be a matter of dispute and open to different explanations. There are certain preconditions in the absence of which the great industrial and economic transformation would have been impossible. Without all democratic changes in the British government, law, and society that allowed greater freedom of thought and expression and individual protection under the law to pursue their individual interests, the Industrial Revolution would not have taken place in Britain. Another critical factor that is overlooked in this critical transformation was the division of the world, colonization, and exploitation of the resources of subjugated nations. This enabled the formation of massive private wealth from plundering the colonized territories and creating both unprecedented demand for more and new goods and services and at the same time a massive amount of investment in new ventures and production.

Besides these points, there were some specific characteristics in the British economy and society that allowed the roots of industrialization to spread in England. British society after the glorious revolution allowed critical and creative thinking. Most great thinkers and scientists during the period of transition were from Britain – Francis Bacon, Isaac Newton, William Harvey, Thomas Hobbes, John Locke, David Hume, Adam Smith, and many others. The Industrial Revolution rested on the back of freedom of thought that allowed to be creative, to be imaginative in innovation and discovery in ideas, science, technology, institution, and organization. As a result, science and empirical knowledge were applied systematically in the organization of society and economy (Deane 1967: 1).

Deane remarks that the Industrial Revolution "grew up on a basis of coal and iron" (Deane 1967: 76). One of the most ingenious methods of transport was invented in England during this period. It utilized most effectively the comparative advantage that Britain enjoys from its rainwater, rivers, and coasts. The canal age is dated from 1760 to 1840. Within this period an extensive canal network of about 6,500 km navigable inland waterways was constructed in Britain, most specifically in England, that connected the big cities and British ports to coasts. As with any momentous economic invention and discovery, the burst of investing craze in canal construction came between 1791 and 1794. Mass and heavy speculative frenzy engulfed the canal market in Britain. The expectation of soaring returns catapulted Ponzi investors and the poor to jump in turbulent waves of wild speculation. During this period 42 canals were built. Whoever wanted to get rich invested his money in canal projects. Many of these projects were never materialized (Kindleberger 1984: 198 and Beggs-Humphreys et al. 2006: 40).

The pre-industrial economy was clamped, in the main, in a system of a monocracy of production. It was dominated not only by fathers passing their skills and techniques of production to their sons but also by the agricultural sector. Most households lived at or below subsistence levels. The production level was barely adequate and if minority households produced surplus products, there was neither a well-established market nor a culture of exchange to trade the surplus produce. That limited the scope and scale of innovations in methods and organization of production and exchange. The Industrial Revolution transformed all these aspects of the economy and society. Instead of monocracy of production, it introduced a plethora of possibilities in production, in agricultural, commercial, and banking sectors.

The Industrial Revolution paved the way for a significant portion of the population to depart from "the kind of domestic industry which was an off-season activity of agriculturalists and went into full-time manufacturing in factory and workshop" (Deane 1967: 138). This move not only altered the pace of economic growth but uprooted the landless and smallholder peasants from the rural areas and dragged them into cities. It was this population that formed the dispossessed proletariat class. The Industrial Revolution congregated the workers and the machines and housed them under one roof. The Industrial Revolution altered the place of the agricultural sector from being dominant into a secondary position.

> By 1881, as Britain began to draw a large part of its food supplies and raw materials from overseas, the agricultural industry accounted for only about a tenth of gross national product and by 1901 its share had fallen to near 6 percent.
>
> (Deane 1967: 189)

Among other changes the Industrial Revolution brought about were the increasing application of science and technology in the production for the market and the mass production of goods and services for mass consumption – for national and international consumption.

One critical factor in the rise of the Industrial Revolution in England was its population. The population of England and Wales from 1700 to 1741 was about five million people and by 1800 it doubled to about ten million people. These changes transformed the nature and culture of work. New innovations provided more opportunities for people to enter types of employment that were traditionally not being considered meritorious. Making money substituted traditional restrictions in the choice of job. The first impact of the Industrial Revolution was on the cotton industry. This was due to Hargreaves' invention of the spinning jenny and Arkwright's water frame. In its first phase, the forerunners of the Industrial Revolution demonstrated a great deal of charitable attitude. As good Samaritans, they created factory villages to house their workers and treated their workers relatively altruistically. Jedediah Strutt (1726–97) and Richard Arkwright (1732–92) built cottages to house their workers. With increasing transformation of business class moral standards and conducts, the industrial economy took a pitiless turn. Relentless rivalry in making profit became the ultimate end and the term of moral reference. This happened some years after the cancellation of Arkwright's patent (1785). It was the Boulton and Watt steam engine that initiated the second phase of the Industrial Revolution. In the year that Arkwright's patent was cancelled, the steam engine was used in spinning mill opening the way for large-scale production.

The Industrial Revolution was a long and slow process that cannot be described by any single change or a short span of time. Among many other things, it created industrial workers, including men, women, and children. Strutt and Arkwright employed women and children too. But in the second phase of industrialization, the number of women and children employed increased considerably. All workers, regardless of age and gender, worked in shifts for 12–16 hours a day (Deane 1967: 381). As more and different products and services were added into the categories of goods and services, new sectors were added to the economy, which required different methods, techniques, machines, organizations, skills, and processes. This in turn divided the jobs into a great many types of employment. The process, however, has not created a homogenous working class as it is characterized in Marx's classic industrial proletariat. E. P. Thompson in *The Making of the English Working Class* comments that this "class did not rise like the sun at an appointed time. It was present in its own making … There were tailors here and weavers there, and together they make up the working classes" (Thompson 1968: 9). The working class demonstrated its power first as an organized and incontestable social, political, and economic force in Britain in 1834. It was in this year that under the leadership of Robert Own, The Grand National Consolidated Trade Union began its activities and about a half-million of workers joined the Union (Deane 1967: 150). The power of workers has, as an organized social force, steadily increased with the development of industrial economies and it has been a major contributory factor during economic disorders and political revolutions ever since.

The industrialization of Britain was a revolutionary process. Evidently, every major event in its construction was over-exploited. One of the prime movers of industrialization was the invention and application of new technology. In the nineteenth century, the catalytic technology that triggered widespread economic and social change was the rail industry. In W. W. Rostow's assessment, the UK rail industry and the network were the most important economic force in the first stage of industrialization of the British economy. In his reading "the introduction of the railroad has been historically the most powerful single initiator of take-offs." He gives three reasons for this understanding. It reduced the cost of transport and created new products and markets. It created an additional export sector and stimulated the development of other industries (Rostow 1960: 302–303). The British railways industry began with the operation of George Stephenson steam locomotives on the Stockton and Darlington railroad in 1825. The 1824–25 is marked as railway mania. This "speculative bubble" was generated by the application of this new technology. Subsequently, it "prompted the publication of prospectuses for more than 70 lines, 40 of which reached the parliamentary stage, but the boom ended after a commercial crisis in December 1825 dampened the enthusiasm of investors and only one major scheme was completed" (McCartney and Arnold 2003: 821). The second railway boom and bust in the nineteenth century in Britain was in the 1840s. It reached its peak in Britain between 1845 and 1847. The occasion is known as "railway mania." It is "characterized by the large-scale appearance of speculative capital in the market for railway shares" (Deane 1967: 160). Parliament approved 805 route mileage in 1844. On average investment in railways in the early 1840s was about £4 million. It reached £30 million in 1847 (McCartney and Arnold 2003: 822).

## Banking and money economy

The modern industrial economy could not be other, but a money-dominated economic system. Without progress and the spread of the banking system, forms, institutions, and functions of money, industrialization would not have happened. Money is one of the critical constituents of modern economies. However, there is no consensus among economists as to what money is. The obvious case in support of the absence of a consensus among economists about the meaning of money is the multiplicity of forms of money that are in current use and a great many archaic forms that have been perished. There is a split view on which forms can be included in the category of money and which forms can be excluded. For example, within the Solomon Islands people used dogs' teeth as a form of money (Einzig 1951: 70–71). But there is nothing in a dog's teeth that is to be found in new forms of money. Therein lies an intransigent difference of opinion among economists. Either new forms are money and a dog's tooth is not, or a dog's tooth is money and new forms of money are not. One can say the same for most of the outdated forms of money. The simple fact is that most forms of money have retarded from circulation and many new forms are added to circulation over time. The crux of the matter is that not all economists accept all forms of money as being money, and in each specific period, different forms of money are classified as true money but in another period, or place, they are barred from being money (Karimzadi 2013).

The temple of money in modern economies is the central bank. All central banks are a product of an economic disorder. The central banks have been established to overcome some of the economic disorders of their time at different specific geographical locations. In this section, we will limit our analysis to the case study of the Bank of England. The first central bank was Severiges Riksbank that was established in 1668 in Sweden. The next central bank was the Bank of England that was founded in 1694 and the one after was the Bank of Scotland that was established in 1695. The national central bank of Spain was founded in 1782 and the central bank of France in 1800. Few other European nations, the Netherland, Austria, Denmark, and Norway, also founded their banks in the nineteenth century. Japan and the United States were the latecomers in this respect. The central bank of Japan was established in 1882 and the US Federal Reserve System in 1913.

A complex developed economy is inconceivable and unworkable without a multifaceted and interdependent monetary, credit, and financial system, institutions, markets, and instruments. The central bank is situated at the heart of it all. The formation of central banks is a process that is contingent on various social, economic, and political factors. No central bank is perfect or the same. The other leading central banks were modelled on the Bank of England. After England's glorious revolution, the public finances were ruined due to continuous wars (the Jacobite wars and the war with France) and William III lavish spending on his adventures. In the 1690s, the King was badly short of funds. He went to London merchants for help. The Parliament in 1692 considered different options of paying off the war debt. William Paterson (1658–1719), a Scotsman and a member of the Merchant Taylor's company in the City of London, submitted a proposal to pay public debt. His proposal with some alteration was accepted in 1694. So, he gathered several city merchants who collectively contributed £1.2 million and loaned that to the king. Paterson became the founding director and other subscribers comprised the governor's body of the bank. What Paterson set up was a private company and its subscribers were its shareholders. In return for lending money to the crown, the subscribers were granted Royal Charter. Being listed in the Royal Charter, the company became a limited-liability institution which can issue banknotes and trade in government bonds.

Paterson's plan was ahead of its time. There was no limited liability bank then. The next act in England that allowed the formation of a limited liability company was the 1720 Act. This act made it possible for British railway companies to be established. The most defining period that shaped the development of company law in England was from the 1820s to the 1860s. The *Economist* on 18 December 1826 commented that

> the economic historian of the future may assign to the nameless inventor of the principle of limited liability, as applied to trade corporations, a place of honour with Watt and Stephenson, and other pioneers of the

> Industrial Revolution. The genius of these men produced the means of which man's command of natural resources was multiplied many times over; the limited liability company, the means by which huge aggregations of capital required to give effect to their discoveries were collected, organized, and efficiently administered.

In a series of company acts during this period limited liability became the standard of company law in England. This invention enhanced the process of democratization of investment in the economy. Under the limited liability principle, the owners, i.e., the shareholders of a corporation, were not responsible for the company's debt to the extent that all their assets outside the company to be taken in the event of insolvency. The company assumed a separate legal entity distinct from the managers and owners of the company. The liability of each shareholder became limited to the nominal value of capital invested in the company. These company acts paved the way for the flourishing and proliferation of private and public limited companies.

The Bank of England was the first limited liability company in the banking sector. The bank has evolved in time and has passed many eventful storms. Its form, functions, and structure, they all changed over time. What was considered to be money when it was set up and the functions it carried as a bank have never remained the same. The only valid form of money when the bank was founded was money that had intrinsic value. Gold was the principal form of money. After three years of its formation, it competed with the South Seas Company. This company was also approved by a Royal Charter. To protect the South Seas Company from any other competitor, in 1696 Parliament disallowed the formation of any new joint-stock company. The Bank of England, as a joint-stock company, was a competitor of the South Seas Company. It was a monopolistic company. It had a monopoly over trade in Spanish colonies in South America. One thing that the company and the South Seas Company shared was, in effect, buying government debts – the funds the government had spent for a couple of decades earlier. The company banked on its overestimated prospects. By 1719, the company was holding 11.7 million national debt. The debt conversion scheme for the prospect of overstated profit from future profit in the early 1720s put the company in direct competition with the Bank of England. The company increased its holding of national debt to £43.2 million. Due to these exaggerated claims, the company share price increased from January to March 1720 from £128 to £330. Its share price continued to increase and reached its peak in June to £1,050 and then it crashed in October 1720.

In the crisis of 1783, for example, the August balance of bullion in the bank showed a reserve of under £600,000 – lower than the level when the cash payments were suspended in 1797. It must be noted that the crisis of 1783 was the aftermath of the American War (Deane 1967: 173). When the Bank of England was founded, there was an established custom that the goldsmiths issued and endorsed bills of receipts for the deposit of gold coins.

These receipts were redeemable for full-body gold coins. The receipts were promissory notes that promised to pay the bearer on demand the amount of gold stated on the receipts. Gradually these gold-linked receipts evolved and changed instead of the gold coins. They were used to withdraw deposits; they were transferred from one economic agent to another and were redeemable for gold coinage in different goldsmith banks. The Bank of England, immediately after its foundation, issued handwritten receipts to its depositors of gold, an obligation to pay back on demand the bearer of receipts the equivalent amount of gold deposited in the bank. The bank receipts to its depositor were the first form of banknotes. The gold-linked banknotes evolved into different denominations in subsequent decades and centuries.

In the initial phase of the gold standard, known as the gold circulation standard, gold coins predominated the circulation. As promissory notes grew in popularity and replaced gold coins in circulation, the gold circulation standard evolved into the gold exchange standard. In this type of monetary system, the issue of any banknote (bank receipts) is tied to the stock of gold deposited in a bank. In the same manner, the first Bank of England's notes were receipts that represented the actual amount of gold deposited in the bank. In 1797, the Bank could not fulfil its obligation of paying its depositors gold on demand. It did not exchange bank's notes on demand for gold. The Bank Restriction Act (1797) suspended specie payment for 21 years until 1821. The war against France started in 1792. The cost exceeded the entire income of British people by the year 1794. The Bank's coin and bullion were reduced, and people started hoarding their silver and gold coin. There was no other option for the bank than to suspend the payment of gold on demand (Poovey 2003: 8).

Again, to fund Wellington's troops, the Bank turned to Rothschild for help in 1814. In a run on the Bank in 1825, the bank turned to the House of Rothschild for assistance. Rothschild landed a ship in Falmouth injecting 150 kg of sovereigns in a single day into the bank's treasury. The 1826 Country Bankers' Act allowed the bank to open branches in provincial cities and in the 1833 act banknotes above £5 became officially legal tender in England and Wales. The 1844 Bank Charter Act prevented new banks to issue their own money and drew a strict rule between the gold held in the bank and the banknotes. It made a rule that the gold held should exceed the banknotes issued and circulated.

The nineteenth century is not only the century of the industry, but it is the century of paper money and banking too in Britain. It was in this century in Britain that the paper money and banks replaced the position of gold and land. The fact is there is a considerable lag in the creation of wealth by land or precious metals. Banks and paper money opened a new form of credit system for new adventures and misappropriation of wealth. Indeed, with new forms of money, the new ways of misinformation and misappropriations were invented. Alongside the invention of any new form of paper money, there were many ways of forging them. In a similar manner that the extremist profit-seekers clipped, scared, and mixed the metallic forms of money – in the same way, they exploited the paper forms of money or the credit system. This resulted in frequent monetary and banking crises in Britain. Among much-noted banking crises were in the years 1825–26, 1837, 1847, 1857, 1866, and 1878. The period that hits the banking system most was between 1840 and 1866. From 1844 to 1868, 291 banks were established but only 49 of them survived after 1868 (Poovey 2003: 22).

The 1840s is a decade that stands out among other decades in Britain in the nineteenth century. It is known as the "Hungry Forties." The title fits the Irish famine. Ireland was a colony of Britain and that exacerbated the widespread famine and hunger in Ireland when it happened. Phytophthora infestans destroyed the potato crop in Ireland. As a result of this and British colonial policies, the Irish population declined drastically. According to the 1841 census, the Irish population was 8,175,124 and in the 1851 census, it dropped to 6,552,385. The death toll of the potato blight is estimated to be over one million people (Kinealy 1999: 247). The potato blight was widespread in Europe during this decade. The combination of this tragedy with the economic and social policies of the despotic regimes in power resulted in a flood of social unrest spreading all over Europe. The flame of the unrest caught the small states of Germany and Italy and toppled the French and Hungarian states. The English statesman and novelist, Benjamin Disraeli (1804–81), published his novel *Sybil, or The Two Nations* (1845) describing the growing gap between the rich and the poor in England. Karl Marx and Friedrich Engel published, perhaps their most read book, *The Communist Manifesto* on 21 February 1848. The next day, on 22 February 1848, the French revolution started. This booklet reflected the economic, social, and working conditions of the industrialized society of England. But its appeal and drawing power were in its visionary and prophetic foresight.

The 1840s was also a decade of intense debates on monetary matters in which Robert Peel's Bank Charter Act (1844) settled the debate between Bullionists and anti-Bullionists. The debate rotated on forms of money, on real and representative forms of money. The controversy was on the effects of representative forms of money on inflation and the balance of payments. The generally accepted form of real money when the Bank of England was founded was a gold coin. A bimetallic monetary system (silver and gold) was proposed in 1717 under the supervision of Isaac Newton. But towards the end of the eighteenth century, the generally accepted form of money consisted merely of gold coin. Side by side to this the Bank of England country banks' notes were backed by gold. Bills of exchange and bank deposits were used for wholesale transactions. In 1793 the Bank's specie reserves were drained due to the war with France in the same year. The bank reduced its banknotes. In February 1797, the French landed a small troop in Wales. The landing of the French troop precipitated the run on banks' deposits. Given the circumstances, the representative form of money was the second best option and the escape plan. However, the idea and the deed were not new. Adam Smith entertained the idea that other forms of money can be as effective as a medium of circulation as the intrinsic forms of money and John Law applied this idea in his scheme. Under the Scottish banking system, notes were exchanged for real bills. Banks exchanged notes so long as the bills were credible. The advocates of anti-Bullion doctrine were of the view that there would not be an oversupply of banknotes without greater demand for trade and commerce. Any excessive issue of notes would return to banks in exchange for the bills.

On the other side, the Bullionist argued that paper notes are not real money and should not be convertible to gold on demand. This view was backed by the "Bullion Committee" report in 1810. The report related the cause of inflation at the time to oversupply unbacked note issues. Something that David Ricardo in several articles and pamphlets referred to as the guilty party. This debate reached its climax in 1844. Under the shadow of Ricardo's reputation, the Bullionists won the contest. Subsequently, the Bank Charter Act of 1844 made the Bank the de facto monopoly issuer of notes. It introduced a strict rule between the issue of notes and the gold reserve.

By the last decade of the nineteenth century, the Bank of England was not only a state bank, a bank of one national economy, but a bank of the largest empire and a world bank. It demonstrated this power in relation to the Baring crisis of 1890–95 and the bank's investment in Argentina. The Barings, the oldest merchant bank in Britain, was older than the country of Argentina. The bank was established by a German family in 1762. Argentine gained its independence from the Spanish Empire only on 9 July 1816. Argentina's war of independence began in 1806. The independence war gathered momentum in 1808 after Napoleon Bonaparte deposed King Ferdinand VII and installed his brother Joseph as the king of Spain. The invasion of Spain shook the Spanish Empire's power to its core. By the 1880s Argentina was the most upcoming country in South America.

Argentina was portrayed as the "United States of South America." The state and local governments encouraged foreign investment and competed vigorously to attract more investment to their every state. The plan was to transform Buenos Aires into the "Paris of South America." This was a decade of high immigration into Argentina. It is hardly necessary to mention that during this period there were considerable advances in telecommunications, refrigerated cargo, shipbuilding, and long-distance transportation. In addition, interest rates were relatively low. The Bank of England discount rate remained under 3 per cent for most of the 1884–88 period. The two most important destinations for British investors, both private and public sectors, during the 1880s were, in the first place, in the United States and, in the second place, in Argentina. Almost half of all British investment overseas in 1889 was in Argentine. By 1890, the British invested £80 million abroad, which was equivalent to 5.5 per cent of the gross domestic product (GDP) of the country (Clapham 1944: 324). The Argentinian government encouraged foreign investors to invest in the railway sector and the government guaranteed interest payments. In the case of defaults or insufficient revenue, the government promised to pay the difference. The three-quarters of British investment in the railways' sector in 1890 in Argentina were guaranteed under this scheme.

The House of Baring heavily invested in Argentine railroads, land, and many different utilities. Moreover, the bank was involved in the underwriting of Argentine state bonds extensively. Three-fourths of Baring' loans in 1890 went to Argentine and Uruguay. Baring House between 1888 and 1890 invested £13.6 million in Argentine. This was the largest amount of capital invested in one country then. The second largest amount was £4.5 million (Kornert 2003: 189). The culmination of several internal and external factors eventually brought the largest and oldest merchant bank down in 1890. The collapse of the bank was against the background of the economic downturn in both Britain and Argentine between 1888 and 1889. The Bank of England raised its rate from 2.5 per cent in April 1889 to 6 per cent by December 1889. The worsening situations in succession ceased the inflow of capital into Argentine, leading to the Argentine government effectively defaulting on its external debt. The presidential coup in the same year aggravated the situation even further. In 1890 the inflation rate in Argentine plummeted to 17 per cent and the Buenos Aires Water Supply and Drainage Company Limited went insolvent. A large segment of the loan to this company was underwritten by the House of Barings. The national government could only finance about 30 per cent of its expenditures out of its revenues. Its deficit was about 70 per cent in 1890–91. The financial situation of the provinces was considerably worse. The House of Baring was in serious trouble. On 8 November 1890, the head of the House, Edward Baring, reported his difficulties to William Lidderdale, the governor of the Bank of England, and desperately pleaded for assistance from the bank to rescue his company.

The Bank of England loaned the House about £9 million to meet its most immediate obligations. It also encouraged and made other banks to take part in the rescue. In the intervening period, the assets of members of the Baring family were sold to pay for the "toxic" assets. The Bank of England acquired the assets that remained unsold. The timely intervention of the Bank of England saved the House and reduced the risk of the crisis spreading to the rest of the banking and financial system. Britain's oldest merchant bank was sold to the Dutch bank ING for £1 a century later in 1995. One of Baring's trader, Nick Leeson, in the Singapore branch single handily brought the bank down. He bet on Japanese financial instruments that included bonds, equity, and options. While the bank capital was $600 million his bets escalated to $30 billion. His enormous desire for making untold profit bankrupted the bank spectacularly.

## Great wars, revolutions, and depressions

The Bolsheviks seized the power in Russia on 25 October 1917. In November of the same year the revolutionary government exposed the details of the Sykes-Picot Agreement (Johnson 2016: 229). In 1915 the British, the French, and the Russian Empires conspired to divide the Middle East between their empires. The negotiations between the representatives of Britain, Mark Sykes (1879–1919), the French, Francois Georges-Picot (1870–1951), and the Russian foreign minister, Sergey Dmitrievich Sazonov (1860–1927), started in November 1915. The plan was to dismember the decadent Ottoman Empire and divide its territories between their own empires. The agreement concluded in May 1916 and became to be known as the Sykes-Picot Agreement.

The Ottoman Empire was founded by Osman I in 1298. It became one of the most powerful empires in the fifteenth and sixteenth centuries. The Ottoman Empire was the reign of Sultans, terror, and absolute power. By the mid-nineteenth century, the empire lost its mighty power and was reduced to "the sick man of Europe." The Bolsheviks left the Sykes-Picot Agreement immediately after the revolution. Italy substituted the place of Russia. Following the downfall of the Ottoman Empire in 1922, these three European empires divided the Arab world and apportioned it between themselves. The present artificial boundaries in the Middle East and its surroundings are the manufactures of this imperial colonial agreement. The social, economic, cultural, military, and human costs of this policy for the nations that were affected by this policy are inestimable. The arbitrary boundaries drawn created artificial countries that could only be governed by means of extreme ideology, militarism, and religious fanaticism. The human and economic resources of this region were, in the first instance, diverted into the fight against these empires. After these empires left the region, such resources have been employed in preservation of the legacy of these empires. That is the artificial boundaries that they have left behind and the despotic states that they had implanted. The exit of the British, the French, Italians, and others from the region was merely in form and not in substance. It only reinstated the old colonial establishment in a different garb. The European empires passed their colonial geopolitical construction to a political structure that was their own construction. A political construction that was based on the policy of divide and rule and made up of monarchism, theocracy, and dependency on external powers to maintain and safeguard each of these artificial and undemocratic countries. A full analysis and ramifications of the Sykes-Picot treaty and its human and economic costs are beyond the scope of this chapter. We will only refer to one example to illustrate the depth of the matter.

Both Iraq and Syria are colonial constructions. Like virtually all countries in the Middle East, their borders were drawn artificially. The British concocted the state of Iraq in 1921 and selected King Faisal I (1883–1933) as its ruler. The borders of this arbitrary state were drawn to include purposefully about 80 per cent Arab Muslims. Over half of which were Shia, but the political power was handed to minority Arab Sunni Muslims. A segment of Kurdistan was also hacked from the main body of the Kurdish nation and was annexed to Iraq. This comprised about 20 per cent of the Iraq population. There were also a significant number of Assyrians, Jews, and Turkmen that were included in this boundary. The whole thing was a textbook divide and rule strategy. A colonial scheme that its tragic saga will never end so long as the region stays the same as it is. It was Faisal's allegiance to the British Empire and not a democratic mandate that brought him to power. The entire history of Iraq is a perfect example of instability, despotism, autocracy, theocracy, and reign of terror. If we disregard all the brutalities and economic mishandlings of other rulers in the region and select only two of Saddam Hussain's wars, one with Iran and another the invasion of Iraq by the United States in March 2003, we can reveal the depth of irrationality and immorality of this colonial construction. The total economic costs of eight years war with Iran (1980–88) are estimated to be around $159 billion. The human toll is estimated somewhere between 550,000 and 1,040,000 people (Murray and Woods 2014: 242). The cost of the Iraq invasion only to American taxpayers is estimated to be about three trillion dollars (Stiglitz and Bilmes 2008). The number of Iraqis killed within four years of invasion is estimated to be between 392,979 and 942,636 victims.

Along the same line, Syria was created. British troops occupied Damascus and Aleppo in 1918. In 1920, Syria went under French control. What has kept Syria subsequently has been a brute force. The British and French colonial rulers cobbled about 70 per cent of Arabs, about 10 per cent of whom are Alawites and rest Sunni Muslims, about 10 per cent of Kurdish, 5 per cent of Turkmen, about 4 per cent of Assyrian, and the rest from other ethnic and religious groups. This was a toxic mixed bag ready to descend into bloodshed at any moment. Its entire legacy of this tattered colonial design has been nothing but coercion and carnage. The French controlled Syria until 1940 when France itself fell a victim of the German occupation. It was in 1946 the French troops eventually left Syria. The government that the French installed was deposed by the Syrian army. From that day the army became Syria. The army seized power three times only in 1949. The last military coup d'état was in 1970. Hafez al-Assad (1930–2000) seized power and ruled Syria with Iron fist for 30 years. After Hafez al-Assad's death his son, Bashar al-Assad, succeeded him as another ruthless ruler of Syria.

The Arab Spring that started in December 2010 was a continuation and accumulation of the same resentment against the artificial boundaries that needed the authoritarian regimes to safeguard such boundaries. Given the way things stand, there will always be a state of the outpouring of popular discontent in these boundaries. It just needs to be ignited one way or another and this was what happened in the Arab world in late 2010. Mohamed Bouazizi, a 26-year-old Tunisian street vendor, set himself on fire as a mark of protest against the way he had been treated by the government officials on 17 December 2010. It ignited mass protests throughout the Arab world. The first protest started in Tunisia in December 2010. The continuous protests toppled the Zine al-Abidine Ben Ali government in January 2011 in Tunisia. In Egypt, Hosni Mubarak was ousted from power in February 2011. In October 2011 Muammar al-Qaddafi, the Libyan dictator, was captured and killed. People also ousted the Yemeni dictator. There were also protests for greater freedom and democratic rights in Bahrain, Oman, and other Arab countries. The economic, social, and human costs of these events are unimaginable. In this regard, we take the case of Syria to show the cataclysm that has fallen on the people in Syria.

Demonstration against the Assad regime and for democracy also started in 2011 in Syria. The Islamic Regime of Iran and Russian oligarchy came to his support. The case of Syria is not short of a disaster in every sense of the term. *The Telegraph* (15 March 2016) estimated the Syrian civil war death toll to be about half a million and people fleeing Syria more than seven million. The UN estimated the cost of conflict to the country around $388 billion (Financial Tribune 11 August 2018). If we take into account the cost of involvement of other countries, Arab and non-Arab countries, the human and economic costs of just the Syrian conflict are truly startling and inconceivable.

The long-term economic, social, and psychological consequences of conflicts of this nature are impossible to measure. The twentieth century was the century of the most catastrophic wars. Over 90 years, from 1900 to 1990, there were 237 wars. Due to these wars, on average one million army personnel per year were killed. The total civilian and non-civilian death toll during the century is estimated to be 250 million persons. That is 700 individuals were killed every day (Ryan 2007: 404). The two most destructive wars took place in the twentieth century. The death toll from combat in the First World War is estimated to be about eight million (Lightbody 2004: 268). The total economic costs are worked out to be in the region of $338 billion (Hardach 1981: 286). The number of peopled killed in the most estimates is about 55 million in the Second World War. But when we look at the broader amphitheatre of the war and include all countries of the Soviet Empire, China, and the Philippines, the death toll exceeds 60 million (Lightbody 2004: 268). In Nail Ferguson's estimate, 2.4 per cent of the world population was killed in the Second World War (Ferguson 2001: 37). Only the military costs of the war are estimated to be one trillion dollars in 1940-dollar value (Dugger and Peach 2009: 117). But these are only a fraction of the actual costs of wars. In these wars an unknown number of people went missing, many millions were wounded, and many millions became homeless and displaced. The infrastructures of the war-torn countries usually are destroyed, and their production capacities are drastically diminished. Their potential economic and social progress in the time of the violent disorder is unaccounted for and the adverse psychological impacts of the war do not end with the end of the war but will linger on for many decades to come.

The two political upheavals that affected the world's social and economic events in the twentieth century were the rise and fall of communism and fascism. Most certainly these were not simply random and unrelated events. Their effects were wide-reaching. The worldwide impact of these seismic and traumatic events is hard to envisage. They shaped the contemporary world order and economy. These upheavals vandalized the inner core conscience of humanity. The Russian Revolution was a product of the First World War. It occurred towards the end of the war in October 1917. The Bolsheviks led by Vladimir Lenin (1870–1924) seized political power in Russia. The Nicholas II (1868–1918) abdication from the throne on 15 March 1917 marked the end of the Romanov dynasty in Russia. The Russian empire was large – covering Siberia, the Caucasus, and central Asia. After the end of the Second World War, the imperial power of Russia was extended to eastern and central Europe. The Bolsheviks consolidated the power in the one-party political system by 1920. The leader of the revolution, Lenin, suffered three debilitating strokes in 1922 and 1923. The first stoke was in May and the second in December 1922. The third stoke was in March 1923, which physically and mentally incapacitated him. Joseph Stalin (1878–1953) won the power struggle among the Bolsheviks and succeeded Lenin as the unquestioned leader of the Soviet Empire.

The apocalyptic era of Stalin lasted for over three decades. Stalin ruled the Soviet Union with an Iron fist. The violence reached an endemic level during his reign. Under his headship, peace and war lost their meanings. The atrocities committed are the same if not more in peacetime as in the wartime. He ordered the systematic killing of many millions of people all over the Soviet Empire both in peace and war times. His system of slave communism consisted of an extensive network of labour camps in forms of collective farms, industrial workshops, and forced labour camps for the exiled dissidents. In the Great Purges that were launched in the 1930s, 1.2 million members of the communist party were arrested. Only 50,000 of them were released between 1936 and 1939. Most of them died from starvation and forced labour. The rest, 600,000, were executed. The policy of "purification," consumed the lives of about seven million peasants in collectivized camps. It is estimated that in networks of forced labour camps, Gulags, 12 million have perished. Overall, it is estimated that during Stalin's rule, from 1924 to 1953, 20 million Soviet criticizes were murdered (Heidenrich 2001: 7).

The event of the Russian Revolution rippled throughout the world. By the end of the Second World War about one-third of the human population were under totalitarian Marxist-Leninist system. The historical deterministic approach that followed these political upheavals and the traumatic events in the countries that experienced the communist autocracy has not been considerably different from that of the Soviet Bloc. Theocracy and communist monocracy descend from a common root. In the former setup, God is the absolute ruler, but he does not rule directly. He rules through his unbreakable laws. The self-appointed class, the clergy, is the custodian who executes the God's commands. Under God's headship, the fate of everything is sealed forever. It is predetermined and what is meant to happen is written in one's destiny and will happen. In the latter case, in a communist theocracy, the self-appointed class, assembled in the communist party, follow and enact the predetermined natural and unescapable course of history. They act in accordance with the laws of historical materialism. The historical necessity determines what it meant to be. This strict canonical tenet, expressed mystically or pseudo-scientifically, is the licence that gives power to the theocratic and the monocratic governments to do whatever they wish. One is sanctioned by the command of God and the other by the laws of historical materialism.

The theocratic and communist monocratic states, without exceptions, have relegated human beings to the means to achieve some invented ends. As a means, in our first case, if they have perished it is because it is written in their fate and in the second case, it is due to irrevocable laws of historical materialism. This is how state-sponsored violence, bloodshed, extreme forms of cruelty, and destruction have been so easily carried out and justified in the name of the god or deterministic historical laws. After the Russian Revolution, the Chinese revolution in 1949 was the second most important communist revolution in the twentieth century. The revolution led to victory by Mao Tse-tung (1893–1976). Under his reign, an indirect consequence of communist party policies in the 1950s, several millions of Chinese people lost their lives. Most from famine and the rest were executed or perished in forced labour camps. During Mao's Cultural Revolution, 1960–70, about two million Chinese were killed. Over the period of his entire rule, 1949–79, it is estimated that over 27 million people were killed in China (Heidenrich 2001: 7). Under the Khmer Rouge rule, in Kampuchea during only four years 1975–79, over one and half million of the Kampuchean population were killed. In the same manner under the Mengistu Marxist regime in Ethiopia, about 1.2 million Ethiopian people lost their lives (Kissi 2006: xiv).

The Soviet totalitarian regime, in part, was also a catalyst for the decades of conflict between west and east and the rise of the fascist movement in the 1930s. These events have had far-reaching implications on world social, economic, and political arrangements and performance. As an outgrowth of this conflict, there was the arms race between the Western bloc led by the US and the Soviet Bloc led by Russia. We need to refer merely to a couple of examples to discern the incredible costs of an arms race between these two blocs. The military-industrial complex on both sides of the conflict was among their most protected industries. The cost of the cold war (1948–91) for the US is estimated at about $13.1 trillion (Accordino 2000). The Soviet's statistics are not reliable as almost every information under the Soviet Empire was treated as the state secrets. Nevertheless, a careful study of military expenditures of the Soviet Union under the leadership of Leonid Brezhnev (1906–82) clearly reveals the place of the military-industrial complex within the Soviet Empire economy. Brezhnev was the longest-reigning Soviet leader after Stalin. He was in power for 18 years. On average – only during his reign – the military expenditure was between 25 per cent and 30 per cent of the Soviet Union GDP (Hirts 1997: 167).

We will never be able to know the hidden costs of the arms race between countries. Again, with citing a couple of examples we can show the scale of the folly in the arms race. The fact of the matter is that most weapons produced are not used in war. If they are used, they cause inestimable destruction. If they are not used and kept for quite a while, they become obsolete.

This means the waste of scarce resources either way. But the cost does not end here. The wastes generated from some weapons such as chemical and nuclear weapons that must be stored and disposed of. In relation to the topic of our analysis one example suffice to explain the extent of the cost and risk involved in the production of such weapons. According to W. R. Cullen, "more than 1 million tons of chemical weapons were dumped into global seas, oceans, and lakes between 1945 and 1970." Half dumped by Russia and one-tenth by the US, it was estimated that the cost of destruction of chemical weapons up to the year 2003 for Russia was about $6–10 billion and about $24 billion for the US (Cullen 2008: 267).

The Russian Revolution created a global ideological divide between the rulers of all countries. No ruler was left uninvolved in this divide. You were either in the camp of capitalism or in the camp of communism. This divide got wider as more countries joined the communist camp. The confrontation and rivalry between these two camps fostered mutual hate against each other that eventually led to the collapse of the Soviet Empire in 1989. But the adverse economic and social impacts of this divide were wide-ranging and global. Either side used the most destructive and inhumane means to defend the regimes that expressed loyalty to its side. Propaganda, deception, conspiracy, violence, and coups were the normal tools to change regimes to realign the regimes to the east or to the west. By the end of the Second World War, the Red Army occupied and annexed the Eastern and Central European nations to the Soviet Union, which led to the intensification of mistrust, political and economic polarities, and confrontation between two leading powers, the US and the Soviet Union. From the 1950s onwards each power initiated and engineered several coups in different regions of the world. Among the Soviet-sponsored coups we have the coups in Egypt (1952), Iraq (1958), Syria (1966), Peru (1968), Libya (1969), Somalia (1969), Sudan (1969), Benin (1972), Ethiopia (1974), Afghanistan (1978), South Yemen (1978), and a few others (David 1986). The CIA was more successful in the pursuit of this scheme. It plotted and supported considerably a larger number of coups in different parts of the world. Among CIA-supported coups were Iran (1953), Guatemala (1954), North Vietnam (1958), Laos (1973), Haiti (1959), Dominican Republic (1961), Ecuador (1961), Brazil (1964), Indonesia (1965), Greece (1967), Bolivia (1968), Uruguay (1969), Bolivia (1971), and Chile (1973). This is neither a complete list of the US-sponsored coups nor does it include the cover operations of the CIA in the affairs of other undemocratic regimes.

All these regimes and governments that were authorized through coups or were undemocratic but found themselves in either camp during the cold war were repressive regimes. These regimes were militaristic, despotic, and corrupt. Space does not allow us here to investigate each case separately. Instead, we shall look at a few cases to demonstrate the destructive and murderous nature of orchestration of this policy and its long-term implications. Our first case is 19 August 1953 in Iran. The British and the CIA were behind and masterminded this covert action. The CIA codename was TPAJAX and

MI6 codename was Operation Boot. The democratically elected Prime Minister, Mohammad Mossadegh (1882–1967), was overthrown from power because Britain and the United States found Mosaddeq political and economic policies as a serious threat to their economic and strategic interests in Iran. Mossadegh nationalized the Anglo-Iranian Oil Company in March 1951. In 1914, the British government acquired 51 per cent of the company shares and they were in total control of the company by 1935. The share of Iranian was increased from the profit in 1950 but it was less than what the company paid in the form of tax in Britain (Etges 2013: 59). The nationalization of the Anglo-Iranian Oil Company did not go well with the British ruling establishment. Because of that they sponsored a coup ousting the democratic government of Mossadegh on 19 August 1953. The return of the repressive and despotic monarchy, the Mohammad Reza Pahlavi government, brutally suppressed all forms of democratic activities for over two and half decades which contributed to the 1979 revolution and the fall of the political power to the hands of fundamentalist Shia clerics (Gasiorowski 1987: 261).

Iranian economy and society retreated under the clerical Shia regime. A brief comparison of the economy under two regimes displays the scope of the retrogression. From 1960 to 1976 the average economic growth per annum in Iran was 9.8 per cent. The consumer price index on average was 5.7 per cent and the country's per capita income rose by 7 per cent. The rate of exchange of dollar to Toman in March 1979 was $1 to 7 Toman. The Toman to dollar exchange rate plunged $1 to 16.000 Toman in 2019. The official statistics of the Islamic regime are totally unreliable. But even according to such misleading data the inflation rate during the entire life of the Islamic regime on average has never dropped from double digit. From the theocratic standpoint, the economy is a minor matter. Everyone is the victim of their blind fate. The economic position of a person is beyond their control. Human destiny is predetermined by the divine will. No matter what one does, one will end up with one's fate. This was the view of the Shia cleric, Ruhollah Khomeini (1902–89), the founder of the Islamic regime of Iran, about the economy. The reality of this outlook hit shortly after the revolution. Khomeini's response to people's demand for improving their economic conditions was in his speech in Qom on 24 August 1979. He seized power only in February 1979. This is what he said about the economy only about six months after the victory of the revolution. He said, "economics is a matter for the donkey. Our people made the revolution for Islam" (quoted from Arjomand 2009: 56).

Unable to move with time and improve the economic, social, political, and legal conditions of people, the Islamic regime resorted to violence and religious fanaticism. The regime initiated the war with Iraq in 1980. The regime initiated its nuclear programme from the fear of the internal uprising and of exporting Shia Islam abroad. The whole plan from its start to its end was an epic disaster. The cost of sponsoring terrorism and Shia fundamentalist abroad is hard to estimate but the cost of the Islamic regime nuclear programme is estimated to be around $100 billion (Wright 2014: 53).

Under the Islamic regime, the Iranian population more than doubled. It was 37 million in 1979 and in 2019 it passed 82 million. The Shia clerics aimed to create "twenty million soldiers of Islam" to spread Khomeini Sheism throughout the world. The number of individuals that were executed for "political crimes" up to 2002 is estimated to be about 120,000 individuals (Ganji 2002: 103). In July 1988, Khomeini set up a death squad committee to massacre the political prisoners who had served their prison sentence or nearly completed their prison sentence. The "death committees" hanged over 30,000 political prisoners only in the second half of 1988. Even Hossein Ali Montazeri, who meant to be Khomeini's first successor, expressed opposition to this policy. He revealed that within two weeks of implementation of this policy 3,800 political prisoners were executed (Lamb – Telegraph 4 February 2001). For nearly 40 years of Islamic rule, the 2018 Misery Index has ranked Iran 15 out of 126 countries of the most miserable country. Transparency International (2017) has ranked it 130 out of 175 countries as one of the most corrupt countries in the world.

It is impossible to calculate the exact human, economic, and environmental costs of the conflicts of the superpowers of the East and the West blocs post-Second World War. The resources and human power allocated for the security of their despotic allies are incalculable. Here we only suffice to look at two cases. The first was the conflict in Vietnam and the second one the Afghan conflict which is still ongoing. Both cases were the theatre of combat and the big show of strength between the US and the Soviet Union military capabilities. Let us take two examples of such destructive contests. These are the examples of the Vietnamese liberation war and the Afghanistan war. These wars were among the most bloody and prolonged wars of the twentieth century. Not long after Vietnam's war against French colonialism, it plunged into the middle of a conflict between the United States, the Soviet Union, and communist China, and a civil war between the North and South sides of Vietnam. These wars engulfed Vietnam for three decades, from 1945 to 1975. In line with President Harry Truman's foreign policy, he declared in March 1947 in his address to Congress that the United States would intervene wherever that is under threat of falling to communism. This intervention that took place from 1960 to 1975 until the fall of Saigon and reunification of South Vietnam to North Vietnam has cost all sides of conflict great human and economic costs. The death tolls for Vietnamese are estimated at about 850,000 and 47,000 for US nationals. The economic cost of this conflict is estimated at about $500 billion (Hedges 2003: 4).

The Soviet Union's relationship with Afghanistan went for a long time. Soviet's influence in Afghanistan went as far back as Mohammad Zahir Shah's reign. Mohammad Daud Khan (1909–78) assumed many high responsibilities under Zahir Shah's time in power. But at the same time, he was a sympathizer of the Soviet system. As the occasion arose Daud seized the moment and overthrew the monarchy in Afghanistan in 1973. Under Daud's regime, the scope of Soviet influence became greater. The followers of the Soviet Union took advantage of this situation and launched a coup against the Daud regime in April 1978. The People's Democratic Party of Afghanistan, the Khalq faction, headed by Nur Mohammad Taraki (1917–79) seized the power. The Taraki government was weak and restricted by the Soviet interests and Marxist instructions. Added to these limitations were the ruling groups' internal fighting, Afghanistan's extreme social and religious conservatism, and the extreme hostility of West against the pro-Soviet regime in Afghanistan. The speed of disintegration of its backed regime in Afghanistan alarmed the Red Army. Consequently, the Soviet Union invaded Afghanistan in December 1979. The Soviet invasion has contributed to a protracted war, and the spread of Islamic fundamentalism and terrorism.

The human costs to Afghans, both military and civilian, from 1978 to 2002 are estimated at about 1.5 million people. In addition, millions of Afghans have been displaced internally and about six million of them became refugees (Bhatia and Sedra 2008: 20; Thackrah 2009: xxii). The economic cost of the Afghanistan war is estimated at the 2011 price to be about $600 billion (Swanson 2013). In June 1989 Nikolai Ryzhkov, the former prime minister of the Soviet Union from 1985 to 1991, announced that the economic cost of Soviet Union involvement in Afghanistan war has been about $70 billion (Defence Journal 1995: 5). In pursuit of its policy of "containment" to counter the Soviet aggression, the consecutive US administrations carefully selected their allies from the most despotic, fundamentalist, and violent states and Islamic extremist groups. Pakistan and Saudi Arabia became their closest allies. Saudis provided the finance and Pakistani army and security apparatus set up Jihadist factories and supplied Islamic suicide squads and Islamist terrorist groups. Al-Qaeda was one of these Islamist groups. Osama bin Laden, the founder Al-Qaeda, was initially an ally of the US government. Later he turned against his former ally and organized and carried out thousands of terrorist attacks against the US and its allies. He masterminded the 9/11 suicide attacks on the World Trade Centre and Pentagon in 2001. The attack on the World Trade Centre resulted in 2,995 fatalities and $82.8–94.8 billion economic damage to the New York City (Strindberg and Warn 2011: 93).

## Hyperinflation and economic depression

All forms of exchange economies, except the exchange of gifts, are the monetary economy. Money is the principal actor in a monetary economy. There is no consensus among economists about the definition, essence, forms, and functions of money. Experts' views differ considerably about what constitutes money (Karimzadi 2013). The absence of a consensus about what constitutes money, its essence, forms, and function results in a failure to reach appropriate and consistent policies in a money economy. Despite one's best intention the identification of the nature of monetary disorder and crisis would be incorrect and making any prognosis either will be inadequate or completely erroneous.

Monetary economies differ in respect to what form or forms of money are used as generally accepted medium of exchange. The ramifications of money on the economy when there is no generally accepted medium of exchange, or there are several media of exchange, or two mediums of exchange is materially different. In an exchange economy where there are too many forms of money, the scarcity of one form appreciates the value of the form that is short in supply relative to other forms of money. Forms of money can come in ones that have intrinsic value – wheat, barley, rice, cow, gold, silver, and so on. Ones that come in forms of the symbol of cultural, social, religious, political, and legal expression such as the cowrie shell, dog's teeth, religious images, fish bones, token money, paper money, or electronic forms. The essence of money is exchange. Money without exchange is like life without oxygen. In the absence of an exchange of economic goods and services, there is no money. Exchange of economic goods and services, not the exchange of gifts, is the beginning of money.

The fundamental economic, social, legal, cultural, technological, institutional, and political conditions, processes, structures, and organizations differ for invention and application of different forms of money. The social and economic conditions when the simplest forms of money were in use are fundamentally different from the most sophisticated monetary economies. If we put aside the act of exchange that all forms of money have in common, the next fundamental attribute of all forms of money is the ownership. All forms of money are owned by individuals, rulers, states, and monetary institutions. Money without an owner does not exist. As a general characteristic, all forms of money are not equally efficient to perform the same functions equally effectively. All forms of money cannot be supplied at the same time, in the same space, transported and stored in the same way. The value of all forms of money can appreciate and depreciate but not in the same manner. All forms of money, one way or another, express economic, social, psychological, cultural, and legal values of commodities and services. In relation to the quantity of the generally accepted medium, if there are more goods and services offered for exchange, the higher will be the demand for the generally accepted medium of exchange. No matter the form of money is a cow, coins, note, or credit money.

The potential velocity of circulation of all generally accepted forms of money is not the same. On one hand, we have the stone money or big animals with very low-velocity circulation and on the other hand, we have electronic money with a very high potential velocity of circulation. The value of some forms of money, most specifically forms of money with intrinsic value, is determined not only by the demand and supply of those forms but also by the cost of production of such forms. All generally accepted forms of money acquire an attribute that detaches them from their real function as a medium of exchange. The money came into existence under very specific economic, social, legal, and technological conditions and structure. Humans were the creator of these conditions. As such money is a human creation to improve their conditions of life. But generally accepted forms of money perform two types of work. One is its true job and its real functions. In its second role, it is demonetized. Not in the sense that it loses its intrinsic value but in the sense that it would be detached from its essence. It would be alienated from its real environment and functions. The estrangement of money from itself has given money an autonomous life of its own. In its autonomous role, money rules over its creator. It has parted from its creator and operates independently from the common will of its creator. In this capacity, it becomes the paragon of power, prestige, intelligence, beauty, and culture. Money can assume the upper hand over its creator and substitutes the conscious management of life with the precarious imperatives of money.

In any economic exchange, there are five sides to the story. There are the counterparties in the exchange, the sellers and the buyers. There is the good or the service to be exchanged. The fourth and the fifth agents are the medium of the exchange and the price respectively. If there are more on the demand side than the goods available, all other factors are given, the price will go up. The higher the monopoly control of the goods and services, the higher the price. In reverse, the more goods and services are supplied the lower will be the prices. Apart from these two sides, the price is determined by the costs of production and all factors that determined the costs of production. Let us for the sake of argument take all the factors cited as given, suddenly there is a major discovery as in the case of discovering substantial gold money when a gold coin is the principal form of money. In this case, there will be more gold coins in relation to the earlier period. More coin in circulation reduces the value of gold money and increases the price level. An example of this was the discovery of the new world and the influx of precious metals, in particular silver, from Mexico and Peru to certain parts of Europe. In the parts most affected prices rose by 300–400 per cent in the sixteenth century (Flynn 1983: 157). This fact can be applied to all generally accepted forms of money. Given all other economic conditions and factors remain constant and there is a considerable supply of a form of money, the value of the oversupplied form of money will decrease and prices will increase.

Let us assume that a monarch owns this form of money. The ambitious monarch wants to conquer the neighbouring countries and is short of finance. He decides to debase the coins by mixing the gold coin with other less valuable metals. In this case, the value of the gold coin depreciates and the price of goods and services will go up. This rule can also be applied to all other forms of money. The result would be the same if counterfeiting forms of money are the prevalent forms of money. The monopoly of demand, supply, and forms of money pushes the prices up. The more resources and power are concentrated on fewer individuals in an economy, the higher the prices will be. The more the rulers are subsumed in ideological dogma and away from the course of events and the requirements of the changing environment, the higher the prices will be. The public trust in the supply, demand, forms of money, monetary authorities, and the state is another factor that undermines the value of the medium of exchange and the price of goods and services. When all these elements accumulate in one period, it is then we have the extreme of the price turbulence and the collapse of the generally accepted forms of money. It is when we get hyperinflation.

The fluctuation in the value of money between various forms of money is different. The fluctuation is less extreme in forms of money with intrinsic value than in a token, fiat, or fiduciary forms of money. Extreme and sudden fluctuations in the value of money, i.e., hyperinflations, are the product of the latter forms of money. The prime example of hyperinflation in the twentieth century was during the interwar (1918–39) period. A slight oscillation in prices, a rise or fall in the purchasing power, is a permanent state of monetary order. There are no panaceas for this. Likewise, slight upward and downward trends in the velocity of circulation of the money stock are a permanent order of the fabric of advanced monetary arrangement. Ordinarily, excesses of demand and supply, the lags between the two, misguided economic policies, natural and technological constraints, and severe short-term social and economic changes compel prices to keep changing. The extreme excesses on either side cause chronic inflation or deflation. The first half of the twentieth century was marked by monetary turmoil in much of the industrialized world. From the onset of the First World War to the end of the Second World War was a period of extreme monetary disorders and loss of complete confidence in the currencies of several nations. This was, in part, "the result of the destruction of the vanquished countries' productive capacities, and their governments' resort to the printing presses to finance rehabilitation and reparation payments" (Brenner 1983: 94).

The war altered the old setup. The breakdown was thorough. It was no longer possible to go back to the old way of conducting the economy and the state. The gold standard had reached its ultimate limits. The amount of gold available to the issuing bank notes fell drastically. The notes in circulation far exceeded the gold reserves in the banks' disposals. To finance the expenses of the war, the reconstruction programmes, and to cope with the growing public demand for more jobs, states resorted to printing machines to finance their budget deficits. The none-fiat currency was in short supply. Inconvertible paper money was the inevitable answer to the perilous situation. The desperate states took the chance and exploited the opportunity in extreme measures. Here we refer to several cases in different times that exploited the issue of fiat money in its most extreme form. Our first case is the post-First World War inflation in Germany. In 1922 and 1923, the German state issued fiat money to the extent that it became worthless. As a result, the wholesale price index from December 1922 to November 1923 increased by "100 million percent" (Samuelson and Nordhaus 1995: 579). At the end of World War II, Hungary encountered a similar situation. The price index rose sharply to 400 quadrillion pengos between June 1945 and July 1946 (Borhi 2004: 149). In the midst of its disintegration, Yugoslavia experienced the worst hyperinflation in the entire history of its existence. From April 1992 to January 1994, prices kept rising at an accelerated rate. In January 1994, the inflation rate was 313,000,000 per cent (Champ, Freeman and Haslag 2016: 369). Zimbabwe, under the long-time dictator, Robert Mugabe, in 2008, experienced the most extreme case of hyperinflation ever recorded. Mugabe ruled Zimbabwe for 37 years. He practically destroyed the Zimbabwe economy. The highest monthly inflation rate in Zimbabwe was in November 2008. It was about 79,600,000,000 per cent (Zeidan 2018: 8).

The First World War and the formation of the Soviet Union broke three prevalent barricades of the world economic and political order. The first impact of these events was to reveal the beginning of the end of the global economic, military, and political supremacy of the British Empire. After the war concluded, not only Britain's imperial domination weekend but it was practically ended. From 1915 onwards the biggest empire and creditor in the nineteenth century turned to its former colony to borrow money to finance its war expenditures. As Britain's imperial domination receded, two new world powers begin to emerge. This marked the end of an epoch in world economic, political, and military order. The second effect of these events was a change in the nature of the imperial domination itself. For a long time, imperial domination used to be by means of invasion and conquest. The rise of the US and the Soviet Union's global economic, military, and political dominance ended the antiquated colonial practice.

Among key factors that contributed to replacing indirect with direct subjugation were as follows. One important factor was the Bolsheviks' rhetoric. Prior to the revolution, the Bolsheviks argued for the right of independence. Lenin advocated the right of self-determination. He preached a system of socialism that could "achieve complete democracy … the complete equality of nations …[and]… the right of oppressed nations to self-determination, i.e., the right to free political secession" (Lenin 1935: 267). In the midst of the Russian Revolution and the heat of the moment, only one nation succeeded to take advantage of this principle. In 1809, Russian invaded Finland. This ended Swedish colonial domination over Finland and replaced it by Russia. Finland declared independence soon after the outbreak of the Bolshevik revolution on 6 December 1917. It was the only nation kept in Russian captivity that was saved from the Soviet Empire.

Along the same line, the Bolshevik peace negotiation at Brest-Litovsk in December 1917 endorsed and centred on the principle of self-determination. In point 3 of the negotiation agenda, we read that "national groups not enjoying political independence before the war to be guaranteed an opportunity to decide freely by means of a referendum whether to adhere to any given State or to be an independent State" (Raic 2002: 179). This tactical gesture was in stark contrast to their chief doctrine of the unity of the world proletariat and the spread of revolution throughout the world. In the same spirit of all universal political ideologies and religions, the Bolshevik communism commanded all nations to be under one banner and creed. The third most significant ramification of the war and the Russian Revolution was the departure from one superpower into two superpowers. The US and the Soviet Union replaced the British Empire as the economic, political, and military powers of the world. These opposing poles of power grew a dynamic hostility that contributed to much of destruction and construction of the world economy till the collapse of the Soviet Empire in the 1990s.

The rivalry between the US and the Soviet Union began in the early 1920s. The Americans saw the Russian Revolution as a "the great red menace" and "the red scares." In 1919 there were 3,300 labour strikes in the US. Four million workers took part in these strikes. These movements alarmed the American ruling establishment of possible loss of their "way of life" (Norton et al 2015: 590). The red scare hysteria on one side and the biggest social engineering on the other side divided the world into blocs for most of the twentieth century. The US came out of the First World War in better shape than all others involved in the war. Its liberalism both in political and economic spheres was also ahead of other acclaimed democratic nations. In every other respect, the US was ahead of others. The "Roaring Twenties" started in 1922 in America. Also, the requirements of the war led to many technological innovations and improvements. The use of electricity became widespread, transport and communication were drastically improved all over the American states. One of the major changes in America was the mass application of advertising on radio and in cinemas. Consumer goods were increasingly standardized and were produced for mass consumption.

Technological advances paved the way for the invention and innovation of new consumer goods and methods of management and production. Among the top in demand for such goods were the radio, car, telephone, cooker, and washing machines. Frederick W. Taylor (1856–1915), an engineer, published his *Principles of Scientific Management* in 1911. In this book, he described his method of management of workers to improve their productivity and to maximize profit. This method of management became to be known as Taylorism. Henry Ford (1863–1947), the founder of the Ford Motor Company, applied Taylor's scientific method of management in his car production. This method standardized the production of the car, increased productivity, and made Ford's cars affordable to masses. In 1908 Ford's Model T cost about $1,000 and its much improved Model A only cost $300 in 1927. The ownership of the car in the 1920s increased from one car for every 15 individuals to one car for every five individuals.

Besides, the Republicans' economic policy in the 1920s was dominated by the policy of less government and more private initiatives. The policy was wrapped in the old casket of laissez-faire and balanced budget policies. That being said, this was certainly not a hands-off policy. The government actively intervened in the economy and deregulated the economy. It reduced the rates, opposed workers' associations and unions, and introduced many anti-trust policies. Andrew W. Mellon (1855–1937), the US secretary of the treasury (1921–32), argued for giving "tax breaks to large corporations." In doing so he believed "that money can trickle down to the general public, in the form of extra jobs" (quoted from Garfinkle 2006: 95). Mellon reduced the marginal tax rates for the top earners from 73 per cent to 25 per cent (Williams 2010: 234). President Calvin Coolidge in his inaugural address in 1925 argued that he was against high rates of taxation "because they are bad for country ... and ... because they are wrong" (quoted from Streissguth 2007: 356). The two sides of Coolidge's economic policy were incompatible. On one hand, he advocated tax cuts, a balanced budget, laissez-faire, mass marketing, and advertising, and on the other side, he restricted foreign trade with high tariffs. In 1920s advertising emerged as a big business. The total expenditure on advertising was $2.3 billion in 1919. By 1929, it increased to $3.4 billion. Coolidge recognized the central importance of advertising in mass consumption. In 1926 he said that "mass production is only possible where there is mass demand. Mass demand has been created almost entirely through the development of advertising" (quoted from Klein 2001: 109).

The US central bank was established in 1913. This was a response to the widespread run on the banks in 1907. On 24 October 1907 banks nationwide virtually halted credit payments (Noyes 1909: 188). It was on the background of this event that the 23 December 1913 Act decreed the formation of the Federal Reserve System of the United States of America. The Federal Reserve System consisted of 12 regional central banks. The system was established as the lender of last resort. It was set up to meet the requirements of the banking system in hard times and to prevent banking and financial panics and credit drain in American markets (Sprague 1914: 213). This in turn added on the false hope. That is with the ultimate remedy there is no fear and limit to lending. In the US the credit system, institutions, and instruments expanded noticeably after the formation of the Federal Reserve System. Along with this, the culture of fear of being in debt was fading and people rushed to buy durable goods such as cars and new appliances on the basis of buy now and pay later in the hope that the Federal Reserve System would be there to provide any level of liquidity as required. Credit expanded as if there was no limit in the supply of money and wealth creation. From 1922 to 1928, the US GNP increased by 40 per cent, the per capita income by 30 per cent, the industrial production by 70 per cent, and the corporate profits by about 60 per cent. The GDP grew by about 4.7 per cent per annum from 1922 to 1929 and the average unemployment rate for this period was 3.7 per cent. During the same period, the number of workers increased by 11 per cent and industrial workers' real wages by 20 per cent. Within the period of four years (1925–29), the number of manufacturing went up from 183,900 to 206,700. In the course of three years (1926–29), the production of cars went up from 4,301,000 to 5,358,000 (Galbraith 1992: 31).

In the 1920s less than 1 per cent of the American population owned some type of equity security. The 1 per cent who owned shares and were among the wealthiest people in America benefited from the wild rushes to buy and sell shares. The wild peak in stock prices made the richest richer. The value of the Dow Jones Industrial Average in 1929 was six times higher than it was in 1921 (Eugene 1990: 67). The rapid expansion in the prices of stocks took unprecedented form in 1928. According to Galbraith, "the nature of the boom changed ... the true speculative orgy started in earnest ... when men sought not to be persuaded of the reality of things but to find excuses for escaping into the new world of fancy" (Galbraith 1992: 40). The prices of stocks and shares soared. The bull market was already underway. In November 1928 Herbert Hoover (1874–1964) was elected as the president of the United States. When Hoover was elected the bullish market was already underway. But the odds were against his overly optimistic outlook. His great confidence soon went downhill into great despair. As Galbraith has put it "in 1927 the increase began in earnest. Day after day and month after month the price of stocks went up" (Galbraith 1992: 37). As the market was building momentum, the less creditworthy borrowers joined the market. The momentum sowed the seeds of its own failure.

The market boomed. It hit all-time highs and broke all past records. At its height on the New York Exchange 8,246,740 shares passed hands (Galbraith 1992: 62). The farther the market dispersed its tentacles the less creditworthy economic agents joined the speculative escapade to buy and sell at a high profit. At the peak of the stock market, the prospect of getting rich attracted eager individuals from all walks of life. Many mortgaged their homes and sold bonds to buy shares. The carnival of getting rich quick was in full swing. Any sound in a boozed-up crowd is melodic. Individuals with no borrowing capacity or very poor credit standing borrowed money to buy securities, using the securities as collateral to borrow more money in order to buy more shares on their margin accounts. In the march of making a killing unknown billions of dollars were drawn from banks and relocated to brokers' books to manage the margin accounts. The temptation of the speculative lure of buying securities at the fraction of the price of the underlying assets on borrowed money and making a high profit has no boundaries. This is this desire that ends in what Galbraith described as "a mood of exhilarant optimism and wild speculative frenzy" (Galbraith 1992: 29).

In the US, by August 1929, about 300 million shares had been bought on margin (Streissguth 2007: 301). The voices of those who considered the stock prices unsustainable were silenced by an avalanche of powerful vested interests in business, in the state and by the force of mainstream economics. John Moody (1868–1958), a financial analyst, writing in 1928, described the state of the US economy as unique in history. He was right in his description but wrong in his conclusion. He wrote that "nothing now to be foreseen which can prevent the United States from enjoying an era of business prosperity which is entire without equal in the pages of history" (Shiller 2015: 130). However, he was wrong to conclude that the same level of prosperity would last forever.

Charles Amos Dice (1878–1969) in his book *New Levels in Stock Market* published in September 1929 was categorical in his prediction about the US economy and stock market. He projected the US economy as advancing beyond the troubled years of the past, to a new age of perpetual growth and prosperity. Dice wrote that the American economy had entered into an era of "new world industry," a "new world of distribution," and a "new world of finance." He saw the bull market as a reflection of economic fundamentals and believed that there would be no limit to the new era of stock prices and rapid economic growth in America. Irving Fisher (1867–1947) was one of the most prominent economists in the 1920s. His prediction about the stock market crash was completely wrong. His guess not only damaged his public reputation but also cost him eight to ten million dollars in the crash (Galbraith 2017: 241). In August 1929, Fisher took the view that the stocks were still undervalued and predicted that the earnings and dividends would continue to go up. In his view, the fundamentals were too strong to prevent any major contraction in real output. This, he argued, was due to unprecedented improvements in the economy caused by exceptional innovations in science, technology, institutions, markets, and management. Fisher was overly optimistic. In August 1929, he said that "stock prices have reached what looks like a permanently high plateau" (quoted from Poitras 2011: 177). After the crash, in 1930, he also persisted that his "impression has been and still is that the market went up principally because of sound, justified expectations of earnings, and partly because of unreasoning and unintelligent mania for buying" (Fisher 1930: 53).

The wild rush had to crash. Signs of the crash were ignored. Antidepressant policies are not effective when there are little understanding, miscommunication, and much reciprocal mistrust between economic agents. The stock market went hyperactive and that was considered as a natural and balanced working of the system. This antidote fuelled the speculative craze. When the end came, the crash was harp and swift. The selling started and nobody knew how or dared to stop it. It came on 28 October 1929. The stock market fell by 13 per cent on that day. On 19 October the S&P 500 fell from 283 to 225. It dropped by 21 per cent (Farmer 2014: 125). The great crash was followed by the Great Depression, which lasted for about ten years. The unemployment rate was 8 per cent in 1929 in the United States. It increased to 24 per cent in 1932. Among the industrialized countries, unemployment rose to about 30 million (Stewart 1991: 129). By 1933 about 13 millions of American working population had lost their jobs (Galbraith 1992: 186). By 1932 the output of capital goods dropped to a quarter and industrial production to half. Between 1929 and 1932, the housing prices nationwide also fell on average by 30–40 per cent (Congressional Oversight Panel 2010: 90).

## Empires and the Frankenstein states

Empires fall but not without leaving a trail of destruction. The most palpable and concrete toxic residues left behind after their breakdown are the artificial borders and the Frankenstein states that they fabricate. The economic, political, legal, cultural, and environmental costs of such toxics cannot be underestimated. The cost of this legacy is rarely counted in the study of mainstream economics. To form a better understanding of this important issue, we shall merely look at one case study. The case in point is the collapse of the British Empire and what it has left behind. The jewel in the crown of the British Empire was India. The Indian misfortune began with adventurous British merchants who went to India as far back as 1600. One aftereffect of this venture was the formation of the British India Company. Over time the company became too rich and powerful for its part as a trading company. It set up its own army and became the instrument of imperial conquest. In 1757 during the Battle of Plassey, it seized a significant portion of Bengal. Following the Indian revolt in 1857, the British government ended the rule of the East India Company and the Mughal Dynasty.

Suffice it to say that the interest of a subjugated nation and its colonizer is a gulf apart. It is also plain to see that the imperial subjugation and economic rationality cannot be compatible. The occupation and subjugation of nations are usually carried out by force. After the conquest, we need hardly say, the imperial rulers deploy all sorts of unscrupulous means to penetrate their power in order to destroy the resistance of the subjugated people. They systematically apply policies that can subdue the conquered nation and gradually make their institutions, economic and legal infrastructure, cultural and moral norms, political associations, art, language, and music to be reliant on the plans and wishes of imperial rulers. In applying these strategies, the imperial rulers paralyze the actual and potential capabilities of the subjugated subjects. Such costs are hardly ever perceived in mainstream economics let alone being measured and accounted for.

One such policy is divide and rule policy. British imperial rulers applied this policy most effectively in India. The deadly effects of this policy persist to the present day. This policy is most lethal in the war of religions. India is one country where there are "so many religions and sects functioning side by side" (Woodburne 1923: 387). The diversity of religions is a testimony of religious tolerance but it is also a venomous cocktail that can in certain circumstances be exploited. This is what the British colonial rulers did in India. The British used the most objectionable elements of religion and used religion to perpetuate their imperial power.

The spread of Islam in India was after the Turkish Ghaznavid invasion of India. Shah Tughlaq (1351–85) used the art of bribery as an economic incentive to seduce the Indian population to accept Islam. He declared that "I encourage my infidel subjects to embrace the religion of the prophet, and I proclaimed that everyone who repeated the creed and became a Muslim should be exempt from jizya [Tax]" (quoted from Dasgupta 1993: 45). Some Indians converted to Islam to be exempted from paying taxes and also to escape from the servility of caste discrimination. The religious card, in particular the rift between Hinduism and Islam, played a crucial role in the British policy of divide and rule in India. This role was much intensified as India was getting closer to its independence. A historical landmark in the escalation of this policy was the establishment of the Indian National Congress on 28 December 1885. This political association attracted many progressive and secular Indians from all walks of life and religious beliefs. The Indian National Congress frightened the British colonists and alarmed them of the risk of their vulnerability.

To counter the Congress movement, the British found no more effective weapon in India than Islam. They began to support systematically the Indian Muslims to widen the rift between Hindus and Muslims. They backed Sayyid Ahmad Khan (1817–98) to form the All India Muhammadan Educational Conference in 1886. This forum was not a medium only for religious education. It was also a carrier for the British divide and rule policy. In the following decades, the British employed this medium as the vehicle for reinforcing the British colonial rule in India. The leaders of Indian Muslims emboldened by the British reassurance called for special representation in councils for Muslims in 1906. G. J. Elliot-Murray-Kynynumound (1845–1914), the 4th Earl of Minto, the Viceroy of India (1905–10), accepted their request. The scheme segregated the Indian Muslim population from the rest of the Indian population. It granted a special right to Muslims to have separate electorates and additional seats. Lord Minto's wife, Mary Caroline Grey (1858–1940), welcomed her husband's decision and wrote in her diary that the act destroyed the risk of "sixty-two million people [Indian Muslims] from joining the ranks of the seditious opposition" (quoted from Menon 1957: 10).

All was not lost. These were the preliminary steps taken for a far-reaching application of the divide and rule policy in India. The British colonial rulers wanted to counter the influence of the Indian secular liberation movement. For that purpose, they created the All-India Muslim League on 30 December 1906 in Dhaka. Under the pretext of safeguarding the rights of Indian Muslims, it was an agency of British colonial machine to promote religious bigotry in India. The first article of the Muslim League clearly states the main objective of the party. The first priority of the party is said: "to promote among Mussalmans [Muslims] of India, feelings of loyalty to the British government" (quoted from Agarwal 2005: 159). M. A. Jinnah (1876–1948) was the longest-serving leader of the Muslim League before the partition of India. He was from a Gujarati merchant family. Originally a follower of Hinduism, he converted to Islam after his grandfather, Poonja Gokuldas Meghji, converted to Islam. Jinnah, a Hindu name, also changed religion from one sect of Shia Islam, Ismaili Khoja, to a mainstream Shia religion. His lifestyle was everything but Islamic. He embraced the lifestyle of a British colonial elite, drinking alcohol, eating pork, and speaking English at home. When he died in 1948, his funeral observed as a Shia Muslim at home and as a Sunni Muslim in public. George E. Jones, who interviewed Jinnah several times, described him as "a Machiavelli in the amoral sense" (Jones 1948: 112). Louis Mountbatten (1900–79), the last viceroy of India, described him as a "lunatic," a "psychopathic case," and "an evil genius" (Hussain 2006: 352). Jawaharlal Nehru (1889–1964), the first prime minister of India after Indian partition, described him as "a man full of arrogance and pomposity … essentially uncultured … [has no] a single intelligent or enlightened idea in his head." Nehru also pointed out that he had "never come across any man who had less humanity in his character than Jinnah" (quoted from Panigrahi 2004: 33).

Jinnah's political career started in 1910. He joined the Indian National Congress and three years later, in 1913, he left the Congress for the Muslim League. From 1916 to his death, he presided the League. Jinnah followed the central line of the League policy of one India under control of the British Empire until the end of the Second World War. The rise of fascism in Europe, in the background, also inspired the Indian Muslim leaders to search for racial justification to divide the Indian Muslims from the rest of the population. At the height fascist movement in the 1930s, Chaudry Rahmat Ali (1897–1951), an Indian fundamentalist student in Cambridge, coined the term "Pakistan" in 1933. The term is a fabricate that has no real base. There was no and there is no nation in this name. It is a highly obnoxious and xenophobic designate that divided the Indians into "clean" and "unclean" people. The term is a compounded noun. It is composed of the term "Pak," which in Iranian languages means "clean." It's second part, "Stan" means the "Land" or "Location." Thus, "Pakistan" means the land of "clean people." Opposite to this designate stands Hindustan (India), which literally means the land of Hindus. To Indian fundamentalist Muslims, Hindus were regarded as "Najis" (filthy). This is the root and the intention behind this loaded fake acronym. Pakistan's school textbooks portray Hindus as "unclean" and "inferior" to Muslims (Pervez 2013: 123).

The outbreak of the Second World War in 1939 heightened the anti-colonial feelings in India, and the demand for independence got louder and stronger. V. A. John Hope (1887–1952), the Viceroy of India (1936–43), approached the leader of All-India Muslim League to sabotage the Indian's mass uprising. It was during the war that the British establishment acknowledged the inevitable. Wounded deeply from the war, the British did not want to lose all their influence in the Indian subcontinent. Losing the whole of India was tantamount to losing their political, military, and economic influence in Asia. The future destiny of India fell into the hands of Archibald Percival Wavell (1883–1950). He was a British colonial officer who served in the First World War. In 1939, Wavell became the commander in chief of British troops in the Middle East. While serving in the Middle East, he became aware of the region's strategic importance to the world powers. From 1941 to June 1943, he was the commander in chief in Southeast Asia, then moved to India, where he served as field marshal and viceroy of India until 1947. Wavell was a die-hard colonist and a trusted man of Churchill's inner circle with extensive experience of serving the empire. To many British, Winston Churchill (1874–1965) was a Great War leader. However, his battle against Nazi Germany, by no means, was a battle for racial equality. Churchill, two years after the 1945 Nuremberg laws, in 1947, addressed the Palestine Royal Commission. In his address, he remarked these words:

> I do not admit for instance, that a great wrong has been done to the Red Indians of America or the black people of Australia. I do not admit that a wrong has been done to these people by the fact that a stronger race, a higher-grade race, a more worldly-wise race to put it that way, has come in and taken their place.
>
> (quoted from Lagadec 2012: 78)

Churchill served twice as a prime minister of the British Empire: the first time from 1940 to 1945 and the second time from 1951 to 1955. His deep-seated faith in the superiority of British to rule was central to the subsequent act of the partition of India.

Empires in every form operate on the basis of social Darwinism. The principle of hierarchy of inferior and master race is entrenched in the very psyche of those who reach the seat of empire. Churchill was not an exception in this respect. The British rulers in India saw Indians as being "incapable of self-restraint, self-discipline, or self-help, let alone self-rule" (Herman 2008: 31). In the 1943 Bengal Famine, 3.5–3.8 million Indians perished as a direct result of Churchill's secret war against Indians (Mukerjee 2010). Churchill's response to the famine was with utter contempt. By 1940, Churchill could see the biggest empire was slowly crumbling before his eyes. He saw India as the cause of the break-up of his cherished empire. He expressed his private feelings about India and Indians to the secretary of state, Leopold S. Amery, and the Viceroy of India, Archibald Percival Wavell (1883–1950). Amery recalls that in September 1940 Churchill said, "I hate Indians. They are a beastly people with a beastly religion" (quoted from Ghose 1993: 111). Churchill's remarks about M. K. Gandhi (1869–1948) are equally disdainful and spiteful. On Gandhi's visit to London, he commented that "a seditious Middle Temple lawyer of the type well-known in the East, now posing as a fakir, striding half-naked up the steps of the Viceregal palace to parley on equal terms with the representative of the King-Emperor" (*The Times* 24 February 1931).

The British imperial establishment and, at the head of it, Churchill, were determined not to let India break free unharmed. The Raj viceroy, Wavell, met Churchill on 29 March 1945. Churchill admitted the inevitable. He suggested dividing India into "Pakistan, Hindustan, Pricestan, etc" (quoted from Panigrahi 2004: 99). Churchill and his party were defeated in the July 1945 general election. Labour Party won 393 seats, the absolute majority, and the Conservatives only 213 seats in the House of Commons. Clement Attlee (1883–1967) became the British prime minister. Churchill's defeat at the poll did not diminish his influence on the old order. Wavell met Churchill again after his general election defeat on 3 August 1945 when Churchill advised him to "keep a bit of India" (quoted from Ankit 2011: 49). Britain needed a servile parasitic state after dismembering India in the region for its military and strategic ambitions. It was no coincidence that Bernard L. Montgomery (1887–1976), British military chief, greeted the idea of partition with enthusiasm. Britain had the plan to use the "airfields and ports in northwest India," i.e., Pakistan as its military base (Sarila 2008: 27).

To mutilate India and "keep a bit of it," they did. Two provinces of India were the subject of division, Bengal and Punjab. To this end, a Boundary Commission was set up, consisting of four members from the India National Congress and four members from the Muslim League. Cyril Radcliffe (1899–1977), a British lawyer, chaired the commission. Radcliffe had no knowledge of India. On 8 July 1947, he arrived in India and was given the task of dividing India by 15 August 1947. From Bengal, Justice C. C. Biswas and B. K. Mukherji represented the National Congress and Abu Saleh Mohamed Akram and S. A. Rahman represented the Muslim League. On Punjab's side, Justice Mehr Chand Mahajan and Teja Singh represented the Congress and Din Mohamed and Muhammad Munir represented the Muslim League. The two sides quarrelled with no result in sight. In the end, in a matter of a few minutes, Cyril demarcated the boundaries of the two provinces of India. The Province of Bengal was divided into East and West parts. The eastern part was renamed as East Pakistan. Province Punjab was also divided into two parts. West Punjab was renamed as West Pakistan. The population of East Bengal at the time of partition was about 44 million and the population of West Punjab about 20 million. The two parts, the East Bengal and West Punjab, were about 1,000 miles apart (Segal 1991: 213). The human cost of the partition is estimated to be from 200,000 to 2 million people. The number of people being displaced is estimated to be about 15 million (O'leary 2012: 44). Radcliffe, after observing the carnage following his hand in the partition, refused to accept the fee of £2,000 for the time that he worked for the Boundary Commission.

The creation of the Islamic State of Pakistan from its inception to this very day has been a catalogue of disasters. Pakistan was the first imperial fabrication of an Islamic state. The base upon which this artificial state was constructed was the principle of divide and rule. British divided India and passed what they hacked from the body of India to their most ingratiating subservient Indian class. Up to 1857, the British Raj army recruited its personnel predominantly from the upper-caste Hindus. Most of the conscripts were from Bengal. But the Raj army mutiny changed the British policy of the recruitment. They looked for more compliant mercenaries. The peasants from north western India, mostly from Punjab and Muslim, and from the tribes of Gurkhas and Garhwalis fitted well to this description (Herman 2008: 30). The shift of the recruitment of mercenaries from Bengal to Punjab is vital to understand the British plan to divide India. In the 1857 revolt against British colonialism, Bengali soldiers were behind the uprising. In this mutiny, the Punjabi mercenaries took the side of the British and crashed the uprising (Soherwordi 2010: 6). The role of Punjabi soldiers in crashing the 1857 Indian uprising was critical. They proved their royalty to the British officers. Appreciative of Punjabis role in suppressing the mutiny, from 1857 British altered the composition and the setup of their army in India (Collen 1907: 19).

By the turn of the twentieth century, the British colonial army in India was transformed completely. It became dominated by Punjabi mercenaries. The Punjab population was then only 10 per cent of the Indian population. Most of these mercenaries were recruited from the northern regions of Punjab (present-day Province of Punjab in Pakistan), from such districts as Rawalpindi, Attock, Jehlum, and the Pakhtoon areas that are adjacent to Punjab (Soherwordi 2010: 8–9). Prior to the 1857 uprising, the British army in India was called the Bengal army. By 1929 there were very few solders recruited from Bengal. Out of the population of 45 million, 7,000 military personnel were from Bengal and Punjab with a population of 20 million contributed 349,000 mercenaries to the British Raj army. By 1929, 62 per cent of the entire British colonial army in India was Punjabis. In the First World War, 100,000 Punjabis served in the war who fought in most fields of the war under the British command (Soherwordi 2010: 12–14).

The allotment of the army after the partition of India is a vivid reflection of what Pakistan is today. Its share of the British colonial army in India was over 30 per cent. That is, 140,000 out of 410,000 military personnel, 40 per cent of the navy, 20 per cent of the air force, and 35 out of 67 battalions (Hewitt 1992: 26). Considering that East Bengal (East Pakistan) with a population of 44 million had virtually no army left and the allotment of the Indian army after partition was only between India and West Punjab (practically West Pakistan). The population of West Punjab during the partition was about 20 million and the Indian population in 1950 was 358 million (Sanderson 1995: 25). This indicates that 20 million (Punjabi Muslims in West Punjab) inherited over 30 per cent of the British colonial army in India and the 358 million inherited less than 70 per cent of the army. It was this well-established colonial design that laid the foundation of Pakistan, in which it manifested its forthcoming theocratic, bloody, and despotic legacy since its foundation. Pakistan is not a nation. In its essence, it is the mercenary army.

The British Empire was the biggest and most sophisticated empire that the world has ever known. Its falls have caused as much harm as its rise. Its harms are still ongoing in some parts of the world but hidden from the public consciousness. The creation of Pakistan is one of these hidden disasters. The term "Pakistan" was an invention of a twisted religious cult. The designate has no real national base. A "Muslim Nation" is merely a myth. Indians in all parts of India, including its provinces of Bengal and Punjab, adhered to a wide variety of religions. Pakistan, as a Muslim nation separate from India, is a blatant fallacy. It is a sacralization of falsehood. We have noted earlier that Pakistan was formed out of Indian provinces of East Bengal and West Punjab. The incorporation of Sindh and the Pashtun areas to Pakistan was also done deceitfully and in an underhand manner.

The noun "India" is derived from "Indus." Hindu and Hind are originated from Sindhu and Sindh, respectively. The fact of the matter is Sindh is "the root Part of India" (Falzon 2004: 78). Sindhi political leaders joined their forces with the All-India Muslim League in late 1938. In 1939 the first riot between Muslims and Hindu took place in Sindh. The most noted Sindhi leader who cooperated with the Muslim league was Ghulam Murtaza Syed (1904–95). He was instrumental in directing Sindh away from India or Independence in the 1940s. Sindhis were deceived. G. M. Syed soon after the creation of Pakistan in 1947 realized his big mistake. Soon after the first Muslim-Hindu riot in Sindh, during the year of partition, 1.4 million of Hindus were forced to leave their ancestral homeland and went to the other side of the artificial border that the British created. Sayed described the state of Pakistan as being unnatural. In 1972, he set up Sindhu Desh, a Sindhi political party, and called for the Independence of Sindh from the domination of the Punjabi-Mohajir axis (Siddiqi 2012: 88). Syed for his opposition to Pakistan as a political entity has spent over 30 years of his life in Pakistan jails.

The border disputes between Pakistan and Afghanistan began with the formation of Pakistan. The only country that opposed the admission of Pakistan to the UN and voted against it in September 1947 was Afghanistan. The history of this long-standing dispute goes back to 12 November 1893. On this day and year, Mortimer Durand (1850–1924), British India's foreign secretary, signed an agreement with the King of Afghanistan Abdul Rahman Khan (1844–1901) and divided the Pashtun territory into two parts. One part was annexed to British India. The Afghan king sold out the Pashtun land for a 50 per cent increase in his subsidy from Britain. The line that divides the Pashtun homeland is known as the "Durand Line" and it is about 1,600 miles (Cavanna 2015: 78). In order to quell the unrest in the region under their control, the British divided the annexed region into two separate jurisdictions. These two district areas are called the Federally Administered Tribal Area (FATA), which covered the region along the Durand Line, and the Northwest Frontier Province (NWFP). Abdul Ghaffar Khan (1890–1988), the most eminent Pashtun political leader, had spent considerable time in British prisons for his opposition to the British Raj and for putting an end to the Durand Line treaty. He allied with Indian Congress to win the 1937 and 1946 elections in the NWFP. Ghaffar Khan called for the termination of the Durand Line treaty and restoration of Pashtun independence. At the time of partition both Pashtun regions under Indian Raj control, the NWFP and FATA areas, were deceitfully annexed to Pakistan.

Ghaffar Khan and his party, the Khidmatgars, continued their opposition to the Durand Line and campaigned for the return of Pashtun areas to Afghanistan. It was not yet a year passed after the creation of Pakistan, in June 1948, Pakistan authorities arrested Ghaffar Khan and from 1948 to 1965 he spent about 15 years in Pakistani jails. Pashtun under the leadership of Ghaffar Khan was the close allies of the Indian Congress and Gandhi. Religion played no part or a minor part in their political struggle for independence. The fear of Pashtun breaking away from the colonial geopolitical construction of Pakistan alarmed the Pakistani political, religious, and military establishment. By 1960, they decided to fix the Pashtun problem by investing in Islamic extremism and in rejuvenating the most backward Pashtun's traditions, customs, and culture.

In his autobiography, Ghaffar Khan commented living under the colonial rule of the Punjabi Muslim of West Punjab as follows:

> The British had never looted our homes, but the Islamic Government of Pakistan did. The British had never stopped us from holding public meetings or publishing newspapers, but the Islamic Government of Pakistan did both. The British had never treated the Pakhtun women disrespectfully, but the Islamic government of Pakistan did.
>
> (quoted from Chitkara 2003: 27–28)

There is not a monolithic cult in any religion. Islam is not an exception. There are hundreds of different Islamic cults. The Islamic cult of Punjabi rulers of Pakistan is one of the deadliest cults in Islam. It is the most lethal weapon in the hands of the state of Pakistan. The constitution of Pakistan is drawn from the divinity of this sect, to which end history has grossly been fabricated and it is claimed that Pakistan was "established for the first time when the Arabs led by Muhammad bin Qasim occupied Sindh and Multan" in the eighth century (Hasan 1980: 11).

In this conquest, the subjugation of India is celebrated. The Muslims under the pretext of holy war waged jihad to colonize India. Global jihad by means of violence has not only been a key determinant in an expansion of Islam but it is one of its founding principles. The main drive behind the creation of Pakistan is buried in the central tenet of Islam. That is global jihad. Little wonder that "the jihadi mindset is being taught through the textbooks of compulsory subjects in government institutions from class one to university level" in Pakistan (Weidemam 2004: 59). Pakistan is a murderer of truth. Even its state title, the "Islamic Republic of Pakistan," is fake. The idea of a republic and an Islamic government that is subject to divine injunctions is self-contradictory. The unlearned and apathetic class is bewildered by the phenomenon of Pakistan. The disorientation of this class both inside and outside Pakistan is due to the myopic vision of history. Their astigmatic visualization of history misdirects their quest to tell apart truth from lie and right from wrong. Undiscerning, they fall into the teleological quagmire of whatever we have at present is natural and right.

The state of Pakistan was incubated in religious animosity. The British colonial rulers of India were the architecture of this undertaking. The intensity and order of magnitude of the religious animosity fostered in India to an extent that a section of the Indian population denounced their ancestral identity, nationality, culture, language, and values. The Pakistani theocratic state and army have been using Jihadist groups to safeguard their deceptive existence. The Punjabi rulers of Pakistan were neither the victim of the British colonial rule nor they are the victim of Islamic extremism. They were patronages of the British Empire in India. Throughout much of its existence, Pakistan has been the centre of a breeding ground for Islamic jihadists and terrorists. In the early 1970s, Zulfikar Ali Bhutto's government organized fanatic Islamic groups and sent them to crash the Bangladesh freedom movement. His chief of military staff, Zia-ul-Haq, in a coup seized power in 1977 and in 1979 he hanged Bhutto. Zia joined the British Army in 1943 in India. His reliance on Islamic fundamentalism was overt. Zia came to power at the time when the Americans started their holy war against the Soviet army in Afghanistan. This was a blessing in disguise for Pakistan and its rulers. Under the pretext of the fight against Soviet communism, Zia and his army with the financial support of the US and Saudi governments organized numerous fanatical Sunni groups in Pakistan. Many who took part in Zia jihad came from the Arab and other Muslim countries. Zia was killed in a mysterious air crash in August 1988.

Benazir Bhutto (1953–2007), daughter of Ali Bhutto, became the prime minister of Pakistan in 1988–90 and 1993–96. On both occasions, she was dismissed by the military. It was under her government that the jihadist network of madrassas was established and promoted. Her interior minister, Naseerullah Barbar, organized various jihadist Sunni groups to carry out terrorist activities in Afghanistan and Kashmir. In 1994, Barbar set up the Taliban group out of Afghan refugees who were indoctrinated in religious schools organized by Jamiat Ulema-e-Islam of Pakistan. Taliban and Mullah Omar are Benazir's creation. To the Pakistan army, Benazir became a liability. Benazir was killed on 27 December 2007 in a suicide bomb attack in Pakistan.

Pakistan has been the main sanctuary for the most Sunni Jihadi groups and it will remain the centre of most Sunni fundamentalist groups in the future. The fact of the matter is that its survival depends on such groups. The formation of over 40 jihadist groups in Pakistan, including Hizbul Mujahideen, Lashkar-e-Taiba, Jaish-e-Mohammed, the Haqqani network, Taliban, Al-Qaeda, and many others, is the natural progression of a baseless national identity that rests on fabricated history, demented religious delusion, and deceit. The grisly act of self-harm, Islamic suicide terrorism, has been thriving in Pakistan. The security forces of Pakistan have been nurturing and training the clandestine Islamic agents and suicide squad to an industrial scale. Most of the horrendous suicide attacks in Afghanistan, India, and on opposition parties in Pakistan have been masterminded by Pakistan's various security and religious groups. Pakistan cannot survive without harbouring, recruiting, and sponsoring Islamist extremists and terrorism.

The bigger partner in the creation of Pakistan was East Bengal. The population of East Bengal at the time of the creation of Pakistan was twice as much as West Punjab. The East Bengal was also an intellectual driving force for an Islamic state. In contrast, West Punjab was one of the main centres of British Raj bureaucracy, a territory for recruiting mercenaries for the Raj army, and the highbrow of Islamists who were most loyal to the rule of Empire. The conflict between the two parts of Pakistan was inevitable. M. A. Jinnah, the first Governor-General of Pakistan, without any consultation with other nationalities that joined Pakistan in 1948, ordered that the Urdu language be the national language of Pakistan. He directed that "Urdu and only Urdu" must be the national language (Bianco 2010: 158). It is ironic that Jinnah himself chose to speak English in his home, not his maternal language, Gujarati, nor Urdu, but imposed the Urdu language on both sides of Pakistan, where Urdu was the first language of only 4 per cent of the population (Khan 2017: 122). The Urdu speakers, by and large, were those who were displaced during the partition and from the political elites in West Pakistan. As the Bengali language was the language of the majority population of Pakistan and was a very developed ancient language, the Bengalis in East Bengal asked their language to be given equal status to Urdu as the national language of Pakistan. The language movement, 1948–52, in East Pakistan continued relatively peacefully until 21 February 1952. On this day, Pakistani security forces attacked Bengali students' demonstration, injuring many and killing five protesters. Among the dead was a nine-year boy (Schendel 2013: 1982). The UNESCO, in 1999 in memory of these victims, has declared 21 February as International Mother Language Day. The Bengali resentment against Punjabi rulers of Pakistan after this event grew year by year until the Bangladesh Holocaust in 1971.

Ten years after the creation of Pakistan, the *Economist* described it as shifting between "the grotesque and macabre" (Economist 11 Oct 1958). This comment was made four days after the first military coup in Pakistan. On 7 October 1958, General Ayyub Khan seized the power in Pakistan. His tight military rule lasted until he was made to abdicate power in 1969. After Ayyub Khan, the political power went to another military general, Yahya Khan. Realizing that direct military rule was difficult under the circumstances, he promised a general election, which was held in January 1971. The East Bengal (East Pakistan) won 167 seats out of total seats of 300 in both East and West Pakistan. This represented about 56 per cent of the total votes from both parts of Pakistan. West Punjab with 86 seats secured only 29 per cent of the total votes. According to the election results, the Awami League in East Pakistan won the absolute majority. But the colonial rulers of Pakistan, 29 per cent in Punjab, were determined to keep the power to themselves. They used everything in their power to stop Bengalis to form the government.

The red herring claim, the liberation Muslim from the yoke of Hindus, was discredited in the 1970s. It became too obvious that Islam was merely a pretext in the creation of Pakistan. The Bengali bloody struggle for independence revealed the true face of the whole scheme. It was not Islam but the British Empire that created Pakistan. Since the whole scheme was groundless, Pakistan crumbled. The biggest partner broke free. The Bengalis were no more equal Muslims. The Punjabi rulers of Pakistan preached the most reprehensible racist remarks about Bengali Muslims in East Pakistan. In 1969 General Ayyub Khan described them as being evolved from the "downtrodden races" (Kiernan 2007: 573). General Yahya Khan, who succeeded Ayyub, on 22 February 1971 instructed the Pakistani army, in case Bengalis do not consent to their domination, to kill three million Bengalis so that "the rest will eat out of our hand" (quoted from Payne 1973: 50). In genocides, it is impossible to know the exact extent of the ghoulish deeds done and even the death toll. In the case of East Pakistan, it is estimated that in the course of 267 days, the Pakistani army killed 1,247,000 Bengalis (Rummel 1994: 331). About 40 million Bengalis were displaced, ten million sought sanctuary in India and the other 30 million were displaced internally. All over East Pakistan, the Pakistan army and their collaborators set up "rape camps" (D'Costa 2011: 103). To one estimate, the number of Bengali women being raped by Pakistani soldiers is between 200,000 and 400,000 (Brownmiller 1993: 81–83). East Bengal declared its independence on 26 March 1971 from Pakistan but it has not yet recovered fully from the destruction and the grotesque treatment that they suffered from the hands of the Pakistani army.

In colonial geopolitical jurisdictions, justice, democracy, freedom, rule of law, and human rights have been abused since their inception. Crime against humanity in such pseudo dominions is the norm. The world has, out of convenience, desensitized to such geopolitical constructions. The bloodshed, genocide, and corruption are regarded as a matter of course. These characteristics are perceived as ingrained in oriental and Asiatic disposition, culture, religion, and mind-set. The common misperception rests on the view that "it is a fact; therefore, it is natural." Another mistake that reinforces the severity of this error is that all these colonial geopolitical constructions are projected as homogenous historical nations. The case in question is Pakistan. The horrific acts of crime and the deliberate destructions that the state and army of Pakistan have committed have not just investigated and the perpetrators of crimes brought to justice but they have been praised, honoured, awarded, and promoted for their atrocities. The perpetrators of the Bengalis Holocaust in their return to West Pakistan were not brought to justice but they were deployed to Baluchistan to continue the massacre of Baluch people with complete impunity. Before we go any further in addressing this subject, we need to understand the background of Baluchistan's ill-fortune.

Baluchistan is located on the plateau of Iran. The Baluch formed their first national state in 1666. The Baluch independent state lasted over two and half centuries until the British invasion of Baluchistan. A year after the invasion of Afghanistan in 1938, the British imperial army invaded Baluchistan on 13 November 1839. With the intensification of Baluch continuous revolts, armed struggle, and resistance against British colonial rule, the British decided to divide Baluchistan. Major General F. J. Goldsmid (1818–1909) drew the first line, the Goldsmid Line, in 1871, dividing Baluchistan into two parts, the western and eastern Baluchistan. The British continued to control the eastern part and the western part of Baluchistan was given to the Qajar, the rulers of Persia. The second artificial line was drawn in 1893. H. M. Durand (1850–1924) drew the "Durand Line," as a result of which the northern part of Baluchistan was annexed to Afghanistan. These divisions were forced upon the Baluch nation and were drawn without Baluch will and consent.

At the outbreak of the First World War, western Baluchistan was liberated from the Qajar dynasty. J. Ramsay has captured the Baluch sentiment against

Qajar colonial rulers in western Baluchistan. On 25 January 1927, he wrote that "there is not a vestige of Persian authority existing, nor has Persia any means of asserting her theoretical claims to sovereignty over" western Baluchistan. "Not only has the country under discussion (western Baluchistan) slipped out of Persian grasp, it has been so hostile to Persia" (quoted from Breseeg 2004: 185). A year later, in 1928, Reza Mir Panj (1878–1944), the Persian military dictator, invaded and annexed western Baluchistan to Persia. We must also add that it was and it has been Russian strategic ambition to have access to warm water in the South, an outlet to the Persian Gulf. British feared the advances of the Bolsheviks to central Asia – expecting that the Russian would march beyond central Asia. The disintegration of the Qajar dynasty increased British mistrust about the Russian plan. To keep the Bolshevik at bay and avert their threat against British India and the Persian Gulf, the British needed a ruthless dictator to patch things up in Iran. Reza Mir Panj fitted the requirements of the job. He was uneducated. Harold Nicolson (1886–1968), a British diplomat who was born in Tehran in 1926, described him as a "secretive, suspicious and ignorant" man (Ghani 2000: 388). Another British diplomat, Robert Vansittart (1881–1957), in 1933 described him as a "bloodthirsty lunatic" (Zirinsky 1992: 639).

Reza Khan in his youth worked for the European commissioners as a horse hostler in Tehran (Ludington Daily News: 26 April 1926). He seized power in Persia in a coup on 21 February 1921. The coup d'état could not have succeeded without the British approval and support. The British interests could not be served better without a strong central government and without restoration of order in Persia. Reza Khan's ideal political system, the "one-man system," was compatible with the British colonial strategy in the region (Adel, Elmi and Taromi-Red 2012: 15). To this end, the British backed Reza Khan to rise to power (Zirinsky 1992: 658). In the course of about four years after the coup, Reza Khan ascended to the positions of commander in chief of the army, the minister of war, and the prime minister of Persia. Finally, on 12 December 1925, he crowned himself as the king. In the 1920s, he consolidated his power. In the 1930s, he established a close relationship with Nazi Germany (Goldschmidt 1991: 213). Inspired by Nazi's ideology of pure race, on 21 March 1935 in reference to the Aryan race he changed "Persia" to "Iran," which means the "land of Arians."

From the date of the British invasion of Baluchistan to their departure, the British imposed many treaties unilaterally on the Baluch nation. Besides drawing the "Goldsmid Line" and the "Durand Line," other treatises that forced upon the Baluch nation were 1839, 1854, 1863, and 1876 treaties (Baloch 1987: 127–43). These treaties in succession stripped the Baluch national sovereignty bit by bit and restrained the political, legal, cultural, and economic development of Baluchistan. The British kept their semi-colonial rule in eastern Baluchistan until their departure in 1947. The Baluch struggle to attain full independence took a modern form in the 1920s with the establishment of the Anjuman-e-It had-e-Baluchistan – The Association for Unity of Baluchistan (Baloch 1987: 151–57). The political model that this group of Baluch intellectuals and political activists aspired to amounted to no less than a social-democratic political system. The quest for the unity of Baluchistan and the attainment of full independence formed the core values of their political struggle. Baluch was inspired by the 1917 Russian Revolution and the Indian independence movement. In post-colonial Baluchistan, they wanted to establish a secular constitutional democracy based on the principle of one person one vote. The Baluch representatives attended the Bolsheviks Congress of the Peoples of the East in Baku on 1 September 1920. The Congress described the cases of Baluchistan, Afghanistan, and India as being "under 'paternal' case of British Imperialism" (Stenographic Report 1977: 111).

As Baluchistan preserved its semi-independence status and the British could only stay in Baluchistan according to the agreements that the British imposed on Baluchistan, the Baluch by mid-1930s decided to regain their full independence through legal means. For this purpose, the state of Baluchistan under the leadership of Khan of Kalat employed an Indian lawyer, M. A. Jinnah, who became the founder of Pakistan. The only reason for employing M. A. Jinnah was to represent and to defend the Baluchistan case to British authorities for independence. From about the mid-1930s to 1946, Jinnah was an official lawyer of the state of Kalat. For the time period, about ten years, that Jinnah was the official lawyer of the state of Baluchistan and in addition to his regular fees he was provided gold equal to his body weight. During the period that he worked as the state of Kalat lawyer, he learned all the weaknesses of the political establishment of Baluchistan and its economic and strategic importance.

The Baluch constant demand to retain their full independence compelled the British authorities to look at the case of Baluchistan, for which purpose General R. C. Money (1888–1985) in 1944 studied the constitutional position of Baluchistan and its relationship to Britain. The verdict of his findings was that the Baluch nation was an independent nation. The British in the end yielded to the demand of the Baluch national state full sovereignty. The British signed the Standstill Agreement on 4 August 1947. This agreement, which was also signed by the representative of the state of Baluchistan and Mr Jinnah as the forthcoming general governor of the state of Pakistan, returned the full independence to Baluchistan. Following the Standstill Agreement, Baluchistan under control of Britain reclaimed its independence on 11 August 1947. The news of Baluchistan independence was reported in the *New York Times* on 12 August 1947. Three days later, on 14 August 1947, India was officially divided and the artificial state of Pakistan was created. The partition put West Punjab, due to its historical ties with the British colonial bureaucracy, on a much stronger position compared to other parts that were annexed to Pakistan. West Punjab inherited a significant fraction of the Indian Raj army, administration, and resources.

Pakistan invaded the first democratic state in Baluchistan. Pakistan was created on 14 August 1947 and its army invaded and annexed eastern Baluchistan on 27 March 1948. Baluch resistance against occupation was prompt and has continued to the present day. Pakistan has carried out six major military operations in Baluchistan ever since: in 1948, 1958, 1965, 1971, 1999, and the last one started in 2002. In the 1970s operation that lasted from 1973 to 1977 about 15,000 personnel from Pakistani were killed in Baluchistan. The Baluch death toll just in this conflict is estimated to be over 25,000. The Pakistani army, state, and religious establishment have disappeared, killed many thousands of Baluch, and have displaced over a million of them only in their latest military operations in eastern Baluchistan. Most Baluch victims are carefully selected from those individuals who oppose the Punjabi Muslim army rule in Baluchistan. The Baluch who is targeted is from the secular and most informed section of Baluch society. The bodies of many of these victims have been found after years and months of being disappeared in different parts of Baluchistan. Signs of gruesome torture appear on the bodies of all of the victims. Bodies of many victims are buried in unknown mass graves. Three of such graves were discovered in Tootak, Khuzdar district of Baluchistan, on 17 January 2014. Pakistan has also tested its "Islamic nuclear bombs" on 28 May 1998 in Baluchistan. Eastern Baluchistan under Punjabi Muslim colonial rule has become one of the most deprived, devastated, and militarized areas in the world. One of the American scholars, Selig S. Harrison (1927–2016), who has studied the case of Baluchistan, has described the situation in Baluchistan as a "slow genocide" of the Baluch nation (Harrison Oct 2006).

Besides all these atrocities and destructions, the state of Pakistan has been in constant conflict with India. It has waged five major military confrontations with India since its creation. The first war was in October 1947 and Pakistan was only created in August 1947. The largest built-up troops and tanks after the Second World War was the 1965 Pakistan and India war. In the 1971 war, East Bengal (Pakistan) was liberated. The whole scenario of India would have been very different if the British rulers did not rush to divide India on the demagogic religious sectarian ground. M. A. Jinnah by the time of the division of India was suffering from acute tuberculosis. As the first Governor-General of Pakistan, he made Karachi its capital city. Immediately after the creation of Pakistan, the real power shifted to the Punjabi army, bureaucracy, and the religious establishment. Jinnah died in September 1948.

Pakistan from its very foundation began to eat itself from within. This macabre business started with M. A. Jinnah, the founder of Pakistan, and Choudhry Rahmat Ali, the inventor of the term "Pakistan." M. A. Jinnah died in total neglection of his creation and Choudhry Rahmat Ali was thrown out of the country only after a few months of being in the country. Choudhry with high hope and great expectations left England for Pakistan in April 1948. As a son of the Muslim Punjabi feudal, he had already lost his land and property inheritance, which were located in East Punjab. In October 1948, Liaquat Ali Khan (1895–1951), the first prime minister of Pakistan and the successor of Jinnah, confiscated all his belongings and expelled him from Pakistan. Rahmat Ali returned to England and died lonely and in poverty on

3 February 1951 in Cambridge. His body was discovered a few days after his death. His former college arranged his funeral on 20 February 1951 and paid the expenses for his burial (Venkatesh 2018 Herald). The first prime minister of Pakistan, Liaquat Ali Khan, was also shot dead in the same year on 16 October 1951. In the first ten years of its existence, Pakistan sacked and replaced seven prime ministers. Within this period Pakistan army elevated itself as the undisputed rulers of Pakistan. This started with the military man, Iskander Mirza (1899–1969), declaring himself as the first president of Pakistan on 23 March 1956. Mirza was ousted by his army commander, Ayyub Khan, on 27 October 1958. Ever since Pakistan practically has been run by military men. All prime ministers of Pakistan, except the military rulers, were either dismissed or killed by the army or their associates. Zulfkar Ali Bhutto's government was overthrown in a coup by his chief of army Zia-ul-Haq in July 1977. Two years later, on 4 April 1979, Bhutto was hanged to death. The military dictator himself was killed in a mysterious plane crash on 17 August 1988. Bhutto's daughter, who served two terms as prime minister, was murdered during her political rally on 27 December 2007.

## The generations of wars

The generation that has suffered so much in two of the greatest wars cannot see the world in the same light as the generations who have not experienced the wars. This generation could not live in the same way as their ancestors. The incredible destruction and suffering conditioned them to work extra hard to compensate their lost times. This conditioning is multifaceted. The most important element of this conditioning was the general consensus not to repeat the same catastrophic wars. This was the generation that worked long hours doing any job that they got hold of it without belittling what they did. This was the generation that believed that there is a better way of living than what they and their parents experienced. The two great wars and many wars of liberation taught them that peace is possible and it is under a peaceful and cooperative environment that there can be progress and prosperity. In this section, we shall look at some of these economic, political, legal, institutional, cultural, and technological conditionings that transformed the advanced nations into democratic welfare-state economies.

The two great wars, the Great Depression, the Russian communist revolution, and the rise of fascist governments exposed convincingly the inability and inapplicability of the conventional economic theory. The conventional economics was out of touch with the new realities of the ever-changing national and global economic and political orders. The competing economic doctrines were well tied with powerful patronage of vested interests in government, in academia, and in business. On the other extreme side of the spectrum were the Marxian command economy and the Fascist totalitarian economics. Besides, their relative irrationality and ineptness, to a various degree, were undemocratic. The search for a more effective and applicable economic instruction resulted in Keynesian economics. John M. Keynes (1883–1946), the most influential economist of the twentieth century, published his monumental work *The General Theory* in 1936. One of the two most important messages of the book is that the prolonged unemployment is not natural. To this end, he explained the causes of prolonged unemployment and articulated eloquently how to end unemployment. The second most important message of the book is that the economic theory postulated in the book is consistent and compatible with liberal democracy. The emphasis here is not on the validity of the theory in its explanation, prediction, or application but on how quickly it was commended generally by mainstream economics and policymakers and applied enthusiastically both by the left and right political spectrum. The point that we should pay close attention to is the reason that in a short space of time the majority of economists and policymakers in advanced industrialized economies followed and applied Keynes's prognoses and prescriptions. Moreover, what is the secret that they in no time convinced the majority of their citizens about the efficacy of Keynes's theory? There was no mystery in that. This was an extraordinary time. Most people were open to the idea of liberating themselves from war, poverty, and uncertainty. In this sense, the Keynes's economic ideas were viewed positively and worked well when all the stakeholders wanted them to work irrespective of their validity.

The other elements that have contributed to Keynes's success were the treatment of the economy as a mechanical machine. The pledge that if you study the economy carefully and learn about its different components in the same way as in a mechanical machine then the economy can be managed and be directed to the desired outcomes. With the timely application of proper macroeconomic policies, anticipated macroeconomic objectives can be achieved. Keynes's economics had its time. As it became the benchmark of conventional macroeconomic theory, it became many things to many people. Embedded in the approach that treats the economy like the machine is the inescapable track that confines economic activities, trends, directions, events, and outcomes as something that is predictable precisely. By predicting these elements then we can manage the economy and be able to avoid economic malfunctions and distresses and can channel the economy into long-lasting economic growth and full employment. Keynes himself was less optimistic about this approach. The by-product of treating the economy as a machine that its operation can be predicted and adjusted was the rapid mathematization of economics. The rapid technological innovation and adoption of information technology in storing data, in assessing data, and in forecasting economic trends based on past data have served in a big way the trend to narrow down the depth and the scope of real-world economy to the language of mathematics.

The generation gaps are unavoidable. But the distance between those who defeated fascism and witnessed the atrocities of Stalinism and their parents was among the widest generation gaps. This was the generation that experienced the most extreme form of human cruelty and deprivation. The propensity to seek a better life is instinctive. It is an inborn force that cannot be measured by any mathematical notation. Changes in masses' beliefs and expectations collectively, rightly or wrongly, can bring great social, political, and economic transformations. All revolutions and mass religious movements, as well as political and ideological movements such as fascism, communism, anti-colonialism, and liberal democracy were movements of this nature. The generation who lived through the great wars, the Great Depression, fascism, Stalinism, and colonialism did everything in their power to break free from their nightmare. What they witnessed was too horrendous. So, it was not hard for them to imagine and seek a better life. It was this mass passion of unity of purpose that after the Second World War we began to see serious attempts being made to apply and implement social and liberal democracy in several countries that were affected by the factors cited above. The social groups that suffered the most – workers, women, soldiers, and other low-income groups strongly motivated to improve their economic, social, and economic conditions – worked long and hard to bring a real change in their living environment and the level of well-being. Keynes was the economist of that generation.

Other elements in this social and economic periodic table were the restoration of international monetary order. In July 1944 the Bretton Woods conference was held. At the end of the conference, a number of international monetary and economic institutions were set up. These institutions were the World Bank, the International Monetary Fund, and the International Trade organization. The chief objective of the conference and creation of these institutions was to restore stability in exchange rate movements and the global monetary system. The conference replaced the gold standard to a form of a fixed exchange rate regime that these institutions were made responsible to observe and uphold. It replaced the gold standard with a form of fixed exchange rate regime to be compatible with Keynesian prescript of the state management of the aggregate effective demand. Another element was the introduction of the welfare state. The alternative worldview offered a different perspective. A vision that argued that political freedom is not achievable without the basic economic freedom. In other words, political freedom, economic efficiency, and social justice are compatible. The fusion of these determinants in the right order, time, and place is said to be the building block of greater productivity, cohesion, unity, inclusion, cooperation, stability, harmony, peace, and progress. It was argued that political liberties without basic economic security, i.e., security in the provision of basic needs, is not liberty. Individual liberty remains an empty gesture without the security of basic economic needs. This is all the more the case if economic insecurity is not the fault of the individuals. The welfare state is intended to free, protect, and promote social, political, and economic liberties. It is intended to free individuals at their times of greatest need from economic insecurity. The provision of education, social insurance, health services, old-age pensions, and unemployment benefits were real steps taken to promote equality of opportunities.

The institution that consolidated many of these elements was the United Nations. Yet, the designate is a misnomer. The United Nations (UN) from its formation to the present day is an assembly of the world states. There are many stateless nations that do not have their representatives in the UN. Nevertheless, the UN is the most familiar international institution. No other institution quite like it exists. The main motive for its creation was world peace. But as long as there have been wars there has been the quest for peace. The UN was a by-product of the two world wars. The immediate challenge at the end of the Second World War was to restore world peace and trade. The most influential thinker behind the idea of multilateralism, international governance, and world peace was A. Kant. In his short treatise, *Essay on Eternal Peace*, which was published in 1795, he argued that war is inherently destructive and undesirable and must be avoided by all means. Most importantly, in this brief discourse, he proposed his argument for the eternal world peace. Kant wrote:

> a war of extermination – where the destruction of both parties along with all rights is the result – would permit perpetual peace to occur only in the vast graveyard of humanity as a whole. Thus, such a war, including all means used to wage it, must be absolutely prohibited.
>
> (Kant 2003: 5)

His concrete proposal for this purpose was a federation of states. A jurisdictional institution that would safeguard international order by resolving the international conflicts and settling disputes between member states by means of arbitration.

The forerunner of the UN was the League of Nations, which was set up by the victors of the First World War in 1919. This was a voluntary association of 63 states. The principal aim of the League was "to develop cooperation among nations and to guarantee them peace and security." The League did not only fail to maintain universal peace but failed to avoid the Second World War. The war gave birth to a new world law and order. It produced institutions to match the new order. The UN was the product of the war and the construction of the victors of the war, most specifically the United States. The last day of the League of Nations was 18 April 1946. This was the day that the United Nations was born. The primary objective of the UN was to prevent wars to the scale experienced in the two great wars. To this end, it produced one of the most important universal social, political, legal, and economic contracts in history. The charter of the United Nations is mainly a construction of American, but most of its elements are Keynesians. The chief purpose is maintaining peace and security in the world.

The prerequisites to achieve the desired results, i.e., the world peace, security world order, and governance, were taken essentially from Keynesian economics and policies. On 10 December 1948, the United Nations General

Assembly proclaimed and adopted the Universal Declaration of Human Rights. This document reflects Kant's teaching on the equal worth of every person, "the politics of equal dignity," and global eternal peace. But the charter adopted Keynesian economics and policies to achieve such desired objectives. Virtually in all 30 articles of the charter, we can find the influence of Keynes's economic system. The articles that show Kantian influence the most are articles 1, 2, 3, 7, 15, 18, 20, and 21. Article (1) declares that "all human beings are born free and equal in dignity and rights. They are endowed with reason and conscience and should act towards one another in the spirit of brotherhood." In Article (2) we read that "everyone is entitled to all rights and freedom ... without distinction of any kind, such as race, colour, sex, language, religion, political or other opinion, national or social origin, property, birth or another status." All these and other articles are the prerequisites for eternal peace.

Although these are said to be necessary preconditions for peace, they are not sufficient. In an attempt to complete the number of prerequisites, the charter adopted Keynesian economics and policies. Article (23) reads, "everyone has the right to work, to free choice of employment, to just and favourable conditions of work and to protection against unemployment." Article (55) states that

> everyone has the right to a standard of living adequate for the health and well-being of himself and of his family, including food, clothing, housing, and medical care and necessary social services, and the right to security in the event of unemployment; sickness, disability, widowhood, old age or other lack of livelihood in circumstances beyond his control.

In Article (26) it is added that "everyone has the right to education. Education shall be free, at least in the elementary and fundamental stages."

At the start of the First World War, the European empires and their colonies, the metropoles, and the peripheries encircled about 85 per cent of the land of the whole earth. The Universal Declaration of Human Rights broke new ground for oppressed people and nations. It was a new dawn that opened a new horizon for new possibilities against social, economic, and political injustices. The Declaration denounced the legitimacy of imperial dominance. It condemned imperial dominance as being immoral. In the course of three decades after the publication of the Declaration, the intercontinental empires were dissolved. This global anti-bondage movement diminished significantly the racial and cultural pecking order that was an integral part of the socio-economic and political system of colonialism. The physical space of the empires receded quickly and direct conquest and appropriation of land lost its moral pre-eminence.

Two other social and political upheavals that discarded the old order and shaped the new order were the gender equality movement and the trade union movement. Needless to say, half of the human population are women.

This half of the human race has been deprived of their most basic rights from the distance time. Virtually all religions were founded by men and spread by men. Equally, all rulers and war leaders have been men. The men, by and large, have been the owners of wealth in its different forms. Furthermore, for millennia women were excluded from learning. Aristotle, the most influential philosopher for over 2,000 years, wrote how to exclude women from social and economic life and to dominate them. From antiquity, motherhood, giving birth and rearing children, has been perceived as a weakness, not as a woman's fortitude, tenacity, and compassion. All sorts of prejudices and violence against women fossilized over a long time that has formed a discriminative cultural, social, political, religious, and ideological orientation that is still ongoing. These prejudicial conditions for a very long time were deemed to be interminable. Patriarchal societies are discriminatory. The etymology of patriarchy here is used to mean a power structure where the male members of society dominate and subordinate the female members both in private and public spheres.

Full gender equality does not even exist in the most advanced liberal democratic societies. Women are paid less for the same job as their male counterparts. Full equality of rights and opportunities for women for the most part of the world is a distant dream. Equality between men and women will diminish not only violence against women but overall violence in society. It will empower women and allow them to have equal access to education, economic resources, employment, health, political power, leisure, and recreation. One of the most basic demands of women, the right to vote, was granted first in New Zealand in 1893. It was followed by Australia in 1902. The Indigenous Australian, however, had to wait another 60 years to be granted the universal right to vote in federal elections. The Scandinavian nations were the next on the list who granted women the right to vote. Finland was first in 1906, then Norway in 1913, then Denmark and Iceland in 1915. The Soviet Union and the Netherlands granted the same right in 1917, the US in 1920, Britain in 1928, France in 1944, Japan in 1945, and Switzerland in 1971. In the case of undemocratic countries, especially in theocratic states, discrimination against women is institutionalized. Any pretence of adhering to or complying with international standards about the rights of women is only on paper. We need hardly say that full restoration of gender equality and rights, women's full citizenship, their participation, and empowerment enhance the economic growth, prosperity, and well-being of every nation. That is something rarely seen in the analysis of mainstream economics. What can we call the situation when the rights of half of the population are infringed and they are barred systematically and legally to utilize their full potential? Is it not a form of chronic economic crisis?

The Industrial Revolution occurred first in England. The revolution transformed British society into an industrialized society. The formation of trade unions and workers' associations was a by-product of industrialization in England. One important characteristic of the process of the Industrial

Revolution was the accumulation and concentration of large capital into the hands of a small number of daring individuals who set up factories and employed a large number of wage-labourers under one roof. This emerging class of people used machines to produce commodities for mass consumption. The mass production for mass consumption changed the workplace, the assembly of production, and the nature of work. It brought a large number of workers under one roof. The assembly of a crowd of labourers under one roof necessitated strict work discipline, the division of labour, and the application of machinery. The industrial factory production also broke the link between the ownership of the means of production and workers and created its own social classes, the industrial capitalist, and the industrial working class.

The conditions in which the process of industrialization took place paved the way for the formation of workers' associations and unions to fight for their basic rights. One cannot sufficiently understand the nature of economic disorder and crisis by overlooking the position that the workers and their institutions hold in advanced industrialized economies. Workers' organizations, associations, and unions have a significant bearing on the development of the economy and economic policies of developed democratic countries. To this end, our coverage of the trade union movement will be limited to the British experience. The first unions in Britain gradually appeared in the eighteenth century. The path of development of unions, as one can expect, was a hazardous venture. Even to this day for workers to assert their demands collectively in the organized union is a perilous venture in many countries. The pioneers of workers' association, endured hostility, used their own time and resources to set up and to guard their unions. The unions were set up first and foremost for the emerging working class to reassert their identity as a social group with a common interest. Their bound was the conditions in which they worked and the common treatment they received collectively from their employers. Their conditions of living were so bad that they all shared the desire to improve their poor living conditions. Instinctively, the home to improve the conditions in their workplace and the demand for better pay was trade unions.

The repeal of the Combination Acts prohibited trade unions in Britain in 1824. A significant landmark in the history of British trade unionism was in 1851. It was when the Amalgamated Engineering Union (AEU) was formed. The AEU was a national union made of the merger of nine smaller unions. This event was also a landmark in both British and world trade union history. In Britain, it was the first national union in the modern sense and the beginning of rapid rise in union membership, and it also set a precedent for the world trade union movement to follow. Another major event in the history of the British trade union movement was the formation of the Trade Union Congress (TUC) in 1868. It was an expression of growing power, organization, and increasing demand for the rights of the working population.

The period from the mid-nineteenth century to the outbreak of the First World War, we have the statutory recognition and the formation of many national workers' unions in Britain. The statutory recognition transformed those unions that fulfilled the legislative requirements from voluntary institutions into legal entities that could work on behalf of their members. In the second half of the nineteenth century, the unions increased their membership, improved their organizations, and adopted sophisticated strategies to improve the rights and working conditions of their members. The membership of the unions was increased from 700,000 in 1889 to about 2,000,000 in 1900. In the course of two years, from 1889 to 1891, the membership of the unions was doubled (Brodie 2003: 27 and Lovell 1977: 21). Another period of rapid expansion of membership of the unions was from 1911 to 1914. Their total membership increased from two million to four million. Again, it was doubled by the end of the First World War to eight million (Hobsbawm 1967: 358). The trade unions demonstrated their power in the General Strike of 1926 when the TUC opposed the wage cuts and called the strike. This strike was a turning point for the union movements and the advanced industrialized economies. The General Strike started on 4 May and ended on 12 May.

## The pandemic of globalization

The Marxist doctrines of universalism, continuous revolution, and the dictatorship of the proletariat failed in a big way. These dogmas were applied, to varying degrees, in the Soviet Empire, in the eastern and central European nations, in China, in Cambodia, in Ethiopia, and in Afghanistan and a few other countries. The consequences of the failure of Marxian social engineering have been horrific. The idea of the dictatorship of the proletariat was endemic. It had a universal appeal. It was infectious just like any fashionable addiction despite its obvious harms and manifestly ill-founded rationale. The social endemics, either way, as in wearing a cap backwards or as in unfounded social engineering, share a common denomination. The vast majority of people follow the crowd blindly. In these matters, most people are dispositioned to believe and adhere to blind allegiance to an act without having a clear understanding of what they do. In the sphere of social order, ideas are more infectious than reality. All religions, invariably, fall into this category. Each lays claim to ultimate truth. By definition, each counters the validity of all other religions. Ideas that cannot be validated scientifically are of this nature. The Marxian universal dictatorship of the proletariat is in the same set. Such ideas can be fashionable without being right. Partly, because they can serve certain social, political, economic, and cultural vested interests but mainly it is due to the disposition of the masses' blind trust to follow the crowd.

The economic ideas that rest on analytical truth are essentially the same. Likewise, they can be infectious without being correct. All schools of thought in economics, more or less, lay claims on analytical truths. The virulent drift: the more people believe in a theory, not because it is true but because it is infective, the more people will follow the theory that is more tradeable. The popularity of Keynesian economics, just like Marxian economics or other prevailing schools of thought in economics, despite their differences and disagreements, shares pretty much this common ground. Unlike religion, in economics economic doctrines are proposed to be applied in the real world and the real world keeps changing. Fixed economic ideas that rest in the past and are meant to be applied everywhere and always cannot stand the test of time and the ceaseless changing conditions. On the same basis, the Marxian and the Keynesian ideas went out of fashion. The growing doctrine that changed the intellectual climate from the 1970s onwards was the doctrine of globalism. This doctrine not only challenged the central ideas of Keynes and precipitated the decline of Keynesian economics but also under its pretext so much has been rejected and done. It is safe to say that globalization has been the topic of the last four decades. Possibly, more has been written on this topic than any other topic in social science disciplines in these past decades.

All happened, good and bad, claimed to be caused by globalization. Nobody knows what globalization is but everyone knows the good or its bad attributes, effects, and contributions. Globalization is an example of an endemic idea. The idea is infectious not because it is right or true but because it is in harmony with the mob mentality. It is in conformity with the habit of mob conduct that the more people jump on the bandwagon of the mantra because others doing the same the more will be chanting the same hymn. There is no consensus on the definition of globalization. Every trait ascribed is contentious. Here we refer only to the most central features that have been attributed to globalization. Generally speaking, globalization is defined as the "growing interconnectedness and interrelatedness of all aspects of society" (Jones 2006: 2). It is also defined as the end of national states. The differences that exist with different definitions of globalization are in the degree of emphasis that each definition puts on some aspects of either the causes, the effects, or the attributes of what is called the global village. Some put more emphasis on the interconnectivity of interactive forces, some on internationalization and integration of markets and national economies, some on the liberalization of international trade and free trade, some on cultural integration, some on the disappearance of time and geography as a result of the revolution in information technology and communication, and some on the pace of change. Each claim can be credited with some truth or with being suggested in good faith but the overall verdict is not affirmative and cannot be conclusively proven.

All in all, the idea of globalization is a self-serving delusion in this day and age. From the countless definitions offered, it is difficult to determine exactly what globalization is. One thing that is clear is that behind any action or idea there is an intention. The pretext of globalization has served certain political and economic beliefs and interests. The doctrine was fundamental to proponents of the unrestrained market system that was prevalent in the advanced Western world in the last decades of the twentieth century. The reality of marketing the idea was as simple and as stark as that. As the spectre of globalization became fashionable, the pandemic spread like a fire that engulfed the informed and the uninformed. Central to the myth of globalism is its deterministic power. That is, it is detached from humans. The supremacy of globalism is equated to something supernatural that has wrecked human power, ability, control, and reason. Humankind is doomed eternally to the command order and requirements of globalization. Globalization makes history and it is this supernatural force that determines all human conditions.

The reality is that there are no two nations or artificially demarcated countries that share exactly the same laws, economic development, political system, institutions, culture, technology, level and standard of education, level of equality of opportunity, regulations, natural resources, landscape, and the list is endless. So long as there are any remnants of colonialism, the question of national borders will, in the very least, remain unresolved for the nations that are undemocratically locked up in one or another form of colonial boundary. There is yet a significant segment of every continent, in particular nations of Asia and Africa, which are deprived of their actual borders. Colonial boundaries are immoral, illegal, and undemocratic. They are imposed by the force of the sword. Those insist on preserving such borders are the autocratic elite rulers of these colonial geopolitical structures. Under such colonial borders, people of colonized nations are deprived of their liberty, democracy, rule of law, and economic development.

The idea of globalism has served the multinational companies well. It endorsed monetarism and neoliberal economics and all undemocratic states and colonial geopolitical constructions. The belief, fundamental in the spectre of globalism, is that it has ended national borders. The hallmark of existing time, it is proclaimed, is the demise of the nation-states. In a globalized world, there is a universal realignment of the free movement of capital and labour to every corner of the globe. This assertion implies that there is an acceptable level of harmonization of rights, regulations, and responsibilities; institutions; working conditions; business environment; political, economic, educational, cultural, and moral objectives; infrastructures; taxation; among most of the countries. The fact is it is not the harmony that is prevailing in our time but the discord, which will always prevail so long as there is economic disorder.

Globalization is a self-serving myth. Like many myths, it serves certain social groups. In the real world that we currently live, the world population is about 7.7 billion. It is worryingly high and is increasing alarmingly. Around 50 per cent of the world population lives on less than $5.50 a day. About 780 million live below the international poverty line. By January 2018 only about half of the world population had access to global mobile internet. In all colonial geopolitical constructions, undemocratic countries, totalitarian states, Islamo-fascist states, and the states run by the autocratic oligarchy, access to the internet is limited to the ruling establishments, to certain ideas and information, and used for their propaganda purposes. The nations that are under dominations of such states either do not have access to the internet or if they do, access to the internet is limited to certain restricted information. By and large, the internet in colonial geopolitical boundaries is not used as a tool for progress, harmony, education, and development but as a tool of repression.

There are too many examples of the geopolitical constructions and the countries that fall under this category, namely China, Russia, North Korea, the Islamic states of Pakistan, Iran, and most of the Arab world.

The idea of globalism that lacks road, air, and sea connection in the major parts of the world is merely a conjecture. We can only find an adequate combination of the road, sea, and air connection in selected parts of the developed world. The rest of the world, depending on their economic development, lacks such connections. Global harmonization of the key factors such as weather, natural resources, access to sea, values, customs, history, culture, religion, scientific and technological invention, discovery and innovation, education, distribution of income, equal opportunity for different social and gender groups, national identification and expectations will never be fully achieved – no matter how far and fast the technology advances. The requirements of all nations or even different regions of the world cannot be reduced into a common identity, shared beliefs, problems, and quality of living. Different nations live in the different natural environment, have lived for hundreds and thousands of years forming different histories, languages, cultures, the system of existence, ways of perceiving life for themselves and others, and have undergone through many wars to safeguard and establish different political, economic, social, and legal norms and systems. It is only in totalitarian military systems that will compel such differences into a unified entity. The least common denominator in such matters will be dictated by the dominant nation.

Three main factors that are considered as the main pillars of globalism are political, economic, and technology. Political globalism requires a global political constitution. This, in turn, requires a global supranational state with its three distinct branches of the global executive, the legislative, and the judicial. Neither a global supranational government with its branches exists nor is desirable. A global government neither upholds liberty nor improves efficiency. The risk of global government is global totalitarianism. Like universal religions and universal ideologies, i.e., communism, a world outlook of this kind fossilizes the world in one kind of vision. In a mono-vision that inevitably ends in the might is right. At present, there is one example of regional political integration. The European Union is a unique case. It was formed in 1957 after six European nations signed the Treaty of Rome. The aim of the Union was to create a common market. The new members joined the Union in 1981, 1986, 1995, 2004, 2007, and 20013. The members of the Union reached 28, including the UK with a total population of about 500 million people. The majority of British electorate voted to leave the EU in June 2016. Officially, the UK left the EU in January 2020. The rationale behind the formation of the Union was not economic but political. All members of the Union have suffered from many wars and occupations throughout their histories. In the twentieth century, they experienced two world wars, fascism, and communism. The Union was formed to end the recurrence of the same catastrophic conflicts. It was believed that joining a common market to trade goods and services freely would reduce the risk of further wars. Over time economic and other objectives were added into the list of the Union. The Union has gradually been distancing itself from just being a common market and heading more to being a supranational state.

Formation of any economic and political union is in itself a negation of globalism. A common market frees trade for most of goods and services among the member countries and restricts trade with the rest of the world. Second, in the case of the European Union, contrary to the United Nations charter and to the Lisbon Treaty of the right of self-determination, the Union openly violated this democratic right. The Kurdistan region under the Iraq boundary held a democratic referendum for independence on 25 September 2017. The referendum was held in an open and democratic atmosphere and 93.25 per cent of Kurdish people cast their votes for independence. But the European Union sided with all undemocratic states in the region and opposed the Kurdish democratic votes and the right to be independent. Likewise, they opposed the Catalonia independence from Spain. Catalonia held their referendum on 1 October 2017. The Spanish government suppressed the Catalonian democratic and peaceful demand for independence. Many leaders of the Catalonian independence movement were arrested and imprisoned by the Spanish government. The EU supported the Spanish undemocratic policy and actions. Their treatment on the result of the British referendum has equally been equally dismal. The British public participated in a referendum held on 23 June 2016 to decide whether they would remain in the EU or leave. With the turnout of 72.2 per cent, 51.9 per cent voted to leave and 48.1 per cent voted to remain in the EU. The democratic mandate of majority vote came to nothing to the EU elites. In the global financial crisis of 2007, the EU bluntly overruled the sovereignty of the Greek nation and its democratic mandate.

Globalism is a hands-off approach. Quitting is not only limited to the economy but extended to many other areas, as in human rights, the right of self-determination, in law and culture, and so on. As if there is nothing we can do or can stand against globalism. Everything that should succumb to the market was the rallying cry of the advocates of globalism. The market is the remedy of everything. A free market is a fallacy. No market exists in a social vacuum. Markets are products of certain time, locations, historical processes, institutional frameworks, cultural backgrounds, technological, legal, and ethical constraints, and boundaries of nations. Globalism was also intended to repudiate the Keynesian economics.

Keynesian economics aided the trend to mathematize economics. The rationale behind this movement rests on the belief that the future can be predicted if the right mathematical approach is applied to collecting past data accurately, processing data correctly and putting them into appropriate mathematical models, and taking advantage of the advances in information technology in storing large data and processing them at the right time and place. Given all these stages undertaken correctly then we can forecast future economic trends, events, and outcomes and then accordingly adopt policies to direct the economy into desirable directions. In other words, the remedy to economic problems is the proper use of the right mathematics. That is, the correct use of correct mathematics would solve the economic problems in time. This worldview confuses one of the most pivotal underlying economic problems with one form of language of understanding. Communication by means of mathematical notations and models is not the cure but only a circumscribed method to describe, discuss, and explain the maladies and solutions to economic problems. Thus, the realm in which this approach finds the economy and society is in the realm of analytical truth. It projects the past into the future by the means of analytical truth. What became to be known as the "Phillips curve" is of this nature. A. W. Phillips (1914–75), a New Zealander, whose background was engineering, worked for the Royal Air Force as an engineer during the Second World War. The Japanese army captured him and kept him in a prison camp in Indonesia for three and a half years. After his release, he went to the London School of Economics where he completed a degree course in sociology and then turned to economics. It was at the London School of Economics that he published his most famous article in 1958. The article was published in *Economica* in which he looked at the statistical data of unemployment and money wage rates in Britain for the period of 1861–1957. From these data, he observed a relationship between the level of unemployment and the money wage rates. The Phillips curve stirred much interest among economists and policymakers for most of the second half of the twentieth century.

The growing interest in this relationship fitted very well with the prevailing economic orthodoxy of the time. Many papers were published to confirm the relationship. On the basis of this trade-off, any level of unemployment corresponds to some inverse level of inflation. So, going for a lower level of unemployment inescapably meant going for a higher rate of inflation. The promoters of the trade-off saw it as a natural law. However, a close and deeper study of the supposed relationship could reject its universality even at the time when the article was published just by looking at the Swedish economy. From 1950 to 1955, the inflation rate in Sweden was 5.4 per cent and the unemployment rate was 1.8 per cent. The unemployment rate stayed at 1.8 per cent while the inflation rate decreased from 5.4 per cent to 3.7 per cent during 1955–60. The inflation rate stayed the same 3.7 per cent in 1960–65 while the unemployment rate decreased from 1.8 per cent to 1.5 per cent in the same period (Bohlin 2014: 123).

As far as the world economy goes, the 1970s and 1980s were transitional decades. There was a drastic rise in the price of the main source of energy in the early 1970s. The price of crude oil skyrocketed within a decade. In 1970 the price of a barrel of crude oil was less than $2 per barrel. It increased to $3 in October 1973 (Santos 1991: 156). By January 1974, it increased to $10.50 per barrel. The rapid run-up in crude oil prices coincided with the start of the war between Egypt and Israel in 1973. The Organization of the Petroleum Exporting Countries (OPEC), dominated by the Arab world, imposed an embargo on oil exports to those countries that supported Israel and laid an embargo on the companies that did not follow their terms. As a result, the price of crude oil per barrel increased to $20 by 1978.

This was a decade (the 1970s) in which Britain descended into a prolonged and protracted economic stagnation and inflation. The country hit its rock bottom of its past imperial standing and was reduced to the "sick man of Europe." Its share of manufacturing goods in world trade fell from 25.4 per cent in 1950 to 9.1 per cent in 1973. The inflation rate escalated and reached 24.2 per cent and the unemployment rate shoots up to 1.7 million (Parker 2006: 9). These developments lined up a serious challenge against Keynesian economics. The ascending economic orthodoxy, monetary and Austrian economics, attributed the problems of the 1970s to Keynesian economics policies. The rising tide of self-regulating laissez-faire economics and the growing sway of non-interference economic consensus laid the groundwork for the accession of the Thatcher administration in Britain and the Reagan administration in the US in the 1980s to power. Their governments embraced the monetarists' economic prescriptions that were first applied in Chile under the military regime of Pinochet.

In 1970, Chile's Socialist Party under the leadership of Salvador Allende (1908–73) was elected. Allende was a medical doctor who began his political activities in the 1930s and was among the first founders of the Chilean Socialist Party. The democratically elected Allende government was in its third-year presidency on 11 September 1973 that a US-backed coup overthrew his government. Allende was killed during the coup. General Augusto Pinochet (1915–2006) seized the power and imposed his reign of terror until he relinquished his presidency in 1990. Pinochet was a mass murderer. The bodies of Chilean supporters of Allende, other human rights, and political activists are still being discovered at the present time. It is estimated that during the 17 years of his military rule, about 3,186 people were killed and disappeared (Bassiouni 2011: 698).

Milton Friedman (1912–2006), the leading proponent of monetarism, was an economic advisor of American Presidents, President Richard Nixon and President Ronald W. Reagan. His ideas also inspired Mrs Thatcher, the British Prime Minister's social and economic policies. Friedman was a successor of Chicago School. He embarked on his opposition to Keynesian economics during the early days of the triumph of Keynesianism. Friedman opposed the fixed exchange rate system, regulation of markets, income policies, minimum wage and rent controls, and fiscal policy. He advocated a balanced budget and limited operation of monetary policy and put the blame for the stagflation in the 1970s to Keynesian policies. From the 1960s onwards, as the core of his monetary policy, he advocated his "k-percent rule." He recommended a policy of a constant rate of growth in the money supply (Rivot 2016: 228–30). By adopting this rule, he maintained, the prices can be stabilized and inflation can be kept at a desirable level. This rule required the stock of money, in Friedman's parlance, to be kept in the range of 2 to 4 or 5 per cent per annum. In 1975 Friedman met General Pinochet in Chile. In his return, Friedman on 21 April 1975 wrote a letter to Pinochet advising him to administer a "shock approach" to Chilean economy to control inflation in Chile. He wrote, "if this shock approach were adopted, I believe that it should be announced publicly in great detail, to take effect at a very close date" (Friedman Letter to Pinochet 21 April 1975). These shock treatments that Friedman recommended to the military dictator were privatization of nationalized industries; elimination of income policies; price and wage control; deregulation of markets and trade, particularly deregulation of financial markets and foreign trade; elimination of welfare state; and a massive reduction in public expenditures. These shocks were designed, planned, and executed by Chilean economists who were graduated from Chicago School during the 1950s and 1960s.

In the US, two short spikes in inflation rate were in 1974 and 1979. To have a better sense of these inflationary distresses, let us take the last year of the 1960s decade as the basis for comparison. The US average unemployment rate this year was 3.5 per cent. That corresponded with a 6.2 per cent of inflation rate and a GDP growth rate of 3.1 per cent. By 1974 the GDP decreased to −05 per cent and the inflation and unemployment rates increased to 12.3 per cent and 7.2 per cent respectively. In 1979, the inflation rate crept to 13.3 per cent, the GDP fell to 3.2 per cent, and unemployment moved up to 6.0 per cent. The simultaneous rise in inflation and unemployment rates clearly discarded the Phillips' curve orthodoxy. The "stagflation" became in vogue. Many prevailing economic ideas were revisited and discarded. One was the Bretton Woods agreement. In July 1944, 44 countries were gathered in Bretton Woods, New Hampshire in America. Keynes was the main source of inspiration behind the agreement. The allied representatives met to reform the international monetary system and introduce a monetary order to boost international trade and restore the global monetary and economic stability. The Bretton Woods agreement introduced an international monetary system whereby the US government agreed to remain on gold exchange standard, agreed to fix the dollar to gold, and exchange $35 for an ounce of gold. It was also agreed that other currencies should fix the value of their currencies to the dollar but could float within a permissible ceiling and floor of 20 per cent above or below dollar parity. On this basis, the British pound was set at US$4.80 per one British pound.

Many factors contributed to the collapse of Bretton Woods's exchange rate system. The first sign of its demise appeared on 15 August 1971. On this day the US authorities withdrew from their unilateral commitment to buy and sell gold at $35 an ounce. This act, in turn, ended the fixed price for gold. The breakdown of the Bretton Woods system was completed on 19 March 1973 when the United States and other advanced developed nations left the system. The international monetary system that replaced the fixed exchange rate regime was not by design nor a random accident. Its advent was contingent on the new global economic environment. It was a departure from Keynesian orthodoxy. Most economic ideas, right or wrong, are passing fancy. The latest fad in economics in the 1970s was the monetarist school of thought. The free-market economics was in vogue. It was this economic trend that was gaining upper hand over other competing schools. Like any form of fashion, the tantrum was copied and disseminated by means of mimicry and most economists within the mainstream frontier changed their faith and taste and became adherents to the heat of the moment. A fixed exchange rate system was discarded because of the faith in the unregulated market economy. In the same way, as in any other market, it was argued, the value of each currency should be left to the market to be determined.

One of the key factors to the demise of the Bretton Wood system and the rise of neoliberal economics was the occurrence of stagflation that many industrialized economies experienced in the 1970s. From 1950 to 1973 the world trade had increased by 7.2 per cent (Simai 1994: 222). United States' share of world trade in 1950 was 15.7 per cent. Its relative share of world trade decreased to 13.7 per cent in 1975 and it kept decreasing ever since. Japan's relative share of world trade, for example, in 1950 was 1.5 per cent. It increased to 7.3 per cent in 1975. By 1970s the relative share of the world trade of other emerging countries was rising with great speed. In 1975 the EEC relative share of world trade rose to 20 per cent (Aggarwal 1985: 31).

In the post-Second World War, the US engaged itself in virtually all right-wing military coups and the wars. On average, the annual US defence budget during the cold war was about 7 per cent of its GDP (NIC 2012: 102). If we set aside the US expenses in the Korean War, the monetary cost of the Vietnam War alone, according to Melvin Laird, is estimated to be in the range of US$236 billion (Duong 2008: 223). The US involvement in the Vietnam War lasted about two decades, from the mid-1950s to mid-1975s. The legacy of the Vietnam War was not just limited to its economic costs. The Americans lost 58,000 of the army personnel and over 300,000 of them were wounded. The economic costs to Vietnamese are difficult to estimate. The death tolls for the Viet Cong are estimated to be about 1.1 million, the number of Viet Cong wounded to be 600,000, and the number of people who were missing during the fighting is estimated in the rage of 330,000. The civilian tolls are estimated at about one million (Wiest 2009: 83). Wars cause the national debt to increase. The US national debt was $50 billion at the beginning of Second World War. By the end of the war, the federal debt increased to $250 billion. It only increased by 50 billion to 300 billion in 1962. As the Vietnam War heightened, the US national debt increased drastically to $432 billion by 1972. It reached to $914 billion by 1980. Despite the new right getting into power in the 1980s and their hostility to deficit spending, the US national debt between 1980 and 1985 increased to $1,800 billion and it went up to $2,614 billion by 1988.

The Eurodollar market was developed in the course of the Vietnam War. As European nations came out of the Second World War, the economy of many of them was totally devastated. The Americans feared that the war-torn people of these nations living in abject poverty and despondency may seek salvation in communism. George C. Marshall (1880–1959), who was the US

Army Chief of staff during the war and had experienced the scale of destruction of the war, became the US secretary of the state in 1947. In his address on 5 June 1947 at Harvard University, he suggested that the US government should assist Europe financially to recover from the war. The US Congress approved the plan and President Henry S. Truman (1884–1972) signed the financial aid plan to Europe on 3 April 1948. As a result, the US government donated $12 billion to 17 western and southern countries of Europe, including Turkey, within a period of five years (Kumar 2012: 142).

Another contributory factor was the Treaty of Rome. The treaty was signed on 25 March 1957, which created the European Economic Community (EEC). Over time more countries joined the community. The EEC has evolved into the present-day European Union. The Community created a regional customs union. Because the EEC diverted trade away from the US in the late 1950s, the US multinational companies increased their foreign direct investment in Europe. That has augmented the number of dollars invested in the EEC countries.

One of the inadvertent consequences of the formation of the eastern communist bloc was the growth of the Eurodollar market. Eurodollars were US dollars that were deposited outside the judicial control of the US government. By the end of the Second World War, the United States was the undisputed world economic and military power. It was the US that dictated the terms of the Bretton Woods exchange rate system that raised dollar to the world supreme vehicle currency. After the war, pound along with weakening economic and political position of Britain kept depreciating. From the time of the Bretton agreement to 1949, the pound sterling was devalued by 30 per cent (Windecker Jr 1993: 361). The dollar became the international currency. For their major exports, the communist bloc was paid in dollars.

The Soviet Bloc led by Russia initially deposited the dollars earned from their exports in the United States. As the tension between two blocs increased, to evade the freezing of their dollar deposits, the eastern communist regimes began to transfer their deposit to the Soviet-owned banks in London and Paris. In addition to this, the US authorities introduced a number of regulations in the 1960s and 1970s that restricted the scope of the US capital markets. Besides, in the 1960s, the US authorities were alarmed with their growing balance of payment deficits. To remedy the situation, they introduced three laws to control the flow of capital abroad. In 1964, they introduced the Interest Equalization Tax. This tax intended to discourage foreigners to borrow in the US capital and money markets. The second law was the Foreign Credit Restraint Programme that was introduced in 1965. The aim of this law was to control the American lending institutions lending money to foreign borrowers. The 1968 law, the Foreign Investment Programme, attempted to control the domestic corporations using their dollars at home to fund investment abroad. On top of all these restrictions, the Regulation Q fixed the highest rates on the domestic deposits. All these restrictions hard-pressed the domestic credit markets, resulting in a rise in the domestic interest rates in 1968–69. The domestic investors turned to the Eurodollar market as the return to their deposits in this market was relatively higher.

The other impetus that has boosted the Eurodollar credit markets in the 1970s was the sharp increase in OPEC oil revenues and the rise in the US current account imbalances. The revenues of the OPEC countries increased by about 15 times from 1970 to 1975. It increased from $7.9 billion to $115.8 billion (Warnok 2005: 10). The members of the OPEC countries were underdeveloped, had a relatively small population and market, poor infrastructure and financial institutions, and were very repressive. The revenues of such magnitude could not be absorbed within their small and undeveloped markets. A significant amount of this revenue, therefore, found its way either officially or unofficially in the Eurodollar credit markets. Compared to the US domestic dollar, the Eurodollar was safer and offered higher yields. As a result of this, the syndicated Eurodollar credits were formed as the mediators between the countries with a balance of payments surplus and the countries with a balance of payments deficit. The sharp rise in oil prices also affected the balance of payments of the industrialized economies. The US current account deficit reached $100 billion in 1984 and $150 billion in 1987 (Oatley 2016: 226).

As oil prices plummeted into double digits in a matter of a few months, many oil-dependent countries, particularly among the less developed countries, faced a severe balance of payment difficulties. The sharp rise in oil prices increased the cost of production for most of the output produced domestically or imported into these countries. In tandem with high inflation, most of these countries submerged in political turmoil and military dictatorship. The three regions most affected were Latin America, East Asia, and Eastern Europe. The Eurodollar credit markets and banks recirculated the surplus funds of the OPEC countries to these regions and some other third world countries. By the end of the 1970s, the Latin American borrowings were about $29 billion. By the end of 1978, it had increased to $159 billion. About 80 per cent of this debt was sovereign debt. The largest portion of this debt, about $89, went to Mexico and Brazil. With regard to the Eastern European countries, the gross debt at 1987 prices for these countries increased from $8.4 billion in 1970 to $77.1 billion in 1979. The same amount of debt has been estimated for the East Asian and Pacific countries too (Zloch-Christy 1987: 33). By mid-1986, the LDCs and the Eastern European countries owed the banks an estimated amount of $424 billion (Economist: 1987: vol. 302). Above all else, in 1970 the interest payment on LDC debt was about 0.5 per cent of their GNP. It increased to 2.8 per cent by 1984 (Hogendorn 1996: 194). With this sharp rise in interest rates, the highly indebted countries began to default on their interest payments on their debts.

By the end of 1983, the external debts of LDCs that imported oil approached US$900 billion, amounting to one-third of the GNP of non-oil-producing, less developed countries. The annual interest payments of the LDCs came to $150 billion, which was about 25 per cent of hard currency from their exports (Goldstein 1985: 119). These countries were drowned in foreign debts and their debts eventually went up to US$1.28 trillion (Rahnama-Moghdam 1995: 11). Mexico defaulted on its debt repayment obligations in August 1982. The burden of sovereign debts forced many LDCs to reschedule their debt repayment obligations. Most of the indebted LDCs multilaterally renegotiated and rescheduled their debts by 1985.

The Eurodollar credit market is an unregulated market. This characteristic of the market aided its rapid expansion. It has created a sanctuary for illegal and criminal transactions and a mighty and immeasurable mobile global capital. The size and the lightning speed, the rapid inflow and outflow of capital, can lead to speedy economic expansion but its rapid outflow can also be very destructive. In the main, it undermines the domestic macroeconomic policies and democratic control and accountability. Lack of regulation and control has acted as a catalytic agent in the growth of international money markets. Money market financial instruments such as repurchase agreements (Repos), international interbank lending, bankers' acceptance, and certificate of deposit (CD) emerged in parallel to the domestic money market instruments. The total euro currency (gross) in 1964 was estimated to be 14.9 billion. Since then, it grew by about 17 times to US$248 billion in 1974. It went to 7,1161.8 billion in 1994, to 19,198.6 billion in 2004, and to 28,495.2 billion in 2014 (Pilbeam 2018: 103).

The Eurodollar market has been a safe harbour for global money laundering. Lack of transparency and accountability in the market have enabled international criminals, corrupt officials, and terrorist organizations to conceal the illegal sources of their funds through money laundering. The actual sources of funds can be disguised when the funds are transferred into legal financial institutions and the Eurodollar credit market has acted as one of the foremost intermediaries in laundering such funds and converting illegally obtained money into something that appears legal. The Bank of Credit and Commerce International (BCCI) was one of these mediators. It was a hideaway for professional fraudsters, arms merchants, international criminals, the world dictators, Islamic groups and the states, drug traffickers, and many Arab Sheikhs. The CIA director, Robert Gates, referred to the defunct BCCI bank as the "Bank of Crooks and Criminal International" (Hiatt 2007: 92).

Agha Hassan Abedi (1922–95), a Pakistani banker, founded the BCCI in 1972. The BCCI used the Eurodollar credit market to cover its illicit activities and clandestine operations. The BCCI was a "bank within a bank." The bank used the Eurodollar market for laundering money from drug trafficking, from arms sales and for bribing government officials (Windecker 1993). During the Iran and Iraq war in the 1980s, the BCCI was the medium through which the Islamic regime paid for receiving the anti-tank missiles from the United States. The Islamic regime came to power on 11 February 1979. In the same year, on 4 November 1979, the followers of the regime seized the US embassy in Tehran. After storming the embassy, they held 66 American hostages. The regime from its early days began to carry out organizing proxy Shia fundamentalist groups and the policy of hostage-taking at home and abroad. One of these proxy groups is Lebanon's Hezbollah. In the 1980s, the BCCI mediated between different groups in the business of arms for a hostage – trading the US anti-tank missiles for the release of American hostages held by the Hezbollah in Lebanon. The money was transacted through the BCCI bank. The BCCI also facilitated multi-million dollar arms transactions for Arab terrorist groups and for Palestinian groups such as the Abu Nidal group (Windecker 1988: 360).

The BCCI was the main refuge for the funds raised by the sale of narcotics worldwide. It was the biggest drug money laundering vehicle. One of its customers was General Manuel Noriega (1934–2017), the former military dictator of Panama. After the collapse of the BCCI, it was discovered that Agha Hasan Abedi, who was in charge of the bank until 1990, and his assistant Swaleh Naqvi, whom Abedi appointed as the director of the bank in a long successive and well-calculated policy, bribed state officials, ministers, central bankers, and important officials of regional and international organizations to attract more deposits into the bank and to cover up their illegal activities. The BCCI network was wide-ranging and far-reaching. It included the officials of the African Development Bank, the officials of the central banks of Peru, Nigeria, Senegal, and the Ivory Coast export and import officials (Windecker 1988: 360). By 1980, the bank operated in 73 countries. It had 40 branches and employed 14,000 staff. The end of the bank came in July 1991. The British officials seized about $20 billion bank's assets. The actual losses of 800,000 of the banks' depositors are unknown. In one assessment, it is estimated at about $15 billion. As the bank collapsed, its founder returned to Pakistan where he was protected until his death.

The 1970s and 1980s big bang revolutions in the United States and the United Kingdom facilitated the expansion of the international capital market. In domestic markets, financial markets are among the most regulated markets and will always remain among the most regulated markets. Trust lies at the heart of these markets. No regulation can replace trust in credit markets. Trust is the opposite of knowing what one exactly does. It is wrapped in the world of make-believe. Regulations are only partial compensation for the fiduciary element for the credit held in pledge. There is a strong incentive to breach trust in the credit markets. First, the element of not knowing can conceal the activities of financial intermediaries and second the rewards can be very high in misappropriation and breach of fiduciary duty. Liberalization of financial markets stretched the entry for profiteering and shady deals. The first Big Bang financial deregulation was in 1975 in the United States. It began on 1 May 1975, when the New York Stock Exchange implemented a set of reforms to liberalize and increase the competitiveness of the exchange. Among many notable reforms was the abolition of fixed commissions' rates on the traded securities. Similar reforms were also introduced – about a decade later, in 1986, through Big Bang deregulation – to the London Stock Market and more than a decade later, in 1997–99, Japanese Big Bang financial liberalization took place. These reforms aimed at structural changes in structures, organization, operations, and functions of the market. Following the New Stock Exchange deregulations, the London Stock Exchange Big Bang, on 27 October 1986, eliminated fixed brokerage commissions, altered the structure and ownership of the trading firms, allowed a greater number of firms and economic agents to trade, got rid of floor trading, and introduced a screen-based system of trading. The Japanese Big Bang deregulation was implemented over two years from 1997 to 1999. In the same way as in London and in New York, the Japanese Big Bang abolished the fixed commissions on securities transactions and opened the market to more market participants. Other leading Stock Exchanges, one after another, implemented similar reforms in the years ahead.

The implications of the Big Bang deregulations were deep and wide. These reforms were not confined to the same market or to the domestic market. The effects of these changes were wide and global. As was noted earlier, the Eurodollar markets are outside the boundary of control and regulation of any domestic market. Thus, the Eurodollar markets took advantage of the liberalization of financial markets. In addition, the commercial application of information and telecommunication widened the scope, scale, and speed of transactions in these markets. The structural reforms, liberalization, and application of information technology enhanced the competitiveness of these markets. The increase in the number of participants and the abolition of fixed commissions on securities decreased costs of commissions and the bid-ask spread. As a result of this, financial markets became the most profitable markets compared to other markets, i.e., the goods markets. The income of top earners in these markets escalated sky-high. Partly because in a more liberalized market high-income groups have relative comparative advantages. Besides their higher incomes, they are better known in the market, political establishment, and media and have access to a larger number of expertise and connections. There was an increasing gulf between the incomes of employees and the management of firms in financial markets. The management created all sorts of remuneration schemes to benefit from. The liberalization allowed firms, non-specialized firms, or individuals to assume multiple functions. The same firm could represent a client and their counterparty in a deal. The division of functions between different types of bank started to disappear. A commercial bank assumed the functions of investment and vice versa. Physicists and mathematicians went for the posts in financial markets and designed financial products that neither had they known their economic and social implications nor the manager and customers could understand the complexities of these services and financial products.

To recap, the 1970s was a decade of stagflation, the collapse of the Bretton Wood fixed exchange rate system, the financial big bang, and the triumph of monetarism. This was a game-changing decade. It was a turning point for adjusting incomes, prices, and returns on real and financial assets to the cost of inflation. Likewise, it was a watershed decade for the growth of securitization of risk instruments. Besides indexing, from the 1970s onwards in order to counter the risks of change in prices and incomes, there was an extraordinary rise in derivatives markets and products. Neither the idea of derivative nor the practice of derivative transactions was new. Aristotle (384–322 BC) in his book *The Politics*, writing about Thales of Miletus, had captured the essence of the idea of trading in derivatives.

As the forerunners of these markets, we have the Amsterdam Bourse, which was established in 1611. In its financial derivatives, commodities, equities, and government bonds were traded. Joseph Penso de la Vega, in his book *Confusion de Confusiones* (1688), described such traded derivatives as "time bargains." The shares of the Dutch East and West India companies (1602–1621) with standard printed futures and options contracts and a set of rules were traded on the Amsterdam Bourse. Financial derivatives were also traded in London, at the Osaka Rice Exchange in Okinawa, Japan in the eighteenth century, and in the Chicago futures wheat market in the nineteenth century. In modern times, the United States led the way. Chicago Mercantile Exchange (CME) began trading in derivatives in the early 1970s followed by the Philadelphia Stock Exchange and London International Financial Futures Exchange (LIFFE) in 1982. The rest of the other exchanges in different countries followed thereafter.

The term "derivative" is used, indicating that the future prices of both real and financial products are derived from the current prices of commodities, currencies, interest rates, equities, bonds, and so on. The main types of derivative products are classified as forwarding contracts, swaps, financial futures, and traded options. Forward contracts are arrangements between economic agents who borrow or lend an agreed sum of money at agreed rates for some time in the future for the transactions to take place. Swaps are agreements between different counterparties to exchange two different forms of payment obligations. The two main types of the swap are an interest rate swap and a currency swap. The financial futures and options, in reality, occupy most of the derivatives markets. Financial futures are agreements between different counterparties to exchange a specified number of commodities, bonds, equities, currencies, and bills at a fixed date at a predetermined price. A futures contract indicates the amount of the security, the exchange on which the contract is traded, and the delivery date. Unlike the futures contracts, the options contracts give the holders the right but not the obligation to buy or sell an underlying asset at a predetermined price. The two basic types of options are the call option, the right to buy a financial product later, and the put option, the right to sell a financial product later at the predetermined price. For the extra right attached to traded options, the counterparties in trade pay a premium called margin when options are bought. The thing that enchanted investors in this market is the asymmetrical profit/loss profile of the options. That is, one could combine the downside protection with unlimited upside potential of traded options and avoid the risk of loss of changes in prices and rates of return and also take advantage of high profit.

However, one cannot lose sight of the derivatives' paradox. To restate, the future prices of assets are never certain. That explains the types of economic agents that will participate in these markets. In reality, all economic agents participating in these markets are speculators. Taking part either as speculators or as hedgers is the belief that each side is convinced to know the direction of price or interest movements and for that, they gamble and back up their judgement with their money. The received wisdom that speculators use the derivatives markets to take risks and the hedgers to avoid risks is only one side of the truth. The establishment of exchanges reveals the speculative nature of both sides. The exchanges confirm and guarantee the derivative contracts. After this is done, an exchange assumes the defaulting parties' obligations. To limit its exposure, an exchange requires that each counterparty make an initial deposit with the exchange, i.e., the margin. In case a contract involves a party making a loss greater than the initial margin, further deposits, i.e., variation margin, are required on a daily basis from the losing party. The variation margin mirrors the potential loss associated with the contract. The marking to market is calculated at the end of each day on the basis of the settlement price to limit the exposure of the exchange.

The vested interest was on the side of the growth of the derivatives markets and products. It overstated the hedging element of derivative instruments and underrated the speculative part. Very few were concerned about the latter. One among these few dissident voices was the *Economist*, which on 14 May 1994 warned that "there are fears that derivatives fuel financial-market uncertainty by multiplying the leverage, or debt-based buying power, of hedge funds and other speculators-an uncertainty that could if the things went wrong, threaten the whole of the world financial system."

## Conclusion

Since the rise of commercial and industrial economies from the seventeenth century, there has been a steady rise in the accumulation of excesses in trade. This trend has moved side by side with the extreme division of employment, the culture of ultra-individualism, and dependency – giving favour to money as a mark of glory. By belittling knowledge and humanity, the safeguards against unexpected are curtailed. Once addicted to money and not relying on dependable knowledge and mortality, the result will be captivity to our herd temperament.

In the Latin American sovereign debt crisis of 1982, many states in this region saw no limit to the cheap loans of the Eurodollar international capital market. In the absence of any democratic openness and accountability, many states in this region kept borrowing as if it had no end. The heads of this binge borrowing were Mexico, Brazil, and Argentina. Within seven years, Latin American sovereign debt quadrupled. The world economy in the late 1970s was not what it was a few years earlier. The world recession compounded with high inflation, political instability, and depreciation of currencies that these countries were experiencing pushed the interest rates on bond payments for these countries. The interest rate got to the point that these countries could not honour their bills. Mexico was the first Latin American country that unilaterally announced that it was no longer able to service its foreign debt. The Mexican Finance Minister Jesus Silva-Herzog in August 1982 reported that his country had severe difficulty with its cash flow. Thus, Mexico was the first Latin American country that defaulted on its sovereign debt and this aggravated the situation and led other Latin American countries in a similar situation to default on servicing their foreign debts. At the time of announcing their inability to pay off their debt, Mexico's foreign debt was about $80 billion (Ghtak 2003: 378). By the end of 1982, Mexico was experiencing zero economic growth – left with virtually no foreign exchange reserves, $6 billion current account deficit, 17 per cent of GDP public sector deficit, 100 per cent inflation rate, clogged domestic financial markets, no access to new foreign loans, a sharply depreciated Peso, and a climate of distrust and political instability (Heredia 1990: 327). Other Latin American countries that were no longer able to service their heavy foreign debts also defaulted on their sovereign debts as Mexico.

The political trend in the 1980s came to the aid of the Eurodollar market. The market originated as an unregulated market. No authority, domestic or international, had close control over it. The political trend in the 1980s encouraged this development further. This made the management of the domestic economy harder and the implementation of macroeconomic policies considerably less effective, resulting in greater economic uncertainty and instability. Losing control over domestic currency created a promising background for criminals, arms and drug trades, and the reinvention of the junk bond market. The individual who reinvented the junk bond market in the 1980s was Michael Milken. Investment-grade bonds are those that are backed by the assets and the cash flow of the company. The junk bonds are low-grade and high-yield bonds that pay high interest rates. These bonds are issued by financially insecure companies that are not backed by the assets and cash flow of the company. In 1981 about $1.6 billion junk bonds were issued. This increased to $16 billion in 1984 and to about $33 billion in 1986. The market collapsed in 1989 with a total default of about $20 billion. In the midst of the Latin American sovereign debt crisis and the excitement of junk bond frenzy, global stock markets crashed. On Monday 19 October 1987, the Dow Jones Industrial Average fell by 508 points. In a single day, the market lost about 23 per cent of its total value. The FTSE 100, within two days of the crash, plummeted by 501 points (Roberts 2008: 53).

The rapid progress in information technology and its application in commerce, most specifically the invention of the World Wide Web and its extraordinary spread in its application worldwide, compounded with unrestricted mobility of Eurodollar currency spread like a pandemic in the 1980s and 1990s. From 1990 to 1995, the economic growth rate of East Asia, the Pacific Rim, in particular, Thailand, was 9 per cent, for Indonesia 8 per cent, for South Korea 7.8 per cent, and for Malaysia 8.9 per cent. The net private capital inflow to Asia in 1990 was $19.6 billion; in 1991 it was $34.1 billion; and for 1993, 1994, 1995, and 1996, $57.7, $66.4, $95.1, and $100.5 billion respectively. This decreased to $3.2 billion in 1997 and to minus $55.1 billion in 1998. This drastic and instantaneous outflow of capital was made possible due to the internet communication global network and the runaway, unbridled, and lawless Eurodollar markets. The Thailand currency, Thai, collapsed in July 1997. Quickly the exchange rate crisis in Thailand spread to other Asian countries and beyond. In the same year, the value of Thai depreciated by 44 per cent, the Indonesian Rupiah by 52 per cent, the South Korean Won by 43 per cent, the Malaysian Ringgit by 33 per cent, and the Philippine peso by 29 per cent (IMF Oct 1998). The flight of capital during the 1997–98 Asian crisis is estimated to be over $100 billion. The currency crisis led these economies into a deep recession with the economic hardship reminiscent of the 1929 Great Depression. The economic hardship and the depth of the crisis were aggravated by the plague of the domination of autocratic states, the scourge of despotism, lack of accountability and democratic transparency, rule of democratic law, domination of ill-reputed family, political and military businesses than the creditable meritocratic economy. In addition, the weaknesses of financial institutions, instruments, and legal framework and over-abuse of moral hazard plunged the real estate, the stock market, other asset prices, and the overall economic activities.

The Asian financial turmoil quickly spread to Russia and Brazil. In November 1997, the Central Bank of Russia defended the Russian rubble losing about $6 billion of its foreign exchange reserves. On 23 March 1998, Russian President Boris N. Yeltsin (1931–2007), not out of the ordinary of his erratic character, dismissed his entire government. The cause was the dire economic situation that Russia was in. The political instability did not help the situation. By 18 May 1998 the Russian government bond yields rose to 47 per cent. The annual yields for the year 1998 went by more than 200 per cent. Subsequently, the Russian currency stock and bond markets collapsed on 13 August 1998. On 17 August, Russia lost its battle against the external capital markets. It devalued its currency and left its value to be determined by market forces and defaulted on payment of its domestic and foreign debts. In the course of January to August 1998, the Russian stock market lost about 75 per cent of its value. By the end of 1998, the real GDP fell by 4.9 per cent and by the end of 1999, the rubble was depreciated against the US dollar by 70 per cent (Chiodo and Owyang 2002: 12–14 and Letiche 2007: 4). From the mid-1970s, Brazil suffered from chronic inflation. The currency crisis then spread to Brazil. There are five periods of inflationary spiral in Brazil from 1970 to 1994. During the first period (1970–74) the average inflation rate was 20.9 per cent, in the second period (1975–79) the average inflation rate per year increased to 46.5 per cent, in the third period (1980–84) to 148 per cent, in the fourth period (1985–89) to 707.4 per cent, and in the last period (1994) to 6,100 per cent (Tullio and Ronci 1996: 635). The Brazilian economy during the 1980s stagnated. The real per capita income for the years 1980–90 was close to zero. The GDP growth in 1990 was minus 3.10 per cent. Brazilian government introduced a new currency, the real, to end the decades of economic stagnation and hyperinflation in Brazil. The real was introduced in July 1994. The new currency (the real) was pegged to the US dollar, one real to one dollar, which was equal to 2,750 Cruzeiro Reais, the old currency. The Brazilian Central Bank defended the value of the real to the US dollar during 1994–99.

The Brazil GDP grew by 5.33 per cent in 1994, 4.42 per cent in 1995 but it decreased to 2.21 per cent in 1996 and then increased by 3.39 per cent in 1997. In 1997, a year before Brazil's currency crisis, foreign direct investment increased by 140 per cent compared to the year before. By the end of 1998, the real went under considerable speculative pressure. In December 1998, the real/dollar exchange rate was 1 dollar to 21 real. By February 1999 it decreased to 1 dollar to 90 real. For the rest of the year 1999, the real appreciated in value and remained 1 dollar to 84 real. In the course of the two years of the currency crisis, Brazil's GDP decreased to 0.34 per cent in 1998 and to 0.47 per cent in 1999. Then it recovered in the year 2000.

# 3 Crypto-economy and trade cycle

## Introduction

No major technological invention is the work of one person. In this sense, there is not any unique and independent technological breakthrough. All inventions that have revolutionized human societies are the work of many generations of human curiosity and knowledge. The technological inventions that resulted in the Industrial Revolution were of this nature. The most profound technological invention of the late twentieth century in terms of its potential, scope, scale, and speed of application and transformation of human societies and economy is the World Wide Web (WWW). In its short history, it has cut short space and time and connected the world. The web compressed the time and space into an instant click. A click of little importance on its own, in turn, has transformed the economy and the way we live. The invention and application of the web have opened a horizon with unlimited functionality. One of the earliest known accounts of the web is by J. C. R. Licklider (1915–90). In August 1962, in his memos, while he was at the Massachusetts Institute of Technology (MIT), he described an image of a global technological network akin to the internet. In his memos, he used the phrase "Galactic Network" to describe his vision of a global network of computers that one could transfer and retrieve information instantly. This vision came to fruition for the first time on 3 October 1969. The two computers separated by 350 miles, one at the University of California and the other at Stanford Research Institute in the United States, transmitted the first word. The word was "login" (Beranek 2000: 55).

For the first time in October 1972, Robert Kahn at the International Computer Communication Conference introduced the new system of internet networking to the public. In March of the same year, Ray Tomlinson (1941–2016) wrote and sent the first email. The internet was well established in the most advanced economies by the mid-1980s. Internet was broadly used in particular among the communities of researchers and academics. The system, however, disconnected from different clusters of computers and different mail systems. The major breakthrough came in 1989 with the invention of the World Wide Web (WWW). The British computer scientist, Tim

DOI: 10.4324/9781003346357-4

Berners-Lee, invented the web. Without any doubt, this is one of the greatest human inventions of all time. The network connected the world instantly. It opened a universal university and library that put in the disposal of every individual who has access to the network. The WWW created a global market and economy. Its extraordinary growth and application in a very short time have been for many factors but among the most important have been its worldwide reach, its unlimited functionality, and growth, and most of all, it was due to the altruistic vision of its inventor. The invention is not privately owned. It is not patented. It was Berners-Lee vision that it should be used as a global public good.

The focus of this chapter is on the crypto-economy. It is about the ebbs and flows of the emerging electronic economy. Most specifically, it is about the rise of e-credit and the wax and wane of the earliest stages of the global e-credit markets. The internet economy is a new dawn, a stage of economic development. A new chapter in human history with new generations experiencing a new life in a new world. The changing economic and technological conditions, however, require new ideas, new justifications, new institutions, new legal frameworks, and a new world order. All these changes would take place to lend legitimacy for being the first to capitalize on the fortune of doing things in the ways that have never been done before.

This chapter is divided into five sections. The first section presents a brief review of the major economic, political, and technological events that took place in the last three decades of the twentieth century. It surveys the main events that transpired and marked the beginning of the crypto-economy. The second section, "The new right and the old left," will delve into the battle between the left and the right in economic, political, and philosophical ideas that cast its dark shadow over most parts of the twentieth century. This section provides a synopsis of the extreme forms of these ideological positions. Both right and left extremism are interlocked in totalitarianism. The battle of Fascism on the side of the extreme right and communism on the side of the extreme left was over the world hegemony. The reign of the Nazi Empire was destroyed in the mid-1940s and the Soviet Empire collapsed at the end of the 1980s. The third section will discuss the causes of the 2007–2008 global credit crunch. This crisis is placed in the category of the first crypto-economic financial crisis. The fourth and fifth sections will address the main innovations in financial products, markets, and institutions that cultivated and brought forth the global credit crunch.

## The last decades of the last millennium

By all accounts, the twentieth century was a very eventful century. It was a century of revolution, world wars, liberation, the welfare state, atomic bombs, and the first human landing on the moon. The subject of our inquiry in this section is the most important events of the last three decades of the century. The most monumental event of these decades, as we have pointed out in the introduction, was the invention and application of the internet. A wonder that became the gold rush of the 1990s. Like any epic invention, the internet marvel spread quickly. The online businesses mushroomed and the well-to-do, the knowledgeable, the daring, and the deluded all rushed to seize the circumstance and make the most of this potential good fortune. Worldwide, there were 15,000 World Wide Web sites in 1994. Two years later, by mid-1996, the number of sites increased to 250,000 (Ho 1997). It was among these sites that the pioneers of e-commerce have emerged. By mid-2019 over 4.5 billion people use the WWW worldwide. The dot.com rush in the 1990s was one of those excesses that are usually experienced after any great invention or discovery. In the United States in the course of three years, 1997–2000, the technology stocks increased over fivefold. By February 2000, the internet sector comprised 6 per cent of the US market capitalization of public companies and 20 per cent of publicly traded shares. The returns on the internet sector's shares increased by 1,000 per cent from 1998 to February 2000 (Ofek and Richardson 2003: 1113). The speedy surge in the dot.com bubble soon imploded. As a result, most of the dot.com companies were trapped in the overvaluation of their shares, which could not be sustained, and went out of business. The total loss of the dot.com stock market bubble burst is estimated to be at about US$4 trillion (Ghosh 2006: 15). The collapse of the dot.com market was short-lived. The e-commerce sector ever since has been the fastest growing global sector, in terms of both B2C and B2B divisions. Amazon and eBay were among the pioneering dot.com companies that outlived the storm and subsequently led the global e-commerce sector to what the market is today.

In addition to what has been said, in the last three closing decades of the twentieth century, there were five major political events with worldwide ramifications, which had shaped the course of the regional and global economic disorders and crises. The monetary costs of these events are hard to measure. The first event was the occupation of Afghanistan by the Soviet Union in 1978. In April 1978, the government of Mohammad Daud Khan was overthrown by the pro-Soviet officers of the Afghan army. The Marxist government in Afghanistan was very weak and gravely disunited. In order to prevent the pro-Soviet Union government from crumbling, the Russian communist leaders sent 30,000 Soviet troops to Afghanistan on 24 December 1979. Eventually, the number of Soviet troops increased to over 100,000 military personnel. The implications of this invasion have been far-reaching and its detrimental aftereffects would last a very long time. The most obvious effect of this transgression was the justification of a greater arms race by both sides: the Soviet Bloc and the US and their allies. Many billions of dollars were wasted in this way. To defeat and expel the Soviet troops, the US and its allies supported and organized the most ill-informed, bigoted, violent Afghan, Pakistani, and Arab Islamist groups. The collective term used for these groups was the "Afghan Mujahidin." Osama bin Landen was one of these Islamist mercenaries.

The invasion of Afghanistan reinforced the grip of the Russian communist empire over the nations and the states that were under their domination. Side by side with the increasing military achievements of religious fanatics and their backers and sponsors in Afghanistan, the Russian empire hardened its hold over its puppet regimes on the periphery. At the same time, the US and its allies in the West increased their support for the most repressive right-wing and theocratic regimes throughout the world. The combined misdoings of the West and East powers decimated any form of progressive, rational, democratic, and humane political campaign and activism, particularly in developing nations. Such movements were liquidated systematically or were completely marginalized. The Islamic fundamentalist beast was born in the midst of strangulating the enlightened objectivity on one hand and protecting and promoting ignorance, bigotry, idiocy, hypocrisy, and violent fanaticism on the other hand.

The first toxic Islamic state is Pakistan. There is a good reason for this. It is a baseless state and the first Islamic state that was created by the British Empire. The British divided India and created Pakistan. The cruel irony is that there is not a nation in this name. No nation calls itself a "clean" nation! The two sides of India that the British divided to create Pakistan were East Bengal from the Indian Province of Bengal and West Punjab from the Indian province of Punjab. At the time of partition of India, the population of East Bengal was about 44 million, and the population of West Punjab about 20 million. Pakistan, in reality, became the Punjabi Muslim army, and political and religious establishment in West Punjab. This was the same clandestine network of Indian flatterers who have forsaken their motherland India and became loyal to the invaders of India including the British colonizers. Pakistan was lame from its birth. From its very day of foundation, Pakistan has never seen a day of stability or being free of extreme violence or bigotry. The fact is there will be no Pakistan without militarism, Islamic fundamentalism, extreme violence, and corruption. The baselessness of this artificial state became too obvious when its principal founder, East Bengal, after a very bloody war, separated itself from Pakistan on 26 March 1971. This was, in effect, the end of Pakistan. But the Punjabi army of Pakistan came to rescue itself with Zia-ul-Haq's military coup on 5 July 1977. The Zulfikar Ali Bhutto government was overthrown and Bhutto was hanged on 4 April 1979.

Iran became another site for depositing Islamic fundamentalism of a different kind from that of Pakistan. The monarchy in Iran was toppled on 11 February 1979. The abolition of the Pahlavi dictatorship took place in a popular rebellion that lasted about six months. Shah could not crash the popular rebellion and subsequently was ousted from the throne. Iran quickly descended into a state of chaos. The social and economic progress that took place in the two decades earlier dissipated in no time. In the 1970s, Iran was the third largest producer of oil and by 1976 it had the fifth largest army equipped with the most sophisticated hardware from the United States (Venn 2002: 23 and Patrikarakos 2012: 25). By the late 1970s, Iran also was recounted in the rank of the major industrial economies. It was only one of very few countries in the Middle East where people enjoyed a certain degree of personal freedom. At the time of the downfall of the Pahlavi dynasty Iran was the soldier of region. The colonial geopolitical structure of Iran in its present form is tight-knit with dictatorship, militarism, violence, and religious fundamentalism. These elements are the indivisible parts of Iran in its present form. As it is, Iran is a misnomer. It is a term applied to an artificial boundary that does not accurately denote. Contrary to general usage, Iran is a plateau where Iranian nations, such as the Baluch, Fars, Lur, Gillaki, Mazandarani, Afghan, and Kurdish, have inhabited it for millennia. In its current format, Iran was created in the 1920s with the help of the British Empire. Ever since it has been dominated by the Persian state. It is their domination that Iran has remained synonymous with Persia.

Dictatorship and colonial geopolitical structures are inseparable. Such political structures cannot survive without absolute power. Invariably, political authority in these arbitrary boundaries is allotted to a tyrannical ruler or a single-party rule or a small clique of oligarchs or clerics. Changing one government to another under a colonial geopolitical structure would only alter the form of dictatorship. The downfall of the monarchy and the rise of Shia theocracy in Iran merely changed the form of dictatorship. The fact is history is not determined by reason. History does not have a conscious mind. It is oblivious and indifferent to our follies. So, it does not always progress. Under flood of ignorance and lack of liberty, it can regress. Human follies can be avoided by means of freedom of thought, rationalism, and humanism in an open and democratic environment. Those who succeeded over the steering wheel of the 1979 revolution in Iran were deprived of such attributes. The revolution was led by a medieval figure with a spiteful plan. The upcoming medieval Shia state of Ruhollah Khomeini was the worst of all possible worlds. That being said, the transition of political power to another unenlightened clan in Iran was compatible with the second-best aftereffect of the Iranian revolution for both the Eastern and Western powers. In their estimate and experience of the history of ecclesiastics in Iran, it was believed that it was easier to manipulate a narrow-minded clergy than a broadminded and democratic state in Iran. Hence, in less than no time, the American abandoned one of their closest ally in the Middle East and the Soviet Union (Russia) was among the first countries to recognize the Shia theocratic state of Iran.

Islamic fundamentalism is inherently militant and violent. It has been recorded cold facts of its entire history. The militancy of Islamic fundamentalism has taken different forms, under the umbrella of either Sunni Islam or Shia Islam. The essence of all forms of militant Islamic fundamentalism is the same. The fundamentalist Shia clergy seized the political power as the monarchy was abolished in Iran on 11 February 1979. From the very day of coming to the throne, the Islamic State of Iran initiated a cycle of violence that has not ended to this day. After the Shia clergy seized the power, the frenzied fanatical

Islamic revolutionary mob lashed through the streets of cities and towns, confiscating the assets of what they perceived to be the supporters of the former regime, lynching the less lucky ones at the site and arresting thousands of others only suspected of being un-Islamic. The captives were divided into those who died under toured, those who were brought to show trials, those publicly executed, and those who encountered summary trials and execution. As the Islamic regime consolidated its power, it turned against the intellectuals, the Marxists, socialists, free thinkers, other nationalities such as Kurds and Baluch, and others who were demanding the rights of self-determination, as well as women and the religious minority groups. The regime justified all its crimes against humanity under the banner of God and Islam.

In enforcing its harsh medieval Islamic codes, as women are perceived in Islam to be incomplete human beings, i.e., half men, the Islamic world turned its wrath against half of the population of Iran. We must bear in mind that women in Iran played a critical role in the revolution and the victory of the revolution. Immediately after the revolution, they were forced to be wrapped up in thick black cloth from top to toe. In keeping with Islamic norms that women are incapable of making decisions for themselves, they had to be accompanied by their fathers, brothers, or husbands outside the house. The religious militias roaming the streets terrorized women if they observe any slight disobedience of their Islamic dress code. Tens of thousands of women were arrested, imprisoned, sprayed with acid, and executed by the regime to administer and execute its Islamic penal code. In compliance with its Islamic law, the Islamic regime introduced and protected the child marriage and violated the most basic rights of children, most specifically the rights of female children. The girls were segregated from boys and barred from many sports activities and professions such as being a judge in a court. The regime removed all the civil and political rights that women in Iran were granted in the former regime.

A tight group of followers of Khomeini seized the US embassy in Tehran in November 1979 and took 66 American hostages. The Islamic regime of Iran extended this policy to outside Iran by employing other fanatical Shias to take hostages of Western nationals and others, either to keep them in captivity for many years or to kill them. A policy that all Islamic extremists and Jihadist groups all over the world mimicked the Shia regime of Iran and exploited it in pursuit of their aims. On 14 February 1989, the head of the Islamic regime of Iran issued an edict and called for all Muslims to kill Salman Rushdie, a British writer, wherever they found him for writing his book, *The Satanic Verses*, which was an indispensable constituent of this policy. The response of the democratic and progressive camp to the incident was either implicitly siding with the edict, deceived by the regime's anti-imperialist rhetoric, or their response was so feeble that it meant nothing. The complicity of enlightened and democratic camp emboldened different shades of Islamic fundamentalism in different parts of the world to commit all sorts of crimes with impunity. Islamic extremism in Iran was a catalyst to the revival of Islamic fundamentalism in the rest of the world. A caricature of this model was copied in Afghanistan by the Taliban; in Algeria by Algeria's Islamic Salvation Front victory in 1991; in Sudan by the Islamic State of General Umar Hassan al-Bashir; and in Turkey, Iraq, and Egypt with the victory of Islamists. The canonical of Iran has been responsible directly for organizing many Islamic extremist groups in Iraq and Lebanon such as Hezbollah. The Islamic State in Syria and Iraq (ISIS) was, not in a direct way but covertly, a by-product of the Islamic regime of Iran. It has been the principal cause of the sectarian war among the main sects of Islam (Sunni and Shia), in particular, in the Middle East. This regime deprived the people of their most basic civil, political, and human rights. It imprisoned, tortured, and killed tens and thousands of most informed and conscientious people in Iran and caused about four million of the most educated Iranian to leave their homeland. What is the cost of all this and how all these events can be looked at as being outside the sphere of economic disorder and crisis?

The duel between two dominant political and ideological perspectives of the twentieth century ended in the late 1980s. After a sustained back-and-forth battle and war of words between the East and the West, the dominant political ideology in the West won the contest. The New Right reign supreme in the 1980s and eventually prevailed over the Soviet Union ideology. By the end of the 1980s, the Soviet Empire collapsed and its reign of terror was out of the way in the eastern and central Europe. As a result of the termination of this confrontation, the global political and economic landscape has changed. In 1979, the British public elected their first woman prime minister, Margaret Thatcher. In the United States, Ronald Reagan was elected as the president on similar radical political agenda. However, the triumph of the New Right politics in the 1980s was not accidental. This was a heterogeneous political movement that had one foot in classical political economist laissez-faire economics and the other in Austrian School hostility towards socialist economic planning as it was practised by the Bolsheviks after the demise of the Tsarist Empire in 1917. One school of thought in economics that thrived by opposing socialist central planning unfailingly was the Austrian school. Ludwig von Mises (1881–1972), one of the founders of the school, in an article in 1920, argued that rational economic calculation under socialist central planning was not possible. As a result, under socialist planning, economic resources cannot be allocated efficiently – stressing that socialism is inherently flawed because it is a product of human design and it is impractical. He maintained that a planned socialist economy "cannot be realized because it is beyond human power to establish it as a social system" (Mises 1998: 676). Mises went on to say that socialism is impractical not because we lack technical methods of measurement but "is due to the absence of constant relations" (Mises 1998: 56).

Members of each school of thought in economics tend to adhere to the school's core principles. These principles are the ones that are laid down in the main by the architectures of each school. Deviation from central beliefs usually among the members of the school is a matter of degree of over- or under-emphasizes than straying from the core ideas. As an example, for Mises, the most erosive economic system was the Soviet command economy. For his student, Friedrich Hayek, it was the Keynesian management of aggregate demand. For Milton Friedman, it was the over-supply of money and Keynesian deficit spending. All three descend from the same caste, the new right economics. The ideological lineage of the core principle from which they deduce these inferences was the belief in the free-market economy and their intense hostility towards the socialist central planning. On this account, Keynesian welfare state economics was viewed as a form of socialist planning through the back door.

Friedman attributed the outbreak of stagflation in the 1970s to Keynesian economics and economic policies. The three most sinister means in the realm of ideas to tip the balance in favour of one conjecture against a countervailing supposition and the censure of the latter by the former are God, nature, and science. The word of God is final. To this very day, the heretics in the theocratic states are put to death for not submitting to the word of God. Stalin killed millions of nonconformists in the name of Marxist-Leninist science. Friedman in his defiance of Keynesian teaching used the agency of nature and became the adviser to Chile's mass murderer General Augusto Pinochet. When nature is the article of faith, humankind cannot do much but to obey its command. Human beings cannot impose their will on nature. They must do and act upon the commands dictated by nature. Any effort to change the course of nature would be futile. The laws of nature are immutable and nature knows best. The destiny of the natural world is in its own hand. The Physiocrats and the classical economists, by and large, were longing for a harmonious natural order in society similar to the seemingly celestial harmony. In their ideal vision, they extended their conviction of natural order as the basis of the natural world to their idyllic economy. Physiocracy literally means the rule of nature. The doctrine of laissez-faire was an outgrowth of this faith which was passed down from the natural law tradition to these schools.

Nature is for the best. It cannot be other than it is. Friedman's repudiation of Keynesian macro-management of aggregate demand was a descendant of this much dated natural order doctrine that is used as the basis for the positive laws. His concepts of the natural rate of unemployment, output, and interest rate were a derivation of this antiquated tradition. Natural laws are immutable, by implication, so one cannot eliminate the natural rate of unemployment. Thus, any attempt to violate this rate by Keynesian policies or any other policies would be futile. In the long run, the Phillips curve is stable at the natural rate of unemployment, and the Phillips curve is compatible with any level of inflation. Violating the natural course of the natural rate of employment can only cause higher inflation and unemployment. In Friedman's theology inflation is the cardinal sin and the greatest sinners of all are the Keynesian policymakers. The chief problem is inflation and the cause of inflation is the excessive expansion of the money supply due to Keynesian deficit financing. Friedman maintained that inflation "is always and everywhere a monetary phenomenon, produced in the first instance by unduly rapid growth in the quantity of money" (Friedman 1968: 18). His remedy to curb inflation was to prevent Keynesian policymakers from overspending. The economic stability can be restored by controlling the rate of growth of the money supply and leaving the rest to the market to do its natural adjustments.

The faith in the New Right economics rests on five cardinal tenets. Most of these tenets are to be found in the physiocrats and the classical economists' writings. These tenets were expressed for different contexts, time, and to serve different objectives. Nevertheless, the groundworks for these tenets in the New Right garb are laid in the writings of Austrian and Monetary schools of thought. These tenets coalesce around the following assertions: (a) the world of the economy is composed of individuals and an individual is the only indivisible particle in the domain of economy. (b) The individual is an "acting man." Since individuals act the focus of the economy must be on an individual. (c) The "facts" in natural and social sciences are not the same. Human sciences begin with intention, purpose, and plans. Thus, facts in social sciences are what individuals think and believe. Individuals' actions are only known to each individual. Each individual's intention, choice, and understanding are subjective. Economics is the creation of individuals' subjective valuation of goods. The only unit that makes choices within the orbit of the economy are individuals. Thus, the central mission of economic analysis should be the study of individuals' intentions, plans, and purposes. Mises remarked:

> the concept of man is, above all else, also the concept of the being who acts. Our consciousness is that of an ego that is capable of acting and does act. The fact that our deeds are intentional makes them actions. Our thinking about men and their conduct, and our conduct toward men and toward our surroundings in general, presuppose the category of action.
> (Mises 1978: 15)

(d) One guiding light that triggered the age of reason and provided the means to break away from medieval times was the idea of the natural law. The progression of this law in particular to natural liberty set off this historical departure. But the natural liberty in classical liberalism is expressed in the context of individual liberty. This form of individual liberty is qualified within the framework of freedom of thought in a free society. In the new right economics, natural liberty is delineated within the confinement of the framework of a free-market economy. There are three overriding implications to the latter perspective. First, the latter approach either denies the existence of society entirely or considers it as being insignificant. Either way, liberty is taken out of the scope of society. Mrs Thatcher, the first woman prime minister of Britain, in her interview with *Woman's Own* in

1989, declared that "there is no such thing as society." Even if it is admitted that there is a society, it is said to be inconsequential. I. Kirzner states:

> Society is made up of numerous individuals. Each individual can be viewed as independently selecting his goal program … and each individual adopts his own course of action to achieve his goals. It is therefore unrealistic to speak of society as a single unit to allocate resources … Society has no single mind.
>
> (Kirzner 2007: 35)

In any case, in denial or in the form of society being inconsequential, it is individual that is the prime mover. Second, political liberty, i.e., individual liberty, stems from the institution of the market. From this inference, we are led to believe that individual liberty emanates from the market and not from the democratic rule of law in an open and democratic society. Third, this inference has also got a fatalistic epistemological implication. That is, it detaches humans from the market. The market becomes the omniscience and the people the nescience – negating in a sense one of their own central article of faith that an individual knows best how to serve their interest. In this relationship, the market is the subject and humans are passive predicates. There is a problem in this view of knowledge. The market takes the place of an animate conscious intelligent entity whereas the individuals are a blind crowd of bystanders.

In this view of the market, not only market is the source of knowledge but it is the basis of human ethics. It is the maker of human ethics. Let us delve a little deeper into this subject. Central to the moral codes of human conduct is the principle of justice. On account of the fact that the market knows best and is the sustainer of the spontaneous order, it is inferred that the market allocates the scarce economic resources most efficiently. It follows then that justice can be served best by the free market. That is, market treats individuals most fairly because the free market rests on mutually voluntary exchange. Any undertaking in a free market can be just since economic agents who take part in the exchange are treated fairly on the basis of their voluntary participation. The aspect of being just, which is also credited to the market, is based on a mistaken belief that each exchange in the market is mutually beneficial. On this ground government intervention in the economy is regarded as a cardinal sin. It is said that government intervention would do more harm than good. Besides, all forms of government are considered to be alike. Mises argued that the best government is the least government. Murray N. Rothbard contested that "no government interference with exchanges can ever increase social utility … whenever government forces anyone to make an exchange which he would not have made, this person loses in utility as a result of the coercion" (Rothbard: 2011: 323).

In neoliberalism's ideal world, a free competitive market is the best of all possible economic systems. The market is the basis of the optimum allocation of scarce resources and the upholder of individual liberty. The unregulated free market system is imperative for economic efficiency and freedom. The free market is tallied with modern Western civilization. It is the code word for the emancipation of the individual ego. Hayek emphatically stipulated that the price mechanism (market system) came into being on its own. It is a "spontaneous order" that arose out of unintended consequences of individuals' actions. Had it been consciously designed, it "would have acclaimed as one of the greatest triumphs of the human mind" (Hayek 1980: 87). The ideologues of this train of thought were stricken by fear of the Western civilization (i.e., the market) being on the brink of collapse. The threat that they saw was the collective movement. The crusade was manifested in different denominations, ranging from communism to Nazism to Keynesianism.

In his acclaimed book, *The Road to Serfdom* (1944), Hayek recounted tellingly the danger of Western civilization sliding ever more into slavery. The book was written with the object to warn the men of means and goodwill that the threat to Western civilization (the market economy) was imminent. This was a top-rated book that described the road to serfdom and totalitarianism through the aqueduct of planning. With the publication of this book, the New Right hostility against Soviet Union central planning and other types of planning was all-out and full-fledged. The two sides, most specifically the communist side and the new right side, were drifting more and more apart into two extreme opposing global ideological standpoints. To secure self-assurance and ease of mind, the new right retreated more and more to religion, political, social, and cultural conservatism, and the diametrically opposite side to the extreme Marxism. Concurrent with the ascent of the new right, the far left was degenerating expeditiously. The New Right triumphed in the 1980s when the elected Anglo-America administrations complemented each other political ideology in their commitment to new right policies and their hostility against communism. The victory of the new right order co-occurred with the demise of the Soviet Empire in the late 1980s.

## The new right and the old left

The Russian communist empire in the 1980s was the sick man of Europe. The Soviet Empire carried with it over seven decades of political repression and the death of many millions of people. It invaded and colonized many nations. Finally, it reached its impasse in the 1980s. In the last dying days of the empire, the rulers of the empire were old and out of touch with the new realities and demands of the younger generations. The Marxist rhetoric lost its initial reverence. Wherever the stock of Marxian ideas was applied in a system of a one-party state, they were over-exploited. The Soviet state propaganda and coercion became less effective, particularly after the invention of the internet. Gorbachev's reforms were a tacit admission of the system failure. Leonid Brezhnev (1906–82), who ruled the Soviet Empire, died in November 1982. After Brezhnev, another old guard from the politburo of the Russian communist party, Yuri Andropov (1914–84), became the general secretary in 1982. Andropov died in 1984. His successor, Konstantin Cherenkov (1911–85), only ruled the Soviet Empire from 13 February 1984 to 10 March 1985. The empire had its day. One problem on top of another with no hope of recovery plunged the empire into chaos and a chronic crisis. The crisis of leadership went hand in hand with inept propagandas, social, economic, and cultural stagnation, arms race, poor harvests, the rise of alcoholism, scarcity of the most basic necessities, costs of Afghanistan war, the Chernobyl disaster in 1986, and the 1988 earthquake in Armenia. The soviet difficulties were endless and critical.

Mikhail Gorbachev was elected as the general secretary of the communist party of the Soviet Union in March 1985. He initiated a series of economic and political reforms under the flags of Perestroika (restructuring) and Glasnost (openness). These reforms did not only rescue the empire but triggered its dissolution. As the pervasive climate of fear and suspicion fettered away, the empire fell apart. One symbol of the empire after another began to disappear. One of the most visible icons of the empire, the Berlin Wall, was knocked down in November 1989. By the end of December 1991, the Soviet Empire no longer existed.

The Soviet Empire was based on an absolute ideology. All such forms of ideology are imperialistic by nature. A nation armed with this worldview uses its power against its neighbours and will conquer and colonize them. The conquest can be in the name of God, civilization, and race or even in the name of science. As the genetic code of the empire rests on the principle of universalism, there can be no limit in its imperialistic ambition. The collapse of the Soviet Empire also proved that the open, rational, democratic, and humane path is the least violent and destructive passage of transition from a repressive regime to a democratic system. Nicolae Ceausescu (1918–89), the leader of Romania (1965–89), like most dictators, underestimated the force of the democratic movement in the Soviet bloc. His regime only lasted until 25 December 1989. Ceausescu and his wife, Elena, were arrested and executed. The Serbian empire was a mini communist empire. An empire that was hidden under the name of Yugoslavia. The Serbians ruled Macedonia, Montenegro, Bosnia, Croatia, and Slovenia. As these nations demanded their democratic rights, the Serbian rulers resorted to violence. Hence, the war of independence lasted for about ten years, from 1991 to 2001. The death tolls to this conflict for the period of 1991–95 are estimated to be about 200,000 people. The number of people wounded is estimated to be about 250,000; the number of refugees, including those who were internally displaced and those who left the country, is said to be over four million people. The economic cost – the loss of assets and destruction of infrastructure – is estimated to be about between US$15 and US$20 billion (Whitehead 2009). Several leaders of Serbia, including Slobodan Milosevic (1941–2006), the former President of Yugoslavia, were arrested and put on trial at The Hague on charges of crimes against humanity, genocide, and a war crime. Milosevic was found dead in his cell at the UN tribunal detention centre on 11 March 2006 in The Hague.

It is a fact that empires cannot last forever. The artificial colonial and imperial boundaries are inherently irrational, undemocratic, inhumane, and illegal. One pivotal precondition for long-lasting peace, security, democracy, and prosperity is the removal of colonial boundaries. Getting rid of the Berlin wall not only united the German nation but also removed the possibility of war between the two sides of the German nation. The dissolutions of the Czechoslovak federation and Yugoslavia are great lessons in history to learn from. Both colonial geopolitical structures were the legacy of the First World War. It was this war that crashed the Ottoman, the Russian, and the Habsburg empires. As a result, new borders were drawn and new countries were created. As the Habsburg Empire ended, both these two arbitrary countries were forged, each as a unified nation. Czechoslovakia was formed on 28 October 1918 with the consent of the allied powers.

The Czechs and Slovaks shared long historical, cultural, and linguistic ties – the latter being the weaker partner. The Czech as the dominant nation, before long, augmented their hegemony over the Slovaks. The ascendancy of the exercise of power in the course of time alerted a section of the Slovak intellectuals of their dwindling national rights. In due time, a mode of thought was formed among these intellectuals that opposed the idea of Czechoslovakism. The perspective that this group put forward was the distinct national identity of the Slovak nation. Slovaks' longing and the call for a separate nation go back to 1861. This view was first brought to the public arena by the Slovak People's Party. The proponents of an independent Slovakia opposed the core tenet of Czechoslovakism. That is, homogenization and fusion of the two nations into one unified national identity. In effect, this was coequal to the assimilation of Slovak to the Czech nation. Czechoslovakia was at the mercy of the extreme political events in Europe. From 1938 to 1945, the country was under the occupation of Nazi Germany and from 1948 to 1989 it was under the domination of the Soviet Empire.

Gorbachev's reforms triggered the breakup of the Soviet Union. These reforms were followed by mass demonstrations against the totalitarian communist rulers in countries under Soviet domination in the eastern and central Europe. The continuous and increasing waves of dissent against the former regimes led to the collapse of one communist regime after another. The most successful transition was in Czechoslovakia. Given the difficult circumstances of the time, the transition was rational, humane, democratic, and peaceful. The general elections in Czechoslovakia were held in June 1990. The majority of seats in the Federal Assembly went to the opponents of the former regime. Vaclav Havel (1936–2011), the former political dissident and playwright, became the president of Czechoslovakia. The open political arena created an environment where both the Czech and Slovak masses and intellectuals could express their views and questioned the irrational, undemocratic, inhumane, and unjust ideas, and practices of the former regime. Many of the political taboos that were taken for granted either out of ignorance, fear, or vested interest were hammered out by intense open debates. It was not too long that the conflict embedded in the colonial construction of Czechoslovakia resurfaced one more time. The Slovaks were resolved to end the colonial hegemony of the Czechs but Czech insisted on maintaining their domination. The conflict escalated.

The Czech and Slovak breakup is a case of deep moral judgement. The gravity of the mishap is very high. The disagreement between those who hold the colonial power and those who want to break free is a very delicate balance. If the right steps are not taken at the right time by the right political leaders from either side of the conflict the end outcome would be nothing short of total disaster. The resolution of the conflict between the Czechs and the Slovaks stands out as an exemplary resolution for the nations that are still consigned behind the colonial bars. The political and civic leaders of both nations resorted to free debates and discussions to resolve the conflict. The priority was given to democratic consent. Subsequently, on 1 January 1993, Slovakia gained its independence peacefully by mutual assent. The Czechs accepted and approved the democratic right of the Slovaks as a separate nation. But this was not what happened in Yugoslavia and in Russia.

As Gorbachev's reforms failed, Yugoslavia and Russia went downhill into extreme violence and repression. Under the existing geopolitical construction, their relapse into dictatorship was inevitable. The bloody events ensued were due to the Serb and the Russian who wanted to preserve their colonial authority at any cost. The critical distinction between Czechoslovakia, Yugoslavia, and Russia can be summed up in two factors. First, in Czechoslovakia, there was a long historical trend for the restoration of civic and democratic rights. The Prague Spring of 1968 was an outburst of this trend. From January to August 1968, many harsh and repressive rules were abated in Czechoslovakia. The reformist government of Alexander Dubcek (1921–92) introduced a series of liberal reforms that granted a set of political, economic, cultural, and civic rights. To the Soviet rulers what Dubcek did was sacrilegious. Dubcek was denounced as a heretic and his reforms were stamped as counterrevolutionary. Nevertheless, the reforms allowed the citizens to think, speak, and write not in total fear and also to travel freely. The Soviet officials decided before it spiralled out of control to send their army to Czechoslovakia. Hence, the Soviet army invaded Prague on 21 August 1968, removed Dubcek from power, and crushed the Prague Spring movement.

Another and even greater expression of a democratic trend in Czechoslovakia was the Charter 77. On 1 August 1975, in Helsinki, representative of 35 countries signed an agreement called the Helsinki Accords. Czechoslovakia was one of these countries that signed this agreement. The agreement requested the 35 signatory countries to "promote and encourage the effective exercise of civil, political, social, cultural, and other rights." On the back of this agreement, the civil and human rights activists in Czechoslovakia compiled and published the Charter 77 in January 1977. The Charter initially endorsed and signed by 242 civil rights activists. It is declared in the Charter that "basic human rights" in Czechoslovakia exist "only on paper" and "the right to freedom of expression" in the country is "purely illusory." The Charter stated its principal object as "the respect of civic and human rights" in Czechoslovakia and "throughout the world" (Kraus 2007). In October 1979, the six leaders of the civic group, including the co-author of the Charter, Vaclav Havel, were tried and sentenced to up to six years in prison. Vaclav Havel was sentenced to four and a half years. After the fall of the Soviet Empire and the collapse of the communist regime in Czechoslovakia, the civic and human rights activists that compiled the Charter 77 came to power. In the case of Russia and Yugoslavia, such a democratic trend and charter did not exist. The changes in the latter countries were mere formalities. The same hard-line ideological communists were shuffled between different political posts to safeguard the same old status quo political order.

Gorbachev's economic and political reforms were ended by the August 1991 coup. The coup ousted Gorbachev from the seat of power for a very short time. The coup failed but it brought down Gorbachev with it. After the coup, Gorbachev was merely a discredited figurehead with no authority. Boris Yeltsin (1931–2007), who defied the coup, emerged the central figure of the dying empire. Yeltsin was through and through a political demagogue and an alcoholic. It was him that sent the Russian troops to Chechnya in December 1994. In the course of the seventeen months of being in office, he appointed five prime ministers. The last one was in August 1999. It was Vladimir Putin, a former KGB officer. Not long after, on 31 December 1999, Yeltsin promoted Putin as the acting president of the Russian Federation. Putin has achieved everything that could be expected from a KGB officer. He crashed the Chechenian rebellion. The human cost of the Chechenian war according to official sources for the period of 1994–96 is estimated at about 30,000 Chechenians and 4,300 from the Russian army. The economic cost for the same period is estimated at about $5.5 billion (Pain 2001: 7). Putin repeated the Chechenian tragedy in Syria. He flared tension between Abkhazia (1999) and South Ossetia (2008) and paved the way to their session from Georgia.

In the closing decades of the twentieth century, China also discarded its frightful Maoist cult. The new leaders of the communist party of China chanted the new right hymns in Maoist garb. The two extreme autocratic systems of the right and the left were reconciled through the dictatorship of the market forces. The difference between the right dictatorship in Chile under the Pinochet regime and the left dictatorship in China was only in their forms. In essence, both types of dictatorship have enforced the faith of market order by any unscrupulous means obtainable. Deng Xiaoping, the Chinese leader after Mao, articulated the new right economics in an old Chinese saying. He expressed the principle of freedom of economic incentive by reciting the old proverb that "it does matter whether the cat is black or white as long as it catches mice, it is a good cat" (quoted from Holmes 2009: 42). There is not much difference between this vision of the economy and the vision of the economy that Milton Friedman prescribed to Pinochet, the Chilean military dictator. Pinochet slaughtered many thousands of Chileans for executing the white cat vision of the free-market economy and Deng Xiaoping massacred many thousands of Chinese students in Tiananmen Square on 4 June 1989 for carrying out his red cat vision of the free-market economy.

The entire history of China has been a successive nexus of tyrants and despots. Its current political and economic system, by and large, is the legacy of the nineteenth and twentieth centuries' attempts to escape from complete mayhem. In the course of the first opium war (1839–42) and the second opium war (1856–60), China descended into a colony of the European imperial powers. The eviction of the colonial invaders did not improve the conditions of the Chinese general public much. The new masters on the throne went down along the same path as the former rulers of China. The number of Chinese killed during the period of the Chinese nationalists' rule (1912–49) is about 10,214,000 people (Rummel 1991: Preface). The death rate precipitated after the Japanese invaded China in 1937. Nanking, then the capital city of China, fell to the Japanese imperial army on 13 December 1937. Japanese ruled China to the end of the Second World War. Their atrocities against the Chinese public had no bounds. Within six weeks of the fall of Nanking, Japanese soldiers murdered about 260,000–300,000 Chinese and raped about 20,000 women (Brook 1999: 284). The number of military death of Chinese in the Second World War is said to be about 2.2 million.

After the war, the influence of the Chinese communist party in China increased rapidly. On 1 October 1949, under the leadership of Mao Tes-tung, the Communist Party assumed power in China. The same old episodes of mass murders continued under communist rule. The number of victims of the communist rule, including the victims of the Chinese Cultural Revolution (1966–76), is estimated at about 38,702,000 people. Not long after Mao Tes-tung death, Den Xiaoping (1904–97) came to power. His economic reforms in the 1980s transformed the Chinese economy. These reforms, as we referred to earlier, were revisionary and contrary to Marxian economic principles. He introduced free-market exchange on the principle of private ownership of means of production and the state's total grip of society. The autarky of mind revived in different forms. Chineses were allowed to think as far as they could make money and remained submissive to the communist party faith and hierarchical order. After many decades of experiencing mass murders, starvation, destruction, and humiliation, for the generation of Chinese who were allowed to make money and keep it, it was a very liberating dream. Masses of Chinese hurried to cash in on the opportunity given before it was too late. This has been the drive, more than anything else, for the transformation of the Chinese economy.

Gorbachev's reforms were only a spark in the circuit of the Soviet Empire. Nevertheless, this small flash of light broke the circuit of the Soviet Empire and caught China, the second largest totalitarian empire. In the spring of 1989, Chinese students from a number of universities began their peaceful protests, demanding democratization of the country in line with the ones

Gorbachev had introduced in the Soviet Union. This movement grew and other social groups also joined the movement. The centre of the movement was in Beijing but in other cities such as Shanghai, Xian, Chengdu, and Nanjing people of diverse backgrounds joined the protest against state corruption and demanded greater political and individual freedom. Gorbachev visited Beijing on 15 May 1989. His three-day stay in China encouraged more Chinese to join the movement. It also exposed the protest to the outside world but left not much leeway for the Chinese totalitarian political system. There were only two ways out of the quandary, either to crush the protest or to end the Chinese totalitarian empire. The Chinese leaders devotedly went for the massacre of the protesters. The number of victims of the Tiananmen Square massacre can never be known. An estimate put the number to at least 1,000 people (Uekert 1995: 32).

The Tiananmen Square massacre is a hallmark in the Chinese communist empire. In the aftermath of the massacre, the Chinese rulers saw no limit in getting rich, in dealing with a great mixture of despotic states to exploit their natural resources and in staying in power by any means. After the Second World War, it was the US government that armed and protected all right-wing dictators of the world and communist Russia that armed and protected all totalitarian communist regimes. After the collapse of the Soviet Union, these roles have shifted. China has emerged as the principal protector of most despotic and criminal regimes by bribing them and Russia has taken the second position by arming the most brutal states. The greatest barrier to the democratization of the regions that are left behind in respect to human rights violations, lack of freedom, and rule of law in the present and near future is the totalitarian state of China and the oligarchic state of Russia. The human and economic costs of these states and other undemocratic states are simply inconceivable.

## The 2007–2008 credit depression

Many factors have contributed to the global credit crunch of 2007–2008. As in all matters of great calamity, the initial response tends to be simplistic and cast down into a convenient sacrificial lamb and a sin-eater. In consequence, the true causes of the malaise are underestimated and overlooked. Frequently, the ideologues, the authors, and the prime movers of the scheme are acquitted from the misdeed. Most often not only the real contrivers, the crafters, the driving forces, and the executors are exonerated but recompensed for their deceit and oversight. Not only the academics, the policymakers, and the Capitan of the calamity are let off of the hook but they are promoted to higher positions to remedy something that they were the root cause of it. Much in the same way, the architectures of the global credit crunch were given the post of the healers of their own syndrome.

At the 1997 conference of the Labour Party, Gordon Brown, the finance minister of Great Britain, boasted that under his watch the time for the boom and bust business cycles is over. Instead of "a stop-go, boom and bust economy," the British economy would grow continuously. Gordon Brown was enchanted by Alan Greenspan's seeming success in the United States of America. Greenspan, while he was the Board of Governors of the US Federal Reserves (1987–2006), credited his apparent achievements to his faith in pursuit of self-interest and the free market economy. As a strong believer in Smith's "invisible hands," he thought that the rational pursuit of self-interest is not just a virtue but it is a self-regulating mechanism. Self-interest brings the best of human nature, prevents economic anarchy, and engenders collective economic progress and prosperity. One year after Greenspan retired, the 2007 global credit crunch occurred. Gordon Brown was still in his job by that date. The event proved that they were wrong.

There is no and there will be no general consensus in the economic literature on the credit crunch of 2007/2008. The prevailing view prior to the crisis ran counter to such a likelihood. The very few individuals who questioned the conventional wisdom were taken no notice of and were side-lined. Those very few individuals who questioned the received wisdom were in much disadvantageous position. They could not tell when the expansionary cycle would end whereas their opponents were on the top of the cycle and were making names and money. The prevailing situation and the past and the present data were on the side of those who were making a lot of money. The judgement of the minority, even though it was correct, could not be applied as an exact form of instruction for action. Unless one could state the exact date of the economic meltdown the view would have no buyer. In the case of the credit crunch of 2007/2008, much like any other economic and financial crisis, nobody knew exactly the time and place of the crash. It is only with the wisdom of hindsight after the event a growing consensus of opinion about the exact time of meltdown can be formed.

The 2007–2008 credit crunch was a global phenomenon. Its key determinants are also said to be global. Among these determinants we have the innovation and application of information technology, a revolution in financial markets, flexible exchange rate system, financial disintermediation, and deregulation of markets (Cassis 2013: 47). Greenspan testifying before Congress in 1997 acknowledged these changes as necessary steps for the "modernization" of financial markets – affirming that these measures were necessary for the restoration of "a more efficient financial system." These alterations in his evaluation removed the "outdated restrictions that serve no useful purpose." Furthermore, these required adjustments have increased "economic efficiency" and allowed "banking organizations to compete more effectively in their natural markets" (Inquiry Report 2011: 35).

Global imbalances in production, consumption, and savings are a fact of life. These imbalances can be improved but cannot be removed entirely. Throughout human history with changing social, natural, and technological conditions and political power such imbalances have shifted from one region into another. One example of this shift in recent decades has been the shifting of production to countries with comparative cost advantages in labour and raw materials. China has been at the forefront of the wave with its ever inflated savings from its export-led economic growth. Chinese and the rich Arab states of the Gulf have taken advantage of the world currency and the largest economy and have channelled much of their surplus savings into the US credit markets. The huge inflow of capital from these sources and others combined with the Fed purposive monetary policy of low interest kept the rates of interest low for a considerable time in the United States before the crash. The availability of cheap credit soared the demand for consumer goods and the steady increase in demand kept the asset prices snowballing (Huertas 2011: 13). The Islamist 9/11 terrorist attack and the dotcom crisis also pressed the leading central banks to go for cheap debt rates.

One effect of financial liberalization and technological innovations was the development of derivatives markets. These markets expanded rapidly in parallel to greater deregulation and integration of global financial markets, ever-increasing fluctuation in asset prices, exchange rate fluctuation, and trade opportunities. There are four basic types of financial derivatives. These are forward and futures contracts, the traded options, and the swaps. The futures and options contracts are the two most primary types of financial derivatives. For greater clarity of argument let us divide the markets into the present and the futures markets. This is because the past is done, and bygones are bygones. The past markets are gone. The only possible markets are the current and upcoming markets. The derivatives market is the trade between these two markets. The future prices of derivative instruments are derived from the current prices of the underlying assets. Derivatives can be traded both on organized and OTC markets. Their promotion, by and large, has been as protection against economic instability and as hedging and risk management instruments to counter the effects of adverse price volatilities. The underlying principle of financial derivatives is the same as the one Aristotle described two and half millennium years ago.

Thales in Aristotle's account relied on his knowledge of stars and took the risk of hiring out all the oil-pressed equipment in Miletus and Chio with only paying a small percentage of the price of the underlying asset. Believing that if he is right, he will make a lot of money but if he is wrong, he will only lose the small percentage of the price of the underlying asset that he paid to hire the oil-pressed kit in his vicinity. To the most participants of derivatives markets today, Thales's approach can be seen as mumbo-jumbo. His knowledge of the estimate of the future prices is classified as no more of somewhat quackery knowledge. The fact of the matter is the contemporary traders' knowledge in trading derivative instruments is not much superior to that of Thales forecast of future prices. The only difference between the two is that the art and language of persuasion for the modern trader is much more sophisticated than in Thales' time. The modern trader has in his disposal the output of the academics, the elaborate and elegant mathematical models, the intricate media and information technology, and the well-versed backing of the commercial and political establishment. The judgement of Thales to the modern trader at first instance seems very naïve and too primitive. But after we remove the labyrinthine of complex modern society and economy layer by layer the judgement of modern derivative traders is not as orderly, accurate, and authentic as it is generally believed. Their knowledge of modern traders, at long last, falls to one's belief of future prices. It is based, in the same way as in Thales' case, on one's faith among many possibilities. Faith, by its very essence, is way off of being reliable. Substantiated knowledge and faith are two separate things. The greater the number of traders who share your faith in the direction of the future prices of the assets in question the greater the probability of confirmation of your belief. Likewise, this is equally applicable in the case of Thales' faith in his mission. Joseph Penso de la Vega, a seventeenth-century commentator of derivatives in his book *Confusion de confusiones* (1688), called the derivative products the "time bargains." Moreover, the future prices of assets are never certain and for this reason, all economic agents taking part in derivatives markets are speculating on their future directions.

Warrant Buffett, in 2002, described derivatives as "financial weapons of mass destruction" (quoted from Irons 2019: 188). The Buffett dramatic catchphrase may be over the top. Nevertheless, it became the proclamation of the post-mortem faith healers of the derivatives markets after the 2007 global credit crash on the grounds that the derivatives were blamed by many for causing the crash. For the apostles of these markets, derivatives are perfectly good. For the opposing side, they are perfectly bad. Both sides are unaware of the unintended consequences of good and bad derivative transactions. A bad transaction may turn good and a good transaction can turn bad. Besides, derivative instruments can be used, moderately, by farmers, corporations, importers, and financial institutions by entering into certain derivative contracts to protect themselves from unforeseen violent fluctuations in future prices, exchange rates, and interest rates. The excess use of derivative is when most of the derivative contracts are not for hedging but for short-term speculation.

There is not one narrative about the global financial meltdown of 2007–2008. Economists, market practitioners, and policymakers disagree on different causes and effects of the crash. On such matters, there can never be one universally accepted description. The only universal agreement is the disagreement that will have no end. But among all these disagreements, there will always be one prevailing narrative. In the totalitarian, autocratic, and theocratic, this narrative is the state narrative. In democratic societies, the prevailing narrative is the most convenient narrative for the vested interest among the academic world, the political arena, the media, and those who have the power and pulse of the economy under their thumbs. The prevailing theory of the global credit crunch begins its tale at the dawn of the twenty-first century. The story goes that as the global economy entered the third millennium, it had only left the cradle of the crisis. It had only left behind the 1997-98 Asian and the Russian financial crises. Not only that, but the global economy in the second half of the

1990s also experienced the first internet gold rush. The internet quickly and spectacularly changed modern societies and economies. The overly optimistic market gradually created a euphoric trend in the online commerce sector that resulted in the dot.com bubble. The bubble burst on 10 March 2000. This was followed by the US stock market crash on 20 March 2001. In 2001, the US endured the deadliest Islamic terrorist suicide attacks in its history. On 11 September 2001, 19 members of Al-Qaeda hijacked four American civil airplanes. They crashed the two airplanes into the World Trade Towers in New York, one into the Pentagon in Washington, D.C., and one plane crashed in Pennsylvania. The death toll of this deadly attack is estimated to be over 3,000 people (Bauer 2007: 422).

The Fed was alarmed over the gloomy situation, and in order to quell any deeper economic slowdown and widespread recession, it decreased the base rates time and time again. The Fed funds rate in the mid-2000 was 6.5 per cent. By the beginning of 2004, the Fed benchmark rate was decreased to 1 per cent. In the period from 2002 to 2004, the Fund rate vacillated within the orbit of 1–1.75 per cent. This is the period where we have the housing and real estate boom in America. The direction of the Fed rate was reversed in 2005. The rate was increased to 2 per cent and then kept rising, reaching 5.25 per cent by mid-2007 (Nayak 2013: 21). The period of cheap credit is argued to be one of the central factors that caused the 2007–2008 global financial crisis.

The outflow of capital is said to be another primary cause of the credit crunch. One source of the outflow was the collapse and disintegration of the Soviet Empire. Another source was the South-eastern Asian countries. This was due to the 1990s financial crises in these countries. The two other sources, as we referred to earlier, were the Chinese and the rich Arab savings. The main magnet for this capital was the United States of America. The savings in the Middle East rose to over one trillion US dollars from 2003 to 2008 (Persaud 2011: 98). This huge volume of savings was far greater than what was recycled in these countries. This was also a time of great political and social instability in this specific region. The flight of capital from Russia to the US for the period of 1992 and 1996 is estimated to be about $50 billion (Claesseus, Oks and Polastri 2000: 38). For the period of 1992–1999, it is estimated to be around $150 billion (Cooper 2003: 15). The total capital fleeing only from the four Southeast Asian countries, Indonesia, Malaysia, the Philippines, and Thailand, is said to be in the range of $658 billion (Beja Jr 2009: 23). Chinese holdings of the US securities in 2002 were $124.4 billion. It increased to $236.2 billion in 2004. By February it was over $1.25 trillion (Bernbach 2016). Adding the flight of capital from the rest of the world, in particular from South America and Africa, to this centre of gravitation is argued to have resulted in imbalances of the global net capital inflows.

There was a period of reorientation of real interest rates in advanced industrialized countries in the years preceding the 2007/2008 global financial crisis. Japan went into a prolonged economic depression in the 1990s. From the mid-1990s to 2000, interest rates in Japan fell to very low levels. From early 1999 to August 2000, the minimum lending rate dropped to zero. The Bank of England base rate was 7.25 per cent in 1997. It was reduced to 4 per cent in 2001 and from 2002 to 2006 it remained at an average of 4.4 per cent per annum. The European Central Bank's official rate was 2.25 per cent on 9 November 2001. It remained under 2 per cent by the end of 2005. The US Fed funds rate on 16 May 2000 was 6 per cent. It was reduced to 3 per cent on 2 October 2001, to 1.75 per cent on 6 November 2002, to 1 per cent on 30 June 2004 and by 2006 it was kept under 5 per cent. It is this period of low interest rates, easy lending, lax financial regulations, and the recycling of massive capital inflows that are blamed for the 2008 financial meltdown.

According to this view, the new financial practices and innovations were the effects of the vast amount of savings, the low rate of returns on fixed income government securities, and the great uncertainty that surrounded the return on stocks after the attacks on the twin towers. One fact remains unchallenged, and that is there was a lot of cheap money. Everything to do with the debt finance became the vogue. It became trendy to turn the cheap money into a high return. All sorts of debt appeared on the market. Consumers financed their ever-increasing expenditures by borrowing. Their borrowing kept breaking the historically high levels over and over again. There was no foreseeable limit to the leveraged buyouts. The US housing market was at the centre of this borrowing and spending spree. The period in question here is from the first quarter of 1998 to the second quarter of 2006. In most industrialized countries, except Japan and Germany, during this period there was an unprecedented inflation-adjusted increase in the housing prices. For this period home prices in Japan and Germany decreased by 25.6 per cent and 11.4 per cent respectively. The highest increase was in Ireland (131 per cent), followed by the UK (112.2 per cent), Spain (108.6 per cent), Switzerland (107 per cent), and France (102.2 per cent). For Australia, Denmark, and Sweden, the inflation-adjusted price increase was close to or above 80 per cent. For Belgium, Canada, Finland, Italy, the Netherlands, New Zealand, and Norway, home prices increased by more than 50 per cent. For the same period, the US home prices increased by 49.9 per cent (Cohen, Coughlin, and Lopez 2012: 361). The data cited above raises one important question and that is if an increase in housing prices in the US for this period was considerably lower than in many other countries, why was it that the financial crisis started from the United States of America?

The Americans lived on credit. The recycling of the huge volume of capital that had made its way into the hands of consumers, particularly the home buyers, was one of the underlying causes of the housing bubble in the US. This sharp rise in US household debt during 2003–2006 is mostly attributed to mortgage and the home equity line of credit (HELOC). These two forms of household debt increased from $3.3 trillion in 1999 to about $10 trillion by 2008 (Haughwout et al. 2019: 33–34). The 2007–2008 crisis is dubbed as a credit crunch – implying that the root cause of the crisis was the credit but most specifically housing sector credit in the US. The actual offender is said to be the subprime mortgage. In Britain and subsequently many other countries, the housing sector went under considerable changes from the beginning of the 1980s with the coming into power of the Thatcher government in the United Kingdom. The Conservative Party under the leadership of Mrs Thatcher opposed not only a state-centred economy but the traditional conservatism in Britain. Thatcher in one of her speeches defined the core tenet of her Conservatism as the belief "in popular capitalism … in property-owning democracy" (Thatcher 1997: 262).

Thatcher's "property-owning democracy" was not a new way of thinking. The Russian Bolsheviks, except for a very general puffed up idealistic economic order, did not have any clear view of their socialist economy. By discarding the economic theory that was applied in the most advanced industrialized economies, they continued fumbling around with their idealistic fantasies. Eventually, they settled down for the soviet command economy where the resources were centrally planned and the economic priorities were set and monitored by the communist party. One of the conservatives' responses to this type of administration of economy was the property-owning democracy. The genealogy of the phrase goes back to a Scottish Journalist and Unionist MP, Noel Skelton (1880–1935). Skelton argued in order to eradicate the appeal to socialism and prevent workers from joining the communist movements, the Conservatives cannot go far without some drastic political and economic reforms. His alternative to bring the rise of Bolshevism under control was the "property-owning democracy." This alternative economic system is organized around property and characterized by small agricultural holdings, profit sharing, and cooperative management (Ortolano 2019: 222). Thatcher's government adopted the property-owning democracy as the pinnacle of her core political ideology. This core principle was not better implemented in any of her economic policies than her housing policies. In 1980, a year after coming to power, the Housing Act was passed by the Parliament, and enacted and put into force on 3 October 1980. The Act launched Thatcher's scheme of the "right to buy." The Act allowed tenants of council homes to buy their homes at discounted rates. The transfer of the state-owned homes into private ownership was the largest and most publicized Conservative privatization scheme. By 1992, 1.7 million council homes were sold off to the private owners, adding over £24 billion to the state's coffers (Parker 2009: 433). The privatization programme took off from Britain in the 1980s and it spread to the rest of the world in the following decades. But it took a different form in the US and was an important contributory factor in fuelling the property price mania, which ended in the 2008 credit crunch.

The orthodoxy of reversing nationalization policy quickly spread to the rest of the world. It became a remedy for all economic ills. Tables were turned. The state-centred economy became the source of all social and economic evils and privatization of public enterprises is the only panacea to do away with all the economic ills. Privatization was the cause of action.

Provided that the antidote, privatization, is administered correctly, the economy can be returned to health and economic ills on all fronts can be cured. The states, ranging from liberal democratic to extreme despotic, theoretic to communist totalitarian, all opted for this policy. It all went down in the name of economic justice and efficiency. This all happened in the name of helping the lower social groups. In the US economy where the public sector does not hold a similar position as in nations with many decades of social democratic or communist domination, the policy of privatization took a different form. The essence of the policy, however, stays the same. This policy was implemented most clearly in the housing sector of the economy. The homeownership was the beginning and the end of the neoliberal economic policy for dismantling government regulations and a pious wish for individuals at fringes of the society to get rich quickly.

Before proceeding further, it is necessary to say a few words about the proportion of disposable income that is used for consumption. The largest proportion of the disposable incomes of the population in each country is used in consumption. The more advanced and wealthier a country is, the lower the marginal propensity to consume (MPC) of its population compared to less developed and poorer countries. But for those who can afford to buy a house, one of the biggest items in their consumption basket is the payment of the mortgage. In 2018, the median mortgage and rent burden as a share of disposable income was above 30 per cent in Finland; around 30 per cent in Norway, the Netherlands, Denmark, and the UK; and above 25 per cent in Australia, Switzerland, Canada, Spain, and France. For the US, it was above 25 per cent of the gross income. For Germany, Japan, and Ireland, it was more than 20 per cent (OECD 2019). This small sample adequately reflects the proportion of households' income that is used for their housing expenditure in the developed world.

## Altruistic or self-serving subprime mortgage

The main thrust of the mortgage is democratic. However, like other good economic instruments, a mortgage can be misused and abused. The core idea behind a mortgage is that if a household or an individual wishes to buy a home, they can – even if they do not have sufficient savings to pay the price of the home at once. Some forms of mortgage, not as a functioning market, existed even in ancient times. The six primary requirements for the rise of the phenomenon of the mortgage have been the presence of division of employment, production of surplus product, private property ownership, the law that allowed the exchange of privately owned assets, increase in the urban population, and the institution of market. As a functioning market, the mortgage market is a product of industrialization and the developed market economies. In its most basic form, the mortgagee with a deficit saving will go to a mortgage provider institution, i.e., a bank. If the candidate meets the specific conditions of the mortgage offered, the bank provides them with the loan to purchase the house. The mortgage lender protects its loan, in case of default, by the right to repossess the home to recoup its debt. Thus, a mortgage is a legal contract between the lender of mortgage and the mortgagee. The contract sets out the terms and conditions of the mortgage, the obligations of the borrowers and lenders, the amount of credit, the interest on the mortgage, the monthly payment of the mortgage, the renewal of the mortgage, and so on.

The mortgage markets and instruments have evolved over time. The legal and institutions in which these markets operate and the instruments that are traded are not what they were in the same country and vary across countries. The term "mortgage" literally means "dead pledge." The terms "mort" and "gage" came from old French into the English language in the fourteenth century. The words stand for "dead" and "pledge." The term was used for one form of pledge whereby the pledgee, the Pawnee of the land, kept the return from land irrespective of the payment of a debt. The term mortgage corresponded to a dead pledge because the control of land was passed from the owner of the land to the pledgee and the return on land went to the pledgee than to the owner of the land. Like most terms, over time, the term "mortgage" has lost its original meaning. It does not designate what it did in the past. The term "mortgage" as a legal term that kept its meaning today came into use in the mid-fifteenth century. Mortgage stood for money borrowed on interest to buy a property. The origin of the mortgage as an economic act goes back to a lien upon the property. In every society based on the division of employment, a class structure, and established private property ownership, a charge, a claim, or a security on property one way or another had existed. Claiming a form of security upon purchase of property purchased on credit has evolved over time to the present-day modern complex mortgage markets.

To pledge collateral to secure a loan goes back to ancient times. All sorts of assets, forms of protection against default, have also been used. The borrower defaults on the loan payments, which, in many cases, has resulted in the enslavement, imprisonment, or execution of the person liable for the payment. A mortgage cannot exist without liability. It is a deed with an attached set of conditions. A mortgage contract is a legal deed. It pledges land and a lien upon real estate with a proviso that the land and the real estate go into control of the pledgee. Given the period of time, the pledgee would pay to the lender of the land a certain amount of money in a specified time period until the contract reaches its redemption date. Upon default the contract becomes inoperative and the lender is entitled to repossess the land. A mortgage dead on land is only a pledge when the pledgee takes the possession and the transaction is a pawn. In the event that the pledgee does not take possession the pledge of land is hypothecation. The economic agents borrow money from mortgage institutions to buy a home or other real assets. The mortgage institutions put the terms and conditions of this contract in the paper, in a mortgage deed, which they keep. The mortgage contract specifies the terms and conditions of contract and how much of the principal and interest the holder of the home should pay each month and in the event of default who will get the home.

The major difference between the ancient and the contemporary mortgage contracts is that the latter contracts can be used as financial securities. These are self-serving mercenary contracts. They cross over the financial institutions worldwide as fortune hunters. In the event of default, whoever has the mortgage contract in their possession will get the home. These layers upon layers of selling and reselling of the mortgage securities, i.e., lending and re-lending, takes the contracts farther and farther away from the initial borrowers and lenders. The practice in itself is not new but the number of times the mortgage security has changed hands around the globe is very recent. This practice of selling and reselling mortgage securities got out of hand and led to the formation of the subprime mortgage market. A functional mortgage market has limits and direction. If an economic agent does not have a well-paid permanent job, good credit history, and sufficient collateral security in a workable market, they would not be able to get a mortgage. The practice of low-risk and high-return trend that started some years before the credit crunch replaced the traditional mortgage market. The housing market altered in such a way that the rate of return in investing in the purchase of a home surpassed the rate of return on equity, bonds, and other assets. The higher the demand for homeownership, the bigger the housing bubble became. The more bets on the continued increase in house prices, the greater the return on buying homes compared to the rate of returns on other assets. This process of a self-fuelling surge in demand for home purchase catapulted the home prices through the roof in many industrialized economies. To secure a greater portion of bonanza, under such circumstances, all sorts of claims by the upright and the swindlers will be made about their new discoveries and innovations. These claims are expressed in grandiose expressions and are marketed by flamboyant characters ostentatiously in a very garish and splashy manner in order to entice rather than to inform.

One of these showy innovations in the mortgage market was the Mortgage-Backed Securities (MBS). This market was initiated by big financial institutions. These institutions securitized mortgages. They bought numerous mortgages of varying amounts and risks, bundle these mortgages together, and then sold them around the world. The MBS were presented as a great innovation. This was a new discovery of the finance alchemists. A new panacea that transmuted the illiquid assets into liquid securities that secured higher returns for its investors. Like other securities, the MBS changed hands from one investor to another until the initial transactors became irrelevant. The question is, why the MBS succeeded to generate higher returns and allured many to invest in this market? The higher return was not an illusion. The market participants, both from the demand and the supply side, were making good money out of this market. For those who were making good money and those who looked at the past data, investing in MBS proved to be a safe and very rewarding investment. Home prices skyrocketed and yet kept increasing.

The policymakers, media, and academic establishment overwhelmingly were behind the trend. They either encourage the trend or did everything in their power to safeguard the status quo. For the mortgage holders, if the worst came to worst in the case of mortgagee's default, they could repossess the house and sell it at the market price.

The MBS was not an insulated case. Different tentacles, claws, paws, arms, limbs, antennas, sensors, and fangs of the market supported each other to push the home prices into ever-higher levels. Every element of the market benefited from the housing bubble. One of these elements that profited from the buoyant MBS market were the credit rating agencies such as Moody's, Standard & Poor's, Fitch, A.M. Best, and others. The moral stance of the credit rating industry, on paper at least, is drawn from the protection of consumers' rights. They were founded to be the voice of consumers and to encourage the efficient functioning of the financial markets at large. With this moral weight on their side, it was expected from them to moderate the information asymmetry between investors and financial institutions, to enforce voluntary regulation in the credit market, to cut the cost of borrowing and lending by increasing efficiency, accountability, and transparency in the market, and hence to perform a public function. The house buyers were enticed by higher returns and a belief in the point of no return and were assured by credit rating agencies that the mortgage-backed securities are safe bets to invest. In such circumstances, no one could dare to denounce the commonly held view. The investors were enchanted by the glitz and opulence of those who got famously rich so quickly doing the same bets and intoxicated by the information supplied by the credit rating agencies, the pundits, and governments about the promising future ahead.

A credit rating company can be a public service if it provides objectively and independently a consistent standard comparison of the debt obligations and the issuers of debt. Independent agencies, in the case of mortgage-backed securities, would offer impartial and reliable information on the risks associated with tranches of mortgage-backed securities and the issuers of such securities. By assigning accurate, objective, and independent credit risk, both the issuers of the securities and the investors in securities can evaluate the level of risks attached in each tranche and then act upon it. But the whole scheme of credit rating agencies rested on a lopsided foundation. The problem with such an economic institution is internal. It is inherent to the institution of the market itself. The fact of the matter is that there can be no market in the absence of pursuit of self-interest. The pursuit of self-interest is one of the most critical forces in the absence of which the market regresses and stagnates. But at the same time, each market is composed of two forces with conflict of interest. Thus, the market would cease to exist if all of the interest falls on one side of the conflict. Without recognition of these facts, there can be no practical and viable solution to matters of this nature. The problem with the fiasco of the credit-rating agencies in the equation of the 2007/2008 global credit crunch was that the weight of interest skewed much on the sides of financial product providers and credit agencies. These institutions relied on each other and were mutually reinforcing and promoting their reciprocated interests. On the opposite side to this joint taskforce were the customers. The subprime mortgages were designed in the name of marginalized customers but not to serve the interests of these customers. The credit rating agencies' top priority was not to help the investors to find out the actual risks associated with each risk but to misinform the investors by giving high credit ratings such as triple-A or triple-B to very risky debt instruments.

The reliance of investors on credit rating agencies increased with greater intricacy and expansion of the credit markets. The grades, from the highest to the lowest, did not reflect the actual risk associated with different financial products. In the same way, other grades gave the investors a false sense of security. The rating was misleading. Incorrect ratings benefited the rating agencies and the issuers in the short run. It boosted the sale of the securities. The rise in demand for the financial products generated larger profits for the issuers and sellers of the products. Not only that but it also increased the value of securities. This self-fulfilling mutually rewarding policy between the rating agencies and the security issuers created a parasitic web of beneficiaries that lived merely on fees. The credit-rating agencies were paid by issuers of the securities rather than the buyers of securities. The conflict of interest existed between customers, on one side, and, on the other side, the credit rating agencies and the issuers of securities. For this reason, the rating agencies could not be partial. It was in the interest of the agencies to collude with the issuers against the interest of customers.

The problem was structural. Not just that, the problem was not restricted to the miss-rating of securities. The agencies heavily relied on past data as being science-based knowledge. The forecast based on the past charts and data up to the time of the collapse of markets can give no other information than the prospect of higher demand and prices. This method of forecasting rests on inductivism. In this method, the past is projected into the future. However, the future is never the same as the past. David Hume in the eighteenth century had discussed the knowledge that is constructed by the means of the inductive method. He demonstrated that the inductive knowledge lacks universality. Along the same lines, Bertrand Russell (1872–1970) used his example of the inductivist Turkey to mock the inductivist proof. Concluding from his experience of being fed every morning at a certain time, the trusting Turkey was expecting the same on Christmas day. Instead, the time he expected to be fed on Christmas day, he was beheaded. Besides, tracing the origin of all credits passed through different hands and institutions, serving different purposes at different times and places, is simply impossible.

Around the time when there is an increasing demand for more securities, any hesitation means losing money. Reluctance to act on time means your competitors gain greater market share. It was in this contest of who makes most of what was on offer that lenders created more and more of MBS securities. For additional securities, they needed more mortgages. In simple terms, the mortgage lenders had to lend to those economic agents who were below the standard required in the past. This is what they did. Lowering the established standards in society requires compliance with the prevailing social, economic, legal, moral, and cultural norms. Making loans to economic agents with very poor credit history had to have its legitimacy to fulfil the above requirements. The tidal waves of credit creation overstepped such requirements. The result was the subprime mortgages. These credit instruments were introduced as very noble innovations. For the idea to gain some sort of legitimacy, the motive was prescribed as altruistic, an act of generosity to help the poor to own a house and create a home-owning democracy.

Angelo R. Mozilo, the co-founder of Countrywide Financial Corporation, and its former chairman with the slogan of "we house America" promoted this market. Before long, he became a man of mark, venerated in the circle of finance. Mozilo presented himself as a public-spirited saviour, champion of the poor and minority groups. He became the tycoon of subprime mortgage markets. His corporation was America's biggest mortgage lender. The Country Financial Corporation, in the name of affordable loans to low-income or even no-income borrowers, "issued close to $100 billion in sub-prime loans" (Hanson and Essenburg 2014: 51). However, his greed for money outpaced his sanity. Right after the downfall of the market, he went out of favour. The biggest mortgage lender in America collapsed. The Countrywide borrowed $11 billion in August 2007 to pay for its toxic mortgages. The end came on 11 January when the Bank of America bought the Corporation for $4 billion in stock. The former chairman of Countrywide Financial when the market was in full swing described himself "as a tough guy, a son of a bitch" (Forbes Nov 2000). In his email to Sambol on 17 April 2006, he wrote that "in all my years in the business, I have never seen a more toxic product." Mozilo was not the only one behind the steering wheel of the toxic finance who knew about the scale and scope of toxic products. All those at the helm of the world finance were fully informed of the facts.

The dominant culture of finance is making money by every means. Making money, not the people, is the end. To make money in every way is the end. People are only the means for this end. In this order of priority, humanism diminishes to ashes. It is no wonder that there has always been wide support for the deregulation of financial markets from the leaders of this industry. The doctrine of laissez-faire, the faith in the unfettered pursuit of private profit as a form of natural economic order, is much stronger in this sector than in any other permissible sector of the economy. In financial affairs, legal and moral principles and instructions are seen as secondary and coercive measures that spoil the stewardship of rational profit-seeking individuals. The ethic of the world of finance is based on social Darwinism. In mimicking natural science and Darwin's theory of evolution by natural selection, the advocates of unregulated financial markets aim to give the practice of unrestricted making money by any means a scientific validity. The finance environment is seen as a natural ground of competition and a ground of social Darwinian war of attrition. Financial markets are projected as a great battlefield of natural selection that is locked in a perpetual and relentless vicious struggle for life and death. In this conflict, the inferior, weak, and unfit individuals and markets are eliminated and the fittest survive and rule. This is what they call natural progress, and the elites, the Capitan of finance and the leading companies, are the fittest since those who survive by employing any means are innately superior. Financial Darwinism rests on a cult of personality. Those individuals who arise on the top employ any means to get there. However, their position is secured by a herd of blind worshipers who idolize these individuals in order to be considered in their leaders' good book. The mob chastened in this sect would elevate their leaders to the pantheon of gods and who can rule supreme. At the core of financial Darwinism, we have the ideal of eugenics. Eugenism is logged in the heart of unethical finance. The practice shows its bare bones during financial crisis. One of these elites, an idealized captain of finance, who ruled supreme was Dick Fuld. He was the last chairman of Lehman Brothers, then the fourth largest investment bank in the US.

Henry Lehman (1822–55), a German immigrant, founded Lehman Brothers in 1844. Dick Fuld started his working career in 1969 and worked for Lehman Brothers for over 39 years. In November of 2003, he became the chief executive of the company. To those who worked under him, he was known as the "Gorilla … the scariest man on Wall Street" (Irwin 2009: 78). In 1993 the company was in the loss of $102 million. From the time that Fuld became the chief to the end of 2007, the turnover of the company went to $4.2 billion and for one year his earnings as the head of the company exceeded $70 million (Irwin 2009: 78). He was obsessed with self-adulation and a star in the financial world. His employees feared him and others who were seeking his income and position envied him. Fuld ascended to a cast of personality and was simply untouchable. His words were the last commands. A speech in one of the company's internal videos is most illuminating about his pathological narcissistic personality. The tone and the temperament of speech are sadistic. His speech reminds one of the rant and rave of a deranged dictator. He addressed the traders who, in his view, were trying to bring down the prices of the company stocks. He said he would "rip out" their hearts and eat them "before they die" (quoted from Freese 2020: 210). Autocracy in its every form is hinged on a personality cult. It is often tinted with a morbid and frightful tone of preaching. All tyrants are egomaniacs. They are driven by religious vows and do all they can to conquer and reclaim what is perceived in their opinion to be lost. They suspect everyone and live under the constant shadow of fear.

The house prices kept decreasing in the US but Lehman Brothers under command of Fuld continued to originate subprime mortgages. From the fiscal year 2006 to the end of the fiscal year 2007, Lehman Brothers doubled its holding of real estate assets and securities, raising it to $111 billion. The firm was in a very precarious situation. Any rumour could destroy it. The financial tsunami crashed those firms that were most exposed. In September 2008, Lehman Brothers filed for bankruptcy. Its toxic assets amounted to $630 billion. This was the biggest victim of the credit crash and the largest of a brokerage firm in the US with 25,000 employees worldwide (Irwin 2009: 81).

The subprime mortgage was an era of lax home loan and economic boom that has made almost anyone qualified to be a mortgage holder. This was a period when mortgage providers were more concerned about selling a greater number of mortgages than the requirements of payment. The mortgage providers were ready to offer their service even if you could not afford to pay the interest on the loan. The highest monetary authorities also encouraged this policy. The leading central banks were independent institutions by this time. An independent central bank, it was believed, would end the boom-bust cycles in the economy. In contrast, they did not only end the era of boom-bust cycles but fuelled the housing market boom as other parties in the steering position of the economy did.

The competition in mortgage loans steadily reduced the standard of requirements. Individuals with very poor credit history, low income, or no steady income were provided with a mortgage. The next thing to the subprime mortgages was the predatory loans. This was a scheme designed with the intention of deceiving and entrapping the subprime mortgage borrowers. The terms, condition, and high costs were set so insidiously that subprime mortgages were steered cunningly to default on their mortgages in order that the mortgage lenders repossess their homes. The target of subprime loan providers was low-income groups. In the US, the main targets were poor African-Americans and Latinos. Across America in 2006 and 2007, 27.6 per cent subprime loans went to Hispanics, 33.5 per cent to Blacks, and 10.5 per cent to Whites (Nguyen and Pontell 2011: 9).

## The predatory financial products

Lending on usurious interests is a gripping habit-forming. The more money one lends at higher interest rates, the stronger will be the desire for lending more at higher rates. Parasitic and mercenary loan dealers do mushroom at the time of great uncertainty and freakish economic activities. Predatory financial products flourish under these circumstances. Very attractive phrases are used to conceal the facts about these products. The collateralized debt obligation (CDO) is one of these products. The CDO is a generic term. These are leveraged loans that designate one type of asset securitization. Different financial institutions take part in this market. Investment banks structure CDOs and pension funds, insurance companies, hedge funds, and commercial banks use them in their portfolios of assets for hedging. The Special Purpose Vehicle (SPV) issues CDOs. Each CDO is linked with a particular SPV and different SPVs issue different CDOs in the capital markets. The height of the CDO market was in 2006. It was in this year that globally over $550 billion CDOs were issued (Bouteille and Coogan-pushner 2013: 283).

The collateralized debt obligation is a misleading term. On the surface, a CDO is a hedge investment. It is intended to protect one's returns on certain assets from the risk of losing value. The least it could do, as a risk management strategy, is to offset the exposure to the crippling adverse price volatility, i.e., retaining a relative safety against any loss. Either way, as in what the term conveys or as in the intention behind the product, the information stipulated in the designate is misleading. The CDOs are engineered debt securities. These are by-products of data handling and sophisticated information technology. The CDOs are credit derivatives. The real intention of packaging different debts into tranches is three things. It means the propagation of credit from the same loan. That is, breeding more loans from the same loans. It means increasing the overall debt and the leverage ratio in the economy. The problem is not the creation of credit from credit but not knowing the limits of the proliferation of credit from one loan. Creating credit from the same loan oblivious of its limits will precipitate the risk of the credit crunch, as the greater the leverage ratio in the economy, the greater the number of interest rates charged. The CDOs, as in credit derivatives, detach series of debt from their original debt. There is not a dependable way to detect and know the original source of such debt instruments. These instruments seem to work so long as the economy is expanding and asset prices will keep rising. But this period cannot go forever. Any serious setback in the economy can be very destructive. Third, the CDO market contrary to widely held views is primarily a speculative market.

Another hermetically sealed and mystic term is the Credit Default Swap (CDS). The financial alchemists of JP Morgan in the mid-1990s brewed and engineered this financial instrument. It was the invention of a young team of driven individuals with strong mathematical backgrounds, eager to strike it rich with their new invention. They fudged this financial wizardry disinterested in its unintended effects. The CDS was introduced to redistribute credit risks. There are two sides to this derivative contract: the seller of a CDS and the buyer of a CDS. In the event of default, the seller of a CDS, a bond, or any other type of loans will recompense the buyer of the loss. The CDSs were marketed as an insurance policy that guarantees protection against risk. Initially, banks used it to transfer credit risk exposure, and soon it found its way to the portfolios of the rest of participants in the financial markets. The two elements of a CDS contract are the company, i.e., the reference entity, and the credit event. The two sides of the contract are the protection purchaser and the protection seller. That being said, a CDS works as follows: the loss that occurs as a result of a credit event in any particular reference instrument is paid to the protection buyer by the protection seller. For this protection, the protection buyer agrees to pay regular periodic payment to the protection seller. The contract gives the buyer the right to receive the face value from the protection seller in case of a default. The advantage of a CDS to the seller of protection is to have access to liquidity and cheaper money.

On the face of it and intuitively, a CDS is a very attractive financial instrument. When it works, it makes good money. The market for CDS financial instruments took off very quickly after its invention. The global value of the CDS market in 1998 was estimated to be around $300 billion and JP Morgan owned about $50 billion of this amount (O'Malley 2015: 150). The notional value of the market increased to $62 trillion in 2007. This meant that the face value of underlying assets of the CDS market that year was $8 trillion more than the world GDP, which was about $54 trillion (Nanto 2009: 30). The CDS market is blamed, as one of the contributory factors, for the global credit crash of 2008. It is blamed for being a high-risk financial instrument and for the misconduct of the stakeholders in the market, i.e., for mishandling of the market. It is held responsible for its complexity and lack of knowledge of most participants in the market, including the regulators. It is blamed for encouraging greed and creating a very obscure and esoteric market that made it hard to see what goes on behind the scenes. Above all, the CDS enabled many financial companies such as JP Morgan to keep some of their debt off the balance sheet. These companies sold trillions of tranches of derivative securities worldwide, composed of loans of every credit ratings (Ferrell et al. 2010: IX). When the tide was reversed, these companies found themselves to be in very serious difficulty. The mishandling of their debt instruments caused the worldwide tsunami that its ripples were felt in every corner of the global financial system.

The CDS market encouraged the subprime mortgage market. One critical factor in the sharp rise in the volume of CDOs was the invention of the CDS financial instruments. The CDS emerged seemingly as insurance protection for the subprime mortgages and the CDO market. The world's largest insurance company provides insurance protection for these securities. The fact that the largest company provided insurance protection meant that the public and the smaller companies considered these securities to be safe. American International Group (AIG) prior to the 2008 financial crisis was the largest insurance company and the largest issuers of CDS in the world (Wolff 2012: 55). The American Asiatic Underwriters, later renamed to AIG, was founded in 1919 in Shanghai. Judging from its size one could not get a safer insurance provider at the height of its glory. At the outset of the crisis, the company had over 80,000 employees in 130 different countries (Ciment 2010: 29). The company provided insurance protection to over 100,000 entities worldwide. Its policyholders, just in America, were more than 375 million. The face value of this market alone amounted to $19 trillion (Rosenberg 2010: 9). Yet, the company invested heavily in toxic debts. It issued too many securities covered by credit default swap. As the housing market plummeted, the largest issuers of CDS were caught in the tentacles of its bad debts. The world's largest insurance company became one of the world's largest bailouts. On the brink of its collapse, in September 2008, the Fed authorized a bailout package of $85 billion and seized the control of the company to prevent its bankruptcy and the ultimate havoc that it might have caused throughout financial markets. The AIG reported a record loss of $7.8 billion for the first quarter on 9 May 2008. On 7 August it reported $5.4 billion for the second quarter and for the third quarter a loss of

$24.47 billion. In total, the AIG bailout came to $153 billion, the largest recipient of the bailout funds in history (Rosenberg 2010: 9).

One financial instrument, which is assigned as the fundamental cause of the 2008 global credit crash, is over-the-counter derivatives. The global financial crisis unwrapped many inner conundrums of the over-the-counter (OTC) derivatives. An OTC derivative is privately negotiated through a dealer contract between two counterparties. It is a trading contract that takes place outside any intermediary, i.e., an exchange. Among the OTC securities traded are different types of exotic derivatives, exotic options, swaps, and forward agreements. Just like other types of derivatives, the value of the OTC derivatives is determined by the price of the underlying assets. The derivative products that were traded directly over-the-counter basis had two major drawbacks. First, these trades took place outside a centralized exchange. This was a territory with no jurisdiction, and one's reach went as far as the range of one's hegemony in the global market. This meant that the OTC derivatives markets, by and large, were unregulated.

In the same way that the 1929 Great Depression was the tipping point for major financial reforms such as the Glass-Steagall Act, the 2008 global credit crunch was a critical juncture for the re-examination of activities of financial markets and institutions. The post-2007–2008 crisis period resulted in two notable financial legislations to regulate financial markets in general and the OTC derivatives markets in particular. In the US, it was the Federal legislation, the Dodd-Fran Wall Street Reform, and the Consumer Protection Act. This law was enacted on 21 July 2010. In Europe, it was the European Market Infrastructure Regulation (Regulation No 648/2012, EMIR), which came into force in August 2012 within the EU member states (McBride 2010 and Alexander 2019: 275). These regulations are mandatory. The overall aims of these regulations are to reduce the range of cross-border shadow trading and banking, manage the scope of tax evasion, and mitigate systematic financial risks and the level of financial volatility. With respect to the OTC derivatives markets, these legislations intended to remove the loopholes in the market. Hence, the OTC trades are subjected to a level of standardization required for derivatives that are traded in centralized exchanges and electronic trading settings. That is, they are subjected to capital requirements, the exchange, and clearing obligations. The compliance with these regulatory requirements is intended to improve transparency, price discovery, and to control the unregulated growth of the OTC derivatives markets. The number of outstanding OTC derivative contracts worldwide in 1990 was about $3.45 trillion. By the end of 1994, 1999, and 2004, it increased to $11.3, $88.2, and $248 trillion respectively (Tsingou 2006: 168). The global notional amount outstanding at the end of 2007 increased to US$516 trillion and it kept increasing to $683 trillion in the first half of 2008. Thereafter, the crisis caught the OTC sector and the contracts started to fall (Scalcione 2011: 29).

Northern Rock was the signifier of a global credit crunch in Britain. The origin of the bank goes back to 1850. It was founded when a group of shopkeepers in Newcastle upon Tyne set up a mutual building society. Over years many small and big building societies were merged with the Northern Rock in the northeast regions of England. For most of its history, the society remained a mutual business organization, owned by its members, deposited the savings of its members, and provided mortgages to its buyers. In 1997 all that changed. The Northern Rock building society became a bank. It was demutualized and was listed on the London stock exchange. By July 2007 it became the fifth largest mortgage lender in Britain. The extraordinary growth of banks from 1997 to 2007 and their ultimate downfall are closely linked with one individual, Adam J. Applegarth. He joined the bank in 1983 and became its chief executive in 2001. Over the course of ten years, 1997–2007, the bank's loan portfolio went up from £16 billion to £101 billion. Its share of the UK's residential mortgage increased from 6 per cent to 20 per cent. The bank also adopted a very aggressive policy of mortgage lending, i.e., six times a homebuyer's income and 125 per cent of the value of the home (Das 2011: 200). The bank's share of the UK home loan market increased to 14.5 per cent by 2006. In the second half of the same year, its profit increased by more than 50 per cent and its share price by 25 per cent. By mid-2007, it had 800,000 customers in its mortgage list. Its mortgage lending during the first half of 2007 amounted to £17.4 billion, 37 per cent more in the course of a year (Gilbert 2010: 118).

Prior to 1997, the bulk of Northern Rock liabilities consisted of retail deposits. The bank changed its loan model. It moved away from retail deposits and relied more and more on the wholesale money markets and the securitized markets as the main sources of its liabilities. One function of banks is the maturity transformation of loans. They borrow short-term loans and lend medium- and long-term loans. However, the retail deposit market and short borrowing in money markets and long lending in capital markets are not of the same nature. Nor are the implications of the sources of these borrowings and lendings the same. Northern Rock aggressively added to its assets by rolling over large-scale short-term borrowing in the money markets. The more it kept its distance from retail deposits and relied more on overnight, short-term borrowing, and mortgage-backed securities, the more it became exposed to interest rate shocks and the drainage of liquidity in the system. For the years 2005 and 2006, about 50 per cent of bank's short-term wholesale money market borrowing had less than one-year maturity. Its total liabilities in June 2007 consisted of 23 per cent retail deposits, 44 per cent securitized notes, and 25 per cent short-term wholesale money market borrowing. The remaining portion consisted of covered bonds and other securities (Whitehead and Scanlon 2012). Northern Rock's funding structure was not sustainable in the long run. Its leverage in 2007 was between 60:1 and 80:1. To make the matter worse, the bank did not hold many of its mortgage loans on its balance sheets (Chick 2020: 357).

Taking advantage of arbitrage opportunity of lower interest rates on short-term loans and the higher interest rates on long-term loans can work well in limited circumstances. Provided that the economy is expanding, the external situation stays the same and the rates of interest on both short- and long-term loans remain unchanged, then the arbitrage opportunity runs relatively well. But the financial system by its very nature is a fragile setup. It rests on precarious layout, on trust. Any meaningful economic shock can disturb this fragile order. Northern Rock was exposed to a major economic shock and an increase in interest rates. The first ripple in an economic downturn is not the most damaging incursion but it is most destructive to the heavily indebted firms. As the first wave of the credit crunch hit the Northern Rock, the rush for the exit had trickled to every fibre of its funding structure. The bank's debt-maturity mismatch was exposed. The bank's depositors lost confidence in the bank. The depositors rushed and queued outside the bank to withdraw their deposits. The decline in house prices in the US ignited the mistrust through financial markets. Northern Rock was one of its first victims. The highly leveraged and highly dependent institutions on short-term wholesale money market securities were among the first casualties of the credit panic. The money markets' stream of liquidity froze and Northern Rock was exposed. As the sources of short-term financing were drained, it turned to the Bank of England for help. Robert Peston, then the BBC's business editor, broke the news of the bank's financial difficulties and the Bank of England rescue plan on 13 September 2007. The run on the bank followed in the ensuing days. The bank's clients panicked and formed long queues outside banks' branches to withdraw their savings. The last run on a bank before Northern Rock run in Britain was in 1866 with Overend Gurney. Northern Rock was nationalized in February 2008.

Those top executives who brought their financial institutions to bankruptcy in Britain also did well during the crisis. The ratio of the pay to top executives compared to their employees in 2007 in Britain was 98:1. The top ten executives received £70 million in 2006 and £140 in 2007. Their pay increased to £170 million in 2008. During the worst year of FTSE's performance, 2008–2009, the directors of 100 leading companies had a 31 per cent increase in their salaries. When Adam Applegarth left Northern Rock, he was paid £750,000 and got £2.5 million for his pension (Pugh 2012: 388).

It is difficult to establish the origins of historical events exactly. Precise dating based on the chronology of absolute dates is nearly impossible. By the same token, there is not a generally accepted fixed date of the origin of the 2007–2008 global credit crunch. Several timelines and dates of the origin of the crisis have been suggested that link the first signs of the crisis to a few years before 2007 (Hutter and Lloyd-Bostock 2017: 68). The problem of the historical chronology of the origin of the crisis is something that will never be established to a fixed date that can be accepted by all scholars. On this issue, there will always be different shades of opinion. The real visible signs of financial difficulties that most scholars refer to as the starting signs of crisis are summer 2007. It was then that the early doubts and concerns were raised on the possibility of the upcoming major financial crisis. On 3 April

2007, New Century Financial in the US filed for bankruptcy. In June 2007, the Bearn Stearns' two hedge funds announced huge losses. On 18 August 2007, Baden-Wuerttemberg Landesbank rescued Sachsen Landesbank, another German bank, from collapsing. On 9 August 2007, BNP Paribas, a French investment bank, stopped three of its hedge funds from working. In the UK, Northern Rock collapsed on 13 September 2007. The common link between these institutions and the subsequent financial institutions that either collapsed or experienced great financial difficulties was the mortgage market. These institutions relied either on the subprime mortgage or the wholesale money markets or on both markets to fund their mortgage lending.

In the case of 2007–2008 global credit crunch, September 2007 was the point of no return. The global financial system is so interconnected that the domino effect became global in a very short time. The ripples did freeze the short-term funds, cascading a chain of reactions and events that advanced into a full-blown global financial crisis. The crisis began in the private sector and in 2010 it spread to the sovereign debt crisis. Countries most affected by the sovereign debt crisis were in Europe. The ratio of public debt to GDP of Greece, the most affected country in 2010, was 136.6 per cent. In Italy, Ireland, Portugal, the UK, and Spain, the ratio was 118.6 per cent, 98.7 per cent, 85.1 per cent, 78.8 per cent, and 63.6 per cent respectively (Subacchi 2011: 72). It is virtually impossible to estimate the lasting adverse effects of such events as the global liquidity crunch on both actual and potential economic growth, investment, income, employment, education, health, welfare loss, and people's confidence. These effects will be long-lived and the estimates offered by various sources only provide a partial picture of reality. In August 2009, the International Monetary Fund estimated the total cost of the credit crunch to be about $11.9 trillion (Sun et al. 2011: 2). In 2010, the total cost of bailing out different financial institutions was estimated to be about $65 trillion (Hain 2015: 53). In June 2009, the World Bank reported about a 3 per cent contraction in the world economy (Das 2011: 9). The global unemployment increased from 172 million in 2007 to 200 million in 2012 (Hasmath 2015: 1). The highest number of unemployed was among the economically active youth, 15–24 year-olds. The number unemployed within this age range was 81 million at the end of 2009. The rate of unemployed in this age group was 11.9 per cent in 2007 and it increased to 13 per cent by 2009. The region that was most affected was the European Union. The rate of unemployed in this group was 6.7 per cent in March 2008 and by May 2009 it increased to 8.9 per cent (Padua 2014: 69).

## Conclusion

It is widely believed that the global liquidity crunch started in 2007 with the collapse of the subprime mortgage in the United States. Subsequently, the credit crunch crisis spread into the rest of the major financial centres. The contagion was rapid. It quickly progressed into the banking and the public debt sectors. Financial motives are infectious. These motives can be negative or positive. One way or the other, they are infective. The most tainting of all motives is the motive of striking it rich. The virulent of making a fortune by any means and with the least effort is irresistible. It comes as a no surprise that the exultation of having the golden touch, the prospect of which amounts to great power and influence and rank, has no boundaries. The drive, vigour, and aptitude would quickly be rounded in order to preserve the power, standing, and glory of the past. But the speed of catching in the case of the financial panics is even more lethal. Financial panics spread like wildfire. This is because those who have made a fortune tend in despair to freeze the time. Deploy all efforts and bid to salvage their fortunes and to avert the unfolding disaster. But the instincts for self-preservation and the attempts of getting out of the crash would exacerbate the process and precipitate the speed of fall. This will in turn stir up greater chaos and self-inflicted financial losses. The purpose to reclaim the past fortunes and restore order does not save the past fortunes. Quite the opposite, it acts as a catalyst that triggers greater self-doubt, uncertainty, and over-pessimism that aggravates the gloomy outlook of business downturns.

During the period from the dawn of 1970–2007 – in the run-up to the global financial crisis – the world of finance had undergone a series of fundamental changes in its structure, forms, functions, and institutions. This radical transformation has reshaped the world of finance. This is the gestation period of the crypto-economy. An emerging economic order that is based on internet technology and electronic communication. The crypto-economy is a new stage in economic development. The exponential growth of the internet is changing the overall structure of the global economy, albeit we are in the earliest stages of the process of crypto-economic development. The economic potential of crypto-economy is immense. The transition from one phase of crypto-economic progress to the next is rapid and its eventual implications are difficult to foresee. The 2007–2008 crisis was the first major crypto-economic crisis.

Due to this transition to the new economy, many of the old economic practices were discarded or rewritten, reworked, and re-engineered. At the turn of the decade, in 1972, the Bretton Woods system of fixed exchange rates collapsed. The price of crude oil per barrel in 1970 was about $3. By 1973 it increased to $12. The period of the economic prosperity of high employment and a low inflation rate of the post-war was over in many industrial economies. In the 1970s, many Western industrialized economies experienced a condition of the simultaneous increase in inflation and unemployment. A combination of high inflation and unemployment, known as stagflation, defied the cornerstone of the Keynesian economic policy. The stagflation ended the supremacy of the Keynesian era. The demise of Keynesian welfare state economy was followed by the resurgence and the revival of the Monetarist and the Austrian schools of economics. Most specifically, the downfall of Keynesian economics reincarnated the quantity theory of money and laissez-faire economic policies. Equally important in the rise of the new era was the 1976 big bang in the US financial services industry and the 1986 big bang in the British financial sector. The big bangs introduced the biggest deregulation reforms in the financial services industry in the second half of the twentieth century. These reforms widened the pattern of liberalization in the financial sector. The growth of the supply-side economics, the monetarist, and the Austrian schools improved with the arrival of Mrs Thatcher's administration in the UK in 1979 and Reagan's administration in the United States in 1981.

These leading countries adopted supply-side economics. The changes were many and far-reaching. The revolution in information technology, combined with the deregulation of financial markets, the third world debt crisis, financial disintermediation, the invention of the internet and its wide variety of applications, the digital age and the rise of e-commerce, and the collapse of the Soviet Union empire, all these changes united by other less visible changes have created a new world economic order. As these changes were disseminated across the world, they have unleashed seismic waves of change in the global social and economic order. This is the age of rapid change. The fast-changing world requires swift adaptability. But human understanding is lagging behind the accelerating pace of change. The world of finance is not an exception to this general direction. The financial sector has been one of the fastest changing sectors of the world economy in the last few decades. There has been an ever-increasing integration of domestic financial markets with the global market. Capital markets have experienced the greatest transformations within a relatively short period of time.

In the last few decades preceding the 2007/2008 global financial crisis, the banks and mortgage lenders engineered very complex mortgage loans. Some terms and conditions of these loans were hidden under coatings of quackery terms and phrases. The mortgage rates for some mortgage loans were set in a way that it was difficult for ordinary people to take in and grasp the unintended consequences of their decisions. The toxic loans benefited every stakeholder, the lenders, the securitizers, the brokers, the market makers, and the mortgagees for several years. The culture of the toxic market prevailed because the market worked for the conductors and the key drivers of the market in the short run.

The increasing recruitment of physicists and mathematicians in the financial world from the early 1980s exacerbated the opacity of many financial products. They did not only improve the "degree of predictability" (Nayak 2013: 255) of markets but made them mistier. Joining these markets was not for an ulterior move. The highest paying occupations were in this sector. At the top, the high ranking executives and CEOs in this sector were and are among the highest paid jobs in the economy. Both cash and bonuses are the sector-driven. They are determined by the captain of the industry. The implications of this system of pay are given as follows: first, the top executive of the industry will decide how much they deserve. Second, the increase in the pay of executives in one competitive firm would spread to the rest of the sector. This often occurs under the disguise of retaining financial wizards and preventing the flight of talented executives. Third, the culture of bonus-driven remuneration promotes taking high risks, undue and hasty short-term decisions, and extreme greed that can be very rewarding in the short term but very damaging in the long term. In the event of an economic downturn when the failing companies file for bankruptcy, their CEOs and top executives who have not prepared their companies for such days and who are responsible for poor decisions, planning, and badly executed decisions and plans will leave their companies with lavish pay packages. A striking example of this in the 2008 financial crisis is referred to as "fat cats" CEOs (Balkin 2008: 200). For instance, Dick Fuld, former chief executive of Lehman Brothers, received $485 million from 2000 to 2007. The final pay to Stan O'Neal, chairman of Merrill Lynch in 2007, was $161 million. John Thain, the CEO of Merrill Lynch, was paid $83 million before he left the company. In the same year, Chuck Price, the Citigroup's chief, left with $38 million, and Barclay's president, Bob Diamond, total pay amounted to £36 million (Siam-Heng and Wei 2009: 70).

# 4 Over-trading, trade cycles, and crises

## Introduction

One cannot lose sight of survival instincts in the living species. The most basic natural drives are the instincts of reproduction and self-preservation. These instincts cannot by themselves be taken to imply a definite distinction between humans and other living species. The striking and most distinctive features of the human species, in comparison with other living beings, are their capacity to invent and discover and to communicate their findings and inventions to each other. These facts raise a question of great importance. Humans not only can invent things that are real but can invent imaginary things and thoughts in imaginary worlds. They can dream, fantasize, and envisage the best and worst of all possible worlds, and can live in false hopes and thoughts. They can invent myths and fairy tales. One of the human's mythical inventions is God. No other living organism has got a God. Humans have invented it. Belief in the supernatural has a far-reaching significance to the conduct of human life. Its invention was one of the most defining chapters in the development of human comprehension of the world and life. The human vision of the world and life before the invention of God and religion is dominated by natural instincts. Their response to the world was perfectly natural. They viewed the world and life through the lens of nature itself. Natural calamities – drought, famine, flood, earthquake, volcanic eruption, tsunami, typhoons, pestilence, and hostilities between rival communities – were interpreted as a natural course of events and order of things. Good times and bad times were entirely natural so were the wax and wane of the times of plenty and scarcity. There is no more to the economy than its highs and lows over the course of time. Nothing in an economy is permanent. The highs and lows in the economy will never leave human species. Economic fluctuations caused by natural events or by human folly were in the past and, in different forms, are at present time. They will be with us in the future. It is all the more important to be clear about such matters as being indispensable to our deeper understanding of the economy to be able to protect ourselves against the unexpected.

This chapter is divided into seven sections. In the first section, we shall look at how humanity departed from their self-inflicted blind conformity and

DOI: 10.4324/9781003346357-5

have made headway to the world of objective understanding. The transition occurred due to the force of circumstances. The mastery of divinity gradually degraded and complied with the mastery of humans. The rise of economics as a scientific discourse owed much to this transition. The Age of Enlightenment was instrumental in the departure of economics from a theistic and divine affair to a worldly matter. Instead of faith in destiny, the early modern writers in economics relied on factual information in search of personal gain and in pursuit of national interest. They have narrowed the main area of their quest down to trade. The central focus of the second section is on over-trading. In a nutshell, it is on abnormal trading. This fact has been recognized by all schools of thought in economics. Mercantilists related the source of wealth and power to trade. They were aware of different systems of trade and knew that in the former times the rudimentary trade systems and policies had existed and were aware that there is no everlasting regularity in trade. This means trade cannot be the same during normal times, times of peace and prosperity, and times of natural, economic, and social disorders and disruptions. By the same token, the physiocrats could not dismiss such possibilities even after regarding trade as a "sterile" activity. To believe otherwise would be to fly in the face of the plain facts. Land is the centrepiece of physiocrats' economic theory and yet trade is not excluded from their overall belief in a natural order. Free trade is consistent with their laissez-faire system. There is a natural order in trade and any interference in this natural order would side-track trade from its natural course. Irregularities in the ebbs and flows of trade reroute the trade from its normal orbit of circulation. In Smith's work, the propensity to exchange is one of human's inborn impulses. Free trade is inbuilt in Smith's idea of natural liberty. In his account, specialization, division of labour, and free trade, all in one unimpeded, are the real causes of the expansion of the wealth of each nation. The irregularities in trade, over- and under-trading, are possible but not at once in all sectors of the economy.

All other members of classical political economy have also drawn attention to over-trading. In Ricardo's interpretation, the removal of capital from one employment to another is the cause of over-trading. In James Mill's account, over-trading is due to the disproportional production of different goods in different sectors of the economy. According to J.S. Mill, it is caused by merchants' speculative orders. On this issue, Malthus was ahead of his contemporaries. His theory of under-trading is a part of his broad ideological perspective. It is an integral constituent of his general standpoint on the human pecking order and their perpetual struggle for food and shelter. In his big picture, the lack of effective demand is the cause of under-trading that can be ameliorated by the consumption of landlords and their servants. Classical political economists have also brought to the notice that overextension of credit may also lead to over-trading. In the third section, we will show how three trends came together to finalize one era in economic ideas. Side by side, they acted as catalysts of immense power in transforming the medieval social, economic, cultural, legal, political, and institutional norms. The impetus that sparked this revolutionary change was the ideas of the natural order, progress, and human struggle for a better life.

Aligned with these real economic and social changes, we have the birth and evolution of the theory of economic crisis. The task of the fourth section is to delve into the very core of the theory of economic crisis, which rests on a set of suppositions. First, that there is not plenty in nature's mighty feats. Second, the ideological divide between those who considered the social and economic hierarchy as being in harmony with the natural order and those who question such social and economic relations. For the latter, poverty in the midst of plenty is not natural. Poverty can be alleviated or even can be eradicated entirely. The concept of capitalism lies at the very centre of this divide, which we shall explore in the fifth section. In this section, we shall reflect on the original model of capitalism and how other forms of capitalism are standing apart from the original model. The last two sections, (sixth and seventh) will disclose the economic and social settings in which the models of capitalism have been laid down. In these two sections, we will tie together the loose ends of the argument presented in this chapter. To this end, we shall explain how all conventional theories of the business cycle and economic crisis are anchored to the concept of capitalism and are subservient to either defending or attacking the presumed economic system.

## Parting with self-imposed blind faith

There is not only one god. In polytheistic religions, multiple gods consist of celestial bodies, atmospheric phenomena, geological structures, rulers, animals, and different types of tokens or idols. These deities are the defining measure of good or bad and true or false for their devotees. With the passage of time, some communities cut down the multiple deities into two super beings. One notable conception of dualism is in the Zoroastrian religion. The two supernatural powers are tied up in a constant battle for the supremacy of good and evil. The malevolent deity is in charge of all malicious things and the benevolent one is in control of the good world. One God was invented much later in human history. Monotheism is mainly a creation of Semitic religions. It was in this ritual tradition that one absolute deity was invented. Everything depends on this all-powerful being – the creator and destroyer of everything everywhere and always.

Admittedly, there has always been some form of catechism in every human settlement. Faith in divinity, in practical life, is not people's central concern but it is the prime target of clerics and the theocratic states. When it comes to the practical life even most devoted individuals to deity prefer a full stomach to idle chatters and hopes hailed from any form of divinity. In cases where religious instruction is the overruling force, the world and everything in it would be viewed through the lens of religious teaching. Human knowledge and rights, science, art, culture, law, economic life, social relations, rules of conduct, one's conscience, all would be pressed under one set of convictions. The world and everything in it would not be seen for what it is but for what religion says it to be. Except for some isolated individual cases, the heretics here and there, human societies until the Age of Enlightenment were tied up to their specific religion or religions. The first most serious contest against the supremacy of religion came during the Age of Enlightenment. Kant singled out this era as the time when humanity was "leaving his self-caused immaturity" and have assumed responsibility for their way of life (Kant 2013). Much in the same way, Enlightenment has laid the groundwork for the foundations of modern economics as it was laid out in Smith's monumental work, the *Wealth of Nations* (1776).

In respect of the economy, one of the concrete accomplishments of this period was the insight that the economy is not entirely out of human control. It is not merely a hostage of the providence. Our economic circumstances and standing are not predestined. The economic arena and relationships are not stationary. In contrast, they can be understood and improved. Along with other developments such as the triumph of reason over myth, modernization over impoverishment, free will over fate, cause and effect over despair, the age of predestination and miracles in economics was over. The world became intelligible, changeable, recoverable, and amendable. In moving away from the domination of non-scientific understanding into a scientific view of the world, the cause-effect relationships played a crucial role in attaining knowledge and in determining and consolidating the scientific methodology. In the chain of cause and effect, one seeks a reason behind the causal nexus and, in effect, casts aside the divine will.

Embedded in the causal link is a firm belief in a structured world. A real world that is governed by the principles of causation. This means all events, matters, and phenomena in the world emerge, develop, and change according to the successions of a chain of cause-and-effect interconnections. So, no deity is the cognizant here. The agent of knowledge and the prime mover is the human being. Adopting the law of causality was the leading light and the guiding thread in breaking ties from the former pseudoscientific methods of inquiry. It was this open and sceptical inquiry that allowed Hume to refute even the validity of *a priori* knowledge based on causal relations. For this reason, the causal connection information marches as far as its circuit of constant conjunction. Yet, without the knowledge of cause-and-effect connections we cannot function because the causal connections "are the foundation of all our thoughts and actions … upon their removal … human nature … immediately perish and go to ruin" (Hume 1974: 216). Apart from that, the causal connections will allow us to "go beyond evidence of our memory and senses" (Hume 1990: 25).

Objective knowledge is sovereign. It is real knowledge, a work of true and valid science. Actual knowledge cannot be attained under the dominion of any forms of divinity. Liberty from all forms of a deity can ensure the supremacy of objective knowledge. Real knowledge is dependable and can be applied. Its application can improve our socio-economic conditions. The early modern writers in economics were conscious of this fact. Consequently, they deserted the kingdom of divinity and probed into the real wonder of trade to plan and implement trade policies. In patterns of buying and selling, in trade, they saw continuous variability. They saw not a straight line but a broken line in trade. Trade was not a straight and neat line of succession of buying and selling. The pattern of trade in reality is not regular, uniform, fixed, stable, and monolithic. It is irregular and constantly changing. This is something that could not and cannot be overlooked. With the expansion of trade, the rate of variabilities in the chain of trade tends to intensify. The early modern writers in economics tried to find out the causes and effects of these irregularities in trade. Thus, they were aware of the occasional tide of over- and under-trade in their contemporary commercial societies.

Whatever there is, broadly speaking, can be divided into living and non-living things. Much like the non-living objects, the living things are very diverse. Just as inanimate objects are classified into groups with similar properties, the animate organisms too are put in different classifications of hierarchies of general and specific features. Humans, animals, and plants are living things. Biogeochemists reckon that there are 25 known elements that are essential for life (Crowe and Bradshaw 2014: 346). All living organisms are composed of cells, which in turn are living matters. All living things need nutrition to obtain energy and for growth. They break down food to release energy to move. They eat, grow, reproduce, get rid of waste, and sense and respond to stimuli. The living things eat, breathe, and have a lifespan. Their lifecycle phases of development consist of birth, growth, and death. These are essential elements of life. These basic chemical and biological elements are indispensable to life. In order to be supplied with the basic needs of food, air, water, habitat, and shelter, living things depend on non-living things. The interactions of animate and inanimate beings shape the environment in which they habitat.

There are so many factors that have made life, as we know it, possible on the earth. For instance, life on the earth would be impossible without the earth's unique atmosphere, sunlight, greenhouse gases, water, oxygen, ATP (adenosine triphosphate), microorganisms, and so on. These factors are vital for life. Life and human society would not exist without these basic primary conditions and factors. However, there is not much we can do about such matters. Granted that such conditions are in place in the right proportion, humans and other living things can continue their existence. There are elements that we can alter to improve our social and economic conditions. Human beings are social beings. One individual can live as long as the basic necessities of life are provided for them. But driving people to live in complete isolation would wipe out the human species in the long run. Humans construct societies, economic systems, legal and political systems, institutions; form moral habits and values; acquire knowledge; invent technologies; and discover the unknowns not only to survive but also to improve their well-being. All these things were not the same a thousand years ago as they are now or will be in the future. On such matters, there is much that humans can do and have done to change their conditions of life. For example, if the whole reality of human life were a ceaseless war, humanity would have been exterminated by now. So, they can do something about it.

Along the same lines, no individual can survive without the provision of a series of biological necessities. The basic biological requirements for life are air, water, food, shelter, excretion of toxic substances and waste products from the body, and right temperature and pressure. No individual can survive without these basic requirements. At its most elementary level, economics is about eating, drinking, breathing, discharging waste products, and shelter. No individual is exempt from these necessities. Given these biological necessities are in their place, an individual can survive a lifetime without society, language, culture, reproduction, moral, legal, political, and aesthetic values, and structure. In the long run, however, the human species cannot survive without these key requirements. Hence, the natural necessities make up the essence of the economy and the secondary requirements of life. That is the fabric of the economy; the means of adaptation, reproduction, and survival. Secondary requirements are the means, the mechanisms by which human species adjust to their changing environment.

Human beings are also bearers of a set of inherent propensities. Among them, we have the capacity to reason, to learn and self-reflection, to invent, to be sad or happy, to be pessimistic or hopeful, to lament or rejoice, to hate or love, to have free will, and to feel sympathy. There are general propensities that we acquire through learning or are imposed on us. Any child is born anywhere is a product of their time and place. They are born with one natural baggage that determined their inborn natural propensities and the rest comes from one's conditions of life and upbringing. The minute a child is born, there is another baggage that contains the specific conditions of time and place that are imposed on them. Individuals have no choice in these matters. Parents and society discard this package on them. Immediately after they are born, they are burdened with the parents' ideas, values, social class, the prevailing culture, religion, rules, and regulations of the place and the time. As people are born with the capacity to learn, reason, and exercise free will, they can adopt different general propensities given their degree of access to education and the level of freedom in their society. As people have free will, there is a purpose and intention behind anything they say and do. All economic disorders and crises are cumulative interactions of all these elements in a given time and place. The way the human crises are expressed, economic or otherwise, will be manifested in one form or another human action.

## From trade to over-trading

Trade occupies a central place in economics. This was the focus of economic analysis of the pioneering schools of thought in economics. Mercantilists were the first in the early modern times who centred their economic studies on trade. The power and prosperity of a country, they said, is in trade. Starting from the assumption that trade is a zero-sum game, they argued that trade needs to be regulated. It should be directed to ensure a favourable balance of trade by encouraging "inflow of treasure" and discouraging imports of goods. This is how the wealth and power of a nation can best be served. The physiocrats, a more structured and orderly school, took issue with this train of thought and logic. The economy in physiocrats' account is a part and parcel of the general natural order of things. Trade, albeit a "sterile" activity, is not outside of this order. In its most natural form, free trade is consistent with the laissez-faire law. In this form, trade stimulates specialization and reduces the cost of production, and encourages cooperation among nations. Different nations can export their surplus products and import goods that they cannot produce cheaper in their countries.

Trade is also central to the works of classical economists. Adam Smith, the founder of classical economics and father of modern economics, in his pioneering book, demonstrated the indispensable position of trade in the market economy. He showed how specialization and division of labour are closely interlinked with both domestic and international trade. Besides this, how trade causes the wealth of nations to expand or contract. In both his major works, Smith put trade the focal point of his idea of "natural order." Trade is said to be in the nature of humankind. In his *Moral Sentiment*, human conduct is grounded on three pairs of natural predispositions. One of them is "the habit of labour and the propensity to exchange." The other two pairs are "self-love and sympathy" and "the desire to be free and a sense of propriety" (Barber 1970: 25). In the *Wealth of Nation*, this natural motive is referred to as the "propensity to truck, barter, and exchange one thing for another" (Smith 1986: 117). Smith tried to connect free trade to his idea of natural liberty. He defended this link with the truism that you should not produce goods at home if they cost you less to buy from abroad. That is, each individual or a country should specialize in the production of goods and services that they have an absolute advantage. David Ricardo was not content with Smith's absolute advantage theory of trade. He presented a more compelling theory of trade and demonstrated that trade can be mutually advantageous even if one party has got the absolute advantage in the production of both goods traded. Ricardo proved that there is a base for trade as long as the ratios of comparative cost of producing goods differ between two countries. That is one side in trade can produce a good or service for a lower opportunity cost than its counterparty country.

There is one thing that unites the advocates and the opponents of free trade. Both camps concede to successive ebbs and flows in trade. It is in these ups and downs and back and forth of trade that different interpretations of economic disorder and crisis are founded. In the early modern time, the position of trade in upcoming European nations was captured by Nicole Oresme (c.1320–82), a fourteenth-century French writer. He held trade as a privilege venture for all members of a community. Thomas Mun (1571–1641), like the rest of mercantilist writers, sought the source of the wealth in trade, most specifically in foreign trade (Gomes 2003: 9). For the physiocrats, even though trade was considered a sterile undertaking but without free trade (laissez-faire) their system of natural order was incomplete.

What the pioneering authors of modern economics did was to integrate trade into the natural course of things. The passing abundance and scarcity or prosperity and famine were the integral workings of the economy. It was not out of this world to have more trade at the time of prosperity and less at the time of shortage. The pioneering economists also pointed to the rise and fall of trade that is not caused by natural calamities and referred to such trade fluctuations as over- and under-trading. William Petty categorized such cycles as "dearths and plenties" (Petty 1899: 43, vol. 1). For Smith such abnormalities in trade are the errors that occurred "both among great and small dealers" and he related the cause of this to "when the profits of trade happen to be greater than ordinary" amount (Smith 1864: 177). This kind of irregularity in trade has been recognized by all denominations in economics ever since. In its most basic sense, trade as a linear process defies common sense. The spasmodic nature of trade is something that cannot be unnoticed for too long. Jean-Baptiste Say (1767–1832), who is typically represented as the exponent of perfect market and economic order, also admits to the irregularity in the trade. Say finds the fault in the interruption of the trade from its normal course of trade in either the good in question has been over-produced or other goods have been under-produced. Say states:

> the glut of a particular commodity arises from its having outrun the total demand for it in one or two ways; either because it has been produced in excessive abundance, or because the production of other commodities has fallen short. It is because the production of some commodities has declined, that other commodities are superabundant.
>
> (Say 1971: 134–35)

David Ricardo (1772–1823) accepted the possibility of the "sudden changes in channels of trade" and sought the cause of these "temporary reverses and contingencies" in trade in "the removal of capital from one employment to another" (Ricardo 1846: 159). Moreover, he did not dispute the likelihood of "universal glut" in a single market on the basis that "there might neither be demand for and an additional quantity of such commodities, nor profits on the employment of more capital if men ceased to consume, they would cease to produce" (Ricardo 2006: 199). Ricardo shared the opinion of his close friend and motivator, James Mill (1773–1836), on this point. James Mill had also addressed the same issue and pointed out that "the quantity of any one commodity may easily be carried beyond its due proportion, but by that very circulation is implied that some other commodity is not provided in sufficient proportion" (Mill 1965: 84–85). In his book, *Elements of Political Economy*, he states there is no guarantee that the supply and demand in the market would always match. He stipulated that

> though it be undeniable, that the demand, which every man brings, is equal to the supply, which he brings, he may not find in the market the sort of purchaser, which he wants. No man may have come desiring that sort of commodity, of which, he has to dispose.
>
> (Mill 1821: 191)

Thomas Tooke (1774–1858) linked the cause of "over-trading" to the "extension of credit" (Tooke 1844: 88) and Robert Torrens (1780–1864) related the glut in production of one commodity to delay and stagnation in the production of other commodities – asserting that "a glut of a particular commodity may occasion a general stagnation and lead to a suspension of production, not merely of the commodity which first exists in excess, but of all the commodity brought to market" (Torren 1821: 414).

The belief in temporary economic disorder is not unusual among proponents of classical economists. John Stuart Mill's account of "over-trading" is not materially different from his predecessors. He is just more explicit on the subject where he says

> there may be, at some given time, a very general inclination to sell with as little delay as possible, accompanied with a general inclination to defer all purchases as long as possible. This is always actually the case in those periods which are described as periods of general excess. And no one, after sufficient explanation, will contest the possibility of general excess, in this sense of the word.
>
> (Mill 1844: 70)

The cause of "over-trading" for Mill is merchants' "speculative orders" that encourage manufacturers to increase their production. This enticement would embolden the manufacturers to borrow and expand their operation till the whole speculative trend will end in over-trading.

Thomas Robert Malthus (1766–1834) and Jean Sismondi (1773–1842) were the two eminent scholars of this period (eighteenth and nineteenth centuries) who went one step further in their accounts of the causes of economic fluctuations and over-trading. Marx was inspired by Sismondi and Keynes by Malthus in their theories of under-consumption and insufficient aggregate demand. Malthus and Sismondi, from two opposing ends, detected some intricacies in the emerging economic system that were overlooked by their contemporaries. For the rest what was taking place was in line with the natural order of human progress. Only slight abnormality (occasional over-trading) did not concern them much. For both Sismondi and Malthus, the economic malfunctions were an integral part of the system. Sismondi drew attention to the increasing wealth of the rich. He held that by production or by an appropriation of the wealth of the poor the rich get richer. Either way what the rich would do comes right down to over-production and under-consumption – noting that this type of economic order and arrangement is not sustainable and is doomed to fail one way or another.

Malthus's conception of human nature and society was opposite to that of Sismondi's political standpoint. He considered humankind as species that are in "perpetual struggle for room and food" and the "recurrence of misery" was an inextricable part of this order. Thus, the prevention of "the recurrence of misery" is not in our power to remedy. It is "beyond the power of man."

The higher classes are not only the cause of the problem but are necessary to lighten the misery and the "histories of mankind are histories only of the higher classes" (Malthus 1986: 15, vol. 1). The "menial servants are absolutely necessary" because they "make the resources of the higher and middle classes of society efficient in the demand for material products" (Malthus 1986: 32, vol. 2). Under-consumption is the cause of the market gluts. Malthus enquired "where are we to look for the consumption required" to minimize the effects of this problem. Two classes are qualified for his requirement for this purpose: "the unproductive labourers of Adam Smith" and the "landlords and persons of property" (Malthus 1836: 406). Just like Sismondi, Malthus saw the inadequacy of demand for goods as the cause of the imbalances between aggregate demand and aggregate supply. His other suggestion to mitigate this disparity was "the employment of the poor in roads and public works, and a tendency among landlords and persons of property to build, to improve and beautify their grounds, and to employ workmen and menial servants" (Malthus 1986: 342, vol. 2).

## Consolidation of three trends

The end of the mercantilist, the physiocrat, and the classical era brought three trains of thought into a single track. Time, from the early written works, has been described as either advancing continuously into the future or going around in a circle, or following a natural order that is manifested in an endless struggle of opposite forces. Directing these three trends of thought into one direction has transformed the course of economic ideas. In addition, it has stimulated intellectual curiosity on economic fluctuations and their possible causes. The cyclical and linear times are the dominant views about the direction of time. We find an explanation of the cyclic conception of time in ancient Greek literature, in Hindu, Zoroastrianism, the Chinese, and the Aztec religions. In this account, time is conceived as a ceaseless march of unbroken cyclical repetitions. We find the clearest description of cyclical time in Hinduism. In the Hindu theory of Yugas, manvantaras, and Kalpas, it is said that "the cosmos passes through cycles within cycles for all eternity." In Rg Veda, the year is compared to the wheel of time.

In monochromic reading of time, time is linear. It is unbroken, which begins from infinity and goes on forever. There is one way to go, one-way street nonstop progress into the future. The time here is teleological, it advances into an improved and a desired state. The progress can be in the form of knowledge, moral or material improvements. That is, time consists of configurations of transformation, a tapestry of patterns. Human history is advancing stage by stage into its perfection. We find this view in the work of Hesiod (700 BC) and Toynbee in ancient times. In the sixth century BC, Xenophanes placed the time in hands of Gods who concealed it from the sight of humans, and "in the course of time Through seeking, men find that which is the better" (quoted from Kane 2010: 117). In Protagoras's view, humans break away from ignorance not at once but in time. It occurs gradually by acquiring knowledge, which enables humans to improve their culture and conditions of life. Thucydides demonstrated how the Greeks progressed from barbarism into a great civilization. Plato's distinction of perfect and imperfect worlds is of this nature. For Plato, everything in the real world is the imperfect representation of their forms in the world of ideas. In *The Statesman* and *the Law*, he describes the stages in which human progress unfolds – how their advances to higher stages of living and knowledge will come about. In *Politics*, Aristotle states that these advances are achieved by means of reason. Against this backdrop, he divided human history into four stages of socio-economic formations. A history that begins with kinship, then evolves into a village, a confederation, and then to a political state.

The enduring relevance of the teleological outlook of time has never waned. It continued to be an influential stimulus in every emerging empire. Lucretius (born 94 BC), a Roman Epicurean thinker, in his work, *On the Nature of Things*, showed how the world has evolved from nothing into tangible matters and then to its present form. Lucius Annaeus Seneca, another Roman philosopher, assigned knowledge as the carrying device of human progress. A ladder with its stages of progress that will improve with time. The maker and the conductor of this form of time are human. It is human "ingenuity" that creates and innovates things. Language, farming, navigation, and civilization are among these inventions. In view of these abilities (intelligence, power, and skills), Seneca envisaged a perfect human society that is in making. A time that "will come when mental acumen and prolonged study will bring to light what is now hidden" (quoted from Nisbet 2009: 12). The belief in a linear progression of history was not restricted to Ancient Greco-Roman thoughts. It was also central to the Hebraic faiths. But history in Hebraic faiths has a beginning and an end. History goes through different stages till the last day of judgement. In *The City of God*, St Augustine writes that it is education that advances the human race into higher stages and gradually will raise them "from earthly to heavenly things, and from the visible to the invisible" world (Augustine 1952: 307).

The idea of progress took off at full force in the seventeenth century in Europe. It was wrapped in aspiration of modernity. Modernity was not only desirable but said to agree with the laws of nature. Bernard Le Bovier de Fontanelle (1657–1757), a French essayist in his work *Digression on the Ancients and Moderns* (1688), argued about the supremacy of modernity over former societies. Fontanelle held that while the human mind and its capacity to reason have not changed, their conditions have improved with modernity. So, modernity is a preferred choice rather than turning back to former poorer living conditions.

There was a fundamental shift in the economy of a part of Europe in the sixteenth and seventeenth centuries. A sea change that was in stark contrast to any other period in history. Life and economy were not what they had been in the past. This fact bewildered the inquiring minds of the great thinkers of the period. The quest for the causes of the sweeping changes was the main impetus for uncovering the hidden truth. One of the unsettled questions was whether the changes were accidental or natural. This is how the old and new ideas clashed. The emerging ideas challenged Aristotelian physics, which led to the triumph of Newtonian Physics. For the leading thinkers of the time, the Newtonian cosmic order set the stage as the template and working model of true science to be followed. It became the blueprint and conceptual tool to explain the inner nature of things and society. Newton described his method of natural philosophy as "discovering the frame and operations of nature and reducing them … to general rules or laws – establishing these rules by observations and experiments, and thence deducting the causes and effects of things" (quoted from Westfall 1980: 632).

The apparent successes in natural philosophy set an example for moral philosophy. Likewise, various scholars in moral philosophy adopted Newton's methods and models to discover the laws that govern human social, economic, and moral conduct and order. Implicit in this confession was the tacit admittance to the totality and singularity of nature and society. That is both nature and society share a common underlying framework and order. Just as much as nature is governed by natural laws, society and human nature, in the same way, are regulated by the rules of nature. The whole universe and everything in it were encircled in a mechanistic world and a deterministic reality. A unified world that its incontrovertible truths can be discovered, classified, and described in mathematical and causal laws and language. The legacy of Newton superseded his actual achievements. His physics became the prototype of scientific work. The impact of the Newtonian revolution was such that every other discipline seeped their inquiries into the Newtonian worldview. Most specifically, in the realm of social sciences, every effort was made to emulate Newtonian physics. The preoccupation of the emerging social scientists was to generalize on par with Newton's laws. In order to place their findings on an equal footing to that of Newton's laws, they required four sets of qualifications. These are, first and foremost, embracing natural order; second, classifying wherever it is required into specific stages and discovering laws of each stage; third, placing the cause and effect as the driver of the scientific method to uncover exact truths; and, finally, expressing the discovered natural laws and orders in mathematical language. This is how natural regularity embedded in nature and society can be discovered, explained, and predicted.

By the mid-eighteenth century, the leading scholars embraced history as a natural process. A process that has evolved naturally from a primitive stage to an advanced stage. The colonists' experience of meeting different people from different nations in America, Africa, and Asia provided the evidence in the proof of their assertion. These nations and people had different cultures, values, institutions, political and legal frameworks, and levels of economic development. Somehow these very visible differences had to be articulated either for the sake of learning or for the sake of granting licence to colonial conquest of the world. The idea of "natural" was a by-product of the cosmic natural order. Human societies had definite origins, evolved into different forms, and advanced into contemporary modes. This was a view expressed by the early modern scholars such as Samuel Pufendorf (1632–94) and then steered on the course to its most extreme dead end by Karl Marx. Initially, the uninitiated common observers spoke of the stages of human progress into savage and civilized societies. In the mid-eighteenth century, this view has come of age.

R. J. Turgot (1727–81), one of the principal members of the physiocratic school, in his *A Philosophical Review of Successive Advances of Human Mind* in 1750 and in his *Plan for Two Discourses on Universal History* in 1751, divided the entire human history into four stages of development: the hunter-gatherer period, the pastoral period, the agricultural period, and the commercial period. Human history became an organic process. The impact of this approach was far and wide. The social and economic processes were viewed in a smooth, mechanistic, and deterministic manner. History was constructed into definite stages. The purpose of constructing history into definite and fixed periods of time was to show the inevitable laws of progress. In Turgot's *Universal History*, the four stages of history are dominated by four methods of provision of subsistence and the social classes, i.e., by hunters, shepherds, husbandmen, and merchants. Each period has its distinctive modes of subsistence, culture, customs, institutions, legal and political framework, art, and moral values. The driving forces that propel one stage to advance and defeat the vanquished stage are art and science. It is the progress in art and science that transforms societies from one stage of development into a higher stage of development.

Almost every notable scholar in the eighteenth century had something to say about the different stages of transformation of human societies and the causes of the transformation. In 1763, Quesnay and Marquis de Mirabeau (1715–89), in their Philosophie Rurale, have identified four human social formations. These are hunting, pasturage, agriculture, and commerce. Manifested in this identification of series of the progressive development of social and economic transformation, there is the interplay of three inner-driving determinants. One of the critical factors is the belief in social orders that are dynamic and are subject to transformation. The second fundamental driving force is the systematic quest for the cause or causes behind the evolution and transformation of social formations. The third driving force is the general optimism and trust in social and economic progress and the dream of a more advanced society in the future. The moving force, the cause, the "essence" and the "root" of social transformation for Quesnay and Mirabeau is the way human "subsistence" is supplied.

Quesnay and Mirabeau held that every "moral and physical parts of which society is constituted derive from this and are subordinate to it. It is upon subsistence, upon the means of subsistence, that all the branches of the political order depend." Other aspects of life, i.e., arts, science, law, government, agriculture, trade, and industry, are "subordinated to the means of subsistence.

This is the fundamental force to which is due to everything which men cultivate, navigate and build" (quoted from Brown 1984: 107). By all manner and means, the idea of social and economic evolution and transformation was interpreted during this period. Nicolas de Condorcet (1743–94), a student of Turgot, was deeply inspired by his teacher's outline of the stages of social change. In his *Sketch for the Historical Picture of the Progress of the Human Mind* (1794), Condorcet divided social orders into ten separate periods. His first stage is the age of hordes, hunting, fishing, and gathering. In his division, each social order has got its own inner laws of development that has made human progress inevitable. Western Europe, in his classification, was in the lead. It had reached stage 9, the highest level of civilization. The last stage, the tenth epoch, is yet to come, which will be the age of perfection, perfect equality, freedom, and justice. In this stage, all inequalities will disappear and society guarantees each person all the rights conceivable. At this stage, "the sun will shine only on free men who know no other master but their reasons; when tyrants and slaves, priests and their stupid or hypocritical instruments will exist only in works of history" (Condorcet 2012: 130).

By the mid-eighteenth century, constructing the history into successive epochs and the end of it to a perfect society was a trendsetting idea. Scholars, both in the mainstream and at the fringe, took part in this debate. One of these figures was Etienne-Gabriel Morelly (1717–78). He was an obscure French thinker. Very little is known about him but his ideas greatly impacted the subsequent socialist and communist movement in Europe. His book, *Code of Nature*, was published anonymously in 1755. For about 50 years, it was believed that Diderot was the author of this book. Morelly in this book upholds that human beings are not "born vicious and wicked." It is "the circumstances of life in this world" that "inevitably predispose" them to "perverseness." This is due to living in an "unnatural system" in a system that is dominated by a "vulgar morality." Morality is the central concern in Morelly's thought. He divides morality into scientific and unscientific morality. True morality is good morality, a scientific morality that is based on rules of mathematics. True morality grants results that are as valid as in mathematical equivalence. In a similar way, Morelly maintained, as in "mathematical Equations" morality is "truly susceptible of the clearest proofs" (Fried and Sanders 1964: 18–31). In his worldview, whatever is natural is meant to be good and the natural system is the one that is governed by true morality. In a system of true morality, there are fundamental natural laws that are discoverable by reason and can be conveyed by the language of logic and mathematics. Whenever these laws are discovered, we can construct a perfect society and economy. The form that this ideal society will take is communism. In this ideal society, there is no private property. No one will be allowed to "own anything," every person will be "a public person," and "every citizen contribute to the public weal in accordance with his strength, his talents, and his age; these will determine his obligations, in conformity with the Distributive law" (quoted from Fried and Sanders 1964: 18–31)

All other leading French writers of the enlightenment such as Rousseau (1712–78), Voltaire (1694–1778), Diderot (1713–84), and Montesquieu (1689–1755) subscribed to one or another form of stages of economic and social progress. So, the accepted wisdom about the world and human nature stemmed from their preconception of the stages of human progress. It should be noted that for Montesquieu the force behind progress in his three stages of history is the law. These three stages of history are the society of hunters, farmers, and merchants. In the first stage, people lived like herds and the legal basis of society is barbarism. In agrarian societies, the legal basis is despotism and in commercial societies it is liberty. In the *Spirit of Law*, book two, chapter 12, Montesquieu makes a distinction between the "liberty of commerce" and the "liberty of the merchant." Commercial societies are very complex and require complex laws and government to maintain law and order, liberty, and social and commercial contracts. The right setting for this type of society is a civil society that rests on social and commercial contracts. It is for this reason that in "countries of liberty" commerce is "less impeded by laws than in the countries of servitude" economic settings (quoted from Pangle 2010: 116).

The three foremost German thinkers of the Enlightenment who addressed the internal potential of human societies to improve and advance were Kant, Johann Gottfried Herder (1744–1803), and Hegel. The prime mover, central to Kant's thought, that hoists a society from a lower stage to a higher stage of development is the intellect. Kant in his short essay, *Idea of a Universal History from Cosmopolitan Point of View* (1784), describes human progress to higher levels as being embedded in human natural capacity. In this natural capacity, there is an end destined to be achieved. In the first thesis of this essay, he writes, "all the capacities implanted in a creature by nature are destined to unfold themselves, completely and conformably to their end, in the course of time" (Kant 1914: x). In the third thesis, Kant refers to the human capacity to reason as the means by which this end can be realized. In this thesis, we read that

> nature has willed that man should, by himself, produce everything that goes beyond the mechanical ordering of his animal existence, and that he should partake of no other happiness or perfection than that which he himself, independently of instinct, has created by his own reason.
>
> (Kant 1963: 13)

Kant reveals the nature of the hidden plan in thesis number 8 of the essay. In this thesis, he says

> the history of mankind can be seen, in the large, as the realization of Nature's secret plan to bring forth a perfectly constituted state as the only condition in which the capacities of mankind can be fully developed, and also bring forth that external relation among states which is perfectly adequate to this end.
>
> (Kant 1963: 21)

Johann Gottfried Herder, who was taught by Kant in his *Outline of a Philosophy of History of Man* (1784), affirms the stage by stage of human social and cultural headway as an imminent necessity. The locus of the stage-by-stage progress is deterministic. The ultimate purpose of human society is to move upwards into perfection in improving human knowledge, happiness, culture, institutions, and legal and political capabilities.

As was noted above, for Montesquieu the prime mover in human progress is the idea of liberty. This idea is constituted in the positive laws. The realization of liberty in the context of positive law comes from intellectual progress. We find variations of this tradition in the work of the German philosopher Georg Wilhelm Hegel (1770–1831) and the French sociologist, August Comte (1798–1857). Human progress in their worldviews is manifested in intellect and ideas. For Hegel, it is manifested in the progression of "self-consciousness" of the spirit/mind. It is the "evolution of spirit in time" and the ultimate goal of Geist (spirit, mind, soul) is freedom. Freedom is realized in successive stages; in subjective spirit (as in the life of the individual), in society (as in ethics), and in absolute spirit (as in the world history in general). Science of logic is a progression to a definite goal. There is rationality in the progress of history. History moves forward to a specific end. In Hegel's teleological account of history, "reason rules the world." Reason and history are inseparable. History has a purpose. Its goal is the consciousness of freedom. If the progress directly corresponds to this end, then the progress is rational. The "world Spirit," Geist, opens its mysteries through human consciousness. These mysteries are embedded in every society's culture, in their philosophy, religion, and art. The ultimate purpose of the progression of history is "absolute spirit" (Perperzak 2001: 601).

Progress in history in Hegel's grand system is a unified triadic dialectical process. This is due to the antagonism between "matter" and "spirit" in his scheme. History is at war with itself. It is this war within that drives history on the way to full consciousness and freedom. The concrete reality, however, is the hindrance to get to this end. The unity of opposites acts in both directions. History moves forward because of the dialectical unity of thesis and antithesis. The end result of the unity of negation is synthesis. History contains within itself its own contradiction and all contradictions eventually will give in to a higher stage of historical development. Similarly, the new stage will tread the same route as the one before. Hegel applied his theory of consciousness of freedom to world history. He identified three stages of human history. The first stage is the "oriental world," the pre-Greek period, which he classified as the tyrannical age. In this period only the ruler, the despot, is free. The rest of the population knows no more than being ruled by a despot. The second stage is the Greek and Roman periods. In this period what are classed as citizens also are free. In the third stage, to which only the Germanic people have reached in Hegel's mind, all people are free. Thus, in the first stage the consciousness of freedom is limited to one ruler, in the second to a few, and in the third to all. In Hegel's grand spirit, the drivers of world history are the "world-historical individuals" who knowingly and unknowingly change the tides of history and carry it step by step forward. The ultimate end of the journey of world history is the absolute idea. History ends in this "system of totality." In this circle, we also have August Comte, the French sociologist who treats history as a progression of human intellect. His three stages of intellectual development are theological, metaphysical, and scientific (positive science). In his classification, only natural sciences have reached the top end.

Human progress from a less developed into a more developed society was equally central to the work of Scottish writers of the Age of Enlightenment. It was pivotal to Smith's economics. In his *Lectures on Jurisprudence* (1762–63), Smith divided human development into four stages: "the Age of Hunters," "The Age of Shepherds," "the Age of Agriculture," and "the Age of Commerce" (Gaukroger 2016: 261). John Millar (1735–1801), another distinguished figure of Scottish enlightenment, wrote that human beings' first struggle is to acquire their "means of subsistence." It began with "catching or ensnaring wild animals, or by gathering the spontaneous fruits of the earth." Then it progressed to "taming and rearing cattle, and of cultivating the ground." In time, "as men have been successful in these great improvements … the various branches of manufacture together with commerce … are introduced" (Millar 1979: 176). Adam Ferguson (1723–1816), another key figure of the Scottish enlightenment in his foremost work, *An Essay on the History of Civil Society* (1767), divided the natural history of human societies into three stages. In the first stage, the savages' period, there is no property ownership; in the second stage, in the barbarians' period, there is property but no law. In the final stage, the polished – the civil society, there is both property and laws. William Godwin (1756–1836), a leading member of the English enlighten movement, in his book *An Enquiry Concerning Political Justice and Its Influence on General Virtue and Happiness* (1793), drew attention to the final and perfect stage of human societies. Human affairs at this stage are conducted voluntarily. There will be the complete annihilation of all the ills of society. In this complete spontaneous order, perfect equality and justice will rule. In this classless society "there will be no war, no crime, no administration of justice … and no government. Besides this there would be no disease, anguish, melancholy, or resentment" (quoted from Heilbroner 2011: 77).

## No poor on nature's banquet

When Marx arrived on the scene in the mid-nineteenth century, the idea of the viability of an idyllic society and perfect order was widely acknowledged. By this time the idea of progress was a commonly accepted theory. Equally, there was a broad acceptance of the issue of each historical period having its own definite economic, social, moral, cultural, legal, and political relationships. For some it was subsistence and for others the intellect (ideas) was the driving force of the change. Nonetheless, a transformation of a lower social order into a higher social formation accounted for much of the scholarly writings of the time. In addition, Newton's cosmic order was the model of knowledge that all looked up to and hoped to achieve a comparable authority in their field. Newtonian physics offered a stable, balanced, and orderly universe. An automated and self-winding cosmos that was predictable. All serious scholars aspired to this model. Newtonian physics formed the definitive benchmark for any theory that claimed to be scientific. Newton presented a tidy world, an orderly and independent world that is regulated and governed by the laws of nature. These laws can be discovered by scientific methods and managed in the interest of humankind. This was the only model that social and moral thinkers yearned to adopt in their studies of society and economy until the publication of Darwin's seminal book, *The Origins of Species* (1859).

Darwin's natural selection was a ground-breaking theory. This work closed the door to the theistic claim of creation found in the book of Genesis. In Genesis, God created the earth and all sorts of life in it at once and in their fixed and complete forms. Darwin presented a diametrically opposite theory. The Darwinian natural order is an evolutionary, adaptive, and transmutation process. It is a theory of descent from the variability, the struggle for survival, adaptation, and extinction. Darwin's revolutionary book, *On the Origin of Species*, was published in 1859. In this book, Darwin gives details of the evolution of species by natural selections. The work of one economist, Thomas Malthus, had an influence on Darwin's theory of natural selection. Malthus published his famous essay, *Essay on the Principle of Population*, in 1798. The central theme of the *Essay* is human's constant "struggle for existence." This was an idea in line with Darwin's scientific findings. Malthus built his theory on two assumptions. First, "food is necessary to the existence of man." Second, "the passion between the sexes is necessary, and will remain nearly in its present state." He then concluded that "the power of population is indefinitely greater than the power in the earth to produce subsistence for man. Population, when unchecked, increases in a geometrical ratio. Subsistence only increases in an arithmetical ratio" (Malthus 1985: 70–71). The germ of this idea is that the increase in population is much greater than the earth's capability to supply food for an ever increasing number of human population. Therefore, the "struggle for existence" is inevitable. Malthus blamed, what he called the lower classes, for being the guilty party for their over-reproduction. In the second edition of his *Essay* (1803), Malthus writes in "a world already possessed" there is no room for a poor child being born. "At nature's mighty feast there is no vacant cover for him. She tells him to be gone and will quickly execute her own orders" (Malthus 1803: 531). It was this pitiless directness of Malthus's teaching that earned him the title of the prophet of the "dismal science."

Darwin read Malthus's *Essay* on population in October 1838. In his *Autobiography*, he says this was "fifteen months after" he had started his "systematic inquiry" about the evolution of species. He goes on to say:

> being well prepared to appreciate the struggle for existence which everywhere goes on, from long-continued observation of the habits of animals and plants, it at once struck me that under these circumstances favourable

> variations would tend to be preserved, and unfavourable ones to be destroyed. The result of this would be the formation of a new species. Here then I had, at last, got a theory by which to work.
>
> (Darwin 1887: 68)

After the publication of Darwin's seminal work, the analytical structure of economic ideas, irrespective of their differences, has been dominated by both the Newtonian cosmic order and Darwin's theory of evolution. In respect to Darwin's influence, let us see his influence on the works of Herbert Spence (1820–1903) and Karl Marx. Darwin's influence on these two formidable opponents is rooted in their imitation of the Darwinian natural order, organic change, and transformation. They interpreted the language of Darwin's theory of evolution and natural selection in their visions of society and economy. In their grand design, they share a naturalistic outline with an inherent order that is firmly grounded in their systems. How things work is viewed to be the same in both nature and society. The two realms essentially share a common natural structure. Their categorization of human history into ring-fenced periods stems from this prearranged grand scheme of things. So do the causes of the transition of society from one historical period to another.

Spencer coined the phrase "survival of the fittest" in 1864. It was he and Alfred Russel Wallace who persuaded Darwin to substitute the phrase "natural selection" with the "survival of the fittest" in the later editions of his book (Darwin 1866: 227). Spencer adopted this mantra to give human societies a biological reality. Something that matched well with his racialist position. This is how he justified his preference for his own saying. He noted that the "survival of the fittest which I have here sought to express in mechanical terms, is that which Mr. Darwin has called 'natural selection,' or the preservation of favoured races in the struggle for life" (Spencer 1921: 530). Elsewhere, Spencer commented that the "survival of the fittest implies multiplication of the fittest" (Spencer 1891: 444). From this angle, he claimed that the evolution of human societies and the evolution of species conform to laws that are natural.

Spencer distorted the theory of natural selection by applying it to the evolution of human societies, economic relations, and social development. The implications and repercussions of misuse of this theory were deep and wide. By naturalizing the superiority of certain social classes, races, gender, and cultures, it made inequality, exploitation, and colonial conquests compatible with the natural order and the laws of progress. Natural laws govern everything and natural selection is a law of nature. The misfits (natural or social) are ill-suited to their environment. The law of the survival of the fittest would get rid of the weak and unwanted at the earliest possible time. Spencer insisted that "all excess and all deficiency must disappear; that is, all imperfection must disappear" (Spencer 1868: 79). This was an echo of Malthus's verdict that he added to his second edition of *Essay* in 1803 that the economy is a locked room for the rich.

There is a toxic morass of hierarchy in every step of the labyrinth of the revelation of the survival of the fittest. In this frenetic wilderness, the adaptable and unadaptable, suited and ill-suited, strong and weak, have and have not, the dispensable and the wanted are at each other's throats. On the strength of this savagery, it is said, humans and their societies would progress. Spencer purported that "progress is not an accident; not a thing within human control, but a beneficent necessity" (Spencer 1865: 58). While Spencer and Marx's ideas are poles apart, they share the inevitability of social progress. Marx's organic theory of society, like Spence's theory, is teleological with one big difference. In Spencer's prognostic war of the survival of the fittest, the weak is the victim that will perish, whereas in Marx's war of class struggle it is the weak who will revive, improve, and succeed.

Marx's society is a social organism. Each human society has definite laws and orders. The laws are susceptible to being discovered by the means of dialectical methods. Marx compared his law of "value" to Newton's universal law of gravity (Böhm-Bawerk 1949: 105). Marx's law of motion of human societies has many similarities to the Darwinian natural selection theory. Engels first read the *Origin of Species* a few weeks after its publication. Being much impressed by it, he recommended it to Marx in December 1859. After reading the book, in January 1861 Marx wrote a letter to Ferdinand Lassalle, in which he praised the book as an "important" book that could serve him "as a natural scientific basis for the class struggle in history" (Marx and Engels 1942: 193). To Engels, he wrote that the book "contains the basis in natural history for our view" (Marx and Engels 1942: 126). In the late 1860s, Marx commented that "nothing ever give me greater pleasure than to have my name linked onto Darwin's. His wonderful work makes my own absolutely impregnable. Darwin may not know it but he belongs to the Social Revolution" (quoted from Spargo 1910: 200). Engels in his speech at Marx's graveside in 1883 also reiterated the common thread between Marx and Darwin, one in discovering "the law of development of organic nature" and the other in discovering "the law of development of human history."

Most of all, Marx was much enchanted by Hegel's teleological history. Regarding history, Marx was essentially a Hegelian student. His escape from Hegelian universal history was merely a partial rupture. Marx paid tribute to Hegel for discovering the "correct laws of the dialect" but criticized his mentor's idealist method. Marx described Hegel as a "mighty thinker," as his teacher, and pointed out that "the mystification which the dialectic suffers in Hegel's hands by no means prevents him from being the first to present its general forms of motion in a comprehensive and conscious manner" (quoted from Likitkijsomboon 1992: 413-14) – inattentive of the fact that false reasoning (bereft of implementation to any reality) has no head. With this qualification, Marx's analysis of economy and history took off. Hegelian dialectical and teleological history consists of the progression of unity of opposites to the "absolute idea." The succession of the unity of opposites, in Marx's historical materialism, advances eventually into an absolute perfect society.

In Marx as in Hegel's dialectic of world history, history has an ultimate goal to fulfil. In Marx's materialistic conception of history, the entire human history passes through five distinct successive socio-economic formations. Each of these formations consists of "mode of production" and "the social relations of production." The economic relations are the "base" and the social relations of the production are the "superstructure" of each mode of production. The economic order, the base, is always the primary determining factor. The technical forces of production are the engine of change. They are the dynamic forces that are foiled from their natural progress by the social relations of production. The material mode of existence, the means of production, determines the consciousness of people in each mode of production.

Hegel's universal history consists of two main concepts. The realization of the idea of reason is the first one. The second one is that this realization is achieved in a succession of national spirits by world-historical heroes such as Napoleon. In Marx's universal history, this ultimate goal is communism and his heroes are the oppressed masses that struggle for their emancipation from exploitation. Marx described the essence of his historical materialism in his *Critique Political Economy* (1859). In discussing this process, he says "in the social production of their existence, men inevitably enter into definite relations, which are independent of their will, namely relations of production appropriate to a given stage in the development of their material forces of production" (Marx 1971: 20). With this qualification, Marx and Engels divided their various modes and relations of production into five stages of development.

The first stage is "primitive communism." These "early communal societies" are completely egalitarian. The resources are owned commonly and there is no class structure or hierarchy and no state. This mode of production, somehow, dissolved and gave way to the slavery mode of production. The transformation came from the

> continued increase of production and with it, the increased productivity of labour [that] enhanced the value of human labour-power. Slavery, which had been a nascent and sporadic factor in the preceding stage, now became an essential part of the social system.
>
> (Marx and Engels vol. II – 1962: 312)

In the slave and slave-owning mode of production, the "slave did not sell his labour-power to the slave owner, any more than the ox sells its services to the peasant. The slave, together with his labour-power, has been sold once and for all to his owner" (Marx and Engels vol. I – 1962: 83). In the slavery system of production, the mode of production is based on slavery. Slaves and tools of production are stitched into one and the same relations of production. The slave masters are everything and the slaves are nothing.

In Marx's historical materialism the course of history is determined by material forces and relations of production. The stress is on the method of production. This is his starting point, free of external influence, which shapes the social, legal, cultural, political, religious, and aesthetic aspects of any society. Class struggle is another driving factor in Marx's historical materialism. The class struggle is limited to the class-based modes of production. Its advent was with the advent of slavery mode of production. The slave owners and the slaves are the two dominant classes of this system and relations of production. The slave owners own all the means of production, including the slaves. It was this struggle that ended the slavery mode of production and dragged history forward to the next mode of production. In their *Communist Manifesto* (1848), Marx and Engels declared that the history of "existing human society is the history of class struggles" (Marx and Engels 1990: xv). On the role of the ruling class in the society, in their *German Ideology*, we read that they do not only own the means of production but their ideas are also:

> the ruling ideas, i.e., the class, which is the ruling *material* force of society, is at the same time its ruling *intellectual* force. The class which has the means of material production at its disposal has control at the same time over the means of mental production.
>
> (Marx and Engels 1991: 64 – Italics in the original)

Central to Marxian socio-economic transformation is the relentless class conflict. The revolutionary change emanates from the combined interworking of the class struggle and technological changes (means of production). The feudal mode and relations of production were born inside the slavery system. It then defeated slavery and the nobility (the landlords) and the peasants (the serfs) formed a higher social and economic formation with its unique common laws. Under this mode of production, the feudal lords are "in possession" of the "means of production" (Marx 1984: Capital vol. 3: 790) and the peasants are the "bondage" and "tied to the soil as its accessory" (Marx 1975: 777). It is in the nature of the exploited class to rise and emancipate itself with the passing of time. Because each dominant class at the same time is "its own grave-diggers." As much as the slavery mode of production fosters its own grave-digger, the feudal society fosters its own undertaker, the capitalist mode of production. Capitalism grows "out of the economic structure of feudal society" (Marx 1964: 133). On this reading, this process took place when the producers (the peasants) became "wage-workers," emancipated "from serfdom and from the fetters of the guilds … on the other hand, these new freedmen became sellers of themselves only after they had been robbed of all their own means of production" (Marx and Engels 1996: 706).

Marx rose to prominence, in the main, for his analysis of what he called the capitalist mode and relations of production. The durability of his name, at large, is also down to his work on capital and capitalism. His capitalism is not only the point of reference of his devotees but also a declaration of faith for his adversaries. The term "capitalism" has become the benchmark for his defenders and opponents alike to compare all other stages of social and economic evolution in human history. It is the seat of every theory of the business cycle and economic crisis. Marx's account of capitalism rests on only one event in history, the first Industrial Revolution. A watershed event that started in the mid-eighteenth century and lasted until the mid-nineteenth century in England. By the time Marx became interested in the industrial economy, it was a bygone era. Old times are bygone forever. It is not possible to ignore the British Industrial Revolution as an epoch-making event in history. This was a turning point in human history, a momentous and historic achievement, a decisive break from the old times. The old society's economy, culture, technology, institutions, and legal, moral, and political relationships took a new form. Full credit goes to Marx for his original insights, understanding, and treatment of this tipping point in human history. However, what he has deduced out of his observations and analyses of this landmark event is patently unfounded. Capitalism is a fossilized period in Marx's historical materialism and the clearest vindication of his theory of history. Other modes of production, pre- and post-modes of production, are filtered and extracted through the spectacles of his capitalism.

The two classes at war in capitalism are the bourgeoisie (the capitalist class) and the proletariat (the working class). The capitalist class owns the means of production and is the master of the working class. The proletariat class consists of wage-labourers who have nothing to live on but their labour power to sell. Here we have a mode of and relations of production that is grounded on private property ownership. A system that turns everything into a commodity, produce merely for exchange. The labour-power, the most precious assets of workers, becomes the most treasured possession of the capitalist class, the source of the wealth of the capitalist system. The industrialist capitalist class exploits productive labour through the "extended reproduction" of capital. Something, which is inherent in the very structure of the system that is simply unstoppable. The reproduction of capital only ends with the end of the capitalist mode of production.

The capitalist mode of production like any other class-based mode of production is naturally a self-dissolving system. It suffers from its natural laws of development. The contradiction between capitalist relations and its forces of production takes the system one step at a time to its own destruction. The concentration of the means of production on one hand and socialization of labour on the other hand at last reach a point where they become incompatible with their former confined structure. In the meantime, in the course of capitalist development, the working class would be organized and becomes conscious of its historical role to lead the collapse of the capitalist mode of production.

Marx asserted that "the fall of bourgeoisie and the victory of the proletariat are equally inevitable" (Drennen 1972: 83). Besides, this is the last class-based mode of production. The next and final stage is classless communism. This is a mode of production where "there will be an association in which the free development of each is the condition for the free development of all"

(Marx 1988: 158). In the end, humanity achieves its ultimate historical goal that entire humankind lives on the principle of "from each according to their ability, to each according to their contribution." But in order to break completely from the capitalist habits, there is a need for a transitional period – a "period of the revolutionary transformation." A stage of "a political transition in which the state can be nothing but the revolutionary dictatorship of the proletariat" (quoted from Machan 1987: 194).

Marx was convinced that through his dialectic and historical materialism he has discovered the template of social and economic development in general and the DNA of capitalist production in particular. His works are focused on capitalism. He looked at the past and the future in his image of capitalism. Marx's capitalism at its core can be cut to his symbolic expression of the circuit of industrial capital. The circuit starts with the money capital (M). The industrial capitalist invests M productively when they buy the commodity inputs: the labour power (LP) and means of production (MP). The LP and the MP are put in the production process (P) and at the end of the production process, new commodities (C′) are produced that is greater in value than the initial commodities inputs (C). The industrial capitalist then exchanges his commodities C′ with money M′ to realize his surplus value. C′ is the surplus value in commodity form and M′ is the surplus value in money form because M′ is greater than M. The difference between M′ and M is the surplus value, the staple food of capitalist existence. This is what all industrialist capitalists do in different productive sectors of the economy.

## The original model of capitalism

The original model of capitalism is Marx's prototype capitalism. In this model, labour alone is the only productive factor of production, which creates surplus value. The wages that workers are paid are less than the value of the commodities they produce. Workers are paid a subsistence wage, the minimum required for their daily survival. The surplus value is created in production, which will be realized in the money form in the sphere of exchange. It will then be divided between different capitalist classes. Among different capitalist classes, it is the industrial capitalists who are the productive ones. The industrial capitalists appropriate the surplus value first and then share it with money lending capitalists for the money they have borrowed, with merchant capitalists for circulating their commodities, and with land-owning capitalists for the land they have rented from them. So, the surplus value will be "split up into various parts. Its fragments fall to various categories of person, and take on various mutually independent forms, such as profit, interest, gains made through trade, ground rent, etc" (Marx 1983: Capital vol. 1 – 529).

Marx's account of capitalist mode and relations of production at its best is a description of a textile factory system in England in the mid-nineteenth century. In the course of the eighteenth century, there were a number of successive innovations and improvements of cotton-spinning machines in England, which transformed England into the factory of the world. John Kay invented a wheeled shuttle in 1733. In 1767, James Hargreaves developed the spinning jenny and two years later Richard Arkwright added the water frame to this spinning jenny. Other inventions were followed one after another to complete the process of the Industrial Revolution. Edmund Cartwright invented the power loom in 1785. An American inventor, Eli Whitney, later on, invented the cotton gin in 1793. In England, it was Richard Arkwright who set up the spinning machine, the factory system, and, with this, revolutionized the manufacturing textile industry in England. Before his adaptation of the factory system, the cottage industry dominated production in England. The production in the cottage industry was on a small scale and employed very few skilled workers. With patenting his spinning frame in 1769, Arkwright assembled the first factory that produced goods at a large scale and employed over 300 workers. The number of workers increased to 800 in 1789. By 1850, there were about 250,000 power looms in Britain, the most dominant industry in the British economy at that time. Marx's vision of capitalism is based on this industry at this specific time in British history.

Factories changed the landscape of England drastically. It centralized the location of the work. Besides, except for retaining a few skilled workers (engineers), it de-skilled the rest of workforce. The factory rules were very strict and extremely harsh. There were no health and safety provisions at work, and no job security and welfare protection. The air in the mills was thick with cotton dust and it was kept hot and humid to make sure threads do not break. These conditions led to all sorts of diseases, especially byssinosis. The factory system has also altered the patterns of work. Due to the process of de-skilling and the simplicity of tasks performed, women and children were added to the army of spinning mill workers. Daily hours of work were long and industrial accidents very common. There were no or very few laws to protect the workers' rights. The factory owners did not even comply with these lame laws. Many of these owners were members of Parliament or had very close relations with the members of Parliament where their factories were located. The state was basically under their thumbs. The factory inspectors were merely shadowy figures, poorly paid, and easily bought and corrupted by the factory owners. These were the conditions that put England ahead of the rest of the world in the manufacturing industry. By 1850, when Marx turned his attention to a serious study of the economy, the British economy was the most advanced manufacturing economy in the world. It was the factory of the world. With 1.8 per cent of the world population and 0.16 per cent of the world's landmass, half of the world's output of cotton textiles was produced in Britain. As the largest and most powerful empire, it prevented other leading European colonial nations to trade freely in its colonies. Its supreme economic power and military might dictated the world trade. This was the image that Marx had about his capitalism.

Marx, indeed, is one of the most influential thinkers of the world. He is credited as one of the great thinkers whose ideas have, right or wrong, shaped the modern world. He has left an enduring legacy on a wide range of disciplines from history to sociology, economics, and politics. Marx is best remembered for his analysis of what he called the capitalist mode of production. This has been his greatest impact. On the basis of this belief, many revolutions have taken place and much blood has been spilled. The world of communism was erected on his vision. Ironically, his arch enemies have also come to be devoted to his capitalism. As in any faith, what the prophesiers of faiths profess is not what their apostles follow and do. Likewise, the time and the place of their oracles are never the same as when their disciples try to impose them on others. Capitalism was one thing to Marx but it is another to his apostles and yet another to his foes. Capitalism, Marx's greatest legacy, has become a universal faith. It, virtually, has left no one to be indifferent about it. You are either on its side or not. But the common denominator is capitalism. Marx's devotees' crusade is to defeat it and his adversaries and sceptics are fighting to defend and reform it. The thing that is mystifying is that the idol that is either venerated or despised is bygone. Another inexplicable issue tied to this deceased idol is that almost all variation of economic crises begins with this mirage.

Thus, understanding this lasting legacy of Marx's ideas is fundamental in understanding contemporary theories of economic crises. The adoption of a belief, in this case, capitalism, consciously or unconsciously obscures the horizon of our understanding of ever-changing economies and human societies. It limits the scope and the effects of our diagnoses to cure the modern-day social and economic ills. As in Plato's allegory of the cave, this vision has chained us in a pothole called capitalism, in which reality is a castle in the air. We only can see the world through this preconceived faith. But the reality is something else. So long as we remain in this pothole, we cannot realize our errors. The right salvation is to break the chain and to leave the pothole for our own good. In Kant's green-tinted glasses, the objective reality is not the one that is seen through the glasses. Marx's capitalism is the tinted glasses through which all accounts of economic crises are observed. Both his friends and foes filter modern societies and economies through his glasses. But the reality is different from what Marx has described capitalism to be.

In all schools of economic thought, from Marxian and after, "capitalism" is held as a long-established fact. Everyone is either for or against it. Those who are against current dominant economic order associate all evils of modern non-communist societies and economies to capitalism. Those in favour of market order attribute all strong points of advanced democratic economies to capitalism. It was not just Marx who dedicated his time to the study of capitalism. The central theme of the works of Max Weber (1864–1920), Werner Sombart (1863–1941), and Joseph Schumpeter (1883–1950) is on this subject too. In their approach capitalist system is also an incontestable fact. Much of their attention, however, was directed at explaining the driving forces of different stages of development of capitalism. Unlike Marx, for Weber, the rise of capitalism was not due to material forces. It was due to protestant ethics. Sombart started with Marxism and then dropped it for the German Historical School and eventually, he became a sympathizer of Nazism. His work is an attempt to lay bare the psychological behaviours of entrepreneurs at different stages of capitalist development. Schumpeter was fond of capitalism and was much beguiled by it but lamented its collapse through its own successes.

Capitalism is the received wisdom in which various ideas of business cycles and economic crises start with. Early economists referred to the occasional occurrence of under- and over-trading, which were self-correcting. Under- and over-trading were transitory, which did not cause the collapse of the economic system. Economy returned back to its natural equilibrium position in the shortest possible time. For Marx, the economic system itself is a self-annihilating mechanism. The trade fluctuations, the business cycles, and crises are integral parts of its very existence. The classical economist also foresaw not the end of their contemporary economic system but saw a time that it stops developing, a stationary state. Classical economists pointed to the law of diminishing return, the tendency of the rate of profit to fall, and the law of the population growth – all of which testify to their explicit recognition of economic change and implicit acceptance of intermittent disorder in the economy.

To the early socialist and social critics, the problems of the emerging economic system were too obvious. The radical philosopher and economist, Sismondi, pointed to over-production as one characteristic of the emerging commercial and industrial economy. He noted that the social setting of the system is such that it produces more goods than its real producers, the workers, can afford to buy. This was what Malthus also found in his study of the economy. But for the same symptom, they offered two different types of prognosis. Malthus's prescription was to avoid such economic disorders by maintaining "a body of unproductive consumers" to keep up the level of effective demand equal to the supply of goods. The socialists' prognosis was broader. It consisted of considerable social, economic, legal, and political reforms. The thing that either side did not think of was to design and suggest a new economic system instead of what they had. William Stanley Jevons (1835–82) placed his contemporary economic setup as natural as the cosmos or as a bridge that can be explained by means of pure science. No wonder his trade fluctuation theory is naturalistic. It stems from the Sunspot irregularities, which cause good and bad harvests.

Once the metaphor "capitalism" has entered common usage, every type of trade fluctuations has been enclosed in it. Most interpretations of economic cycles presuppose capitalism as the vessel in which economic fluctuations take place. Marx was a pioneering member of this trend. Another interpretation is by one of Marx's contemporaries, Clement Juglar (1819–1905), a French physician and statistician. In 1862, Juglar published a book on business fluctuations using time series, identifying three phases of a periodic cycle: the time of prosperity, crisis, and liquidation. In Juglar's view business cycles "arise out of the behaviour, the activities, and above all out of the saving habits of the population, and the way they employ the capital and credit available" (quoted from Landreth and Colander 2002: 417). Juglar predicted

7–11 years for each cycle to occur. Mikhail Tugan-Baranovsky (1865–1919), a Ukrainian statesman and economist, built his theory of the trade cycle on the works of Marx and Juglar. In his PhD thesis, *The Industrial Crisis in England*, which was published in Russia in 1894, he linked the periodic recurrence of prosperity and economic distress to the nature of capitalist production caused primarily by intermittent over-investment.

Another Russian economist and statistician, Nikolai Kondratiev (1892–1938), published his work on long waves of fluctuation of the trade first in 1922. He revised his initial trade cycle theory in 1926. Kondratiev's cycle lasts about 50–60 years and the upswing of each cycle is about 25 years. The two phases of each cycle are expansion and contraction. Kondratiev held that in the phase of expansion recessions are sporadic and in the phase of contraction recessions are frequent (Mason 2016: 33). In his account, the causes of long business cycles are technological inventions and capital investment in the sectors of the economy such as railroad and car. As a devoted Bolshevik, his target was capitalism. With backing from this study, he intended to demonstrate the capitalist system's incurable contradictions and the historical inevitability of its collapse. The cruel parody had it that he was accused of being the fifth column of the very "capitalism" that he despised so much. Kondratiev was one of Stalin's purges simply for airing his opinion about long waves of recovery and expansion of developed economies. His prediction was not palatable to Stalin's monocratic agenda. The total and immediate meltdown of the capitalist system was what Stalin wanted to hear. But it was not what Kondratiev's business cycle predicted. Above all, Kondratiev's extrapolation could not feed Stalin's propaganda machine. Nikolai was arrested in 1930 and sentenced to eight years in 1931. In 1938, he was tried again and murdered on fabricated charges. In a similar fashion as in the Kondratiev study, Joseph Kitchin (1861–1932) investigated fluctuations in the commodity prices, bank clearings, and short-term interest rates in Britain and the US for the period of 1890–1922. His cycles are shorter. From this study, he discovered three activities that were moving together in successive cycles. Each cycle is about 40 months. Kitchin identified two types of cycles: the minor and the major cycles.

In October 1917, the Bolshevik seized the political power in Russia. This was a landmark in the history of economic crises. The seizure inaugurated the foundation of a new empire, the Soviet Empire. The event seemed to have confirmed Marx's prophesy. It seemed that the collapse of the capitalist system was inevitable, which also convinced Marx's followers of the logical necessity of communism. However, the opponents of Marx went armed from head to toe to defend their capitalism. This event gave birth to two imaginary idols, capitalism and communism. Both were held sacred, venerated, and worshiped like any holy deity. All sides were oblivious of one important fact. It was not the inevitability of the system to collapse and for communism to be born but the contingent conditions that led to the fall of the Tsar's Empire. The Tsarist Empire collapsed not due to the inescapable inevitability of laws of historical materialism, i.e., the fall of capitalism and the rise of communism. Tsar Nicholas II was an absolute monarch believing in the divine right to rule. He ruled with an iron fist and his government was corrupt and ineffective and his opponents were better organized and more determined in achieving their aims.

In addition, the First World War bankrupted the regime. By 1917, the fatigue of war and social unrest spread to every corner of the Russian empire. The Tsar house was cut off from the outside world. He was segregated and stranded in his absolute power, parasite existence, and the infatuation of Rasputin oracles. He was in trouble when the Petrograd garrison refused to fire on people in February 1917. The Russian generals and leading politicians forced him to abdicate the throne. At the same time, there were at front lines soldiers who kept rebelling against their terrible conditions, peasants were seizing common lands, and workers were taking control of their workplace. Furthermore, the Russian colonies were in turmoil. Many were striving to end the Russian colonial rule and others demanding for greater self-rule. Above all, Vladimir Lenin disregarded Marx's instruction on historical materialism. In a timely manner, he seized the moment, and at the time when the provisional government was vulnerable, he overthrew the government. The Bolshevik seizure of power took place when Russia was one of the least developed economies in Europe. It was predominantly an agrarian economy and a feudalistic society.

From the formation of the Soviet Empire to its collapse, theories of the economic crisis were locked up in two ideologies: capitalism and communism. On each side, the other side things were not right. The opposite side was inept, immoral, wasteful, disorganized, unproductive, unfit, and destined to fail. Thus, both sides looked for any clue imaginary and real to show the presence of an economic crisis on the opposite side. On the capitalist side, the market economy is described as the most stable, efficient, and just system of production and distribution. The economic crises were merely abnormal activities. The system is perfect but its natural course from time to time is distorted by external forces such as the state, regulations, monopoly power, trade unions, cultural restrictions, lack of education and training, and outside factors. Those who find the capitalist system an imperfect system but viable have tried to reform its defects and make it adaptable.

Keynes was not alone in his attempt to save the capitalist system. Schumpeter also referred to some defects of the system. The failings that are not terminal. But Schumpeter, in the end, sided with Marx's dim view of the self-destructive nature of the system. Marx celebrated the defects of the system while Schumpeter lamented such defects. Its fall, according to Schumpeter, is due to its own "creative destruction" oddity. This idea was not an entirely novel one. Marx used a similar analogy to demonstrate the dynamism and the end of the system. Schumpeter's "creative destruction" is a process whereby the capitalist system "incessantly revolutionizes the economic structure from within, incessantly destroying the old one" and "incessantly [creating] a new one" (Schumpeter 1942: 83). The innovators are the entrepreneurs who seek new economic opportunities to exploit. What sets each gale of innovations is consumer demand for new goods and what fuels the creative destruction is the fierce competition among the entrepreneurs who enter the markets to exploit the emerging opportunities.

## From trade cycle to economic crisis

The prevailing view in economics before the Wall Street crash adhered to the teaching that general depression is not possible. The traditional theory maintained that a trade cycle is possible but not a general economic meltdown. The Great Depression was the proof to the contrary. It was at this juncture that we have the link between the trade cycle and the economic crisis. Keynes concluded this link. After these events, three trends persisted their presence in the theory of economic crisis. But all these three trends have one thing in common and that is capitalism. To the old school, despite giving in to the events, they did not go too far from their initial view about the efficacy of their preferred economic system. They treated economic crises more like turbulent irregularities that gave no cause for concern. Their version of capitalism is self-automated. It would correct itself, penalizes those who overstep its rules, and will reward those who comply with its requirements. Provided that the markets are left to their own natural devices, such distortions are self-healing and markets would return to their natural equilibrium positions. All transactions at market equilibrium prices in perfectly competitive markets will lead to an optimum outcome. At a market equilibrium condition, the optimum results are achieved for all stakeholders. The resources will be allocated most efficiently, and the common good will be served most effectively. As one can expect, in this ideal world, yielding to the idea of the fall of the system is not short of committing heresy. It meant conceding defeat, giving in to the irrevocability of the 1917 Russian Revolution and the inevitability of Marx's historical materialism.

Paradoxically, the two greatest economic crises have occurred in the largest and the most advanced economy of the world. The first one was the 1929 Great Depression and the second the 2007–2008 global credit crunch. With any event, there is a background and a context attached to it. These crises occurred at the back of some major social and economic transformations in the US economy. The 1929 Wall Street crash occurred at the end of the "roaring twenties" in America. The rapid expansion of the American economy in the 1920s was in part a defiance of the Soviet Empire's deterministic theory of history. It was a contest to show the superiority of "Capitalism" over "Communism." In the 1920s the US economy was the most dynamic economy in the world. Europe was practically paralyzed from the effects of the First World War. The whole continent was in turmoil, tied up in the most extreme ideological battle of Nazism, Fascism, colonialism, and communism. Their economies, in general, were in the doldrums and plunged into an extraordinary level of hyperinflation. The British Empire, which for over two centuries ruled the world, was broken and was passing its closing days. Its colonial superiority was dissipating rapidly by each waning year.

In the 1920s, the US economy was almost doubled. It was a decade of great optimism, and economic, social, cultural, and technological change in America. An era of advertising and the rise of mass consumerism. It is the decade of the expansion of electricity, cars, and chain stores. Women were guaranteed the right to vote in 1920, more people lived in cities than in rural areas. The Women workforce joining the labour market and their greater economic independence transformed the traditional patriarchy and family structure of American society, extending the personal, economic, and sexual freedom of American people. In the meantime, credit institutions and instruments developed and became more sophisticated. The decade changed the way of life in America. The trendiest of all activities was to get rich quickly and America was getting more affluent every year. Getting rich in a very short space of time led to reckless speculation, which peaked at an all-time high in August 1929. The New York Stock Exchange crashed on 29 October 1929. The crash was the beginning of the worldwide great economic depression.

The main share price indexes in the New York Exchange fell by 30 per cent (Bailey 2005: 239). The number of banks was 43,633 in December 1929. By December 1933, this number went down to 15,015, a fall of about 39 per cent (Calomiris 2013: 166). Taking the year 1929 as the base year, the real GDP at the height of the Great Depression (1933) decreased to 73.4 per cent, the unemployment rate increased from 2.9 per cent in 1929 to 20.9 per cent, and the stock prices decreased to 46.2 per cent in the US. In Great Britain, for the same period, the unemployment rate increased from 8 per cent to 15.4 per cent and share prices decreased to 74.3 per cent (Crafts and Fearon 2010: 287). The Great Depression, in effect, caused a paradigm shift in mainstream economic thought. It was a radical departure from the position of adherence to the idea of the business cycle and shifting a step forward in the reception of economic crisis as a reality in modern advanced industrialized economies with highly organized markets. This seismic shift was not limited to conceptual revision but to a change of focus and emphasis. It is the first time that mainstream economics acknowledged economic crises as a real possibility that is entrenched in the very structure of the industrialized economies. Not just as in the form of a business cycle or over-trading and some peripheral irritations in the system but as a serious defect that, if not treated at right time, can destroy the system itself. Keynes led this battle. By 1931, he recognized the severity of the crisis and declared that the world economy was "in the middle of the greatest economic catastrophe" (Keynes 1971: 343).

Keynes's response to the 1929 Great Depression has five interrelated facets. First, he was the first leading member of the mainstream economics who grasped the gravity of the situation. Second, Keynes saw the turn of events as something that was more than just a normal business cycle. Something that was considerably more serious than a self-sustaining business cycle. He perceived it to be so serious a threat that it could end European civilization.

Third, the course of events following the great crash deepened his stand against the efficacy of laissez-faire economics. Fourth, his quest was to rescue what he felt to be on the verge of its demise. Lastly, he scanned, assessed, and offered his resolutions under a preconceived economic system designated as capitalism. This was conceding to Marx's conjecture of "capitalism" but unlike Marx, Keynes wanted to rescue the beast.

In his article, *The End of Laisses-Faire* (1926), Keynes wrote that despite many "extremely objectionable" elements of capitalism, if it is "wisely managed" it "can probably be made more efficient for attaining economic ends than any alternative system yet in sight" (Keynes 1972: 294). On this matter, Marx succeeded in converting his opponents to his faith. His "capitalism" was no longer the cardinal tenet of the confession of faith of his disciples but an article of faith of his opponents too. For his part, Keynes succeeded to take the business cycle a step further and raise it to a widely accepted economic reality. That is, crisis is sealed in the very laws of the inner logic of the prevailing system and the relations of production. Keynes's teaching downgraded capitalism from a perfect economic order to a system that is prone to crisis.

All ground-breaking social, economic, political, cultural, technological, and scientific events are a product of cumulative activities and changes that take place over time. Some contributory factors play minor and some major roles in the process and the event of change. Some facets of social and economic transformations are easily detectable, some are hard to make sense, and some we may never know. As much as the Great Depression was the product of such cumulative causes, effects, processes, and events, the global credit crunch of 2007–2008 was also a product of its cumulative historical factors. It came against the background of the fall of Keynesian economics and the collapse of the fixed exchange rate system. The economic and financial climate in which the global credit crunch was incubated and hatched out was after the aftereffects of the financial big bangs in the 1970s and 1980s in the US and Britain and the rise and domination of the new right economics in the political arena. It was in the shadow of the invention of the internet and its worldwide application and the collapse of the Soviet Empire. The 2007–2008 global financial crisis also originated in the US and spread to the rest of the world. Unlike the Great Depression that lasted about ten years, the duration of the 2007–2008 crisis was less than five years. The impact of the global credit crunch compared to the 1929 stock market crash was more widespread. In 2009, when the crisis was at its peak, the real GDP of the advanced countries, taking the year 2007 as the base year, decreased to 97.3 per cent, the unemployment rate from 5.4 per cent to 8 per cent, and the trade volume to about 85 per cent (Crafts and Fearon 2010: 286).

One can see the essential elements of a none-Marxian sketch of the economic crisis in W.C. Mitchell's (1874–1948) book, *Business Cycles* (1913). In his following works, Mitchell elaborated his core argument about the cyclical fluctuations in an advanced industrialized economy. Mitchell's work on the business cycle was published about two decades earlier than the publication of Keynes's *General Theory*. But Mitchell's theory remained in the tradition of business fluctuations that are self-clearing. Mitchell considered business cycles as an unanswered question, a "working hypothesis" that its nature, working mechanism, and effects can be revealed with greater study and collection of evidence in the future. As in Marx and Keynes's theories of crisis, Mitchell traces the origin of business cycles to the rise of monetary economy. Mitchell states it is when "the uses of money have reached an advanced stage in a country that its economic vicissitudes take on the character of business cycles" (Mitchell 1927: 75).

In Mitchell's account, business fluctuations occur in industrialized economies because different businesses and industrial sectors are exceedingly interdependent. The industrial, commercial, financial, agricultural, and services depend on each other. They grow and decline because of the high interconnection and symbiotic activities that exist between them. The catalyst of the cyclical fluctuation in this symbiotic relationship is profit. The prospect of more profit means more business activities and less profit means less economic activities. Business expansions and contractions move along this line. Hence, the cumulative changes and interdependent interactions of different businesses and sectors of the economy are the causes of the business cycles in the economy. The driving forces of the fluctuations in the economy are cumulative and internal. Each phase of the cycle will generate the next phase. The whole cycle begins with the revival of the economy and then it "develops into full prosperity, prosperity gradually breeds a crisis, the crisis merges into depression, depression becomes deeper for a while, but ultimately engenders a fresh revival of activity, which is the beginning of another cycle" (Mitchell 1941: ix).

A prototype cycle begins with the revival of a key sector in the economy. The recovery stimulates the more sluggish sectors and then spreads to other markets. The future prospects of higher profit will lead to higher employment, causing wages to rise steadily. Higher incomes are followed by more consumption and investment. This trend, in turn, escalates the restocking of inventories and demand for factors of production. In parallel to the escalation of economic activities, the credit market would expand. Prices, wages, and profit continue to rise with the expansion of credit. Along with the increase in demand, the cost of all factors of production will go up. Succeeded by those businesses that started late and due to starting later they encounter higher costs. They pay higher prices for less efficient factors of production. The rising costs reduce their actual profit and dampen the prospect of higher profit. This climate alters the market temper. The very time when prices, costs, wages, and business and consumers' indebts hit new heights, the economy reverses its direction. Down the line, goods cannot recover their original selling prices. Business and consumers' optimism evaporate rapidly. Consumers save more and buy less and producers invest less with more unsold goods in their hands. The debtors fail to pay their debts and the creditors refuse to lend. The end result is falling prices of goods and services, mass liquidation, and bankruptcy. Pessimism spread in both supply and demand sides of the economy. Many firms go out of business and many workers will be laid off. The aggregate income and investment will drop drastically. In time, as the pessimistic outlook gives way to an optimistic outlook, the future prospect of profit growth sets in and triggers the next cumulative upswing.

Mitchell's business cycle model rests on three key presuppositions. The economy is a money-using economy, which hinges on private enterprise and decentralized decision-making relations of production and distribution. From his first major publication in 1913 to his last works on the business cycle in the 1940s, Mitchell relied heavily on factual data, and on detailed empirical data to track the path and uncover the uncharted secrets of each cycle. Burns and Mitchell define a business cycle as "a type of fluctuation found in the aggregate economic activity of nations ... a cycle consists of expansions occurring at about the same time in many economic activities, followed by similar general recessions, contractions, and revivals" (Burns and Mitchell 1946: 1). The duration of each cycle lasts from one to twelve years. As each cycle is self-adjusting, the downturn and revival are embedded in each cycle. Mitchell's business cycle was not yet developed into a theory of economic crisis.

The point of departure from this position was the 1929 Wall Street crash. This was an unprecedented event in the history of industrialized economies. The two notable economists who had some leverage and were adversely affected by the stock market crash were Irving Fisher and J. M. Keynes. Fisher was the foremost authority in the business at the time of the crash. On 22 October 1929, on the eve of the crash, Fisher reported that all is well and good. The fundamentals and the stock prices are safe and sound. Two days after this prediction, the stock market crashed. Fisher lost all his investment including his house and Keynes lost a significant portion of his wealth in the crash (Payne 2015: 82). The magnitude of the crash was such that one could not pass over it. The intensity and effects of the crash were far greater than any other in the past. The conventional theories of the business cycle failed to explain and predict the great crash. The personal experience of these two leading economists was another factor that drove them to think of an alternative theory. In the light of reconsideration of the events that took place and re-examination of their former views, they proposed their alternative theories of economic booms and busts that transformed the former theories of business cycle into the prevailing theory of economic crisis.

Fisher presented his alternative theory in his 1933 article, *The Debt-Deflation Theory of Great Depressions*. Fisher called his alternative his new "creed" of business cycle theory. His "creed consists of 49 'articles' some of which are old and some new" (Fisher 1933: 337). In this "creed," Fisher has kept the most essential part of the neoclassical theory, the equilibrium point as a natural position of the economy. The problem that causes crisis is a deviation from this natural position. But the state of equilibrium:

> is so delicately poised that, after departure from it beyond certain limits, instability ensues, just as, at first, a stick may bend under strain, ready all

> the time to bend back, until a certain point is reached when it breaks. This simile probably applies when a debtor gets 'broke,' or when the breaking of many debtors constitutes a 'crash,' after which there is no coming back to the original equilibrium.
>
> (Fisher 1933: 339)

Fisher held that the deviation from equilibrium in the great crash was so long that its return to its initial position caused "economic frictions" – concluding that such frictions can be absorbed as "any 'free' oscillations about equilibrium" will "tend progressively to grow smaller and smaller, just as a rocking chair set in motion tends to stop" (Fisher 1933: 339). In this article, Fisher further noted that the "deviation from equilibrium" can end into "the great booms and depression" if the business disturbances are "sufficiently great" (Fisher 1933: 340).

Fisher maintained that "big disturbances" cannot be explained by "over-production, under consumption, over-capacity, price-dislocation, mal-adjustment between agricultural and industrial prices, over-confidence, over-investment, over-saving, over-spending, and the discrepancy between saving and investment" (Fisher 1933: 340). These factors, either individually or collectively, cannot explain "the great booms and depressions." These are merely subordinate factors. At their place, the determining factors of economic crises (the great booms and depressions) are "over-indebtedness" and "deflation." Strictly speaking, the crisis begins with indebtedness and followed by deflation. The journey of a typical economic crisis begins when the state of equilibrium is broken. Then the "general economic equilibrium is disturbed by … over-indebtedness" (Fisher 1933: 341). After this, the path of crisis goes through nine phases, given the opening shock is not remedied on time. In Fisher's account of economic crisis, the cause of indebtedness can be many factors. But the prime mover that triggers the process of indebtedness is the "new opportunities to invest at a big prospective profit … such as through new inventions, new industries, development of new resources, the opening of new lands of new markets" (Fisher 1933: 348).

At this juncture, it deems appropriate to take a look at Soddy's observations on economic crisis. Frederick Soddy (1877–1956) was a British chemist and a forward-looking thinker who had great faith in science as the only true human liberator. He hoped that science, in its full glory, would work everything out for the best in the end. It has to be said, however, that for Soddy science was not on an equal footing with scientists. In his frame of reference, the problem was not science but scientists themselves. The problem was the way scientists deployed science, and the way scientists debilitated the sphere of efficacy of science. For case in a point, he pointed to scientists' antipathy in regard to the social, economic, and ethical consequences of their scientific activities. As far back as 1915, Soddy cautioned the world against nuclear war and its cataclysmic consequences. After winning the Nobel Prize in 1921 for his contribution to Chemistry, he devoted most of his time to the study of what he perceived to be the root cause of all human problems. In the search of a solution, between 1921 and 1934, he wrote four books on economics. Unlike his contributions in Chemistry, these works were ignored almost entirely. The cause of this reaction was readily discernible, as the centrepiece of these works was fundamentally at odds with the mainstream thinking at the time, which was riddled with misguided convictions and an unquestioned faith in the hegemonic economic discourse. It was not surprising that he did not receive a better reception from the leading economists, given the dominant culture of that time. In a very pejorative manner, his economic ideas were disregarded and dismissed as being outlandish, alarmist, and inconsequential.

However, time for good or ill is a refutation of itself. This is the case with Soddy's basic message. The thrust of Soddy's economic argument has not withered away into the lapse of deep-rooted prejudices. His mission has not receded from view. What is noteworthy of his economic ideas is not their originality but his perceptive glimpse of future events and difficulties. He was an anticipator who was swimming upstream against a body of thought that had failed the test of time. He cautioned scientists and economists about their shortcomings and the dire consequences of their theories and policies. With the First World War and hyperinflation that followed the war, this triggered a shift in direction of his scholarly pursuits. He considered that the cause of these two events was connected to the ruling economic theories and policies, and scientists' undiscerning and inattentive attitude to the consequences of their theories, discoveries, and innovations. In startling contrast, Soddy in a fit of defiance spoke of such failures and in doing so he paid the price by being banished from the circle of conformists.

Soddy's principal economic ideas have been revived after his death. Here we shall briefly discuss his ideas that have remained relatively influential. The central component of Soddy's economic thinking was his distinction between the real wealth and the illusory wealth. This breakdown is a constantly recurring theme in Soddy's economic arguments. In his distinction, money and debt are not seen as real wealth. They are a form of deceitful wealth. Something that he takes as a matter of course, which he defines as the "ruling passion of the age." An obsession that recourses to economic progress and development by converting "wealth into debt in order to derive a permanent future income from it – to convert wealth that perishes into debt that endures, debt that does not rot, costs nothing to maintain, and brings in perennial interests" (Soddy 1933: 25). From these tacitly assumed stipulations, Soddy seeks his ultimate path of salvation, his Holy Grail in economics. Energy cuts down to the root of every economic activity and Soddy puts it in the forefront of his economic system as the ultimate form of real wealth. In its most discernible form, the origin of wealth is caused by the interactions between energy and matter. Soddy argued that the laws that determine "the relations between energy and matter" are fundamental "in pure science." As an equal measure, these laws are crucial

> in the whole record of human experience, and the control, in the last resort, the rise or fall of political systems, the freedom or bondage of

> nations, the movements of commerce and industry, the origin of wealth and poverty, and the general physical welfare of the race.
>
> (quoted in Scheer 2005: 3)

Soddy offers two inextricably linked solutions to human problems. One solution is in nature's hands and the other in the hands of humankind. In the first instance, the fundamental question is "how does man live?" Soddy says, "by sunshine." From this response, Soddy deduces the inference that real wealth constitutes "the humanly useful forms of matter and energy" (Soddy 1943: 6). On the side of human, he seeks the ultimate panacea in science and scientific progress while he is mindful of the fact that science is a mixed blessing. It can be misused.

Soddy is a disciple of Ruskin. His concept of wealth was influenced by Ruskin's moral prescription that "there is no wealth but life." John Ruskin (1819–1900) was a British polymath, an artist and social critic who questioned the moral foundations of industrialized countries. He was of the opinion that contemporary developed societies know the price of everything and the value of nothing. It is this outlook within which Soddy built his argument about wealth. For Soddy, no energy means no human activity. That is, human life without "sunshine" is simply impossible. Be that truism as it may, equating sunshine (energy) to wealth is a problematic issue. The gifts of nature, in many forms, can exist in the absence of humans. The Sun, the earth, and all other elements that they are furnished with are natural gifts that cannot be confined exclusively to what can be termed as wealth. Wealth is a human activity and the exclusion of the human factor from the equation of wealth is meaningless. Furthermore, all schools of thought in economics somehow include land in the body of their economic analyses either as the only source of wealth or as one of primary factors of production. Soddy's parochial view about scientific inquiry, which he limited to natural sciences, seems to be the cause of taking a very broad and elusive idea of wealth.

Soddy is right about the overriding power of nature over human life. Economics as one of the most fundamental human endeavours cannot function independently from nature and the laws of nature. It was this commitment to nature and ecology, the facets of Soddy's writings, that stirred much interest in his works and that revived some of his economic ideas from the 1960s onwards. With the rise of ecological economics and the increasing awareness of environmental matters by the general public, Soddy's message became more inviting and relevant. In the same way, the outbreak of stagflation in the 1970s made Soddy's views on money and credit less disagreeable. Stagflation echoed Soddy's forewarning about the main trend of the age. A period in history that he marked as being ruled by the passion of debt. Moreover, the expansion of debt means the expansion of virtual wealth. The two types of wealth comply with two different sets of rules. The virtual wealth as in forms of debt is "subject to the laws of mathematics rather than physics. Unlike wealth, which is subject to the laws of thermodynamics, debts do not rot with old age and are not consumed in the process of living" (Soddy 1926: 70).

Money and banks, for Soddy, are at the heart of economic problems. This is due to the fact that virtual wealth increases faster than real wealth. This trend will continue until the gap between the two types of wealth cannot be bridged. Eventually the system will break down, which will then be succeeded by economic crisis, bankruptcy, and violence. The contention here is the supply of money. Most specifically, it is about how money enters the economy and how its quantity can be regulated. A topic that brought forth much heated debate between the monetarists and Post-Keynesian economists in the closing decades of the twentieth century. Monetarists asserted that money supply is exogenously determined and Post-Keynesians claimed that it is endogenously supplied. Neither of the views, however, were original. The currency school and the banking school in the nineteenth century had debated the same concern. As already pointed out, it was also one of Soddy's main concerns when he refers to the inflationary spiral of virtual wealth as the main obsession of the age. Soddy held the banks responsible for this crescendo. That is, banks are in a position to accept deposits and lend out other people's money at interest. Soddy correctly argued that banks are not money lenders in the traditional sense of the word. Money lenders lend their own money, whereas banks control and lend other people's money. Therefore, in fractional reserve banking, Soddy maintained, the desire for lending and re-lending other people's money is insatiable. Much irritated by the role of banks in the economy, he commented that banks start "with nothing … of their own, they have got the whole world into their debt irredeemably, by a trick. This money comes into existence every time the banks 'lend' and disappears every time the debt is repaid to them" (quoted in Shakespeare 2007: 81).

Soddy at the cost of his reputation went against the current thinking of that time. All in all, he was partially right in his main ideas while his opponents were precisely wrong. Soddy was a believer in a state of permanent disorder. Whenever "a problem [is] solved," he would argue it would not be a problem anymore. It would be "dead." Moreover, on these grounds, "a world without problems to be solved would be devoid of science" (Soddy 1912: 18).

## Two crises and three illusory capitalisms

Capitalism is many things to many people. It is many things to the competing followers of Marx and it is many things to different opponents of Marx. Capitalism, as it is widely held, is much like a faith. That was not what Marx was intended it to be but every universal ideology carries an element of faith with it. The messianic message of Marx is not an exception. It is a prophet-centric edict. Capitalism is one of Marx's chief oracles. All history, the past, and the future revolve around this new faith. This outlook has instigated two classes of misconceptions. It has instituted a myriad range of capitalist denominations. Capitalism has emerged as a holy ghost that appears in different sorts of vision. But nowhere one can place exactly the very idol, the common model, which is venerated by some and despised by others. What we have is a range of faith-based sects that adhere to a golden calf that is not real. To the most devoted followers of capitalism, it is a perfect entity and it is eternal. To the sceptics, it is a faulty and untrustworthy economic system that needs to be saved by directing and managing it prudently. To those haunted by it, it is a demon that should be destroyed at the earliest opportunity. Side by side with this divergence in views, we have the configuration of two accounts of economic crises. In its most basic form, the crisis is either self-correcting or treatable, and the crisis is incurable and can in the end kill the bearer of crisis.

Marxian capitalism is unnatural and forbidding. The system destroys itself through its own crises. The second type of capitalism is the prevailing view. It has two sides. On the first side, each crisis can treat itself. On the second side, capitalism is said to be inherently unstable but it is treatable. In the case of Marx's theory, the crisis is an internal matter and is caused by natural laws of motion of class-based modes and relations of production in history. In this account, the motion of history forward is unstoppable. All class-based modes and relations of production will expire in the end. Communism is the only mode of production that lasts forever because it is a harmonious society. In other modes of production, there is a class struggle that is the cause of their destruction. Class conflicts cannot be reformed and remedied. It eliminates itself. Marx credited himself for discovering this "law of motion" in history, most specifically the law of motion of capitalist mode and relations of production.

Marx described the working of the factory production in England. Factory production created a new social setting that led to the first Industrial Revolution in history. It was this social and economic setting that Marx defined as a unique historical mode and relations of production. Max's capitalism is this mode of factory production. A very harsh business world where numerous factories were competing ferociously to make as much profit as possible. It was this struggle for the survival of competing factories and the struggle of the dispossessed working population to stay alive that Marx assigned as the law of capitalism. This was a world of unfettered competition to make as much profit as possible and to survive. Marx reflected that competition is an inescapable external force that each capitalist is exposed to. This external force intensifies the essence of capitalist production, which is the production of maximum surplus value. To this end, competing capitalists trample any acceptable moral values. This constant accumulation of capital on one hand for the reproduction of capital and the rise of the reserve army of labour on the other is one-way traffic. The tipping point of this path of no return is over-production on behalf of capitalists and under-consumption on behalf of unemployed and dispossessed workers. Capitalism without profit has no future. Eventually, the rate of profit in the capitalist system falls so low that the system would be unsustainable. This is because it is in the nature of the system to overdo its reproduction of capital. Morbid obesity is the end result of the working of this system. Something that is due to its irresistible accumulation of capital.

Marx cannot be faulted for observing and reflecting the intense competitive factory production system in nineteenth-century Britain. His account of the economic crisis rests on this harsh working environment. His theory is kept within the confines of the factory production and relations during this period. His long-lasting legacy has become a part of accepted wisdom in economics. Capitalism was his invention but the true followers of his invention are his opponents. Marx was the first economist to point out that the system, capitalist mode of production, is inherently prone to unrelenting crises. In that framework, he developed the most elaborate theory of economic crisis by that time. The footprint of Marx's theory of crisis can be traced to all prevailing non-Marxian theories of economic crises today. The widespread reception of the none-Marxian theory of crisis can be credited to three primary factors. The first one was the experience of the 1929 Great Depression. The second factor was the inability of the established orthodoxy to explain and offer workable policy prescriptions about the Great Depression. The third factor was the publication of Keynes's *General Theory* and its immediate endorsement and adoption by the mainstream economists and the policymakers. Keynes intended to persuade "economists to re-examine critically … their basic assumptions" and he managed to fulfil this goal (Keynes 1967: v).

The cited three factors were instrumental in assent to a non-Marxian economic crisis. In a non-Marxian economic crisis as in the Marxian crisis, the base on which the crisis rests is capitalism. There are two types of capitalism in Keynes's stand. These are laissez-faire capitalism and the managed capitalism. From his point of view, laissez-faire capitalism is undesirable because it "is not intelligent, it is not beautiful, it is not just, it is not virtuous – and it doesn't deliver the goods" and it is prone to economic depression. This sort of capitalism hinges on the maxim of "the paradox of poverty in the midst of plenty" (Keynes 1971: 377, CWK, part 2). This type of capitalism is not compatible with economic stability and full employment, whereas the managed capitalism is viable and not destined for self-destruction. Its downfall is not inevitable provided it is managed intelligently. Keynes laid three preventive measures down to preserve the latter form of capitalism. His first safety measure is the departure from unfettered capitalism (laissez-faire capitalism) and the economic theory behind it. The reason is that the theory behind it is antiquated and does not correspond to the modern age. Keynes compared the theory that backs up laissez-faire capitalism to the "Euclidean Geometers" who operate "in the non-Euclidean world" (Keynes 1967: 16). His second cautionary means is bypassing Marxism – keeping away from Marxian prescriptions. He contended that the contemporary economic problems do not come near to Marx's instructions and remedies. Keynes relegated Marxism to a form of "religion." He was so baffled by it and said how "an educated, decent, intelligent son of Western Europe" finds Marx's ideas "his ideals" (Keynes 1972: 258). His third pre-emptive step to shield capitalism from collapse is the active government intervention in the economy. Because the government is the only institution that can save the "existing economic forms in their entirety and as the condition of the successful functioning of the individual initiative" (Keynes 1967: 380).

Facts of life and Keynes's revolt defeated conventional economics temporarily. Up until the 1929 great crash, the concept of the crisis was a peripheral voice echoed only by a few quirky economists and was a shadowy vision that haunted the common wisdom. The great crash made it real and served as a point of departure from the traditional theory. It helped the mainstream economics to drop out of their self-regulating and self-adjusting economy and to come to an understanding that the economy is prone to uncontrollable fluctuations. No longer after this critical episode, the crisis has been perceived to be an unnatural occurrence. Economic crisis entered the common usage as a composite process, a fusion of many tangled positive and negative feedbacks in the course of economic activities of developed economies. The economic crisis is viewed as an inextricable process with blended reactions that would quicken the pace of economic growth and the rate of economic contraction. Such a possibility became incontestable. Even the most loyal disciples of free-market economy came to this realization and began to recite from the same tune. A typical crisis starts with some sort of distress in the economy. The distress feeds on itself; if left unchecked, it will finally turn into a panic. The negative feedback gets bigger and bigger and eventually forms a stampede that can be very destructive.

The most refined exposition of this theory of economic crisis is by Charles P. Kindleberger (1910–2003) in his classic book, *Manias, Panics, and Crashes: A History of Financial Crisis* (1978). Kindleberger has drawn his interpretation of the anatomy of a typical financial crisis from the works of Mitchell, Fisher and Keynes, and Minsky. We have looked at the accounts of Keynes and Fisher before. Hyman Minsky (1919–96) developed his "financial instability hypothesis" as early as 1957 (Keen 1995: 607). Over the course of his academic life, he revised and expanded it. Like Keynes, Minsky takes capitalism as the base on which he has constructed his theory of economic crisis. In his approach, economic crises are caused by the "internal dynamics of capitalist economies" due to the instability that is rooted in the very fabric of the system. Minsky's capitalism "oscillates between threats of an imminent collapse of asset values and employment and threats of accelerating inflation and rampant speculation" (Minsky 2008: 6). The internal dynamism of the system is such that it cannot all by itself take care of its defects. The extreme fluctuations in capitalist setups are a result of the system's insatiable hunger for profit. A motive that is reinforced, on the word of Minsky, by the system's dynamic mechanism of innovation, economic growth, and its fragile financial structure.

Minsky links stages of economic activities to different financial regimes in a capitalist economy. The first phase is the replacement stage. In this phase, the economy is on its way to recovery. The trigger for the replacement phase is a reassuring expectation that the economic agents with wealth and position feel for the future profit. A sense that is full of promise. Something that inspires confidence like a new innovation, a discovery, or a new market. In this phase, the borrowing regime is dominated by the hedge borrowers. These are groups of borrowers whose business can cover the principal along with the interest payments. The next stage is the period of the economic boom. The finance regime during this period falls, at an increasing rate, to the hands of speculative borrowers. In this financial regime, the borrowers, in an event of an economic downturn, can only cover their interest payments, not their principal obligations. The next stage, the period of euphoria, is dominated by the Ponzi borrowers. These are the borrowers who in the event of an economic contraction are unable to pay either the principal or their interest obligations. Their borrowings are carried out on the expectation that the value of their assets will increase. This period and financing regime is not sustainable for long and the bubble that is caused by over-borrowing and over-lending will burst soon. Minsky termed his "first theorem of the financial instability hypothesis" as the one:

> that the economy has financing regimes under which it is stable, and financing regimes in which it is unstable. The second theorem ... is that over periods of prolonged prosperity, the economy transits from financial relations that make for a stable system to financial relations that make for an unstable system. In particular, over a protracted period of good times, capitalist economies tend to move from a financial structure dominated by hedge finance units to a structure in which there is large weight to units engaged in speculative and Ponzi finance.
>
> (Minsky 1992: 7–8)

Minsky is a faithful student of Keynes. On his most fundamental beliefs, he stands on his teacher's shoulders. Like his mentor, Minsky distrusts the capitalist system but firmly believes that it can be managed by the government using the right stabilizing economic policies in good time.

Kindleberger divides economic crises, broadly, into commercial, industrial, monetary, banking, fiscal, financial, local, regional, and international types. There is not a great deal in his "anatomy of a typical crisis" that is not addressed in the works of Mitchell, Fisher, Keynes, and Minsky. What is novel in Kindleberger's account is his succinct narrative. His originality is in his forensic analysis and in his call for an international lender of the last resort to monitor the world financial markets. As in Mitchell's description, in Kindleberger's depiction, a crisis is set off by a major event, usually a path-breaking invention, discovery, war, revolution, or a drastic policy shift. These are momentous events that alter the "horizons, expectations, profit opportunities, behaviour" of the economic operators (Kindleberger 1996: 34). The far-reaching external causes of displacements can be "war, revolution, restoration, change of regime, and mutiny." Their corresponding internal causes are "monetary and financial displacements" that have a significant impact on the direction of the economy (Kindleberger 1996: 36).

These historic changes are accompanied by new opportunities. Exploiting these prospects in time will set in motion a general feeling of optimism that is an upward spiral. The outbreak and spread of optimism sparks economic revival, which activates investment, consumption, output, and employment. In the course of the revival of the economy, profit and prices of certain goods and factors of production begin to rise. The rise in prices and the anticipation of rising in profit stimulate further economic activities. Profits will keep rising as long as the cost of wages and overhead lags behind the increase in general prices. In the meantime, economic actors keep borrowing and the lending institutions keep lending for the fear of not being left behind. The increasing demand for credit for new investment, consumption, and speculation will expand the credit system, institutions, and instruments. All these changes transport the economy to the point that most economic activities are overdone, overstated, overworked, and over-inflated.

In the first stage, in the stage of economic revival, speculation is well disposed. It is palatable and digestible and generates more output and employment compared to its latter destructive phase. In the last stage of the business cycle, speculation engenders more speculation. It happens because of the "inherent instability of credit," a characteristic that was well-understood by earlier economists. In the end, it is the "inherent instability of credit" that causes "manias and crashes" (Kindleberger 1996: 59). During the economic boom, the overriding vision about the future "hope" is "boundless" (Galbraith 1992: 42). The "high tide of prosperity" at the time of economic ramp-up conceals the truth (Galbraith 1992: 44). In this phase "pure speculation" has the upper hand – a situation when buying for resale rather than use in the case of commodities, or for resale rather than income in the case of financial assets is the name of the game (Kindleberger 1996: 13). Ultimately, the increase in pure speculation turns the economy "away from normal, rational behaviour" and submerges it into the state of "'manias' or 'bubbles'" (Kindleberger 1996: 13). It is against this background and the overheated economic climate that the "valuable objects" will give way to the "delusive ones" and the "swindlers and catchpenny schemes" will proliferate (Kindleberger 1996: 14).

Every economic upswing has got its downturn. The speculative boom cannot go forever. Parallel to the worsening passion of speculative bubbles, the "interest rates, the velocity of circulation, and prices all continue to mount" and not for too long "a few insiders decide to take their profits and sell out" (Kindleberger 1996: 15). Possibly, "some professional traders" begin to sell because they think the time has come when there is "no money with which to carry stocks on margin" (Galbraith 1992: 63). The excessive gearing becomes more apparent as days go by. At this junction, the markets rush for liquidity. At this time, the mass stampede cannot be avoided. Everyone with real or financial assets dashes to get out of their assets into money. The rush for liquidity precipitates the fall in goods and securities prices. The deeper the distress, the deeper the decline in the asset prices. The assets that were overpriced will be quickly knocked down and go under-priced. As the panic is spread to more markets, prices decline further. The endemic of bankruptcy spreads from one sector of the economy to another. Financial panics are infectious. This is because the:

> panic feeds on itself, as did the speculation, until one or more of three things happen: (1) prices fall so low that people are again tempted to move back into less liquid assets; (2) trade is cut off by setting limits on prices declines, shutting down exchanges, or otherwise closing trading; or (3) a lender of last resort succeeds in convincing the market that money will be made available in sufficient volume to meet the demand for cash.
>
> (Kindleberger 1996: 15)

## Conclusion

There is hardly any economics textbook nowadays which does not begin with L. Robbins's definition of economics. Robbins in his *Essay* (1932) defines economics as "the science which studies human behaviour as a relationship between ends and scarce means which have alternative uses" (Robbins 1952: 16). This definition is taught as a self-evident truth, a hard fact that is demonstrable universally. This definition was proposed when the Great Depression was at its deepest end. Robbins was a proponent of the Austrian school. In this tradition, the market order is the supreme economic order. Markets are self-correcting mechanisms. It was from this frame of reference that in the Great Depression, Robbins placed his trust in the markets, as all proponents of free markets did, to heal all. Robbins held that given that the prices of all factors of production are flexible, markets sooner or later will find their equilibrium positions and clear away the excesses and shortages in each market. It was because of this conviction that during the depth of the Great Depression in 1934, he prescribed wage reduction to remedy the problem of the vast army of unemployed of the day. He recommended that "a greater flexibility of wage rates would considerably reduce unemployment" (Robbins 2007: 186). Implicit in the very essence of this teaching, which is the teaching of prevailing economics, is the economic disorder. The market here is perceived as the perfect example of economic efficiency and coordination. But markets are hostages to infinite ends and scare means. The battle between the two opposing sides is an uneven contest.

Times of plenty and times of scarcity are not some of the great discoveries of economists. Its history goes back as far as human history. In the work of nature, we have the good times and the bad times. The times that are hospitable for agriculture, hunting, fishing, and gathering fruits and the times that are too hot or too cold, too rainy or no rain at all. There are times of flood, an outbreak of pandemics and wars, blights, pests, fire, the eruption of volcanoes, and earthquakes. The ancient Egyptian referred to seven lean years and seven fat years. In ancient China, the decline in population corresponded with the removal of each dynastic power. Usually, each of these bloody conflicts was followed by famine (Cyrus et al. 1993). Every relatively well-populated society has experienced occasional monetary disorders. These disorders have been either adopting a new generally accepted medium of exchange, debasing of coins, or the misuse of the credit system. The code of Hammurabi was one of the ancient times' urgently needed social and economic reforms. Such thorough and penetrating reforms are usually carried out against the background of severe social and economic turmoil. Hammurabi was the king of Babylon from 1792 to 1750 BC. His code is the most comprehensive legal code of the time that provided the debtors, consumers, traders, and workers with legal protection. As long back as the sixth century BC, the farmers of Attica in ancient Greece became insolvent due to their excessive borrowing. Solon, a Greek poet, and statesman implemented his monetary reforms against this backdrop. He cancelled the farmers' debts and ended the execution of insolvent debtors. The city of Rome went through a boom-and-bust period in the real estate market in 33 AD. The credit expansion fuelled the boom and exacerbated the bust of the business cycle. To stabilize the land prices, the emperor Tiberius introduced a rescue package that those who were affected adversely by the crisis received interest-free loans (Elliot 2015).

Normal times and times of hardships caused by adverse weather conditions, outbreaks of war, social and political unrest are some things that cannot go unnoticed in any community. Long before any sign of the theories of economic crisis, cataclysmic natural, social, political, religious, and economic troubles had taken place and had been the subject of many heated debates and controversies among the contemporaries. The early economic commentators and the pioneering economists were fully conscious of such matters and their intended and unintended consequences. It stands to reason to claim that the experience of tulip mania, the John Law's monetary experiments, the Mississippi speculation, and many other forms of poverty, economic malpractices, usury credit systems, inflationary spirals, and inconvertibility of money problems were matters that were known to any reasonably informed individual social and political thinker of Europe from the sixteenth century onwards. From mercantilists to classical political economists, trade is the focus of their studies. They all referred to the rise and fall of trade. Irregularity in trade or interruption of the trade from its normal course was not alien to the pioneering writers in economics. Even though trade was conceived as an integral constituent of natural order just like order in the Newtonian universe, it was not believed to stay undisturbed always. In Newton's world, the order, the equilibrium, is maintained by self-regulation natural laws. In economics, the equilibrium position is attained through the invisible hand. Economic equilibrium is not a permanent position. If an economic disequilibrium position is possible, which there is a general consensus of opinion about it, then trade disorder is unavoidable. The disturbance in trade according to the adherents of the invisible hand is adjusted automatically. But the mismatches of supply and demand in a market entail trade disorder.

Classical laissez-faire order and their national background instigated an ideological clash between two traditions. The German intellectuals took a stand against the British economy and economists. Britain was the most developed economy and was the most powerful empire of the time. With its largest number of colonies and the most outstanding economists and most comprehensive economic theories, it ruled the world; whereas Germany was divided, underdeveloped, and poor. Under these conditions in Germany, both the Marxian school and the German historical school were established. These schools rehabilitated classical economics into an ideology that served either the British economic interest or the bourgeoisie class. The German historical school opposed the classical economics free trade theory as the instrument of the British Empire's economic, political, and military power to assert its hegemony over the world economy. Friedrich List (1789–1846), one of the founders of the German historical school of economics, compared the British classical theory of laisses-fair as "a maxim which sounds no less agreeable to robbers, cheats, and thieves than to the merchant" (quoted from Gray 1957: 231). Marx characterized classical economists as the representative of bourgeoisie economics.

Marx's capitalism is widely endorsed as a self-evident truth. Capitalism is a multi-layered preconception. At its primary level, we have Marx's model of capitalism. The rest of the layers are the extension of this particular model. It is one model that does not fit all other models. However, all widely accepted business cycle and economic crisis theories rest firmly on this multi-layered presumption. Capitalism is the icebox in which all shades of economic fluctuations are kept frozen. It is the filter through which the theories of the economic crisis are trickled. It is the shield that protects each variation and secures blind adherence to something that is only imaginary. Blind devotion to capitalism as the final resting place has entered the theory of economic crisis into a persistent vegetative state. Capitalism has been cloned into tinted glasses that every proponent of economic crisis is wearing to observe the economy by the colour of their tinted glasses. The contemporary developed economies are filtered through these tinted glasses. The Marxian economic crisis is seen in red-tinted glasses. This type of glasses is not taken off to the end of capitalism. Those who look at the economy with yellow-tinted spectacles, see the economy as an unsettled economic relation that can be treated and put right. Those who look at the economy with blue-tinted spectacles wish the system is left alone to sort out its sporadic maladjustments. The implication of these trends is a configuration of two worlds. The real world and the world that is seen through different coloured tinted worlds. Unless we remove these tinted spectacles, capitalism, we would not be able to see different stages of development of economies in different parts of the world as they are and understand the nature of economic crises, their effects, and how to deal with their effects with appropriate economic policies.

# 5 Economic crises and human propensity to extremism

## Introduction

Humans are the most complex living species on the earth. The human brain is not only the most developed biological organ in the human body but it is also the most complex thing in the known universe. What we can or cannot know and everything good and bad we do are closely related to our brain. With this brain, we reason, create languages, plan, and invent things; wonder in our imagination; decode mysteries; think, feel, and act. Our brain is the storage of our memories and the collector and filter of our knowledge, sensations, sentiments, and emotions. It is the warehouse of our instincts and creative power. We eat, drink, act, and pass down our genes to the next generation on the part of self-preservation. These things are done instinctively. We undertake and do such activities on impulse. Imprinted in us from birth are the instincts of fear, hate, love, pleasure, pain, shame, anger, sympathy, passion, curiosity, laugh, and the capacity to learn, reason, imagine, and plan. These capacities and capabilities are survival instincts, which are displayed naturally. We do not acquire instincts. We have them. They are not acquired through learning or experience but are genetically hard-wired fixed capabilities that are built into our very being. We are born with these natural capabilities. As a case in point, a mother's maternal instinct is a spontaneous reaction to nurture, nurse, and protect her child at the cost of her own life.

All living organisms and species are equipped with the instincts of self-preservation and pass on their genes to the next generation. However, humans are not merely the prey of their instincts, but they are also the subject of their own conscious and unconscious making. They can shape their environment and way of life by learning and experience. Humans imagine goal-directed plans and execute them. Such activities are driven by pre-planned intentions. Humans can imagine, think, and plan before acting. They evaluate in advance the reactions of others to their acts and anticipate the outcome of their conduct. Humans are furnished with a boundless and fertile imagination. We can imagine an unreal world and can live in it. Aside from living in a fantasy, we defend it, kill for it, and are killed for it. We are armed with the most evolved intellectual capacity and cognitive abilities of all living species. We

DOI: 10.4324/9781003346357-6

are equipped with faculties to learn, reason, understand, and communicate abstract ideas. We are self-aware, have a conscience and cooperate with others, and plan and invent real and imaginary objects and thoughts. In addition, we can be motivated and act with intention and manipulate and adapt to new environments.

Human intellect cuts both ways. This remarkable faculty is a double-edged sword that can be used for good and evil. Therein lie the crux of the matter, the extraordinary human potential, and the root of humans' self-caused and self-inflicted problems. Simply put, human intelligence can be used for the advancement of both good and bad. An intelligent human can be a dreadful person or an upright amiable individual. An intelligent person can intentionally plan to harm, torture, kill, exploit, or enslave their fellow human beings. They can intentionally mislead, lie, control, manipulate, intimidate, loot, embezzle, or steal consciously and wilfully. The opposite also holds true. An informed and moral person knowingly plans to do good deeds. This trait is not restricted to one group of people. It presents itself in all walks of life and employment. The most fully developed intelligent person can choose their intelligence either way. They can be constructive or destructive. Be that as it may, they can be the most savage and ruthless individual or one of the most humane and conscionable people of the day.

We employ our intelligence purposefully. Utilizing our cognitive capabilities of learning, reasoning, language, experience, memory, perception, imagination, and problem solving can be placed in service of a combination of different purposes. They are directed first to serve our primal inborn instincts, then to what is considered as the requirements of pursuing the goal of self-interest and the compliance with the rules and customary practices in the given society in which we live. There is an element of selfish motive in our basic natural instincts. It is the fear of death and pain. One's self-preservation and the defence of one's offspring, or satisfying one's hunger and thirst, or defending one's sanctuary to be safe from the elements, fall into the category of self-interest and self-love. In all these matters, we have the factor of ownership. Each person lives their own life. The life of each person belongs to one person. This self-ownership is demarcated as self-preservation, in the sense that one's strength, abilities, intelligence, desires, wishes, dreams, and interests belong to that individual and no one else. In an extreme scenario, it is the ownership of self, i.e., the instinct of self-preservation that the priority falls to the right of self-defence and self-protection. Saving one's life comes first instead of saving the life of a murderer or an assailant. The natural right of self-preservation justifies the right of resistance and taking the assailant's life rather than being killed by the assailant. Other forms of protection – food, drink, and shelter – are complementary constituents of one's instinct of self-preservation. Complete deprivation from these primary rights also ends one's life.

Thus, self-interest and private ownership are integral elements of rights of self-protection and self-defence. As humans are the most intelligent species, this incredible power, as stated earlier, can be used for good or bad. On either side of this equation, this propensity can be pushed to its extreme. In plain words, the propensity of extremism is embedded in every human activity, in anything that people do and believe. The economic crisis is an expression of the propensity of human extremism in one or many sectors of the economy. In this chapter, we shall explore several sides of this trait of humanity in economics.

This chapter consists of five sections. The first section ponders on the root cause of extremism in economics. It sheds some light on the issue of whether the economic order is the overriding factor of economic crises or the fault rests elsewhere. Does the culpability rest at the door of economic order or human nature itself? This section disentangles a fundamental paradox between the economic orders and the architects of economic orders. The riddle is on the prime mover. Which of these two agencies is the key factor? Which one holds sway and rules the roosts, the creator or its creation? The focus of the second section is on the human propensity to extremism in general. In this section, we shall argue that the propensity to extremism, both negative and positive, is to be found in all human beings. The section will also touch upon different kinds of human extremism, addressing the problem in all its manifestations. The third section is concerned with monotheism as the extreme end of beliefs. It reflects on its claim to absolute truth. The only truth is the exclusive right of only one power and authority. The fourth section provides a selection of extreme human mistreatments to ponder on the fact that most of such mistreatments are overlooked in human history. This section will also look at the critical implication of this calamity in human social and economic development. Most victims in this category are usually selected from the informed and critical section of society, which means that in their absence the society regresses and stagnates. The final part, fifth section, dwells on the role of ideology as the breeding ground for extremism in economics. It looks at the enabling environment in which ideologies create a nesting place for blind conformity and fanaticism.

## The root cause of the economic crisis

In any type of economic crisis, there is a long list of facts at the back of the calamity. These facts are neither exhausting nor sufficient as the only causes and consequences of any given type of economic crisis. There are some facts that are common to all economic crises and there are facts that are unique to each crisis. Economic crises, except those caused by natural disasters, are a characteristic of a relatively large population permanently residing in different locations. The behaviour of a large population inhabiting one location is not the same as a few individuals or a family dwelling in the same location. The coordination and synchronization of production and distribution of economic needs in a well-developed and populated society are much more complex than in a small social unit. The larger the human population, the more complex its economic activities, coordination, and synchronization of production, distribution, and exchange must be. With higher social, economic, technological, cultural, legal and institutional development, people's needs change and get more varied and complex. The greater the division of labour and employment in an economy, the more complex the coordination, management, organization, and harmonization of its different parts. The more complex and varied the types of property ownership, the harder it will get to accommodate the different economic interests in an uneven playing competitive society. The greater the division of markets and the types of goods and services produced and supplied, the higher the mismatch between potential buyers and sellers. More to the point, if there were only one individual and one state and one form of ownership, it would not be so arduous to match and coordinate the different economic interests. However, in a condition of total dictatorship and monopoly of resources, everything will be done on the behest of a single command.

In the present-day economies where most goods and services are supplied not for the suppliers' own consumption but for sale, the supply and demand would not necessarily meet at the same point in time at equal quantity, amount, or size. The truth is that the resources in the world are unevenly distributed. Different parts of the world have different climates. There are parts of the world that are cold, and other parts are hot or temperate. There are parts of the world that are mountainous and other parts are flat. There are parts of the world that are wet and green and others that are dry and desert. The socio-economic history of different parts of the world is also different. There are some parts that are more developed and other parts that are less developed. To add further complexity to already intricate connections and relationships is peoples' diverse cultural, religious, moral values and expectations. There are parts of the world that are trapped in the old colonial and dictatorial structures and there are parts that are liberated and democratic. There are parts of the world where people are better educated and there are parts of the world where the level of education is very poor or is of no consequence.

There are the rich parts of the world and there are the poor parts of the world. There are parts of the world where half of the population, women, enjoy greater freedom and equality of opportunities, and there are parts of the world where the half of the population are denied their most basic rights. There are parts of the world where the economic infrastructures, and social, political, and legal institutions are developed, and in other parts they are underdeveloped and simply dysfunctional. There are parts of the world where monetary institutions and instruments are developed and in others they are not. Finally, individuals brought up in the same environment are not exactly alike. There are those who are friendly, altruistic, and honest, and those who are inconsiderate, stingy, and intemperate. There are individuals who are open-minded, upright, and hardworking and there are individuals who are unconscientious and corrupt. There are individuals who are arrogant or conceited and there are individuals who are attentive and courageous. All these internal and external and many other important contributory factors do influence economic disorders and crises. Suffice it to say that some of these factors contribute more to the gestation, scale, scope, and effects of crises than others.

Over the past three centuries, the evolution of the idea of business cycle into economic crisis has touched many of the observations made above. Implicit or explicit acceptance of economic crisis as an incontestable fact after the 1929 Wall Street crash and after the publication of Keynes's *General Theory* was a step in this direction. In the wake of those events all established schools of thought in economics have given their consent to the possibility of economic crisis. As far as culpability is concerned, different non-Marxian schools of thought have blamed different factors and agents as the chief cause of economic crisis. There are those who assign the blame to the economic system and shift the responsibility to the government to remedy the situation. On this side, the system is argued to be naturally unstable and calls for the government to rectify the excesses of the system. There are those who lay the blame on the government, on regulations, on trade unions, and on all obstacles that are put in front of the unfettered market system. Although they concede that the economic system is prone to crisis, they place the fault not in the economic system itself. From this perspective, the system is not at fault. The buck here is passed to the outside interferences that eject the economy from its real orbit and displace it from its natural path. With this end in view, markets are held as the self-correcting medium.

With that in mind, let us take the case of the Austrian school monetary theory of cycle for example. In their view, the implementation of monetary policy does not only remedy anything but dislodges the credit markets from their normal conduct. It causes the market rates of interest to go above or below natural rates of interest. Driving off interest rate from its natural rate causes inordinate demand or supply of investment and consumer goods. The same principles also apply to other factors of production. Constraints on their regular course would drive them away from their natural rate, which is the cause of the crisis in their specific market. The monetarists equally lay the blame on the interferences in the natural course of the market mechanism. Milton Friedman (1912–2006) held the incorrect application of monetary policy responsible for the cause of the Great Depression. For the monetarists, there is one exception in interfering in the free working of the markets. This is to do with inflation because "inflation is always and everywhere a monetary phenomenon, produced in the first instance by an unduly rapid growth in the quantity of money" (Friedman 1968: 18). From this point of view, economic crisis can be avoided if inflation is controlled. By controlling the supply of money to a fixed rate annually in line with the long-term growth of output, the market forces adjust the rest of economic activities according to their natural course. The most natural and fitting economic system, advocated from this perspective, is the free market economy. It is the capitalist economy, which is built on private ownership, the pursuit of self-interest, free competition, and the state balanced budget. Intervention in any of these components would evict capitalism from its natural order and cause economic disorder in the system.

For Marx and in Marxian teaching, capitalism and crisis are inextricably linked. Capitalism and crisis of Marx and capitalism and crisis of the mainstream economics are not one and the same thing. Nor are capitalism and crisis among different types of mainstream economics. It is to be noted that the economic crisis in all its various interpretations falls back on capitalism. The central error in this line of reasoning is that except for Marx's prototype capitalism, other variations of capitalism are legendary. Both the devotees and hesitant critics have accepted capitalism as a matter of faith. For some, capitalism is a delightful fairy tale and for others, it is a frightful beast. Anything good or bad is associated with it depending on which creed one follows. Different interpretations of capitalism are neither consistent within the same creed nor among different creeds. The interpretations are offered in such a manner as if the system is detached from the very people who have created the system. The system has got its own laws and behaviour in such a way that it is disconnected completely from its makers.

In view of the foregoing, theories of economic crises treat the crisis as if it is caused by an economic system. Oddly enough, they address to a system that has got its own mind, body, and behaviour separate from the people who created the system itself – as though the system administers itself and is bound by its own laws. In relation to the economic crisis, the root of the crisis is the system and not the economic agents that are the creator of the system. This is scientifically insupportable position. Economic crises, putting natural disasters aside, are products of human beings as much as different socio-economic, cultural, political, legal, technological, and scientific developments are their products. There must be something in human beings that leads humanity to such extreme behaviour in their activities. This element of extremism must be in the maker; doer, mover, and shaker of the system in the first place for the system to behave at a certain time normally and other times abnormally. The socio-economic, political, and legal, cultural conditions and technological, institutional, and scientific development either accelerate or decelerate such behaviour but are not the root cause of extreme fluctuations in the economy.

Human nature is an untenable concept. There is not a common agreement on this subject. So, forming a consensus on this issue is not possible. From one perspective, it can be viewed as the essence, the innermost defining string that links all human species. That is something, which is common to all human beings. In human biology, we find many things that are common among all people. They are living beings. For their survival, they eat, drink, breathe, and reproduce. All human beings have a genetic makeup. But we find all these elements in other living things too. Moreover, the genetic makeup of all human beings is not the same. Only 99.9 per cent of the genetic makeup of people is the same. Thus, human nature cannot be defined by biology alone. It may be claimed that human nature is that they are social beings. This element is not also unique to human beings. There are other social beings besides human beings. It may be claimed that human nature is that they are political beings. The fact of the matter is one individual can live alone without being involved with any form of politics. In addition, being a political animal is not a constant thing that is all the same. The same reasoning applies for seeking the nature of human beings in the culture of their environment.

One other thing that is common to all human beings is the capacity to learn. But this capacity is not exclusive to humans. This capacity, to a lesser degree, also exists in some other animals. Nonetheless, this capacity is the greatest in the human species. Human beings are exceptionally intelligent living beings. Their capacity to learn, create, and invent surpassed all other species. They have the capacity to reason, self-realization, self-awareness, self-deception, and self-delusion. All these aspects are mutually interconnected and evolved and have shaped the human species and their ways of living. Humans created languages, arts, science, societies, economies; discovered new lands and means of sustenance; and invented technologies, myths, deities, cultures, and institutions.

The idea of what constitutes human nature is one of the long-standing wonders that humanity has struggled with since the dawn of time. It is divided into three categories. Either human nature, whatever it meant to be, is good or evil or it is neutral. Human nature is thought to be the inner-most essence of being a human in all its various forms. In Hinduism this inner-most nature of humans is good. In the Iranian nations' ancient religion, Zoroastrian, there is a purpose for being a human and that is to fight against evil and defeat it. This constitutes human nature. In the Abrahamic religions, Judaism, Christianity, and Islam, human nature is wicked. Their three prophets were sent to guide their people to choose between good and evil. If the essentials of human nature were good, then there would be no need to send such messengers to guide them into the right path. We are also told that God created all goods and evils in the first place. The fate of everyone and everything is sealed before they are born. So, the idea that humans are inherently good or evil is not compatible with God's act of sending his messengers to lead people to his path. It is important to bear in mind that consistency has never been the mission of any deity.

In the choice to do good or evil, Judaism's explanation of the nature of humanity is more ambiguous than the other two of its sibling religions. Genesis (1:26, 27:5:1, and 9:6) says that humans are created in the image of God. A perfect deity that is the paragon of goodness but also the author of all evils. In the *Torah*, Genesis 8.21, we also read that the "will of man's heart is evil from his youth." In Christianity, it is due to the inherent wicked nature of humanity. Adam and Eve, the first two humans, committed the original sin. As a result, all humanity has been implicated by this sin. In Islam, if we put all its reading about apocalyptic elements of the preordained destiny, the second coming of Christ, the resurrection of the dead and final judgement, hell and heaven – and Islam as the last religion and Mohammad as the last messenger – all point to the evil nature of humanity. What constitutes the nature of humanity is fundamental to what everyone says and does. This subject has engaged the minds of the greatest thinkers since the beginning of time. Thucydides, the ancient Greek historian, described human nature as violent and argued whatever has occurred in history will happen so long as human nature remains the same (Apfel 2011: 147). For Mencius, an ancient Chinese writer, human nature is good. As for his fellow countryman, Xunzi, human nature is evil. This was also one of the key topics of debate during the age of enlightenment. In Hobbes and Locke's views, humans by nature are selfish and competitive and for Marx and Durkheim, it is social and altruistic. For most proponents of the enlightenment, humans are inherently good. They are born equal with an innate moral compass. This distinction is the first step to form an opinion on human and human nature.

## Human propensity to extremism

The dispositions that are attributed to humans, such as good, bad, violent, selfish, competitive, individualistic, cooperative, wicked, cruel, benevolent, fanatical, bigoted, compassionate, caring, mean, generous, rational, and irrational, and much more, all carry some elements of truth. Because people are intelligent and have the capacity to reason and communicate their creativity, findings, inventions, discoveries, and beliefs, then this capacity of being intelligent and their power of reason can be employed for all human propensities, good or bad. One of these propensities, which is the object of this chapter, is the human propensity to extremism good or bad. In every human activity, there is this propensity to extremism. If we take each human activity, we find abundant evidence in proof of this fact. In this section, we shall try to select some cases and examples to show the manifestation of this propensity in humans. As we know, one vital human activity is economic activity. In this activity like other human activities, we have the propensity to extremism. Economic crises are acts of propensity to extremism in economics.

The simple fact is, there is no limit to human folly. One of the human follies is the propensity to extremism. To clarify this point let us consider several examples. It is not unnatural to cover oneself with cloth to protect oneself from extreme cold or extreme heat and sun. In Islam, it is taken to its most extreme level. There are Muslim women who, either by the force of religion, the force of tradition, the force of surrounding, the force of faith or sheer belief or not knowing any better, are covered head to toe in black garb in extreme temperatures of up to 50 centigrade at the certain times of the year in certain places. The extreme reverse side of this irrational conviction is the one when somebody decides to live naked in freezing temperatures to prove their strict belief or otherwise.

Body mutilation and modification have a long history. It is found in all societies and all cultures. The practice can be wilfully and deliberately or it can be by peer and cultural pressure or religious rituals. The oldest recorded types of body mutilations are tattooing and piercing. Ear-piercing is the most common one that is practically everywhere. Ear and nostril piercing are also mentioned in the Bible. The ancient Egyptian mummies have tattoos on them. Such body modifications must have started with one dot of tattoo and gradually extended to all parts of the body being covered by tattoos. Piercing may have started with nostril piercing and then widened to include all sorts of piercing such as ear, labret, lip, tongue, gentile piercing, and so on. Body mutilation for whatever motivation it may be, aesthetic, ritual, or cultural, like the rest of human activities, can be extended to its extremes. In terms of piercing and tattooing, they can be applied to all parts of the body. Scarring all over the face and body is another form of body mutilation as it is practised in the Abyei region of Sudan. It can be in splitting lips, tongues, or enlargement of the lower lip as it is practised by women in the Mursi tribe of Ethiopia with their lip plate. This could be in the form of deforming and sharpening one's teeth as it was practised among the Bagobo in the Philippines or cutting the tips of one's fingers off after the death of one's relative in Dani Village in New Guinea. The practice can be in the form of stretching one's neck as it is practised among the Kayan Lahwi tribe in Myanmar. Extreme practice of body mutilation can be applied to genital mutilation as it is practised for all Jew and Muslim devotees and some women Muslims. In modern prosperous societies, surgical body mutilation has become a large industry, which is a derivation from the same extreme customary behaviour.

The crux of the matter is that any human activity has the potential for extremism. This includes from most basic and vital activities like eating, drinking, sleeping, sex, love, and hate to more complex activities like the quest for knowledge, invention, discovery, the state administration, and living in a society. With a few examples, we shall show how the propensity to extremism in these activities is manifested. Let us take consumption first. The most obvious cases in this respect are either eating too much or eating too little. In the first case, it can lead to morbid obesity, and in the second case to anorexia nervosa. There is a right amount of food intake that corresponds to the right proportion of body weight to the height that is measured by the body mass index (BMI). Obesity is caused by excessive intake of carbohydrates and sugar over considerable time for someone who is inactive and does not do sufficient exercise to burn the excessive calorie intake. Anorexia can be a result of a binge eating disorder or severely restricting the amount of food one can eat. Self-starvation is in the form of bulimia, bingeing, and purging, whereby the person eats too much food and then vomits to get rid of the food intake. Excesses are not just confined to food. It applies to all articles of consumption, from clothes, shoes, and jewellery, and so on. In all these matters, people can have too much or too little of what is necessary for each function.

In the case of drinking, even drinking too much water can kill. As people get more affluent, they will have less plain water intake and more sugary drinks. For many, fizzy drinks with high sugar contents have substituted water as their normal drinks. This trend has reached the point that some individuals are addicted to such drinks that need medical treatment. Perhaps, most fitting example in this regard is alcoholic beverages. On one extreme position, alcoholic drinks are totally prohibited. On the other extreme position, there are those individuals whose entire lives revolve around drinking intoxicating liquor. This analogy can also be applied in the case of substances for which a small dose of each can be found in the normal diet of most people. There are those who suffer from oversleeping and hypersomnia, and those who suffer from sleep deprivation. There are those who exercise excessively and there are those who do not exercise at all.

Historically, sexual relationships between people have been one area of human relations that the propensity to extremism has been too conspicuous. Extremism in sexual relations has manifested itself in either limiting the sexual orientation to a specific group, to heterosexuals, or persecuting or even killing homosexuals, lesbians, and others with different sexual orientations. Or at the other end, we have the state of celibacy, a state of being totally sexually abstinent. In one or another form, celibacy existed in all major religions. Celibacy is practised to this day among Catholic priests. Quite the opposite extreme is polygamous marriages, where usually a rich and powerful man can have as many women as he wishes and treat them as his private properties. Islamic rulers' harems and Chinese rulers' concubines fall in this category. Chinese imperial rulers kept hundreds of concubines in their castles. The Muslim rulers and Sultans were especially famous for their harems where they kept many women for their sexual gratification. It is said that Fatah Ali Shah Qajar who ruled Persia (1797–1834) had over 1,000 women in his harem.

In every culture and nation, there is a story of uncontrolled feelings of romantic love, lust, desire, and intense feelings between two lovers. This hysterical emotion is presented perfectly in Nizami Ganjavi's (1141–1209) tragic story of Layla and Majnun. This was originally a story from Arabia. William Shakespeare adopted his renowned tragic play, Romeo and Juliet (1590s), from earlier dramas. Many argue that he adopted it from a work of the Italian author, Masaccio Salernitana. The lineage of this tragic story can also be found in ancient Greek writings. The crux of this tragic story in its all historical variations is the same. In the story of Layla and Majnun, they fall madly in love. Layla becomes ill and dies. Majnun finds out about Layla's death and goes to her gravesite, where he dies from his uncontrollable grief of losing his lover and his main purpose in life. In Shakespeare's Romeo and Juliet, Juliet fakes her death to use this plan to be with her lover. Romeo unaware of the plan believes that Juliet is dead. The passion of finding Juliet play-act as if she is dead is so strong that Romeo takes his own life. Then Juliet wakes up and finds Romeo's body next to her and finds the sight unbearable, so she too takes her life. This extreme devotion has got two inseparable sides to it. The first one is that one side of the relationship defines their life in terms of the death of the other one. This is the side of complete love and devotion for one another. The other side is the complete hate and revulsion. When these lovers find that their lovers are no more, it is this feeling of complete self-hate and revulsion that pushes them to take their own lives.

We can find the extreme unity of love and hate in the acts of Japanese Kamikaze pilots during the Second World War, the Islamic jihadist suicides, the practice of Sati or Suttee in India, and the practice of Aztec human sacrifice to their deities. The intensity and devotion of Japanese pilots were such that they volunteered to fly their planes deliberately and crash them against American warships and being burnt alive in the act. Japanese kamikaze pilots resorted to crash-dive, out of their fanatical devotion and loyalty to Emperor Hirohito (1901–89). One side of embracing death in these suicide crashes was their divine Emperor but on the other side, with the same intensity, they hated what they perceived to be their enemy. This unity of intense adoration and hate readily prepared them to crash into American warships and as the result to be killed and kill many from the opposite side. It is estimated about 5,000 Japanese Kamikaze pilots were killed in these deliberate suicide crashes.

From its origin, suicide has been one regular method of eliminating the perceived enemy. The Muslim groups in Iran and the Islamic regime of Iran after the 1979 revolution deployed this method extensively. The Islamic regime has organized many proxy groups in different countries and all these groups have relied on this method to achieve their jihadist goal. The best-known group in this category is Hezbollah. The other centre of training for Islamic suicide bombers in the last few decades has been in Pakistan. For the last four decades, Pakistan has been the centre of the deadliest Sunni fanatical groups in the world. One of the ethnic groups that the Punjabi army and rulers of Pakistan most effectively exploited in their suicide factories has been the Pashtuns. These individuals are used against all opponents of the Pakistan army inside and outside Pakistan in Afghanistan, India and in Kashmir. Among the Jihadist groups that were trained and were protected in Pakistan was the notorious Islamic terrorist group Al-Qaeda which was led by Bin Laden. It was this group that organized 19 Islamic jihadists to attack several well-known sights in the US. On 11 September 2001, 19 members of Al-Qaeda hijacked four American airplanes. Two of the planes were crashed into the World Trade Centre in New York, one crashed into the Pentagon, and the fourth one crashed into a field in Pennsylvania. It is estimated that over 3,000 people were killed during these crashes. Here again, we see the two opposite poles of extremism. On one hand, we have immense devotion to Al-Qaeda and its leader and on the other hand the diabolic hate against America and American people and their way of life.

In its different form, the same intensity of devotion and rejection was expressed in the Sati or Suttee practice in India. This practice was not widespread. Nevertheless, it was practised until the nineteenth century in India. It was the custom for the women of a small section of society to self-immolate after the death of their husbands. Burning oneself indicates extreme devotion either to their husbands or to the idea that they were chaste wives but at the same time, it bears the sense of extreme hate that the power of death overcomes the power of life. This practice was outlawed in 1829. Human sacrifice is something that was and is still practised in some religions. The Islamic suicide bombers are one form of the practice. Another form was in the form of feeding gods by the Aztec. This practice was performed in the Aztec city of Tenochtitlan from the fourteenth century to the sixteenth century. In this practice, the victims were skinned, dismembered, and fed to their gods. One of these gory practices involved ripping the victim's heart while he was alive and passing the heart while it was still beating to their gods. They did this because of their devotion to their gods and religions. The Aztec human sacrifice is only a different variation of the killing of humans for extreme religious beliefs. Aztec killing in its essence is not different from burning at the stake for religious motives. The Church burnt alive Giordano Bruno (1548–1600), the Italian philosopher and astronomer, on 17 February 1600 for advocating the heliocentric theory of the universe. Bruno was one of the most original thinkers of his time. The Roman inquisition act of burning Bruno alive to death is not much different, in its essence, from what happened to Theo van Gogh (1957–2004), the Dutch director. An Islamist fanatic slit his throat on 2 November 2004 for his critical artistic works. There are countless similar examples in history that believers of religions committed terrible atrocities on each other or on non-believers out of their intense and deeply held convictions.

In patriarchal societies not only the deities, their messengers, and their religions are male-dominated but every other aspect of society including the family is closely monitored by men. In extreme cases, in these societies, women are reduced to the private property of men. The existence of women are defined by men's beliefs, customs, social status and privileges, legal, political, economic, and cultural powers. Gender inequality and sexism in these cultures are perceived as God-given norms. Men violence against women is rooted in such societies, and it is manifested in many forms; in total control over females' activities, in wife abuse, and in the form of honour killing. The killing of wives, daughters, and sisters in the name of honour is an expression of extreme hate towards the victims and intense admiration towards the men' social, cultural, and religious privileges and status. This gruesome passion in some cases has risen to such a height that the victims of rape are also being killed by the male members of the family in the name of honour.

Among many early human obsessions, God and religion are the two most notorious ones. Gods and religions are human creations. In the beginning, we have primitive gods and religions. Like the rest of all other human activities, they are driven to their extremes. Since its inception, all sorts of things have been used as gods. There is an endless list of gods. The list includes the planets, the stars, the sky, the clouds, rains, wind, hurricanes, thunder, mountains, animals, ancestors, kings and queens, symbols, metaphors, magic, witchcraft, ghosts, spirits, abstract ideas, and so on. All these forms of gods have attributes that are supernatural. Their power is unmatched in human capabilities. These super-beings are assigned the task of doing the things that humans cannot do. Under this self-deceptive pretext dwells a false sense of emancipation from whatever we are unable to do, achieve, or have. Superstitious emancipation is degenerative. It deprives one of the liberties of critical observation, thinking, imagination, and actions.

Gods and religions have evolved in different phases of human development to comply with the desires and wishes of the rulers and the struggle of the masses to escape from their unbearable conditions. Humanity invented so many gods and so many religions to compensate for their deficiencies, vulnerabilities, frailties, and ignorance. In the course of time, the multitudes of gods and religions are reduced to one universal deity with all the attributes of former gods and to one religion with the power of all former religions put together in one and the last messenger with whom human history ends. In this blind alley, one cannot put a foot outside what is the last and the only god, religion, book, and messenger. Their instruction and commands are final. Every aspect of humanity, life, death, pain, hunger, feelings, aspiration, thought, reason, belief, will, desires, happiness, love, hate, and relations is locked in this dark and insulated cage. This conviction stands above everything else. It is superior to everything else. Its goal is to conquer the world and convert everyone to this rigid monocratic authority. Here we have all power and an absolute totalitarian system that has unqualified control over everything.

This was the advent of the first universal totalitarian faith. In this creed, not only is everything under complete monopoly of one God, one religion, one book, and one messenger but these authorities are absolute and eternal. Many faiths have gone extinct throughout history after the formation of universal religions. Over time many gods and religions have withered away. The successive competition and concentration of gods and religions, roughly, can be classified into three general stages: animism, polytheism, and monotheism. In the first stage, anything goes. Beliefs are not limited. Practically, anything can be a deity and an object of veneration. As people outgrown from this phase of revision of religion, we have the rise of polytheism. The transition from this pluralistic stage where the choice of belief and an object of worship is almost a personal preference to polytheism was a radical transition. Here we have higher gods and religions, which have not only limited the personal preference but the demand of these higher powers is greater over their devotees. These high powers not only demand total submission but regular offers by the prayers. The offers usually manifested in various forms of sacrifice such as in the form of wealth, animals, or human life. During the transition from the phase of eclectic deities to polytheism, we have the syncretistic deities that incorporated many attributes of different local gods and goddesses.

For instance, in ancient Greece, there were several gods and goddesses that were responsible for different things. The most important gods and goddesses were members of the same family and were in a cloud on the top of Mount Olympus. The king of gods, Zeus, controlled the weather and was the God of thunder and the sky. His wife, Hera, was the queen of the gods and was responsible for marriage and family. The brother of Zeus, Poseidon, was the God of sea and earthquake. Zeus's other brother, Hades, was the God of Mount Olympus and the dead. His son, Hermes, was the messenger between the gods. Another son, Apollo, was the God of music, art, and so on. There was a division of labour between a definite number of gods. The Romans after the occupation of Greece also followed the Greek tradition and adopted a limited number of gods and goddesses some of which were borrowed from the Greeks and were given the responsibility of certain tasks to do. In ancient India, we also witness this family hierarchy of gods. On the top is the Brahman. Following the Brahman are deva and devi. These are gods and goddesses that represent different aspects of Brahman. For instance, Vishnu is the creator and maintainer of the world and Shiva is the destroyer of the world. The son of Shiva, Ganesha, is the God of knowledge, wealth, and success. Krishna is the God of love and compassion, and Rama is the God of virtue and truth. Hanuman is the God of perseverance and physical strength, and Lakshmi is the goddess of wealth and prosperity. Durga is the mother of all goddesses and the guardian of the righteous and the destroyer of evil. The other tasks are divided between the rest of the different gods and goddesses.

In other ancient societies, we also observe a similar trend. Among the most popular gods and goddesses in ancient China, we have on the top the Dragon as the bearer of Yin and Yang that was responsible for the restoration of balance and justice in the society. In turn, Shanti was the God of law, order, and justice. Guanyin was the goddess of mercy and compassion, and Yan Wang was the God of death and the afterlife. Caishen was the God of wealth, and Zao Shen was the God of the kitchen. We also have Chang'e, which was the goddess of the moon, P'anku, the God of creation, and Niu Lang and Zhi Nu, the God and goddesses of love. In addition, there were other gods and goddesses who were less important with fewer responsibilities. At the stage of polytheism, there is still a choice of homage, devotion to different gods, and call for help from different entities. The next step in the evolution of beliefs from polytheism to monotheism was the belief in dualism that occurred in the Iranian plateau among Iranian nations. Zarathustra was the founder of this faith. His dates of birth and death are unknown, but it is generally believed that he was born sometime in the seventh century and died in the sixth century BC. His teachings reflect closely the teaching of Indian religions, most specifically the teaching of Durga. As noted above, Durga was the mother of all goddesses and the guardian of the righteous and the destroyer of evil. In Zoroastrianism, the religion that Zarathustra founded, the central tenet is the battle of two universal opposing forces. These are Ahura Mazda (wise lord) and Angra. Ahura Mazda represents the good and Angra represents the evil. This battle will continue until the triumph of good over evil. In the Avesta (the Zoroastrian scriptures) and Gathas (the older hymns), we read that Zarathustra received his vision from Ahura Mazda. The central message of the vision was to call Zarathustra to preach the truth. The highest truth and light is Ahura Mazda, the lawgiver that has the power to end the darkness and bring the light.

Ahura Mazda is the kingdom of justice and light. In the Gatha, it is described as the top authority and the centre of nature that is worthy of the highest veneration. Moreover, it is the creator of the earth and heaven. The dualism of Ahura Mazda (the wise lord) and Angra or Ahriman (the evil spirit) is the foundation of Zoroastrian cosmology and ethics. Gods and human beings are subject to these dualistic forces and kingdoms. In one we have justice and truth and in the other the rule of lies. These dominions cannot go in a continuous battle forever. Eventually, good (truth, justice, and light) triumphs over evil (lie and darkness). That would be the end of the dualistic cosmology and ethics. At the end of this dualistic deity, we find the roots of monotheism. As much as the gods, in the dualistic dominions, have the choice between good and evil, human beings have the same choice. Everyone is responsible for their own fate. Those who do good deeds and remain righteous would be rewarded immortality and eternal integrity. Those who lie and do evil things would be condemned to the most miserable life that cannot be reversed for all eternity. In this division also lies the root of the monotheists' two afterlife worlds, heaven and hell. As the fate of everyone is decided after life, the judge who decides the reward and punishment is the Ahura Mazda. After death, the soul of everyone passes the Cinvat, the Bridge of the Requiter. Those who have done good deeds will be awarded everlasting happiness, joy, and light while those who have committed evils will suffer misery, horror, and darkness forever. The monotheist religions were inspired by Zarathustra teachings.

## Monotheism, the extreme end of beliefs

The designation, monotheism, is associated with believing in one God. Henry More (1614–89) coined the term "monotheism." Judaism is said to be the first monotheist religion. The ancient Israelites, however, had a system of the plurality of deities. Sargon II, the Assyrian king, defeated and occupied the kingdom of Israel in the eighth century BC. While his troops looted Samaria (the capital city), they found different statues, which represented different deities that the Israelites were worshiping. These were real and visible deities. After Assyrian destroyed the Kingdom of Israel in 720 BC, the Israelites embraced Yhuh as their main god. The transformation from polytheism to henotheism was the next step in this long process of inventing one God. In the Old Testament, we have the belief in henotheism. This is a situation where there are many deities but one of them is the most powerful one. There is competition between the most powerful God and other deities but not to the point of consolidation of all power in one or the other side. This demonstrates that the ancient Israelites worshiped more than one deity. Their two notable gods were Ei and Yahweh. Ei occupied a higher position than its rival Yahweh. Yahweh was the God of a tribe in the southern Levant and Arabia. It is worth mentioning that the early Jew Rabies were the all power-full beings, the God of gods, and absolute rulers. The first account of one and only one God is an inscription in a tomb in Khirbet Beit Lei. The writing says that "Yahweh is the God of the whole country; the mountains of Judah belong to the God of Jerusalem." In the book of Deuteronomy, the same theme is also repeated where it says "Hear, O Israel, Yahweh is our God, Yahweh is one." But here we do not have any reference to the invisible and abstract God. The concept of all-powerful and intangible being had evolved in the course of time among the ancient Hebrews. It was this incorporeal solo God, all on his own, who revealed himself to Moses. In God's commandments to Moses, he says, "I am the Lord, your God."

The idea of a Supreme Being that is the totality of everything good and evil, known and unknown is what Judaism, Christianity, and Islam have adopted. With these religions, the concept of God is driven to its most extreme point. This invisible entity is said to be infinite, eternal, immanence, immutable, omnipotent, omniscient, omnipresent, merciful, and perfect in every other sense such as beauty and justice. It is said that he has created everything. He is the author of everything and the destroyer of everything. He planned all horrific wars, diseases, sufferings, starvation, earthquakes, repression, torture, and death. He knows all that but, at the same time, he is merciful. This hidden power is self-sufficient. But the most opulent structures are built for him. He is perfectly self-reliant but needs his subjects to worship him. He has heaven and hell, the hell for torture, and the heaven for idleness, leisure, and sexual indulgence. The destiny of who goes where is sealed from the beginning. His types of torture to inflict pain are eternal and unbeatable. His victims are burnt in fire or fried in boiling oil forever. In heaven, the lethargic sex maniac idle men who are intoxicated with overeating, drinking, sleeping, and sex will also hold on to the same lifestyle forever.

Monotheism by its very nature is an extreme belief. Like any totalitarian universal creed, it considers only one group of people to be right and virtuous or even to have the right to live. Only their strict followers fall in this group. Absolute truth is in their monopoly and the God is on their side. With such power, you are never wrong. This leaves open the door for abuse of power in all sorts of ways. Perhaps that is why the three religions in this category, Judaism, Christianity and Islam, have been the most violent and destructive religions in history. These religions have not only been at war with each other but at war within themselves. Throughout their history, they have caused inconceivable suffering, loss of human lives, and destruction. They have been among the most destructive weapons in the hands of dictators and the empires. Their holy wars have lasted for millenniums. For the same reason for over two millenniums, the Jews were discriminated against, displaced, tortured, and killed. The mass murder of Jews during the Nazi's final solution was also of the same nature. The Nazi cult is also a monotheist cult. It is an ideology of the supremacy of one group of people over everything else.

At the height of its power, when the holocaust was at full speed, the Pope and the Muslim Mufti revered and endorsed Hitler's murderous machine.

The Nazis murdered six million Jews, young and old, men and women, in their extermination camps. This religious hatred still goes on in some parts of the world. The wars of crusades between the Christians and the Muslims are another example. It took place between the eleventh and fifteenth centuries and caused inconceivable death and destruction on both sides. The largest empires used these religions in their conquests and subjugation of other nations. Various types of Christianity were employed in the enslavement of people and nations in America, Africa, and Asia. As a result of such colonial conquests, some nations and their people have completely been annihilated. Islam soon after its foundation launched a bloody conquest of its neighbouring nations. In a couple of decades, it destroyed all civilizations in the Middle East and in Iran. The Muslims eventually invaded India. The creation of the Muslim state of Pakistan is a legacy of this invasion.

Islam is the most extreme end point of the monotheist creed. It has assigned to itself one God, one religion, one prophet, one book, and one people. This means there is no other gods but one and this is the God of Islam. There is no other true religion but Islam. The rest are renounced as a heretic and demonic. The likely result under this circumstance is either that you convert to Islam or that Islam will fight against you. Mohammad is the last prophet, the last messenger of God. Those before him had their times and have lost their validity and authority. He is the king of all prophets. So, whoever renounces his commands and defects to Islam deserves to get killed. This is the prevalence of this harsh and extreme type of monotheism that the Islamist jihadists endorse in justification of their atrocities.

When it comes to sacrifice, gods are the greediest of all greedy beings. One principal pillar of all religions is their devotion to their gods. It seems that the more fanatical this devotion, the happier the God turns out to be. Devotions have been carried out in all sorts of ways: by the sacrifice of humans, animals, self-harm, or leading a hermetic lifestyle. The human sacrifice, in one form or another, has been practised in different parts of the world to various gods. It was practised in China during the Shang Dynasty (1600–1040 BC). The act is mentioned in the Hebrew Bible among Israelites. It was practised in Vedic India around 1500–600 BC. Evidence from the ancient city of Ur in modern Iraq about 4,660 years ago also shows the evidence of this practice. It was practised in the ancient Maya by using the prisoners of war as the offering to their gods. During the Chimu Empire in modern-day Peru, in Chan Chan in the fourteenth and fifteenth centuries adolescent women were buried with the king. The Aztec is another well-known case in this regard. There have been group sacrifices as the one that occurred in Jonestown, Guyana on 18 November 1978. In this collective sacrifice, 914 members of the temple took a cyanide-laced fruit and committed suicide. In the same way, the Islamist suicide bombers see their sacrifice as an offer to their god.

Another form of offering to consecrate to the God is the sacrifice of animals. The most extreme of this practice is by the Muslims on Eid al-Adha. This is a religious day that Muslims celebrate by killing millions of animals primarily goats, sheep, cows, and camels. This practice is drawn from the Genesis tale when God tested Abraham by asking Abraham to sacrifice his son Isaac for him. Self-denial is another extreme form of sacrifice for gods. There are different degrees of self-abnegation. The most common of which involves evading real life and following a celibate, solitude, and reclusive life. These individuals choose a hermitic and mendicancy life. Ascetic living is austere and puritanical. It is a life of abstinent, solitary, pray, and meditation and it is known by various names such as mystics, hermits, monks, nuns, abbots, dervish, or others. One type of another such reclusive lifestyle is to serve gods, which has been practised all around the world. These are individuals who retire from normal life and live as loner or in a very reclusive community. The tradition of such monastic sects or individual hermits has existed in China, in India, in the Middle East, and in Europe. There were sects that followed the laws of Moses very strictly and pursued a solitary lifestyle. Eremite was a form of recluse existence that the earlier Christiane followed. In India, this practice came in the form of ascetics, yogins, and seers. In other parts, it has been practised in the form of monks, dervishes, and so on. These individuals seek refuge either in a desert, forest, mountain, or a sacred place to keep themselves far away from the rest of the society. For instance, Tibetan monks spend three years, three months, and three days in their training in the hermitage. Individuals who chose to live in seclusion depend on others for means of living. They support themselves from donations, begging, a patch of land of their monastery, or whatever they find on the earth.

The extreme devotion to gods can be expressed in the form of self-harm. The self-harm can be expressed in the form of refraining from eating and drinking for a certain period. Fasting or starving oneself is practised in most major religions – Judaism, Christianity, Islam, Hinduism, Buddhism, and Taoism. The better-known type of self-emaciation is in Islam that one month in the year is imperative that all adult Muslims fast. In this self-maceration ritual, children are also encouraged to take part. In the Coptic Christian sect, 240 days in a year are for fasting at different times. Religious devolution is also expressed in self-harm. In the case of Christianity, the devotees have been practising the act of crucifixion in different parts of the world. In Shia Islam, during Muharram, many followers flagellate themselves with chest-beating, with chains, and slashing themselves with knives and swords. Such horrific acts in some cases are also performed on children.

The collective attributes of the God add up to totalism. It is a complete deadlock and an absolute dead end for any thought or act to go further away than that. It finishes up to outright bondage and total control, the extreme of extremism. There will be no more and less to this final offer and the last word. This is the invincible weapon that the proponents of gods are armed with. The universal ideologies, fascism, Marxism, colonialism, racism, and scientism, have much in common with this unyielding authority and can be fitted well in this ordinance. Their truths are absolute truths, which are imposed on others by any means. On the other extreme are those who claim to know nothing. By implication, that means anything goes. The word "scepticism" is derived from the Greek word "skeptikos," which means "an inquirer." Scepticism is a remedy of dogmatism but in its extreme form, it is the saviour of dogmatism. Questioning the reliability of any claim or a widely accepted belief as it is purported to be true is a very healthy practice of freethinking. However, in its extreme form, nothing can be known or done.

The pre-Socratic Sophist philosopher, Gorgias of Leontini (483–376), was a founder of this extreme view. For him "nothing exists." But "even if something exists, nothing can be known about it; and even if something can be known about it, knowledge about it can't be communicated to others" (quoted from Christian 2002: 200). The idea that "nothing exists" is a contradiction in terms. This means there is something that can be known and be communicated. The other side of extreme sceptics is extreme cynicism. Everyone can be cynical about some aspects of life: the prevailing customs and conventions, beliefs, social and economic arrangements. Diogenes of Sinop (404–323 BC) adopted this extreme view. He rejected all traditional and conventional ways of life in his time. He considered family as unnatural and tried to live a natural life without wife, possession, house, income, and friends. For Sinop possession of any unnecessary material is a luxury. So, he discarded all his possessions and lived as a pauper. Sinop slept in a derelict place, lived off begging, and broke every etiquette by his plain-talking, fearless actions and urinating in public. His motto was to live in totally unrestricted freedom.

Nihilism and anarchism are derivations of extreme cynicism and scepticism. Nihilism is the most extreme of all these beliefs. The basic tenets that underlie nihilism and anarchism are the same as in their overindulgence in extreme scepticism and cynicism. In Gegias' maxim "nothing exists." In this extreme cynicism, any social, economic, legal, conventional, institutional, and cultural restrictions and regulations are denied. The idea of absolute freedom consists of total freedom from possession, family, state, and conventions. That is, the freedom to live according to nature, freedom of self-sufficiency, and freedom to do and say without any fear and limit, free from customs, values, cosmetic appearance, desires, fears, emotions, and superfluous needs. A life that is anything more than the bare minimum of existence is seen as illusory and unnecessary. Diogenes applied this code of belief to the extent that he regarded even shoes as to be unnecessary and walked barefoot on hot days and in the snow. Nihilism is the last step of this conviction. The term is derived from "nihil," which is a Latin word that means "nothing." The term reappeared in the eighteenth century. It appeared in F. L. Goetius work *De Nonismo et Nihilismo in Theologia* (1733). D. Jenisch also used it in his work in 1796. A more developed version of it was used in a published work by Friedrich H. Jacobi (1743–1819) and Johann G. Fichte (1762–1814). The term came to general usage after Ivan Turgenev, the Russian novelist, published his novel *Fathers and Sons* (1862), where Bazarov, the central figure in the novel, plays the role of a nihilist.

Nihilism is not a monolithic train of thought. The idea has evolved into its many varieties of forms. The core principle in all its variations is the same.

That is the world is meaningless. The world and life amount to nothing. There is no meaning and purpose in any aspect of life. The inner logic of a nihilist precept is total despair and rejection of the prevailing order of things. It is the rejection of the world as it is and the prevailing social, economic, political, ethical, and cultural order. The world and life in the final phase of Nihilism are completely apocalyptical, which spares no point worthy for living. It is at this stage that followers of this creed choose death by suicide. The extreme opposite of ending life in this way is taking extreme measures to stay alive, including sacrificing the lives of others to stay alive. All tyrant rulers use any means, including murder, to stay in power and live longer. It is said that Genghis Khan (1162–1227), the founder of the Mongol Empire, invited a Taoist master by the name of Qui Changchun to bring him a life-prolonging drug. It took Qui about four years and 10,000 km to get to the Khan. The Khan's first question was about life-prolonging medicine, to which he was disappointed by Qui's reply. By some miracle with this direct response, Qui did not become one of his 40 million victims. The Mongols invaded Baghdad, the seat of power and learning in the Arab world, in 1258. They burnt down 36 libraries and slaughtered as many people in the city that the stream of blood reached as high as their horses' knees (Green 2009: 39). Many of Genghis Khan's ancestors pursued the same policy of extreme brutality. Sultan Mehmed III (1566–1603), the Ottoman Emperor, killed his 19 siblings, including infants, to prolong his reign and as a matter of fact his life (Fukuyama 2012: 221).

The other extreme side of cynicism is Anarchism. The term is derived from the Greek term "anacho" which means "without authority." The idea existed in one form or another since ancient times. In its all forms, modern and the old, it rests on a few common principles. On the top, it stands on the belief in human good nature. The good nature, usually taken as unconditional, cannot be fully utilized and expressed unless there is absolute individual freedom. Such freedom would not be carried into effect unless all signs of authority and tyranny, i.e., government, laws, competitions, coercion, and private property, are removed. Proudhon wrote, "society seeks order in anarchy" but anarchy is about "the absence of a master, of a sovereign" (Proudhon 1994: 209). Anarchism is a form of extreme liberalism. It seeks a natural social order in a dreamland. Paradoxically, this natural order is their own mental construction. Something that anarchists revolted against it. In this imaginary construction, there is not any form of authority, competition, coercion, and property. What we have is a complete libertarian utopia that promises absolute and unqualified individual liberty. Opposite to this form of extreme liberalism, we have all extreme clusters of tyrannical political authority, ranging from the theocratic to fascist, imperial, colonial, proletarian dictatorship; absolute monarchy; oligarchic regimes; and any other undemocratic political orders.

Anywhere we look at we can see the behaviour of human propensity to extremism. Collectivists want to go to the end of collectivism by any means and at any cost. The individualist in the same way pursues their agenda in the same manner so do the imperialists, the colonists, the fascists, and the fundamentalists. This tendency is expressed in different ways and at different times. The practice of infanticide has existed in all human societies. That is, the murder of a new-born child for various forms of folly. These include economic, cultural, religious, or having children out of incestuous sexual relations and wedlock or because of children having some form of disability. In China and Japan, the unwanted female infants were drowned. In ancient Greece and Rome, some disabled new-born children were left on dung heaps to be eaten by wild animals. The Kallas of Madurai in India practised female infanticide and it was also practised among the Netsilik Eskimo and Kung of the Kalahari. Among the Tikopia of Polynesia, it was the father who decided which infant to be killed and which infant to stay alive. Infanticide in modern times has been practised in a different way and with a different justification. Two commonly known are the eugenic policies that began in the early twentieth century and practised widely by Nazis' systematic policy of extermination and sterilization of disabled persons and those social groups that they regarded as being undesirable. This policy was also practised in the name of improving hereditary traits and in preventing the birth of people who were deemed to be genetically unfit. Many countries including the Soviet Union, Australia, the United States, Japan, Canada, Sweden, France, Brazil, Britain, Belgium, and France employed this scheme. The Chinese one-child policy also falls into this category. This policy was introduced in the late 1970s and ended in 2015. As a result of this policy, many children, mostly female infants, were killed because the parents feared being persecuted by the authorities or instead of a girl, they wanted a boy.

One of the lavish parts of human history is human cruelty to each other. The most systematic form of cruelty is manifested in the hands of organized states. All undemocratic states are guilty of the most macabre and grisly inhumane acts throughout human history. The forms and nature of these acts are too many to count even during the rule of only one dictator. Dictatorship operates on the principle of indentured servitude and the enemy. Whoever serves and obeys the dictator are insiders and the rest are the real and perceived enemies. In dictatorial regimes, the circle of the accessories gets smaller and smaller over time. To silence their enemies all dictators resort to all sorts of means for this purpose. The most obvious means is throwing their opponents in jail. The autocratic political system rests on fear, conflict, and death. If their opponents have no fear of prison, all dictators resort to harsher and harsher means of punishment. The most extreme means of punishment is the death penalty. In this regard, the undemocratic systems and cultures have been awfully innovative in their invention of cruel means to this end. They mysteriously disappeared their opponents, poisoned, target killed, burned alive, or collectively gassed or buried them alive. In this gory world of extremism, there is no limit to inhumanity. In its most extreme form of this dreadful ritual, the victims are killed under systematic torture.

All undemocratic states and cultures have opted for this method of punishment. The types of torture are limited to the torturers' imagination. To name just a few forms of torture, Brazen Bull was used in ancient Greece, the Judas Cradle in ancient Rome, Ling Chi in China, boiling slowly in east Asia and England, heretics' folk, rack and head crushers used by the Spanish inquisition, and the rat torture used by the Dutch in the seventeenth century and by South American military dictatorship in the twentieth century.

The two gruesome types of torture to death, crucifixion and death by stoning, were originated in the Middle East. Crucifixion was invented by the Assyrians and Babylonians. It was put into practice widely by the Persians in the sixth century BC. Alexander of Macedonia adopted it and introduced it in Rome. In the hands of Roman, it became a common mode of punishing their enemies. The death by stoning has also a long history. It is mentioned and sanctioned in the Old Testament. The death by stoning was adopted and applied by both the Jew and Muslim rulers. All Islamic states have been using this method widely to this day. After the 1979 revolution in Iran, the Islamic regime of Iran employed this grisly method of torture to death extensively against its opponents. The more commonly known victim of crucifixion was the Jesus of Nazareth. He was a Jewish preacher who was unhappy with the Roman colonial rule in his homeland and the corruption within the Jewish religious establishment. His revolt against what he considered to be unjust alarmed the rulers of Judea. The Roman rulers and the Jewish vested interests considered his activities a threat to their power and interests. Subsequently, Jesus was arrested, put on trial, and crucified. This brutal act brings to light two sides of the human propensity to extremism. On one side we have extreme inhumanity and on the opposite side the extreme humanity. The extreme inhumanity in this act is manifested in the extreme delight of the perpetrators of the crime and on the opposite end the extreme humanity of Jesus for standing up and enduring enormous cruelty for what is right. The ineffable humanity of Jesus was to such an extent that he endured the extreme pain, humiliation, and death for what he believed to be just and right.

Another comparable historical example that has been immortalized was the death of Socrates (469–399 BC). Socrates was one of the three greatest ancient Greek philosophers. A teacher of Plato and best known for his method of inquiry of constant questioning to reveal the limitation of our knowledge. The long-haired, unwashed, and barefooted philosopher with no possession and power became a threat to the rulers, religious establishment, and their gullible followers in Athens. He was accused of corrupting the young minds and for not honouring the Athenian gods. For such charges, he was sentenced to death. At the age of 70, he realized this was the time to choose between life and death. He decided that an unexamined life and a life without questioning and free-thinking do not worth living. His burning feeling for seeking after truth far surpassed his consent to submission and indignity. Socrates drunk the hemlock that his executioners prepared for him instead of submitting to their will.

## Atrocities – consigned to oblivion

Most extreme human mistreatments in history are either neglected or forgotten. For this group of people, history is a blank space. Their names and existence are erased from the clock of time. All efforts are made to distort the history and to delete such instances from memory. In cases of this kind, the victims are usually kept in solitary confinement in secret detentions. Completely cut off from the outside world, in full isolation they are tortured, killed, and buried. Regarding this subject, I can speak from personal experience. I was a political prisoner in my teenage. I saved my life with the help of another fellow political prisoner who planned and successfully executed our escape from the prison. The friend who planned the breakout was captured not long after our escape by the security forces of the Islamic regime of Iran and was executed. For over four decades, I have actively been pursuing my human rights and political activism, mostly in exile. The next case of extreme human mistreatment that I will recount is from my first-hand personal experience. The account is based on the fate of a victim who I came to know from the day he was abducted and followed his tragic tale day by day to its sorrowful end.

This tragic tale is about one Baluch teenage political activist. Nasir Dagarzai was only 17 years old when he was abducted by the Pakistani army from his house in a town in eastern Baluchistan. He was abducted with his three friends on 24 January 2010. The other three Baluch activists abducted were Rasool Baksh, Abid Saleem, and Mehrab Baluch. On 27 January 2010, the bodies of Nasir alongside Rasool Baksh, his age, were discovered in their hometown, Panjgur. At the time of the discovery, Nasir Dagarzai was still barely breathing. He was shot in neck and his legs and unconscious. His family did all that they could to keep him safe for four months. For the second time, Nasir was abducted on the way to hospital on 23 May 2011 by the Pakistani Fronter Corps (FC). Almost one month and a half later, on 17 July 2011, the bodies of three Baluch political activists were found at the western bypass area of Quetta. One of these bodies was the body of Nasir Dagarzai and the other two were the bodies of two Baluch youth political activists, Maqgsood Qalandarani and Murtaza Sarparah Baluch. Hardly any bone was left in one piece in their bodies when these bodies were discovered.

Radio Gwank interviewed Nasir at the time when he was recovering from his first ordeal. In this interview, he described the details of his and his friends' abduction on the first occasion. He told the interviewer that Pakistani army broke into his house abducting him, Rasool Baksh, Abid Saleem, and Mehrab Baluch. In the secret location, where they were taken, he saw a few more captives who were hanged upside down. Nasir recalled an old army man entering the room with a knife. Right away, the old man went by the side of Mehrab and without hesitation he cut some flesh from Mehrab's thigh. He then turned to Nasir and slashed Nasir's chest. While the old man was cutting Mehrab's thigh and slashing Nasir's chest, a young soldier was hard at work on crucifying Abid Saleem. After rubbing salt on Nasir's wounds, the old man left the room. When Nasir regained consciousness, he saw Abid Saleem and Mehrab were given electric shocks. The last thing that Nasir recalled of this torture room was being whipped with a purposely made belt with iron bolts on it. Nasir went on to say:

> The next morning … they broke Mehrab's arm first, then Saleem's arm, and after that my arm. By this time Rasool Baksh was dead and his body was hanging by the ceiling … Then … we were taken in a jeep and after a short drive we were lined up in front of twenty army men. The commander addressed his squad by saying that: 'these Baluchi are infidels. They are fighting against Allah and his prophet. They get their orders from Israel and India that is why killing them serves Islam.' Then they shouted 'Allaho Akbar,' and fired at me.
>
> (Radio Gwank 2011)

One will never know the extent of suffering that this teenager endured during his second time in captivity. Even thinking about it is simply incomprehensible. In the course of four to five months, Nasir experienced the worst of all possible inhumanity. The trauma is told in his own words. His ordeal during the second time is a forgone secret. The fact is this horrific case is not uncommon in colonized nations. The example of Nasir is only the tip of the iceberg of extreme barbarity that Baluch political workers are subjected under the colonial rule of Punjabi army of Pakistan. The fate of all Baluch political and human rights activists who are captured and disappeared by the occupying security forces of the Islamic states of Pakistan and Iran cannot be other than what Nasir's harrowing experience.

To come to the point, in delving deeper into any aspect of life we can see human propensity to extremism. There is not any activity in human life that is not prone to extremism or it has not been driven to extremism. All beliefs and ideologies can be driven to the point of absurdity. The empires start with the occupation of one nation or a segment of one nation and then there is no limit in their imperialist ambition until their ultimate collapse. The state is meant to protect the security of the citizens and restore law and order. Yet, a state turns into an empire. To rule as far or as long it is possible is the intention of any tyrant ruler. An emperor keeps subjugating new nations and draw new artificial borders. When empire collapse, they leave a trail of toxic parasite states behind that are accountable to nobody. An archetype of such a state is the Islamic state of Pakistan. In these colonial geopolitical structures, the aim of the state would never be the pursuit of humanism, liberty, welfare, happiness, freedom, and justice but the protection of the interest of the clandestine ruling establishment and the artificial colonial borders. In policing their Frankenstein state, they commit the most inconceivable irrational acts and crimes imaginable.

The human propensity to extremism can manifest itself in every extreme act and behaviour. Opposite of pathological liars are those who never lie. There are those obsessed with cleaning and there are those who never wash. Many run from society and are reticent, and those who are too outgoing recognize no social barriers. Some are too secretive and there are those who never keep a secret. Some are too timid and there are those who are too brave. Many do not do any physical exercise and constantly eat and lose their body shape, and others do too much exercise and use anabolic steroids to change the shape of their bodies. Some are too mean and there are those who are too generous. The hoarders keep hoarding and the incorrigible spender keeps spending. The compulsive gamblers live in taking risks and the pusillanimous dread any risk. The adventurous adventures to their death and the hidebound may not go anywhere. On one extreme, the moral bearings are strictly observed and on the opposite extreme, we find no scrupulous compliance. One is killed for their freedom and one kills to prevent liberty. One takes their life for the protection of the life of another and one kills others out of their fear of imaginary enemies.

A malignant narcissist intoxicated with a sense of self-importance expresses no or very little empathy towards others while an extreme altruist has no life of their own but life for others. A dictator creates their own prison intending to have their own absolute freedom safeguarded but deprives the rest of population to have any freedom. Some experiment on animals and there are those animal lovers who kill to prevent cruelty against animals. Some are poaching endangered animals and there are those who protect endangered animals at the cost of one's life. The absurdity is extended to the point that there are those who pay an extortionate amount of money for a small piece of the bone of these animals for some imaginary medicinal use. Extremist anti-abortion individual aims to save a life but go as far as to kill the doctor who does the work of abortion under the law even if the foetus is a result of rape. We have the misogynists and, on the opposite side of it, we have the misandrists. We have one for kicking a ball or for landing blows on their opponent's head paid millions of pounds, and someone who saves life but gets no more than the minimum subsistence level.

Education is generally perceived as a positive thing. For many, this is the only way to break from poverty and illiteracy. For most, it is a key factor in the development of culture, economy, and civilization. Undoubtedly, no society would flourish without the acquisition of knowledge. But education has its extreme side to it too. Once, Haim Ginott (1922–73), a High School Principal in America and a holocaust survivor, sent a letter to his newly appointed teachers. In the letter, he said,

> I am a survivor of a concentration camp. My eyes saw what no man should witness: Gas chambers built by learned engineers. Children poisoned by educated physicians. Infants killed by trained nurses. Women and babies shot and burned by high school and college graduates.
>
> (quoted from Mitchell 1980: 14)

In Ginott's letter, there is a terrible truth. That is, one determining pillar of the dictatorial and totalitarian political systems is educated individuals. The strength and prolongation of such systems depend more on the educated fabric of the system than one dictator who is the head of the system. Preservation of modern dictatorial, colonial, and totalitarian regimes, by and large, is due to this section of society. It is from this section of society that the legitimacy of the system is formulated and is traded. They invent the most horrific instruments of imprisonment, torture, and repression and create and train an army of fanatics and murderers to defend their possession. For the Nazis, they have invented a superior race, and for the communist the historical inevitability of their rule. It was the educated class in Iran who saw the picture of Khomeini on the moon first and made the gullible crowds believe it devotedly. It is from this section of Indian Muslims who fabricated the idea of an Islamic nation and divided India.

It was the educated class that invented the nuclear bombs in the Second World War. The Americans feared that German scientists could have the bomb first, because they heavily invested in research and development of the bomb. The German scientists, in this respect, were a step ahead of their counterparts in other countries. They had discovered nuclear fission in 1938. The atomic bomb was invented and used in the name of defending the free world. On 28 December 1942, Franklin Roosevelt (1882–1945), the US president, authorized the formation of the Manhattan Project. In this project, the brightest nuclear physicists in America were gathered and led by Julius R. Oppenheimer (1904–67) to invent the deadliest and most destructive weapon ever in human history. The oxymoronic propensity to extremism in this act, on one side, is supposedly the brightest minds of the world and, on the other side, is their invention of the deadliest weapon till then in human history. How come the brightest become so unwise that they could not discern the cost of their idiocy? On 16 July 1945, the first nuclear bomb was tested and in April 1945 the war ended in Europe. The first nuclear bomb was dropped over the city of Hiroshima on 6 August 1945 and three days later the second bomb on the city of Nagasaki. The total death from these two nuclear blasts and subsequent exposure to nuclear radiation is estimated to be over 300,000 individuals (McGarry and Walklate 2019: 97). Yet, in the same field but the opposite extreme we had the heroism of up to 600 Ukrainian helicopter pilots who flew over the Chernobyl Nuclear Power Plant in 1986 to minimize the impact of the disaster. Chernobyl was the world's worst civilian nuclear disaster. About 30 pilots subsequently died as a result of exposure to nuclear radiation. After the US, eight other countries have acquired nuclear weapons. Among them is the rogue state of Pakistan. The economic costs of acquiring nuclear bombs and maintaining such weapons go many billion dollars that could have been used more productively for the well-being of the citizens of these countries or elsewhere.

Things become trendy but all the rage is not exclusive to wearing a cap backwards. Going into fashion encompasses all aspects of life, i.e., ideas, beliefs, culture, and theories. The list is endless. All these aspects can and have been driven to their extreme ends. As in beliefs, to religious fundamentalism, as in ideas, to fascism, totalitarianism, and anarchism, as in economics, to an idealization of pure market economy or pure communist economy, as in aesthetic, to mutilation of the body or forcing a people of a nation to wear different clothes from their national costumes and adopt a different language from their mother tongue. Mustafa Kemal Ataturk (1881–1938), the military dictator and founder of the Turkish Republic, forbade the Turks to wear Turkish costumes and adopted the European dress code. Equally farcical was that soon after adopting the European dress code, the imitated dress code pretended to be the original dress code of the Turkish nation. Due to artificial colonial borders drawn, a segment of the Kurdish nation ended up under the control of Turkey. The Kurdish population was not only forced to dress code to look like the Turk but to discard the Kurdish language and speak Turkish.

Another moronic example of this nature took place in Iran. Reza Khan Mir Panj (1878–1944), a Persian military dictator and a contemporary of Kemal Ataturk, assumed political power in the 1920s in Iran. He too followed the same derisory policy in Iran as Ataturk had done in Turkey. The Persians were forced to discard their traditional clothes and to adopt the European dress code. Then the European dress code purported to be the Persian traditional dress code, and all other nations under the Persian colonial rule such as the Kurds, Baluch, Arab, Turkmen, Turk Azerbaijanis, and others were not only forced to change their dress codes to European dress codes but to discard their languages, cultures, and values and adopt the Persian language and the way of life. For about 1,000 years, foot binding was practised in China. In this practice, young girls' feet were wrapped very tight to the extent that their arched were broken. A very painful practice that had left the girls being disabled and limited their ability to move. Despite all its adverse effects, foot binding was revered and it was a symbol of status and a badge for getting married to higher social classes. This practice was only officially banned in 1911 in China.

Thus, every aspect of human life can and is driven to extremism. We know that the planet earth does not belong to one species. But it is the human species that have driven millions of plant and animal species to extinction and many more are in danger of extinction. We have poisoned the atmosphere, depleted the earth of its natural resources, and deforested many areas of the world. Millions of people were hunted through repeated genocides or evicted from their homelands. History is distorted by the sage apologists. The natural boundaries of nations are unreal but Frankenstein's boundaries and states are real. We have created monstrous cities with monstrous buildings that can only function in prosperous times. With any protracted decline in prosperity in these human settlements, these skyscraper cities fall into ghost superstructures, in which affliction has never been experienced in human history. It must be stressed that demolishing and repairing these mega-tall superstructures even in time of prosperity is a herculean task. All cities will pass their golden years and decline. In their old age and continuous economic decline, demolishing and repairing these gigantic cities dominated by monstrous skyscrapers is only an idle hope.

In Europe, the fever for witch hunting started from the mid-fourteenth century up to the eighteenth century. From the early fourteenth century to 1650, it is estimated that in Europe between 200,000 and 500,000 people, mostly women, were implicated as witches and were either hanged or burned at the stake (Ben-Yehuda 1980: 1). The witch hysteria was more widespread in Germany and Switzerland compared to other parts of Europe. In St Maximin, in Germany, with a population of 2,200 between 1572 and 1590, up to 500 confessed under torture to be witches and were burned at the stake. In Switzerland between 1400 and 1782, the number of people accused of being witches and subsequently hanged or burned at the stake is estimated to be 80,000 people. Most of the victims of the witch craze were women.

Needless to say, that trade is a vital factor for economic development. But the extreme end of trade is the trade in illicit drugs and trafficking of people, especially trafficking of women and children. Slave trade is another extreme form of trade. Suffice it to mention that the slave trade did not start with the transatlantic slave trade. Its roots go back to ancient times. In Africa, the institution of slavery was endemic before the European put their foot in the continent. In Congo to the present day the Pygmies, the oldest Indigenous people of central Africa, are treated in the most inhumane manner. The Bantu ethnic group, who migrated from south west of Africa, not only enslave the Pygmies but also keep them as pets.

In 1984 Josef Fritzl (born 9 April 1935), an Austrian father, kidnapped her own daughter, Elisabeth Fritzl (born on 6 April 1966). He held her in his cellar for 24 years in the town of Amstetten. Josef apparently a normal dedicated family man began raping his daughter when she was only 11 years old. Elisabeth went missing on 28 August 1984. Her father carefully planned her abduction. During the 24 years of captivity, her father forced her to watch pornographic films and then raped her as a result of which she gave birth to seven children under the cellar horrific circumstances. The Austrian police discovered Elisabeth on 26 April 2008.

Greed is a desire. It is an insatiable craving, some kind of starvation, yearning, hunger, thirst, and passion that has no boundaries. No one is free from this. We are all endued with a certain degree of it. In its most natural state, greed reveals itself in the act of self-preservation. On one extreme one possesses one's body and life and at the other extreme one employs all means to possess everything else, including the lives and bodies of others. It has been out of this extreme greed that we have enslaved the earth and almost everything in it – as if the whole planet and all species in it are created to serve humans. The tendency to possess everything and have a monopoly over everything has created social classes and the states with more power and wealth and others with less or no power and wealth at all. At the very extreme end of this power and wealth relationship, the oppressed and the dispossessed in the course of history have on and off resorted to revolt against their social and economic conditions. But a revolution in itself is another form of extremism. This behaviour is an extreme act of human behaviour since the oppressed classes cannot express their grievances rationally, humanely, democratically, legally, and peacefully. Suffice it to say, extreme human behaviours cannot be executed calmly, calculatedly, judicially, and mindfully.

Baron d'Holbach in 1773 in his cautionary note has reminded us that one thing that the "revolution men" do is that they are "guided by fury." One thing that they do not consult is the reason (Stromberg 1994: 15). This cautionary note is not far from the fact of the matter. I need hardly say that all violent revolutions take place in very traumatic social conditions. The turns of events and circumstances are so fast and hyped up in a fiery rage that only the extremes appear attractive and gratifying. Political revolutions stir up humans' deepest hostility and passion. The fanatical revolutionaries are only blinded by the power of mob rule and by the state of anarchy and can do anything in the names of their ideals. One of the prime movers of revolutions is liberty, to be emancipated from the former tyranny. Madame Roland (1745–93) and her husband Jean-Marie Roland de la Platie're (1734–93) took part in the 1789 French Revolution and soon after the revolution they became the sacrificial victims of the revolution. They were among the first victims of the revolution who were convicted and executed on a charge of treason to revolution. It is said that at the very last moment, at the foot of the guillotine to be executed, she cried out these last words: "O Liberty, how many crimes have been perpetrated in thy name" (Smyth 1855: 95).

In the 1979 Iranian revolution, I merely attended a few demonstrations that were organized against the monarchy regime in my hometown. In the early days of the revolution, it was the ideals of freedom, justice, and equality that I was attracted to like most of those who took a part in the revolution. At the last stage of the revolution, at the time of precipitous mayhems, these ideals were substituted with a frenzied rage of revenge, violence, and destruction. The mobs attacked everything that was somewhat associated with the former regime. Among them were the King's palaces. One of these palaces was the Niavaran palace. Mahwash Aminzadeh, a middle-aged woman, used to be one of the maidservants in this palace. The revolutionary mob caught her and took her around the streets while she was beaten viciously from every side, and in the end, they burnt her alive. The only evidence of this barbaric act is a picture taken of her by a France Press journalist. In this picture, we see the victim with her bloody face with the picture of Hossein Salami on her right side with a knife. Hossein Salami became the head of the Islamic Revolutionary Guard of Iran in 2019.

## Embedded extremism in economics

Modern economics as a discipline of inquiry, of its own accord, is a byproduct of the age of enlightenment. From its very foundation, it was divided into different schools and sub-schools of thought. That being the case, there is no economic theory that is universally accepted or can be applied always in any place in the world at any time. In the realm of economics, as in any of human endeavours, economic activities and ideas can be driven to their extreme edges. The facts of life with which economics deals are not addressed discretely from one's allegiance to certain societies, cultures, ideas, and moral compass. Indeed, there is a point of central concern in every economic school of thought, which is puritanic and is revered. Like in any system of thought, belief, ideology, or theory, this golden calf can be driven into its most extreme bounds. It is this central concern in each school that is driven to its most extreme leeway. The thing that is presupposed tends to be the central concern of each school of thought. For instance, mercantilists equated economics to precious metal. These metals are said to be "the avenues by which power and strengths" of each nation were achieved (Gray 1957: 79).

To the Physiocrats it is the land. The ultimate source of wealth and well-being is land. Quesnay, the founder of the school, maintained that land is "the source of all the wealth of the State and of the wealth of all citizens" (quoted from Galbraith 1988: 52). For classical economists, the end in any economic activity is the pursuit of self-interest. Smith has captured this end in his often-cited passage where he says

> it is not from the benevolence of the butcher, the brewer, or the baker, that we expect our dinner, but from their regard to their own interest. We address ourselves, not to their humanity but to their self-love, and never talk to them of our own necessities but of their advantages.
>
> (Smith 1986: 119)

Marx wrapped up all economic activities in labour. In his capitalist mode of production, he buried it in one form of labour, the labour power of industrial workers. To German historical school, this ultimate intent is the state. The state is not only the end but it is "the centre of all things, and consequently all wealth, all production" and all consumption (Gray 1957: 221). Adam Muller (1779–1829) wrote that the state "is not merely a fundamental human need; it is the supreme human need" (quoted from Mills 2002: 84). To the marginalist school, it is the decision of the economic agents, which is made at the margin (O'Connor 2014: 15). That is, in the case of consumers it is made at the marginal utility and in the case of producers it is made at the marginal cost.

For neoclassical economics, the end is the market equilibrium. The point where the rational economic agents make their rational choices and reach a balanced agreement that all sides of transactions maximize their self-interests. At the equilibrium price, supply equals demand, and markets are clear. This is the point of rest where the economic agents maximize their utilities and profits and the resources are said to be allocated most efficiently. The institutionalists put institutions at the centre of their economic theory. It is the institutions that determine every economic activity, shape, and direct human societies through humans' collective actions. Humans act collectively and their collective actions not only guide individuals' actions but liberate each individual:

> from coercion, duress, discrimination, or unfair competition, by means of restraints placed on other individuals. And collective action is more than restraint and liberation of individual action – it is an *expansion* of the will of the individual far beyond what he can do by his own puny acts.
>
> (Commons 1943: 15 – italics in original)

For Keynes and Keynesians, economic policy is central to their economic theory. Keynes argued that the ultimate object of his "analysis is to discover what determines the volume of employment" in order to remedy the problem of unemployment by adopting and applying appropriate practical macroeconomic policies. He further noted that unemployment is a short-term problem, which requires an immediate solution. Keynes backed this supposition up with one of his best-known sayings that "in the long run, we are all dead" (Keynes 1971: 65). In view of the foregoing, he argued that this objective can be achieved by timely application of macroeconomic policies, most specifically fiscal policy. The Austrian school has an unfettered free market as the cornerstone of their system of thought. The free market covers everything. It is a natural process, which promotes the best order and results. The institution of the market is not the work of deliberate design but it results from a spontaneous order where individuals of their own accord and freely pursue their self-interest. The unfettered market is idealized to such an extent that it takes the place of everything, including the total denial of the existence of society. This is also the ideal economic order of the monetarist. However, for the monetarists, there is a fundamental and underlying problem in the economies of present times that prevents this ideal economic order from operating naturally at its full capacity. The problem is the unrestrained money supply, which is against the natural order of the economy. For the Post-Keynesian it is the instability of the capitalist economy caused by uncertainty and for behavioural economics, it is human psychological motivations.

In all these perspectives, there is one overriding preconceived idea. There is a controlling presupposition that stands above all considerations in each school and it is the driver and the growth lever of the school. This focal foregone conclusion is the centre of the field of inquiry of each school. As in god, this defining idea is kept sacred. All and everything known and unknown in economics is strained through this filter. The governing presupposition is the end of the line, the measure of the broad-based agreement within and disagreement with the adversaries. This one-way approach has got one target insight at the expense of everything else. The monocratic goal that all schools of thought have in common is the root of everything. The almighty desire in all dominant schools of thought in economics is economic growth. In all these schools, economic growth is the measure of everything else in the economy and society. Everything else is sacrificed or neglected to this end. Any growth in the economy by any means is viewed as the factual confirmation and consistency of the theory in question – regardless of the context in which this illusory economic growth may have manifested itself. Such shadowy economic growth to a certain degree is found in all slavery-dominated systems of production, under serfdom, imperial powers, and under the captivity of the cruellest Sultans, monarchs, and megalomaniac narcissist dictators. In modern times, there has been economic growth in Stalin's totalitarian system of the Soviet Union; in Hitler's fascist Germany; in communist China; and in all imperial nations, their colonies, and all colonial geopolitical structures that have been under the yoke of the left, right, and theocratic dictators. At certain periods of time of the Islamic fundamentalist rule in Iran, Pakistan, and Afghanistan, we have witnessed the growth in the economy under their control. Such growth has occurred under all cultures, political systems, legal, institutional, social relations, and historical period.

To this end, the totality of economic ideas can be narrowed down into two trends of thought. The shades of opinion that embrace capitalism as the most effective means for economic growth and the range of views that are anti-capitalism. The anti-capitalists do not deny economic growth in capitalism but are convinced that in their varied alternative systems economic growth will be greater and more balanced. In this denomination, capitalism is a system that is based on exploitation and poverty. Virtually all currents of economic thought are fixated with capitalism. They are habitually captivated by it and have remained obsessed by it. The common ground and thread is capitalism for all currents of thought in economics. There are those who are pro-capitalism and there are those against it. Capitalism is the basis of the divided loyalties. It is the lens from which the ideals of each school are defined and filtered. As a result, little attention is paid to the central problems of modern economies. Even there is no consensus about capitalism, which is the point of convergence of all dominant trends of thought in economics. The failure to reach consensus is not due to the lack of intelligence but it is due to either idolizing or cursing something that does not exist in reality. It is merely a preconceived belief that is crystallized in hate and devotion to a specific ideological persuasion.

This being the case, all economies are judged in the light of their growth. The economy of an independent democratic nation, in this respect, is aligned with the economy of a colonized nation. Let us consider the Sykes-Picot agreement to explain this subject matter in more detail and shed some light on the absurdity of bringing a democratic economy to the same level as a subjugated and overbearing economy. The British, the French, and the Russian Empires plotted a plan to break the Ottoman Empire. They signed this agreement in 1916. The main objective of the agreement was to dismember "the sick man of Europe." The 1917 Russian Revolution prevented Russia to fulfil its task in this agreement. But the other two empires ripped the Ottoman Empire to pieces and divided most of it between themselves by drawing many arbitrary borderlines and creating several arbitrary countries. For the sake of argument, Iraq and Syria are among these colonial geopolitical structures. One of the nations that were sacrificed from this scheme was the Kurdish nation. Kurdistan was divided into several parts. Two parts of which were annexed to Syria and Iraq. Kurdish society has been incapacitated ever since. Kurdish people have been living in a state of perpetual war from that time. But the right, the left, and the religious have congratulated themselves on any economic growth that has been made in Iraq and Syria – oblivious to the actual economic and human costs that these artificial boundaries are loaded with. Picture this possible world. An independent Kurdistan where its society is marked by open and civic life. Its political system is characterized by free and fair elections, separation of powers, rule of law, free expression, belief, association, and well-developed and progressive property rights. It is under such conditions that the actual and the potential of people can most effectively be utilized with the least cost. Economic resources and human potentials cannot be utilized under one form or another colonial boundary or under any tyrannical despotic state. Mainstream economics is indifferent to such matters.

For the purposes of this discussion, let us take another example. It was obvious that the British Empire would not leave its jewel in the crown, India, without harming it. At this junction, it is worth to point out that even Keynes did not question the British colonial rule in India. This factor has never entered the design of his economic theory. At the time when Indian independence was unavoidable, Churchill declared "to keep a bit of India." As a result, two provinces of India, the Province of Bengal and the province of Punjab, were divided. This was how the British rulers invented East and West Pakistan in 1947. In a way, the British colonial rulers of India created the first fundamentalist Islamic state by dividing India into two parts. Soon after its creation, Pakistan in the name of Islam incorporated some parts of the Pashtun regions that the Durand Line in the 1890s separated from Afghanistan and annexed into the Indian Raj. In 1948, the Pakistani army occupied eastern Baluchistan and annexed it to Pakistan. In the mainstream economic theory, the Baluch economy has no distinct entity. It is lost in the arbitrary state of Pakistan. Thus, all actual and historical potentials of the Baluch nation are overshadowed by this fake political entity. Pakistan is an archetypal colonial geopolitical structure that is dominated by the Punjabi Muslim military, political, and religious establishment. To the prevailing economic schools of thought, Pakistan is not any different from any free and democratic nation such as Sweden or the Netherlands in its claim to nationhood. Furthermore, they assume that the economic conditions and behaviour of a Baluch under the occupation of the Punjabi Muslims of Pakistan are the same as with the Punjabi colonial rulers and as with the Dutch or Swedish people in their countries. This perspective hangs in the air and is misleading. It is deceptive and deception is unscientific and it is the root of irrationality.

## Conclusion

Most of the mainstream economic ideas were contemplated at the time when women had no or very little legal rights. Any economic theory that overlooks the actual and potential abilities, contributions, and rights of half of the population can be no other but misguided and ill-considered. Economics, as a discipline, by and large, has paid little attention to the harmful human activities on environment. The land and all its contents and conditions have been taken for granted, as a free pack that is inexhaustible. There is no or very little account of the destruction of the environment: depletion of natural resources, deforestation, extinction of certain species, and long-term calculation of such costs in all of the prevailing economic theories.

Economics is a human phenomenon that is indispensable to human existence. The very human life hangs on the economy. Without eating, drinking, and shelter, life is not possible. Economic activities are not the work of solitary individuals. Robinson Crusoe economic man does not exist. Economic activities as social actions are dynamic. These activities are very complex that deal with complex human beings. The economic crisis is an expression of one activity of these complex social beings and their social interactions. The economic crisis is not separable from the human constitution, their configuration, temperament, and their social activities. It is one of many human follies and frailties that manifest themselves in their actions. There are acts of extreme behaviour in all human activities. These acts take place in different times and places. One form of such acts is conveyed in economic activities. It can be expressed in production, distribution, and technology, in economic institutions, instruments, organizations, management, infrastructure, policies, ideas, relations, regulations, and culture, or a combination of some or all of the above issues put together.

Modern economies are very complex, which are coordinated on an extreme arrangement of division of labour and employment. We depend on others for virtually all economic needs. This dependency is worldwide. The most basic economic items of consumption, i.e., a pair of shoes, are not a work of one person or one place anymore. Its production involves complex division of labour, skills, knowledge, multiple industries, and raw materials that are drawn from a vast vicinity of the globe. The extreme interdependency of economic agents in contemporary economies is a by-product of the enormous human population, the establishment of very complex institutions and cultures, very developed technologies, international trade, and the division of the globe into different states of diverse legal structures. All these aspects of the economy are interdependent. None of which exists or functions in isolation. If we add to this list other facts of economic life such as limited resources, insatiable wants, desire for domination, curiosity, the law of diminishing returns, the asymmetry of information in economic exchange, the presence of a moral hazard, the rise of monopolies, undemocratic governments, money and monetary malfunctions, misunderstanding, mismanagement, ideological battles, wasteful expenditures (i.e., atomic bombs), lack of transparency and accountability, artificial borders and colonialism, the degradation of the environment, natural disasters, absence of gender equality and equality of opportunity, religious fundamentalism, wars, mass migration, the increasing ageing population in the world, and many other factors then we can form a much more informed understanding of economic disorders and crises and be able to adapt more effectively in this perilous fast-moving world.

The preoccupation of currents of thought in economics with capitalism is composed of very diverse shades of opinion. One side of extremism in this broad spectrum of ideas is an outright endorsement of the status quo and on the other extreme end sanctification of a dogmatic stance for the sake of sustaining a faith. Giving up vested interest or a venerated belief is not an easy thing. The spectre of capitalism is such a matter. It serves well certain vested interests and certain faiths. Ideology encompasses both sides of this phenomenon. So, the pursuit of knowledge is forfeited to this end. Priority is given to vested interest and the defence of opposing faiths instead of reason and objective analysis of facts. In the chain of ends and means, the end is capitalism. The end justifies the means. The battle is either to use any means in its protection or to use any means in its destruction. For most of the twentieth century it was this battle, the war between the capitalist West and the communist East, which claimed the lives of many millions of people, wrecked the economies of many nations, and blighted the lives of so many more, leaving them destitute.

After the Bolshevik revolution in 1917, the Western power headed by the US, in the name of defending capitalism, supported the most brutal right-wing dictators by providing them with economic, military, and diplomatic assistance. In the same way, the Soviet Bloc headed by Russia, in the name of destroying capitalism, supported equally most corrupt and ruthless left-wing dictators. The Soviet Union collapsed in 1991. The world gasped with a sigh of relief when it happened. For about four decades, the world was waiting for the nuclear war between these two sides. With the collapse of the Soviet Empire those holding to capitalism as their end thought they reached their end. The collapse was viewed as self-authenticating their long-held belief in the superiority of capitalism to communism. The victory of capitalism was announced and celebrated as a forgone conclusion. In two opposing positions, the pro- and anti-capitalist positions, the result was the victory of one faith over another, and not the domination reason over folly.

# 6 Coping with unknowns and human follies

## Introduction

Economics as an intellectual discipline is a by-product of the age of enlightenment. It can be dated to the mid-eighteenth century, most specifically to the publication of *The Wealth of Nations* in 1776. It took several decades after the publication of this momentous book for economics to emerge as an independent practising intellectual inquiry. Malthus is said to be the first professional political economist. The first professor of political economy was in the nineteenth century. It was during this century that economics was advanced into a discrete academic specialism. In 1825, Nassau W. Senior (1790–1864) became the University of Oxford's first professor of political economy. The first professor of political economy of another prestigious English university, Cambridge University, was Alfred Marshall. He became a professor in 1885 and it was Marshall who created the first faculty of economics at Cambridge University in 1903.

It may safely be said, economics as an academic discipline and specialism and as a profession is a relatively new division in the academic world. This does not necessarily imply that before economics became a discrete mode of thought, there was no economic change and growth. There has always been economic growth in different times and circumstances, and under the direction of different political systems. There was economic growth under the slavery system in ancient Egypt, under the bondage system of imperial China, and under the system of serfdom in imperial Russia. The point is that in all social and political formations, from time to time, there has been one or another form of economic growth. All empires and their colonies, ancient or modern, without any exception have experienced occasional economic growth. In our time we have had economic growth under the administrations of the fascist, communist, religious fundamentalist, conservative, and liberal economists. The fact of the matter is that the unprecedented economic transformations and growth in the last few centuries are not entirely due to the intellectual specialism of economics as a discrete academic discipline and the practice of economics.

DOI: 10.4324/9781003346357-7

The rise of economics as an autonomous field of inquiry was part of a much larger social, political, legal, cultural, intellectual, and scientific movement. It was a by-product of the greatest revolutionary movement that fought for the freedom of reason. A movement that has transformed the intellectual landscape and dislodged the entrenched old ideas, institutions, and culture, and shifted the disciplinary perimeter from superstition to mundane reality. Economics had to break free from the past to emerge as an independent distinct discipline. In achieving this end, economics followed the path of natural sciences. It has imitated the natural sciences by breaking away from the dark ages of myth, blind faith, and superstition. The birth of modern economics took place when it broke from the authority of deities, sacred books, and ancient writers. The formative years of economics as an independent intellectual discipline began with scepticism against the two traditional sources of ideas in economics: theology and ancient Greek philosophy. It had to get away from theology, which it did.

Instead of seeking answers from ecclesiastical texts, modern economics became a worldly field of study to serve earthly wants. As an academic field, economics outgrew from its former canonical and literalist crust. It shed its old skin and adopted a secular approach. As a dynamic and viable discipline, it had to leave a casual and haphazard method of study and investigation and adopt a rational, systematic, and critical approach of inquiry. It has opted for the use of reason and scientific inquiry of cause and effect as the means of true understanding, authority, and legitimacy. Economics has become a dominant subject in social sciences. But when we dig deep down, in spite of all these successes and popular belief, economics lags behind some social and moral sciences in its true achievements. Contrary to the generally held view, economics is not at the top of the pecking order in social sciences. In this chapter, we shall argue that economics is not the jewel in the crown of social sciences. Economics is left behind other social sciences, most specifically political science, ethics, and law. Moreover, many achievements in economics are due to these fields of study and other scientific disciplines in natural sciences rather than economics' own making.

This chapter is divided into nine sections. The first section, "Digression from fatalism," sketches an outline of the efforts of many thinkers of the age of enlightenment and the later writers to depart from humans' predetermined fate. By doing so, they have liberated humankind from the dominion of divinity. At the core of this departure was the emancipation of knowledge from monopoly of clergy. That is, counter to things being preordained from eternity, each individual is capable of knowing, understanding, acquiring, accumulating, and applying knowledge. This section also addresses the sources from which knowledge can be acquired and the demarcation criteria used to set apart valid from invalid knowledge. The second section, "Every person can acquire knowledge," recounts the process in which human knowledge has reclaimed its rightful place. It was rescued from the grip of the deities, clerics, and the ancient texts and resumed to each and every individual. Knowledge was democratized. That is, each person with the help of their sensory organs and brain is capable of learning and reason. In addition, this section takes a close look at the empiricists' and the rationalists' accounts of the ultimate source of knowledge and shows how in both cases the human knowledge is in the capacity of each individual. As each person has the faculties of senses and mind, each person can acquire the knowledge of sense data by means of inductive reasoning, and immutable knowledge through the mind by means of deductive reasoning. Put it briefly, each individual can acquire and apply knowledge. In this section, we will also say a few words on how such developments have influenced the progress of different scientific research methods and the dominant methodology of research in mainstream economics.

The third section, "Perfect and imperfect truths," is broadly concerned with the distinction between contingent and analytical truths. This section provides a summary of arguments about particular and universal truths and the sources from which truths are derived. The necessary universal truths belong to the perfect world that is only revealed by means of pure reason and deduction. Such truths are truths of reason that are necessary and universal. These truths are true in all possible worlds and their contradiction is impossible. In contrast to necessary truths, contingent truths are truths of facts. These truths are uncertain and do not exist out of necessity and the opposite of these kinds of truths is possible. In different possible worlds contingent truths can be different. This section will wrap up by explaining the significance of this division of truths for economic theories and policies. The fourth section, "Liberty and pursuit of self-interest", is devoted to the development of appropriate prerequisites and circumstances for individuals to secure their personal, civic, political, moral, and economic liberties. By regaining the mastery of knowledge and reason, an individual came of age. An individual could know, act, and hope. This optimistic outlook also extended to human nature. By nature, it is said, humans are good. This section also explores the interactions of all these achievements and their effects on human progress. The means used to achieve this end have been through clarity of moral obligation, the pursuit of self-interest, education, reform, and revolution.

The fifth section, "Economics of might is right," traces the propensity to extremism of selected influential thinkers of the ancient and modern times. The purpose of this selection is to demonstrate that the propensity to extremism is inside each and every one. The leading thinkers of the modern age advocated humanism, freedom, justice, science, rationalism, and progress but at the same time, for example, they dismissed the rights of women and the rights of the people of subjugated nations. Along with this, it comments on how the economic discourse that has come to dominate economic thought has been filtered through the aforementioned developments. Most specifically, it digs into the rise of capitalism as faith and how the fate of humanity by dominant schools of thought in economics has been interlocked with the fate of capitalism. The sixth section is on the fixed known and the changing unknown. In this section, we shall question the hierarchy of superior and inferior scientific disciplines. By the same token, it is contended that economics as a discipline of social inquiry, despite the general belief of being more scientific than other social sciences, is debatable. Over and above, this section will investigate the main roots of this confusion and will address the universal truths that are drawn from regularities or by sole virtue of the meaning of terms and those truths that are contingent on the ever-changing conditions and circumstances. Finding these truths by any of these competing approaches does not make findings of one approach more scientific than findings of the other approach. In this section, we shall explain how seeking truths, either way, can be dragged into extremism.

In the seventh section, "Permissible and impermissible boundaries," it is argued that humans are a social, political, cultural, moral, and aesthetically driven species. Owing to the fact that they have the capacity to learn and reason, humans operate beyond animal instincts. They plan and set ends consciously and execute them wilfully. The eighth section probes into several instances of extreme arrangements and dispositions. The primary point of the section is the idea that human beings cannot survive in extremism. By virtue of this fact, there is an inextricable relationship between extremism and human imagination and the foundation of moral bearings. The final section, "The end, the means and adaptability," discusses the co-dependency of these elements with the standards of right and wrong and the standards of true and false. In view of this, these elements are as important in economic activities as in any other human endeavour.

## Digression from fatalism

The modern scientific achievements, including in economics, are due to the accomplishments of the age of enlightenment. The enlightenment period started roughly from the seventeenth century and its journey has not ended yet. From one perspective, its first phase was over by the Second World War. This period of transition is important because there was a serious attempt to break from the past. Europe initiated the movement. The break from medieval Europe symbolizes this era. Despite all its successes and the shaking up of the basic fabric of society, the first phase of the age of enlightenment did not achieve all its intended goals. Some relics of the past have lingered on long after the start of the movement and some are still to be found more or less in all human societies. In spite of all the setbacks, the age of reason has left its long-lasting marks on every aspect of human societies and laid the foundations of the new world. One of the greatest contributions of the age has been the rise of independent thinkers. These thinkers altered radically conventional ways of learning and acting. They observe the world objectively as it is. This reading of the world and the way of thinking detached itself from the old sacred and ancient texts, the ecclesiastical beliefs, and the rulers' commands as the sources of truth. The objective truth was what they were looking for. Needless to say, the battle that these free thinkers initiated was a risky journey. In this section, we shall see how some disciplines have been more effective in achieving the goal of scientific objectivity. A goal that all academic fields aspire to and lay claim to. By all academic subjects, objective knowledge is counted as the hallmark of science and the epitome of correct and credible research. In this section, we shall investigate the claim and position of economics in this hierarchy.

In a historical movement of this enormity, there are many contributing factors. One of these factors was the contention about human nature. To almost all religions, human beings are inadequate, incapable, and ignorant. Religions stand on this very foundation. Otherwise, there is no motive for inventing gods, religions, and the search for prophets. Those who endorse and uphold these inadequacies follow a religion or a rigid ideology. The whole discord between the free thinkers with their opponents then can be summed up to human nature. In relation to this issue, the all-important question is the question of authority. Who has the primary authority over a person? Is it the person itself or is it another authority? Europe, which was the cradle of enlightenment, for about two millennia was dominated by the Christian doctrine of the Fall. The Original Sin is an integral part of this doctrine. The idea of the Fall goes back to the story of Adam and Eve in the *Old Testament.* Adam and Eve disobeyed God's command and hence fell from the grace (Armstrong 1999: 144–45). Ever since this Fall, it is said that the fate of each individual has been locked in the Original Sin. So, each human is born sinful and has a sinful nature. That is, by nature we are bad and beyond redemption. This domain is the realm of destiny. In the dominion of fate, there is no free will. There is not much a person can know or do from what has already been written in their destiny. The free thinkers of the age of reason rejected this doctrine.

One of the most effective ways to defeat this view was a very mundane idea. This was the idea that each individual is equipped with a capability to know. Each person has the capacity to acquire knowledge. John Locke (1632–1704) remarked that the brain of a child at birth is a "blank slate." This meant that the Original Sin could not be true. Following this inference is the extrapolation that humans by birth (by nature) are not bad. Therefore, the empty brain of a child can be filled with knowledge, which can be used for good. That is, they acquire knowledge and the sources of acquiring knowledge are achieved through sensory experience. Locke on explaining this issue assumed the mind to be a white paper "void of all characters, without any ideas." He then asked:

> How comes it to be furnished? Whence comes it by that vast store which the busy and boundless fancy of man has painted on it with an almost endless variety? Whence has it all the materials of reason and knowledge? To this I answer, in one word, from EXPERIENCE.
>
> (Locke 1994: 311)

George Berkeley (1685–1753), another empiricist and a Bishop, considered Locke's ideas very dangerous. The danger was atheism. If the ultimate source of knowledge is sense experience, then each individual is the final authority on their knowledge. Thus, there is no need for relying on the authority of any deity for anything. In order to uphold his religious belief, Berkeley denied the existence of the material world. As for the world of ordinary objects, he purported that these are the "truths" in our minds. These objects "are so near and obvious to the mind that a man need only opens his eyes to see them" (Berkeley 1820: 26). Objects and bodies are merely collections of ideas that are perceived by the mind. Ideas exist in the mind and to exist means to be perceived by the mind. Following this reasoning, Berkeley concluded that there is nothing more than ideas in the mind.

Hume was another leading forerunner empiricist of the early modern age. He was an atheist and his contributions to human knowledge have lasted the longest. To him, the ultimate source of knowledge is also from sensation. Hume divided human knowledge into two categories. The first one is about the relations of ideas, the knowledge in logic, mathematics, geometry, and definition statements. In this form of knowledge, the knowledge stays the same always and everywhere. For example, a right-angle triangle cannot be anything else but a right-angle triangle, or as in definitional statement such as a bachelor cannot be anything except an unmarried man. These are analytic claims that are true by definition and justified *a priori*. In truths of this nature, they are true by necessity and their denials would imply a contradiction. The second type of knowledge is about matters of facts. These are synthetic and *a posteriori* claims. There is no necessity in such knowledge. Their denial would not imply a contradiction. The matters of fact, such as "the Sun will rise tomorrow," or causal relations are of this nature.

The only certain knowledge for Hume is the analytic truths. All the rest are uncertain, even the sunrise and sunset tomorrow. Hume remarked that "*the sun will not rise tomorrow*, is no less intelligible a proposition, and implies no more contradiction, than the affirmation that it will rise" (Hume 1854: 31 – Italics in original). The conviction that a night is followed by a day, he argued, is based on our past experience and "what is possible can never be demonstrated to be false" (Hume 1962: 294). This is because the:

> probable arguments are built on the supposition, that there is this conformity betwixt the future and the past, and therefore can never prove it. This conformity is *a matter of fact*, and if it must be proved, will admit of no proof but from experience. But our experience in the past can be a proof of nothing for the future, but upon a supposition, that there is a resemblance betwixt them. This therefore is a point, which can admit of no proof at all, and which we take for granted without any proof.
>
> (Hume 2007: 138 – Italics in original)

The same inconclusive relation also exists in causal relations. In the cause-and-effect relation, we can never infer the existence of one object from another, unless they are connected together. Hume used the analogy of a billiard ball to demonstrate the inconclusive outcome of the causal connections. He commented that imagine,

> a billiard ball lying on the table, and another ball moving toward it with rapidity. They strike; and the ball which was formerly at rest now acquires a motion. This is as perfect an instance of the relation of cause and effect as any which we know, either by sensation or reflection.
>
> (Hume 1993: 129)

In this case of regular succession, Hume extrapolated, one cannot conclusively prior to action say that the first ball will hit the second and the motion of the first is caused by the first ball.

Hume argues that it is not from our reasoning that we expect and believe that the motion of the second ball is caused by the first but from our experience of the past instances that we have observed the motions of the balls in similar acts. That is one "cannot penetrate into the reason of the conjunctions." One can "only observe the thing itself, and always find that from the constant conjunction the objects acquire a union in the imagination" (Hume 1974: 95). The reason for our conviction of cause-and-effect connection is "only by our experience of their constant conjunction." Hence, "the past may be no rule for the future, all experience becomes useless and can give rise to no inference or conclusions" (Hume 1875: 33). This problem became to be known as the problem of induction. That is, inductive inferences are inconclusive and cannot be justified by deductive reasoning. Hume's problem of induction caused Immanuel Kant to be "interrupted" from what he described as his "dogmatic slumber." It was this problem that Karl Popper also made his mark as one of the most influential philosophers of science of the twentieth century. Popper asserted famously that "I think I have solved a major philosophical problem" (Popper 1971: 167).

Like Hume, Popper maintains that sense experience is the ultimate source of knowledge and that "there is no such thing as induction by repetition in logic" (Popper 1971: 172). Popper then goes about to frame the actual problem by trying to explain how we may be able to justify inductive inferences. In step with Hume's proposed objection, inductive reasoning cannot be answered because we cannot rely on induction. Reliance on induction is just impossible. For the reason that inductive reasoning is hypothetical reasoning that is corroborated by successive induction in agreement with common sense. On this ground all inductively approved established theories can be proved to be false with a counter-instance. Therefore, in Popper's view, "all theories are hypotheses" that can be "overthrown." They are "conjectures," developed by accumulating confirming instances, data and observation, and sheer repetition.

Popper sought his solution to the problem of induction in his deductive logic – a hypothetical deductive method, starting with the premise that all general theories are conjectures and remain conjectural no matter how many supportive instances are being collected. So, no general theory can be proved to be true with this method. The growth of scientific knowledge is based on sense experience, conjectures, hypotheses, and guesses. But all hypotheses and conjectures are not of equal merits. They are not alike in justification, veracity, and validity. It is here where Popper draws his demarcation line between real science and pseudo-science. In his demarcation, true scientific theories are testable and pseudo-science theories are not. A genuine scientific theory is falsifiable because it "speaks about reality" but "in so far as it is not falsifiable, it does not speak about reality" (Popper 2002: 316).

The most imminent pioneering thinker of modern science who refuted the traditional sources of truth was Francis Bacon. He questioned the prevailing research methods that dominated scientific inquiry during the Middle Ages. It was customary during this period to search for truth in the sacred books or the work of ancient philosophers. Bacon rebutted this practice as a degenerative and futile approach. Instead, he suggested a method of direct observation of the real world and experimentation. By means of systematic empirical studies, human knowledge can progress and with knowledge, one can achieve great things. Because "knowledge is power." Bacon described different scientific research methods in his allegory of ants, spiders, and bees. In comparing their specific line of work, Bacon commented that the traditional scientists:

> have been either men of experiment or men of dogmas. The men of the experiment are like the ant, they only collect and use; the reasoners resemble spiders, who make cobwebs out of their own substance. But the bee takes the middle course: it gathers its material from the flowers of the garden and field but transforms and digests it by a power of its own.
>
> (Bacon 1999: 128)

Bacon's methodology of research has influenced the scientists of his age and the works of successive scientists to the present day. The break from digging in the ancient scriptures for the truth to the study of real nature and life was a major step in the transition from the old superstitious age to the modern scientific age. Galileo likened the universe to the "great book" that

> we cannot understand it if we do not first learn the language and grasp the symbols in which it is written. The book is written in mathematical language, and the symbols are triangles, circles and other geometrical figures, without whose help it is impossible to comprehend a single word of it.
>
> (quoted from Kline 1982: 46)

The points to be considered here are two: the source from which knowledge can be acquired and the language in which the true knowledge can be expressed.

## Every person can acquire knowledge

Advocating sense data, which includes experiments, as the ultimate source of knowledge was a critical step in liberating human knowledge from the monopoly of deities and the ecclesiastics. In an indirect way, it was tantamount to saying that each person can learn and deities are no longer needed. This was dissent from the unyielding and monocratic world of clerics. Knowledge was no longer an exclusive entitlement of gods and their associates but it is in hands of each individual. Every person is endowed with necessary requirements to acquire knowledge. The freehand, the exclusive right and licence of Gods, and the clerics vanish as soon as this privilege is granted to each individual. The empowerment of each individual to know independently unleashed the march of knowledge, learning and insight against inability and ignorance. But this was only a spark. It was only one half of the story. The other half was the contributions of the rationalist school that we shall explain next.

Before moving on to the contributions of the rationalist school, it is worth saying a word about the drawbacks of empiricism and its ascendency as the dominant methodology of research in mainstream economics. As it was repeated several times earlier for the empiricists, the ultimate source of all knowledge in this school is from sensory experience. Traditionally, it was believed to come from the five sense organs: visual (eyes), auditory (ears), tastes (tongue), smell (an olfactory – nose), and touch (skin). Biologists have discovered two other sense organs. The vestibular sensory system regulates the orientation and position of the body and head. It regulates body motion, posture, and spatial orientation. The proprioception sensory system controls the conscious and unconscious movements of muscles and limbs in 3D space as in balancing on one leg or walking without looking at one's feet. These are sensory organs that we know with the current progress of human knowledge. There could be other sensory organs that we do not know and are possibly not discovered yet. That said, there are other living species that have the same sensory organs. Take a horse as an example. A horse has all the sensory organs listed above. So, what makes a human different from a horse in relation to human knowledge? A horse uses its sight, hearing, taste, smell, touch, and sense of orientation. If it does not, it will not function and die. If it experiences pain by somebody mistreating it in a specific location, it will try to avoid that location. This means, the horse is aware of being mistreated and knows where it will be mistreated. The same applies to many other living species. Therefore, the question is why a horse with the same sense organs is not capable of forming and accumulating knowledge as a human does. The short answer to this question is that the horse does not have the human brain.

The human brain is the most evolved brain among the living species. It is the most complex wonder of the known universe. With the help of this brain, human beings can reason, invent a language, construct societies, and have the moral compass. But can the human brain be detached from its sensory receptors and still work? Is it self-contained and self-reliant? If it were autonomous and self-sustaining, then human knowledge could only be the product of the human mind. This is a subject that we shall return to in our coverage of the views of the rationalist school. There are two issues that we need to clarify at the outset before we answer the questions raised above. Let us in the interest of clarity consider a hypothetical scenario. Let us assume we have the first human. There is no other human except them. Furthermore, let us assume that all sensory organs – the visual, the auditory, taste, smell, touch, the orientation senses – and other unknown sense organs of this individual are out of working order. In this counterfactual situation, we can categorically confirm that acquiring any knowledge cannot be possible if these senses are out of order completely. All the more serious than that any living species in similar conditions would perish in no time. Let us take another conjectural case. Let us assume a new-born baby lacks all the sensory organs. Without the help of his parents and society, this baby would die immediately after birth without being aware of anything. The conclusion that we can draw from this scenario is that there can be no human knowledge without human sensory organs.

The next question that we need to ask about human knowledge is: can there be knowledge without the human brain? Can the sense organs on their own and each in isolation create knowledge? Imagine someone who is born without a brain? This individual will not only be born without any knowledge but they will also not be born alive. Thus, human knowledge is the work of both human sensory organs and the human brain. It is through the interaction and the interdependency of the two that human knowledge is acquired and formed. The important factor we need to draw attention to here is that all empiricists seek the source of knowledge for sense organs and all rationalists regard the brain as the source of the creation of knowledge. In both cases, human knowledge is specific to each individual. When we limit knowledge to individuals only, it means each individual is naturally equipped with functional sensory organs and a brain to acquire certain knowledge. It also means, with respect to knowledge, each person is detached from the past and after dying, nothing will be left of them individually. In biology, we are told that the human DNA is passed down from the past generations to the next generations. The genetic information is passed between generations. In a similar way, though not of the same magnitude and certainty, the work of all sense organs and brains has been passed down through the generations since the beginning of human history from one generation to the next. Each human generation inherits all the sense experience of the past generations and the work of their minds. Each child born does not learn everything detached from the experience and knowledge of the past generations. Knowledge heredity is not genetic information but more vaguely is from the accumulation of the sense experience and creation of minds of the past generations. A child is born not only with the baggage of genetic information but also with the baggage of experience and knowledge of the past generations.

There are two issues worth explaining at this junction. The first one is Popper's claim about solving Hume's problem of induction. The second one is inductive reasoning as the dominant method of research in mainstream economics. Popper's main concern was about the progress of human knowledge. To this end, he drew a demarcation line between science and pseudo-science, differentiating the territory of scientific from non-scientific knowledge. He strived to explain the method of research that practising scientists employ to advance scientific knowledge and the criteria used to validate their theories. Going along with Hume, he questioned the validity of a theory by means of repetition of instances that occurred in the past. That is, he doubted the validity of inductive reasoning – of moving from collection of past data and observations to the prediction of the future effects. From this reading, he concluded that all theories are conjectural no matter how many times they are confirmed and reaffirmed. Thus, theories based on induction cannot guarantee certainty. No matter how many instances confirm a theory, the theory cannot rationally be justified – concluding that the true mark of a scientific theory cannot be confirmation but falsification. On this account, all theories remain conjectural. A bold conjecture that can be falsified is the true mark of scientific theory and this is Popper's solution to the problem of induction.

Despite Popper's valuable inputs to the debate on the problem of induction, starting with a bold conjecture is not the solution to Hume's problem of induction. For practical purposes, Hume also referred to the customary belief that is formed out of ordinary expectation informing one's opinions. In other words, he did not think that peoples' brains and most certainly the learned brains are empty slates. Those who use inductive reasoning are well indoctrinated and carry very sophisticated baggage that is full of all sorts of beliefs, ideologies, moral and religious convictions, social-cultural prejudice, and personal experience. Nobody conducts systematic research with an empty brain. As we have indicated above, a new-born baby the day they are born will be loaded with their parents' and society's values, expectations, and culture, let alone a well-trained scientist who is educated in the received wisdom of their society.

In all branches of modern economics that involve prediction and forecasting, it is the induction method that runs the show. The basic cannons of this method are the systematic collection of data from different economic indicators of past events and using sophisticated mathematical models to forecast the future based on the past data. This is done on the expectation that the past will be repeated exactly in the future. The fact is no matter how accurate the information and data collected from the past is, they are still in the past. The past is bygone and will never be the future and there is no way that we can insert the certainty of deductive reasoning in such matters into inductive reasoning. We shall explore the latter points further next in the rationalist account of knowledge.

One question from the beginning of human history must have been the distinction between humans and animals. This was a question that the ancient thinkers, most specifically the ancient Greek philosophers, delved into systematically and tried to answer. For the purpose of our discussion, we shall merely refer to the points that are relevant to the subject of our analysis. The two distinct differences that they referred to were the ability of human beings to know the truth and their ability to reason. That is, humans can acquire and apply knowledge. One of the primary barriers that was needed to be removed in this respect is whether the ability to know the truth and the knowledge of truth is innate or is acquired from sense data. Socrates with his method of dialogue demonstrated that those who claim to know do not know what they claim to know. Plato applied Socrates' method of revealing the truth in *Meno*. His quest for knowledge was for universal knowledge, the type of knowledge that is not acquired by sense data. In both *Meno* and *Phaedo*, Plato talks of a previous life. Some kind of reincarnation and rebirth that he believed people do experience. The knowledge that people had in a previous life, Plato asserts, remains in one's mind, and by means of Socrates' method, one can recollect the knowledge buried deep in the soul of each individual. So according to Plato, we possess innate knowledge. Whereas animals do not have knowledge but instinct, human knowledge is innate knowledge. Animals cannot reason and rely on their instincts and humans can reason and due to having a rational faculty use concepts and construct abstract ideas.

Plato gives an example of a young shepherd with no former mathematical instruction to reveal a truth that he had not learned from anyone in support of his claim for innate knowledge. The writer of the dialogue also implicitly wants to show the difference between the young shepherd and the most sophisticated animal. After applying the identical method for the animal, the result would not be the same. Even Plato does not accept the view that all knowledge is innate. He only considers certain forms of knowledge to be innate. In his example, some definitions and geometrical relations were explained and the boy guided, with the help of given information, extrapolated and predicted, without relying on sense data, the next steps in this relation. For Plato, there are truths that are beyond the sense experience, eternal truths that cannot be formed by sense data. With his innate idea, Plato has opened a long-lasting debate about the source of knowledge that has no final ending. Aristotle, his famous student, rejected his teacher's theory of innate knowledge and argued that the starting point of knowledge cannot be other than sense data. Moreover, conceptual knowledge is only possible through teaching and humans are social animals and humans learn language through their social interactions. It is from the work of this teacher and student and the back and forth of their accounts of the transient and the universal truths that we have the earliest systematic explanations of such division. The implication of this division is crucial in understanding the nature of economics.

Plato's theory of Forms and Aristotle's division of *a priori* and *a posteriori* propositions are of much consequence to the later developments of contingent and analytical truths. Plato in his dialogues talks of two worlds: the real world and the world of ideas. The real world is the physical world. It is the world of objects, animals, plants, and so on. Let us take a horse that exists in the real physical world. For Plato, this horse is a particular horse. There are other horses that are taller, smaller, fatter, skinnier, stronger, weaker, younger, older, male, female, of different colours, and so on. This is only a particular horse. It is not exactly the same as other horses. Our horse cannot represent other horses because all other horses are different from each other. From his account of the variation of particulars, Plato deduced that particulars are conditional, transitory, and imperfect. Therefore, human knowledge about particulars is provisional and imperfect. However, there is something that puts all particular horses in one boundary and that is the Form of the horse or the idea of horse that represents the concept of horseness. The Form of the horse includes all particular horses in the past, present, and future. Thus, the knowledge of Form, the idea of the horse, is absolute, timeless, unchanging, and perfect and is the manifestation of the essence of being a horse. Particulars are momentary and change in varying circumstances whereas Forms are universal and immutable.

Here we are not interested in the validity of Plato and Aristotle's arguments. The point of exposition of their arguments is merely to highlight the evolution of the debate about contingent and analytical truths. Aristotle offered a different version of this division in his *Organon*. For him, human knowledge is composed of *a priori* and *a posteriori* analytic propositions. The *a priori* analytic knowledge is similar to Plato's Forms. They make up the essence of matter, timeless and infallible. This is the quality of sameness that is found in all different particulars that connects all members in one group. Our knowledge of *a priori* analytic is universal and we acquire this knowledge by means of deductive reasoning and intuition. The structure of this form of knowledge is orderly and complete. The order is necessary and the conclusion cannot be other than what it is in the premises of the proposition. This is a constant form of knowledge that is outside the realm of sensory experience and cannot be from what it is. An *a posterior* proposition, however, is a sensory experience knowledge. It is momentary and changes with circumstances, representing particulars. This form of knowledge is not timeless and contingent on specific accidents and conditions. This is our knowledge of the real world. The knowledge that we acquire by means of our senses is unreliable and therefore cannot be qualified as true knowledge. This is because sense data stays at appearance. It does not penetrate deep into the essence of matters. The *a posteriori* knowledge is inaccurate, transitory, and is only the source of our beliefs. True knowledge is certain and beliefs are uncertain.

Rene Descartes (1596–1650), through a pretended dream and a thought process, tried to prove how attaining certain knowledge is possible. In this mental exercise, he assumed that all his faculties were in the grip of a demon with one exception. The demon could not stop him to think. The evil demon controlled his thoughts but not his ability to think. Descartes was allowed to have false thoughts but not the thoughts that he wanted. On this ground, Descartes doubted everything that he had believed up to that point except himself and the act of thinking. These two things that he could not doubt, the very act of thinking and the person who did the act of thinking, were Descartes's first steps to demonstrate the attainability of absolute knowledge. Descartes coined his most famous dictum, Cogito ergo sum (I think, therefore I am), "as proof of the reality of one's own mind." From this dictum he deduced his certain truth. He doubted everything but he could not doubt his existence and his thoughts. This is an *a priori* type of knowledge that is obtained independently from sense experience and observation. His inference is deduced by means of deductive reasoning that is not liable to verification and falsification. What we have here, according to Descartes, is the absolute truth. Absolute because it "has within it the pure and simple nature in question; that is, whatever is viewed as being independent, a cause, simple, universal, single, equal, similar, straight and other qualities of that sort" (Descartes 2004: 23).

In Cartesian epistemology, true knowledge is the work of the mind. One obtains such distinctive knowledge by means of rigorous deductive reasoning. The absolute truths are clear and universal. They are immaterial, merely the derivation of our intuition and soul. Our knowledge of sense experience is not reliable because the senses can deceive us. So, he concluded, "it is prudent never to trust entirely those who have once deceived us" (Descartes 1988: 96). In contrast, distinct and clear knowledge is the product of the mind. This form of knowledge cannot be doubted. Irrespective of the validity or invalidity of Descartes's argument of obtaining absolute knowledge by means of deductive reasoning, his argument was the complementary part of the attempt made to liberate knowledge from the grip of the god, the clergy, and the ancient sacred and non-sacred texts and return it to individuals. Just like the empiricists who argued that the ultimate source of knowledge is from sensory data that each individual is equipped with, Descartes as the father of modern rationalism argued that each individual can think, therefore they exist and hence are capable of obtaining clear and distinct knowledge. This belief, despite its validity or falsity, side by side with the empiricist account of knowledge, liberated human knowledge from the monopoly of religions and ancient scriptures and made it a democratic endeavour that any individual is capable of seeking and acquiring. Since everyone has the faculties of senses and mind, they can acquire knowledge through sense data by means of inductive reasoning, and through the mind by means of deductive reasoning.

## Perfect and imperfect truths

Benedict Spinoza (1632–77) was an enigmatic Dutch philosopher, and a very high-minded individual who worked for several years as a grinder of optical lenses to earn a living. Spinoza offered a general critique of Cartesian theory and rejected Descartes's method of doubt as a valid means of discovering the truth. The Amsterdam Sephardic Community expelled and excommunicated him for his unorthodox religious views. In every respect, Spinoza was an original thinker and a pioneering member of the rationalist school in the seventeenth century. His influence during his short life was minor. His book, *Ethics*, was published shortly after Spinoza's death in 1677 where he has applied Euclidian geometry in the ethical principles. Just like Descartes, Spinoza was searching for universal truths and started with a set of self-evident axioms and then step by step built upon his self-contained deductive argument. Spinoza's starting point in the construction of his grand theory is Descartes's definition of substance. His reason for this selection is that substance "is in itself and is conceived through itself" (Spinoza 1963: 1). God is his perfect example of substance.

For Spinoza, there is a totality of everything that can be summed up in nature. The whole reality is one substance. The underlying substance is made up of "modes," objects that make up different aspects of the underlying substance. In this single underlying reality (nature/god) everything exists out of necessity. Everything is necessary. In this way, Spinoza tried to show the contrast in his system of modality between necessity and contingency and arrive at the conclusion that everything that exists in nature is out of necessity. There is nothing contingent and the whole order of things that exist in this single reality is necessary. God's creations are perfect and he could not have produced them "in any other manner or order than that in which they were produced" (Spinoza 1963: 26).

The god/nature is perfect. There is a reason for everything. Reason and contingency are two opposing processes. One is out of necessity and the other is not. A perfect world has an essential nature with essential parts, the truths of which are universal. The method of discovery of such truths is tightly linked with the method of pure reason, deduction. The sense data is inadequate in this respect. This distinction was one of the areas that aroused much interest to the German philosopher, Gottfried W. Leibniz (1646–1716). Spinoza and Leibniz met in November 1676 and it is clear that Leibniz was aware of Spinoza's views. One of the areas of influence of Spinoza's ideas on Leibniz is this distinction. Nevertheless, Leibniz went deeper into the matter. For Leibniz, there are things that happen to be true or false, and there are things that are meant to be true and false by necessity. In his division, we have the "truths of reasons" and the "truths of facts." In other words, there are propositions of facts and truths that are necessarily true. The truths of facts and the truths of reasons stem from two different sources. The source of the former is the intuition of sense perception and the source of the latter is the intuition of intellect. By means of sense perception, we acquire the truths of facts but the truth of reason is neither acquired nor validated by means of sense experience. The truths of reason cannot be untrue while the truths of fact can. The truths of reason are true in all possible worlds and the truths of fact can be different in different possible worlds. The truths of reason are necessary truths and necessary truths "can be demonstrated from the resolution of the terms, that is, which are necessary or virtually identical" (quoted from Sleigh 1972: 16). Such truths are "the eternal truths ... [that] ... their truth is understood [*a priori*] by the infinite mind alone, and they cannot be demonstrated by any resolution" (quoted in Sleigh 1972: 16–17). The opposite of necessary truths is "impossible or virtually contradictory."

In contrast, contingent truths are different. They exist in the transient and uncertain realm. These truths "are true at a certain time." They "would exist contingently if certain things were supposed" (quoted from Sleigh 1972: 16–17). There is no "common measure" in contingent truths. A contingent truth, "never arrives to infinity … it never arrives at demonstration however much you may resolve the concepts" (quoted from Sleigh 1972: 16). Another way that Leibniz expresses this relationship is the relationship between the predicate and the subject. He asserts that "in every true affirmative proposition, necessary or contingent, universal or singular, the concept of the predicate is in some way contained in the concept of the subject" (quoted from Sleigh 1972: 15). Necessary truths are identical propositions. The predicate and subject in such truths are one. In contingent truth, we can never reach the identity as in the proposition of A being A. The reason for that in the case of contingent truth is "even though the predicate is really present in the subject, nevertheless by whatever revolution you please of either term, indefinitely continued, you will never arrive at demonstration or identity" (quoted from Sleigh 1972: 16). The necessary truths "can be resolved into identical propositions" (quoted from Sleigh 1972: 15) because the opposite of such truths and knowledge is impossible. The necessary truths are *a priori* truths that are acquired independently of experience and whose premises are self-confirming, whereas contingent truths are truths that are derived from the experience, so their verification also depends on experience. The necessary truths are true in all possible worlds and contingent truths in a specific world. The latter truths are "true in virtue of the way the world is actually constituted" (Sleigh 1972: 2). We can prove necessary truths but cannot prove the contingent and existential laws. In this regard, Leibniz says even if:

> someone were able to know the whole series of the universe, he still could not state the reason of it, except by having undertaken the comparison of it with all other possible universes. From this it is clear why a demonstration of no contingent proposition can be found, however far the resolution of concepts be continued.
>
> (quoted from Sleigh 1972: 17)

The two categories of truths noted above can be termed as the epistemological truths and the semantic truths. The latter truths are true by convention, by definition, and virtue of the meanings of terms used in the expression. The epistemological truths are truths that correspond to reality. An equilateral triangle has three equal sides and angles, and red is a colour are examples of necessary truths that are true by virtue of their definitions. The statements, in this case, are complete and inclusive. Spinoza, a descendant of Portuguese Jews, was born and died in Amsterdam is a contingent truth. This is an example of epistemological truth, which under different circumstances might not have been exactly the same. Spinoza's ancestors could have stayed in Portugal and he could have been born in that country. In this case, absolute certitude cannot be guaranteed.

The subject of the division of truths into different categories was one of the highly debated topics of the age of enlightenment. One philosopher who has made the greatest contribution to this debate was Immanuel Kant (1724–1804). Kant, arguably the greatest thinker of the enlightenment era, argued against the findings of former Empiricist and Rationalist schools. On the source of knowledge, he argued, both schools take no notice of some aspects of the acquisition and forms of knowledge. He agrees with the empiricists that "all our knowledge begins with experience." But he goes a step further by stating that "it does not follow that it all arises out of experience" (Kant 1929: 41). Furthermore, he says, "experience teaches us that a thing is so and so, but not that it cannot be otherwise" (Kant 1929: 43). Given that these two statements are true, Kant goes on to explain the distinction between what he terms as "pure and empirical knowledge." His two general categories of the sources of knowledge are the *a priori* and the empirical knowledge. *A priori* knowledge is "independent of experience and even all impressions of the senses." In the case of empirical knowledge, it is "*a posteriori*, that is, in experience" (Kant 1929: 42–43). The *a priori* knowledge is no "knowledge of this or that experience, but knowledge absolutely independent of all experience" (Kant 1929: 43). To add to the complexity of his scheme of knowledge, Kant divides *a priori* knowledge into different types. There is a tainted and there is an untainted *a priori* knowledge. Untainted *a priori* knowledge is the one "when there is no admixture of anything empirical" and tainted *a priori* knowledge is the one that after its original acquisition from experience it does not rely on experience and is acquired independently of experience (Kant 1929: 43).

The former type, the absolute *a priori* knowledge, carries the property of "strict universality." This type of knowledge is pure and has "no exception" and is "valid absolutely *a priori*" (Kant 1929: 44). The two determining prerequisites of Kant's pure *a priori* knowledge are "necessity and strict universality." Among examples of pure *a priori* judgement are the statements that 2 + 2 = 4 and that every cause has an effect. These judgements, according to Kant, can be known through pure reason. In an absolutely *a priori* judgement, the judgement is detached from the world of appearance, "in a realm beyond the world of the senses." We acquire this type of knowledge by means of intuition and reason. These types of knowledge are outside the boundary of experience and for that reason, they cannot be "contradicted by experience." Knowledge of pure mathematics falls under this category. Pure mathematical propositions are "always judgment *a priori*, not empirical; because they carry with them necessity, which cannot be derived from experience … the very concept of which implies that it does not contain empirical, but only pure *a priori* knowledge" (Kant 1927: 52).

Broadly speaking, for Kant opposite of *a priori* knowledge, we have *a posteriori* knowledge. This type of knowledge is transitory and lacks the attribute of "necessity and strict universality." These types of judgements are "arbitrary extension of a validity holding in most cases to one which holds in all," which are not universally valid. For further clarification of this division, Kant has introduced two more concepts in his theory of knowledge. These are the analytic and the synthetic judgements that broadly correspond to *a priori* and *a posteriori* knowledge. Moreover, in his account of knowledge, we have *a priori* analytic propositions and *a priori* synthetic propositions. Mathematical propositions fall under the category of *a priori* analytic knowledge, where such knowledge is not acquired and demonstrated by means of senses but by means of intuition and deduction. However, in natural sciences, we have examples of *a priori* synthetic knowledge. He refers to two laws of Newton's physics to demonstrate his *a priori* synthetic knowledge. These are the laws that "in all changes of the material world the quantity of matter remains unchanged; and that in all communication of motion, action and reaction must always be equal" (Kant 1927: 54). Kant goes on to say that not only are these propositions are:

> necessary, and therefore in their origin *a priori*, but also synthetic. For in the concept of the matter I do not think its permanence, but only its presence in the space which it occupies. I go outside and beyond the concept of matter, joining to it *a priori* in thought something which I have not thought in it. The proposition is not, therefore, analytic, but synthetic, and yet is thought *a priori*; and so likewise are the other propositions of the pure part of natural science.
>
> (Kant 1927: 54)

The *a priori* analytic judgement is the product of pure reason, whereas the *a priori* synthetic judgements are a derivation of both *a priori* and *a posteriori* knowledge. A good example of *a priori* synthetic judgement is matter. In this distinction of different types of knowledge, we have two types of universal laws or judgements. The first one is the one we acquire by means of *a priori* analytic judgement and the second one by means of *a priori* synthetic judgement. The first type has no exception and it is "valid absolutely *a priori*." In this case, the predicate belongs to the subject and can be demonstrated by the means of deductive reasoning. The other types of universal laws and judgements are the ones derived from *a priori* synthetic judgements. In *a priori* synthetic judgements, the predicate does not belong to the subject. The universality, in this case, is derived from experience by means of inductive reasoning. Kant went along with Hume on this point. That is to say, the validity of this type of universality cannot be proven "through induction." One "can properly only say … so far as we have hitherto observed, there is no exception to this or that rule" (Kant 1927: 44).

The purpose of the brief summary of the sources of knowledge presented above, most specifically the contributions of thinkers of the age of enlightenment, is neither meant to confirm nor refute but to demonstrate that they are all share a common ground. The core idea from which human knowledge is considered to spring from is the idea that humans are rational or that they have the capacity to reason. By virtue of having a faculty to reason, being able to reason, humans are capable of acting rationally. The implications of this inference are profound and path-breaking. The first critical implication of this conclusion is that rationality is an innate property that each human is endowed with. The second ramification following the first implication is that on the grounds that each human has got the faculty to reason they are equal. Due to this fact individually and collectively they can acquire objective knowledge to improve their conditions. Knowledge is a liberating force. It is a power by which humans can go forward and progress.

In Kant's system of epistemology, humans are different from other animals. Animals act entirely on their instincts. Their way of life is determined by their instincts. Humans, in addition to animal instincts, have the capacity to reason, so their mode of living is not predetermined. Due to their power of capacity to reason, they can set ends and can freely choose the end or ends in life and pursue those ends. Therefore, humans for the reason that they possess a rational faculty the way in which they live is not fixed. It is pliant and open to change. Kant does not, in his assessment of humanity, preclude free will. He allows a certain degree of free will, the power to choose among alternatives and do otherwise given established restraints in one's life. But a rational agent can only utilize their capacity to reason when they are free to exercise one's rationality and free to act and behave accordingly. Humans are self-transforming because of this capacity. A fulfilled human is one who is free and exercises their faculty of rationality freely. The faculty to reason cannot function fully and effectively unless the rational agents are free to use their faculty of reason at liberty.

In view of the above considerations, what is epistemically problematic in mainstream economics are two entwined presuppositions. The economy is presupposed to be in the realm of analytic truth and inductive reasoning is applied to reveal the facts of the economy. The economy is assumed to work according to the principles of analytical truth but the dominant method of knowing is induction. That is, the truths of the economy are likened to the truths such as we find in a right-angled triangle with one of its angles being equal to 90 degrees, or in the fact that number 2 is lower than number 3, or in the tautological statement of a "promise is a promise." These truths are universal and exist in all possible worlds, always in all places. By means of deductive reason, given one side of the truth, we can forecast without failing the other side. But this is not what we have in economics. Economic truths are not analytical truths. This is not how economies work. Economies are based on contingent truths. Economies are the hostage of their time and locations. Such truths are subject to all sorts of natural, social, economic, moral, technological, political, legal, cultural, institutional, and psychological conditions. Economies are never the same. They are constantly changing as the circumstances change. Applying inductive reasoning to forecast future economic events is bound to fail because the future is never the same as the past. Extrapolating the past into the future is tantamount to no change. This was the problem that Hume repudiated in his theory of the problem of induction in the eighteenth century. On account of Hume's dissent, we cannot predict economic activities based on past data and trends. Inductive reasoning cannot conclusively establish any future outcome. Moreover, the accuracy and validity of inductive inference cannot be justified by deductive reasoning. By means of inductive research, we cannot extrapolate deductive predictions.

The basis for knowledge and progress in mainstream economics entails an unresolved misperception. Besides the misunderstanding that we have referred to above in terms of the confusion between the analytical and contingent truths and the problem of induction, there are other epistemological issues that are not sufficiently clarified and considered in the study of economics. Economics as a discipline has remained an ideological venture. In this respect, there is an affinity between religion and scholarly endeavours in economics. Religions are formed on strict instructions. The basic cannons of each religion are intransigent instructions. They are locked in the past and carved in stone in the sacred texts. To the devotees of religions, their scriptures are uncompromising and must be followed and applied verbatim as much as the faithful economists strictly follow and apply the sacred writings of their school. Besides religious or ideological instructions, let us consider three other types. One of these examples is computer programming. These are instructions given in the form of codes to computers in order to perform certain tasks and solve certain problems. The instruction manuals that come along with a technical device that explain how to set up or operate the equipment are of this nature. For instance, the instruction manual for assembling a greenhouse or the instruction manual for operating a juice extractor. In the same category of the instruction manual, we can have a bridge blueprint that is drawn by an architect. The economy has not got a fixed blueprint. It has not got pre-prepared instructions that one can read and follow step by step and then set it up as in a technical device, or assemble it as in a greenhouse, or build it as in a bridge. But this is how the economy is treated in mainstream economics. There can be no one perfect blueprint for the economy. Any proposed economic master plan, at best, is a rough sketch, which will never correspond to the future economic arrangements and bare facts of life. For this reason, the template of such a plan is adapted from a little bit of the present and past knowledge. The working model of any economy in its past, present, and future forms is never the same. All economic blueprints are about the future. They are applied in the future when the layout is not what it was when the rough ideas were proposed and were drafted in their preliminary forms. But a plan that is drawn by an ancient Greek architect for a bridge can be applied in its very minute details at the present or in the future. Thus, economic instructions are different. They are the recipes of the contingent truths.

The economic theories that claim universality are in the domain of analytical truths. These theories either define, discuss, or report an economic issue.

They are either explanatory, expository, descriptive, declarative, predictive, or prescriptive instructions. These theories are suggested to be applicable to all places and all times. The fact is economic instructions are not analytical truths. They are merely a derivation of past experience of economic activities, good and bad, of certain locations and times. Economic theories are partial abstractions of the past economic realities in specific places and times. They are not general abstractions of universal economic activities. Of necessity, learning from the past is important for building up our defensive skills to cope and be more adaptive to the ever-changing economic environment. But the past economic problems will never occur in exactly the same way in the future. Besides, economics knowledge is not confined to abstract knowledge. In every aspect of economic activities, production, exchange, distribution, organization, management, and policies, there is an element of practical knowledge that economic theories cannot conquer. Such learnings and concrete skills can only take place during that specific activity. Consider trade. In modern developed economies, there are no or very negligible number of economic agents who are self-sufficient. We are all dependent on trade. A trader, from a sole apple trader in a village to the trader of the most complex financial instrument in the biggest exchange, learns and develops their trading skills more through their direct ongoing engagement with their specific trade. This type of experiential knowledge cannot be acquired just in abstracted theory. In the same way, one cannot learn how to swim or ride a bicycle by reading the instructions on how to swim or to cycle.

## Liberty and pursuit of self-interest

The step taken to liberate knowledge from divinity and clergy and returning it to each individual was a big step in emancipating economics as a separate academic discipline. This was a major step forward in the democratization of knowledge, which paved the way for other major changes in the subsequent transformation of modern societies and economies. Greater democratization of human knowledge laid a strong base for other basic human rights. The modern free and democratic societies and economies would not have been possible without this significant breakthrough. One aftereffect of mastery of each individual on their knowledge and reason was the supposition of the goodness of human nature. Francis Hutcheson (1694–1746) argued that sympathy and fellow feelings are innate. In Rousseau's "state of nature" people are pure, innocent, and compassionate. Given that the human by nature is not wicked but innately kind and benevolent and is capable of learning and changing, then the forerunners of the age of reason argued there must be other hindrances that stop people from utilizing these capabilities.

With this outlook, powers such as god, religion, and government were brought down from the realm of the unintelligible into the real world. Hume argued that as much as fairy tales are the works of the imagination and the concoction of creative writing, the invention of gods and religions is a fabrication of human fantasy. Religions are inventions of humans as much as the states are. Hume maintained that God's attributes are drawn from our sensory perception. The attributes of Gods as being omnipotent, omniscient, omnipresent, and others are some of the over-exaggerated traits of humans. These are of the same kind as when in a caricature of a person we see some of their features are overdone. Hume considered fear and hope as the origin of the invention of religion. This human-made activity is sanctified by its inventor and then it takes precedence over its creators. Humanity invented supernatural powers to compensate for their fear, ignorance, and feebleness.

The French revolutionary philosopher, Marquis de Sade (1740–1814), puts religion as one of the central oppressors and the cause of human submission and ignorance. The adage that religion is "the opium of the people" was his invention. Voltaire likened the "truths of religion" to the loss of "the power of reason." In 1764, he also noted that whoever believes in "absurdities ... shall commit atrocities" (quoted from Tremblay 2010: 143). Pascal commented that people, "never do evil so completely and cheerfully as when they do it from religious conviction" (quoted from Avise 1998: 205). Feuerbach held that God is what people want to be and people created gods in their own images. Furthermore, in religion, "only what it holds sacred is true, whereas to philosophy [reason], only what holds true is sacred" (Feuerbach 2018: 11). Marx who was much influenced by Feuerbach on this subject reaffirmed Feuerbach saying that "man makes religion; religion does not make man" (Marx 1973: 13). Religion for Marx is, "the sight of the oppressed creature, the heart of a heartless world, and the soul of soulless conditions. It is the opium of the people" (Marx 1994: 57).

The quest for reason not only calls for the democratization of knowledge but also calls for the democratization of belief. In contrast to the belief in reason, the belief in religion is rigid and autocratic. Embedded in the core being of religion is intolerance, the rejection of all other religions and beliefs. This has been one of the main causes of religious wars. Each religion claims to be the sole holder of absolute truth. By definition, religions cannot tolerate each other or other beliefs. Among the most intolerant religions are the monistic religions. The proponents of the Age of Enlightenment plea for the democratization of belief. The confrontation between these two firmly opposed worldviews was unavoidable. From the perspective of the exponents of reason, a person's belief is a personal matter. Each person is capable of forming their faith and conviction. This perspective opted for common well-being, tolerance, moderation, and secularity instead of the pursuit of dogmatism, bigotry, and wars. Locke in the *Letter Concerning Tolerance* (1689) renounced the religious course of coercion and persecution. He cautiously reasoned that even if:

> the magistrate's opinion in religion be sound, and the way that he appoints be truly evangelical, yet if I be not thoroughly persuaded thereof in my own mind, there will be no safety for me in following it.
>
> (Locke 2003: 232)

Voltaire in his *Treatise on Tolerance* (1763) pleaded for the practice of tolerance and freedom of conscience. He raised the position of tolerance to the "first law of nature." He said toleration is "the prerogative of humanity. We are all steeped in weaknesses and errors: Let us forgive one another's follies" (quoted from Yarlagadda 2017: 34). In defence of freedom of belief, word has it that he daringly testified that he can disagree with everything one may say "but will defend to the death" their "right to say it" (quoted from Haworth 1998: 39). Gotthold Ephraim Lessing (1729–81), a German dramatist in his play *Nathan the Wise* (1779), used a parable to show how tolerance between different faiths is the prerequisite for peace and the common good. The critical message in this quest for toleration is that each individual is predisposed to being right or wrong in their beliefs. Thus, it is one of the most basic natural rights of each individual not just to uphold correct views but also wrong and unorthodox beliefs. The liability of being wrong and the security in holding wrong beliefs is the most basic of all rights in safeguarding the freedom of thought.

The universalist religions as much as universalist ideologies are essentially totalitarian. They are imperialistic and strive to conquer and overpower everything and everyone by any means. The more power they acquire, the more people they dominate and coerce to convert to their own creed. By making religion and belief a personal matter, the proponents of the age of enlightenment succeeded to achieve three critically important goals. The advances of the age have restricted the power of religion in many spheres of life, from political, economic, cultural, ethical, and intellectual power. This separation created an environment conducive to greater tolerance and the necessary conditions to confront religious cruelty. Most importantly, it created an enabling climate for morality to get out of the exclusive domination of religion and become one's own birth-right entitlement. In doing so, this for its part then has facilitated greater dissemination of freedom of thought and conscience.

Escaping from the grim vision of the nature of humanity generated a supportive environment that encouraged hope, optimism, and a collective dynamism for change. It put emphasis on human potentials, the potential to learn, improve, and be good. Against full utilization of human nature and capabilities, the advocates of enlightenment saw three major barriers. These were identified as unrepresentative government (absolute monarchy), state theocracy (union of state and religion), and the lack of freedom. Undemocratic government and the absence of freedom were viewed as being against natural law. Religion, in particular the unity of religion and state, was viewed as being the worst of all possible worlds, because it was said that it is a major cause of ignorance, superstition, and fanaticism. Locke in his *Two Treatises of Government* laid the foundations of modern representative democratic states. In this work, Locke pointed out that before the formation of the state people lived in the "state of nature" when the earth did not belong to anyone – when there was no private ownership of land.

The origin of ownership in Locke's account is nature. From natural ownership stems all other types of ownership that are unnatural. By the law of nature, for example, each person owns their body. By virtue of this fact, each person should own the product of their own labour. Thus, each individual has the right to ownership. So, these types of ownership are natural. In the next stage, we have the transition of the state of nature to the formation of the state and property ownership. Under the law of nature, people are free. As an individual's self-preservation and security are also in the nature of humanity, the state of nature is not capable of providing this security for ever-expanding human communities. For this reason, people invented states for their collective security and survival. The state in itself is a necessity but not its absolute power. Its authority should not come from its own or divine authority. Locke held that neither the gods nor the absolute rulers can determine the legitimacy of the government. The right of authority only belongs to the people and if people find that this right is violated people have got the right to overthrow that government. This was an important step in removing the state from the realm of divinity and absolute authority and passing the ultimate authority to the individual – a right that each individual can exercise by taking part in the choice of their political authority.

But this right in itself is not sufficient for a government and an economy to be democratic. The majority of people are not always right. They can be wrong. They can elect a theocratic government, a fascist government, a totalitarian communist government, an oligarchic government, or any other type of autocratic government. This is where the contribution of Montesquieu on the rule of law came vitally handy for breaking away from long-lasting undemocratic political systems and the formation of democratic states. Montesquieu and other leading thinkers of the enlightenment pointed to two central sources of the laws of undemocratic states. These laws stem from sin and blind obedience. Under this political climate, any defiance of authority was correlated with the transgression of divinity and the authority of the rulers. In addition, the prevailing legal system in this political setup is arbitrary and its penal system has the criminal law as its common law. The legal system does not make a distinction between a political nonconformist and a common murderer. Montesquieu in one very influential book of the modern age, *The Spirit of the Laws*, demonstrated that representative government without rule of law cannot protect the democratic rights of people. That is without the rule of law there can be no freedom. Moreover, the right to equality before the law cannot be guaranteed unless there is a division of power between different organs of the state. In any other form, all the political power will be concentrated in the hands of one individual or authority, which is the cause of tyranny. Montesquieu reasoned that liberation from tyranny is only possible when the state power is divided between the executive, legislative, and judicial branches of the state. Protection of life and freedom is possible only when the judicial branch of government is independent. Hence, a democratic constitution with cited preconditions can defend and maintain individual liberty.

Savagery has been a universal practice throughout human history. It is widespread among undemocratic political systems, old and new. As a normal practice, for the first time in human history, it was seriously called into question by the thinkers of the age of enlightenment. Cesare Beccaria (1738–94), an Italian criminologist in his booklet, *On Crimes and Punishments* (1764), questioned the validity and efficacy of the system of punishment that is based on torture and capital punishment. He described the whole terrible acts of torture and capital punishment as "cold cruelty." Beccaria contested the use of torture to extract a false confession. He cast doubt on the credibility of evidence extracted under torture and called the verdict of the court to take one's life as state murder. Reasoning from this fact that under torture the victims are coerced to confess to something they have not done and incriminating the suspect based on evidence obtained from a false confession is inherently immoral and must be illegal. In such penal systems, the fundamental principle of justice is wilfully violated. Beccaria was professing that at the core of the fundamental principle of justice is the maxim that "for in the eye of the law, every man is innocent, whose crime has not been proved" (Beccaria 1813: 74). The accused is presumed innocent until their guilt is proven. The essential conditions for this procedure to be implemented correctly are that it must be free of confession under torture in a free and independent court of law. The precept of the presumption of innocence is more than just dispensing the fundamental principle of justice. It is also freedom from torture, freedom from insecurity, and respect for the sanctity of human life.

Humans are social beings. Throughout their history, they have created unique communities that share the same land, history, culture, language, specific social and economic relations of production, moral codes, legal system, and some kind of collective sympathy. In other words, in its most advanced form, they have developed a sense of nationhood. Within these human gatherings in different parts of the world, some occupy very large tracts of land, some have very large populations, some are developed, and many are much smaller, weaker, and less developed. One of the main concerns of the age was the legitimacy of law. The age of reason also overlapped with the age of colonialism. The European powers in the name of economic prosperity, the spread of Christianity, rivalry, and "civilizing" the uncivilized conquered the world and subjugated many nations. As a result of European colonialism, for the most part, many nations of the world were exterminated. In consequence, the native people of many other colonized nations have been reduced into small minority groups. Johann Gottfried von Herder (1744–1803), a German critic, found the colonial law as being unjust. In his book, *Outline of a Philosophy of the History of Man* (1784), he questioned the legitimacy of the double standards in the law of nations – one law for the occupiers and another for the occupied. In view of this, he argued that colonialism is contrary to the principle of one law for all nations.

Herder contended that when stronger nations occupy and subjugate other nations, the aggressive nations deprive the colonized nations of "their country," which means they "deprive them of everything" (Herder 1803: 303). The colonial rule and arbitrary drawing of artificial borders by colonial rulers and the creation of Frankenstein states raise a fundamental issue about the legitimacy and enforcement of a law that hitherto has not been paid due attention by scholars. Rationally and morally speaking, no law has got any legal authority and legitimacy unless it is approved and declared by the representatives of a free nation who are elected in a free, open, and competitive political environment based on the principle of one person, one vote in their democratic legislative chambers, i.e., in the parliaments of a free nation. For clarification of this point let us consider India when it was a colony of Britain. The colonial laws that were made in London and were enforced in India had no moral and legal legitimacy in India. For the same reason, the colonial geopolitical constructions that were decided and created in London by the British colonial rulers by dividing different nations and creating numerous Frankenstein states have no moral authority and legal legitimacy. Among the archetype of these colonial political structures that have been fabricated by European empires during the First and Second World Wars, just to name a few, are Pakistan, Iraq, and Syria. Several nations were divided to create these freakish countries. The Punjabi Muslims were put in charge of Pakistan and the Arabs in charge of Iraq and Syria. The laws made by Punjabi Muslims in Islamabad or the laws made by Arabs in Bagdad or Damascus are colonial laws. These laws are imposed on the nations under their control. On the strength of the same reason that the British colonial laws in India were illegitimate and lacked moral authority, in the same way, the laws of nations in charge of colonial geopolitical constructions cited above over the nations under their control lack legitimacy.

That said, it is the only freedom that ensures the legitimacy of law. Jean Jacques Rousseau (1712–78) purported that "man is born free and yet is universally enslaved" (Rousseau 1764: 3). He identified two main causes of human enslavement: "power" and "cowardice." The "power first made slaves and cowardice hath perpetuated them" (Rousseau 1764: 6). Rousseau renounced all forms of slavery. Slavery, he said, is unnatural "as no man hath any natural authority over the rest of his species, and as power doth not confer right" (Rousseau 1767: 10). Colonialism is a form of slavery. It is the collective enslavement of a whole or a part of a nation irrespective of whoever may be the culprit. The offender, the colonizer, can be any nation or its ex-colony. Both acts are unjust, and justice and slavery are not compatible. In Rousseau's words, they are "contradictory and reciprocally exclusive of each other" (Rousseau 1764: 16). The unjust authorities, be that a slave master or a colonial state, would not last unless they convert their "power into a right of command" and "people are compelled to obey … but as soon as they are in a capacity to resist, they do better to throw off the yoke of restraint" (Rousseau 1764: 4). Slavery decimates human potential. It is in freedom that human potentials can be put to use. Human nature is entwined with freedom. By depriving humans of their liberty, you deprive them of being human. That is:

> to renounce one's natural liberty, is to renounce one's very being as a man; it is to renounce not only the rights but even the duties of humanity …

> Such a renunciation is incompatible with our very nature; for to deprive us of the liberty of the will, is to take away all morality from actions.
>
> (Rousseau 1764: 12)

By means of this reasoning, the proponents of the enlightenment have justified the revolts of the oppressed against all forms of authorities that deny their natural rights. Revolt against the absolute power of religion, the king, slavery, and colonialism. The ideas of the writers of the age influenced the French revolutions and the American anti-colonialist movement and the independence war. These revolutions in turn reaffirmed the validity and the limitations of the ideas of the proponents of the age of reason. American independence revealed one of these drawbacks. It was noted that just permission for free speech is inadequate for obtaining full freedom. When free speech and freedom of association and assembly come hand in hand, their unity is a more powerful instrument against absolutism and tyranny. The advocates of the age of reason were, by and large, optimist thinkers. They had great faith in the power of humanity to change on grounds of having the capacity to reason. One such power was the power of revolt against the unjust authorities and restoration of legitimate representative authority. But even such direct actions could not succeed unless it was an informed action. These thinkers had great faith in the power of education. By means of education and resistance against ignorance, superstition, and tyranny, human beings are capable of constructing ideal societies that are free of pain, hunger, and conflict. They were strong believers in human goodness and ability. By changing the human environment, they believed, one can change human conduct and their conditions of living for good.

To the most extreme optimists, only a perfect human society was acceptable. Morelly was one of those over-optimistic authors. His proclamation entitled *Code of Nature* (1755) is about communism, his ideal type of society. Morelly had a firm conviction in the goodness of humanity and the power of reason. This being the case, Morelly held that the construction of a perfect society is inevitable. Since no person is "born vicious and wicked" and the "very make-up" of every person is formed "by the circumstances of life in this world." In the right conditions, people become good and moral. With the help of science, we can change everything including human morality. True morality is discoverable by true scientific methods and can be defined by mathematical language. Morelly asserted that "as with mathematical Equations, such Reasoning, avoiding and eliminating the false and dubious, would finally make the unknown quantity emerge, that is, a system of Ethics truly susceptible of the clearest proofs" (quoted from Fried and Sanders 1964: 18–31). This is the same method that Spinoza applied in his book, *Ethics*, in defining moral laws. Spinoza adopted the deductive logical method to demonstrate that moral laws are universally applicable. By discovering the fundamental laws of morality, Morelly maintained, we can construct a perfect society. In his *Code of Nature*, he discusses a number of such laws.

In law (3) of Morelly's communism, Morelly describes the central pillars of his perfect society. This law reads that "for his part, every citizen will contribute to the public weal in accordance with his strength, his talents, and his age; these will determine his obligations, in conformity with the Distributive law" (quoted from Fried and Sanders 1964: 18–31).

Another French thinker, Marquis de Condorcet (1743–94), in his *Sketch for a Historical Picture of Progress of the Human Mind* (1794), described the stages of development of human societies. The chief objective of this article is about human progress. He identified ten different stages of development of human societies. In his last epoch, the tenth epoch, we will have the supremacy of reason over superstition. During this stage, human conduct is based entirely on scientific principles. By means of the law of causal necessity, we would be able to discover all fundamental laws of a just society. This perfect society will last forever. It is during this epoch that we would witness "the destruction of inequality between different nations; the progress of equality in one and the same nation; and lastly, the real improvement of man" (Condorcet 2009: 353). These ideas were developed further by Marx who called for direct action, revolution, to create a new society. Side by side with this group of writers, there was another group who advocated further progress by means of education and reforms. This group of writers also deeply held the belief that people are either good by nature or morally neutral. Either way, they can be improved through education and reforms. The utilitarian writers were from this school. Jeremy Bentham (1748–1832), the founder of the school, argued that there are two main forces that govern humans. These are the "two sovereign masters, *pain* and *pleasure*. It is for them alone to point out what we ought to do, as well as to determine what we shall do" (Bentham 1838: 1 – Italics in original). Accordingly, he concludes that by means of education and reforms pain can be minimized and pleasure maximized for the greatest number of people.

It may safely be said that Kant's works had the biggest impact on the ideas of this period. In a number of ground-breaking books, *The Critique of Pure Reason* (1781), *The Critique of Practical Reason* (1788), *The Critique of Judgement* (1790), *The Fundamental Principles of the Metaphysics of Morals* (1785), and his other works, he expounded his central ideas about epistemology and ethics. Kant did not think of the period as a fully fledged enlightened period but a transitional period that is in the midst of "enlightening." An era that Europe entered the age of maturity and the European man was coming of age in two critical realms. These were the realms of knowledge and morality. Kant attested this distinction in his two wonders of, "the starry sky above … and the moral law within" (Kant 1992: 1). In both realms, the individual is liberated from the yoke of divinity. Each individual is in charge of their knowledge and moral bearings, by virtue of the fact that each individual is equipped with a faculty to reason. Thus, rationality is at the core of Kant's theory of knowledge and morality. The only thing agreeable in the end is the reason.

To know, to act, and to hope are exclusive to oneself. Knowledge begins from one's own self, from the sensory experience of each individual in the external world. Because all knowledge begins with our, "senses, proceeds from thence to understanding, and ends with reason" (Kant 1929: 300). Due to the fact that each person is endowed with the faculty to learn and the capacity to reason, they are capable of acting rationally. Thus, the foundation of human morality is also the reason. Human beings, unlike other species, are subject to moral laws on account of having the capacity to reason. The state laws and the moral laws are both subject to reason but the two laws are not the same. In a state's laws, "a man is guilty when he violates the rights of others. In ethics he is guilty if he only thinks of doing so" (quoted from Gerald and et al. 2014: 309). Only a rational being can have this moral consciousness. As rational beings, human beings can formulate their own rules of conduct and go against personal interests in pursuit of what is considered to be morally right. The rational beings that are able to know, act, and hope are an end in themselves. Kant insists that:

> the rational being itself, must be made the foundation of all maxims of actions, never merely as a means, but as the supreme limiting condition in the use of all means, i.e., always at the same time as an end.
>
> (Kant 2012: 49)

Kant's ethics is centred on his moral duties. His moral duties in turn are rested on his categorical imperatives. A categorical imperative is, "one which represented an action as objectively necessary in itself apart from its relation to a further end" (Kant 2002: 44). The supreme rule of conduct and morality in view of this definition is unconditional and applies to everyone, everywhere all the time. This maxim requires each individual to act in a way that it "can at the same time make itself a universal law" (Kant 2005: 95). Therefore, moral law is imperative because it is a requirement that everyone must follow the law and it is categorical because it is applicable to everyone. The act becomes a universal law and is applied everywhere by every individual. Kant's central message in this deliberation is that as a species that has got the capacity to reason, know, and construct rules of conduct and hope, human beings can make themselves. That is, "to be is to do" so social and moral progress is possible and therein lies his answer to the question of hope.

From the mere fact that human beings have the capacity of being rational and to reason, it does not follow that this capacity is always put into effect. Fulfilling this capacity is contingent on one's freedom. Thus, for Kant freedom is the embodiment and objectification of being able to reason, to know, to act (to meet one's moral duty), and to wish. Under coercion, such activities and requirements cannot be fulfilled. From this perspective, each human is the end and the highest good – not God, the religion, the government, or anything else. Each person possesses a free will that in the absence of coercion can utilize one's freedom in their quest to learn and know what is true and false and what is right or wrong and enhance and cultivate one's capacities by freely setting one's own ends. In Kant's view, freedom and free will are the unconditional rights of each individual. If you like, they are inborn natural rights by virtue of being a human. This freedom is not confined only to external coercion but also to internal barriers that one intakes in the course of one's upbringing that undermine one's capacity to reason, to know, or to act morally. Kant raised the position of freedom as "the alone unoriginated birth right of man and belongs to him by force of his humanity; and is independence on the will and co-action of every other in so far as this consists with every other person's freedom" (Kant 1871: 185). It is freedom that makes humans what they are essentially meant to be. It is under the freedom that one can reason effectively, speak freely, set one's own ends, and live life to the fullest with dignity. Kant says that "the public use of one's reason must always be free, and that only can bring about enlightening among men" (Kant 1976: 287).

One of the most striking traits of the age of Enlightenment was the general optimism that was expressed by different writers. There was solid confidence in the power of human reasoning. It made people feel responsible for their difficulties. Equally, it placed freedom and the human capacity to reason as their only way forward for a better and more fulfilling life. The frontrunners of the movement were confident that the laws of nature could be discovered and be employed to serve people's well-being. Many of the scientific and technological achievements at the time confirmed this trend of thought. The wheel of optimism and progress gathered pace over time and spread across an ever greater number of scientific disciplines. Combinations of many technological innovations, scientific discoveries, and colonization of new lands had transformed the medieval economy and society in Europe. These changes opened new gates for personal liberty and the pursuit of personal interest.

Economics as a scientific discipline was also conceived during this era. It gave birth to Adam Smith. The *Wealth of Nations* (1776), Smith's monumental book, is among the ground-breaking books of the age. With the publication of this book, economics became a scientific discipline in its own right. This work was a significant step forward in the democratization of the economy. Smith's *Wealth of Nations* spearheaded the liberty of the economy from the bondage of divinities, religions, and the hollow and crippling rules and customs of the state and society of medieval Europe and passed it to individuals. In the main, during the medieval time in Europe, one did not belong to oneself but to a god, a religion, a king, a feudal lord, or any other power. As complete or partial bondage, their belongings were also not their own belongings. Generally speaking, each individual lived to pass a test, waiting to be judged for their deeds after their death. As the nature of economic activities is such that they are for improving one's real economic conditions of life, this activity was meted out as sinful. With respect to an individual's economic activity, one was not self-governing. The type of property one could have, the economic role one could play, and the profession one could choose were hardly ever made out of free choice.

A Dutch physician, Bernard Mandeville (1670–1733), who lived for most of his life in London, published a poem entitled *The Fable of the Bees* in 1705. An extended variation of this allegory subsequently was published in the form of a book in 1714. The satire shocked the men of god, the puritanical breed, the reputable class, and the old schools. All raised their voice and denounced Mandeville's poem as scandalous banter. In this poem, Mandeville likens a hive of bees to human society and demonstrates how private vices lead to general prosperity and public benefits. He describes how the pursuit of self-interest and pleasure – that is, greed, luxury, and lust for profit; accumulation of wealth and pleasure – can result in general prosperity and an affluent society. Smith consolidated this view and canonized it in the grand order of his economic ideas. In this way, Smith liberated individuals to pursue their economic activities. He expressed this declaration by saying that "it is not from the benevolence of the butcher, the brewer, or the baker, that we expect our dinner, but from their regard to their own interest" (Smith 1986: 119).

## Economics of might is right

The common thread of our inquiry in this book is the idea that the propensity to human extremism applies to every aspect of life. It is in everyone and in every human activity. Aristotle, arguably, is the greatest philosopher of ancient times. By birth, he divided men who are born slaves and those who are born masters. By virtue of their nature, masters are born to rule and the slaves to be enslaved – concluding that slavery is necessary and there is not much the slave can do about it. Likewise, women are born inferior to men and he pigeonholed them as deformed males that are to be ruled by the males. This extreme and harsh opinion and treatment of women and slaves is encapsulated almost in all religions, most prominently in the religions that have drawn many of their doctrines from Aristotle such as in Judaism, Christianity, and Islam.

Even Kant who championed the idea that people must be treated as an end in themselves did not believe in gender equality. He held the view that women compared to men are less capable of making a correct moral judgement. In 1764, he wrote, "the virtue of a woman is a beautiful virtue." In contrast, the virtue of men is a "noble virtue." From his interpretation of the gender hierarchy, he inferred that "women will avoid evil not because it is unjust, but because it is ugly," and therefore they are not "capable of principles" (Kant 2011: 39). For most of his life, Kant believed in the racial hierarchy and European colonialism. In his racial hierarchy, the "white race" is the most perfect race who has "all incentives and talents," and at the lowest level are the Native persons who "are too weak for hard labour and too indifferent for industrious work." For these reasons, Kant asserted that they are "incapable of any culture" (Kleingeld 2007: 574). So long as he remained in this frame of mind, Kant justified European colonialism on the ground that non-White races "weren't capable of governing themselves" (Kleingeld 2007: 577). Only in the last ten years of his life, with the writing of his work *Towards Perpetual Peace* (1795), Kant revised and repudiated his views and rejected the act of colonialism as being immoral.

With respect to the permissibility of gender bias, Kant was not alone. Rousseau argued that in the state of nature everyone is free but when it came to the freedom and equality of women, he asserted that by nature women are subordinated to men – claiming that women do not possess autonomous rationality and they also rely on men for their well-being. He confined the role of women to only being a "wife" and a "mother" and asserted that men can survive without women but women cannot. Basically, a woman in Rousseau's mind is "made for man's delight" (Trono 1994: 54). Simply put, this meant the exclusion of half of the human population from the utilization of their potential and economic activities. Nowhere, as yet, has gender equality been fully implemented. One of the core principles of a democratic system is one person one vote. Women comprise the largest group of people who were previously denied, and are currently denied in many countries, equal rights and opportunities to exert the same influence in their respective societies. Women's suffrage in the twentieth century was a major step in the emancipation of women to acquire the equal right to vote in elections. However, the campaign for gender equality started during the age of enlightenment. One of the pioneering intellectuals of this movement was Mary Wollstonecraft (1759–97). Emancipation of women for Wollstonecraft is not misandry but equality of rights between sexes. She reasoned that it is because "virtue can only flourish amongst equals" (Wollstonecraft 2003: 61).

For Marx discrimination on the basis of gender and discrimination on the grounds of class are intertwined. Marx held that "the degree of woman's emancipation is the natural measure of the general emancipation" (Marx and Engels 1962: 123). J. S. Mill, an economist, philosopher, and contemporary of Marx, was possibly the only leading thinker of the period who advocated unequivocally for full gender equality. Legal subjugation of women, he stated, is not only "wrong in itself" but it is also one of the "chief hindrances as to human improvement" (Mill 1869: 1). Mill undoubtedly was a defender of individual liberty. He advocated that individuals pursue one's own good in their own way so long as each individual does not "attempt to deprive others of theirs or impede their efforts to obtain it" (Mill 2010: 215). When it comes right down to colonialism, even Mill does not consider the same rights for the people of the colonized nations. Mill supported European colonialism (Bell 2010). The implication of this duplicity of position is a matter of much concern in mainstream economics, both its general principles and their actual application. One example of which we shall touch on next.

William S. Jevons (1835–82), one of the principal founders of the marginalist school, and Alfred Marshall (1842–1924), the synthesizer of the neo-classical school, also accepted colonialism as a normal social condition. But the primary premise of their economic idea that laid the foundation of neoclassical economics is a self-interested and perfectly rational individual who maximizes his interest in all circumstances. The time and place are inconsequential for their all-round abstract individual. In their economic theory, this individual is the same always and everywhere. But at the same time, they viewed the colonized people as lesser people. These people will always be less developed and backwards (Blaney 2020). This double-talking about the colonized and the colonizers has been the common trend in mainstream economics from Adam Smith (Williams 2014) to J. M. Keynes. People of colonized nations are left out in their economic order and system of liberty and justice. The question is: how can the people of colonized nations be rational and could maximize their utility and profit when they are regarded as being lower grade human beings who deserve to be subjugated?

The economics of imperial establishments built their economic principles on a preconceived premise that colonialism is a matter of fact and the belief in lower grades humans. In its extreme form, this line of thinking found its natural place in social Darwinism which openly opted for the doctrine of laissez-faire, colonialism, and eugenics. What Winston Churchill, the British prime minister (1940–45 and 1951–55) and a British war hero, said about the colonized people is not far from the dominant view of conventional economics, the economics of the establishment, up to the Second World War. None of these economists saw any problem with colonialism. Churchill publicly admitted that no wrong has been done to the colonialized nations. What has happened to the colonized people was natural as "a stronger race, a higher-grade race or at any rate a more worldly-wise race … has come in and taken their place" (quoted from Addison 2005: 137). It was on the basis of this superiority to rule that when the time for the independence of India came, at the end of the Second World War, Churchill ordered the division of India and asked to "keep a bit of India" (quoted from Khan 1987: 103). Those bits were parts of two provinces of India, the eastern part of Bengal province and the western part of Punjab province, which subsequently became Pakistan. An artificial entity, a colonial geopolitical structure that has been marred from its creation with extreme violence, corruption, religious fundamentalism and militarism. All these elements are excluded from mainstream economic theory.

In Marx's theory of history, capitalism is a definite historical period with a definite mode and social relations of production. This was what he found in England during his time in England. Marx's history is a Hegelian teleological belief that assumes events progress to a specific end. For Marx this historical end was communism. The greatest part that spurred Marx's teleological concept of history was the drastic economic changes caused by the first Industrial Revolution in human history. This historical breakthrough was unprecedented. It transformed the social and economic landscape of Britain completely. This was an era of phenomenal technological revolution, economic productivity, and rapid economic growth, accompanied by new social and economic transformations and problems. It was the selective characteristics of the end period of the Industrial Revolution in England with its economic and social problems that Marx used to define his version of "capitalism." Marx's depiction of the extraordinary changes in technology, economy, society, institution, and law during this period in Britain was only a blurry picture of the reality. More often on such matters, the contents of such a complex picture fade away in time, and instead, empty rhetoric will outgrow and take precedence over the original story. The greatest achievement of Marx was neither his accurate analysis nor his predictions but the conversion of both his disciples and his bitter enemies to capitalism. Both sides believe in capitalism and in their estimates, it is the fate of capitalism that determines the fate of humanity. This rigid fatalistic idea from either side was cemented with the 1917 Russian Revolution. To the Marxists, by all Marxists initially, the Russian Revolution was a confirmation of Marx's teleological theory of history. To others, it was a just cause to crusade against Communism and protect "capitalism" by all means.

History is neither like what Marx imagined it to be nor is the economy the way he described it. "Capitalism" is empty rhetoric that corresponds not to what Marx's critics and opponents believe it to be and not what Marx's devotees wish it to be. History is not an organic species with a fixed DNA. Diminishing human history into some simplistic pre-set time that is destined to a certain end, which is predictable is a big error. But this is the very point upon which the economic theory of different schools of thought stands. Most specifically, this stand has been the prevalent point of departure for dominant economic thoughts after the 1917 Russian Revolution. This point is capitalism, either in its defence or in rejecting it. This was the beginning of J. M. Keynes's economics. Keynes wanted to reform capitalism. In capitalism, he noted, "the most wickedest of men will do the most wickedest of things for the greatest good of everyone" (quoted from Beinhocker 2006: 408). To those committed revolutionaries who wished and acted to abolish capitalism, Keynes declared that in the class war they would find him "on the side of the educated bourgeoisie" (Keynes 1971: 295). Those economists, from the left or the right spectra who call for reform, aim to reform merely one imaginary variation of Marx's capitalism.

Belief in the existence of capitalism is a matter of faith. Its denial is a cardinal sin by those who are brought to hate this fictitious construction and by those who are indoctrinated to love it. The core of Marxists' thoughts, economic or otherwise, is based on this concept. This is their chief template from which they compare the past, the present, and the future. Marxian economics, in particular, since Marx's works has not advanced much. Capitalism is his scripture and the supreme idol. The idol and scripture are untouchable and cannot be rejected. The only venture or progress in Marxian ideas has been on imperialism. The leading proponents of Marx, Karl Kautsky (1854–1938), Rudolf Hilferding (1877–1941), Vladimir Lenin, and Ernest Mandel (1923–95), in their attempt to show that Marx is right have argued that capitalism develops in stages. One of the final of these stages is imperialism. On the other end of the ideological spectrum, Marx's capitalism is guarded by all means. F. Hayek compared capitalism to what is beautiful, to freedom, and the most essential condition for the survival of humanity. He purported that capitalism is "not only a better form of organizing human activity … but it is also the indispensable condition for just keeping that population alive."

Furthermore, it is "an essential condition of the very survival of mankind" (quoted from Barnes 2011: 116). Milton Friedman alleged that "capitalism is a necessary condition for political freedom" (Friedman 2002: 10).

A. Schumpeter described capitalism as "an engine of mass production" (Schumpeter 1996: 281). It is a system of production that produces for the masses and its greatest achievement is the production of cheap goods. He praised the successes of the system but lamented its dynamism as "an evolutionary process," which is the cause of its own destruction. Hyman P. Minsky, a leading proponent of Post-Keynesianism, also argued that the "capitalist economy cannot be maintained … it oscillates between threats of an imminent collapse of asset values and employment and threats of accelerating inflation and rampant speculation" (Minsky 2008: 6). In order to rescue capitalism and to make it to function well, Minsky stipulates that "we must arrange to constrain the uncertainty due to business cycles so that the expectations that guide investment can reflect a vision of tranquil process" (Minsky 2008: 6).

Economic crises are viewed primarily through the lens of the mythos of capitalism. The mantra of capitalism has coloured the discourse on economic crisis. This obsession with capitalism has obscured a critical study and true reading of economic crises. Let us take the example of the 2007–2008 global financial crisis. At the outbreak of the crisis, the monetary and credit institutions and instruments were more developed and sophisticated compared to any time in history. There was predatory lending, some loans were given without verifying income, the credit rating was inflated, and disinformation about adjustable mortgages to serve the interest of mortgage lenders was at top speed. The facts of inflated credit ratings, low-interest rates, and lax lending, the creation of complex securities, the lack of an effective structure of transparency, accountability, and supervision, or even adequate compliance with regulatory requirements did not rise all at once. Neither did the element of moral hazard and the banks taking advantage of shadow banking with opening offshore accounts. There will always be some shady dealings, reckless planning, maturity mismatch, the struggle between those well connected and those less connected, sovereign debts, occasional availability of cheap money, teaser interest rates, new innovations, and strategies based on quackery knowledge in these markets. Over time the size, scale, and scope of markets will change. They get more complex, interdependent, and global. All these changes initially work. If they worked once, then they cannot be the root causes of economic crises.

Consumption is the most basic natural driving force in economics. Consumption in its most basic form is an instinct determinant. It is a natural drive shared by all human species. Its cause is biological. A natural instinct that every individual has. Biological needs – air, food, water, sleep, the urge for procreation, the ability to learn, fear, pain, pleasure, protection against danger, and self-preservation – are natural and instinctual. Such needs are present in us from birth. The basic human needs that are essential for survival are fundamental biological needs that came with humans as a living species.

That is, prior to any form of human social and economic organization. These natural predispositions existed before the formation of the institution of the market and exist in the absence of the institution of the market. The drives, motives, desires, and urges behind consumption to stay alive are natural basic instincts. The development of the institution of the market is not inborn. It is a matter of choice. The formation of markets is historically contingent. Their formation is contingent upon the size of the human population, human settlements, the specialization and division of labour, access to surplus products or production of surplus products, learning about advantages of trade and exchange, and many other needed conditions. The development of a market is a purposeful effort that emerges, provided contingent conditions are in place, through experience and learning. The market is not a natural instinct and the drive and motive behind the market is not a natural instinct. The driving force, the main motive, is to make a profit. The urge to exchange is to mislead the counterparty as much as possible and to make as much profit as possible at the expense of the counterparty.

In a market for tangible goods where the exchange takes place in the presence of counterparties, it is easier to make a more informed judgement. But the financial markets are more aloof and alienated markets. They are detached from the basic exchange of real goods. These markets are very complex, too interdependent, very competitive, and relatively more global. The motive behind these markets is to make as much money as soon as you can by almost any means. Those who take part in these markets do not take part to acquire the basic natural consumption needs. This is the least concern of the real market makers. The central gravitational force in the market is profit. The passion of making a profit and getting rich to the overzealous individual who is eager to strike it rich in no time is irrepressible. Those who operate these markets are obsessed with such ambition. Aggression, chain reaction, and snowball effects are part and parcel of these markets. Trade is agitated and stirred into a frantic activity and can be degenerated into a mob rule. With all the claims of scientific understanding and supervision of these markets, the inner core of these markets operates on the principle of herd instinct. Under the disguise of science, it is the herd mentality that leads the way. As the tempers of trade flares, the fever of higher profit calls the shots. Herd instinct has a power of its own. It is self-fulfilling. The more people join and buy, the more people think it is the right thing to do. Falling blindly prey to the herd action is seeking safety in numbers. Going against the flow, against the dominant mood of the market, and thinking and understanding independently and acting outside the box when it concerns making and losing a lot of money is very hard. Most participants of the market follow the leaders in the pack.

## Fixed known and the changing unknown

There is a general misconception that places economics in a superior position to other social studies. As if it is more scientific than other fields of studies in this category. It is also said that economics is less scientific than natural sciences, e.g., physics. This or a similar pecking order of the disciplinary hierarchy of superior and inferior sciences is misleading. This conviction is misplaced and historically unsupported. To this day there is not one single economic theory that is universally accepted and applied. Almost all terms used in economics are controversial. There is not one instruction, prescription, diagnosis, and medium of instruction in economics that can be applied universally. The life of economics as a modern academic discipline is relatively short. Ever since the foundations of modern economics were laid down by Adam Smith, there have been many schools of thought in economics that disagree on their most basic doctrines. However, the cliché "economists disagree" is not an accurate saying either. The disagreements among economists are disagreements among different schools of thought in economics. In each school of thought, there are some key ideas and basic concepts that the followers of each school would adhere to. The misunderstanding about the disciplinary hierarchy of superior and inferior sciences stems from the confusion of truths that arise out of regularity or are true in virtue of the meanings of the terms in their definition. These truths are fixed. There are truths that are contingent, which are ever-changing with new circumstances. In this section, we shall refute this distinction of truth as the sole criteria of demarcation of the disciplinary hierarchy of superior and inferior sciences or more scientific and less scientific truths.

From common sense data, it appears there are things that are changing; the night becomes the day; a baby grows up, gets old, and dies; the weather keeps changing, one day there is a cloud in the sky and the next day the sky is clear; and so on. There are things, perceived through a common-sense perspective, that appear to be fixed. The sea, the mountains, different species of animals, trees, and plants, the sunrise and the sunset, and so on. The earliest human ideas, to explain the world around them, were drawn from their common-sense experience. The pre-Socratic Greek thinker, Parmenides of Elea (c.515–450 BC), in his poem *On Being*, discusses the nature of existence. He said, "all in one." That is, one can only "speak and think only of what exists" (quoted from Velasquez 1991: 34). The change and "One Being" cannot go side by side. In this static monistic account of reality, there is no change. In Parmenides's opinion, "it is" cannot be "is not." It means it exists and if we cannot think of something, that thing would not exist. If we think of a thing then that exists. But if it does not exist it will not come into our thought. There is no unity of existence and non-existence. What appears as a change is merely an illusion since whatever exists stays forever as it is. In place of this unitary world, Plato presented a dualistic world. He adopted the world of Heraclitus and the world of Parmenides. In Heraclitus's world, everything is in the status of flux and becoming. In his famous saying, one cannot step in the same river twice.

In Plato's dualistic position, Heraclitus's world is a world that is an object of sensuous perception. Knowledge is acquired through sense experience. This is the world of particulars, the finite, the world of instances, the physical world, the changing world, the imperfect world, the realm of ambiguity, transition, doubt, opinion, and beliefs. It is in this world that we have countless particular horses but no single horse bears the full resemblance to any other horse or represents all horses in all possible worlds. Against this realm of many, Plato postulated the realm of the perfect world. He adopted Parmenides's world of "is" for his realm of "Forms." This is an eternal world, the most real and absolute world. The full significance of this world is that it is an abstract world. It is a super-sensory world that moves from the realm of particulars and envisages a realm of essences and absolute reality. This is the world of unity, totality, the world of universals that are timeless and spaceless. That is, the thing that is common in all particular horses – if you like the essence of the horse – is the "idea" of horse and this is the knowledge that we acquire independently of sense experience through pure thought, pure intellect, and reason *a priori*. This worldview has been instrumental in the monistic fallacy of divine creation. In divinity-based creation, a god or gods created the world and whatever exists in it and everything stays the same as they were conceived by these divinities. The Genesis creation in the Bible is a good example of this fallacy. According to this faith and its sister faiths, God created the universe about 6,000 years ago and created humans in his image and the rest of the species in their complete forms, a claim that ran counter to the theory of evolution, scientific discoveries, and evidence.

Plato's dual world of sensuous perception – the world of doubt, belief, and opinion, and the world of absolute reality, certainty, and true knowledge or the sensory realm and the realm of rational cognition – has not died out. It was a chief feature of the quest for truth that coloured the findings of scholars during the age of enlightenment. The division of scholars into the rationalist and empiricist schools pretty much was a continuation of Plato's dualistic realism. Central to the rationalist theory, human knowledge is the work of human mind. The capacity to reason is the work of the mind and it is by means of reason that we acquire knowledge independently of experience that is certain and universally valid. This reality is hidden from appearance and only is detectable *a priori* through reason, intellect, and deduction. This is what Descartes did in his dreams to lay the foundation of knowledge free form doubt. He summed up this thought experiment in his often-cited dictum, cogito ergo sum, or I think therefore I am. The fact that he thinks he exists is something Descartes postulated that he cannot doubt and this certain knowledge is attained independently of sense experience.

The path that Benedict de Spinoza (1632–77) took to demonstrate the attainability of absolute knowledge was also Cartesian. Due to his unorthodox views, he was excommunicated by the synagogue in 1656. Spinoza was a stoic-mannered individual who questioned fanaticism in its every form. He worked as a lens grinder to make ends meet. Spinoza immersed himself in the essence and the nature of the substance of human ethics. The means by which he advances his philosophical treatise is via concepts and deduction. He is interested in certain knowledge, the necessary truth that is derived deductively from the essence of matters. The eternal truths stem from true substance.

This substance is caused by itself. In other words, what we have is the world of "is" or the world of "one." The true substance can only be one substance. In his treatise of ethics, he applies the geometrical order to demonstrate that certain, universally, necessary, and timeless, truths in ethics are possible. Such truths are acquired by means of reason. Human reason is universal. In Spinoza's worldview, every individual has got the capacity to reason. The free individual is the one who applies their capacity to reason and act accordingly. Acting from reason is acting from directives that are not contingent but universal, categorical, and necessary (Shand 1994: 100).

Leibniz based his argument on the premise that it is possible that all fields of inquiry can be refined into one meaningful method of acquiring knowledge with certainty. More precisely, there is one universal method of reasoning and calculation that eradicates all disagreements. This method is the method of reason, and the truth that emanates from this method is the necessary truth. Such truths cannot be otherwise. They are true in all possible worlds. Leibniz hoped to find a universal method to converge the truths of fact into the truth of reason. The truths of facts are not necessary truths. The truths of facts are contingent truths. They could be otherwise than they are. The capital cities of different countries could have been other cities than the current ones. The contingent truths are not necessarily the same in all possible worlds. The sources of knowing these truths for Leibniz differ. The source of truths of facts is sense experience. It is *a posteriori* knowledge that is derived from experience. The truths of reason are *a priori* knowledge that is acquired independently of experience. To put it differently, Leibniz argued that all propositions comprised of their subjects and their predicates. In this respect, all propositions have the same form. But as to the relation of the predicate to the subject, there are two types of propositions. The truths of reason, the necessary truths, fall under propositions that the predicates are contained in the concept of the subjects. The truths of mathematics and logic are of such types of propositions. The truths of reason, the necessary truths or propositions, are unconditionally true and their denial entails a contradiction, whereas the contingent truths can be otherwise and their denial does not imply a contradiction.

To empiricists, by reason alone, we are not able to know what exists. Through experience, we know what exists and our knowledge is limited by experience. But the necessity can only be applied between logical and mathematical relations, the relations of concepts, ideas, and thoughts. The nature of connection in the real world is not necessary but contingent and cannot be discovered by reason but by experience. The truths of facts are the truths of the real world. Locke purports that "all knowledge derives from reasoning about our ideas and secondly, that all ideas originate in experience" (Shand 1994: 114). Berkeley stated that the world is meaningful within the confinement of our experience. The contents of our minds are objects that are perceived by our senses. The ideas are derived from our senses. These sensible objects exist. Therefore, they cannot be unperceived. For Hume too, the source of all human knowledge is sense data. But such data are channelled into two directions: to the memory and to the imagination. The impressions make our memory and the ideas of our imagination. Any connection that appears in the real world is contingent, which cannot be expressed by the language of necessary truth. Hume argued that necessary propositions such as mathematical relations are empty. These relations are merely based on definitions that are devoid of content about the real world.

Kant tried to fuse the rationalists' and empiricists' accounts about human knowledge. In doing so, he gathered the different pairs of propositions that were used by different scholars about human knowledge. For this purpose, he divided these propositions into three primary pairs: *a priori* and *a posteriori*, the analytic and the synthetic, and necessary and contingent statements. In the widest sense, the first parts in the three pairs are types of knowledge that are true independently of experience, or true by definition and should always be true. The second items in the pair are knowledge that is acquired through experience and cannot be known only by the meaning of terms in the statement, and their denial does not imply a contradiction. Setting aside various terms used in distinguishing different types of truth, there is one distinction for which there is a general agreement among scholars from the ancient time to the present day. Russell divided these truths into factual, mathematical, and logical truths. The factual truths can be known to be true *a posteriori*. The mathematical truths are necessary tautological truths that are true independent of experience in virtue of the meaning of the terms used. For verification of such truths, we do not rely on facts of the world but on the meaning of the terms. The truths of reason are deductive statements or relations that are valid or invalid irrespective of their content.

Empiricism and rationalism, like the rest of human activities, can be carried into extremism. In extreme empiricism or outright scepticism, we cannot know anything for certain. The history of this type of scepticism goes back to ancient times. The Greek philosopher Pyrrho of Elis (360–270 BC) was a proponent of this view. In his view, the corpus of what we believe are things that "seem" or "appear" to us. We will never know the inner substance of things. There can be no proof of the existence of anything. The outright sceptics deny any form of certainty. From this perspective, there is not such a thing as the final truth. It is impossible for humans to have certain knowledge. Everything is open to doubt and uncertainty. True knowledge is unattainable. Nothing can be known with certainty either to be true or false. Socrates remarked that he is only sure of one thing and that is "he knows nothing." Gorgias (483–375 BC), a pre-Socratic sophist, held the view that nothing exists. Even if something existed, it would be impossible to communicate it (Kerferd 1955). There were those Greek philosophers who claimed that nothing can be known, we even do not know whether we are able to know. One way or another this position has kept reappearing and in the early modern time, David Hume articulated a more sophisticated version of it (Hume 1854: 331). The implications of this position on human knowledge, irrespective of the embedded contradiction in the proposition itself – not knowing at all but knowing that we do know nothing – have much greater practical implications. Of the greatest importance is the implication that one can do anything without knowing or believing in what he or she does. However, one cannot continue one's life without such convictions. Doubting everything is one side of extreme empiricism and the other side of extreme empiricism is George Berkeley's empiricism. For Berkeley, there is nothing real. All corporeal substances or matter do not have an independent existence. These are only sensible qualities or combinations of sensible qualities that are perceived by minds in the form of ideas. Therefore, human knowledge is limited to sensible qualities and ideas.

On the other end of the scale, we have extreme rationalism. One form of extreme rationalism is solipsism. In the solipsists' world, there is only one thing that exists or allegedly can be proved to exist and that is the mind. Anything outside the mind is not knowledge. There is no external world. No proof of the truth of independent reality is possible. This position was held by the Pre-Socratic philosopher Gorgias and a milder version of it by Parmenides and in early modern times by Descartes. The most extreme end of this position is Gorgias's position that denies any existence and even if something exists, we can neither know about it nor can we communicate it. In Parmenides all reality is reduced to one, or in the case of Descartes to his "cogito ergo sum, I think therefore I am." There is a strong element of solipsism in eastern philosophy from Hinduism, Taoism, and Buddhism. In its different variations, they either see the whole reality in the individual or that what can be known is in one's mind. Other extreme versions of rationalism are obtaining absolute knowledge either by having it already, as in the case of the omniscient God, or by progressing towards it as in Hegel's absolute knowledge. In monotheistic religions, they already have the claim of knowing the absolute. In Hegel's absolute knowledge the mind is on the way towards it. The Hegelian absolute knowledge is "undistorted, unqualified, all-encompassing, free from counter-examples and internal consistencies" (Solomon 1983: 274). It was in the spirit of the Hegelian theory of knowledge that the entirety of human history was divided into a number of predetermined and distinct periods. With absolute certainty, Marx described the absolute inevitability, laws, direction, passage, and journey of these periods.

The two types of propositions are analytic propositions and synthetic propositions. There are two answers attached to each analytic proposition and three possible answers to each synthetic proposition. Let us consider the analytic proposition that "all triangles have three sides." The truth and falsity of this proposition depend only on the meaning of the symbols used in the proposition. It is believed that the truth or falsity of this proposition can be known *a priori*. The proposition lacks factual content so its truth and falsity and for its verification, we do not rely on the evidence of experience. The proposition is either true or false and there is nothing in between. It is necessarily true and cannot be otherwise. Its denial implies a logical contradiction.

Now let us consider the synthetic proposition "the Bank of England is an independent central bank." This is a proposition that expresses a fact about the actual world. It has a truth-value that is different from the logical truths. The truth and falsity of this proposition do not entirely depend on the meaning of symbols to express the proposition. The truth and falsity of this proposition do not depend on an *a priori*. It is determined *a posteriori*, only empirically verifiable. By consulting the empirical evidence, not from the meaning of the terms in the sentence, we are able to corroborate the truth and falsity of this proposition. This proposition is not true in all possible worlds. It is a contingent truth that is true in a certain time and place and its truth and falsity depend on the conditions of a specific time and place. Moreover, the denial of this proposition does not imply a logical contradiction. The Bank of England can and cannot be independent in different possible worlds. As we use language in expressing different propositions, in the analytic as well as the synthetic propositions, the distinction between these two types of proposition is not always certain. Language is not tantamount to the truth. It is an instrument of expression but not a direct representation of the whole truth.

One misgiving with respect to truth is equating language to the expression of the whole truth – as if language directly mirrors all types of truth perfectly. According to Wittgenstein in all forms of human knowledge, there is an element of thinking. These two human activities, language and thinking, are unbreakable. In the same vein, thinking is inseparable from human knowledge. It is an integral constituent of knowledge. In his *Tractatus*, Wittgenstein drew attention to what is thinkable and the limits of our thought. Language is one of the most determining limits in this connection. Our thoughts are incarcerated by the degree of complexity of our language. What cannot be thought cannot be said in language. Besides, with the use of language, we can distort facts. Uttering nonsense is a distortion of facts by language. We cannot say something which cannot be thought. It is by the means of language that we give meaning to the world. The language that goes beyond this and does not stand for the objects in the world is at best empty. There are very few, if any, economic terms that are agreed on by all or have kept their meaning unchanged since they were used originally. Furthermore, it is unthinkable to perceive what the state of any economy will be in many decades ahead. What scientific discoveries and innovations there will be in the future time? Simply put, these and the future social and natural disasters are unthinkable and cannot be expressed by any language.

Instinct is an inborn drive that is common in all developed animals, human and non-human animals. One such instinct is the instinct of self-preservation. An instinct is a behaviour that we are born with. It is an unlearned behaviour that we are genetically programmed with. Non-human animals behave and act mostly according to their instincts. They live, survive, breed, migrate, communicate, and so on, according to their instinctual impulses. Herd instinct is one of these innate drives. These acts, motives, behaviours, and interactions are not done consciously, out of informed choices, free will, deliberation, or by reason and knowledge. In view of the fact that humans live partially by instinct and not completely consciously by reason, knowledge, and free will, their actions can be spontaneous and not necessarily rational. The human herd instinct can be displayed in many human activities. This includes wars and subjugating others, revolutions, economic crises, religious fundamentalism, and so on. But human beings are more complex animals than non-human animals. Humans possess more complex brains. Humans have the capacity to reason and they are self-aware. They construct and use complex languages and construct complex societies, cultures, economies, organizations, and political and legal systems to achieve their ends.

Achieving ends presupposes intention. Ends entail intention and intention comes before ends. Hence, intention in what we say and do is also a unique universal human trait. Before anything being uttered or being done, no one can tell what intention an individual has in mind except the individual in question. Except for instinctive behaviour and actions, all human activities begin with intention. By looking through the window, nobody knows the intention of my act. It could be enjoying the cloud in the sky, observing a cat under a car, gazing at a fly buzzing around and disturbing my concentration, or countless other possibilities. There was a specific intention in my head that no one was aware of except me when I decided to write this book. In economic activities, economic agents entertain certain intentions that no one except those agents is aware of. The intention can be pretend, a make-believe trick, or an authentic fact. Only the individual who intends such acts, behaviour, or speech is aware of it. A seller of an object can pretend to sell the object out of kindness while the intention is cheating or vice versa. The intention of a political leader in issuing a declaration about people's power can be for themselves to obtain absolute power. The most difficult thing to discern in this universal human trait is that human intention can change in a flash and individuals can do and say the opposite of what they had intended to do or say during the sayings and acts. For this very reason, human knowledge about humans compared to human knowledge about non-human animals and the inanimate is more complicated and harder to predict.

On the same line are all mental activities each individual may entertain in one's brain before putting them into words or actions. These may include dreams, plans, hopes, wishes, beliefs, love and hate, and so on. Such matters are not knowable with certainty. An inventor has an image of their invention before the invention is materialized. An engineer first creates an image of a bridge they are about to design and build in their head. An author has a broad plan of their ideas before writing their book. On the grounds that each individual forms an image of what they intend to say or do before it comes into reality, knowing it before it is done is simply impossible. That being said, due to the fact that human activities are in the realm of contingent truths, their acts are always accompanied by unintended consequences.

In addition to intention, we have the human will. This is also a critical element of human knowledge. Opinion on this point differs from those who believe that people have free will to those who believe everything about humans, including their will, is externally determined. The French philosopher, Jean-Paul Sartre (1905–80), argued we are free to choose, i.e., we have free will. In all situations, including the most extreme cases, the choice between life and death, we are free to choose between alternative options in front of us. He held the view that the human is "condemned to be free; because once thrown into the world, he is responsible for everything he does" (quoted from McCartney 2013: 60). This is because people have, as in the case of physical objects, no predetermined essence. Human existence, i.e., "thatness," comes first of their essence, which is "whatness." The defining identity of a human being is what one makes of oneself through their actions.

The choices that we make will make us what we are. We do not have a pre-existing self that Sartre called the "real I." The "real I" is what we make through our choices. This is one extreme position. The fact of the matter is we are born with baggage that is full of a specific geographical location, social, political, and economic environment – history, culture, traditions, moral and religious beliefs, and language – that is not passed to us on the basis of free choice. No individual is born out of free choice. We do not choose our parents. A poor child or a rich child has no choice to choose their parents. Equally, a child who is from a fanatical family and a child who is from a secular humanist family have no choice in choosing their parents. Children have not got free choices. Their lives are determined by the conditions and the environment in which they are born. The choice is also not an inborn predetermined property. A person who is informed, aware of making rational and ethical choices, will make more appropriate choices in an open and democratic society that can serve their society than an uninformed and bigoted individual in a closed and undemocratic society. The choice under such circumstances is not equally distributed. A person cannot alone make oneself detached from their parents and the conditions in which the parents live and what the parents believe from their birth. One is a product of oneself as well as the environment in which they are brought up.

On another extreme end of freedom of choice, we have the position that the human has no free will at all. One group of people who fall under this category are strict believers of deities. This is the view that believes that the fate of every human being is eternally sealed. It is said that there is not much that humanity can do about it. Human knowledge is just an illusion since they cannot change their fate. Another fatalistic vision about human will is purported by the extreme Marxists. In this extreme position, human history is predetermined. It goes through predetermined stages of development and transitions. The engine of change, in this case, is the class struggle, not the free will of the people. All these positions have some influence on the way human knowledge is formed and applied. It either hinders the acquisition of knowledge or reassures individuals about their capacity to learn and make choices that are relatively more free, valid, and ethical. There is not a neutral individual. Every individual is a thinking being, a habitation of boundless imagination, desires, expectations, aspirations, love, hate, happiness, anger, memory, belief, wishes, hopes, despairs, optimism, and pessimism. We can think of things, love or hate them that do not exist.

In the methodology of research, we find extremism in reducing the validity of the research either to deductive reasoning or to inductive reasoning. On one side of the extreme methodology of research, we have the position that restricts true knowledge wholly to deductive knowledge that is expressed by the means of the language of mathematics and logic. Galileo asserted that the language of nature is mathematics. Jevons, one of the founders of the Marginalist school of economics, argued that for economics to become a science it must be expressed in the language of mathematics. The opposite extreme side of this position is the one that limits valid research methods exclusively to inductive reasoning. It is implied that we apprehend the fundamental nature of things merely through inductive reasoning. Essentially, the idea of all these extreme positions leads to one system, a single thought, and one way of looking at matters. The logical positivism that emerged in the 1920s and 1930s was also searching for one unified system of science that can be defined and expressed by one very exact language. Science was reduced to a single form. By this unity of science, they meant that "all branches of scientific inquiry have a common epistemological basis," and "determining the truth or falsity of scientific theories about the nature of the world depends entirely on an appeal to the evidence of experience and observation" – purporting that true science is a unified system of "factual propositions … whose truth or falsity and meaning depend on their being open to the test of the facts of experience" (Shand 1994: 261).

The opposite extreme position of a single valid method of research is the position that anything goes. This is the anarchist methodology of science. This position recognizes no difference between the "vague" and "incoherent … ideologies" and the "highly sophisticated theoretical systems" (Feyerabend 1978: 146). The argument goes that for the reason that in science, "reason cannot be universal and unreason cannot be excluded," it follows that "anarchism is not only possible, but it is also necessary both for the internal progress of science and for the development of our culture as a whole" (Feyerabend 1978: 180). Consider the following scenario. On the one hand, we have a canonical doctrine that precludes women, half of the human population, from economic, political, cultural, legal, and scientific activities. Gender inequality in this case is a divine law and as a consequence, it is holding back women from moving forward. Discrimination based on gender is accepted without any reservation as a sacred principle. Let us now consider an alternative theory, the equality of opportunities among genders. This theory endorses equality before the law and renounces any discriminatory practices between genders. Surely these two doctrines are not equally valid. To suggest that the two are equally significant and have scientific standing is hard to comprehend. This extreme methodology of research position in the first place appears to be against the "fixed and universal rules" in its quest for scientific knowledge. Yet, the slogan of anything goes in the quest for the scientific truth is another fixed and universal rule.

Long-held "scientific theories," many of which lasted for millennia, have been discarded with new theories. Up to the early modern age, it was believed that the earth is flat and is at the centre of the universe. Giordano Bruno was burnt at the stake in 1600 for arguing otherwise. Galileo was humiliated and was imprisoned for questioning this commonly accepted view. For many centuries, it was believed that the universe is composed of four elements, air, fire, earth, and water; space is Euclidean and three-dimensional; the sun rotates around the earth; time is an infinite straight line; the sky is divided into several strata; and the law of causality is universal. These long-held theories were discarded in early modern times. Then came Newton in the seventeenth century with his revolutionary theories of physics, mechanics, and cosmology. His ideas became the benchmark of modern science. It was believed that he discovered the universal truth about space, time, and motion. Einstein repudiated the validity of Newton's hypotheses. Quantum physics has gone a step further by questioning whatever was held as timeless, as in the case of the law of universal causality. Economics has tried to follow the steps that were taken by natural sciences. All schools of thought in economics have been inspired and influenced by natural sciences. The physiocrats adopted William Harvey's discovery of the circulation of blood in living animals, the classical economists the Newtonian mechanics, and the marginalist and neo-classical economics the theory of energy in the nineteenth century. The German historical school, the institutionalist school, and, to a certain degree, the Marxian school of the Darwinian evolutionary biology. As for the rest, we have an amalgamation of all these developments. The issue that needs to be noted here is that people have acted according to such ideas and considered such theories as true and sacred for a certain time period. But in the end, they proved to be wrong. For all advances that are made in economics, there is not even a single theory that is universally accepted. On top of this, there is not a school of thought in economics that its proponents agree on everything they say. If there is any agreement among the followers of each school, the agreement is somewhat more ideological than scientific.

## Permissible and impermissible boundaries

The idea that the market works misses one critical point. It does not plainly tell us what is the market? Any market at any time comprises the drivers of the market. Those who make the market. As a side remark, no market is free. Every market exists with a given society, legal and moral codes, technological, institutional, and economic development, and geographical constraints. The forces of the market operate within such constraints. When they say the market is right, it is right under given constraints. But the meaning of market is right is misleading. From the term "right" we can infer two possibilities. Our first conjecture is that it means it is "just." That is, the market price is just. But no exchange, including the exchange of gifts, is just. We shall return to this subject later. The second thing that we can infer from "right" is that because the market is right and for this reason, people continue to enter the market to buy or sell a particular product or a service. This is one of the illusions of the market. It causes self-deception. The more people buy or sell something, the mere act becomes a self-propelling craze that entices more people to join the trend. This act does not confirm that it is right. It only proves the herd mentality of the economic agents charmed by the vogue. The claim is if the market were not right more people would not take part continuously in the market. The same element of self-affirmation and self-fulfilling prophesy was reflected in salaries and annual bounces of the key drivers of the toxic markets after the liberalization of financial markets in the 1970s and 1980s.

Credit institutions always know more about where the credit goes and to whom but they do not know everything. The innovation of the new credit instruments designed and engineered by physicists and mathematicians preceding the global credit crunch had one predominant aim. That is to make the most money and in the least time, which they did. Contrary to the widely accepted view, the fact that these innovations worked even for short time cannot be the root causes of the financial crisis. The short-term priority in these complex financial instruments also went hand in hand with the model and the aesthetic arrangement of mathematical language rather than the economic implications of these instruments. Those in the top and most of those who operated these products knew very little about the nature of these financial products. The measure of success of these complex financial instruments had nothing to do with the nature of products and their economic implications. The main concern was how much money these instruments could make in the shortest possible time. Inventing a potentially lethal substance and selling it without being aware of the nature of such a substance will always result in a considerable degree of harm. The harm caused will be created when the only measure of success is how much money one can make in the shortest possible time by any means. If this situation is unchecked and it is allowed to rule supreme, it will not be too long after that the unintended effects infect and destroy the very inventor and the beneficiary of the substance.

There is a big loophole in the belief that the market knows best. From this perspective, the loophole is the separation of what makes up the market and the market itself. It is as if the market is a detached entity above those economic agents who make the market. As if it is above the society, customs, and the prevailing traditions that exist in a given time and location. The market is viewed to be above the prevailing legal and moral framework, above the political power, and the level of economic, scientific, technological, and institutional development. A market at any time comprises those who participate in the market and it is controlled by those who are in charge of the market. When it is said that the market knows best, it essentially means those in charge of the particular market, in effect, know more. This is a self-serving faith. It means at any given time whatever decisions are made by those in charge of the market are right on the account that the market as a self-fulfilling mechanism is right.

Human beings are social, moral, cultural, and aesthetically captivated beings. Paradoxically, humans are among the most intelligent but also are the most dependent species. A human child cannot survive without the protection of their parents or their communities for many years. It takes a good many years before a child is able to be independent of their parents but not from the larger community. This community can be a tribal community, a nationality, or, in our time, the global community. Self-preservation is not unique to humans. All living species in perpetuating their lives eat food, drink, and, in one way or another, find a shelter to protect themselves from the elements and danger. The provision of these necessities has not changed throughout the evolution of these species. The economy of non-human living species is constant. They merely adapt to their environment. This is not the case with humans. Human beings change their environment. Their economy is one of the principal mediums through which they change their environment. The base on which the human economy rests is the same with other non-human species. It is eating, drinking, and shelter. But for the provision of these necessities, humans alter their environment and add to their necessities. Non-human species for the provision of these necessities act on natural instincts but humans on their capacity to reason and acquired knowledge. It is not right or wrong for a pack of lions to force a pack of wolves to abandon their hunt or for a snake to occupy the den of other animals. But it is considered to be immoral (wrong) for one group of people to usurp the fruit of the labour of another group or for one group to occupy the land of another group.

Non-human animals are instinctively programmed to preserve themselves from danger. They are not conscious of what they do. To stay alive, they kill other animals and their own species. They defend their territories and occupy the territories of other animals. This is an essential component of their economy. But this economy does not rest on knowing what they are doing. Their surviving arrangements and living orders are neither ethical nor unethical. It is just about adaptation and survival. The human economy is fundamentally different. Any act in the human economy has an element of human knowledge and the human sense of right and wrong, human morality.

Consider there is only one individual occupying the entire planet earth. They have the same capacity and faculty to reason as us. The sense of morality does not apply to this individual. Thus, having the capacity and faculty to reason is not the foundation upon which human morality begins. It is an essential element but not the origin of human ethics. Now, consider there are two individuals living in the same place. From this scenario, we can draw a number of conclusions that are critical in the realm of human morality. First, the earth belongs to itself and no one else. All its contents, including living and non-living things, belong to the earth. Living things come and go. In effect, they rent a small space and a brief time on land. As we noted above, animals drew each other from their territories or appropriate their foods and their acts are neither ethical nor unethical. Therefore, morality is a human attribute. As soon as two humans live beside each other, a relationship between the two emerges that is outside the realm of the relationship of the non-human animal kingdom. This relationship will extend the more people live alongside each other. A great many questions arise about human social life. Is it right for one individual to hurt another individual? Is it right for one individual to kill another individual? Is it right for the stronger individual to confiscate the fruit of the labour of the weaker individual? Is it right for one individual to occupy the sanctuary of another individual and drive them from their land? Above all who owns the land? The stronger ones or the weaker ones? Can the stronger one force the weaker one to work for them? What sort of relationships are these two individuals supposed to have – equal, superior-inferior, or any other? These are elements that we cannot relate wholly to non-human animals but are vital to the social existence, setting, and interaction of humans.

For the first individual, the only individual, the possession of land is irrelevant. But when two individuals live at the same time and in the same place, it becomes relevant. As people are social and cultural animals, this element gets even more significant with larger populations. By owning land or a piece of earth, we mean whatever the earth offers to live on. If the earth belongs to all its dwellers, then each living thing that is born has a share on this planet. This ownership equally applies to each person being born. But that is not the case, humans are the only species that not only deny other species from having a share of the planet earth but systematically evict and deprive other human beings of the land they inhabited. In the course of time, they divided the planet earth between different groups and social classes, and at this very moment there are millions of people that have no possessions, and thousands of babies are born every day who are displaced and homeless. If the earth gives life to a human, then by the very nature of giving birth to its infants, each offspring is entitled to a piece of land as the source of sustenance and to dwell in. Possession or denial of possession of land is a critical factor in the creation of human morality. Land is the most primary factor for human existence and for the formation of the human economy. Without earth, there would be no life, no human, and no economy. Hence, ethics are inextricably linked with the economy.

Self-preservation is a basic instinct among all living species. This instinct stems from avoiding harm or death. In reality, it may involve running from danger, hiding, or destroying the attacker before being hurt or killed. Humans also use their instinct for self-defence. But unlike non-human animals, humans go a step farther than their instincts to achieve their intended ends. They consciously plan to hurt or destroy other human beings, individually or collectively. Human beings, unlike non-human animals, are not satisfied with what they have for consumption and protection even what they have is more than sufficient for their survival. If there is an opportunity to appropriate the livelihoods of those who have less, they do that with planning and intention. The creation of all empires and forceful occupation of one nationality by another, and all the destruction and bloodshed that are involved in such deeds, has not been due to the basic instinct of self-preservation but to deliberate plans that have been executed wilfully. Many communities and nations have been wiped out completely or partially throughout human history from such premeditated onslaughts. In early modern history, the colonization of many nations in America, Africa, Asia, and Europe by relatively more powerful nations was of this nature. The Native Americans and Aboriginal Australians were virtually wiped out from their ancestral homelands, not because of the instinct of self-preservation but deliberately.

Humans, unlike non-human animals, construct prisons, torture dungeons, and invent torture instruments and use them on a mass scale. Gladiators fought to the death to entertain thousands of individuals. The Colosseum in Rome was built to accommodate over 50,000 spectators for this purpose. They do these not out of instinct but on purpose and to express power and for sheer enjoyment. Such misdeeds and atrocities were widespread in the past and are widespread today in some parts of the world. Non-human animals may kill and eat their own kind following their animal instinct but human cannibalism is a conscious and calculated act either in the form of hunting and eating their enemies' flesh or out of some ritual conventions. Cannibalism was practised, one way or another at different times on different continents of the earth. Humans enslave other humans and exploit their labour either completely or partially. They can exclude one group of people from society and give every right, even the right to life to another group. Humans think that they are the master of the earth. Over time fewer and fewer usurpers have been seizing much of the earth and its resources.

Humans create weapons and use them to subjugate, exploit, and kill others. They have the capacity to reason, learn, invent, and use such capabilities for good or evil. We have invented writing. This was great progress in advancing human knowledge and society. But we have also invented weapons and used them in destroying one another. The modern weapons of mass destruction, nuclear bombs, can destroy the whole planet in a very short time. These are purposeful acts. Human beings invent ideas and destroy each other for their ideas. Non-human animals are free from this sort of barbarism. Humans have invented religions and gods and put them at war with each other. The greatest acts of savagery have been perpetrated by the universalist religions and ideologies. The universalist religions were the ideological vehicles of the greatest empires. The war for many centuries between the Christine and Muslim empires was of this nature. On the same footing, we have the universalist ideologies of colonialism, fascism, capitalism, and communism that were imposed on others and have been responsible for the killing of many millions of people and the destruction of many societies. So many people have perished because they did not convert to the religion and the ideology of their invaders. Many were the victims of the holocaust or labour camps because they did not adhere to the Nazi ideology or communism. Non-human animals do not have religion, god, and ideology to kill other animals for not adhering to what they believe or stand by. Humans do. They kill other human beings because they do not share the same beliefs, religion, god, and ideology.

Ethics is not an instinct. Humans are born with some instinct but the sense of morality is not one of them. A new-born child does have a specific code of ethics. They have no sense of right and wrong. Just as a new-born child has no knowledge, a new-born child has no ethical values. What a child has is the capacity to reason and learn. The capacity to reason and learn can be put to serve humanity at large or for other inhumane purposes. The rules of conduct are partially a product of parental upbringing and conditions of society in which a child is brought up, including learning and individual free will. For this reason, every individual who is not suffering from any medical and psychological conditions that impede their faculty to reason and capacity to learn will be programmed with certain moral values, good or bad – a combination of which governs all activities of the individual along with their economic activities. Thus, in every economic activity, there is an element of ethics. Economic agents are not morally neutral, they are ethically programmed. The ethical toolkit can be used either humanly or inhumanly.

Humans set goals as their ends and use humane and inhumane means to achieve their targets. These ends can be economic, social, political, religious, or cultural, or any other end. Among inhumane ends, we have the formation of empires, using every means to destroy and subjugate other people. Dictatorship, the rule of one individual or institution, violates the rights of the majority. Coercive conversion means forcing others to convert to a religion or an ideology by using different means, e.g., violence, legal, economic, social, or cultural. The end could be the formation of economic and social strata and caste systems that create rank, station, class, and race inequality among the people. Selling arms to the most undemocratic states on the grounds that if you do not sell, others do. Bribing the corrupt officials in order to have access to their markets. The list of inhumane targets is endless. These goals are achieved by any means. It can be achieved by means of sheer violence, lies, and deceit. The point we want to make here is that humans unlike non-human animals set goals that can be humane or inhumane. To achieve these goals, they use humane and inhumane means. In the case of humane ends, we have ends that are rational, enlightened, and democratic that are applied in open and democratic societies.

Humans for their survival live in relation to others. This relation is to the natural environment, without which there would be no human. The natural environment with all the species and resources that it contains is the basis of the economic sustenance of all living species on earth. The human species cannot survive individually. Humans are social animals. They have family relations, group relations, national relations, and global relations. Individual self-preservation is defined within the relationship with one another, within groups, and within nations. All human inventions – language, economy, technology, science, government, culture, law, morality, institutions, and religions – are defined in the connection between two primary interactions. These are the interactions between people and nature and people with other. The source of sustaining all lives, including human lives, is the earth. Our relationship to the foremost source of our sustenance is a moral relationship. It is no wonder that economics was born out of ethics (Deane 1980: xiii).

One of the defining human traits is setting a boundary of what we can or cannot do. These boundaries have evolved over time. Irrespective of the elaborate social, economic, and cultural diversities that the early and modern humans have created, they all have this trait in common. The origin of this human quality goes back to the earlier relationship between human and their natural environment and the relationship between humans themselves. From these interactions, some elements of nature and some aspects of life gradually became sacred and hence were protected. That is, who should be honoured and obeyed in the family or the community and what animals to kill and eat and what animals to be saved and revered established certain permissible and impermissible boundaries. In a social context, this relationship was and is expressed in the relationship between parents and their children. In patriarchal social formations, which have dominated human history, it is the father or, in his absence, the eldest brother who holds the primary social, economic, cultural, and legal power over the whole family. This social system is built on gender inequality and the domination of the authority of men over women. It is the man who becomes the chief of the tribe, the religious leader, the king, and, in its most extreme form, the god to be worshipped by everyone. The vast majority of gods, founders of religions, and rulers (kings) in human history have been from the male camp. In matriarchal social formations, the female head of the family holds such powers. In the matriarchal social formations, which are rare in history, the power relations are dominated by a female head. The female head can be the head of the family or a tribe, the overall ruler, the spiritual leader, or, in its most extreme cases, the religious prophet or the goddess of a particular place and group of people.

The realm of ethics, stripped to its most essential and obvious element, can be broken down into two possibilities: either it is a human activity or it is not. Beyond this postulate the quest for ethical inquiry is inconceivable. Therein lie the logical closure and the most basic defining lines of the realm of ethics. If ethics and morality is only a human trait then we can set a number of questions in a definite form. Are we born with certain ethical norms or not? Are these moral codes universal and common among all human beings? Are they set by external agents and imposed on us? Can we acquire moral standards through experience and learning or are they instinctive? The ethical frameworks proposed hitherto all fall within this realm of possibilities. In faith-based morality, the mastermind behind morality is one or another form of divinity. Gods as the maker of everything are the authors of moral structure and the ethical norms of people. The founders of morality in this case are gods and the intermediaries through which their moral commands are delegated are the messengers of gods. In this sequence of orders, human fate is determined in advance. Their destiny is fixed and predetermined. The human moral setting and the outcome of their moral actions are conceived and decided at their birth. Humanity is condemned to its destiny and the will of the providence. In a theistic moral setting, there is no room for free will. What there is, it is meant to be.

The postulates that put humans as the initiators of morality and as the makers and producers of morality can be divided into three broad groups. In the first group, we have those who explicitly or tacitly consider morality as something that each individual is born with. That is, moral foundation, structure, fibre, probity, and the framework are all innate. The human ethical compass is embedded in the human constitution and we can have access to it through our intellect. In this context, moral knowledge is *a priori* and can be acquired independently of experience. There is an element of this sense of morality in all theories of ethics that put the human as the central agent of morality. The major ethical perspectives – virtue ethics, consequentialist ethics, and deontology ethics – put humans as the central agent of ethics and the initiator of morality. Regarding the ways of looking at deeply held ethical values, there are three standpoints. In the first view, morality is internal. It comes from character, from feeling, or in its very extreme form we are internally programmed with our moral values. In the second view, it is said because we have the faculty and capacity to reason and use language – in the same way, we can construct ethical norms and can follow or can change and reject them. In the third position, the ethical standards are the product of external circumstances but humans can change their circumstances, and therefore by changing their circumstances they can change their ethical norms.

We have no economic agent without any ethical belief. Any human economic activity takes place within the husk of an ethical perimeter of right or wrong. The starting question in ethics is whether there is a system of morality comprised of principles with a clear demarcation line between right and wrong. Every moral act begins with an intention, followed by an end and the means to achieve that end. The intention can be egoistic or benevolent – revengeful or altruistic. The end can be the pursuit of self-interest or public welfare. The means can be deception, coercion, and violence, or a rational, honest, and fair medium. The intention can be the quest for knowledge, to invent and discover – the search for happiness or just forming a virtuous character. In all these matters, there is an element of right and wrong and good and bad. No person in sound mind who is brought up in the right conditions and has come to maturity is barren of moral sense. The layout of moral discernment is formed by practical decision-making. The standards and obligations are the blueprints of moral perception. No sane individual is devoid of this capacity and no human action is uninhabited of the spectre of ethical or moral judgements.

Humans can have an image of a better life. Discerning better life carries with it the potentiality of good and bad living – better and worse living. It carries with it the viability of hope and opportunity. Reflecting on what is the best or worst intention, means and ends of conducting one's life is a human activity. Besides natural necessities that are instinctive, humans have created their own customs, cultures, economies, laws, institutions, inventions, discoveries, scientific endeavours, and political and social systems. We find the standards of right and wrong in all these human activities. One cannot act with no moral codes, right or wrong, good or bad. Non-human animals behave and act on their instincts. Their power of choice is restrained by their instincts. They do not act according to their free will. Instead, they are governed by their instincts. They are captive of their natural behaviour and their actions are neither moral nor immoral. But human actions and behaviour are not restricted solely to their instincts. People have the power to choose. A cat kills a sparrow, not because of the sparrow's colour, gender, belief, or nationality but because the cat does it to feed itself. The cat does not invent weapons of mass destruction and organize an army to subjugate the rest of the sparrow population. We do not have an extremist cat but we have extremist humans.

In some non-human animals, we can observe certain behaviours that are more palpable in human ethical conduct. The sense of kinship, the parents taking care of their offspring. In humans, this feeling and obligation are extended to the whole family, the tribe, the nation, and so on. Animals protect their immediate members of their family from danger but the human goes beyond that and protects humans and other species worldwide. The sense of attachment is greater to the closer and intermediate family members and gets less and less as it moves farther and farther away to what is less known and farther away from one's culture, language, belief, and location. Certain obligations and relations are moulded, established, and practised throughout human history from the relationship of kinship and the bond that people have formed between the immediate and the distant descendants. In non-human animals that are social, as in the case of humans, there are mutual needs that are fulfilled by mutual responsibilities. For being social animals, their survival as social animals necessitates cooperation, interaction, interdependency, and duty of reciprocity. When a wolf hunts its prey, it allows all individuals in the pack to eat and the natural bond of reciprocity allows them to eat from the prey that is caught by another member of the pack. It is this bond of reciprocity that is originated from being a social animal that is tied in human cooperation, interaction, and interdependence. The bond of reciprocity is mutually advantageous since the human species cannot survive living alone. Division of duty in fulfilment of reciprocation to serve the mutual needs is the beginning of the exchange, first in forms of exchange of gifts and, in more developed stages of economic development, the exchange of economic goods. In humans, this bond has not only fostered the sense of mutual sympathy but among humans, it is an impetus for recompense, reparation and deceit, and conspiracy.

The human is a living species that has a distinct cognitive capacity of not only self-recognition but the awareness of the world around herself or himself. One is of being conscious of oneself, one's thoughts, feelings, character, deeds, hopes, wishes, dreams, intentions, and behaviour. Moreover, we can express this cognitive ability, the cognition of self-recognition, self-knowing, and self-reflection, in a complex language about who we are, and what we understand and feel about others. We remember, review, reflect, depict, respond, and act on this capacity. We are conscious of ourselves and are able to know what we know. This ability to be conscious of oneself places human in a unique position. Being conscious of oneself means we are aware of our feelings of sympathy, compassion, pity, fellow feeling, goodwill, altruism, sense of caring and honour. We can understand the pain and happiness of ourselves and can self-evaluate and internalize, realize, and reflect it. There is another side to the human ability of self-understanding. It is the ability of the self-conscious feeling of ill will, malice, animosity, hatred, egoism, greed, malevolence, and dishonesty. Unlike humans, non-human animals do not use language that is different from their acts. What people can say is not what they necessarily mean or what they do. Intentionally, they can say one thing and do another thing. There is no unity in what a demagogue, a cheater, a hoaxer, a fraudster, an imposter, a swindler, a gangster, a hypocrite, a crook, dictator, and a criminal say and do. They mislead with intention. A further implication of this deceitful practice is that the misinformed and gullible believe in them and act on falsehood. In doing so, the act will become a reality.

There is in some non-human animals a pack order. These animals live in packs. In this social structure, there is a leader of the pack and the rest of the members of the pack are subservient to the pack leader. The hierarchical social order is instinctive and is meant to benefit the survival of the group. A wolf in a pack will survive longer than one isolated wolf. Compliance with the order of the leader of the pack in non-human animals is a sufficient basis to remain in the pack and share the advantages of the pack. With humans, as soon as a social structure is formed on hierarchy, those above would manipulate their higher social order and intentionally and knowingly plan to make those lower in the hierarchical order weaker and weaker even to the point of enslaving them. With systematic planning, coercion, and violence those at top of the class structure would deprive those who surrendered their freedom and compel them into total submission. Humans invent consciously complex explanations in justifying their deliberate behaviours and acts. They devise other proclamations and precepts to enforce their social and economic hierarchical order. Humans knowingly lie, cheat, steal, rape, murder, and wage wars. At the same time, all people cannot lie, cheat, steal, rape, murder, and be at war. For the survival of their species, they have consciously developed the limits of what they can or cannot do, what is permissible and what is forbidden. That is, conceiving a moral compass of right and wrong, which is a necessity for the survival of the human species.

## Extremism and survival

The human moral foundation rests on the necessity to survive and procreate. In extreme beliefs, behaviours, and conducts, humans cannot maintain their survival. Let that extreme be complete submission to altruism, generosity, and self-sacrifice or a total state of hostility, war, narcissism, misanthropy, lying, double-dealing, bigotry, falsehood, or delusion, or other forms of extremism. The first thing people do in life is looking for food to feed themselves, search for shelter to keep themselves safe from dangers and elements and the next is to spare no effort in the act of self-preservation. All these things are done without much regard for any supreme being or authority. Humans in real life live in the real world. In practice, they are the authority of their own living and the author of their own moral bearings. Therefore, human's moral foundation rests on the actual human mode of existence. The mode of existence, however, has kept changing. In line with changes in the mode of existence, the boundaries of moral standards have also been shifting. To survive, humans unlike non-human animals use both instinct and intellect. It is through the power of their intellect that they modify nature to serve their eating, drinking, sleeping, breeding, and protection from danger. Unlike non-human animals, humans can articulate their discoveries, inventions, fears, hopes, sadness, happiness, pains, anguish, anger, strengths, and weaknesses in complex languages and can pass on their experience and knowledge to future generations. Humans know that nature is far greater for each individual or the entire human species to comprehend fully. They know that their lives are very short in the great scheme of things and it is only the human that for all their inadequacies invents explanations to justify their actions. Ideas on their own lack the limbs to act. With ideas only, without action, humans would perish. The survival of humans depends on individual actions in general and their collective actions in particular. Human existence is a social process. For human collective actions and survival, humans require explanations in justifying what they do. Ideas are formed during this process. These ideas comprise human knowledge in every field of human endeavour.

Many non-human animals amplify, overplay, and disguise their size, appearance, and power to lure their prey or display elaborate appealing rituals to attract a mate. The concealment and the disguise that they display are their natural mechanisms to survive and adapt to their environment. The use of different forms of camouflage and display of exaggerated behaviour in forms of dancing, singing, and changing size and colour is to help them catch their prey or to avoid predation. Such behaviours, undertakings, and moves are to conceal and disguise themselves from being detected, recognized, or to deceive their hunters in the struggle for survival and reproduction. Their mimicking, colouring, dancing, singing, and canny matching to their background are cleverly done and can be aesthetically attractive or displeasing. But non-human animals are not conscious of their artistic activities, both attractive and unattractive. Humans are the only non-human animals that have a sense of aesthetic and artistic appreciation. Humans decorate their bodies to enjoy what they considered as pleasing to themselves and to the opposite sex. They have been drawing, making sculptures, playing music, singing, appreciated and admired nature and animals, written poems, expressed their ideas in beautiful languages, in mathematical and non-mathematical languages. There is not a human being who lacks one or another form of aesthetic appreciation and there are not two individuals who have exactly the same level of aesthetic appreciation of the same thing at once or for each individual to have the same appreciation at two different times in their lifetime. The aesthetic and artistic appreciation and displeasure are correlated closely with human imagination. There is no limit to human imagination. Human imagination is the most distinctive trait of being human and the freedom of human imagination is one of the most natural human rights and the vehicle of human progress.

Human imagination can exaggerate, overstate, magnify, embellish, overplay, and over-dramatize the possibilities. The aesthetic and the work of arts are overemphasized and overstated possibilities. In both nature and human construction whatever is affirmed by any individual as aesthetically attractive or repulsive is something that is exaggerated to the senses of that individual or relation to the way they are brought up. They are the distortion of what one normally has expected and experienced. The most extreme over-inflated sense of the aesthetic is the one that is presented by the monotheistic religions. The two sides of perfection are represented by the god as the most perfect and pleasing side and evil as the vilest and most ugly partner. As in the realm of aesthetics, we have two poles of good and bad; in the realm of ethics these two poles are right and wrong. One of the most extreme forms of right and wrong resides in monotheistic religions. Here, the god is absolutely right and the non-believers are absolutely wrong. Indeed, judging right and wrong, in this case, cannot be but extreme. God is the perfect judge and knows who the wrongdoers are and who the righteous are. The righteous are rewarded with heaven, eternal life of luxury, drunkenness, and sexual pleasure, and the sinful are sent to hell, a perfect place of eternal agony, scorching, and roasting.

Religion by its very nature is extremely hierarchical. Different social classes are ranked and solidified forever. On the top of the pyramid of this class structure is god, the absolute power. Then it is followed by its messengers, the prophets, then the kings if they have not claimed to be the gods themselves, then by a variety of different ranks of priests, then by better-off social classes, and then to the common people, the dispossessed, and finally to the sinners and disbelievers. Among the world religions, Islam is the most extreme of all. It categorically declares that there is one god, Islam is the final and last true religion, and Mohammad is the last and final messenger and prophet. Any digression from this proclamation is regarded as heresy and paganism that deserve to be punished as severely as it can be.

The root of religion rests in the realm of what one can and cannot do. It rests in the realm of what is permissible and what is inadmissible. The authority that sets this boundary is a supernatural being. In the case of law, the boundary of what is legal and what is illegal is not a supernatural being that proscribes and sanctions it. The authority here is human. There are three primary sources of the origin of morality. The first one is the one that takes humans to be good by nature. The human in its essence is good. In the second one, the human in its essence is bad and sinful. In the third one, humans have got the capacity to be moral or immoral. In religion, the fate of each person is predetermined as being good or bad. The doctrine of the Fall in Abrahamic religions is a case in point. Adam disobeyed God in the Old Testament and contaminated the goodness of humans forever. In the midst of many inconsistencies of religion, we are told that human fate is predetermined but, at the same time, we have God's commands that are passed through his prophets to be followed in order to be good. The best known of such commands are the Ten Commandments that God on Mount Sinai proscribed to Moses. The first three commands are about his own absolute power and the rest about what humans must and must not do.

In the course of time, humans have articulated their moral precepts, their principles of right and wrong. These rules of conduct are as diverse as different social formations. In the first place, the moral standing begins with the individual. An individual can have moral convictions that make them a good and virtuous person or a wicked person. In the second group, the ethical requirements are determined by the consequences of an individual action or an authority's actions. In this moral framework, the code of ethics is internalized in a set of outcomes that are not limited to single individuals but to the majority of a given population. In the third case the moral fabric can be extended universally, which includes all individuals everywhere. At its universal level, the ethical requirements and moral imperatives form the basis of the moral fabric that applies to everyone. These moral requirements are universal and imperative. All human beings are brought up with moral standing that is dominated by one of these moral frameworks and bearings or a combination of all these moral standings. We judge every social, economic, legal, and cultural etiquette through the lens of our moral compass. The moral compass is prior to any economic activity we do in any human society.

One long-lasting theory of ethics is Aristotle's virtue ethics. For Aristotle, a virtuous individual is an ethical person. Doing right or wrong is determined by individuals. A virtuous person cannot only have a good life due to being virtuous but he can also serve society. But how one can be a virtuous person according to Aristotle? In Aristotle's worldview, whatever exists must have a function. The function is hierarchical. Above all, everything has a true nature. There is potential in everything to achieve its goal, which is its true nature. So, what makes humans be human? The property that makes a person human according to Aristotle is their capacity to reason. This is the inherent natural potential of humans that can be utilized and developed. So, the ultimate goal of being human is to harness one's capacity to reason. The happiest and best life is one when one's capacity to reason is fully developed. It is when one can exercise one's rational faculties at their best and hence live according to his true nature. A man can live a life to the fullest when he uses his rational faculties and capacity to reason in order to develop his potential in full. But Aristotle's world is a hierarchical world. In this ordered world, all human beings do not possess the same equal faculty of rationality and capacity to reason. There are those who are born slaves and there are those who are born masters. A slave is someone who "by nature belongs not to himself but to another" (Aristotle 1970: 32). He is the property of his master. A slave lacks deliberative capacity and needs to be ruled by his master. In the same way, Aristotle labelled women as "deformed" males and as obedient as slaves to their male masters (Aristotle 1963: 175). The same goes with what the Greeks considered to be barbarians. All these groups, including children, are naturally lacking full rational faculties and capacity to reason and hence should be ruled by their natural masters.

Considering that only natural masters and free men, in Aristotle's view, have fully developed rational faculties and the capacity to reason, then what is the most appropriate moral act that a virtuous person can perform that will make him truly virtuous and happy? The Aristotelian answer is the golden mean. It is the middle point between two extremes. The mean point is not a mechanical or mathematical mean. It depends on the circumstance, the action, the event, the agents involved, and the outcome of the conduct. Aristotle remarks that the golden mean is the "mean between two vices, one excess, the other of deficiency" (Aristotle 2014: 31). For example, cowardice and foolhardiness are two extreme sides of the same human conduct. On one side there is a deficiency, on the other side there is excess. The mean between these two extreme behaviours is courage. Seeking too much pleasure and no pleasure are two extreme sides of the same act but a middle ground between these two extremes, that is moderation within reason, is the mean. The doctrine of mean has been one way or another expressed or applied in all human cultures. The reaction to excess has been the call for moderation, temperance, harmony, fairness, and reasonableness. One of the inscriptions at the temple of Delphi is "nothing in excess." One of the attributes of beauty for Aristotle's teacher, Plato, and for Plato's teacher, Socrates, is the maxim of the mean. Socrates' advice was to "know how to choose the mean and avoid the extremes on either side" (Plato 1875: 516). Plato referred to extremism as the cause of disproportionality, which must be avoided because that is the source of evil. His choice of the ideal state is the "mean between monarch and democracy" (Plato 1895: 67). Buddha, the Indian ancient philosopher, advocated the Middle Way for human emancipation from self-indulgence and self-renunciation. Avoiding the extremes, the golden mean was the primary virtue for the most influential Chinese philosopher, Confucius.

Another long-lasting view of human morality is one that argues that right and wrong are determined by the consequences of what is being done. The consequence or consequences of what being done are determined by the desired end. The reference point to the desired consequence is the greater good. An action is morally right if its outcome maximizes pleasure and minimizes pain. Epicurus (341–270 BC) alluded that moral standing depends on pleasure and pain. Pleasure is the source of good. So, it is ethical and pain is the source of evil. Thus, the ultimate goal for humans is freedom from pain and the pursuit of pleasure. This entails that any human activity that increases pleasure and reduces pain must be desirable. Epicurus divided the pleasure into different categories: the pleasures of the mind and the pleasures of the body. His highest form of pleasure is the state of tranquillity. This form of pleasure is only obtainable when we are content with the simplest form of life and wants. All those extravagances over the basic necessities of life are superfluous. The bare essentials are obtainable by any individual and overindulgence is available to only a few.

One of the central impetuses behind the age of enlightenment was an echo of this sense of morality. This was the foundation of Francis Hutcheson's (1694–1746) moral system. Hutcheson takes benevolence as the basis for his moral sense theory – for the reason that its consequences are good. Hutcheson purported that "that action is best, which procures the greatest happiness for the greatest numbers; and that, worst, which, in like manner, occasions Misery" (Hutcheson 2008: XVI). Jeremy Bentham (1748–1832) is most closely associated with the development of the consequentialist principles of morality. He is commonly regarded as the founder of the utilitarian school. Bentham was convinced that with his system of morality we can calculate the effects of our every action and can tell apart the best and the worst moral action from the effects. Based on the consequences of actions there are alternative moral choices to be made. His yardstick in choosing the right moral action is choosing between pain and pleasure. Like Epicurus, Bentham takes pleasure and pain as the two forces of nature as the chief rulers of all our actions and behaviour. Pleasure is the source of good and pain is the source of bad. Good can be directly or indirectly pleasurable and bad can directly or indirectly cause pain. Right and wrong have meaning in the context of whether they cause pleasure or pain. Thus, the goal of all our actions and government policies should be based on these two self-evident facts. The aim should be to maximize happiness and minimize pain. Bentham wrote:

> nature has placed mankind under the governance of two sovereign masters, pain, and pleasure. It is for them alone to point out what we ought to do, as well as to determine what we shall do. On the one hand, the standard of right and wrong, on the other the chain of causes and effects, are fastened to their throne. They govern us in all we do, in all we say, in all we think.
>
> (Bentham 1879: 1)

It follows that the principle of pain and pleasure is not only the foundation of Bentham's morals and legislation but also the foundation of his epistemology of true and false. John Stuart Mill (1808–73), an earnest disciple of Bentham, found the earlier varieties of utilitarianism, including Bentham's account, to be untenable. In his book, *Utilitarianism* (1861), Mill finds human life to be more complex than a simple pursuit of pleasure and avoidance of pain. He is mindful of the subjective nature of pleasure and pain. These matters are perceived differently by different people at different times. Individuals with different forms and quality of life have different goals in life. The goals that one set and the conditions imposed on one's existence may be superior to those that are commonly perceived as pain or pleasure. Just like Socrates, Mill's motto was the credo that "the unexamined life is not worth living." In Mill's words, it is "better to be Socrates dissatisfied than a fool satisfied" (Mill 1976: 121). Mill preferred a non-conformist life with all its angst and pressure more willingly than to be a conformist and happy. He emphasized:

> In this age, the mere example of non-conformity, the mere refusal to bend the knee to custom, is itself a service. Precisely because the tyranny of opinion is such as to make eccentricity a reproach, it is desirable, in order to break through that tyranny, that people should be eccentric … the amount of eccentricity in a society has generally been proportioned to the amount of genius, mental vigour, and moral courage which it contained.
>
> (Mill 1863: 129)

Henry Sidgwick (1838–1900), in his book *Methods of Ethics* (1874), has offered a more sophisticated account of utilitarian ethics. His account is centred on rational benevolence. From this standpoint, Sidgwick attested that it is self-evident that what is good for one is equally good for everyone. It essentially means that the consequences of an action derived from self-evident rational benevolence would be good and beneficial for everyone. Therefore, such a judgement is ethical. The self-evident axiom to start with in this case is those that are intrinsically good. They are good in themselves. The method used to justify the outcome of justification is a comparative method, the action that leads to the greatest happiness of the greatest number of people means the goal of the action is achieved. Avoiding pain is a self-evident axiom, which means it is good in itself. So is the quest for pleasure. From this, it follows that the self-evident rational benevolence dictates that maximization of pleasure and minimization of pain is good and what is good must be ethical. Since the consequence of happiness is good, the person who performs the act must be a good person, a virtuous person. Their action is ethical. In view of this, the source of ethics is the individual who undertakes the action. It cannot be another being or a deity. This implies that a person, as long as they have not taken any action, is neither moral nor immoral, which indirectly means at birth all individuals are innocent. It is the consequences of one's actions that make a person good or bad and ethical or wicked. A just act, from this perspective, is one that maximizes the pleasure, happiness, and utility of the greatest number of people.

Human rule-based conduct of life goes to the dawn of the human species. We have recorded rules in the earliest inscriptions. The rationale behind regulating human conduct arises out of three possibilities; human beings are wicked, good, or neutral at birth. All these three possibilities imply a rule of conduct. These rules are set either by a deity to guide his subjects or by humans themselves. If the rules are set by humans, then these rules may come from the representatives of the deities, by the clergy or monarchs. These rules may be warranted by collective decisions. In the last place, the source can come from each individual. All codes of law in every society are an interaction of these three possibilities. In common with this universal trend, we have the instructions given to the princes in Ancient Egypt to prepare them how to rule, be prosperous and be happy before 3000 BC. Of like nature, we have the Code of Hammurabi, the Babylon ruler in 1700 BC, the Ten Commandments to Moses in 1300–1400 BC, and many other laws in ancient times. These laws were drawn from well-established customs of the time of each specific area. The basis of most of these laws was retaliatory justice. The Hammurabi code of laws is a collection of 282 rules. One of these laws is the law of "a tooth for a tooth." In the case of two men of equal status, if one of them knocks out a tooth of another, Hammurabi's law asks for equal retribution by knocking out the exact tooth of the person that has committed the offense. The Hebrew edict, "life for life, eye for eye, tooth for tooth," in the book of Exodus is a by-product of the domination of the retaliatory justice of the time in this part of the world.

The first philosophical writings on ethics are by Indians. The Vedas are the earliest Indian writings that date back to the second half of the second millennium BC. The Vedas consist of hymns about how to conduct a moral life. The hymns refer to many gods which are the indivisible parts of the ultimate reality. The universe is the ultimate reality. The whole reality is based on the principle of Rita, the right. The universe has a single order. It is in the right order. The moral order is inseparable from this order. By means of truth, we seek and find what is right. Humans are equipped with the faculty of understanding and can distinguish the truth from deception. The essence of being human is to seek the truth and find out what is right. Therefore, we are enlightened when we know the truth and conduct a moral life. The whole cosmos is an endless transformation and reformation. Human beings and their conduct are an integral part of this process. People are morally neutral when they are born and since they have the faculty to distinguish delusion from the truth and on that basis, they are able to conduct a life that is right. So, it is in our power to choose our moral path. People can choose their goals in life that are right such as moral duty, prosperity, spiritual perfection, and the satisfaction of desires. Following these goals consistently and sincerely makes one be modest, honest, upright, charitable, nonviolent, and amiable. But one also has the capacity to choose a life that is egoistic, false, cruel, violent, fraudulent, and unfaithful. That being so, with the right conduct, we can discover our true nature. Universal laws are eternal. Accordingly, doing good and right would liberate one from living a finite life and deliver them into a life of infinite existence.

In the later centuries, from about the first century BC, Hinduism kept its distance from a philosophical field of study and entered into the realm of religion, mythology, and allegories. The Upanishads set aside the core philosophical principles of original Hinduism. Subsequently, Hinduism was adopted as an instrument of serving the interest of the priests and the ruling class. The establishment of the caste system in India was a by-product of this transformation. Over time many dissident voices were raised against the decline of the original philosophical foundations of Hinduism. The Charvaka School, Jain philosophy, and Buddha took issue with the degeneration of Hinduism. The Charvaka School accused the Brahmans of using Hinduism to serve their interests. This school backed the idea of morality as a private matter. Something that is internally inspired and gratifying. It broke from the traditional belief in eventual spiritual liberation. In accordance with the teaching of this school, the only pleasure one can have is at the present. Jainism stuck to two core principles of the old Vedic tradition. It has placed spiritual liberation as its highest moral quest. Next in order was the philosophy of nonviolence as the only moral means to get to the highest goal. Over time they extended their philosophy of nonviolence to all living species by becoming vegetarian and taking care of all living things, especially when they are sick and injured. Jainism also took an earnest stand against lying and possession.

Gautama Buddha (c.563–483) was another great Indian dissenter. He was unhappy with his life and the way traditional Indian philosophy was eroded. As a prince for the first 29 years of his life, he lived a privileged life in the lap of luxury and idleness. He rejected his old frivolous lifestyle for six years and led an austere life. In the search for the highest fulfilment, he went from one extreme to another. His isolation period also taught him that such a lifestyle is not the solution to the major problems of humanity. It cannot prevent us from getting old, feeling sick, or dying. Buddha learned from this experiment that withdrawing from real life would not solve the real practical problems in life. As an atheist, he considered religion a cause of many problems and miseries. So, his solution to human problems was not a religious but a philosophical one. He sought the solution in each individual. Because morality is an inner power that each individual is equipped with. In view of this, each individual is responsible for their moral duty. There is a place for compassion in each individual that each individual is in charge of. Buddha's practical answer to all major human problems is compassion. It is the compassion of each for all. The end goal of each human is to be free from whatever causes pain and sorrow. In the state of Nirvana, we are free. This freedom can only be obtainable through the means of universal compassion and reciprocity of friendship. By these means we will discover our true moral life, the "middle path," between the selfish egotism and the life of ascetic austerity. This is the middle way between the two extremes of "eternalism and nihilism" (Ellis 2015: 62).

The founders of ancient moral philosophy in China were Laozi and Confucius in the sixth century BC. Laozi advocated his Dao principle, the Way, his supreme principle of moral conduct. A type of moral conduct that was practised among the Chinese population was characterized by acts of simplicity, honesty, and sincerity. The end of a moral life is meant to be in peace with oneself. The moral impulse came from one's own inner nature. A virtuous person can tell apart the worldly goods, status, wealth, positions, extravagance, boasting, and showing-off with a way of living that is modest, peaceful, tranquil, and temperate. Laozi's approach to crime and punishment was tolerance and rejection of the policy of revenge. He preached recompensing "injury with kindness" (Day 1962: 22) – arguing that retribution is a cause of social unrest and chaos. Laozi's contemporary, Confucius, was younger than him but has remained the most influential Chinese thinker of ancient time. Confucius believed in the art of transforming each man into a Junzi through his method of teaching. Junzi is an inner natural quality in each person. But the notion of person is not the same for all individuals. In his rigid hierarchical outlook, all individuals do not have equal positions in society. Each person's role in society is determined by their position. Their disciples, however, have this inner natural capacity that by their teaching can become Junzi. That is, they become a "superior man" and a "superior man shapes the good in man; he does not shape the bad in him" (quoted from Cunningham 2018: 253). Confucius is also said to have proposed a single maxim for a moral life. The maxim that "what you do not want done to yourself, do not do to others" (quoted from Legg 1991: 109). After Confucius, there were other Chinese thinkers who sought the cause of being morally good or evil as an inborn natural thing in each individual. Mencius (c.372–c.289 BC) had a very high opinion of humanity – arguing that by their nature humans are good and would do the right things. It is the bad conditions and poor education that make them lead immoral life. Xunzi (c.300–c.230 BC), however, advocated an opposite view to that of Mencius. Humans by nature, in his view, are egoistic, envious, emulous, and possessive. Seeking profit is an inner human desire that goes with being human. For this reason, we need moral rules of conduct to prevent chaos and violent conflicts between the egoistic and profit-seeking individuals in society.

## The end, the means and adaptability

The morality of doing what is right for no other consideration except because it is right also has its long history. The rules of conduct consist of codes about how one ought to live. This was the core component of the Stoic philosophy. In the Stoic view, human beings are moral. For the reason that humans are the only living being that has the capacity to reason, they can distinguish right from wrong. The capacity to reason is an inner capacity, inseparable from the intelligent agent. It is through correct employment of this capacity that one achieves true wisdom and virtue, which are the ultimate goals of being human. Good and bad are determined by one's capacity to reason and not by passion. A wise person applies their capacity to reason correctly and effectively and differentiates what is good or bad. The highest form of good is a life of wisdom and virtue. This is a life that is under the control of one's reason, not the circumstances or one's passion. As much as one's life is under one's control, one can end it or continue living no matter how difficult and painful it may be.

The conviction in believing in good differs. Good can be considered to be good intrinsically for its own sake or because it is the god's command or for any other agent's sake. The archetype of good as an end unto itself is the Ten Commandments. The laws were sanctioned by the Jewish God. Jesus was raised with these laws and was the teacher of these laws. The source of morality was for Jesus the law (contract) that came from the Jewish God. The New Testament was compiled from this conviction and Jesus' teaching rested on a strong moral sense of right and wrong according to god's command. The basis of his moral standards is the Jewish divine legal system, but he took a stand against the retributory aspect of this system and advocated like Buddha a more compassionate approach of forgiveness, sympathy, and clemency instead of retributive justice. His edict of turning the other cheek was his way of rejecting the path of vengeance. After Emperor Constantine I (c.280–337) converted to Christianity, Jesus' teaching took a different direction. Like Hinduism, it became the vehicle of priests to pursue their economic, social, and political interests and an ideology of the ruling class. Killing and war, instead of clemency, were justified in pursuit of Christian expansion and the expansion of Christian empires. In the centuries that followed, the shortcomings of legal and ethical Christianity were compensated with the Greek philosophical writings and ideas. St Augustine of Hippo (354–430) introduced Plato's concept of the rational soul into Christianity. Humans' ultimate goal became to use one's body to one's ultimate end. That is the union of body and soul, i.e., one's union with one's god. This is what is considered to be ethical and the cause of one's happiness. The idea of original sin was brought to the centre of Christianity's ethical system. Redemption was only possible by God and that required complete submission to God's commandments. In the thirteenth century, St Thomas Aquinas (1225–74) Christianized Aristotle and incorporated his philosophy into the Christian religion. One principal doctrine of Aristotle, as we have noted earlier, was happiness as human's ultimate end. Aquinas adopted this but argued that it can only be achievable in the service of God, the love of God. The right and wrong and reward and punishment are confined to the love of God and acting according to his will.

Except for the axial age, for about two millennia ethics was under the domination of religion. The discovery of a new world was a significant step to break with the past. The discovery of the new world instituted a global upsurge of colonization and conquest. In the course of a couple of centuries, the whole globe was divided between a few major empires. The plague of colonization led to the formation of the richest and most powerful empires in recorded history. The event shifted and displaced a significant portion of the world population to different parts of the world, most specifically to the new world. It led to the formation of a global merchant class who were not confined only to one country, region, or continent to trade. The colonialized people were regarded as less human and hence were exploited ruthlessly. Their natural resources were looted and brought to the metropoles. As a consequence of this historical event, we have some radical economic, social, political, scientific transformations that had accompanied this period. Because of the greater mobility of people and goods to different parts of the world, there were a series of new scientific discoveries and innovations, most specifically in the means of transport, manufacturing, and arms industries. It is during this period that a class of intellectuals was formed with relatively secure income who looked for answers for the problems of the real world. They were looking forward and for them, the past was not the solution. The past was a major barrier to progress forward.

Many thinkers of the period returned to the axial age and revived ancient Greek philosophy. The requirements and activities of the emerging powerful states and merchant class were not compatible with the rigid doctrine of sin and punishment anymore. We find the signs of this incompatibility of the old rule of theocracy with the new world in the work of Niccolo Machiavelli (1469–1527). In *The Prince* (1513), Machiavelli repudiated the prevailing view that the prince's rule is predestined by his deity. It is the prince, Machiavelli declared, who determines how effective his rule is. Machiavelli argued that the prince has not been sent by any deity to impose his command and hence in doing that he proves to be a good ruler. His advice to the rulers is to never trust the public. An effective ruler is one who does not trust the public but can control them. A good ruler is a weak ruler. Machiavelli advised the rulers that they can maintain their power successfully when they "learn how not to be good" (Machiavelli 1950: 75). Hobbes went a step farther than Machiavelli on the issue of the ruler and his subjects. In his view, people should not be left alone without a ruler or a state because in the state of nature people destroy themselves. Since by nature humans are violent and destructive, they need to be prevented from destroying each other. The ruler provides security and for this function, the subject should forego some of their freedom to their rulers.

For Hobbes, humans are self-destructive when they are left alone. The cause of this is human nature. Humans are self-interested and their morality is based on this. This view of human nature was a departure from dominant religious beliefs in Europe at the time. Moreover, this standpoint about human nature laid the foundation of modern economics. Hobbes asserted that things are good or bad, according to "any man's appetite or desire" (Hobbes 1886: 32). Making a distinction between the two is a personal matter. The self-interested human seeks to have more good but there are not sufficient resources to satisfy everyone. Resources are scarce. Naturally, the egoistic individuals compete for limited resources, which causes the "war of all against all" (Welch and Miewald 1983: 54). Under such circumstances, there will be no peace. So, we need a social contract with our rulers to avoid war because each individual cannot enforce any social contract.

In the seventeenth century, Spinoza in Holland and Henry More in England adopted a different approach from the one that had been proposed by the proponents of the Original Sin and by Machiavelli and Hobbes about human nature. In their account, the human by nature is good. In addition, humans have the capacity to reason. With reason, one can also improve one's moral conduct. But the prerequisite for good ethics is science. Given that we employ our capacity to reason, we can formulate and adopt ethical rules that can be as precise, self-evident and as valid as in mathematics. In support of this claim, Henry More remarked that "if it be good that one man should be supplied with the means of living well and happily, it is mathematically certain that it is doubly good that two should be so supplied, and so on" (quoted from Sidgwick 1922: 172). In Hobbes's account, as we have noted above, human nature is fixed. It is a casualty of self-interest. In Spinoza's account, self-interest is not an inflexible desire. With reason, humans can act correctly and be in control of their undesirable conducts and passions. Thus, the debate on morality during the age of enlightenment was liberated from the custody of god and the self-destructive nature of humanity. The responsibility of morality was resumed in each individual and no one else.

Many thinkers of the period questioned Machiavelli and Hobbes's distrust of human nature. In England, the third earl of Shaftesbury (1671–1713) argued that human beings are much more complex than to be defined as merely being selfish. People have all sorts of good feelings: feelings of sympathy, benevolence, generosity, altruism, courage, appreciation, and so on. Human pleasure does not simply descend from egoism but from other feelings too. Besides, egoistic feelings are inferior to other good feelings. Good feelings are virtuous feelings that limit the excesses of the pursuit of self-interest, which clears the way for peace and harmony. Joseph Butler (1692–1752) talked of a higher feeling than self-interest that is unique to the human species. That is, the human conscience, which is entwined with the capacity of humans to reason. Even those thinkers who considered moral judgement to one's feeling, not to one's reason, based moral judgement on the individual than any external source. Moral judgement, from this perspective, stems from a moral sense. It stems from an "amiable or disagreeable" sense (Hutcheson 1971: 224). Hutcheson was the most influential converser of the theory of moral sense of his time. He put forward the argument that what we believe about good and evil derives from our feelings and not from our reason. Our moral sense is an inner sense and that is the source of our moral judgement of approvals and disapprovals. Hutcheson went on to say that

> we are not to imagine, that this moral sense, more than the other senses, supposes any innate ideas, knowledge, or practical proposition: We mean by it only a determination of our minds to receive amiable or disagreeable ideas of actions when they occur to our observation.
>
> (quoted from Cooper 1956: 131)

In the case of moral action, its source is disinterested benevolence. This is the action that at its best it "procures the greatest happiness for the greatest numbers."

Hutcheson's two distinguished fellow countrymen, Smith and Hume, were both influenced by his works on ethics. There is considerable similarity between his theory of the moral sense and Hume's conception of morality. Hume was personally acquainted with Hutcheson and for a short time was directly in touch with him. Like Hutcheson's moral theory, Hume's moral judgement rests on feelings rather than on reason. Hume held that reason alone cannot be the basis of our morality. Morality is merely a practical matter. Morality is not a thought process but a feeling process. Feelings set our ends not our reasons. Reason is the shortest and best way to get to our end. Reason is only the means to the ends that are set by our feelings but it cannot determine what the end should be. Reason cannot alone make one act unless the end motive, desire, or passion is known prior through our feelings as being morally permissible or prohibitive. It has to be said that Hume overrated the role of feeling and passion by suggesting that even reason is "the slave of passions" (Hume 1874: 195). Hence, moral motivation in Hume's account is under the control of our feelings and sentiment. He propounded that it is "impossible, that the distinction betwixt moral good and evil, can be made by reason" (Hume 1874: 239). Hume further stipulated that our moral judgements of approval and disapproval are under the realm of "ought" and not the realm of "is." The former deals with values and the latter deals with facts and one cannot deduce values (ought) from facts (is). In other words, feelings cannot be deduced from reason.

The idea of drawing a social contract between a ruler and his subjects was a by-product of human liberation from the reign of God. It replaced the kingdom of God with the primacy of law. Suspension of the hegemony of the realm of god and theocracy entailed two profound aftereffects. One ramification of this partial break from the captivity of deities was the release of free will from preordained destiny. Humans became responsible for their own moral conduct. The second great impact was secular law gaining ascendancy over the rule of gods. This break from a celestial sphere into a mundane life has had an everlasting impact on the course of human history. Jean Jacques Rousseau (1712–78) saw no evil fixed in human nature. What he called the "noble savages" are innocent and moral people. In Rousseau's view, these are people who were free, benevolent, and very cooperative. The problem started not from humans as being naturally wicked but with the privatization of land. Along this development went the introduction of law, inequality, and corruption. Bypassing the state of nature, according to Rousseau, it does not follow that humanity is condemned eternally to a life of violence, inequality, and repression. By means of reason, they can form civil society and acquire moral freedom.

The triumph of temporal law and morality over the one decided by fate was not a victory of no avail. It brought forth the age of reason that produced the greatest thinkers of the modern time. Kant is one of these great thinkers. Kant acknowledges the influence of two contemporary philosophers on his ideas. The one who exerted the greatest influence is David Hume. His *Critique of Pure Reason*, his crowning achievement, is credited to Hume's "sceptical teaching." Hume's influence is from his discussions on the law of causation and the problem of the rationality of induction. Rousseau is the other thinker who has influenced Kant's moral philosophy. Reading Rousseau's work changed Kant's low regard for the masses, going from detesting them as being ignorant and undeserving to regarding all humans as having equal dignity and personal worth that should be respected.

Human worth stems from being human. Kant contends that passions, feelings, beliefs, actions, and their consequences are not what determine what is morally right. These are not the source and the standard of human morality. The ground for what is morally permissible or mandatory, Kant maintains, "must not be sought in the nature of the human being or in the circumstances of the world in which he is placed, but *a priori* simply in concepts of pure reason" (Kant 1998: 3). Due to this:

> an action from duty is to put aside entirely the influence of inclination and with it every object of the will; hence there is left for the will nothing that could determine it except objectively the *law* and *subjectively* pure respect for this practical law, and so the maxim of complying with such a law even if it infringes upon all my inclinations.
>
> (Kant 1998: 13–14 – Italics in original)

Human moral actions that stem from human reason and the ones that stem from desires are fundamentally different. The former is free and the latter is the bondage of either our desires, passions, feelings, sentiment, or the outcome of actions. There is hardly any likeness between the two sides. The capacity of humans to reason, therefore, is not just confined to human understanding or knowledge. It is the source and the attendant of our moral obligations. At its utmost efficacy, the human capacity to reason, according to Kant, is under freedom. It is in freedom that the human rational faculty is not a captive of any external impediment. The impact of the free functioning of our rational faculty is the highest in freedom. In freedom, humans achieve moral goals. Above all, the only safeguard for freedom is rational action. Just the same, human rationalism remains incapacitated unless it is free to function. Due to the fact that humans are rational beings – an attribute of humanity that applies to every human being – the moral goals that they assign out of reason under full freedom cannot just be confined to each individual's desire, passion, feelings, or the consequence of one's action but form mandatory moral ends for everyone to obey and pursue.

Therefore, the moral worth of any action is determined by a rational being applying one's power of reason in a free environment whose "will" is not confined solely to the individual but can be extended to all rational individuals. The moral merit of the "will" when decided in this way is not for its own sake but it is out of duty. Any other motives outside duty will lack moral worth. Rational will under freedom that is out of duty and applicable universally is the basis of Kant's theory of morality. In an exposition of his ethics, Kant made a distinction between hypothetical and categorical imperatives.

A categorical imperative is an unconditional moral rule of conduct that must be followed by everyone under all circumstances. A hypothetical imperative is an action that is based on one's desires. This is a specific rule of moral conduct. To achieve this desired end, an individual comes upon a number of necessary means that are in one's power. This imperative presupposes three fundamental requirements. The first one is the rational being – a being that has a capacity to reason. This capacity is necessary but not sufficient. When this capacity is applied in a will, which includes both the individual who will and all other individuals, it achieves its end.

Here the moral choice is with the person. An ethical person chooses the ethical maxim regardless of the circumstances. If the desired end is trust, the means to this end is telling the truth regardless of the situation. A categorical imperative is an ethical maxim, which is imperative. It includes everyone. Something that every person must do. It is categorical that is it applies to all times, places, and circumstances. As the contents of these maxims are free from any desire, feelings, or passions, the consequences do not count and change nothing due to the fact that the only content of the moral rule of conduct is the reason. At the pinnacle of Kant's moral conduct is the maxim, "act only in accordance with the maxim through which you can at the same time will that it became a universal law" (Kant 1998: XVIII). This maxim is imperative. That is, everyone must use it as the central moral rule of conduct regardless of its consequences, and it is categorical, that is, it applies to every time and everywhere in all situations. But no action can be moral unless each human is taken as an end, not as a means to achieve a certain end. By virtue of this reasoning, moral reasoning is rational reasoning and each human being has got the rational faculty and capacity to reason and determine their moral conduct. On this basis, each human is an end and not the means to an end. Therefore, Kant professes that a moral act is one where you act in a way that you treat humanity always as an end and never as a means to an end.

Kant's thoughts exerted a considerable impact on the subsequent development of modern democratic societies. His substantive contribution spearheaded a peaceful revolution in ranking each individual as an end. The ramifications of this stand have been far-reaching. In this worldview, each individual has "an intrinsic worth." Something "above all price," which is human dignity that must be respected equally for all individuals. Continuing on this line each individual has a rational faculty and capacity to reason that is autonomous and can learn and decide independently. On these accounts, each individual has the right to freedom, to exercise these faculties at will. They are to be treated as a rational being in the same way that all rational beings are treated, and free to organize their liberal republics. These ideas exerted much influence on the development of human rights organizations and the principles of universal sympathy and cooperation, freedom, democracy, equity, justice, and peace. The United Nations charter was drafted in 1945 on the spirit of Kant's ideas that he expounded in his *Essay on Eternal Peace* (1795). John B. Rawls (1921–2002) is the most noted contemporary student of Kant.

The influence of the works of John Locke, Rousseau, John Stuart Mill, and most specifically Kant's second moral principle of the categorical imperative comprises the basis of Rawls's theory of justice. In his youth, Rawls was deeply religious. He served in the Second World War in New Guinea, the Philippines, and Japan. After the war, much affected by the experience of the war, Rawls immersed his attention mostly to the study of justice.

Rawls tries to show how justice is possible. To this end, he was driven by his religious conviction and experience. In particular, his experience of serving in the war, his observation of the fascist and Stalinist totalitarian political systems, and the 1929 Great Depression, all these events were critical in his life-long interest in the study of justice. The basis of Rawls's theory of justice is Kant's second formulation of the categorical imperative. It is the moral principle that each human is an end in itself and never should be treated as a means. In treating every person as an end, ethical justice will be served and this is the foundation and the backbone on which all other forms of justice, economic and political, can be safeguarded. In Rawls's view justice is a compact conviction that is indiscerptible from fairness. The foundation of both in turn is human reason. By the means of this shared foundation social contracts can be written that would safeguard the moral principle of justice and fairness. This common moral bond is the prerequisite for exercising the universal maxim of treating each individual as an end and never as a means.

Rawls resurrected the Platonic allegory of the cave in a different scenario to demonstrate his case for justice. He called this hypothetical social scenario the "veil of ignorance." It was not the first time that Plato's allegory of the cave re-emerged. The idea of the state of nature that appeared in the works of many vanguards of the age of reason is also modelled essentially on the Platonic allegory. A concept that was central to the formation of Locke, Hobbes, and Rousseau's social contract. Rawls has somewhat adopted Locke's and Rousseau's versions of the idea of the state of nature. Locke adopted this concept in his *Two Treatise of Government* in defining his political contract, obligation, limitation authority and power of the state, and people's right to resist state repression (Simmons 1989: 449). Locke's state of nature resembles the situation of a child at birth that, according to Locke, has a blank mind that will be filled with knowledge by experience after birth. One can detect the likeness of Rawls's "veil of ignorance" to Locke's "tabula rasa" of the mind of a child at birth. In Rousseau's "pure state of nature," people are also like innocent children. Their lives are solitary and dictated by basic natural urges and the desire of staying alive and living in peace. The state of nature is founded upon the natural goodness of humans that is conflict-free, ordered, and happy. As in the aforementioned hypothetical social setting, the core of the "veil of ignorance" is in this tradition. It is also an "original position." In this imaginary social setting, it is assumed that the individuals behind the veil are endowed with rational and moral capacity. One's capacity to reason is rested on one's common sense and enlightened self-interest. Due to these inborn commands, each person is different in terms of one's capability, talent, ends, and goals.

In this imaginary original position, ignorance is bliss. It is a state of innocence in which an individual lacks total awareness. All individuals are free and rational and moral beings. But behind the veil, one is ignorant of one's abilities and the position one occupies in society. In this original position, each individual has equal rights that are compatible to the rights and liberty of any other individual. From this presupposition, Rawls infers that the social and economic inequalities as we find them are arbitrary. These inequalities can be readjusted with a model of redistribution that will be advantageous to the representative of each social group. Inequality should be open to all in the same way – to all economic, social, and political positions. Drawing a social contract on these principles, Rawls argued, would be preferred compared to the prevailing alternatives. Beginning from no knowledge of ability, interest, and status, a social contract can be drawn that is just and fair. A contract that is morally permissible is one that is compatible with the pursuit of enlightened self-interest and political order that is a bearer of freedom, civil liberty, equal rights, and equal opportunity. These are conditions that are necessary for a democratic, just, and egalitarian society, which safeguards the equal worth of morally equal individuals. Rawls maintains, by adopting this level playing field, the fundamental principles of justice can be effectively applied and enforced. These two principles are the principle of equal liberty and the maximin principle. Acting, according to these principles, empowers each person to enjoy equal freedom as any other individual and it will also achieve the maximin principle. In compliance with the latter principle, the economic resources will be allocated such that the benefits of the least advantaged social groups will be maximized.

The question of moral sense as an objective fact or otherwise was also a contentious subject in ancient times. Among the Greek thinkers, Protagoras, Antiphon, and Thrasymachus did think that moral standards are objective facts. All moral precepts, in their opinion, are confined to the given time and place conventions. That is, ethical beliefs are products of humans, living in different times and places. As in the standard of right and wrong, it is "man" that "is the measure of all things." Morality in this sense is relative. Against this view, Protagoras and Herodotus offered a universalist view of morality, which also considered people to be the author of their moral laws. Thrasymachus held that the wealthy and the strong make the laws and justice mean obeying these laws. From this perspective, justice means serving the interest of the rich and strong. The standard of right and wrong is the power and interests of these classes. In this sense, "might makes right." One of the distinctive contributions of Socrates on ethics was his objective account of human morality. The idea that we are objectively capable of distinguishing what is right and then apply it in conducting our lives. A position that was followed by Plato and Aristotle. According to Plato, we know there are many instances of goodness but the true knowledge of goodness is in the Form of goodness. The Form of goodness is perfect and will never change. It is the same with justice. The true knowledge of justice is not relative to any time, place, and custom. It is eternal.

There is a perspective that places history as the cradle of morality. History is the end. From this standpoint, the standards of good and evil are conditional to history. History is the foundation of morality. The human standards of good and evil are dissolved in the ultimate end of history. G. W. Hegel (1770–1831) was an instigator of this view. In Hegel's theory of history, history has an ultimate end. Everything else that occurs in the course of history is for the sake of this end. Human morality is in the service of this mission. All human activities aim at the same end and the ultimate end of history is the progress of the spirit. The underlying principles of human moral conduct are merely an element of attaining this destiny. World history develops into successive stages and this progress is a rational process that follows the path of reason to achieve its ultimate end. The ultimate end of history is the progress of spirit (mind). This progress is a rational advancement to an ultimate end. "Reason rules the world" and it is reason that executes the plan of history to its ultimate end, which is attaining the consciousness of freedom. The progress that serves this aim is rational. The spirit, the nature of which is freedom, discloses itself through the state, culture, art, and religion. The fusion and interplay of all these elements constitute the "ethical life of nation." This progress is realized in a dialectical process where the historical progress begins with a thesis, the thesis creates its negation, and the battle of opposites eventually gives rise to a synthesis, which is a higher stage of the two.

Marx in his theory of ethics retained the historical and dialectical foundations of Hegelian moral judgement. He mixed this Hegelian blend with an element of Thrasymachus's theory of justice. Initially, Marx endorsed Hegel's account of morality almost to the letter. He agreed with Hegel that freedom is the ultimate goal of humanity. An end that could only be realized after the disappearance of private and public interests. In conceptualizing his dialectical materialism, Marx injected in his theory of history one facet of Thrasymachus's theory of justice. In Thrasymachus's theory of justice, it is the natural right of the strong to rule the weak. Being just means serving the interests of the strongest. In Marx's thinking, there are two worlds: the material world and the world of ideas. The latter is a by-product of the former and ethics is one feature of the latter world. The base of the material world is the economy, the economic mode of production. All ideas – political, legal, cultural, ethical, and religious – are by-products of each mode of production. In the class-based mode of production, the "ideas of the ruling class [including the moral ideas] are in every epoch the ruling ideas" (Marx and Engels 1991: 64). It is by the means of class struggle and revolution that human beings achieve their ultimate historical end, which is characterized by full humanity and consciousness. That is the state of communism where social classes will disappear and true human ethics will prevail.

Many followers of Marx took ethics, as Marx did, as a periphery aspect of each mode of production and the class struggle. The one and only purpose in Marxian history is communism. It is the ultimate end that must be reached by any means. Vladimir Lenin (1870–1924), the leader of the Bolshevik Party and the founder of the Soviet Union, considered almost any means as a necessary precept to seize political power to achieve this end. He had no compunction about the end justifying the means (Read 2005: 247). That is, anything was morally permissible to achieve the noble goal of communism. On the basis of this moral reasoning, the many atrocities of Stalin, Mao, Pol Pot, and other totalitarian Marxist regimes have been justified. Herbert Spencer's (1820–1903) theory of survival of the fittest, just like Hegelian and Marxian morality, is a twisted naturalistic morality. But his lever of the moral sense is not history. It is the reverse side of Thrasymachus's sense of morality. In this case, all living species, including the human species, are divided into inferior and superior individuals. The ultimate end here is the complete eradication of inferiors. The superiors have got the right to live and the inferior are meant to perish. It is in the law of nature to improve the strongest and destroy the weak and the poor. Only the fittest "do advance" under the law of nature and "eventually survive." Those who survive "must be the select of their generation." The end in this idea of moral Darwinism is "the survival of the fittest." It is the ultimate goal of nature to weed "out those of lowest development" and to secure "the growth of a race who shall both understand the conditions of existence and be able to act up to them" (Spencer 1851: 378).

One fact always remains. We would not be able to understand and function without having a workable standard for good and evil, right and wrong, and true and false. The standard for such matters is the human itself. The measure cannot be anything else but human – even with objective facts that exist independent of humans. The last judgement of facts is human judgement in believing what is the fact or delusion. The best of human standards will thrive under freedom of thought and imagination. In everything we do there exist these underlying elements of conduct, be it an epistemological judgement or a moral judgement. All matters of human judgements are within the bounds of humanity. But basing one's judgement merely on what is handy, reachable, easily seen, and visible can be delusive and misleading. It is the victim of appearances. It goes and judges by what is easily seen and pronounced. The dominant economic ideas that rely predominately on inductive reasoning, projecting the past into the future, by means of mathematical tools and language as in regression analysis are in this category of judgements. This judgement suffers from mathematical fallacy. It equates mathematical language and expressions to universal truths. By expressing the contingent truths in mathematical language, they do not only copy the past into the future but with this method of research detach contingent truths from their specific time and place and eternalize such truths. Contingent facts are not always what they seem to be. They are more than meets the eye. If they are forgone, they are forgone forever and will not be repeated exactly the same in the future.

The epistemological and moral judgements can also be a prey of naturalistic misconception. Anything assigned as natural can be justified as true and right. For example, tautological truths are not necessarily true or right. Take the general statement, "all humans are born criminal." Socrates is a human. There is one conclusion that we can extrapolate from this statement and that is Socrates is a criminal. The conclusion is logically valid but it is neither true nor right. A logical follow-up to this route is scientism where science dissipates and turns into an object of worship. The logical outgrowth of this trend is what is in vogue will preponderate irrespective of being scientifically proven.

One of these "scientific fads" was the eugenics movement. Almost all strata of society, scientific disciplines, and ideological and political persuasions joined the bandwagon of this cult – from Nobel laureate geneticist Hermann J. Muller (1890–1967) to the author and playwright Bernard Shaw (1854–1950), from Sidney Webb (1859–1947) to John Maynard Keynes, Winston Churchill, and Theodore Roosevelt. Conservatives, liberals, communists, fascists, and scientists, all were advocating selective human breeding. The overriding influence for this movement was Darwin's theory of natural selection. Francis Galton, a cousin of Darwin, coined the term "eugenics" in 1883. On the left, the liberals and socialists supported eugenics in order to improve "the genetic stock of the human race through selected breeding" (Paul 1984: 568). The Nazi's eugenicists used it as a vehicle to bread a pure German race. They all used it to advance their "political convictions and social biases" (Weingart 1989: 260). Eugenics was practised in all developed countries including some underdeveloped countries such as Brazil and Argentina. In Russia, the practice sped up after the Bolshevik revolution in 1917. It became one of the central policies of the Chinese state after the Maoist revolution in 1949.

The means of communication for all human activities is language. The problem is whatever exists and the intention of what is meant to be said are not necessarily expressed with absolute precision. There is always a gap between reality and what is said and written. Language cannot communicate reality and intentions exactly. The logical positivism that developed after the First World War fixated their central doctrine on the relationship between language and factual knowledge. The Vienna circle started logical positivism or logical empiricism in the 1920s. Many members of this circle after the rise of fascism in Europe went to Britain and the United States, generating a worldwide philosophical movement. Broadly speaking, logical positivism was an anti-metaphysical and anti-idealist movement. In their views, real knowledge is factual knowledge and the source of factual knowledge is experience. This implies that by means of language we construct propositions. With these propositions, we describe and try to understand the world. There are three major problems embedded in this link between propositions and reality. First, we acquire our initial input (knowledge) from our experience. This experience in turn is drawn from our senses, and our senses are not reliable sources for providing accurate knowledge. There is an element of illusion in each sense of information being acquired. Second, the information acquired from experience is communicated by means of language in the form of names, terms, propositions, beliefs, and theories. The world and what is intended to be said and understood is never exactly the same as it is conveyed in language. Third, besides these inconsistencies, there is the problem of induction. Inductive propositions cannot be justified by deductive reasoning. In view of these considerations, logical positivists divided true sentences into those that state the facts and the logical truth. Outside this distinction such as for example the metaphysical propositions are meaningless, and logical truths are tautologies. The propositions or statements of facts are only valid if they are verifiable. True knowledge is one that is empirically confirmed. Accordingly, this is the essence of science. If a proposition cannot be empirically verified it is not scientific.

One of the much-talked contributions of the logical positivist school is falsification as the criterion of science. Contrary to what falsification is intended for, in a peculiar way, it is a sort of verification. Karl Popper was the foremost exponent of this theory of the growth of knowledge. Strange as it seems, by falsifying an idea one verifies another idea. In this case, it confirms the problem of inductive reasoning. The problem is that science does not progress by means of induction. The empirical confirmation, at its best, confirms what had happened in the past. Propositions drawn in this way are contingent and cannot be universal and can never be verified empirically by means of induction. Such claims cannot go further than what is already known. Hume raised these issues and addressed the problem of induction. Popper thought he has solved the problem. His solution is in two parts. The first move in his falsification principle is asking the right question, which is missing in the inductive inferences. The second step is that it is only by means of systematic tests and falsification of empirical propositions that we add to the corpus of human knowledge and depart from one problem to the next. This, Popper supposed, is the only firm ground for a potent science.

## Conclusion

Walter Bagehot (1826–77) described the extreme state of affairs in financial markets as when "a great deal of stupid people have a great deal of stupid money … the money of these people – the blind capital … is particularly large and craving: it seeks for someone to devour it, and there is a 'plethora' … it finds someone, and there 'speculation'; it is devoured, and there is 'panic'" (Bagehot 1891: 2). The burgeoning number of economic agents with "blind capital" who pursue their individual self-interest is a transient self-elevating period. As more and more economic agents take this route, more individuals will join them in the act. What we have under such circumstances, like anything in vogue, is a confirmatory bias that is self-actualizing. But the economy does not rise forever to an infinite height. The faster the rotation of the wheel of a "great deal of stupidity," the more severe will be the financial panic and the economic crash. This state of affairs, obviously, is not advantageous to the common good. The economy is not a self-correcting machine. It is not independent of human follies. Economic agents are also not perfect. They are not infallible predictable machines. People do not know everything. It does not necessarily follow from a lack of sufficient knowledge that things are in the right order and are moving on in their natural course. Economic and financial panics and crises are not normal to have a natural course. There is no economy, which is in a position of complete rest. Economies are constantly changing. These changes are a mishmash of those that are planned and those that are unplanned. Some economic decisions go according to the plans and some do not. All economic decisions are not free of defects. There are those decisions that are the causes of the problems and there are economic theories and policies that solve one shortcoming and create another problem. There are employments that create more trades and there are works that destroy jobs.

Humans are the only livings species that invent imaginary myths and kill and be killed for their delusions. Humans can be ruled by their delusions. Dividing human history into preconceived, distinct, and certain economic systems is another form of fantasy. Marx was a very successful prophet in this regard. He thought of capitalism as a transitory system that would eventually destroy itself. His capitalism has become an article of faith for both his disciples and his adversaries. In the credo of capitalism, as in any religion, there are those from opposite sides who hold to their belief with fanatical conviction. In the case of capitalism, the zealot adherents are certain of the presence of the capitalist system of production and distribution and its eventual demise. Their main task is to search and find signs to confirm their faith. The zealot opponents are equally certain about capitalism and its prospects for the future. The system is viewed as a preordained economic order. It is held as one of the greatest human inventions and the most perfect systems of production, allocation of resources, and distribution that has to be protected and preserved in every way. Keynes was also a captive of the same tenet. His crusade was to rescue capitalism. Declaring that if capitalism is "wisely managed," it can be "made more efficient for attaining economic ends" (Keynes 1963: 321).

Economic disorder is a permanent state of affairs. There is no cure for economic disorder and there will be no cure for it in the future. We just do not know what events, inventions, discoveries, natural and social changes, and disasters are ahead of us. The forms of disorders will change but their basic element remains the same. For the sake of clarity, let us refer to a few examples from real life in making this interpretation. The new world was discovered in 1492. Oxygen, uranium, radium, penicillin, and the structure of DNA were discovered in 1774, 1787, 1898, 1928, and 1953, respectively. The printing press, steam engine, the telephone, the personal computer, and the internet were invented in 1450, 1786, 1876, 1974, and 1983, respectively. Their discoveries and inventions, including countless others not on our lists, have a profound effect on the economy. That is only one reason for continuous change. In addition, social and political upheavals and revolutions are erratic events. Nobody knew when the Russian Revolution took place and when the Soviet Union collapsed. Nobody knew the dates of the two world wars or the collapse of the British Empire or many thousands of similar events. The weather keeps changing and pandemics come and go without any warning. The earthquakes and volcanic eruptions, floods, hurricanes, and droughts are not under our control. Improving human knowledge is not constant. It has got its own ups and downs which is unsettling. Over time some institutions, organizations, and technology improve and others go outdated. Human cultures and generations are not fixed into one mode of behaviour. The new generations' demands, expectations, knowledge, way of life, and culture are not an exact copy of the generation before. All these changes and many other possible hidden stimuli are the causes of permanent disorders in the economy.

Mercantilist commentators were the first economic writers of the early modern period. They were well aware of certain excesses of the world of business and finance. These writers pointed to matters such as counterfeiting, debasing of coins, the issue of irredeemable notes, inflation, frenzy speculation, banking and trade irregularities. They neither knew all the factors that had contributed to such economic crises nor had offered the perfect panaceas to prevent such crises from happening again. In this regard, they are not quite alone. Modern economists also do not know all the factors that had caused such events nor agree on the various remedies on offer. These matters are controversial and will always remain contentious subjects. The changing economies create their own unique problems. Modern economies have their own dynamism, complexities, and capricious problems. They create their own excesses. The two most extreme excesses of contemporary advanced economies have been the 1929 great crash and the 2007–2008 global credit crunch. Obviously, many factors have contributed to these great economic crises – factors that are internal and external. There are factors that we have relatively a clear understanding of, there are factors that are partially understood, there are those factors that the future generations will find, and, lastly, there are many other factors that will always remain unknown. Each type of economic crisis has its own causes and effects. We will never know all causes and effects of an economic crisis. If we knew the causes before the event, we could prevent the event from taking place. Looking in the past is clearer than looking into the future. With hindsight, we know more about an event, but the wisdom of hindsight can only partially tell us what has happened; it cannot tell us when the next crisis will take place. With the benefit of hindsight, we can go no further than Russell's Turkey. The future is uncertain and the future markets are going to get more interconnected. Not only will their size, scope, complexity, and importance increase in the future but they will keep expanding and becoming more sophisticated with the expansion and greater integration of the global economy.

Neither economic disorders nor economic crises can be eliminated entirely. There is no complete solution. Those who have promised a perfect paradise have created an impeccable hell, for the reason that human propensity to extremism cannot be eradicated. It can only be mitigated and managed. Moreover, economic activities come under the category of contingent truth. We simply do not know what the future holds for us. The future conditions of life and the future generations are not what they currently are or were in the past. The facts of the matter are that we cannot eliminate human propensity to extremism and we cannot have full knowledge of contingent truths. We do not know, in all their details, the past, present, and future. We know more about the past and present but whatever we claim to know about the future is conjectural. No matter how well-equipped and confident we are about our knowledge of the future, the future is always full of the unexpected. This being said, many of our decisions made in the past and the present are put into practice in the future. Therefore, the past and the present influence the future. But the fact remains that we cannot eliminate our propensity to extremism and our ignorance of the future. With all that said, life goes on and we cannot preclude the unknown future and human nature. The crucial question is the question of survival and our successes and failures in adapting to new circumstances.

Economics is one of the human endeavours where the outcome of its activities lies sometime in the future. Given the contingent character of economic facts, the human propensity to extremism, and the burden of the lack of knowledge about the future, what is the ideal approach to cope with this web of indeterminacy in the world of the economy? Over such matters, we do not have sufficient control. So how can we ensure ourselves against them and mitigate their undesirable effects such as economic crises? On this point, economics as a discipline can learn from other disciplines like ethics, law, politics, and the methodology of science. In ethics, humans are elevated from a means to an end. Each individual has been raised to be equal to another individual as equal ends. In economics, the end is not the human; it is either constrained maximization or any other economic or political goal. In law, we have the development of the rule of law. According to this principle, nobody is above the law. Under the rule of law, everyone is equal before the law. The rulers and the subjects are all equal before the law. The supremacy of law and the equality before the law safeguard the life and liberty of each individual in a fair and inclusive manner. But there is no equality between economic agents before the current economic setups. There are different laws for the economic masters and the vast majority of people. Individuals are not endowed with certain inalienable economic rights. There is not equal treatment of individuals before the economic arrangements and organizations. In politics, we have the development of egalitarian claims for political representation. The legitimacy of the sovereign power arises from the people. The individuals are sovereign. The power of a democratic state flows and emanates from individuals. To prevent the state from the monopoly of power and its arbitrary excesses, the functions of the government are divided into the independent executive, legislative, and judicial branches. The bedrock of the methodology of science is critical inquiry. It is about critical thinking, reasoning, reflection, and objective analysis. This approach can only thrive in an environment and culture that is free, open, and respects the freedom of thought, imagination, and expression. All these elements and the subsequent institutions that are created to maintain these elements are the prerequisite insurance policies for dealing with the unpredictable, the unknown of our propensity to extremism. In the same ways as in ethics, law, politics, and methodology of sciences their former excesses have been moderated, the excesses and extremism in economics can also be moderated with the establishment of democratic economic systems that operate under a democratic rule of law. But such a mechanism is only truly feasible devoid of colonial political structure.

For an economy to develop and to put to use its potential to its fullest, there are certain necessary preconditions that must be in place before creating the circumstances in which the economic agents do their best for each individual and one another. The thing that is possible and can be done is to create an ideal environment for sustainable economic advances to improve conditions of life. In such an environment, in its general sense, we can adapt more successfully to the changing economic conditions and are more prepared to cope with the upcoming economic disorders and crises. This ideal end, at its broadest level, is a democratic economy.

# Bibliography

Accordino J. J. (2000) *Captives of Cold War Economy*, Westport, Praeger.

Adams J. (2003) *The Political Writings of John Adams*: Representative Selections, G. A. Peek Jr (ed.), Indianapolis, Hakett Publishing Company, Inc.

Adams J. (1851) *The Works of John Adams – Novanglus, Thoughts on Government; Defence of the Constitution*, vol. 4, North Charleston, Greatspace.

Adams J. (1797) *Defence of Constitutions of Government of the United States of America, Against the Attack of M. Turgot*, vol. 1, 3rd ed., Philadelphia, Budd and Bartram.

Addison P. (2005) *Churchill – The Unexpected Hero*, Oxford, Oxford University Press.

Adel G. H., Elmi J. and Taromi-Rad H. (2012) *Pahlavi Dynasty: An Entry from Encyclopaedia of the World of Islam*, London, EWI Press Ltd.

Agarwal R. C. (2005) *Constitutional Development and National Movement of India*, Ramnagar, S. Chand and Company LTD.

Aggarwal V. K. (1985) *Liberal Protectionism*, Berkeley, University of California Press.

Alexander K. (2019) *Principles of Banking Regulation*, Cambridge, Cambridge University Press.

Althusius J. (2005) Politics as the Art of Associating, in D. Karmis and W. Norman (eds.) *Theories of Federalism: A Reader*, New York, Palgrave.

Ankit R. (2011) Wavell: The Prophet Maligned, *Epilogue* 4, no. 1.

Apfel L. J. (2011) *The Advent of Pluralism: Diversity and Conflict in the Age of Sophocles*, Oxford, Oxford University Press.

Aristotle (2014) *Nicomachean Ethics*, trans. and ed. by R. Crisp, Cambridge, Cambridge University Press.

Aristotle (1970) *The Politics*, trans. by T. A. Sinclair, Harmondsworth, Penguin Books.

Aristotle (1970) *The Ethics of Aristotle*, trans. by J. A. K. Thomson, Harmondsworth, Penguin Books.

Aristoteles (1963) *Aristotle*, vol. 12, Heinemann.

Arjomand S. A. (2009) *After Khomeini: Iran under his Successors*, Oxford, Oxford University Press.

Armstrong K. (1999) *The History of God*, London, Vintage.

Augustine (1952) *The Confessions: The City of God and on Christian Doctrine*, ed. by R. M. Hutchins, W. Benton, Chicago, Encyclopedia Britannica.

Avise J. C. (1998) *The Genetic Gods – Evolution and belief in Human Affairs*, US, Harvard College.

Backhouse R. E. (2002) *The Penguin History of Economics*, London, Penguin Books.

Bacon F. (1999) *Selected Philosophical Works*, ed. by R. Sargent, Indianapolis, Hackett Publishing Company, Inc.

Bagehot W. (1891) *The Works of Walter Bagehot*, vol. 2, ed. by F. Morgan, Hartford, The Travelers Insurance Company.

Bailey R. E. (2005) *The Economics of Financial Markets*, Cambridge, Cambridge University Press.

Balkin D. B. (2008) Explaining high US CEO pay in a Global Context – An Institutional Perspective, in L. R. Gomez-Mejia and S. Werner (eds.) *Global Compensation – Foundations and Perspectives*, London and New York, Routledge.

Baloch I. (1987) *The Problem of Greater Balochistan – A Study of Baloch Nationalism*, Stuttgart, Steiner Verlag Wiesbaden Gmbh.

Bangs J. D. (2010) Dutch Contributions to Religious Toleration, *Church History*, vol. 79: 3.

Barber W. J. (1970) *A History of Economic Thought*, Harmondsworth, Penguin Books.

Barnes J. (2011) *Children of Liberty*, Bloomington, IN, Xlibris.

Baron M. (1997) Kantian Ethics and Claims of Detachment, in R. M. Scott (ed.) *Feminist Interoperations of Immanuel Kant*, Pennsylvania, Pennsylvania State University.

Bassiouni M. C. (2011) *Crimes against Humanity*, Cambridge, Cambridge University Press.

Bauer M. (2007) Terrorism: September 11, 2001 and its Consequences, in G. Martel (ed.) *A Companion to International History 1900–2001*, Malden, Blackwell Publishing Ltd.

Beccaria C. B. D. (1813) *An Essay on Crimes and Punishment*, London, Printed for J. Almon.

Beggs-Humphreys M., Gregor H. and Humphreys D. (2006) *The Industrial Revolution*, Abingdon, Routledge.

Beinhocker E. D. (2006) *The Origin of Wealth: Evolution, Complexity and the Radical Remaking of Economics*, Boston, Harvard Business School Press.

Beja Jr D. L. (2009) Was Capital Fleeing Southeast Asia? Estimates from Indonesia, Malaysia, the Philippines and Thailand, in C. Rowley ed. *Trade and Capital Flow Among Asian Economies*, London and New York, Routledge.

Bell D. (2010) John Stuart Mill on Colonies, *Political Theory*, vol. 38: 1.

Bentham J. (1838) *The Works of Jeremy Bentham*, Edinburgh, Stevenson and Co.

Bentham J. (1879) *An Introduction to the Principles of Morals and Legislation*, Clarendon Press.

Ben-Yehuda N. (1980) The European Witch Craze of the 14th to 17th Centuries: A Sociologist's Perspective, *American Journal of Sociology*, vol. 86: 1.

Beranek L. (2000) Roots of Internet: A Personal History, *Massachusetts Historical Review* 2.

Berkeley G. (1820) *The Works of George Berkeley*, vol. 3, London, J.F. Dove.

Bernbach J. P. (2016) *Beyond Reason*, New York, Astor and Blue llc.

Bernstein W. (2009) *A Splendid Exchange – How Trade Shaped the World*, London, Atlantic Books.

Bhatia M. and Sedra M. (2008) *Afghanistan, Arms and Conflict*, London, Routledge.

Bianco J. L. (2010) Language Policy and Planning, in N. H. Hornberger and S. L. Mckay ed. *Sociolinguistics and Language Education*, Bristol, Multilingual Matters.

Bilginsoy C. (2015) *A History of Financial Crises - Dreams and Follies of Expectations*, Abingdon, Routledge.

Blaney D. L. (2020) Provincializing Economics: Jevons, Marshall and the Colonial Imaginaries of Free Trade, *Review of International Political Economy*, https://doi.org/10.1080/09692290.2020.1794929.

Bodin J. (1962) *The Six Books of a Commonweale*, trans. by R. Knolles and ed. by K. D. McRae, Cambridge, Harvard University Press.

Bohlin J. (2014) Swedish Industrial Policy: From General Policies to Crisis Management, 1950–1980, in C. Grabas and A. Mutzenadel (eds.) *Industrial Policy in Europe After 1945*, Basingstoke, Palgrave Macmillan.

Böhm-Bawerk V. E. (1949) *Karl Marx and the Close of his System*, New York, H. Wolff.

Borhi L. (2004) *Hungary in the Cold War 1945–1956*, Budapest, Central European University Press.

Bouteille S. and Coogan-Pushner (2013) *The Handbook of Credit Risk Management*, Hoboken, Wiley and Sons, Inc.

Brenner Y. S. (1983) Sources of Inflation: Old and New, in N. Schmukler and E. Marcus (eds.) *Inflation through Ages: Economic, Social, Psychological and Historical Aspects*, New York, Brooklyn College Press.

Breseeg T. M. (2004) *Baloch Nationalism: Its Origin and Development*, Karachi, Royal Book Company.

Brodie D. (2003) *A History of British Labour Law 1867–1945*, Oxford, Hart Publishing.

Brook T. (1999) *Documents on the Rape of Nanking*, Michigan, The University of Michigan Press.

Brown R. (1984) *The Nature of Social Laws: Machiavelli to Mill*, Cambridge, Cambridge University Press.

Brownmiller S. (1993) *Against our Will: Men, Women, and Rape*, New York, Ballantine Books.

Burns A. and Mitchell W. (1946) *Measuring Business Cycles*, Cambridge, MA, National Bureau of Economic Research (NBER).

Calomiris C. W. (2013) The Political Lessons of Depression-era Banking Reform, in N. Crafts and P. Fearton ed. *The Great Depression of the 1930s*, Oxford, Oxford University Press.

Cassis Y. (2013) *Crises and Opportunities – The Shaping of Modern Finance*, Oxford, Oxford University Press.

Cavanna T. P. (2015) *Hubris, Self-Interest, and America's Failed War in Afghanistan*, Lanham, Lexington Books.

Chaline O. and Kowalski J. M. (2018) French Naval Operations, in D. K. Allison and L. D. Ferreiro (eds.) *The American Revolution – A World War*, Washington DC, Smithsonian Books.

Champ B., Freeman S. and Haslag J. (2016) *Modelling Monetary Economics*, 4th ed., Cambridge, Cambridge University Press.

Chick M. (2020) *Changing Times – Economic, Policies and Resource Allocation in Britain since 1951*, Oxford, Oxford University Press.

Child J. (1997) A New Discourse of Trade, in A. E. Murphy ed. *Monetary Theory: 1601–1758*, vol. 3, London, Routledge.

Chiodo A. J. and Owyang M. T. (2002) A Case Study of a Currency Crisis: The Russian Default of 1998, *The Federal Reserve Bank of St. Louis*, vol. 84: 6.

Chitkara M. G. (2003) *Kashmir: LoC*, New Delhi, A.P.H. Publishing Corporation.

Chorafas D. N. (2015) *Financial Cycles*, New York, Palgrave Macmillan.

Christian J. L. (2002) *The Wisdom Seekers: From the Presocratics to the Renaissance*, Belmont, Wadsworth Thomson Learning.

Ciment J. (2010) *Booms and Busts – An Encyclopaedia of Economic History from Tulipmania of the 1630s to the Global Financial Crisis of the 21st Century*, vol. 1–3, London and New York, Routledge.

Cipolla C. M. (2003) *Before the Industrial Revolution*, 3rd ed., London, Routledge.

Claesseus S., Oks D. and Polastri R. (2000) Capital Flows to Central and Eastern Europe and Former Soviet Union, in ed. *European Union Accession Opportunities and Risks in Central European Finances*, Washington DC, The European Commission and the World Bank.

Clapham J. H. (1944) *The Bank of England, A History*, Cambridge, Cambridge University Press.

Clarkson T. and Cugoano O. (2010) *Thomas Clarkson and Ottobah Cugoano: Essays on the Slavery and Commerce of the Human Species*, ed. by M. A. Smith, Broadview Editions.

Cohen J. P., Coughlin C. C. and Lopez D. A. (2012) The Booms and Bust of U.S. Housing Prices from Various Geographic Perspectives, *Federal Reserve Bank of St. Louis Review*, vol. 94: 5.

Collen E. H. H. (1907) The Indian Army: A Sketch of its History and Organisation, *Imperial Gazetteer*, Oxford, Clarendon Press.

Commons J. R. (1943) *Institutional Economics*, New York, Macmillan.

Condorcet J. (2012) *Condorcet: Political Writings*, ed. by S. Lukes and N. Urbinati, Cambridge, Cambridge University Press.

Condorcet A. N. (2009) *Outlines of an Historical View of the Progress of the Human Mind*, Chicago, G. Langer.

Congressional Oversight Panel (2010) *A Review of Treasury's Foreclosure Prevention Programs.*

Cooper W. H. (2003) Russia's Economic Performance: Entering the 21st Century, in J. P. Hardt (ed.) *Russia's Uncertain Economic Future*, London and New York, Routledge.

Cooper B. C. (1956) *An Examination of the Ethics of Francis Hutcheson*, Berkeley, University of California.

Crafts N. and Fearon P. (2010) Lessons from the 1930s Great Depression, *Oxford Review of Economic Policy*, vol. 26: 3.

Crosby Jr A. W. (2003) *The Columbian Exchange – Biological and Cultural Consequences of 1492*, Westport, Praeger.

Crowe J. and Bradshaw T. (2014) *Chemistry for the Biosciences*, 3rd ed., Oxford, Oxford University Press.

Cullen W. R. (2008) *Is Arsenic an Aphrodisiac?* Cambridge, RSC Publishing.

Cunningham G. (2018) *History and Historiography*, Waltham Abby, ED-Tech Press.

Cyrus Chu C. Y. and Lee R. D. (1993) Famine, Revolt, and the Dynamic Cycle – Dynamics in Historic China, *Journal of Population Economics*, vol. 7: 4.

Darwin C. (1887) *The Life and Letters of Charles Darwin*, vol. 1, ed. by F. Darwin, London, John Murray.

Darwin C. (1866) *The Correspondence of Charles Darwin*, vol. 14, Cambridge, Cambridge University Press.

Das D. K. (2011) *The Asian Economy – Spearheading the Recovery from the Global Financial Crisis*, London and New York, Routledge.

Das S. (2011) *Extreme Money: Masters of the Universe and the Cult of Risk*, U.S, Pearson Education LTD.

Dasgupta A. K. (1993) *A History of Indian Economic Thought*, London, Routledge.

Day C. B. (1962) *The Philosophers of China, Classical and Contemporary*, New York, Citade Press.

D'Costa B. (2011) *Nation Building, Gender and War Crimes in South Asia*, London, Routledge.

Deane P. (1980) *The Evolution of Economic Ideas*, Cambridge, Cambridge University Press.

Deane P. (1967) *The First Industrial Revolution*, Cambridge, The University Press.

Defoe D. (1728) *A Plan of the English Commerce*, London, C. Rivington.

De Herrera G. A. (2006) *Ancient Agriculture – Roots and Application of Sustainable Farming*, ed. by J. E. Arellano and trans. by R. Lopez-Gaston, Salt Lake City, Ancient City Press.

De La Vega J. (1996) *Confusiones de Confusiones*, ed. by M. S. Fridson, New York, John Wiley and Sons, Inc.

Descartes R. (2004) Descartes' Methodological Rules – from Rules of the Direction of Mind, in P. Achinstein (ed.) *Science Rules: A Historical Introduction to Scientific Methods*, Baltimore and London, The John Hopkins University Press.

Descartes R. (1988) *Discourse on Method and the Meditations*, trans. by F. E. Sutcliffe, Penguin Books.

Drennen D. A. (1972) *Marx's Communist Manifesto: A full Textual Explication*, Barron's Educational Series.

Dugger W. M. and Peach J. T. (2009) *Economic Abundance – An Introduction*, London, Routledge.

Duong V. N. (2008) *The Tragedy of Vietnam War: A South Vietnamese Officer's Analysis*, Jefferson, North Carolina, McFarland and Company, Inc.

Ederer R. J. (1964) *The Evolution of Money*, Washington DC, Public Affairs Press.

Einzig P. (1951) *Primitive Money in its Ethnological, Historical, and Economic Aspects*, London, Eyre and Spottiswood.

Elliot C. P. (2015) The Crisis of A.D. 33: Past and Present, *Journal of Ancient History*, vol. 3: 2.

Ellis R. M. (2015) *Middle Way Philosophy*, ed. by Omibus, North Carolina, Lulu, Raleigh.

Engels F. (2008) *The Condition of the Working-Class in England in 1844*, New York, Cosimoclassics.

Etges A. (2013) All that Glitters is Not Gold: The 1953 Coup Against Mohammed Mossadegh in Iran, in I. Duyvesteyn (ed.), *Intelligence and Strategic Culture*, London, Routledge.

Eugene N. White (1990) The Stock Market Boom and Crash of 1929 Revisited, *The Journal of Economic Perspectives*, vol. 4: 2.

Falzon M. A. (2004) *Cosmopolitan Connections*, Leiden, Brill.

Farmer R. E. A. (2014) *How the Economy Works*, Oxford, Oxford University Press.

Fell A. L. (2004) *Origins of Legislative Sovereignty and the Legislative State*, vol. 6, Westport, Praeger.

Ferguson N. (2001) *The Cash Nexus: Money and Power in the Modern World, 1700-200*, London, Allen Lane.

Ferrell O. C., Fraedrich J. and Ferrell L. (2010) *Business Ethics – Ethical Decision Making and Cases 2009 Update*, 7th ed., Mason, South-Western Cengage Learning.

Feuerbach L. (2018) *Lectures on the Essence of Religion*, Eugene, Oregon, Wipf and Stock.

Feyerabend P. (1978) *Against Method*, London, Erso.

Financial Crisis Inquiry Commission (2011) *The Financial Crisis Inquiry Report*, Authorised (ed.), New York, PublicAffairs.

Finkelman P. (2012) Slavery in the United States: Persons or Property? in J. Allain (ed.) *The Legal Understanding of Slavery*, Oxford, Oxford University Press.

Fisher I. (1933) The Debt-Deflation Theory of Great Depression, *Econometrica*, vol. 1: 4.
Fisher I. (1930) *The Stock Market Crash – And After*, New York, The Macmillan Company.
Fisher I. (1911) The *Purchasing Power of Money*, New York, The Macmillan Company.
Flynn D. O. (1983) Sixteenth-Century Inflation from a Production Point of View, in N. Schmukler and E. Marcus (eds.), *Inflation throughout the Ages: Economic, Social, Psychological and Historical Aspects*, New York, Brooklyn College Press.
Flynn D. O. and Roper D. (1982) Gresham's Law and the Modern Theory of Demand for Money, *Eastern Economic Journal*, vol. 8: 3.
Freese B. (2020) *Industrial-Strength Denial*, Oakland, University of California Press.
Fried A. and Sanders R. (1964) *Socialist Thought: A Documentary History*, New York, Columbia University Press.
Friedman M. (2002) *Capitalism and Freedom*, 40th Anniversary ed., Chicago and London, The University of Chicago Press.
Friedman M. (1968) *Dollars and Deficits: Inflation, Monetary Policy and the Balance of Payments*, Englewood Cliffs, NJ, Prentice-Hall.
Fryde N. (2001) *Why Magna Carta? Angevin England Revisited*, Hamburg, LIT.
Fukuyama F. (2012) *The Origins of Political Order*, London, Profile Books.
Furet F. (1996) *The French Revolution 1770–1814*, Oxford, Blackwell.
Galbraith J. K. (2017) *Economics in Perspective: A Critical History*, Princeton, Princeton University Press.
Galbraith J. K. (1992) *The Great Crash 1929*, London, Penguin Books.
Galbraith J. K. (1988) *Economics in Perspective*, Boston, Houghton Mifflin.
Ganji M. (2002) *Defying the Revolution*, Westport, Praeger.
Garfinkle N. (2006) *The American Dream vs. The Gospel of Wealth*, New Haven, Yale University Press.
Gasiorowski M. J. (1987) The 1953 Coup D'état in Iran, *International Journal of Middle East Studies*, vol. 19: 3.
Gaukroger S. (2016) *The Natural and the Human Science and the Shaping of Modernity 1739–1841*, Oxford, Oxford University Press.
Gelderblom and Jonker (2011) Public Finance and Economic Growth: The Case of Holland in the Seventeenth Century, *The Journal of Economic History*, vol. 71: 1.
Gerald R. F, Alexander M. M. and Wiggins W. P. (2014) *The Legal and Ethical Environment of Business*, Alphen aan den Rijn, Wolters Kluwer.
Ghani C. (2000) *Iran and the Rise of Reza Shah*, London, L.B. Tauris Publishers.
Ghatak S. (2003) *Introduction to Development Economics*, 4th ed., London, Routledge.
Ghose S. (1993) *Jawaharlal Nehru: A Biography*, New Delhi, Allied Publishers Limited.
Ghosh A. (2006) *Pricing and Performance of Initial Public Offerings in the United States*, New Brunswick, Transaction Publishers.
Gilbert M. (2010) *Complicit – How Greed and Collusion Made the Credit Crisis Unstoppable*, New York, Bloomberg Press.
Gillin J. L. (1919) The Origin of Democracy, *American Journal of Sociology*, vol. 24: 6.
Goldschmidt A. (1991) *A Concise History of the Middle East*, 4th ed., Boulder, Westview Press.
Goldstein W. (1985) The Continuing World Debt Crisis, *Berkeley Journal of International Law*, vol. 3: 1.
Gomes L. (2003) *The Economic and Ideology of Free Trade: A Historical Review*, Cheltenham, Edward Elgar Pub.

Gordon S. (2003) *The History and Philosophy of Social Science*, London and New York, Routledge.

Gould L. A. and Pate M. (2016) *State Fragility around the World – Fractured Justice and Fierce Reprisal*, Boca Raton, CRC Press.

Graeber D. (2012) *Debt – The First 5,000 Years*, New York, Melvillehouse.

Gray A. (1957) *The Development of Economic Doctrine*, London, Longmans, Green and Co.

Green S. (2009) *Good Value*, New York, Grove Press.

Groseclose E. (1961) *Money and Man: A Survey of Monetary Experience*, New York, Frederick Ungar Publishing Co.

Grotius H. (1916) *The Freedom of the Sea*, trans. by R. V. D. Magoffin, ed. by J. B. Scott, New York, Oxford University Press.

Hain P. (2015) *Back to the Future of Socialism*, Bristol, Policy Press.

Hamilton E. J. (1947) Origin and Growth of the National Debt in Western Europe, *The American Economic Review*, vol. 37: 2.

Hanson L. K. and Essenburg T. J. (2014) *The New Faces of American Poverty: Reference Guide to the Great Recession*, vol. 1, Santa Barbara, ABC-CL10.

Hardach G. (1981) *The First World War 1914–1918*, Berkeley, University of California Press.

Harlow C. and Rawlings R. (2006) *Law and Administration*, 2nd ed., Cambridge, Cambridge University Press.

Harris T. (2006) *Revolution: The Great Crisis of British Monarchy, 1685–1720*, London, Allen Lane.

Harrison S. (Oct 2006) Pakistan's Baluch Insurgency, *Le Monde Diplomatique*, http://mondediplo.com/2006/10/05baluchistan.

Hasan M. (1980) *Pakistan: The Call of Islam*, Lahore, Pakistan Publications.

Hasmath R. (2015) Inclusive Growth, Development and Welfare Policy: A Critical Assessment, in R. Hasmath (ed.) *Inclusive Growth, Development and Welfare Policy: A Critical Assessment*, New York, Routledge.

Haughwout A. et al. (2019) Handbook of the Consumer Chapter: Trends in Household Debt and Credit, in A. Haughwout and B. Mandel (eds.) *Handbook of US Consumer Economics*, New York, Academic Press.

Haughwout A. and et al. (2019) Trends in Household Debt and Credit, *Federal Reserve Bank of New York Staff Reports* – Staff Report no. 882.

Haworth A. (1998) *Free Speech*, London, Routledge.

Hayek F. A. (1980) *Individualism and Economic Order*, Chicago, The University of Chicago Press.

Hedges C. (2003) *What Every Person Should Know about War*, New York, Free Press.

Heidenrich J. G. (2001) *How to Prevent Genocide*, Westport, Praeger.

Heilbroner R. L. (2011) *Worldly Philosophers*, 7th ed., Touchstone.

Herder J. G. (1803) *Outline of a Philosophy of History of Man*, vol. 2, Printed by Luke Hansard.

Heredia B. (1990) Interview Jesus Silva Herzog, *Journal of International Affairs*, vol. 43: 2.

Herman A. (2008) *Gandhi and Churchill*, New York, Arrow Book.

Hesiod (1988) *Theogony and Works and Days*, trans. by M. L. West, Oxford, Oxford University Press.

Hewitt V. M. (1992) *The International Politics of South Asia*, Manchester, Manchester University Press.

Hiatt S. (2007) *A Game as Old as Empire: The Secret World of Economic Hit Men and the Web of Global Corruption*, San Francisco, Berret-Koehler Publishers, Inc.
Hirst P. (1997) *From Statism to Pluralism*, London, Routledge.
Ho J. (1997) Evaluating the World Wide Web: A Global Study of Commercial Sites, *Journal of Computer-Mediated Communications*, vol. 3: 1.
Hobbes T. (1886) *Leviathan*, London, George Routledge and Sons.
Hobsbawm E. J. (1967) Trade Union History, *The Economic History Review*, vol. 20: 2.
Hogendorn J. S. (1996) *Economic Development*, New York, HarperCollins College Publishers.
Holbach P. H. T. (2013) *Good Sense Without God: Or Free Thoughts Opposed to Supernatural Ideas*, S.I, South Carolina, CreateSpace Independent Publishing.
Holmes L. (2009) *Communism: A Very Short Introduction*, Oxford, Oxford University Press.
Homer S. (1963) *A History of Interest Rates*, New Brunswick, Rutgers University Press.
Horn J. (2015) *Economic Development in Early Modern France*, Cambridge, Cambridge University Press.
Huertas T. F. (2011) *Crisis – Cause, Containment and Cure*, 2nd ed., Basingstoke, Palgrave Macmillan.
Hughes J. D. (1992) Sustainable Agriculture in Ancient Egypt, *Agricultural History*, vol. 66: 2.
Hume D. (2007) *An Enquiry Concerning Human Understanding*, Oxford, Oxford University Press.
Hume D. (1998) *Selected Essays*, ed. by S. Copley and A. Edgar, Oxford, Oxford University Press.
Hume D. (1993) *An Enquiry Concerning Human Understanding*, 2nd ed., Indianapolis/Cambridge, Hackett Publishing Company.
Hume D. (1990) *Enquiries Concerning Human Understanding and Concerning the Principles of Morals*, 3rd ed., Oxford, Clarendon Press.
Hume D. (1974) *A Treatise of Human Nature*, vol. 1, London, Everyman's Library.
Hume D. (1962) *On Human Nature and the Understanding*, Springfield, Collier Books.
Hume D. and Flew A. (1962) *On Human Nature and Understanding*, New York, Collier Books.
Hume D. (1953) Of the First Principles of Government, in Charles W. Hendel (ed.) *David Hume's Political Essays*, New York, The Liberal Arts Press.
Hume D. (1875) *Essays Moral, Political and Literary*, London, Longmans, Green and Co.
Hume D. (1874) *The Philosophical Works of David Hume*, vol. 2, Thomas Hill Green.
Hume D. (1854) *The Philosophical Works of David Hume*, vol. 1, Little, Brown.
Hume D. (1854) *The Philosophical Works of David Hume*, vol. 4, Little, Brown.
Hunt E. K. (2002) *History of Economic Thought*, 2nd ed., Armonk, M. E. Sharpe.
Hussain I. (2006) *Dimensions of Pakistan-India Relations*, Lahore, Heritage Publication.
Hutcheson F. (2008) *An Inquiry into the Original of our Ideas of Beauty and Virtue*, Indianapolis, Liberty Fund.
Hutcheson F. (1971) *Illustrations on the Moral Sense*, Bernard Peach, Belknap Press.
Hutter B. M. and Lloyd-Bostock S. (2017) *Regulatory Crisis – Negotiating the Consequences of Risk, Disasters and Crises*, Cambridge, Cambridge University Press.
Irons R. (2019) *The Fundamental Principles of Finance*, New York, Routledge.
Irwin T. (2009) *Derailed: Five Lessons Learned From Catastrophic Failures of Leadership*, Nashville, Thomas Nelson.

Israel J. I. (2001) *Radical Enlightenment: Philosophy and the Making of Modernity, 1650–1750*, New York, Oxford University Press.

Israel J. (1998) *The Dutch Republic: Its Rise, Greatness, and Fall, 1477–1806*, Oxford, Clarendon Press.

James VI and I (1986) A Speech to the Lords and Commons of the Parliament at the White-Hall (1610), in D. Wotton ed. *Divine Right and Democracy – An Anthology of Political Writing in Stuart England*, Indianapolis, Hackett Publishing Company, Ince.

Jerome J. K. (2007) *Three Men in Boat*, 1st World Library.

Johnson R. (2016) *The Great War and the Middle East*, Oxford, Oxford University Press.

Johnstone D. (2002) Q and A: Ayatollah Khomeini, in C. Aaron (ed.) *Appeal to Reason – 25 Years in these Times*, New York, Seven Stories Press.

Jones A. (2006) *Dictionary of Globalization*, Cambridge, Polity.

Jones C. (1988) *The Longman Companion to the French Revolution*, Harlow, Longman.

Jones G. E. (1948) *Tumult in India*, Dodd, Mead.

Jones-Hunt J. (2011) *Moses and Jesus: the Shamans*, Winchester, O. Book.

Kane R. (2010) *Ethics and the Quest for Wisdom*, Cambridge, Cambridge University Press.

Kant I. (2013) *An Answer to 'What is Enlightenment?'*, Penguins Books Limited.

Kant I. (2012) *Groundwork of the Metaphysics of Morals*, trans. by M. Gregor and J. Timmermann, Cambridge, Cambridge University Press.

Kant I. (2011) *Observations on the Feeling of the Beautiful and Sublime and other Writings*, ed. by P. Frierson and P. Guyer, Cambridge, Cambridge University Press.

Kant I. (2005) *Groundwork for Metaphysics of Morals*, ed. by L. Denis, Peterborough, Broadview Press.

Kant I. (2003) *To Perpetual Peace – A Philosophical Sketch*, trans. by T. Humphrey, Indianapolis, Hackett Publishing Company, Inc.

Kant I. (2002) *Groundwork of the Metaphysics of Morals in Focus*, ed. by L. Psternack, London and New York, Routledge.

Kant I. (1998) *Groundwork of the Metaphysics of Morals*, ed. by M. Gregor, Cambridge, Cambridge University Press.

Kant I. (1996) *Practical Philosophy*, Cambridge, Cambridge University Press.

Kant I. (1992) *The Cambridge Companion to Kant*, ed. by P. Guyer, Cambridge, Cambridge University Press.

Kant I. (1976) *Critique of Practical Reason, and other Writings in Moral Philosophy*, Philosophy of Immanuel Kant, vol. 1, trans and ed. by L. W. Beck, Garlad pub.

Kant I. (1963) *On History*, trans. by E. L. Fackenheim, L. W. Beck and R. E. Anchor, Publisher – Bobbs-Merrill.

Kant I. (1929) *Critique of Pure Reason*, trans. by N. K Smith, London, Redwood Press Limited.

Kant I. (1927) *Immanuel Kant's Critique of Pure Reason*, trans. by N. K. Smith, Basingstoke, Macmillan.

Kant I. (1914) *Eternal Peace: And other International Essays*, trans. by W. Hastie, World Peace Foundation.

Kant I. (1871) *The Metaphysics of Ethics*, 3rd edn, trans. by J. W. Simple and ed. by H. Calderwood, Edinburgh, T. and T. Clark.

Kaplan L. S. (1956) The Philosophes and the American Revolution, *Social Science*, vol. 31: 1.

Karimzadi S. (2013) *Money and its Origins*, New York, Routledge.

Kean H. (2011) Tolpuddle, Burston and Levellers: The Making of Radical and National Heritages at English Labour Movement Festivals, in L. Smith, P. A. Shackel and G. Campbell (eds.) *Heritage, Labour and the Working Classes*, London and New York, Routledge.

Keen S. (1995) Finance and Economic Breakdown: Modelling Minsky's "Financial Instability Hypothesis," *Journal of Post Keynesian Economics*, vol. 17: 4.

Kerferd G. B. (1955) Gorgias on Nature or That Which Is Not, *Phronesis*, vol. 1: 1.

Keynes J. M. (1972) *The collected Writings of John Maynard Keynes*, vol. 9, Essays in Persuasion, New York, St. Martin's Press.

Keynes J. M. (1971) *The Collected Writings of John Maynard Keynes: Essays in Persuasion*, vol. 9, London, Macmillan.

Keynes J. M. (1967) *The General Theory of Employment Interest and Money*, London, Macmillan.

Keynes J. M. (1963) *Essays in Persuasion*, New York, W. W. Norton and Co.

Khaldun I. (2005) *The Muqaddimah, An Introduction to History*, trans. by F. Rosenthal and ed. by N. J. Dawood, Princeton, Princeton University Press.

Khan A. A. (2017) Language Controversy and Education in Pakistan, in M. Joseph (ed.) *Understanding Pakistan*, London, Routledge.

Khan K. A. W. (1987) *Facts are Facts: The Untold Story of India's Partition*, Noida, Vikas Publishing House.

Kiernan B. (2007) *Blood and Soil – A World History of Genocide and Extermination from Sparta to Darfur*, New Haven, Yale University Press.

Kindleberger C. P. (1998) Economic and Financial Crises and Transformations in Sixteenth-Century Europe, in M. B. Riccardi (ed.) *Essays in International Finance*, no. 208, Princeton, Princeton University.

Kindleberger C. P. (1997) *Economic Laws and Economic History*, Cambridge, Cambridge University Press.

Kindleberger C. P. (1996) *Manias, Panics and Crashes*, 3rd ed., New York, John Wiley and Sons, Inc.

Kindleberger C. P. (1984) *A Financial History of Western Europe*, London, George Allen and Unwin.

Kinealy C. (1999) The Great Irish Famine – A Dangerous Memory? in A. Gribben (ed.) *The Great Famine and the Irish Diaspora in America*, Massachusetts, University of Massachusetts Press.

Kirzner I. M. (2007) *Market Theory and the Price System*, Auburn, Alabama, The Mises Institute.

Kissi E. (2006) *Revolution and Genocide in Ethiopia and Cambodia*, Lanham, Lexington Books.

Klein M. (2001) *Rainbow's End: The Crash of 1929*, Oxford, Oxford University Press.

Kleingeld P. (2007) Kant's Second Thoughts on Race, *The Philosophical Quarterly*, vol. 57: 229.

Kline M. (1982) *Mathematics: The Loss of Certainty*, Oxford, Oxford University Press.

Knoop T. A. (2015) *Business Cycle Economics – Understanding Recessions and Depressions from Boom to Bust*, Santa Barbara, Praeger.

Korab-Karpowicz W. J. (2012) *On the History of Political Philosophy*, London, Routledge.

Körnert J. (2003) The Barings Crises of 1890 and 1995: Causes, Courses, Consequences and the Danger of Domino Effects, *Journal of Financial Markets, Institutions and Money*, vol. 13: 3.

Kraus M. (2007) Did the Charter 77 Movement Bring an end to Communism? *New England Review*, vol. 28: 2.
Kumar S. (2012) *Casino Capitalism*, Bloomington, iUniverse, Inc.
Lagadec E. (2012) *Transatlantic Relations in the 21st Century*, London, Routledge.
Landreth H. and Colander D. C. (2002) *History of Economic Thought*, 4th ed., Boston, Houghton Mifflin.
Lauren P. G. (2011) *The Evolution of International Human Rights*, 3rd ed., Pennsylvania, Pennsylvania State University.
Legg J. (1991) *Chinese Classics*, vol. 1–2, trans. by J. Legg, Taipei, Taiwan, SMC Publishing Inc., CMC.
Lenin V. I. (1935) *Selected Works*, vol. 5, Institut Marksa-Engelsa-Lenina, International Publishers.
Letiche J. M. (2007) *Russia Moves into the Global Economy*, London and New York, Routledge
Lightbody B. (2004) *The Second World War– Ambitious to Nemesis*, London, Routledge.
Likitkijsomboon P. (1992) The Hegelian Dialectic and Marx's "Capital," *Cambridge Journal of Economics*, vol. 16: 4.
Locke J. (2003) *Two Treatises of Government and A Letter Concerning Toleration*, ed. by I. Shapiro, New Haven and London, Yale University Press.
Locke J. (1994) *An Essay Concerning Human Understanding*, New York, Prometheus Books.
Locke J. (1978) *The Correspondence of John Locke: Letters nos. 849–1241*, vol. 3, Oxford, Clarendon Press.
Locke J. (1969) *Two Treatises of Government*, Cambridge, Cambridge University Press.
Locke J. (1948) *Second Treatise of Civil Government*, ed. by J. W. Gough, Oxford, Basil Blackwell.
Lovell J. (1977) *British Trade Unions 1875–1933*, London, The Macmillan Press LTD.
McCartney J. R. (2013) *Authentic Being – Dynamic Creativity*, Bloomington, Xlibris Corporation.
Machan T. R. (1987) *The Main Debate: Communism Versus Capitalism*, New York, Random House.
Machiavelli N. (1950) *Discourses*, vol. 1, New Haven, Yale University Press.
Malthus T. R. (1985) *An Essay on the Principle of Population*, London, Penguin Books.
Malthus T. R. (1836) *Principles of Political Economy Considered with a View to Their Practical Application*, W. Pickering.
Malthus T. R. (1803) *An essay on the Principle of Population*, 2nd ed., London, J. Johnson.
Marx K. (1994) *Marx: Early Political Writings*, ed. by J. J. O'Malley, Cambridge, Cambridge University Press.
Marx K. (1988) *Marx Selections*, ed. by A. W. Wood, London, Macmillan Series.
Marx K. (1984) *Capital*, vol. 3, London, Lawrence and Wishart.
Marx K. (1983) *Capital*, vol. 1, London, Lawrence and Wishart.
Marx K. (1975) *Karl Marx, Frederick Engels: Collective Works*, vol. 37, London, Lawrence and Wishart.
Marx K. (1973) *Karl Marx on Society and Social Change*, ed. by N. J. Smelser, Chicago, The University of Chicago Press.
Marx K. (1971) *A Contribution to the Critique of Political Economy*, trans. by M. Dobb, London, Lawrence and Wishart.
Marx K. (1964) *Selected Writings in Sociology and Social Philosophy*, ed. by T. B. Bottomore, M. Rubel and E. Fromm, New York, McGraw-Hill.

Marx K. and Engels F. (1996) *Karl Marx and Frederik Engels: Collected Works*, vol. 35, London, Lawrence Wishart.
Marx K. and Engels F. (1991) *The German Ideology*, 2nd ed., London, Lawrence and Wishart.
Marx K. and Engels F. (1990) *Karl Marx and Friedrich Engels: Collected Works*, vol. 32, New York, International Publishers.
Marx K. and Engels F. (1962) *Marx and Engels Selected Works*, Vols. 1 and 2, Beijing, Foreign Languages Press.
Marx K. and Engels F. (1942) *Karl Marx and Frederick Engels: Selected Correspondence 1846–1895*, ed. by V. V. Adoratskiĭ and D. Torr, New York, International Publishers.
Mason P. (2016) *Postcapitalism – A Guide to Our Future*, London, Penguin Books.
McBride P. M. (2010) The Dodd-Frank Act and OTC Derivatives – The Impact of Mandatory Central Clearing on the Global OTC Derivatives Market, *The International Lawyer*, vol. 44: 4.
McCartney S. and Arnold A. J. (2003) The Railway Mania of 1845–1847, *Accounting, Auditing and Accountability Journal*, vol. 16: 5.
McGarry R. and Walklate S. (2019) *A Criminology of War?* Bristol, Bristol University Press.
Menon V. P. (1957) *The Transfer of Power in India*, Princeton, Princeton University Press.
Mill J. (1965) *Commerce Defended*, New York, Kelley.
Mill J. (1824) *Elements of Political Economy*, 2nd ed., London, Printed for Baldwin, Cradock, and Joy.
Mill J. (1821) *Elements of Political Economy*, London, Printed for Baldwin, Cradock, and Joy.
Mill J. S. (2010) *Autobiography of J. S. Mill and On Liberty*, Characteristics, Cosimo.
Mill J. S. (1976) *John Stuart Mill on Politics and Society*, London, Fontana.
Mill J. S. (1869) *The Subjection of Women*, London, Longmans.
Mill J. S. (1863) *On Liberty*, 2nd ed., Boston, Ticknor and Fields.
Mill J. S. (1844) *Essays on Some Unsettled Questions of Political Economy*, London, Harrison and Co., Printers.
Millar J. (1979) *John Millar of Glasgow, 1735–1801*, ed. by W. C. Lehman, Manhattan, Arno Press.
Mills J. (2002) *A critical History of Economics*, Basingstoke, Palgrave Macmillan.
Minsky H. P. (2008) *Stabilizing an Unstable Economy*, New York, McGraw Hill.
Minsky H. P. (1992) The Financial Instability Hypothesis, *The Jerome Economics Institute Working Paper*, no. 74.
Mises L. V. (1998) *A Treatise on Economics - Human Action*, The Scholar's ed. Auburn, Ludwig von Mises Institute.
Mises L. V. (1978) *Epistemological Problems of Economics*, 3rd ed., trans. by G. Reisman, New York, New York University Press.
Mitchell J. (1980) Children of the Holocaust, *The English Journal*, vol. 69: 7.
Mitchell W. C. (1941) *Business Cycles and Their Causes*, Berkeley, University of California Press.
Mitchell W. C. (1927) *The Business Cycles: The Problem and its Setting*, New York, National Bureau of Economic Research.
Montesquieu B. (2011) *The Sprits of Laws*, trans. by T. Nugent, New York, Cosimoclassics.

Morrow G. R. (1993) *Plato's Cretan City – A Historical Interpretation of the Laws*, Princeton, Princeton University Press.
Mote F. W. (1999) *Imperial China: 900–1800*, Cambridge, Harvard University Press.
Mukerjee M. (2010) *Churchill's Secret War*, New York, Basic Books.
Munro J. H. (2016) The Technology and Economics of Coinage Debasements in Medieval and Early Modern Europe, in J. H. Munro (ed.) *Money in the Pre-industrial World: Bullion, Debasements and Coin Substitutes*, London, Routledge.
Murray W. and Woods K. M. (2014) *The Iran-Iraq war: A Military and Strategic History*, Cambridge, Cambridge University Press.
Nanto D. K. (2009) *The Global Financial Crisis – Analysis and Policy Implications*, Congressional Research Service.
Nayak S. (2013) *The Global Financial Crisis*, New Delhi, Spring.
Nef J. U. (1943) The Industrial Revolution Reconsidered, *The Journal of Economic History*, vol. 3: 1.
Nguyen T. H. and Pontell H. N. (2011) *Fraud and Inequality in Subprime Mortgage Crisis*, in M. Deflem (ed.) *Economic and Crime*, Bingley, Bright Green Group Publishing Limited.
NIC (2012) *Global Trends 2030: Alternative Worlds.*
Nisbet R. (2009) *History of the Idea of Progress*, New Brunswick, Transaction Publishers.
Norton M. B. et al. (2015) *A People and a Nation, A History of the United States*, 10th ed., Boston, Cengage Learning.
Noyes A. D. (1909) A Year after the Panic of 1909, *The Quarterly Journal of Economics*, vol. 23: 2.
Oatley T. (2016) *International Political Economy*, London, Routledge.
O'Connor D. E. (2014) *Decipher in Economics*, Timely Topics Explained, ABC-CLIO.
Ofek E. and Richardson M. (2003) DotCom Mania: The Rise and Fall of Internet Stock Prices, *The Journal of Finance*, vol. 58: 3.
O'leary B. (2012) Partition, in T. M. Wilson and H. Donnan ed. *A Companion to Border Studies*, Chichester, Wiley-Blackwell.
O'Malley C. (2015) *Bonds without Borders – A History of the Eurobond Market*, Chichester, Wiley.
Oresme N. (2009) *The De Moneta of Nicholas Oresme and English Mint Documents*, trans. by C. Johnson, Auburn, The Ludwig von Mises Institute.
Ortolano G. (2019) *Thatcher's Progress*, Cambridge, Cambridge University Press.
Padua D. (2014) John Maynard Keynes and the Economy of Trust – The Relevance of the Keynesian Social Thought, *Global Society*, Basingstoke, Palgrave-Macmillan.
Pain E. (2001) From the first Chechen War Towards the Second, *The Brown Journal of World Affairs*, vol. 8, no. 1: 7–19.
Paine T. (1894) *The Writings of Thomas Paine*, vol. 1, ed. by M. D. Conway, New York, The Anickerbocher Press.
Palmer R. (1971) *The World of the French Revolution*, London, George Allen and Unwin.
Palmer R. R. (1959) *The Age of the Democratic Revolution*, vol. 1, Princeton, Princeton University Press.
Pangle T. L. (2010) *The Theological Basis of Liberal Modernity in Montesquieu's Spirit of the Laws*, Chicago, University of Chicago Press.
Panigrahi D. N. (2004) *India's Partition – The Story of Imperialism in Retreat*, Abingdon, Routledge.
Park M. (2005) *The Dutch Republic in the Seventeenth Century: The Golden Age*, trans. by D. Webb, Cambridge, Cambridge University Press.

Parker D. (2009) *The Official History of Privatization*, vol. 1, London and New York, Routledge.

Parker D. (2006) Enterprise Sales: Thatcher Leads the Change, in G. Hodge (ed.) *Privatization and Market Development*, Cheltenham, Edward Elgar.

Patrikarakos D. (2012) *Nuclear Iran*, London, I.B. Tauris.

Paul D. (1984) Eugenics and the Left, *Journal of the History of Ideas*, vol. 45: 4.

Payne P. G. (2015) *Crash! How the Economic Boom and Bust of the 1929 Worked*, Baltimore, Johns Hopkins University Press.

Payne (1973) *Massacre: The Tragedy of Bangla Desh and the Phenomenon of Mass Slaughter throughout History*, New York, Macmillan.

Perperzak A. T. (2001) *Modern Freedom: Hegel's Legal, Moral, and Political Philosophy*, Dordrecht, Kluwer Academic Publishers.

Perry M. (2013) *Western Civilization: A Brief History*, Wadsworth, Cengage Learning.

Persaud A. (2011) The Political Economy of Sovereign Wealth Funds, in R. A. Fry, W. J. Mckibbin and J. O'Brien (eds.) *Sovereign Wealth*, London, Imperial College Press.

Pervez M. S. (2013) *Security Community in South Asia: India-Pakistan*, Abingdon, Routledge.

Petty W. (1899) *The Economic Writings of Sir William Petty*, vol. 1, ed. by C. H. Hull, Cambridge, Cambridge University Press.

Pilbeam K. (2018) *Finance and Financial Markets*, 4th ed., London, Palgrave.

Plato (1875) *The Dialogues of Plato*, vol. 3, Trans. By B. Jowett, London, Henry Frowde.

Pliny (1968) *Natural History*, vol. 4, Harvard University Press.

Poitras G. (2011) *Valuation of Equity Securities – History, Theory and Application*, New Jersey, World Scientific.

Polo M. (1874) *The Book of ser Marco Polo, the Venetian*, London, John Murray.

Poovey M. (2003) *The Financial System in Nineteenth-Century Britain*, Oxford, Oxford University Press.

Popper K. (2002) *The Logic of Scientific Discovery*, London and New York, Routledge.

Popper K. (1971) Conjectural Knowledge: My Solution of the Problem of Induction, *Revue Internationale de Philosophie*, vol. 25: 95/96.

Proudhon P. J. (1994) *Proudhon: What is Property*? ed. by B. G. Smith and D. R. Kelly, Cambridge, Cambridge University Press.

Pugh M. (2012) *State and Society – Asocial and Political History of Britain since 1870*, 4th ed., London, Bloomsbury Publishing Plc.

Rahnama-Moghdam M. (1995) Debt Rescheduling in Less Developed Countries: World or Reginal Crisis? *The Journal of Developing Areas*, vol. 30: 1.

Raic D. (2002) *Statehood and the Law of Self-Determination*, The Hague, Kluwer Law.

Read C. (2005) *Lenin: A Revolutionary Life*, London and New York, Routledge.

Reck A. J. (1991) The Enlightenment in American Law II: The Constitution, *The Review of Metaphysics*, vol. 44: 4.

Ricardo D. (2006) *The Principles of Political Economy and Taxation*, London, Timeless Series, Empiricus Books.

Ricardo D. (1846) *The Works of David Ricardo*, ed. by J. R. McCulloch, London: John Murray.

Rivot S. (2016) Why and How Should a Monetary Economy be Stabilized? The Forgotten Lessons of Milton Friedman, in R. A. Cord and J. D. Hammond (eds.), *Milton Friedman Contributions to Economics and Public Policy*, Oxford, Oxford University Press.

Robbins L. (2007) *The Great Depression*, Auburn, Alabama, Ludwig von Mises Institute.

Robbins L. (1952) *An Essay on the Nature and Significance of Economic Science*, 2nd ed., London, Macmillan and Co.

Roberts R. (2008) *The City: A Guide to London's Global Financial Centre*, 2nd ed., London, Economist.

Rosenberg J. M. (2010) *The Concise Encyclopaedia of the Great Recession 2007–2010*, Lanham, The Scarecrow Press, Inc.

Ross S. (2008) *The Industrial Revolution*, London, Evans.

Rostow W. W. (1975) *How it all Began: Origins of the Modern Economy*, New York, McGraw-Hill.

Rostow W. W. (1960) *The Process of Economic Growth*, 2nd ed., Oxford, Clarendon Press.

Rothbard M. N. (2011) *Economic Controversies*, Auburn, Ludwig Von Mises Institute.

Rothbard M. N. (2006) *Economic Thought before Adam Smith*, vol. 1, Auburn, Alabama, Edward Elgar Publishing Ltd.

Rousseau J. J. (1767) *The Miscellaneous Works of Mr. J. J. Rousseau*, vol. 5, London, T. Becket and P.A. De Hondt.

Rousseau J. J. (1764) *A Treatise on the Social Compact; or the Principles of Political Law*, London, Printed for T. Becket and P. A. De Hondt.

Rummel R. J. (1994) *Death by Government*, New Brunswick, Transaction Publishers.

Rummel R. J. (1991) *China's Bloody Century – Genocide and Mass Murder Since 1900*, New Brunswick, Transaction Publishers.

Russell C. (1990) *The Causes of the English Civil War*, Oxford, Clarendon Press.

Ryan C. (2007) Marxism and War, in A. Anton and R. Schmitt ed. *Toward a New Socialism*, Lanham, Lexington Books.

Samuelson P. A. and Nordhaus W. D. (1995) *Economics*, 15th ed., McGraw-Hill. Companies.

Sanderson W. C. (1995) *Population in Asia*, World Bank Regional and Sectoral Studies, Washington DC, The World Bank.

Santos T. M. (1991) Philippine Energy Policy and Problem in a Changing World, in S. Sharma and F. Fesharaki (eds.) *Energy Market and Policies in Asean*, Singapore, Institute of Southeast Asian Studies.

Sarila N. S. (2008) *The Shadow of the Great Game: The Untold Story of India's Partition*, HapperCollins Publisher.

Say J. B. (1971) *A Treatise on Political Economy*, New York, Augustus M. Kelley Publishers.

Scalcione R. (2011) *The Derivatives Revolution – A Trapped Innovation and a Blueprint for Regulatory Reform*, The Netherlands, Wolters Kluwer.

Schechter R. (2018) *A Genealogy of Terror in Eighteenth Century France*, Chicago: The University of Chicago Press.

Scheer H. (2005) *The Solar Economy*, trans. by A. Ketley, London, Earthscan Publications limited.

Schendel W. V. (2013) The Pakistan Experiment and the Language Issue, in M. Guhathakurta and W. V. Schendel (eds.) *The Bangladesh Reader*, Durham, Duke University Press.

Schumpeter J. A. (1996) *The Essence of Joseph Alois Schumpeter*, Reutling, Manz.

Schumpeter (1942) *Capitalism, Socialism, and Democracy*, New York and London, Harper and Brothers.

Schutze R. (2009) *From Dual to Cooperative Federalism: The Changing Structure of European Law*, Oxford, Oxford University Press.
Segal G. (1991) *The World Affairs Companion*, New York, A Touchstone Books.
Shakespeare R. (2007) *The Modern Universal Paradigm*, LPFE.
Shand J. (1994) *Philosophy and Philosophers*, London, Penguin Books.
Shiller R. J. (2015) *Irrational Exuberance*, 3rd ed., Princeton, Princeton University Press.
Siam-Heng M. H. and Wei L.T. (2009) *Destructive Creativity of Wall St. and the East Asian Response*, New Jersey, World Scientific.
Siddiqi F. H. (2012) *The Politics of Ethnicity in Pakistan*, Abingdon, Routledge.
Sidgwick H. (1922) *Outlines of the History of Ethics*, Macmillan and Co.
Simai M. (1994) *The Future of Global Governance*, Washington DC, United States Institute of Peace Press.
Simmons A. J. (1989) Locke's Sate of Nature, *Political Theory*, vol. 17: 3.
Sleigh R. C. (1972) *Necessary Truth*, Englewood Cliffs, Prentice-Hall.
Smith A. (1986) *The Wealth of Nations, Books* 1–3, London, Penguin Classics.
Smith A. (1864) *An Inquiry into the Nature and Causes of the Wealth of Nations*, London, T. Nelson and Sons.
Smith A. (1804) *An Inquiry into the Nature and Causes of the Wealth of Nations*, vol. 2, Hartford, CT, Printed for Oliver D. Cooke.
Smyth W. (1855) *Lectures on the History of the French Revolution*, vol. 2, London, Henry G. Bohan.
Soddy F. (1943) *The Arch Enemy of Economic Freedom*, F. Soddy at Knapp, Enstone.
Soddy F. (1933) *Money Versus Man*, New York, E.P. Dutton and Co., Inc.
Soddy F. (1926) *Wealth, Virtual Wealth, and Debt: the Solution of the Economic Paradox*, London, G. Allen and Unwin, Ltd.
Soddy F. (1912) *Matter and Energy*, New York, H. Holt and Co.
Soherwordi S. H. S. (2010) 'Punjabisation' in the British Indian Army 1857–1947 and Advent of Military Rule in Pakistan, *Edinburgh Papers in South Asian Studies*, no. 24.
Solomon R. C. (1983) *In the Spirit of Hegel*, New York, Oxford University Press.
Spargo J. (1910) *Karl Marx: His Life and Work*, New York, The National Labor Press.
Spencer H. (1921) *Synthetic Philosophy*, New York, Appleton and Co.
Spencer H. (1891) *The Principles of Biology*, vol. 1, New York, Appleton and Co.
Spencer H. (1868) *Social Statics; or, the Conditions Essential to Human Happiness*, London, Williams and Norgate.
Spencer H. (1865) *Illustrations of Universal Progress: A Series of Discussions*, New York, Appleton and Co.
Spencer H. (1851) *Social Statics; or, the Conditions Essentials to Human Happiness*, London, John Chapman.
Spinoza B. (1991) *Tractatus Theologico-Politicus*, trans. by S. Shirly, Leiden, New York, E. J. Brili.
Spinoza B. (1963) *Spinoza's Ethics*, trans. by A. Boyle, London, New York, Everyman's Library.
Sprague O. M. W. (1914) The Federal Reserve Act of 1913, *The Quarterly Journal of Economics*, vol. 28: 2.
Stabile D. R. (2005) *Forerunners of Modern Financial Economics – A Random Walk in the History of Economic Thought*, Cheltenham, Edward Elgar.
Stearns P. (2017) *Tolerance in World History*, Taylor and Francis.

Stenographic Report (1977) *Congress of the Peoples of the East*, Baku September 1920, trans. by B. Pearce, London, New Park Publications.

Stewart M. (1991) *Keynes and After*, 3rd ed., London, Penguin Books.

Stiglitz J. E. and Bilmes L. J. (2008) *The Three Trillion Dollar: The True Cost of the Iraq Conflict*, New York, W.W Norton.

Streissguth T. (2007) *The Roaring Twenties*, New York, Facts on File.

Strindberg A. and Warn M. (2011) *Islamism – Religion, Radicalization, and Resistance*, Cambridge, Polity Press.

Stromberg R. N. (1994) *European Intellectual History since 1789*, Prentice Hall.

Subacchi P. (2011) Europe: From one Crisis to the Other, in P. Savona, J. J. Kirton and C. Oldani (eds.) *Global Financial Crisis – Global Impact and Solutions*, Farnham, Ashgate.

Sun W., Stwart J. and Pollard D. (2011) Introduction: Rethinking Corporate Governance – Lesson from the Global Financial Crisis, in W. Sun, J. Stwart and D. Pollard (ed.) *Corporate Governance and the Global Financial Crisis*, Cambridge, Cambridge University Press.

Swanson D. (2013) *War No More*, ebook, Charlottesville, VA.

Thackrah J. R. (2009) *The Routledge Companion to Military Conflict Since 1945*, London, Routledge.

Thatcher M. (1997) *The Collected Speeches of Margaret Thatcher*, ed. by R. Harris, HarperCollins Publishers.

Thompson E. P. (1968) *The Making of the English Working Class*, Harmondsworth, Pelican Books.

Tooke T. (1844) *An Inquiry into Currency Principle*, 2nd ed., Longman.

Tooke T. (1840) *A History of Prices and of the State of the Circulation in 1838- and 1839*, London, Longman.

Torrens R. (1821) *An Essay on the Production of Wealth*, London, Longman, Hurts, Rees, and Brown.

Tremblay R. (2010) *The Code for Global Ethics: Ten Humanist Principles*, Prometheus Books.

Trevor-Roper H. R. (1959) The General Crisis of the 17th Century, *Past and Present*, vol. 16: 1.

Trono J. C. (1994) *Moral Boundaries – A Political Argument for an Ethic of Care*, New York, Routledge.

Tsesis A. (2012) *For Liberty and Equality – The Life and Times of the Declaration of Independence*, Oxford, Oxford University Press.

Tsingou E. (2006) The Governance of OTC Derivatives Markets, in P. Mooslechner, H. Schuberth and B. Weber (eds.) *The Political Economy of Financial Market Regulation – The Dynamics of Inclusion and Exclusion*, Cheltenham, Edward Elgar.

Tucker S. C. (2018) *The Roots and Consequences of Independence Wars*, Santa Barbara, ABC-CLIO, LLC.

Tullio G. and Ronci M. (1996) Brazilian Inflation from 1980 to 1993: Causes, Consequences and Dynamics, *Journal of Latin American Studies*, vol. 28: 3.

Uekert B. K. (1995) *Rivers of Blood: A Comparative Study of Government Massacres*, Westport, Praeger.

Velasquez M. G. (1991) *Philosophy*, 4th ed., Belmont, Wadsworth Publishing Co Inc.

Velde F. R. (2006) French Public Finance between 1683 and 1726, *Federal Reserve Bank of Chicago*.

Venkatesh K. (26 Feb 2018) All but Forgotten: Choudhary Rahmat Ali, the Inventor and First Champion of Pakistan, *Herald*.

Venn F. (2002) *The Oil Crisis*, London, Routledge.

Vries J. D. (2009) The Economic Crisis of the Seventeenth Century after Fifty Years, *Journal of Interdisciplinary History*, vol. 40: 2.

Warnok J. W. (2005) *Natural Resources and Government Revenues*, Ottawa, Canadian Centre for Alternatives.

Weidemam D. (2004) Pakistan: Self-Perception, Images of History, Concept of the State, in E. Reiter and P. Hazdra (eds.) *The Impact of Asian Powers on Global Developments*, Springer, Verlag Belin Heidelberg Gmbtt.

Weingart P. (1989) German Eugenics between Science and Politics, in *Science in Germany: The Intersection of Institutional and Intellectual Issues*, vol. 5, Chicago, The University of Chicago Press.

Weir S. and Beetham D. (2005) *Political Power and Democratic Control in Britain*, New York, Routledge.

Welch S. and Miewald R. (1983) *Scarce Natural Resources: The Challenge of Public Policymaking*, Sage Publications.

Westermann M. (1996) *The Art of the Dutch Republic 1585–1717*, London, Weidenfeld and Nicolson.

Westfall R. (1980) *Never at Rest*, Cambridge, Cambridge University Press.

White E. N. (1995) The French Revolution and the Politics of Government Finance, 1770–1815, *The Journal of Economic History*, vol. 55: 2.

Whitehead C. (2009) Political Memoirs, Myth, Policy, and the Wars of Yugoslav Secession, *Past Imperfect*, vol. 15, https://doi.org/10.21971/P7OC7R.

Whitehead C. and Scanlon C. (2012) The UK and Europe's Selective Housing Bubble, in A. Bardhan, R. H. Edelstein and C. A. Kroll (eds.) *Global Housing Markets – Crises, policies and Institutions*, Hoboken, John Wiley and Sons, Inc.

Wiest A. (2009) *The Vietnam War*, New York, Rosen Publishing.

William N. P. (2010) *Fixing Everything*, Bloomington, AuthorHouse.

Williams D. (2014) Adam Smith and Colonialism, *Journal of International Political Theory*, vol. 10: 3.

Williams J. (1997) *Money: A History*, New York, St. Martin's Press.

Wilson P. H. (2011) *The Thirty Years War: Europe's Tragedy*, Cambridge, The Belknap Press of Harvard University Press.

Wilson P. H. (2008) The Causes of the Thirty Years War 1618–48, *The English Historical Review*, vol. 123: 502.

Windecker Jr. G. H. (1993) The Eurodollar Market: Strategies and Regulations, *American University International Law Review*, vol. 9: 1.

Wolff R. (2012) *Democracy at Work: A Cure for Capitalism*, Chicago, Haymarket Books.

Wollstonecraft M. (2009) *A Vindication of Rights of Men with a Vindication of the Rights of Women and Hints*, ed. by S. Tomaselli, Cambridge, Cambridge University Press.

Wollstonecraft M. (2003) *A Vindication of the Rights of Men with A Vindication of the Rights of Women and Hints*, ed. by S. Tomaselli, Cambridge, Cambridge University Press.

Woodburne A. S. (1923) The Present Religious Situation in India, *The Journal of Religion*, vol. 3: 4.

Woods W. J. (2009) *Walking with Faith; New Perspectives on the Sources and Shaping of Catholic Moral life*, Eugene, Wipf and Stock Publishers.

Wright N. D. (2014) The Biology of Cooperative Decision Making: Neurobiology to International Relations, in M. Galluccio ed. *Handbook of International Negotiation*, Brussels, Springer.

Yarlagadda R. K. R. (2017) *Life in the Eyes of Thatha*, Pittsburgh, Dorrance Publishing Co.

Zeidan R. (2018) *Economics of Global Business*, Cambridge, The MIT Press.

Zhuo X. (2018) *Religious Faith of the Chinese*, trans. by D. Zhao, Beijing, Springer.

Zirinsky M. P. (1992) Imperial Power and Dictatorship: Britain and the Rise of Reza Shah, 1921–1926, *International Journal of Middle East Studies*, vol. 24: 4.

Zloch-Christy I. (1987) *Debt Problems of Eastern Europe*, Cambridge, Cambridge University Press.

# Index


Abedi, A. H. 130–131
Abu Nidal 131
accountability 4, 130, 164, 257
Adams, J. 49–50
Afghanistan 86, 88–89, 104, 106, 108, 110, 119, 140–141, 144, 149, 234, 255–256
African Development Bank 131
age discrimination 1
Age of Enlightenment 2–3, 42, 45, 55, 64, 179, 181, 192, 194, 259, 262, 280, 285, 288, 318
agriculture 9, 14, 16, 24, 57, 62–64, 72, 160, 190, 194, 210, 212, 221
Ahmad Khan, S. 99
Akram, A. S. M. 102
al-Assad, H. 82–83
al-Bashir, U. H. 144
Algeria 144
Ali, C. R. 100, 111
Allende, S. 125
al-Qaddafi, M. 82
Al-Qaeda 89, 106, 158, 234; September 11 attacks 89, 156, 158, 234
Althusius, J. 34
Amazon 140
American Insurance Group 170–171
American Revolution 40, 45–54, 61, 63–65, 285
Aminzadeh, M. 252
Amos 12
anarchism 242–243, 250
Andropov, Y. 149
Antiphon 330
Applegarth, A. J. 172–173
Aquinas, T. 323
Arab Spring 82–83
Argentina 79–80, 134
Aristotle 7, 11–12, 21, 30–31, 48–49, 117, 133, 156–157, 189, 270–271, 289, 316–317, 323, 330
Arkwright, R. 73, 202
Asian financial crisis 136, 157
Ataturk, M. K. 250
Australia 117, 159, 161, 244
Austrian school 125, 144, 146, 175–176, 221, 228, 251, 254

Bacon, F. 71, 266
Bagehot, W. 334
Baksh, R. 246
balance of payments 78, 128–129
Baluch, M. 246–247
Baluchistan 108–111
Bangladesh 106–107
Bank of America 165
Bank of Credit and Commerce International 130–131
Bank of England 75–80, 159, 173
Bank of Scotland 75
bankruptcy 80, 168, 170, 173–174, 177, 206, 210, 215, 221
Barbar, N. 106
Barclays 177
Baring crisis 79–80
Bear Stearns 174
Beccaria, C. 283
Belgium 159, 244
Benin 86
Bentham, J. 55, 286, 318
Berkeley, G. 263–264, 297, 299
Berlin Wall 149–150
Berners-Lee, T. 138–139
Bhutto, B. 106
Bhutto, Z. A. 106, 112, 141
big bang revolutions 131–132, 176, 209
Bill of Rights (1689) 38, 63, 69–70

bin Laden, O. 89, 140
Biswas, C. C. 102
blind faith 178–183, 260
Bodin, J. 22, 34
body mutilation 231–232
Bolivia 86
Bolsheviks 80–81, 84, 93, 109–110, 144, 160, 205–206, 258, 331, 333
Bosnia 149
Bouazizi, M. 82
Boulton, M. 73
bourgeoisie 200, 223, 292
Brazil 86, 129, 134, 136–137, 244
Bretton Woods 114, 126–128, 132, 175
Brezhnev, L. 85, 148
bribery 98, 130–131, 154
Brown, G. 154–155
Bruno, G. 235, 304
Buddhism 241, 321
Buffett, W. 157
Butler, J. 325

Calas, J. 53
Cambodia 119
Canada 159, 161, 244
capitalism 5, 10, 86, 118, 160, 180, 199–207, 209, 215–218, 223, 229, 255, 258, 261, 291–293, 335; original model of 201–207
Cartwright, E. 202
Catalonia 123
Ceausescu, N. 149
central banks 75–80, 95, 131, 136–137, 156, 159, 168
Chenier, A. 54
Cherenkov, K. 149
Chicago School 125–126
Child, J. 36–37
child workers 73
Chile 86, 125–126, 145, 152–153
China 14, 19–20, 83, 85, 88, 119, 121, 152–154, 156, 158, 187, 222, 231, 237, 240–241, 244–245, 250, 255, 259, 321, 333
Christianity 12, 24–25, 33, 42, 53, 57, 230, 239–241, 263, 283, 289, 296, 308
Churchill, W. 100–101, 256, 291, 333
Citigroup 177
Clarkson, T. 43
class discrimination 1, 55, 196–197, 199–200, 290, 302, 331
Colbert, J.-B. 58
collateralized debt obligation 168–170
colonization 1, 3, 13, 15, 20, 22–25, 28–29, 38, 42, 45–46, 58, 60, 68, 71, 81–82, 88, 93, 113, 116, 121, 141–142, 148, 150–151, 153, 189–190, 207, 241, 247, 249, 255–256, 283–284, 288–291; Frankenstein states 68, 97–112, 247, 250, 284; *see also individual countries*
Columbus, C. 15
communism 84, 86, 88, 94, 114, 122, 127, 139, 141, 148–150, 153–154, 160–161, 191, 198, 200, 203, 206–207, 216, 249, 255, 259
Comte, A. 193–194
Condorcet, Marquis de 55, 191, 286
Confucius 317, 321–322
Coolidge, C. 95
Copernicus, N. 21
corruption 1, 19, 42, 50, 86, 88, 108, 130, 141, 154, 202, 206, 227, 245, 258, 291, 309, 326
counterfeiting 22, 91
Countrywide Financial Corporation 165
credit default swap 169–170
credit rating agencies 164–165, 293
Croatia 149
crypto-economy 8–9, 138–177
Cullen, W. R. 86
Czechoslovakia 150–152

Dagarzai, N. 246–247
Darwin, C. 195–197, 304, 333; natural selection 166–167, 195–197, 333; social Darwinism 101, 166–167, 291
Daud Khan, M. 88–89, 140
de Gouges, O. 56
de Gournay. J.-C.-M.V. 58–59
de la Vega, J. P. 31, 133, 157
de Malestroit, J. 22
Deane, P. 71
debasing coins 21–22, 78
deflation 92, 212
Defoe, D. 36
Deism 42–43
democracy 3, 24–25, 71, 93, 113, 118, 121, 136, 149–150, 152–154, 160–161
Deng, X. 152–153
Denmark 117, 159, 161
Denning, A. 70
derivatives market 133–134, 156–157, 169; over-the-counter derivatives 156, 171
Descartes, R. 37, 271–273, 296, 299
Desh, S. 104

Desmoulins, C. 54
despotism 2, 4, 28, 35, 48, 50, 52, 63, 70, 78, 81–82, 86–89, 103, 136, 153–154, 161, 192–193, 256
d'Holbach, P. H.T. 43, 252
Diamond, B. 177
Dice, C.A. 96–97
dictatorship 3, 129, 142, 149, 151–152, 244–245, 249, 255, 309
Diderot, D. 42, 52, 191–192
Diogenes of Sinop 242
discrimination: age 1; class 1, 55, 196–197, 199–200, 290, 302, 331; racial 1, 100–101, 196, 291; sexual 1, 55–56, 105, 117, 143, 196, 227, 289–290, 310, 317
Disraeli, B. 78
divide and rule 81, 98–99, 102
division of labour 1, 8, 11, 16, 18, 68, 71, 118, 179, 184, 227, 237, 257, 294
Domesday Book 69
Dominican Republic 86
dot.com crisis 140, 156, 158
drug trafficking 130–131, 251
Dubcek, A. 151
Durand, H. M. 104, 108
Durkheim, É. 231

East India Company 23, 65, 98, 133
eBay 140
e-commerce 140, 176
economic crises 4–10, 66, 180, 203, 206–221, 293, 301, 305, 335–338; Asian financial crisis 136, 157; definition of 4–6, 13–15; dot.com crisis 140, 156, 158; global financial crisis (2007) 4, 9, 123, 139, 154–168, 170–177, 207, 209, 293; Great Depression 4, 10, 97, 112–113, 136, 171, 207, 209, 217–218, 221, 228, 329; and human propensity to extremism 10, 224–258 (*see also* extremism); over-trading and 9–10, 178–225; root cause of 226–231; tulip mania 4, 9, 14, 22–33, 222
economic decline 4
economic disorder 4, 6, 8, 75, 144, 228, 338
economic growth 3–4, 13–14, 35, 113, 135, 254–256
economics 3–4, 87, 221, 257, 259–261
e-credit system 8–9, 139
Ecuador 86
Egypt 14, 17, 82, 86, 124, 144, 221, 259, 320
Elliot-Murray-Kynynumound, G. J. 99
Engels, F. 67, 78, 197–199
English revolution 38–40, 75
Epicurus 317–318
Erasmus, D. 24–25
ethics 1–3, 26, 147, 167, 193, 203, 281, 287–288, 296–297, 302, 306–312, 314, 316–332
Ethiopia 85–86, 119, 232
eugenics 167, 244, 291, 333
Eurodollar market 127–130, 132, 134–136
European Central Bank 159
European Economic Community 128
European Union 122–123, 174
exchange rate 87, 114, 125–128, 132, 136–137, 155–157, 175, 209
extremism 1–3, 6, 10, 54, 77, 139, 229, 241, 258, 261–262, 298, 303, 312; embedded in economics 252–256; human propensity to 10, 226, 231–238, 243–245, 247–251, 289, 336–338; Islamic 89, 104–106, 140–144, 156, 158, 234–235, 255; and survival 313–322

famine 9, 17, 29, 78, 85, 101, 178, 185, 222
fascism 3, 35, 83, 85, 100, 112–114, 121–122, 139, 207, 241, 243–244, 250, 255, 259, 282, 308, 329, 333
fatalism 262–266
Federal Reserve 75, 95, 155, 158–159, 170–171
federalism 44–50
Ferguson, A. 194
Ferguson, N. 83
Feuerbach, L. 280
fiat money 20, 65–66, 92
Fichte, J. G. 242
Finland 93, 117, 159, 161
Fisher, I. 97, 211–212, 218–219
Ford, H. 94
foreign direct investment 137
forgery 77–78
France 20, 29, 33, 38, 41–42, 44, 67–69, 77–82, 88, 117, 159, 161, 174, 244, 255; French revolutions 14, 51–56, 61, 78, 252, 280, 285
Frankenstein states 68, 97–112, 247, 250, 284; *see also individual countries*

Franklin, B. 42
fraud 21, 32
freedom of association 3
freedom of belief 2
freedom of expression 3, 38, 71, 152, 337
freedom of thought 3, 71
free trade 23, 36–38, 64, 120, 122–123, 179, 184
free will 17, 47, 56, 181, 183, 263, 277, 287, 300–302, 309, 311–312, 326
French revolutions 14, 51–56, 61, 78, 252, 280, 285
Friedman, M. 125–126, 145–146, 152, 228, 293
Fritzel, J. 251
Fuld, D. 167, 177
full employment 113, 217

Galbraith, J. K. 96
Galileo 266, 303–304
Galton, F. 333
Gandhi, M. K. 101
Ganjavi, N. 233
Gaskell, P. 67
Gates, R. 130
gender equality 1, 3, 55–56, 116–117, 208, 227, 231, 257, 289–290, 303–304; *see also* women's rights
genocide 108, 111, 149
Germany 82, 100, 109, 149–150, 159, 161, 174, 223, 249, 251
Ghaffar Khan, A. 104–105
Gillin, J. L. 38
Ginott, H. 248
global financial crisis (2007) 4, 9, 123, 139, 154–168, 170–177, 207, 209, 293
globalization 69, 119–134
Godwin, W. 194
Goetius, F. L. 242
gold 76–78, 90–92, 110, 114, 126
Goldsmid, F. J. 108
Gong Yu 19
Gorbachev, M. 148–154
Gorgias of Leontini 242, 298–299
Grand National Consolidated Trades Union 73
Great Britain *see* United Kingdom
Great Depression 4, 10, 97, 112–113, 136, 171, 207, 209, 217–218, 221, 228, 329
Greece 86, 123, 174, 236–237, 244–245
Greenspan, A. 155
Gresham's law 21
Gresham, T. 21
Grey, M. C. 99
gross domestic product 79, 85, 95, 126–127, 135–137, 170, 174, 208–209
Grotius, H. 25, 34, 37, 41
Guatemala 86
Guillaume, L. 67
Guillotine, J.-I. 52

Haiti 86
Hamden, J. 64
Hamilton, A. 49–50
Hammurabi 12, 17, 222
Hargreaves, J. 73, 202
Harrington, J. 49
Harrison, S. S. 111
Harvey, W. 71, 304
Havel, V. 150, 152
Hayek, F. 145, 148, 292
Hegel, G. W. 192–194, 197–198, 299, 331
Helsinki Accords 151–152
Helvetus, C. A. 55
Henry, P. 45
Heraclitus 295–296
Herder, J. G. 192–193, 283
Hesiod 7, 11
Hezbollah 131, 144, 234
Hilferding, R. 292
Hinduism 98–100, 102, 104, 187, 230, 241, 320
historical materialism 84–85, 197–201, 206–207, 331
Hobbes, T. 34, 40–41, 49, 55, 71, 231, 324–325, 329
Homer 11
Hoover, H. 96
Hope, V. A. J. 100
human follies 10, 259–338
human rights 3, 108, 123, 125, 144, 151–152, 154, 246, 279
Hume, D. 6, 43, 46, 49, 71, 165, 264–265, 268–269, 276, 278–280, 297–299, 326, 334
Hungary 92
Hutcheson, F. 279, 318, 325–326
hyperinflation 22, 68, 89–97, 136, 207, 213

Iceland 117
imprisonment 1, 59, 70, 123, 143–144, 162, 249, 304
India 98–105, 110, 141, 234–235, 237, 240–241, 247, 249, 256, 284, 291, 320
individualism 134, 231, 244
Indonesia 86, 135, 158

industrialization 7–9, 67–137, 161; banking and money economy 68, 74–80; cradle of 69–74; empires and Frankenstein states 68–69, 97–112; generations of wars 112–119; and globalization 69, 119–134; hyperinflation and depression 68, 89–97; wars, revolutions and depressions 80–89
Industrial Revolution 7–8, 57, 67–68, 71–74, 76, 106, 117–118, 138, 200–202, 216–217, 291
inflation 18, 22, 62, 80, 87, 92–93, 124–126, 129, 134–136, 145–146, 159, 215, 222, 228; hyperinflation 22, 68, 89–97, 136, 207, 213
insurance 170
interest rates 23, 36, 57, 135, 158–159, 161–162, 168, 173, 205, 219, 222, 228, 293
International Monetary Fund 114, 174
International Trade Organization 114
Iran 86–88, 108–109, 122, 141–144, 230, 234, 249, 252, 255
Iraq 81–82, 86–87, 123, 144, 256, 284
Ireland 159, 161, 174
ISIS 144
Islam 12, 57, 81, 83, 87–89, 98–102, 104–107, 111, 121, 130, 140, 230–232, 239–241, 245, 249, 252, 255–256, 284, 289, 308, 315; Islamic extremism 89, 104–106, 140–144, 156, 158, 234–235, 255
Israel 124, 238, 247
Italy 30, 81, 159, 174
Ivory Coast 131

Jacobi, F. H. 242
James II 38–39
Japan 117, 131–133, 153, 158–159, 161, 234, 244
Jefferson, T. 42
Jerome, J. K. 70
Jevons, W. S. 21, 204, 290, 303
Jinnah, M. A. 99–100, 106, 110–111
Jones, G. E. 99
JP Morgan 169–170
Judaism 25, 230, 232, 238–241, 245, 289, 323
Juglar, C. 204–205
junk bond market 135

Kahn, R. 138
Kant, I. 42, 44, 52, 55, 115–116, 181, 192–193, 203, 265, 275–277, 286–290, 298, 326–329
Kautsky, K. 292
Kay, J. 202
Keynesianism 18, 112, 114–116, 119–120, 123, 125, 145–146, 148, 175, 209, 254
Keynes, J. M. 5, 112–113, 120, 126, 186, 206–211, 217–219, 228, 254, 256, 291–292, 333, 335
Khaldun, I. 63
Khan, R. 104, 109, 142
Khan, Y. 107
Khomeini, R. 87–88, 143
Kindleberger, C. P. 218–219, 221
Kirzner, I. 147
Kitchin, J. 205
Kondratiev, N. 205
Kurdistan 123, 255–256

Lafayette, Marquis de 53
Laird, M. 127
laissez-faire system 9, 45, 95, 125, 145, 165, 176, 179, 209, 217, 223
Laos 86
Lassalle, F. 197
Latin American sovereign debt crisis 134–135
Lavosier, A. 54
Law, J. 9, 59–61, 79, 222
League of Nations 115
Le Bovier, B. 188
Lehman Brothers 167–168, 177
Leibniz, G. W. 42, 273–274, 297
Lenin, V. 84, 206, 292, 331–332
Lessing, G. E. 43, 281
Libya 82, 86
Licklider, J. C. R. 138
Lidderdale, W. 80
Lisbon Treaty 123
List, F. 223
Locke, J. 37, 39–43, 46, 49, 55, 71, 231, 263, 280–281, 297, 329
Louis XIV 57–59
Louis XVI 51
Lucretius 188
Lycurgus 47–48

Macedonia 149
Machiavelli, N. 49, 324–325
Macleod, H. D. 21
Madison, J. 51
Magna Carta 63–64, 69–70

Mahgan, M. C. 102
Malaysia 136, 158
Malthus, T. R. 179, 186–187, 195–196, 204, 259
Mandel, E. 292
Mandeville, B. 288–289
Manhattan Project 249
manufacturing 72, 95, 125, 202, 324
Mao Tse-tung 85, 152–153, 332
Marie Antoinette 51–52
Marshall, A. 61, 259, 290
Marshall, G. C. 127
Marxism 5, 84–85, 89, 112, 119–120, 140, 143, 145, 148, 153, 196–203, 215–217, 223, 228–229, 241, 302, 304, 331–332
Marx, K. 61, 73, 78, 186, 190, 194, 196–207, 209–210, 215–217, 223, 229, 231, 253, 280, 286, 290–292, 299, 331, 335
mass consumption 8, 68, 72, 94–95, 118, 208
Mellon, A. W. 94–95
Mencius 231, 322
mercantilism 7, 36, 45, 179, 183–184, 187, 222, 253, 336
mergers and acquisitions 60
Merrill Lynch 177
Mexico 91, 129, 134–135
migration 8, 17, 79, 251, 257, 300
Milken, M. 135
Millar, J. 194
Mill, J. 179, 185
Mill, J. S. 179, 186, 290, 318–319, 329
Milosovic, S. 149
Minsky, H. 218–219, 293
Mirabeau, Marquis de 190–191
Mirza, I. 112
Misery Index 88
Mises, L. 144–147
Mississippi speculation 9, 61, 222
Mitchell, W. C. 209–211, 218–219
Mohamed, D. 102
Money, R. C. 110
monotheism 180, 226, 236–245, 299, 315
Montazeri, H. A. 88
Montenegro 149
Montesquieu, B. 41, 49–50, 192–193, 282
Moody, J. 96
moral hazard 136, 257, 293
More, H. 238, 324–325
Morelly, E.-G. 191, 285–286
mortgage-backed securities 163–165
Mossadegh, M. 87
Mozilo, A. R. 165
Mubarak, H. 82
Mugabe, R. 93
Mujahideen, H. 106
Mukherji, B. K. 102
Muller, A. 253
Muller, H. J. 333
Munir, M. 102
Mun, T. 184
Myanmar 232

Napoleon 62, 79, 198
Naqvi, S. 131
national sovereignty 25, 33–42, 57, 109
natural disasters 4, 9, 13, 16–17, 178, 222, 226, 229, 257, 300
natural selection 166–167, 195–197, 333
Nazism 100, 109, 139, 148, 150, 203, 207, 239–240, 244, 249, 255, 308, 333
Nehru, J. 99
neoliberalism 121, 127, 147–148, 161
Nero 15
Netherlands 67, 69, 80, 117, 133, 159, 161, 245, 256; tulip mania 4, 9, 14, 22–33, 222
New Guinea 232
new right economics 127, 139, 144–146, 148, 152, 209
Newton, I. 21, 71, 78, 189, 195–197, 222, 304
New Zealand 117, 159
Nigeria 131
nihilism 242–243
Nixon, R. 125
Noriega, M. 131
Northern Rock 171–174
North Korea 122
Norway 117, 159, 161

Omar, M. 106
O'Neal, S. 177
Oppenheimer, J. R. 249
Oresme, N. 20–21, 184
Organization of the Petroleum Exporting Countries 124, 128–129
Ortis, J. 64
Ottoman Empire 81, 150, 255
over-the-counter derivatives 156, 171
over-trading 9–10, 179, 182–183, 185–187, 204, 212
Owen, R. 73

Pahlavi, M. R. 87, 141–142
Paine, T. 52

Pakistan 89, 100–108, 110–112, 122, 131, 140–141, 234, 240, 246, 249, 255–256, 284
Palmer, R. R. 47
Panj, R. M. 109
pantheism 25–26
paper money 19–20, 62, 65, 77, 79
Parmenides of Elea 295–296, 299
Pascal, B. 280
Paterson, W. 75
Peel, R. 78
Peru 86, 91, 131
Peston, R. 173
Petty, W. 185
Philippines 83, 136, 158, 232
Phillips, A. W. 124
Phillips curve 124, 145
physiocracy 44–45, 58, 145, 179, 187, 253
Pinochet, A. 125, 145, 152–153
Plato 11–12, 48, 188, 203, 270–271, 295–296, 317, 330
Pliny 15
Polo, M. 20
Polybius 49
Ponzi schemes 72, 219
Popper, K. 265–266, 268–269, 334
population ageing 257
population growth 18, 23, 72–73, 195
Portugal 14, 174, 275
post-Keynesianism 215, 254, 293
potato famine 78
poverty 7, 9, 17, 111, 113, 121, 127, 180, 214, 217, 222, 248, 255
power of appropriation 56–64
Prague Spring 151
Price, C. 177
private property 16, 18, 69, 161–162, 191, 200, 235, 243
privatization 126, 160–161, 326
proletariat 67, 72–73, 93, 119, 200–201, 243
propaganda 86, 121, 148–149, 205
Protagoras 330
Pufendorf, S. 34–35, 190
purchasing power 20, 92
Putin, V. 152
Pyrrho of Elis 298

Qalandarani, M. 246
Quesnay, F. 44, 58, 190–191, 253

racial discrimination 1, 100–101, 196, 291
Radcliffe, C. 102
Rahman, S. A. 102
railway mania 74
Ramsay, J. 108
Rawls, J. B. 328–330
Reagan, R. 125, 144, 176
red scare 94
religion 1–3, 12–13, 16–17, 23, 36, 38–39, 41–43, 81, 84–85, 90, 98–99, 101, 105, 108, 113, 117, 120, 187–188, 222, 235–241, 249–250, 257, 259, 263–264, 269, 272–273, 278, 280–281, 285, 287, 299, 301, 308–311, 315–316; blind faith 178–183, 260; Buddhism 241, 321; Christianity 12, 24–25, 33, 42, 53, 57, 230, 239–241, 263, 283, 289, 296, 308; Deism 42–43; Hinduism 98–100, 102, 104, 187, 230, 241, 320; Islam 12, 57, 81, 83, 87–89, 98–102, 104–107, 111, 121, 130, 140, 230–232, 239–241, 245, 249, 252, 255–256, 284, 289, 308, 315; Islamic extremism 89, 104–106, 140–144, 156, 158, 234–235, 255; religious tolerance 39; religious wars 1, 16, 25, 29, 42, 98; Zoroastrianism 187, 230, 237–238
Renaissance 42
Ricardo, D. 79, 179, 184–185
Robbins, L. 11, 221
Robespierre, M. 53, 55
Roman Empire 12, 15, 49, 62–63, 244–245, 308
Romania 149
Roosevelt, F. D. 249
Roosevelt, T. 333
Rostow, W. W. 74
Rothbard, M. N. 147
Rothschild, N. 77
Rousseau, J. J. 42, 49, 52–53, 55, 192, 279, 284–285, 290, 326–327, 329
rule of law 2–3, 13, 24–26, 33, 36, 39, 41, 47, 56–57, 108, 121, 136, 147, 154, 256, 282, 337–338
Rushdie, S. 143
Ruskin, J. 214
Russell, B. 165, 298
Russia 80–81, 85–86, 93, 109, 112, 122, 128, 136, 140–141, 150–151, 154, 157–158, 160, 205–206, 255, 259, 333; Russian Revolution 83–86, 93–94, 109, 207, 255, 292, 335; *see also* Soviet Union
Ryzhkov, N. 89

Saddam Hussain 82
Sade, Marquis de 280
Salami, H. 252
Saleem, A. 246–247
Salernitana, M. 233
Sartre, J.-P. 302
Saudi Arabia 89, 106
Say, J.-B. 185
Schumpeter, J. 61, 203–204, 206, 293
self-interest 64, 155, 164, 225, 228, 253–254, 261, 279–290, 311, 324–325, 329–330, 334
Seneca, L. A. 188
Senegal 131
Senior, N. W. 259
September 11 attacks 89, 156, 158, 234
Severiges Riksbank 75
sexual discrimination 1, 55–56, 105, 117, 143, 196, 227, 289–290, 310, 317; *see also* women's rights
Shakespeare, W. 233
Shaw, B. 333
Sidgwick, H. 319, 325
Silva-Herzog, J. 135
Singh, T. 102
Sismondi, J. 186–187, 204
Skelton, N. 160
slavery 3, 12, 36–37, 63, 198–199, 251, 255, 259, 284, 289, 313, 316–317
Slovenia 149
Smith, A. 37, 58, 64, 71, 78–79, 155, 179, 181, 184–185, 187, 194, 253, 259, 288–289, 291, 295, 325
social contract 34, 40, 42, 52, 54, 324, 326, 329–330
social Darwinism 101, 166–167, 291
socialism 93, 143–145, 160, 191, 204, 333
Socrates 245, 270, 298, 317, 319, 330, 332–333
Soddy, F. 212–215
Solon 11, 18, 222
Somalia 86
Sombart, W. 203–204
South Korea 135–136
South Sea Bubble 61, 76
Soviet Union 84–86, 88–89, 93–94, 106, 117, 119, 128, 140, 142, 144–145, 148–150, 152–154, 158, 176, 206, 209, 244, 255, 258, 332, 335; *see also* Russia
Spain 14, 24, 30, 35–37, 79, 123, 159, 161, 174
special purpose vehicles 168
Spencer, H. 196–197, 332
Spinoza, B. 25–26, 37, 43, 272–275, 296–297, 324
stagflation 125–127, 132, 136, 145, 175, 214
stagnation 28, 125, 137, 149, 186
Stalin, J. 84, 113, 145, 205, 255, 332
Stephenson, G. 74–75
Strutt, J. 73
subprime mortgages 160–168, 170–174
Sudan 86, 144, 232
suicide 89, 106, 158, 234–235, 240, 243, 245
Sweden 124, 159, 244, 256
Switzerland 34, 117, 159, 161, 251
Syed, G. M. 104
Sykes–Picot Agreement 80–81, 255
Syria 81–82, 86, 144, 152, 255, 284

Tacitus, P. C. 18
Taliban 106, 144
Taraki, N. M. 89
taxation 45, 56, 58, 61–64, 98, 121, 128
Taylor, F. W. 94
terrorism 87, 89, 106, 130, 156, 158, 234; *see also* extremism
Thailand 135–136, 158
Thain, J. 177
Thales of Miletus 30, 133, 156–157
Thatcher, M. 125, 144, 146–147, 160, 176
Thompson, E. P. 73
Thrasymachus 330
Thucydides 231
Tiananmen Square massacre 153–154
Tiberius 222
Toland, J. 26
Tooke, T. 186
Torrens, R. 186
torture 1, 3, 53, 111, 144, 225, 239, 244–247, 249, 251, 283, 308
totalitarianism 3, 35, 84–85, 112, 121–122, 139, 148, 150, 153–154, 157, 161, 236, 239, 248–250, 255, 281–282, 329, 332
trade 6–7, 179, 183–185, 222; crypto-economy and trade cycle 8–9, 138–177; cyclonic ebbs and flows of 7, 11–66; free trade 23, 36–38, 64, 120, 122–123, 179, 184; history of 14–22; industrialization (*see* industrialization); over-trading 9–10, 179, 182–183, 185–187, 204, 212; under-trading 9–10, 179, 182, 185–187, 204
Trade Union Congress 118–119
trade unions 3, 5, 73, 118–119, 228
transparency 3, 88, 130, 136, 164, 171, 257, 293
Transparency International 88

Treaty of Rome 122, 128
Truman, H. 88, 128
trust 20, 34, 61, 86, 91, 94, 97, 100, 109, 119, 131, 135, 165, 173, 190, 216, 219, 221, 272, 324–325, 328
Tugan-Baranovsky, M. 205
tulip mania 4, 9, 14, 22–33, 222
Tunisia 82
Turgenev, I. 242
Turgot, R. J. 190
Turkey 128, 144, 250, 336
tyranny 1, 3, 36, 40, 49–50, 63–64, 142, 153, 167, 256, 285

Ulema-e-Islam, J. 106
under-trading 9–10, 179, 182, 185–187, 204
unemployment 95, 97, 113–116, 124–126, 145, 174–175, 208–209, 216, 221, 254
UNESCO 107
Union of Utrecht 36
United Kingdom 14, 20, 38–40, 80–81, 86–87, 93–94, 98, 101–102, 104–105, 108–111, 117–118, 124–126, 128, 131–133, 141–142, 144, 223, 244–245, 333; big bang revolution 131–132, 176, 209; Brexit 122–123; British Empire 82–84, 98, 103, 105, 107, 141–142, 207–208, 223, 255–256, 284, 335; central bank (*see* Bank of England); English revolution 38–40, 75; and global financial crisis (2007) 154–155, 159–161, 171–174; and the Great Depression 208; Industrial Revolution 7–8, 57, 67–68, 71–74, 76, 106, 117–118, 138, 200–202, 216–217, 291
United Nations 83, 104, 115–116, 123, 149, 328
United States 20, 39–40, 79, 82, 85–88, 93–97, 106, 115, 117, 125–133, 140–141, 144, 155–156, 158, 244, 249, 258, 333; American Revolution 40, 45–54, 61, 63–65, 285; big bang revolution 131–132, 176, 209; Federal Reserve 75, 95, 155, 158–159, 170–171; and global financial crisis (2007) 161, 171–4, 174, 207, 209; and the Great Depression 4, 10, 97, 112–113, 136, 171, 207, 209, 217–218, 221, 228, 329; housing market 159–161, 167, 170, 173 (*see also* subprime mortgages); September 11 attacks 89, 156, 158, 234; Wall Street Crash (1929) 10, 97, 207, 211–212, 218, 228
Universal Declaration of Human Rights 115–116
unknowns 10, 259–338
urbanization 8, 23
Uruguay 80, 86

Vansittart, R. 109
Vedas 320
Vietnam 86, 88, 127
Voltaire 41–43, 52–53, 192, 280–281

Wall Street Crash (1929) 10, 97, 207, 211–212, 218, 228
Wallace, A. R. 196
Washington, G. 42
Watt, J. 73, 75
Wavell, P. 100–101
weapons 1, 85–86, 141–142, 249, 308–309, 312
Webb, S. 333
Weber, M. 203
welfare state 112, 114, 126, 139, 145, 175
Whitney, E. 202
Wilberforce, W. 52
witch hunts 251
Wittgenstein, L. 300
Wollstonecraft, M. 52, 55–56, 290
women's rights 1, 56, 117, 208, 261; *see also* gender equality; sexual discrimination
World Bank 114, 174
World Wide Web 138–140

Xenophon 11, 18
Xunzi 231, 322

Yeltsin, B. N. 136, 152
Yemen 82, 86
Yugoslavia 92–93, 149–151

Zahir Shah, M. 88
Zia-ul-Haq 106, 112
Zimbabwe 93
Zoroastrianism 187, 230, 237–238

For Product Safety Concerns and Information please contact our EU representative GPSR@taylorandfrancis.com
Taylor & Francis Verlag GmbH, Kaufingerstraße 24, 80331 München, Germany

www.ingramcontent.com/pod-product-compliance
Lightning Source LLC
LaVergne TN
LVHW021117300926
849160LV00010B/759
* 9 7 8 1 0 3 2 3 8 6 9 8 0 *